Stanley Marcus: *A Life with Books*

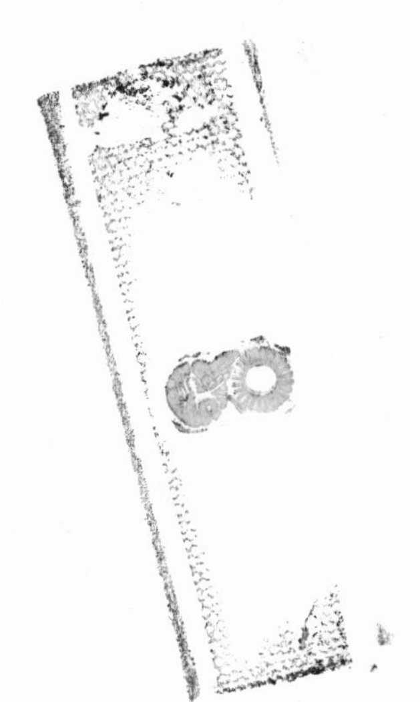

Stanley Marcus

A Life with Books

By David Farmer

TEXAS CHRISTIAN UNIVERSITY PRESS • FORT WORTH

First edition 1993: Still Point Press
Design by W. Thomas Taylor

This edition published by arrangement with Still Point Press and David Farmer

The following publishers have generously given permission to use quotations from copyrighted works: From *Quest for the Best*, by Stanley Marcus. Copyright 1979 by Stanley Marcus. Reprinted by permission of Viking Penguin, a division of Penguin Books USA, Inc. From *Minding the Store: A Memoir*, by Stanley Marcus. Copyright 1974 by Stanley Marcus. Reprinted by permission of Little, Brown and Company. From "America Is in Fashion," by Stanley Marcus. Copyright 1940 by Time, Inc. Reprinted by permission of *Fortune Magazine*. From *Portrait of Max*, by S. N. Behrman. Copyright 1960 by S. N. Behrman. Reprinted by permission of Brandt & Brandt Literary Agents; first published by Random House. From newspaper columns by Stanley Marcus. Copyright 1974, 1984, 1991, 1992 by the *Dallas Morning News*. Reprinted by permission of the publisher.

Library of Congress Cataloging-in-Publication Data

Farmer, David R.
Stanley Marcus : a life with books / by David Farmer.
p. cm.
Originally published : Dallas : Still Point Press, 1993
Includes Bibliographical references (p.) and index.
ISBN 0-87565-147-X :
1. Marcus, Stanley, 1905- . 2. Businessmen — United States — Biography. 3. Authors — United States — Biography. 4. Marcus, Stanley, 1905- — Books and Reading. 5. Marcus, Stanley, 1905- — Library. 6. Neiman-Marcus. I. Title
HF5429.5.D2M3743 1995
381'. .14'092 - dc20
[B] 95-7570
CIP

Jacket design by Barbara Whitehead
Front cover photograph by David Farmer
Back cover photograph courtesy Stanley Marcus

To Carol Farmer

dearest friend, wife, mother of our son,
businesswoman, bibliophile

Contents

Illustrations

Acknowledgements

Few books are ever written without help, and this is clearly one which depended on the interest, cooperation, and graceful sharing of information by a considerable number of people. From the outset I have been grateful to Charlotte and Gould Whaley, who asked me to write about an individual whose accomplishments are so compelling that I could not resist the challenge. The cooperation from Stanley and Linda Marcus has been exemplary, making my task all the easier by granting interviews, providing introductions to other sources, opening files, and even giving the DeGolyer Library at SMU perhaps the largest collection of personal papers ever assembled in this part of Texas.

The making of books should also lead to new friendships, and this is the case with Elizabeth Ann McMurray Johnson, whose experience, knowledge and enthusiasm has helped guide me through interviews, phone calls, correspondence and writing, especially when I began to wonder how I could fit the making of a book into an already full professional life. Colleagues and librarians at Southern Methodist University have also aided the process, particularly Maureen Pastine, David J. Weber, Ron Davis, Marsh Terry, Michael Winship, Betty Friedrich, Kay Bost, Kristin Jacobsen, Page Thomas, Sam Ratcliffe, and Ellen Buie Niewyk. And for the careful checking of facts and for assistance with preparation of the manuscript and letters of permission, I thank Jane Elder, who also brought to the job a refreshingly irreverent sense of humor.

In order to write of a time and place that falls within recent memory, the recollections and perceptions of Stanley Marcus, Evelyn Oppenheimer, Wirt Davis, Jr., Elizabeth Ann Johnson, Leon Harris, Franklin Gilliam, Allen Maxwell, Marvin Steakley, and Andrew Hoyem were of prime importance. My thanks to them and to Jackie McElhaney, who shared her knowledge of sources for Dallas history. I also wish to thank Roger E. Stoddard at Harvard University for providing background information on the course developed by George Parker Winship devoted to the history of the printed book. Especially helpful were members of the Winship family: Peter Winship at SMU, Michael Winship at the University of Texas at Austin, George Parker

Winship, Jr., and Stephen Winship, the latter providing a lively account of his working temporarily at Neiman-Marcus.

As a historian of the book arts, Al Lowman has been particularly helpful, especially in providing information for the chapter on Carl Hertzog. Al generously opened his extensive and well-organized files assembled for his own biography of Hertzog which is presently under way. His was a most unselfish act beyond the call of duty, and I am extremely grateful for the many weeks of research it saved me.

Just as few books are ever written without help from colleagues, even fewer are produced without the assistance of libraries, librarians, and publishers. Thus, I want to acknowledge and heartily thank the following institutions and individuals for offering assistance and granting permission to quote from unpublished and published work: Stanley Marcus, for permission to quote extensively from unpublished correspondence; Robert A. Seal, University Librarian, the University of Texas at El Paso, for permission to quote from the Carl Hertzog papers; June Moll, retired rare book librarian, University of Texas at Austin, for background information on a 1967 rare book exhibit loaned to Dallas Public Library; Sally Leach and Cathy Henderson at the Harry Ransom Humanities Research Center, the University of Texas at Austin, for access to unpublished materials at HRHRC; the J. Frank Dobie Library Trust, P.O. Box 550, Austin, TX 78789, for permission to quote from unpublished letters of J. Frank Dobie. By the wishes of the late J. Frank Dobie, the Trust serves to benefit rural libraries in Texas.

Thanks also to Tom Lea for permission to quote from an unpublished letter to Carl Hertzog; William Koshland, Alfred A. Knopf, Inc., for permission to quote from letters by Alfred A. Knopf, Blanche Knopf, and Pat Knopf; Decherd Turner for permission to quote from his letters to Stanley Marcus; Paul Horgan for permission to quote from unpublished letters to Stanley Marcus, Carl Hertzog, and Tom Lea; John Windle for permission to quote from his letters to Stanley Marcus; Linda J. Long and the Stanford University Libraries for permission to quote from correspondence between Stanley Marcus and John Windle in the John Howell—Books archive; Harley Holden and the Harvard University Archives for quotation of material relating to Stanley Marcus at Harvard; Kate Adams and the Center for American History at the University of Texas at Austin for access to the Walter Prescott Webb papers, the Roy Bedichek papers, and the papers of the Texas State Historical Association; Dorothy Sloan for background on the Book Club of Texas; Ken Ragsdale for background on the Texas Centennial; F. E. Abernethy and the Texas Folklore Society for access to information on J. Frank

Dobie and Stanley Marcus; McFarlin Library, University of Tulsa, for material relating to John A. Lomax; Judith Garrett of the Belo Corporation, and the *Dallas Morning News* for assistance with photo research and for permission to use a photograph; Dr. Turner and the Dupre Library, the University of Southwestern Louisiana, for access to the papers of David Williams.

Finally, I am deeply grateful to my dearest friend and wife, Carol Farmer, for her unending encouragement and close readings of the manuscript in its various stages. In the earlier phases of this project she happily explored the byways of research, traveling with me to Austin, San Marcos, San Diego, and elsewhere to seek new information. Her honest criticism and keen eye for sound writing strengthened this book immeasurably.

Prologue

As the Harvard University senior mounted the steps to the Widener Library, he tried to imagine the course in great books that he was going to attend, "The History of the Printed Book." Having experimented as a child with a toy printing press given him by his mother, he had been drawn to books at an early age. In recent years, he had scouted the antiquarian shops up and down Cornhill in Cambridge for titles of particular interest. He had collected some of what he had found and had resold the rest to support his avocation.

Though his freshman year at Amherst had been marked by social discrimination against him as a Jew, he quickly found Harvard more hospitable and he enjoyed the diverse cultural opportunities of Boston. From the classes of his professors, Bliss Perry, John Livingston Lowes, and George Lyman Kittredge, he carried notes on books to read and ideas to pursue. He learned about "Dr. Eliot's Five-Foot Shelf of Books"—the Harvard Classics readily available on the shelves of his fraternity house. From all these sources, he made lists of books he wanted to collect so that he could reread them at any time. Then he searched through the book shops along Cornhill until he had filled considerably more than five feet of his own bookshelves with a variety of books, including Charles W. Eliot's Harvard Classics, published in uniform binding by P. F. Collier & Son in New York.

His reading, collecting, and book scouting had primed the undergraduate for the course in the history of printing he was now starting. Throughout the course, George Parker Winship would take from the shelves books of great rarity. He would talk about their makers—authors as well as printers—passing the books around the great oak table in the middle of the room so the class could open and examine them and experience for themselves their look and feel. These beautifully printed books were the first published works of Cicero, Copernicus, Dante, Shakespeare, Milton, and other giants of Western learning.

Following each class with Winship, the senior would return to his room at the Zeta Beta Tau fraternity house, where he was president, his head full of thoughts about the writing, printing, collecting, and selling of books. As his graduation approached in 1925, he informed his father that he wanted to devote his life to books, either as a publisher, a fine printer, or an antiquarian bookseller. His father, however, expected all of his sons to join the family business he had established in Dallas in 1907, and would hear of nothing else. A man of considerable persuasion, he convinced his son that a career in retailing would provide far better financial means for collecting than any aspect of the book business.

The undergraduate, of course, was Stanley Marcus. He did join the family business — Neiman-Marcus — and led it to its legendary success. Yet all along the way he never lost his love of books. Indeed, his life with books has been so full that it is hard to imagine how he found enough time to pursue it. And it continues. Even today, at eighty-eight, Stanley Marcus continues to collect and write with the energy of a man half his age. Happily, this attempt to tell the story of his life with books is, therefore, incomplete. Stanley Marcus still proceeds to show us all how to live life to the fullest by filling his own with books that represent a "quest for the best" in writing, printing, and publishing.

Chapter One

The Harvard Experience

Almost fifty years after graduating from Harvard, Stanley Marcus wrote his autobiography *Minding the Store.* In the book he recalled one teacher from grammar school, another from high school, and three from college who had made an enormous difference to him. The first was Miss Edmiston, his grammar school English teacher who encouraged him in his studies. "She was always concerned that I was constantly fidgeting, moving my hands. She admonished me that I was wasting vital energy and that I would lose years of my life unless I learned to conserve my strength. I have never been able to find any scientific substantiation for this warning, but to this day, when I notice myself toying with a pencil or a rubber band, I think back on Miss Edmiston's warning."[1]

At Forest Avenue High School, it was Miss Myra Brown who taught English and coached Marcus in debate. He remembers her leading him through "*Lorna Doone, Wuthering Heights*, and a host of other English classics." This preparation for more advanced reading came in the wake of early avid reading in the Tom Swift series and the Rover Boys series, as well as Charles Dickens and even Sir Walter Scott.[2] At home there was also private tutoring in German until the outbreak of World War I when the study of German language and history was considered unpatriotic.

From his Harvard days, Marcus vividly recalled three professors of English who greatly influenced him: "Perry taught me to love literature in general; Kittredge taught me how to read and understand Shakespeare; Lowes, who gave a course in nineteenth-century English poetry, started back in the twelfth century, so that we could understand the extent and basis of knowledge the nineteenth-century writers possessed." It was from classes with Lowes that Marcus would emerge with notes "of at least a half-dozen books to read and a score of ideas to pursue."[3]

These experiences as a Harvard undergraduate helped set the intellectual foundation for a way of life in which books would play a central role. In looking back, Marcus reflected that "the greatest thing that can happen to any student—and some don't have such good fortune—is to encounter a teacher who unlocks the massive doors of knowledge, suggests the paths of curiosity, and extends an invitation to enter. That John Livingston Lowes did for me."[4]

While Lowes unlocked the doors of knowledge for Stanley Marcus, it was Harry Elkins Widener's bequest, actuated by his untimely death on the *Titanic*, which helped fill Harvard's library shelves with rare books, and George Parker Winship who took them down to place in the hands of his students. The course which Winship taught was "The History of the Printed Book," the description of which was carefully worded to appeal to a select few who wanted to develop their knowledge about books:

> This course is intended for men who are interested in books as objects of art, and who desire to possess or to produce beautiful books. The lectures on the history of printing and its subsidiary crafts will be supplemented by discussions of the characteristic qualities which affect the excellence and the value of any volume. The physical make-up of a book and the conditions governing its manufacture will be explained with sufficient detail to provide a basis for sound judgment of the quality of any piece of work.
>
> The lectures will treat of book production from the period of the illuminated manuscripts to the present time. The work of the men who made noteworthy contributions to the advancement or the deterioration of the art of fine book-making will be studied historically and technically. Considerable attention will be given to the presses which are now producing good work.
>
> The incidental aspects of the subject which affect the collecting of books will be considered. An important object of the course is to train the taste of book-buyers, and to cultivate a well-informed judgment of the value of rare and attractive volumes. The methods by which books of moderate importance are made to seem desirable will be explained. Old and modern examples of good and bad book-making will be shown. There will be opportunities to examine volumes belonging to members of the class and to express opinions as to their fundamental and commercial value.[5]

Winship's course fit perfectly in the scheme of higher education as envisioned by Harvard's president, A. Lawrence Lowell. "College men, it was tacitly understood, were about to assume greater responsibility in national affairs. . . . Intent on raising classroom standards, [Lowell] was equally resolved to banish the weather and sports as the common denominator of American conversation. This accounted for his insistence on what he called self-education, which for Lowell was a lifelong process."[6]

Winship's aim to "train the taste of book-buyers" profoundly influenced a surprising number of his students. Some, such as Arthur A. Houghton, Jr., and Carl H. Pforzheimer, became the greatest collectors of their time. Another, David P. Wheatland, went on to form one of the finest collections ever assembled of books on the history of electricity. He recalled how Winship "sat at the head of a long table and the rest of us arranged ourselves on either side. The marvelous books that appeared at these meetings were in themselves interesting and beautiful, and they detracted from whatever Mr. Winship was saying. We turned pages very slowly and with great care. . . . As I look back on this course I feel that it is one that has given me more lasting pleasure and 'education' than most of the others I took while an undergraduate."[7] Stanley Marcus, too, remembers most the "lasting pleasure" of this course. His reading had already introduced him to many of the great figures in Western thought, so in Winship's course the opportunity to examine closely the *editio princeps* of such works rendered by the great printers of the Renaissance was magical. Marcus still remembers holding the Gutenberg Bible and studying the perfection of its printed pages.

While such great books were slowly making their way around the table, Winship lectured on topics similar to those in his 1926 book, *Gutenberg to Plantin: An Outline of the Early History of Printing*, published by Harvard University Press. Its contents include: The Invention of Typography, The Spread of Printing, Printing As a Business, Printers Encounter the Renaissance, The Use of Pictures, The Decade of Picturebooks, The Learned Printers, The End of the Manuscript Tradition, and The End of the Era of the Master Printers. Later, when "GPW" drew upon his course notes to prepare the Rosenbach lectures in 1940, the results were published as *Printing in the Fifteenth Century,* which he dedicated "to a few score Harvard College students whose attendance at the meetings of that Fine Arts course on the History of the Printed Book between 1915 and 1931 contributed largely to formulating some of the opinions set forth in these lectures."

Winship delivered on the promise to give "considerable attention. . . to the presses which are now producing good work." This meant that Bruce Rogers was discussed in detail as the preeminent figure in American book design. Drawing upon a close personal friendship with Rogers and an intimate knowledge of and appreciation for his work, the educator was at his eloquent best in lecturing about "BR." His lectures marked the beginning of what Marcus called his own "preoccupation with Bruce Rogers," leading eventually to his forming one of the finest Bruce Rogers collections in private hands.

After graduating from Harvard in 1925, Marcus maintained his contact with Winship. Through his former teacher, he learned about books being designed by Bruce Rogers, and he even briefly employed one of Winship's sons, Stephen, at Neiman-Marcus. As Stephen Winship tells the story, he dropped out of college in 1938 after his freshman year and "went off on an open-ended hitch-hiking trip to see and learn about the USA."

> By late November I had reached Dallas and was running a bit short on funds, so I looked for a temporary job and wound up wrapping packages in the N-M basement.
>
> Although I wasn't writing home often, I did give my family a Dallas address and evidently my father informed Stanley of my being there. They contacted me and made me very welcome as a college boy away from home; I recall spending several weekend meals with Stanley and his attractive wife in an exciting house. . . . Stanley also introduced me to his father Herbert, the grand old man of N-M at that time; Herbert made much of me because I could beat his wife at Chinese Checkers (which Herbert couldn't) and they fed me from time to time.
>
> I was smart enough not to let the Marci know where I was working until late March. Herbert from time to time importuned me to seek a career in N-M; finally it got the better of me and I told Herbert what it was like to work in the lower depths of his store. Although I tried to backpedal, he did of course follow up with a visit to the basement to see for himself, which destroyed my *bona fides* with my fellow workers. So I picked up my meager effects and left town for Mexico.[8]

George Parker Winship expressed his gratitude to Stanley Marcus for providing his son a valuable experience. "We have at last heard from Steve, after his experience with what a Christmas rush really means, and I hasten to tell you that his parents are thoroughly appreciative of the opportunity you gave him to learn what he went away to get, and what he never could have gotten in any other way. I also want to assure you that he writes us that he also feels appreciative and grateful, although I infer that he had to make up some sleep before he was certain that this is the way he feels."[9] In the same letter Winship offered Marcus *The Journal of Madam Knight* designed by Bruce Rogers for which he, Winship, had written an introduction.

While Winship articulated the aesthetics of fine printing for Marcus, elsewhere at Harvard H. L. Mencken helped fire Marcus's passion for the defense of freedom of speech. The period in which Marcus grew up and was educated was marked in part by isolationism and intolerance. Indeed, he left Amherst after his freshman year because of its anti-Jewish climate. But this was also the time of the Espionage Act of 1917, under which the mails were declared open for inspection, the time when a Vermont minister was sentenced to fifteen years in prison for praising Jesus as a pacifist, the time when the Socialist leader Eugene V. Debs was jailed, when the governor of Iowa decreed that all telephone conversations must be carried on in English, and when a Connecticut clothing salesman who publicly criticized John D. Rockefeller and capitalism was jailed for six months. By 1924 the Ku Klux Klan counted its membership at four million. In 1925 the Scopes trial caught the attention of the nation, centering on a man who taught his students about Darwin's theory on the evolution of the human species.

Throughout the 1920s and into the 1930s H. L. Mencken was "the country's key social critic," with his *American Mercury* magazine reaching a circulation of 80,500 by April, 1926.[10] In the April 1926 issue Mencken published "Hatrack" by Herbert Asbury, a story with a prostitute as a central character. J. Frank Chase and the Boston Watch and Ward Society sounded the alarm, claiming the story was obscene and suggesting that Mencken, as editor of the magazine, be prosecuted. Chase delivered an address in which he claimed that "obscenity is a short way to the brothel, and the brothel is the entrance to Hell." He spoke of cafes as "the white slave marts of women's purity and the slaughter houses of men's honor." He also directed his invective at the New York publishers who were responsible for reams of immoral literature. For Chase, the evil effect of such literature would spell catastrophe. "A whole High School Class of unwedded mothers may be the result of a lascivious book."[11]

A new feud with the Watch and Ward Society simply fueled Mencken's resolve to fight them every way possible. What was a relatively minor assault by Chase should not go unanswered lest he be encouraged to mount more attacks. Thus, Mencken discussed the matter with Alfred A. Knopf, the publisher of the magazine, and Alfred's father, Samuel Knopf, the business manager. They decided to consult Arthur Garfield Hays, who had been a defense attorney in the Scopes trial the year before. Together they laid a plan for Mencken to go to Boston and publicly sell a copy of the April issue of the *American Mercury*, defying Chase to order his arrest. After all, Chase's agents had been threatening booksellers and magazine dealers around Boston. He had even managed to get one newsdealer arrested for selling "indecent" material. The subject of this attack was a Greek named Felix Caragianes, whose newsstand was located in Harvard Square.

Mencken's plan, announced to the press associations, worked like a well-executed football play. He obtained a peddler's license from the Superintendent of Peddlers in the Boston Health Department. When Chase tried to postpone the meeting with Mencken to avoid buying a copy of the offensive magazine, the editor's attorney countered that they would launch a general sale on the streets of Boston. Thus, at 2:00 P.M. on 5 April 1926 the encounter took place at the intersection of Park and Tremont streets, also known as Brimstone Corner. The afternoon papers were alerted, and when Mencken arrived shortly before the meeting, a huge crowd had assembled, including many Harvard students. Mencken offered the magazine to Chase, who in turn ordered his arrest for purveying "indecent literature."

Word spread immediately through newspapers all over America. Telegrams in support of Mencken began to arrive at the Copley Plaza Hotel where he was staying, and among the first of these was one from Maury Maverick in San Antonio, Texas: "I am with you. Run the jackasses to the cemetery." The graduate secretary of the Harvard Union invited Mencken to be a guest speaker on any date within the next ten days. Before he appeared on the 7th of April, two hundred students had subscribed to the luncheon within the first hour of its announcement. Six hundred students attended, with those unable to secure tickets lining the walls of the Union. Felix Frankfurter presided, and H. L. Mencken spoke about "the joys of fighting for freedom."[12] He told his audience that he had come to Boston "to make these people accuse a man openly in the courts, by laws which are the same for all and known to all in advance. I worked to establish the right of a man accused by this Watch and Ward Society to an open trial in the courts. . . . This sort of thing. . .is going on all over America at present. One advantage it has is that it will put well disposed liberty-loving men on notice. The worst thing in the state, though, is the indolence in the face of such outrages."[13]

Stanley Marcus, back at Harvard for a year in the MBA program, was present at this meeting. To this day he vividly recalls it and attributes to the experience his own life-long commitment "to think, to act, and to judge objectively."[14] The "Hatrack" case and H. L. Mencken's eloquent plea on behalf of freedom of the press gave Stanley Marcus an example and inspiration. When he returned to Dallas, his resolve would be tested by issues as diverse as the attempted suppression of art in the city's museum and the oppression of a high school student with long hair. Stanley Marcus's education at Harvard was complete. Among other things, it had prepared him for a life with books and an intense commitment to the significance of their contents, their aesthetics, and their availability to all who wanted to acquire and read them.

Chapter Two

The Book Club of Texas

With Stanley Marcus, the opportunities which Harvard offered a young man interested in books were unparalleled. He returned to Dallas fired with enthusiasm for books and art, happily renewing the membership in the Book Club of California which his parents had given him earlier. The books and keepsakes issued by the club exemplified some of the best contemporary typography by such important West Coast printers as John Henry Nash and the Grabhorns. Using the Book Club of California as something of a model, Marcus formed the Book Club of Texas to express his interest in typography and graphic design and to promote the growing sense of regional identity prevalent in the state in the late 1920s. But Harvard and the Book Club of California were not the sole factors influencing the development of the Book Club of Texas. Equally important to the shaping of the club and its publications were Stanley Marcus's emerging career at "The Store," his circle of Dallas friends, and the indomitable J. Frank Dobie.

At the store, Marcus soon assumed responsibility for the typography and design of printed promotional materials. Newspaper advertisements, shopping bags, garment boxes, letterheads, and eventually the Neiman-Marcus logo all came under his scrutiny. He persuaded his father that a new look would enhance the store's image with its highly discriminating clientele. As he was designing the new material himself or through ad agencies, his quest for new ideas led him to some of the best graphic artists of his time.

Thus, on a buying trip to New York City he sought out a young designer of promise, Raymond Loewy. As Marcus remembers it:

> Someone told me about a young French designer who had just come to this country who might be able to come up with a design for very little money. I paid him a visit and told him what I had in mind; he reached over, picked up

> a letter, quickly watercolored a rough sketch on the back of it, and asked, "How will this do?" I inquired how much he would charge me and he replied, "Would $75 be too much?" I told him I would have to think about it over the weekend, but I'd let him know the following Monday morning. His name was Raymond Loewy. I got approval from my father, and Loewy quickly completed the finished artwork, which became incorporated into our advertising and labeling for a time. I didn't see Mr. Loewy for about twenty-five years, during which time he had risen to fame as one of the great industrial designers of the world. At a cocktail party in California we met again. He looked at me with a smile and said, "We've both come a pretty long way since that day you called on me and gave me my first commission in America. You know, my prices have gone up quite a bit since then."[1]

On that same trip to New York Marcus also attended an exhibition of work by the great Paris book designer/binder F. L. Schmied. Thanks to Loewy, who had sketched his design on the back of his invitation to the opening of an exclusive showing of Schmied's work, Marcus was given the opportunity to see it. He presented Loewy's invitation at the door to the gallery and enjoyed the show immensely, smiling politely to all those who greeted him as Raymond Loewy!

While his new career expanded his knowledge of design, a circle of new Dallas friends with similar intellectual and aesthetic ideals also shared his interest in typography and printing. In time, many members of this group would play key roles in the establishment of a vital art community in Dallas, some as artists and administrators, others as board members and benefactors of many cultural endeavors, including the Dallas Artists League formed in 1932.

In the late 1920s and early 1930s these like-minded people would gather as a more loose-knit group. They included the Dallas Bohemian set: the artists Jerry Bywaters, Tom Stell, Alexandre Hogue, Olin Travis, and Otis Dozier, architects David Williams and O'Neil Ford, SMU professor Henry Nash Smith, and sports writer Horace McCoy, who also wrote *They Shoot Horses, Don't They?* On Tuesday evenings they would meet to share ideas on topics of mutual interest at the Carl Wyche home on Alice Street in the Oak Lawn neighborhood.[2]

On other occasions they would gather at "The Studio," David Williams's apartment with its large living room anchored at one end by a concert grand Steinway and at the other by an etching press. "The walls were hung with tapestries, etchings, and other art works, and lined with shelves of rare books and prints which [Williams] had collected all over Europe. His was reported to be one of the best rare book collections in the state of Texas.

Stanley Marcus, senior at Harvard University, 1925. Courtesy Stanley Marcus.

Officers

H. Stanley Marcus, *President*
John A. Lomax, *Treasurer*
David R. Williams, *Vice President*
John M. Hackler, *Secretary*

Charter Members

Mr. H. J. Abrams, *Dallas, Texas*
Mr. Frank Altschul, *New York, N.Y.*
Miss Dorothy Amann, *Dallas, Texas*
Mr. Barney Aronoff, *Dallas, Texas*
Mr. Rhodes Baker, *Dallas, Texas*
Mr. Burke Baker, *Houston, Texas*
Mr. L. Richard Bamberger, *New York, N.Y.*
Dr. W. J. Battle, *Austin, Texas*
Mr. R. L. Batts, *Austin, Texas*
Dr. H. Y. Benedict, *Austin, Texas*
Mr. Saml. T. Bledsoe, *Chicago, Ill.*
Mr. Alfred Bromberg, *Dallas, Texas*
Mr. H. L. Bromberg, *Dallas, Texas*
Mr. L. N. Bromberg, *Dallas, Texas*
Mr. R. S. Buddy, *Glen Falls, New York*
Mr. Wm. H. Burges, *El Paso, Texas*
Mr. Bennett A. Cerf, *New York, N.Y.*
Mr. W. H. Clark, *Dallas, Texas*
Mr. Harry I. Cohen, *Houston, Texas*
Mr. J. Irvin Cornwell, *Waxahachie, Texas*
Mr. Harry Benge Crozier, *Dallas, Texas*
Mrs. Wirt Davis, *Dallas, Texas*
Mr. J. P. Dreibelbis, *Dallas, Texas*
Mrs. Mary Pierce Ebie, *Dallas, Texas*
El Paso Library, *El Paso, Texas*
Mrs. Fred F. Florence, *Dallas, T*
Mr. John M. Hackler, *Dallas, Te*
Miss Violet Hayden, *Dallas, Texa*
Mr. Harry Hertzberg, *San Anton*
Mr. J. A. Hosie, *Dallas, Texas*
Houston Public Library, *Houston,*
Mr. L. H. Hubbard, *Denton, Texas*
Mr. J. E. Jarratt, *San Antonio, Te*
Mrs. Henry S. Jacobus, *Dallas, Te*

Mrs. Hobart Key, *Marshall, Texas*
Mr. W. H. Kittrell, Jr., *Dallas, Texas*
Miss Helen Knox, *New York, N.Y.*
Mr. Arthur Kramer, *Dallas, Texas*
Miss Emma Lee, *Galveston, Texas*
Mr. Adrian Levy, *Galveston, Texas*
Mr. Marion Levy, *Galveston, Texas*
Mrs. Benj. F. Lewis, *Dallas, Texas*
Mrs. Polly H. Lobdell, *Dallas, Texas*
Mr. John A. Lomax, *Dallas, Texas*
Mr. W. E. McMahon, *Mexico City, Mexico*
Mr. Theodore Mack, *Fort Worth, Texas*
Mr. Clarence Mallinson, *Dallas, Texas*
Mr. H. Stanley Marcus, *Dallas, Texas*
Mr. John Mayfield, *Austin, Texas*
Mrs. Pearl C. McCracken, *Denton, Texas*
Mr. J. E. Michalson, *Dallas, Texas*
Mrs. L. R. Munger, *Dallas, Texas*
Mrs. Carrie Neiman, *Dallas, Texas*
Mrs. Paul Perella, *Dallas, Texas*
Mr. Donald Rein, *Houston, Texas*
Miss Fannie Ratchford, *Austin, Texas*
Mr. Melrich V. Rosenberg, *New York, N.Y.*
Mr. H. B. Seay, *Mercedes, Texas*
Mr. W. F. Shaw, *Mercedes, Texas*

Mr. Frost

five hundred
printed for dis
rein company o

THE BOOK CLUB OF TEXAS

The Book Club of Texas has been formed for the purpose of fostering arts pertaining to the production of fine books. It will function in two ways: *first*, by the publication of books that will typify the best standards of bookmaking, in regard to subject matter, printing, binding, and typographical design; *second*, by sponsoring exhibitions and lectures pertinent to these interests. ¶ The Club will be governed by a board of eleven directors, who will conduct the club on a non-commercial as well as on a non-profit basis. The Club's publications will be issued at the rate of three or four a year, in limited editions, and will be sold to members only. ¶ Membership, which will be open to book collectors and those interested in the activities of the club, will be limited to three hundred members. Membership will involve no responsibilities other than the payment of the annual dues of $10.00; there will be no initiation fee. ¶ The Club offers its members the opportunity of purchasing books of literary or historical significance in beautiful formats at the actual cost of production. Publication prices will probably vary from $2.00 to $15.00. Members are not obliged to purchase each book, though it is hoped that the outstanding character of the publications will warrant the purchase of each volume. ¶ The Officers and Directors of The Book Club of Texas take pleasure in inviting you to become a member.

First prospectus issued by the Book Club of Texas, 1929, listing officers and charter members. One of 500 numbered quarto-size broadsides printed on handmade Italian paper. Courtesy Allen Maxwell.

TALES *of the*
Mustang

BY J. FRANK DOBIE

ILLUSTRATIONS BY JERRY BYWATERS

1936
THE BOOK CLUB OF TEXAS
DALLAS

Title page from the sixth publication of the Book Club of Texas, *Tales of the Mustang,* by J. Frank Dobie, 1936.

John H. McGinnis on the steps of Dallas Hall, SMU, ca. 1923. Courtesy DeGolyer Library.

For John McGinnis

Whose critical judgement, enthusiasm, and unselfish cooperation made the publication of this book possible.

H Stanley Marcus

July 4, 1932.
Dallas.

Inscription to John H. McGinnis by H. Stanley Marcus on publication of *Miss Zilphia Gant* by William Faulkner (Dallas: Book Club of Texas, 1932). Courtesy DeGolyer Library.

Autobiographies, histories, and books on architecture, art, and design dominated the collection, which included several editions dating from the sixteenth century."[3]

This was the setting in which Stanley Marcus and his new friends would meet. Along with their interest in ideas, in the arts, in typography and printing, they also shared an interest in regionalism. To that end they sponsored the highly successful Alice Street Carnival described by Rick Stewart in *Lone Star Regionalism*:

> Alice Street was only one block long, and unpaved. . . . But on June 29 and 30, 1932, the little sandy street became an outdoor exhibition space for seventy-six artists, an "art carnival" where, to the strains of a Mexican orchestra and "Captain Lucey's colored band," seven thousand people attended to view and possibly purchase works by many local artists and artisans. Inspired by the successful Washington Square art festivals in Greenwich Village, this exhibition marked the arrival of a strong regionalist position on the Dallas art scene.[4]

They also wrote about what they thought, and tested their ideas in a variety of publications. Their most challenging forum was the *Southwest Review*, edited by John McGinnis and Henry Nash Smith in Dallas. With contributing editors who included Mary Austin, B. A. Botkin, Witter Bynner, John Chapman, J. Frank Dobie, and Howard Mumford Jones, the journal enjoyed an erudite and influential role in helping to define what it termed a "new regionalism." Henry Nash Smith wrote the manifesto entitled "Culture" for the *Southwest Review* in 1928, in which he stated that "the culture of Texas must depend finally on one thing: the ability of Texans to relate themselves to their specific environment."[5] A year later Alexandre Hogue, noted member of "The Dallas Nine" artists, stated in an article on Victor Higgins for the *Southwest Review* that the "American artist in general will come of age only when he has the stamina to blaze his own trails through the part of his country in which he lives."[6]

The same year, the editors of the *Southwest Review* asked members of their advisory board to respond to the following question: "Do you think the Southwestern landscape and common traditions can (or should) develop a culture recognizable as unique, and more satisfying and profound than our present imported culture and art?"[7] The responses were affirmative, with Mary Austin leading the way in saying that the "business of interpreting the West in wise and suitable ways of living will be studious and long," but she believed there was a disposition for people to search out what was "native both to themselves and to their land." J. Frank Dobie titled his contribution

"True Culture Is Eclectic, But Provincial," in which he noted that the Southwest had "inherited a turn of idiom, a history, a tradition of character, a flavor of the soil that are highly individual." Stanley Vestal wrote that the Southwest had already "developed a culture recognizable as unique" and that it was "rooted farther back in time than any other regional culture in the United States: it is alive, and we may therefore assume that it is satisfying and profound in its effects."[8]

Marcus added to the momentum for articulating a regional culture in 1928 by gathering ten like-minded people for lunch to discuss the concept of a Texas book club which would publish works of regional importance exemplifying the best precepts of graphic design, much as California was doing. Returning from lunch, he called John McGinnis, who was also the book review editor at the *Dallas Morning News*. He followed the call with a letter outlining plans for the new organization:

> Dear John: Confirming our telephone conversation of a few minutes ago, I am writing you the full particulars about the formation of the Book Club of Texas. At a luncheon today, at which about ten people were present, formation plans were put through for the organizing of the Book Club of Texas, which will publish three or four books a year for members only. These books will represent the highest standards of bookmaking in regard to their typographical design and to their subject matter.
>
> This organization will be conducted on a non-commercial and non-profit making basis, and will be open to any persons who are interested in collecting fine books. At the present time it is impossible to say just what the publication price of these books will be, but in all probability it will vary between $2.00 and $15.00.
>
> As you know, there is no organization of this character in this part of the country. In the east we find the Caxton Club of Cleveland, the Grolier Club of New York, the Carteret Club of Newark, and in the west we find the Book Club of California.
>
> Our aim is to limit the membership to about 300 and we will expect to get this membership from not only the state of Texas, but the adjacent states as well. Anyone, however, at any place may become a member if he so desires. We feel sure that after the publication of our first volume, our membership will be filled.
>
> We hope to have these books produced in Texas wherever the printing facilities are adequate for our needs. In some cases, however, we may have them printed by some outstanding printer in some other part of the country, such as Bruce Rogers, Elmer Adler or Henry Nash.
>
> Toward the end of next week we expect to have a second meeting, at which a larger group of people will be present. At that time we will elect officers and board of governors.[9]

At the next meeting the Book Club of Texas took further shape with the election of officers: Stanley Marcus, president; David Williams, vice-president; John Hackler, secretary; and John Lomax, treasurer. Williams and Marcus would be concerned with the artistic direction of the books. Lomax, "a folklore collector and author-turned Republic Bank trust officer," would look for "literary material worth publication."[10] Hackler, an attorney, would draw up the necessary papers to secure incorporation for the new club as a nonprofit enterprise.

Once the organizational elements were in place, the club created a logo for its colophon. "Since we were proposing to publish material relative to the Southwest, we thought it fitting for the mark to reflect that interest. Accordingly, Williams designed a mark depicting a branding iron with the initials 'B.C.T.' surrounded by the brands of some famous Texas ranches. After all, a branding iron and a colophon served similar purposes, even though one was used to label a cow and the other to mark the origin of a book."[11]

Next came the prospectus. With no tradition of fine printing in Texas, Marcus turned to the Rein Company in Houston, a commercial printing house that had produced a few books and was likely to be responsive to the club's purposes. The result was five hundred numbered quarto-size broadsides on handmade Italian paper.

But even before the official prospectus was ready, the organizers of the club were securing memberships from friends and acquaintances. Lomax solicited a large group of associates in the Texas Folklore Society and elsewhere. His letter to L. W. Payne in the English Department at the University of Texas is characteristic of his approach. "The Club is being adequately fostered, principally under the direction of Mr. Stanley Marcus of Dallas, a young Harvard graduate, who has developed a great interest in rare books in appropriate and artistic form. Will Hogg of Austin is a director of the Club, as are also William H. Burges of El Paso and Dr. [H. Y.] Benedict."[12] At the time of this letter, the Book Club of Texas already had over one hundred paid members.

Lomax's network reached a variety of Texans interested in good books. As this note to his good friend Frost Woodhull shows, he welcomed them all, from retired circus performers to young attorneys with political ambitions, and had a little fun in the process.

> Harry Hertzberg has already come into the Club.[13] Maury [Maverick] has had no chance; although, on your recommendation I am glad to open the doors for him. You applied some strange adjective to him which in your own handwriting I am still unable to make out. I probably wouldn't know the meaning

of the word, even if I could read it. You will keep me wondering what it is; meanwhile, I can't report to Maury what name you have called him.[14]

Should you come to Dallas at any time I would like to show you my home. I built an old fashioned rambling house away out in the trees, eight miles from Dallas, where the owls put me to sleep at night and the squirrels and birds awake me in the morning. You won't hear the clang of a street car or the pop of an automobile. Such seclusion in these times makes possible an undisturbed enjoyment of various liquid refreshments. I would like to take you out there and have you lie in a hammock under the trees and watch the stars through the open spaces with a table at your elbow bearing all that is necessary to make you forget, at least temporarily, the short-comings of life. I really believe you would enjoy it and I know I should.[15]

With the prospectus sent and membership fees providing sufficient working capital for the first book, the time-consuming task of selecting appropriate manuscripts began. Lomax and Marcus, possibly with help from Dobie, at last selected a piece from Yoakum's *History of Texas*, first printed in 1855. Appealing to an interest in Texas history, the prospectus for the new book read: "The Book Club of Texas announces as its first publication the Memoir of Col. Ellis P. Bean written by himself, about the year 1816, with a postscript by Mattie Austin Hatcher. Nothing could be more suitable, it has seemed to the directors, for the first publication than the Memoir of Ellis P. Bean shedding, as it does, a most significant light on the Texas of early days. At the same time, it presents an absorbing and romantic tale told in the piquant language of the semi-illiterate hero of the narrative."[16]

Two hundred copies were produced by the Rein Company of Houston for sale only to members of the club. The octavo volume printed in Monotype Caslon on handmade English paper sold for $9.50 per copy, a relatively expensive book for its time. The illustrations were drawn by David Williams, the skilled architect who was a founding board member of the club.

The choice of the Ellis Bean memoir as the first publication of the Book Club of Texas was inspired. Not only did it fill a gap at the time, it has continued to be regarded as an important source of information on early nineteenth-century Texas history.[17] J. Frank Dobie included it in one of his earliest courses on Life and Literature of the Southwest, procuring additional copies from the Book Club of Texas so the University of Texas Library could meet the demands for it.

Two years had elapsed from the club's conception to this first publication in March, 1930. The difficulty in finding suitable manuscripts, the growing Depression, and busy schedules of those involved all combined to temper the original objective of issuing three or four new books a year. Nevertheless, the club was able to announce for June, 1930, its second publication, a new edition of *Eneas Africanus* by Harry Stillwell Edwards, an epistolary tale of the wanderings of a faithful Negro after the Civil War and his eventual return to his home place. The printer would be Hal Marchbanks in New York City, former owner of a job printing shop in Ennis, Texas, which he left in 1904 to move East where he sought better opportunity to gain recognition.[18]

Though Dobie saw no reason for the club to publish *Eneas Africanus*, since it had already been reprinted several times, his view was not shared by other club members. The book sold more copies than any of the other six titles produced between 1930 and 1937. It was so successful that at the end of the year the Book Club of Texas adapted the map David Williams conceived and drew for the book and sent it to the membership as a broadside greeting "for the approaching year."

The third offering from the Book Club of Texas was *Code Duello: Letters Concerning the Prentiss-Tucker Duel of 1842*, which came as the result of letters made available for publication by the granddaughter of General Quitman, Senator Prentiss's second in the affair of honor. The prospectus for the new book stated that the club was offering *Code Duello* "in pursuance with its policy of delving into the historical 'byroads' of the South and the Southwest." Published for the first time, this series of letters was between "three Southern gentlemen of pre-Civil War days regarding the very delicate subject of a gentleman's honor which could be satisfied only through the fighting of a duel."[19]

Code Duello was designed by William A. Kittredge, one of the foremost typographers of the day. Kittredge had recently completed a new edition of *Moby Dick* with illustrations by Rockwell Kent, which was receiving much favorable notice. Marcus was particularly pleased to secure his services. The book was printed at the Lakeside Press in Chicago. For the first time there was no Texas connection to the design and production of a Book Club of Texas title. Nevertheless, *Code Duello* accomplished something important for the new club by gaining national attention in two respected design forums. First, the American Institute of Graphic Arts in New York selected it as one of the Fifty Books of the Year. Second, Chicago's Society of Typographic Arts gave it an Award of Excellence in its Sixth Annual Exhibition of Chicago Fine Printing.

The club continued to publish books of regional interest with its fourth title, *Miss Zilphia Gant* by William Faulkner. John McGinnis, editor of the *Southwest Review*, brought the work to Marcus's attention. Constantly alert to good writing by little-known authors in the region, McGinnis had written Faulkner for a story to publish in the *Southwest Review*. Faulkner, still struggling for recognition, sent him a typescript that had been rejected by several publishers. The story was clearly of publishable quality, but not at SMU with its Methodist-church affiliation. As time would prove, a story built around a young, secluded, masturbating woman would not go unnoticed by the university's administration.

Marcus found the story well written but too short to be published as a book, so he asked Henry Nash Smith, a member of the English Department faculty at SMU, for a brief introduction. He also asked Smith to fly to Mississippi to meet Faulkner and gain his permission to publish the story as a book instead of a contribution to McGinnis's periodical. As Smith later recalled, the trip was frightful in an "old, corrugated aluminum, Ford, trimotor plane" buffeted by thunderstorms brewed from a hurricane down in the Gulf of Mexico. But he met with Faulkner and brought back the good word. "Mr. Stanley Marcus, Mr. Smith asks me to put in writing my permission to print *Miss Zilphia Gant* in book form. Here it is. He also tells me that it is agreed that all rights to further printing of this story in any form or manner remain with me. With thanks and best wishes in the success in the venture, I am yours sincerely, William Faulkner."[20]

Permission in hand, production moved ahead, with Marcus undertaking the graphic design himself.[21] By May, 1932, Marcus could write McGinnis that publication of *Miss Zilphia Gant* was scheduled for the middle of June, with printing being done by J. M. Colville & Son and binding by the American Beauty Binding Company. He noted that "we have made a careful investigation of printing facilities and feel we should be able to produce a book that will reflect credit upon the Club and upon bookmaking facilities of Dallas."[22]

Inundated with summer commitments, Marcus delayed sending McGinnis a copy of the new book until the fourth of July, but the delay did not keep him from expressing his gratitude.

> Dear Mr. McGinnis—Before leaving for New York I want to express to you my sincere appreciation for all you have done towards making 'Miss Zilphia Gant' possible and at the same time so successful. I have been terribly tied up during the past two weeks with the summer concerts or you would have heard from me sooner. Please don't think me ungrateful. I am sending under separate cover two copies of 'Miss Zilphia,' one of which I have taken the liberty to inscribe. If you write Henry Smith will you be kind enough to tell him that I am holding two copies for him as well, and will give them to him upon his return to Dallas. With best regards, H. Stanley Marcus.[23]

Along with this letter were the two books, one inscribed "For John McGinnis, whose critical judgment, enthusiasm, and unselfish cooperation made the publication of this book possible. H. Stanley Marcus. July 4, 1932. Dallas."[24]

Meanwhile, for Smith the battle had just begun. At the time of publication, he was teaching and traveling in Europe, his return to Dallas scheduled for the beginning of the fall term. When he stopped by the American Express office in Paris to check for mail, he found two letters, the first from SMU President Charles Selecman informing him that he had been fired from his post in the English Department for his association with the publication of a scandalous story by William Faulkner. The other letter was from John O. Beaty, English Department chairman, suggesting that Smith stay in Europe for a year or so until the scandal subsided.

Nevertheless, Smith took the next boat home to confront his accusers, and was placed on leave until the issue could be taken to the Board of Trustees in January, 1933. Marcus mounted a campaign offensive on behalf of the club to make the university's administration reconsider their actions. With the tone of a legal brief, his letter to Selecman made it clear that the implications of the president's judgment of Smith reached beyond the campus to influential members of the community, whose intelligence and feelings were also impugned:

> Whereas, it has been reported to the directors of the Book Club of Texas, that the President of Southern Methodist University, Dr. Charles C. Selecman, has demanded of Mr. Henry Smith, Assistant Professor of English, his resignation from the faculty of the University, and that Mr. Smith has been suspended from teaching classes therein;
>
> And, whereas, it is further reported that this action has been taken by the President at the suggestion of, and with the concurrence of, Dr. John O. Beaty, Head of the English faculty of Southern Methodist University because the said Henry Smith did write at the invitation of the directors of the Book Club the preface to 'Miss Zilphia Gant' by William Faulkner, the Club's most recent volume, published in limited edition for its members in May last;
>
> And, whereas, it is further reported that this book has been characterized by Dr. Selecman or by Dr. Beaty or by both as being wholly foul and its sponsorship as being an unpardonable act;
>
> Therefore, be it resolved by the directors of the Book Club of Texas that if the reports that have been made to members of the board be true, that we deeply deplore the acts and expressions and attitude both of the President of the Uni-

versity and the Head of the English faculty, that we regard their acts and attitude and characterizations as a serious and unwarranted reflection on the directors of the Book Club, as an executive group and as individuals, a reflection on their group and individual intelligence, an imputation against their refined judgment of literary values, as individuals and collectively, a defamation of the delicacy and fine feeling possessed by them as individuals and as a group;

And be it further resolved that the officers be instructed to write Dr. Selecman and Dr. Beaty and request their written expression as to the truth of the reports that have been made, and if it be true, as has been represented, then, that the officers be empowered to take such action as the facts warrant and to defend before the intelligent world, the Book Club, its directors and officers and to discuss the propriety in inviting Henry Smith to write the preface, and the propriety in his granting that request, and the fitness of any and all persons and things that may be involved or associated in the matter.

Yours very truly,
THE BOOK CLUB OF TEXAS
H. STANLEY MARCUS,
President[25]

Through the fall the controversy continued. Members of the club wrote letters supporting Smith, while John O. Beaty solicited support for firing the professor by writing letters full of dark hints of the impending destruction of "all the Christian usefulness of Southern Methodist University." He sent mimeographed letters addressed to "My dear Pastor," about a "situation" which would make SMU "a center for the propaganda of obscenity and degeneracy and to make it the sponsor of a dastardly attack on Jesus Christ." "I wish I could give you full details, but the point at issue involves topics of such a nature that I hesitate to name them in a letter. If you live in or near Dallas or can come to Dallas I shall be glad to give you fuller details."[26] He also told of a trustee, "a prominent Dallas member of the Executive Committee," who, "fearing a little group of Dallas people who have always been hostile to the University, forced the administration to reverse its policy and to surrender to the subversive element."

Not all of Beaty's pastors responded as he had hoped. Harold G. Cooke, Pastor of the First Methodist Church in Paris, Texas, replied:

Now, Professor Beaty, I cannot comprehend the motive that actuated you in sending out such a veiled, damaging, ill-advised and unauthorized communication. You tell us to keep it confidential. You publish to the world what should be handled in executive secrecy. Whatever may have been your motive, you have done the University an irreparable injury. If you are against the present administration, you have made your removal necessary along with the administration that you attack.

I do not know what church you belong to, but such methods as you have employed look more like Frank Norris than anything of the brand of Southern Methodism. You have released in this letter currents of suspicion, distrust, and bitterness that will do lasting injury. I think in justice to Southern Methodist University you should mail out an apology and retraction to every person to whom this letter has gone.[27]

Nor did the SMU faculty endorse his efforts. Eighteen sent a signed statement to Selecman declaring that they wished "to deny and repudiate the charges and innuendoes of the letter as false and unjustified" while also commending "the action of the Administration in retaining Mr. Henry Smith on the faculty of the University."[28] Among the signatories were Herbert Gambrell, H. A. Trexler, and Frank K. Rader.

Finally, at their January meeting, the SMU Board of Trustees reinstated Smith to his full-time position. But the story was not quite over. Beaty refused to allow Smith back into the English Department, thereby forcing the university to move him to the Department of Comparative Literature.

As time would prove, the tempest did no lasting harm to Smith or to Marcus. Smith taught at SMU for several more years, eventually moving to Harvard, then to the University of Minnesota, and finally to the University of California at Berkeley, building a distinguished career all along the way. He and Marcus remained good friends, strengthened by their fight to defend their rights as writer and publisher. In later years Marcus would joke with Smith, saying that he would never have been fired and might still be teaching at SMU had he not agreed to fly over to Oxford, Mississippi, to secure a letter of release from William Faulkner and then write an introduction for the Book Club of Texas.

Meanwhile, amidst the localized controversy over *Miss Zilphia Gant*, news came from New York that it was selected as one of the Fifty Books of the Year by the American Institute of Graphic Arts, making it the second Book Club of Texas imprint to be so honored, and garnering for Stanley Marcus his first national book design award. Less than a decade had passed since his introduction to the world of rare books and typographic design by George Parker Winship in the Widener Library at Harvard.

In 1933, with the aim of further contributing to the cultural climate of the community, the club sponsored free public lectures by notable figures in American arts and letters. Frank Lloyd Wright delivered the first lecture on Tuesday evening, February 28, at the Little Theatre. Marcus opened with an outline of the history and purposes of the club, following which David

Williams introduced the speaker to an audience of several hundred. Wright opened his lecture, titled "My Life and Works," with a poem by Kahlil Gibran expressing the idea that "your house is your larger body." He then made an eloquent plea for his idea of "organic architecture," its character determined by the building materials to be used.[29]

This first public appearance of Wright in Dallas may have marked the beginning of his influence on the Dallas community. Certainly Marcus considered employing him for his own home, as he wrote to David Williams the following year.[30] "Billie and I are thinking of building a house and would like to build a contemporary, functional house, rather than a period one. If you were here, naturally we would like to have you do it, but since you are not, in your opinion is there anyone in Dallas or surrounding cities who is competent to build a frank, sincere, modern home? If there is no one around here, what would you think of Frank Lloyd Wright?"[31]

Williams replied that "as to Frank Lloyd Wright, of course I would like to see one of his jobs in Dallas, but I do not know whether the old 'cootie' would do just the slick sort of modern house which I think you want. If he would stick to the style of the thing such as he sketched out for the people in Colorado, which you remember he called 'The Mesa House' with some modifications to suit the Dallas scene, it would probably be about right."[32]

Marcus ultimately turned to Wright for a design, but found him too inflexible to work with. Nevertheless, Wright did design two Dallas structures, the Kalita Humphries Theatre for the Dallas Theatre Center on Turtle Creek as well as the Gillin House on Rockbrook in the Landsdowne Estates area north of Bluffview.

The next Book Club of Texas speaker in 1933 was Rockwell Kent, noted artist, writer, and book illustrator. There was already in Dallas a keen interest in creating, exhibiting, and collecting original graphic works. A landmark exhibition in November, 1932, by the Dallas Art Association drew record attendance and featured paintings and prints by such contemporary artists as José Clemente Orozco, George Bellows, Wanda Gag, Louis Lozowick, Richard Day, Howard Cook, and Rockwell Kent.[33] Kent was warmly received by the Book Club of Texas audience. Marcus commissioned him to design a bookplate shortly thereafter.

The club's book for 1933 was a memoir by Alexander Watkins Terrell (1827-1912), who served in the Confederate Army as lieutenant colonel of the 34th Texas Regiment and after the war fled to Mexico, where he served as Chef de Battalion with French forces under Emperor Maximilian.[34] Pleased with the work of William Kittredge and the Lakeside Press, Marcus again turned to Chicago for Terrell's *From Texas to Mexico and the Court of Maximilian in 1865*. For the third time in as many years, the American Institute of Graphic Arts selected a club publication as one of the Fifty Books of the Year.

To capitalize on the club's typographic success, Marcus planned a showing of the Fifty Books of the Year, including the most recent award winner from Texas. The exhibit at the Dallas Public Art Galleries opened on Monday, November 21, with an evening lecture on "Modern Book Printing" for club members and their invited friends. It then opened to the public.

Marcus was experiencing success in other realms as well as book production. His responsibilities at the store were increasing. By 1935 he would be Executive Vice-President. The search for new titles continued, but the pace of publishing slackened. To sustain interest in the organization, Marcus developed an innovative cooperative venture with six of the leading book collectors' societies in the country. For the first time, members of any one of the societies could purchase the publications of all the others. The opportunity was first announced to members of the Book Club of Texas in a letter Marcus sent on 26 April 1934. Therein he identified the participating clubs: the Grolier Club, the Club of Odd Volumes, the Caxton Club, the Carteret Book Club, the Book Club of Texas, and the Book Club of California. The arrangement would last for sixty days, with members of all the clubs receiving a joint catalogue of available titles and prices.

When the special catalogue printed by the Grabhorn Press arrived, it listed fifty-seven books grouped according to the club responsible for their publication. The introduction set out the concept: "The books described on the following pages comprise a representative collection of the publications of six leading book collectors' societies of the United States. For a period of sixty days, from May 1 to June 30, 1934, a member of any of the participating clubs will be eligible to purchase the publications of the others. This joint sale of their publications is the first cooperative venture in which these book collectors' clubs have engaged. In nearly every case, it is the first time the clubs have ever made their publications available to any except their own members." The purpose was "to emphasize the common ends to which these collectors' societies have long been devoted, and in particular their important contributions toward the development of the arts pertaining to fine book production."[35]

The Book Club of Texas offered its first five titles. Thus with one innovative stroke, the four-year-old Book Club of Texas was keeping very good company and introducing its work to a highly select group of collectors around the country, including members of the oldest book club in America, The Grolier Club.

Following a two-year hiatus in producing a new work, the club published J. Frank Dobie's *Tales of the Mustang* in 1936. Noted as "a literary highlight of the Texas Centennial observance,"[36] this book was the second club title printed by the Rein Company in Houston. It was set in Garamond type and carried illustrations by Jerry Bywaters. In time, it would become one of the organization's most sought after titles, though it suffered a few bumps with Dobie along the way.

"Mr. Texas," never an ordinary author, bristled at an amateurish attempt at editing by a member of the club's board, but the problem was quickly resolved. Neither was he particularly pleased with the somewhat delicate-looking binding for a book on such a robust subject. Five years after its publication, Dobie had the occasion to inscribe Everette L. DeGolyer's copy and to document his feelings in retrospect: "Friend DeGolyer — This book is supposed to exist for the sake of illustrating and promoting the art of printing. This is good, but I can't keep from damning the violet-half-hidden-from-the-eye kind of binding. Mustangs penned up in such daintiness. Your friend, Frank Dobie."[37]

For its 1937 publication the club produced the first English translation of an important work on Champ D'Asile about the ill-fated attempt by the French to establish a large colony in 1818 near present-day Liberty, Texas. Fannie E. Ratchford, noted rare-book librarian at the University of Texas and one of the earliest members of the club, provided the introduction. Design and printing for *The Story of Champ D'Asile* was done by Walter Goodwin at his Rydal Press in Santa Fe. Goodwin, after ten years with the Philadelphia publisher J. B. Lippincott, had moved to Santa Fe in 1933 to set up his private press, which was best known for producing the Writer's Editions books by Alice Corbin, Peggy Pond Church, Haniel Long, and others.[38] This offering was a most attractive volume, even with the unconventional placement of the table of contents following the introduction.

When *The Story of Champ D'Asile* was published, Marcus and the board had every intention of continuing the organization. Yet heavy demands on their time were increasing and beginning to take their toll. The Depression was subsiding, war in Europe loomed ahead, and professional responsibilities were growing.

When no exciting manuscript prospects were uncovered by the board for several years, Walter Prescott Webb and Carl Hertzog came forward with ideas. In March of 1940 Webb approached Marcus with the concept for a book on Santa Rita, the first well in the West Texas oil field that brought great wealth to the University of Texas. Webb suggested a copublishing arrangement between the Texas State Historical Association and the Book Club of Texas. The subject appealed to Marcus but failed when it bogged down under threat of legal action by some of the principals in the drilling operation.

By then Marcus had decided to close the club and began looking for a grand finale. Tom Lea, Paul Horgan, and Carl Hertzog proposed a *Calendar of Twelve Travelers through the Pass of the North*. Lea had conceived the idea for the book in 1938 because comparatively few people knew and appreciated the history of El Paso, "100 years older than Plymouth Rock and much more interesting and romantic," as Hertzog later wrote.[39] For each of the twelve subjects in the book there would be a full-page illustration facing one large page of readable type. To finance or promote the idea, they needed an expensive "sample." "Not by choice, but as a means to an end, the Hotel Paso del Norte was induced to pay for a series of three drawings to be used as menu covers."[40]

From the zinc etchings needed for the menu covers Carl Hertzog printed some sample pages for the book showing two of the characters, the related text, a title page, and a table of contents. Two of these press proofs were printed in two colors and bound in an appropriate cloth. But because neither Lea nor Hertzog was successful in tapping the wealthy El Paso business community for a favorable response, they put aside the concept.

Then, in the late spring of 1940, Paul Horgan paid Hertzog a visit. Horgan wanted to meet the "printer at the Pass" whose work was by now bringing much favorable attention to the Southwest. He had a keen interest in typography and printing, having designed some of his own work. From San Patricio, New Mexico, where he had been staying with Peter and Henriette Hurd on their nearby Sentinel Ranch, Horgan drove to El Paso. With their shared commitment to the careful production of printed work, their meeting in May, 1940, was pleasant for both Horgan and Hertzog. As the visit progressed, talk turned naturally to projects still in the development stage. No doubt Hertzog showed Horgan the dummy for *Twelve Travelers* with great pride. Not only did Horgan respond with enthusiasm, he was captivated by the concept and the individual historic subjects selected for the book. Soon he and Hertzog were talking about an even more grand production—one for which Paul Horgan would write a more extended piece on each of the twelve pioneers.

Since the cost estimate would take another significant jump with the expansion of the biographical and historical sketches, the need for a patron for the project arose once again. This time Hertzog's sights were directed toward the person in Texas most likely to respond favorably. Perhaps Stanley Marcus would like the idea for the Book Club of Texas.

Horgan returned to Sentinel Ranch fired with enthusiasm and carrying a sample dummy for *Twelve Travelers*. His letter of thanks to Carl Hertzog was full of genuine admiration: "A word to thank you for the very kind reception you gave me, and for the beautiful book. I am certainly delighted to have examples of your creative work in printing, and [rejoiced] to know with my own eyes and meeting that we have so fine an artist in the most basic of civilization's crafts, here in the Southwest." He would send the dummy to Marcus, whom he knew, "with a warm introduction of its merits. It must be published in the style to which you are accustomed."[41]

Hertzog, too, would test Marcus's interest. He wrote in July, and received a reply from Marcus's secretary. "Mr. Marcus has just left Dallas for a few weeks, but he has asked me to write and tell you that he was very much interested in your 'Calendar of the Twelve Travelers'. Would you let me know, for him, the cost of printing 200 copies of this book?"[42] Hertzog replied that he already had seven of the necessary thirteen drawings and engravings (one of which was more than likely being considered for the title page). The cuts, special type, and preliminary work had cost $650, and the balance of the drawings and zinc engravings, along with the typesetting, printing, and binding of two hundred books "in the de luxe manner" would cost an additional $1,200. He emphasized that with Paul Horgan writing the text for the book, its quality and popularity would be all the more enhanced.[43]

In August, Marcus and Hertzog met to discuss the project further, at which time Hertzog offered to omit the earlier expenses and figure the cost from that point forward. Hertzog wrote to Horgan, "He said, 'It's a deal' and I turned pale. Mr. Marcus is going to give up the Book Club of Texas and will make this book a grand finale. It will be a book club publication exclusively. Undoubtedly Mr. Marcus was influenced by the fact that I told him you had agreed to write the text. This is one of the strings tied to the deal so I hope you are not too busy."[44]

Marcus told Hertzog that he needed five hundred copies of a prospectus, for which the printer thought the DeVargas drawing was the most spectacular of those in hand. Thus he asked Horgan to write the copy as soon as possible on DeVargas and enclosed one of the type pages showing the amount of text needed. Then Hertzog informed Marcus that the entire project had been "set in motion," with Paul Horgan agreeing to write the text and Tom Lea delaying work on a mural so he could finish the illustrations for the book. The paper for the prospectus was ordered, although Hertzog was concerned that the oversize format (11 1/2" x 15 1/2") would be a problem in the mail.

Hertzog also gained authorization from the manager of the Hotel Paso del Norte to use the seven characters appearing on their menu covers in the new book. In exchange for the courtesy, the manager of the hotel asked that the Paso del Norte be permitted to use the five additional historical figures being drawn by Tom Lea for *Twelve Travelers*.

Time passed. Hertzog received nothing from Horgan. By the end of October, he wrote a polite inquiry, saying he was "anxious to show Stanley Marcus something as he might cool off or change his mind."[45] Through Peter Hurd news reached Tom Lea that Horgan was making some progress on the writing, but still no word.

Finally, in November Horgan sent his typescript on DeVargas. It was almost four times as long as the sample that Hertzog had sent. Horgan explained that he was unable to say anything useful in the limits of three hundred words and observed that the "textual vitality of the book must be equal to its graphic distinction of both line and type." Horgan then proposed his solution: "Why not double column setting, smallish type, in an overall size to equal the drawing area that will face it; and thus present a sort of period look in the type page, using rubrics in cobalt blue and brick red, and generally Gutenberging the style—the first and most beautiful solution of that treatment I know of. I enclose a rude dummy of what I mean, giving each Traveler his own title page, text page, picture page, and a page for a motto or quote or whatever. . . . Best to you both, and I hope it will be convenient for you to share this letter, which I address to Tom, who I hope will summon Carl."[46]

Hertzog gave a lengthy report to Stanley Marcus in response to his request for an update and also enclosed a copy of Horgan's recent letter and the text on DeVargas. He was enthusiastic over Horgan's suggestion of lengthening the text but expressed opposition to the idea of smaller type in two columns. With the added typesetting and paper, the cost of the book would increase from $6 per copy to $10, "But what a book!" Hertzog added. "For two years I have believed in this project, that Tom and I could do something that would be outstanding and of genuine merit. Now that I have seen what Paul can do with the text, I am doubly sure that we have something."[47]

Marcus didn't respond. As the subsequent weeks passed without a response, Hertzog could feel his beloved and grand project slipping away. Trying to keep it from dying, he wrote H. Bailey Carroll at the Texas State Historical Association seeking advice, but the project was already doomed. Marcus never replied.

The club had come to an end. The increasing demands and responsibilities of the store made a grand finale, especially a complicated one, impossible. Lea and Hertzog would go on to publish *Calendar of Twelve Travelers through the Pass of the North*, regarded today as the finest of all their collaborations, but not for the Book Club of Texas. Lomax and Marcus discussed the idea of the club's ceasing operation and transferring its assets to some other existing organization. Sometime during the late winter or early spring of 1941 Lomax suggested they give the club's unsold book stock and cash on hand to the Texas Folklore Society.

On 18 April 1941 Stanley Marcus wrote his friend J. Frank Dobie, Secretary and Editor of the Texas Folklore Society:

> Upon several occasions I have discussed the affairs of the Book Club of Texas with you, and have indicated that I have felt that our work in the past has somewhat overlapped the excellent work of your Society. It is my opinion that duplication of effort in cultural activities is not completely desirable and that your organization is so well established that it would be better to unite the efforts of the Book Club of Texas with the Texas Folklore Society.
>
> Therefore, to eliminate conflict of effort and in testimonial to your splendid endeavors, I am, therefore, presenting to your organization the assets of the Book Club of Texas, which are as follows:
>
> *Books (at cost)*

Ellis P. Bean	18 @ 10.00	180.00
Tales of the Mustang	53 @ 2.15	113.95
Texas to Mexico	45 @ 4.00	180.00
Zilphia Gant	34 @ 2.85	96.90
Code Duello	16 @ 3.00	48.00
Eneas Africanus	11 @ 2.75	30.25
Champ D'Asile	151 @ 4.40	664.40
		1,313.50

> I am enclosing also a list of the membership of the Book Club of Texas. In view of this transfer of membership, I would like to suggest that you grant to each of the current members of the Book Club of Texas one year's free membership in the Texas Folklore Society in lieu of their transfer of membership.[48]

Shortly afterwards, Dobie wrote to Marcus about the response to his letter at the annual meeting of the Texas Folklore Society. "Dear Stanley Marcus: I wish you could have seen how bowled over and interested and appreciative the members of the Texas Folklore Society were when at the meeting in San Antonio on May 3 your letter . . . was read."[49]

A flyer sent to all members of the Texas Folklore Society announced: "The books listed below . . . have been published by the Book Club of Texas which was organized by Stanley Marcus of Dallas about twelve years ago to encourage and exemplify the art of printing in this part of the country. . . . Formerly, it was almost impossible for anyone who did not belong to the Book Club of Texas to procure one of these books. Now . . . the Book Club of Texas has turned its assets and its purposes over to the Texas Folk-Lore Society. Hence this offer to the general public. Prices have been radically reduced. For such rare items as they are, here are bargains."

And bargains they were! Today Dobie's *Mustangs* may exceed $1,500 and Faulkner's *Miss Zilphia Gant* commands a similar figure. For even the most humble of the offerings, a collector may expect to pay in the hundreds of dollars.

In the final assessment, just what did the club achieve? Twenty years ago Al Lowman, in his book *Printing Arts in Texas,* refrained from making a precise judgment. He observed that the organization was made up largely of people "already dedicated to the printing arts. Whether these small editions fired the ambitions of other printers, or educated a public to appreciate typographical excellence, remains problematical."[50]

Yet today the state is blessed with a number of fine printers, following in the footsteps of Carl Hertzog and mindful of the book club's early attempts to promote their art. William and Barbara Holman established themselves in Austin, where they began to apply the precepts of California fine printing gained in their San Francisco years. William D. Wittliff produced his widely admired Encino Press books, most of which were printed offset rather than letterpress. W. Thomas Taylor works both ends of the technology spectrum. He cheerfully maintains monotype equipment in spite of the fact that the only replacement parts available come from a dwindling and finite supply of old machines sold by others unwilling to maintain them. At the same time, he stays on the leading edge, using computer-set type to great advantage in fine printing, right along with the newest development in photopolymer printing plates. In the Holman family, David Holman has taken over the business following his father's retirement and has carved an enviable niche for himself as the best printer of quality illustration work in this part of the nation. David also produces fine letterpress work. The binding arts are also now well established, with an active Texas chapter of the International Guild of Book Workers, regular courses in book binding being taught at the Dallas Craft Guild, the establishment of BookLab, a custom binding shop in Austin operated by Craig Jensen, and the arrival at SMU of Jan and Jarmila Sobota, internationally acclaimed binders.

But perhaps the best testament to the influence of the Book Club of Texas has been its reemergence since 1988. Following an illustrated lecture on the club given by Marcus, Tom Taylor set about to revive it.[51] With encouragement from Marcus, the new club has published three books and six broadsides to date. All of the fine printers in Texas today are members and many are actively engaged in the club's publications program. Stanley Marcus is Honorary President for Life, with a citation to that effect presented at the first annual meeting of the reconstituted club. In recognition of one of Marcus's book collecting interests, the letterpress citation was printed no larger than the standard page of a miniature book—three inches tall.

Chapter Three

The Dallas Book Scene

When Stanley Marcus returned to Dallas in 1926 he no doubt yearned for the book scene he had grown to know in Cambridge, where antiquarian and out-of-print shops lined Cornhill Street and provided multitudes of fascinating books for town and gown alike. Yet his hometown offered a surprisingly active array of bookshops. In the next three or so decades Marcus would get acquainted with many of the thirty or so bookstores in Dallas offering a wide range of books—new and out-of-print titles, used books, rare and antiquarian books.

Schmalzried's, The Little Book Shop, Aldredge, Cokesbury, and McMurray's Personal Bookshop were around to help Marcus pursue his collecting interests in earnest. Remarkable for their diversity and their excellence, they represent a golden era of book buying and selling in Dallas that is now long passed.

Adolph L. Schmalzried's Book Shop at 911 Main[1] contained the kind of antiquarian stock that drew booksellers and collectors alike to peruse his shelves. His network of book buyers extended far beyond the borders of Texas to include such people as Edward Eberstadt, the noted Western Americana dealer from New York, who first stopped by while on a book-buying trip in the 1930s. Schmalzried knew that Eberstadt was a ready buyer, and when unusual examples of Texana remained unsold after a reasonable period of time, he would offer them to Eberstadt.[2]

Jeff Dykes, noted book collector, bibliographer, and bookseller in retirement from the Department of Agriculture, also had recollections of Schmalzried's. One of Dykes's earliest collecting interests was the Texas Rangers, and it was at Schmalzried's that he bought the first book that started him down this notable path.[3] He recalled that Schmalzried was "good on Texana and had a large stock of old books, including some rarities." Emma Schmalzried worked in the store with her husband, and on occasion he mildly complained about her practice of going through all their recent acquisitions for stock looking for rare Texana to upgrade copies at home, the condition of which she felt needed to be improved.[4]

Still later, Franklin Gilliam, a native Texan who established the Brick Row Book Shop in Austin in 1954, enjoyed stopovers on his frequent buying trips by train in and out of Texas. He knew any visit to Schmalzried's was likely to result in interesting finds and good buys.[5]

The Little Book Shop, founded around 1923[6] and situated in a triangular rental space at the corner of Ervay and Pacific, was a favorite of Stanley Marcus. In the early 1930s it also had a second location in the lobby of the Adolphus Hotel. Its founder, Kate W. (Mrs. Wirt) Davis, whose husband was a principal figure in the Republic Bank, preferred to keep a low profile in day-to-day operation of the store. Its driving force was its manager, Mrs. Polly Harvey Lobdell, who left the book department at Sanger Brothers to join The Little Book Shop in 1926. Characterized as having one of the best book brains in Texas, Lobdell is still remembered by Marcus for her personable service and knowledge of books. Of medium height, Lobdell stood erect, giving the impression of being taller though slightly frail. She wore her iron-grey hair in a bun on the top of her head and chain smoked except when talking to a customer. She knew her customers' likes, dislikes, and abilities as book people, and she regarded Stanley Marcus as a natural born bookman.[7]

Under Lobdell's direction The Little Book Shop maintained a section of rental books, but is most often remembered for its fine selection of trade and rare books.[8] Elizabeth Ann McMurray recalled The Little Book Shop as "a treasure trove of good stuff" that she enjoyed looking through, although she was very busy managing a bookstore at Fair Park during part of the Texas Centennial. And Jeff Dykes remembered one purchase there with particular satisfaction. He stopped by with his daughter Martha Ann to pay his respects to Mrs. Lobdell and to see what he might find to buy before the shop closed in 1938. After finding books for herself, Martha Ann urged her father to purchase what Dykes would later characterize as one of his luckiest buys—William Faulkner's *Miss Zilphia Gant* (Book Club of Texas, 1932) for which he paid two dollars.[9]

On Lobdell's seventieth birthday in 1947 Everette Lee DeGolyer, the noted book collector whose great library of Western Americana now resides at Southern Methodist University, paid tribute to her:

> Dear Mrs. Lobdell: One of the claims that our fair city has to the diamond studded heavyweight intellectual championship of the Black Belt lies in the excellence of our book shops. Any city in which White's *Warfare of Science and*

> *Theology in Christendom* has been issued more than one hundred times, any city in which a copy has been bought on demand and any city which has a book shop which stocks the *Dictionary of American Biography* or the sixty-four dollar dictionary of the University of Chicago Press is justified in such claim.
>
> You have had as much to do with the excellence of these institutions of which I boast as any other person. It may be that you have duller moments when you sell *Texas Brags* or *I Give you Texas* or other of our minor classics but you are an intellectual institution of which we are proud.[10]

Cokesbury's, the largest and oldest bookshop in Dallas, was probably also the best known to the general public. With the waning of circuit-riding preachers, who had ridden the frontier carrying books in their saddlebags for the edification of their parishioners, the Methodist Church looked for new ways to promote "the importance of schools and setting them up and the value of books and making them available."[11] Established in 1899 as the largest of fourteen major bookstores around the country owned and operated by the Methodist Church, Cokesbury's original purpose was to carry on the educational work begun by the early circuit riders.

The name Cokesbury was not given to the store until 1937, when it moved from 1308 Commerce to 1908-10 Main Street. Prior to that time, it carried the names of its principal managers. When managers changed, the store's name changed as well; so to avoid confusion the church renamed the store after two early Methodist clergymen, Bishop Thomas Coke (1747-1814) and Bishop Francis Asbury (1745-1816), both of whom championed the distribution of books.[12]

The store's new quarters in 1937 were impressive. Under Lovick Pierce as general manager, it occupied a new five-story, air-conditioned building on Main Street. Walnut-paneled shelves with broad aisles lined the five thousand square feet of first-floor selling space.[13] John William Rogers, longtime editor of the *Dallas Times Herald* book section, described the setting some years later as a "pleasing intellectual atmosphere which has the quality of a well ordered mind."[14]

By the 1950s Cokesbury, a for-profit business without any tax relief as a religious organization, had moved into the front rank of retail bookstores in America, to the point where Rogers could write that it had been selling "more books than any other retail book shop" in the country.[15] Profits from sales supported superannuated ministers as well as business expansions. In 1956 it announced its third expansion since 1937, three additional floors to the side of the store that faced Commerce Street, giving it a total of eighteen thousand square feet of space (not counting the "penthouse" floor which was designated for the employees' lounge).[16]

Its managers were no small part of Cokesbury's success during these years of expansion. They were Lovick Pierce and his assistant manager and successor, J. F. "Bliss" Albright. Both were savvy bookmen who understood the power of advertising. Throughout the 1930s Albright bought remainder stock at bargain prices from a large book depository in Dallas. He then sold off many of the most desirable titles at a good profit. As the time approached to move into the new building on Main, Albright advertised a series of ingenious sales. In the first sale he featured his more desirable books at half-price or less. Jeff Dykes, who had recently decided to switch from an accumulator to a serious collector of books, regarded this particular event as a lucky break. Dykes took annual leave to attend the sales and bought books by J. Frank Dobie, James K. Greer, G. L. Crocket, and James T. DeShields, among others, all of which appreciated remarkably in his lifetime.[17]

The second sale made Albright nationally famous. In buying bargain-priced remainders, he also accumulated a large stock of less desirable books. These would play a central role in his Removal Sale, which was announced in a series of newspaper ads offering all the books anyone could carry for eighty-nine cents per load. On the morning of the sale, crowds stormed the dismantled store to select their cheap prizes stacked out on trestle tables. People were buying armloads of books which, in Albright's opinion, were better suited as door stops or scrap paper. Older ladies came in pairs so one could pile books in the other's arms, while another buyer surely thought he had outsmarted Cokesbury's by stacking 116 books on a board and staggering just beyond the front door, where he collapsed. Albright accomplished more than getting rid of several thousand unwanted books while making a little profit on them. He used the sale to inform the public that the store was moving into new premises and to demonstrate that Cokesbury offered bargains, and was, above all, in business to sell books.[18]

In addition, Stanley Marcus helped Cokesbury develop some marketing expertise. Because of their mutual interest in books and the art of selling, Marcus and Albright frequently discussed theories of selling. Marcus explained how the sales staff at Neiman-Marcus was trained to lead the customer to other articles of clothing through related elements such as garment style, color coordination, and accessories, thereby introducing the concept of an ensemble that would meet a variety of needs. He believed a similar approach could apply to the selling of books by showing the customer how books of seemingly unrelated subject matter could contain correlative ideas and information that he or she might find useful.

When Albright responded that such an approach might sell articles of clothing but not books, Marcus challenged him to try and offered to present the concept to the Cokesbury staff in several sessions at no cost to the bookstore. Marcus then gave a series of seminars emphasizing the interrelatedness of ideas contained in a variety of books, and showing staff members how they could lead the customer from the book they initially sought to others in and outside their particular field of interest. After applying Marcus's marketing strategy, Cokesbury's sales increased substantially, convincing Albright that Neiman-Marcus's selling theories could also work for bookstores.

Reflecting on Cokesbury's heyday, "Bliss" Albright, manager from 1942 to 1968, later observed that not only did it outsell every other bookstore in the country for a period of time, but he and his colleagues also helped develop local talent. "I got a good many people to write that had never thought about writing books," he said.[19]

Not only did Cokesbury provide inspiration for Texas authors, it also promoted their works before they were discovered in other parts of the country. A good example is the checklist published in 1935 by Whitmore & Smith shortly before the store's name was changed to Cokesbury. The title page reads *Check-List of Books On and About Texas and the Great Southwest and Other Works, Compiled and Published by Whitmore & Smith, 1308 Commerce Street, Dallas, The South's Largest Book Store.* The twenty-eight-page catalogue, which appeared shortly before the Texas Centennial, opens with a foreword by Eugene C. Barker, the noted historian and professor at the University of Texas. It also carried an endorsement from J. Frank Dobie, who said, "Such a list as you are making has long been needed. I recommend both it and you." It then proceeds to offer over fifteen hundred titles by over five hundred authors, including Andy Adams, Mary Austin, Herbert Bolton, Eugene C. Barker, James T. DeShields, J. Frank Dobie, Grant Foreman, Zane Grey, J. Marvin Hunter, Norman G. Kittrell, Charles Siringo, Lota Spell, Ernest Winkler, and Stark Young. Prices ranged from $1 to $10, with most around $2.50 and $3.[20]

Cokesbury's closed its doors in 1983, in a decade that marked the end of an era in trade-book marketing in major cities in America. Remarkable to the end, it managed to compete with computerized retailing chains in suburban malls, such as B. Dalton's and Waldenbooks, far longer than many of its department store counterparts.

Elizabeth Ann McMurray, owner of McMurray's Personal Bookshop from 1938 to 1955, came to Dallas as a recent graduate of the University of Oklahoma in 1936 to manage Karl Placht's Beacon Book Shop at the Texas Centennial. Right in the middle of the Great Depression McMurray was the successful applicant out of hundreds who responded to an article in *Publishers Weekly* about Placht's new venture in Dallas. Her enthusiasm and her natural affinity for books, their authors, publishers, and readers more than made up for her limited book experience as a student employee at the University of Oklahoma Book Exchange.

Little is known and less has been written about the Beacon Book Shop established by Placht in the Electrical and Communications Building at Fair Park. Proprietor of a bookshop by the same name in the Roosevelt Hotel in New York City, Placht had already operated a successful and sizable booth full of books at the 1935 California Pacific International Exposition in San Diego.[21] Placht renewed his exclusive lease at Balboa Park for another year, and when Texas announced plans to celebrate its centennial, he secured a similar contract with a major concessionaire to operate the only bookshop at Fair Park.[22]

Placht was fortunate in hiring Elizabeth Ann McMurray, who was developing a very keen sense about books and people at a very young age. Her hours were long, from ten in the morning until ten at night with barely any time for meals or for depositing the cash generated daily by the store. To help her out the manager of a nearby concession kindly offered to deposit her receipts along with his own. When McMurray learned that the finances of the concessionaire were shaky, she borrowed Calumet Baking Powder cans from her landlady, Alice Acheson, and stashed the daily account tally and money in them until she could make her own less frequent trips to the bank. Her kindly concessionaire neighbor was later tried and convicted for mishandling cash.

Allen Maxwell, longtime director of the SMU Press, editor of *Southwest Review,* and editor of the book page for the *Dallas Morning News,* remembers the Beacon Book Shop with great fondness. Maxwell was still living at home when he landed a job for pocket money at the Texas Centennial as one of the "Texas Rangers," a group of employees dressed in authentic costumes and stationed around Fair Park to welcome visitors and answer questions. Although his Depression-era wages were low, Maxwell applied everything he earned to the purchase of books at the Beacon Book Shop, which he frequented on a daily basis. Maxwell remembers it was small in size but long on a good variety of titles well chosen by its manager, McMurray.[23]

When the Texas Centennial ended, the fair was carried on for another year as the Pan American Exposition. Placht kept his Beacon Book Shop operating for an additional year at Fair Park but without the good services of

Liz Ann McMurray, whose sights were set on her own shop. She had proven herself a perceptive book buyer whose choices caught the attention of crowds of people with diverse interests attending the Texas Centennial. Now it was time to try it on her own. With backing from C. J. Chatman, owner of the Varsity Book Shop in Norman, Oklahoma,[24] and a silent partner, she opened her own business in 1938 at 1330 Commerce, directly across the street from the front door of the Adolphus Hotel. The forty-by-fifteen-foot shop, which rented for $180 per month, was soon filled with books, and within a few years she had paid off her backers.

Jeff Dykes remembered when McMurray first set up shop. He and his wife were headed back to Fort Worth after Sunday dinner with family. While traveling down Commerce they spotted two young people unloading books from a truck and setting them on shelves in a new shop. "They were putting the books on the shelves willy-nilly, so that it was impossible to tell much about the stock. I did spot a copy of Edward E. Hale's *Kansas and Nebraska* (Boston, 1854). Between trips to the truck Elizabeth Ann took my money for it—the first book she sold in Dallas."[25]

Every bookstore has its own personality and McMurray's Personal Bookshop is the one most fondly remembered today for providing books in an atmosphere charged with lively conversation, where one might frequently rub elbows with notable authors and major collectors. Leon Harris, part of the Harris family of merchant princes in Dallas and an accomplished author in his own right, remembers that "in those days Cokesbury's characterized itself certainly as the biggest bookstore in Dallas, and if you include religious books it sold more books than any bookstore around the country. Therefore, when traveling authors came to town they certainly went and bent the knee at Cokesbury's, but as quickly as they could they went over to McMurray's because in spite of the fact that it was a tiny shop, Liz was the one they wanted to see."

Harris thought of McMurray's bookshop as a club. "I never remember *not* seeing Liz Ann. She had an intimate knowledge of hundreds of people in Dallas, so that if you said to her, 'I want a book,' she knew exactly what you liked. If you said, 'I want to buy a book for Stanley or for my mother or for aunt Tillie,' she knew what *they* liked. She had a really catholic taste and stocked anything she thought would interest the people who came into her shop."[26]

In 1980, when asked about her bookshop for an article in the *Dallas Morning News*, McMurray recalled details readily. "There were several happy factors that nudged the shop along in the general direction of solvency, but slowly. One was youth and limitless energy. I was twenty-three. Another was as much interest in the people as in the books they bought. And a third, I am sure, was just plain luck. Dallas was a busy, booming town, and my book shop, shabby though it may have been, was in the busiest, boomingest part of Dallas. The fourth and vital ingredient in the achievement of either solvency or success was the incredibly able and incandescent staff that I was blessed with through the years."[27]

One of the early members of McMurray's staff was none other than Polly Lobdell, who was turned out of her job at The Little Book Shop when Mrs. Wirt Davis closed it in 1938. An acquaintance of McMurray's, who was more a "browser and talker" than a buyer, urged her to hire Polly Lobdell. Although she was just getting started and could only pay a minimal salary, she took on Lobdell, knowing her new employee could bring many former customers into the new shop across from the Adolphus. When Lobdell began working with McMurray, she indeed began calling her regular customers from The Little Book Shop, including Stanley Marcus.[28]

Personal contacts were essential, for the startup of McMurray's bookstore was slow. During the first ten days, sales averaged $8.93 a day. However, McMurray used the time between customers in those early weeks to initiate one of the many types of promotions that would prove beneficial to her business over the years. When someone came in asking for a good book on beekeeping, for example, McMurray produced one from the shelf to the pleasure of the customer, who then left his name and address in case something else came to hand. In response to this opportunity, McMurray generated a list of "every good book on bees, literary as well as instructive, from Cato to Maeterlinck. The customer had not planned to become an expert but the impact of our bibliography and his own curiosity combined to turn a casual interest into a real book collection."[29] Her practice of producing lists for prospective customers developed over the years to include books on such diverse topics as the Five Civilized Tribes, fur-bearing animals, Billy the Kid, organic gardening, Brook Farm, early English books for children, and poker. The results from these efforts ranged from nothing at all or a single small sale, to attracting customers who bought hundreds of dollars' worth of books on a variety of subjects over a period of years.[30]

Stanley Marcus appreciated Liz Ann McMurray's interest in locating special books for her customers, and he called on her to help him select books as gifts for family members, friends, and business associates. Inevitably there were occasions when he felt that a single book would not be enough for a particularly important gift, so he would ask McMurray to assemble a half-dozen to a dozen titles on a subject of special interest to the recipient. If the topic were orchids, for example, fresh orchids would be sent along with the attractively wrapped books. If the books dealt with the subject of honey, Marcus would include a number of unusual honey pots. Creative combinations such as these reflected the Marcus and McMurray genius for promoting books and engendering good will.

McMurray's first attempt at promoting a single book came with the publication of Sam Acheson's *35,000 Days in Texas* shortly after she opened. She had known the Acheson family since she rented a room from Sam Acheson's mother during her summer at the Beacon Book Shop. In collaboration with the Achesons, she developed a select mailing list of Dallas residents most likely to be interested and sent a letter about the new book, a history of the *Dallas Morning News*. The results were gratifying. She had brisk sales to influential people in Dallas who were also learning about her shop.[31]

Her autographing party for George Sessions Perry when *Hold Autumn in Your Hand* was published was the first of many such occasions. As they grew in popularity and assumed a status among the Dallas literati, they had to be moved, alternating between ballrooms at the Baker Hotel and the Adolphus Hotel.

Located on one of the busiest streets in downtown Dallas—the place where everyone went to work, to shop, to eat out, and to find entertainment—McMurray's also had window displays to catch the attention of the casual passerby. Thus, when Max Ball's *This Fascinating Oil Business* was published, she sought out and borrowed a working model of an oil derrick, complete with an electric motor that made plenty of noise. People who were not regular customers stopped to watch the model and some came into the store to purchase books, too. Others who were customers and distinguished members of the petroleum business were pleased to see McMurray spotlighting their industry. She considered books in their field a specialty of the shop. Included in this group of men were Everette Lee DeGolyer, Eugene McDermott, Lewis MacNaughton, Jake L. Hamon, J. C. Karcher, W. J. Morris, Frederick M. Mayer, George C. McGhee, Harry Bass, and W. E. Wrather.[32]

No matter what the focus of window displays or other promotions, there was a smaller group that came regularly to McMurray's. As a matter of fact, they came every weekday at noon simply because they enjoyed the atmosphere in which they could share their enthusiasm for books. The "noon hour seminar" usually took place at the front of the shop where the Southwestern books were shelved, and it included Ramon Adams, the candy manufacturer whose knowledge of the Old West is documented in writings that are consulted by booksellers and collectors to this day. Another of the group was Wayne Gard, a newspaperman whose historical books on the region were well regarded. Dan Ferguson, attorney and Texana collector, also showed up. Joining the group at times would be Stanley Marcus, then interested in books about books and the history of printing, and E. L. DeGolyer, looking for Western Americana.

With individuals like these frequenting the shop, it was not surprising that some of the giants of Texas writing—J. Frank Dobie, Walter Prescott Webb, and Tom Lea—stopped by when in town. Editors and press directors also came—John McGinnis and Allen Maxwell from SMU, Savoie Lottinville from the University of Oklahoma Press, and Frank Wardlaw from the University of Texas Press.[33] Even J. Evetts Haley (who was always ready to express his dislike for Dallas) stopped by the shop on occasion. Such comings and goings also provided Elizabeth Ann McMurray with the news she needed to keep her network of friends informed so they felt part of the bookish activity centered in the lively bookshop. "Evetts was in here between trains for just an hour the other day. He looked fine and it was mighty good to see him," McMurray wrote to Carl Hertzog after one of Haley's visits.[34]

Still others, like J. B. Priestley, the English novelist and playwright, discovered McMurray's on their own as soon as they arrived. Priestley's wife, Jacquetta Hawkes, had gone to Santa Fe to gather material on ancient people and their historic sites, while he came to Dallas to learn about present-day developments in the region for *Journey Down a Rainbow*, their collaborative book of opinions and impressions based on travel around the Southwest. After checking in at the Adolphus, Priestley made his discovery:

> Opposite my hotel, quite small, only one room, was a bookshop, the real thing. Now and again one comes across these small bookshops in America, usually run by women who have a genuine interest in literature, and, like the one I found in Dallas, they are generally places where people drop in for a gossip. There is much to be said in their favour. . . . There is a world of difference between stores operated by sellers of merchandise and shops kept by shopkeepers. Books properly belong to the latter; they are not merchandise. I found some companionable souls in this little bookshop, and popped across all the more often because I took a strong dislike to my hotel.[35]

McMurray had devised the right formula for success, but she never stopped looking for ways to improve her business or to measure its accomplishments. When she told Leon Harris about her concern for continual improvement, he suggested she talk with someone at A. Harris & Company.

> We [the Harris family] had a department store, and department stores are no less addicted to figure analysis than any business. Our sales per square foot were analyzed for every department, and to assemble and analyze this information every store had a resident comptroller. Ours was a very shrewd old man named Rudolph Haas who had gone to work in the late 1880s for my grandfather. He was responsible for exchanging figures with some thirty-five stores from Stearn's in New York to Robinson's. Thus he had assembled figures on all the departments in all the other department stores which were our peers. So Liz Ann said to me once, "I don't know anything about systems, and I may be running this shop entirely wrong. Can you help me, Leon?" I said, "You know, there's this German fellow in our store who understands numbers better than almost anybody I know. Why don't you gather up your figures and come over to A. Harris and talk to him." So she did, and in his strong German accent Mr. Haas said, "Miss McMurray, tell me how much business you do," and she did. "How big is the schtore?" And she told him. "And vat ah your mahkups?" And she told him. Then he said, "Miss McMurray, get out of dis schtore and don't ever talk to nobody like me again. You are doing bedder than any off us. You shouldn't get infected, so get out of here!"[36]

In 1955, McMurray sold her shop to Ralph Gilliland in order to move to Boston with her husband, William Weber Johnson, who had been Southwest Bureau Chief for Life and Time, Inc., and had just accepted a position as chief of the New England Bureau. After nearly eighteen years in business she had one of the half-dozen most famous bookshops in the nation, referred to in the Dallas press as a "local institution, like Neiman-Marcus, if not quite so chic."[37] In addition to her innovative and lively bookselling activities, "Liz Ann," as she was known, had instituted the McMurray Prize awarded by the Texas Institute of Letters for the best Texas first novel, had assisted Everette L. DeGolyer with his Peripatetic Press books, had helped organize the highly successful Southwest Book Fair in 1945, had served on the board of Margo Jones's Theatre-in-the Round, and had housed the theatre's downtown box office in her small shop. In these and dozens of other ways Liz Ann McMurray made significant contributions to the cultural activity of Dallas, and much of her impact centered around books, their writing, making, reading, and collecting.

After her departure, McMurray's Personal Bookshop was managed by Ralph Gilliland and his nephew, William R. Gilliland. They continued the tradition of quality service and assumed key roles in such activities as the Dallas Book and Author Luncheons as well as in the Dallas observations of National Library Week, all of which drew national attention. Bill Gilliland was particularly instrumental in bringing attention to "sleepers" which thereafter moved onto national bestseller lists. These included *The Story of Bridie Murphy* and Jules Pfeiffer's *Sick, Sick, Sick*. During this time he even gave temporary employment to writers like William Goyen and Larry McMurtry.

By the 1960s the book scene in Dallas had changed dramatically from the one to which Stanley Marcus had returned in 1925 and in which he had participated for over thirty years. In 1962 Doubleday bought McMurray's and three years later opened a second location in NorthPark shopping mall, contributing to the general movement of small downtown Dallas businesses to outlying areas.

With the concentration of bookshops in Dallas between the 1920s and 1950s, the promotion of books carried out in a cooperative spirit by bookstore managers, and the support of the local newspapers, Dallas had assumed an important role in the world of books. While bookshops such as Cokesbury's and McMurray's were making a name for themselves and for Dallas in the world of trade-book sales, other stores were also finding innovative and effective ways to promote books. Most large department stores maintained lending libraries as well as substantial book departments with trade books for sale. At A. Harris & Co., Edna Smith developed a book department of significant proportions. Sanger Brothers and Titche-Goettinger also offered similar services, with the former managed by Bertha Prager in its earlier years and the latter managed by Marvin Steakley shortly before its closing in the mid-1970s.[38]

Stanley Marcus was interested in developing a book department at Neiman-Marcus and proposed the idea to his father. However, when they ran the numbers, the sales projections did not justify reallocating highly productive retail floor space for books, which had only a modest margin for profit. Nevertheless, Marcus did use his Neiman-Marcus office to operate the Book Club of Texas throughout most of the 1930s. Then, in 1939 he arranged for Neiman-Marcus to publish a book under its own imprint, Townsend Miller's *A Letter from Texas* designed by Carl Hertzog.

Throughout his years at Neiman-Marcus "Mr. Stanley" would find innovative ways to promote books along with other merchandise, such as children's clothes, distinctive stationery, and fine foods. In these ways Marcus could engage in specialized bookselling without having to develop a book department. When Tom Lea's *The Brave Bulls* was published by Little, Brown in 1949, the book was displayed at several sales points in the store along with silk scarves with a reproduction of an original Lea watercolor, a bullfight scene commissioned by Marcus. The dust jacket of the new book featured art by Lea, but he created a new work for the Neiman-Marcus scarf. Both sold well.

Another Neiman-Marcus promotion involving an author featured Ludwig Bemelmans, the New York restaurateur, raconteur, artist, and creator of the *Madeline* series of children's books. Bemelmans and Marcus became good friends in the 1930s when Marcus dined at his restaurant. After one of his visits to Dallas, Bemelmans wrote and illustrated *Madeline's Christmas in Texas,* which Neiman-Marcus issued for its customers. Still later, Neiman-Marcus introduced the Madeline doll, which is still available.

After Helen Corbitt made the Zodiac Room a renowned restaurant and wrote several successful cookbooks, the stock of cookbooks in the Epicure Shop grew to signicant proportions and accounted for substantial sales. Finally, in 1980 Stanley Marcus arranged for the store to publish another book under its own imprint and feature it in the famous Christmas catalogue. It was a deluxe edition of J. Frank Dobie's *Coronado's Children* designed by Andrew Hoyem, one of the most noted of contemporary typographers and printers in California.

The large department stores with major book departments also drew customers through promotions not available to smaller bookstores. In their sizable auditoriums, Sanger Bros. and Titche-Goettinger scheduled regular appearances of professional book reviewers like Evelyn Oppenheimer. These programs began as monthly events but soon grew in popularity to the point where Oppenheimer, for example, was broadcasting book reviews regularly over KRLD and drawing crowds of three hundred to four hundred people to her weekly appearances sponsored by the department stores in their own auditoriums.[39]

Most of these firms bought significant amounts of advertising space in the two major daily newspapers, which in turn hired active and articulate book review editors. At the *Dallas Morning News* John McGinnis was editor of the book page, assisted by Allen Maxwell, and later by Lon Tinkle. Tinkle succeeded McGinnis as editor and then became book critic when Maxwell was named editor. John William Rogers was book-page editor at the *Dallas Times Herald.*

The buying, reading, and making of books coalesced in the mid-1940s when the book community in Dallas set out to stage a major book event that drew attention from all quarters, especially the publishing center of America, New York City. The occasion was the Southwest Book Fair held at Southern Methodist University in November, 1945.

Book fairs had previously been staged only in major metropolitan areas in the Northeast, such as New York and Boston. The 1945 fair in Dallas, a first for this part of the nation, was approached in its earliest planning stages as a community affair that would place a larger than usual emphasis on books in Dallas and the Southwest. Preliminary plans were made by the *Southwest Review* and the literary editors at the two major daily newspapers for a series of events designed to engage the participation and support of the business community as well as its serious book collectors.

Southern Methodist University would provide the setting for the three-day event at its 2,300-seat McFarlin Auditorium, known widely throughout the community as the location of Dallas Symphony Orchestra performances and notable public lectures. Ties between SMU and the book community were already firmly in place, with the legendary John McGinnis teaching English (his favorite author was Shakespeare), editing a lively book page in the *Dallas Morning News,* editing the *Southwest Review*, and running the SMU Press. McGinnis's assistant was Lon Tinkle, who also taught at SMU. Their connections with authors and publishers placed them in an excellent position to engage speakers like Paul Horgan, Erskine Caldwell, and John Gould Fletcher, who had considerable name recognition. Even the university's president, Umphrey Lee, provided support and participated in the program sessions.

The executive committee was relatively small for such a citywide event. "Bliss" Albright was the chairman, with Elizabeth Ann McMurray, Lon Tinkle, and John William Rogers among the most active of the downtown organizers. At SMU, Elizabeth M. Stover and Donald Day at the *Southwest Review* coordinated space allocation and activities involving the journal, SMU Press, and Fondren Library. When Day moved away before the fair was staged, a young and capable junior administrator at SMU, Willis Tate, was named to assume his role. Destined to become a future president of SMU, Tate distinguished himself through his organizational ability and his skills in dealing with people.

The proposal drafted in May, 1945, called for a three-day fair, with display booths from local bookstores and participating publishers set up on the large stage, in the foyer, and elsewhere in McFarlin Auditorium. Special features would include a variety of "ideal" or model libraries as stimuli to guide book buyers interested in developing a southwestern, a children's, or a church library. Program sessions would feature "a score or more of the most important and most widely discussed contemporary authors" who would each speak for fifteen or twenty minutes.[40]

Related exhibitions in SMU's Fondren Library as well as in the Hall of State

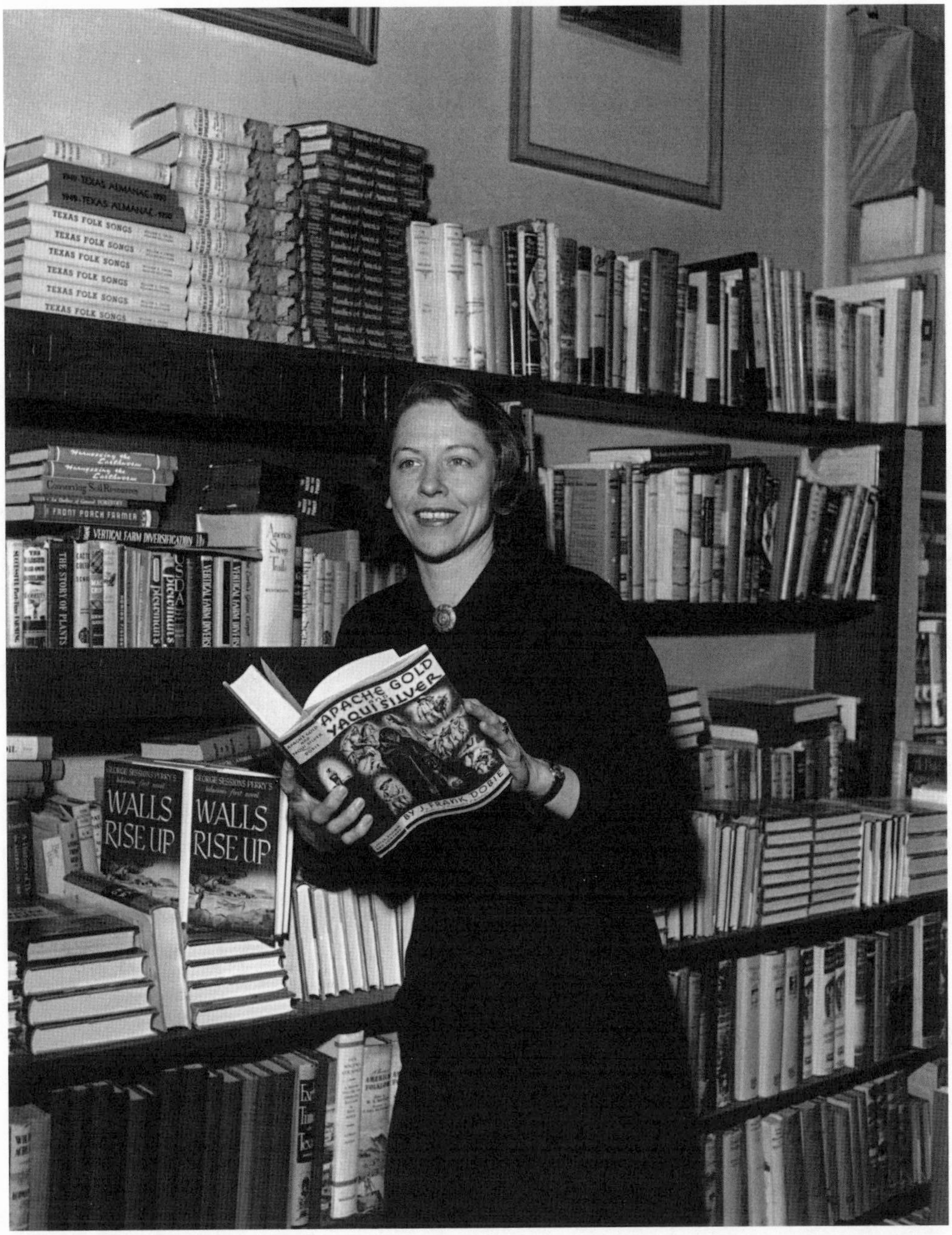

Elizabeth Ann McMurray and the logo for her bookstore, 1939. Photograph courtesy Dallas Public Library, logo courtesy of Elizabeth Johnson.

L-R: J. Frank Dobie, Tom Lea, Percy Johnson, and Angus Cameron in McMurray's Personal Bookshop on publication of *The Brave Bulls* by Tom Lea (Boston: Little, Brown, 1949). Courtesy Elizabeth Johnson.

L-R: Everette Lee DeGolyer, Phyllis Cerf, Bennett Cerf, and Stanley Marcus, Cokesbury Bookstore, Dallas, February 5, 1947. Courtesy *Dallas Morning News*.

Cokesbury Bookstore manager J. F. "Bliss" Albright observes Dallas author and newspaper executive Felix McKnight sign copies of his new book, *The Easter Story*, 1953. Courtesy Allen Maxwell.

Dallas Morning News book editor Allen Maxwell, standing with *News* book critic Lon Tinkle, 1959. Courtesy Allen Maxwell.

Inscribed For:
Stanley & Billie
This biography of
one creative Texan
who proved that excellence
is contagious in a
community inscribed
to two other creative
Texans who have
steadily demonstrated
that excellence is not
geographic or regional
but individual.
Lon Tinkle

Inscription to Stanley and Billie Marcus by Lon Tinkle on the publication of *Mr. D: A Biography of Everette Lee DeGolyer* (Boston: Little, Brown, 1970). Courtesy Stanley Marcus.

and the Museum of Fine Arts on the Texas State Fair grounds were to round out the presentations. These would include exhibits of fine bookmaking, which Stanley Marcus offered to help organize, a display of historical documents, an exhibit of Western Americana from the library of Everette Lee DeGolyer, and books selected for their fine typography.

From this point, organizers rapidly began to gain the support required to make the fair a success. They contacted all the schools in the Dallas area, public and private, encouraging them to send their students to the fair. They sent letters to more than sixty-five publishers, authors, and other organizations outlining plans for the fair and seeking their participation. They also solicited radio and newspaper promotions and enlisted important stores in town to design window displays of books relating to some aspect of their merchandise and include a placard announcing the Southwest Book Fair. The Dallas Graphic Arts Association agreed to provide paper and to print attractive programs with a two-color cover panel of a bright red ferris wheel loaded with booklike figures drawn with little heads, arms, and legs. Then the fair received the all-important endorsement of the Chamber of Commerce with a sponsorship of $10,000, a highly significant demonstration of civic support in 1945.[41]

This was the major level of commitment needed to spark an already energetic group of people. The results of their cooperative efforts were spectacular. Over thirty writers of distinction made appearances, along with forty-eight publishers. Authors included Erskine Caldwell, Harnett Kane, Alan Lomax, Munro Leaf, John Joseph Mathews, and William B. Ziff. Representatives from Bobbs Merrill, Doubleday, Farrar & Rinehart, Alfred A. Knopf, Random House, Simon & Schuster, and Longmans, Green added to the fun. All the visiting authors and publishers were treated to a splendid party hosted by Everette and Nell DeGolyer at Rancho Encinal, their grand hacienda-style home overlooking White Rock Lake. The official souvenir book, *Son-of-a-Gun Stew: A Sampling of the Southwest* (an anthology of writings from the *Southwest Review*, edited by Elizabeth M. Stover), listed all the participants and sold for $1 at the booksellers' cooperative booth. Admission tickets for all three days of the fair were also $1.

A special newspaper supplement published for the occasion featured articles on books—their writing, publishing, and collecting—written by Stanley Marcus, George Sessions Perry, Margaret Cousins, E. DeGolyer, and Fred Gipson, among many others. In his article, "History of Book Making in Texas," Marcus described the recent attention paid to typographic design as beginning to fill an obvious aesthetic gap in the state. Citing some of the

Book Club of Texas' awards from the American Institute of Graphic Arts, he also praised the recent improvement in the appearance of Texas Folklore Society publications. "Frank Dobie," Marcus wrote, "had never given much attention to the appearance of his organization's publications. He was so impressed, however, by the demonstrations in good printing sponsored by the Book Club that he asked the Club to supervise the design of *Puro Mexicano,* the Folklore Society's publication in 1935. Mr. Dobie and his members were so pleased with the results that an increasing amount of attention has been paid to the appearance of the society's subsequent publications."[42] Marcus ended his brief article with a call to arms, typographically speaking, and praise for Carl Hertzog as the one person in Texas "who has the capabilities of being a great bookmaker." He noted Hertzog's production of *A Letter from Texas* for Neiman-Marcus in 1939, *Santa Rita* for the Texas State Historical Association in 1943, and *A Grizzly From the Coral Sea,* printed on his own "because he couldn't resist the opportunity to do a beautiful book written and illustrated by his friend Tom Lea. Hertzog. . .is a good craftsman, he understands the technicalities of book production, he possesses a fine creative style. But for the lack of book work, he has turned back to job printing."[43]

With the success of the Southwest Book Fair came expectations of another event, similar in scope and focus, in the next year or so. Early in 1947 Albright wrote Lon Tinkle inviting him and others from the 1945 executive committee to meet and reorganize for a second Southwest Book Fair. No evidence remains in the files that the needed reorganization ever occurred, but the idea remained alive for nearly a decade. When Bennett Cerf visited Dallas in the spring of 1947, people were still talking about the 1945 fair, so much so that Cerf mentioned it in his "Trade Winds" column in the *Saturday Review*. In 1948, the editor of *Publishers Weekly* sent a hopeful inquiry to Lon Tinkle: "Dear Lon, there is a rumor up here that Dallas will have a book fair in the fall. Needless to say, I very much want the story if there is one. . . . I can't help hoping I would have a good excuse for rushing out immediately and putting one foot on the first train south."[44]

Stanley Marcus discussed the possibilities of having another fair with his book friends, including Lon Tinkle at the *Dallas Morning News*. Marcus tried one last time in 1954 to coalesce interest by writing Jerome Crossman, then president of the Dallas Chamber of Commerce:

> Several years ago the Dallas book trade staged a Book Fair to which were invited authors and publishers for a series of lectures, dinners, and exhibitions. The Fair was a great success, but it entailed a tremendous amount of effort on

> the part of a few people in the book trade and on the newspapers. As a matter of fact, it took so much time and effort that the sponsors of the previous Fair have been loathe to consider a repetition of this event. It seems to me, however, that a Fair of this type is tremendously important in maintaining the cultural prestige of the community and that the booksellers and newspapers should receive some encouragement from the Dallas Chamber of Commerce together with assistance, which can be donated by some of us who would be interested in seeing the Fair repeated. I believe if you would write to Mr. Lon Tinkle, Book Editor of the *Dallas Morning News*, Miss Elizabeth Ann McMurray, McMurray's Book Shop, and to Mr. J. F. Albright, Cokesbury's Book Store, you might stimulate them sufficiently to be willing to undertake another Book Fair.[45]

Following Marcus's suggestions, the president of the Dallas Chamber of Commerce wrote a brief and not altogether encouraging letter, cautioning that the Chamber lacked funds for such an event but "would lend every assistance, especially publicity, towards such a project, should the Book Trade and newspapers undertake it."[46] The move to organize another fair did not catch hold. The scene was changing. Within a year Elizabeth Ann McMurray moved to Boston, not only depriving Dallas of a lively and intelligent figure in its cultural world, but also removing one of the key players in the 1945 Southwest Book Fair. The downtown book and department stores that had been so much a part of the book scene began their migration to the suburbs or disappeared from the scene altogether, and the book review sections of the local papers shrank as the advertising dollars evaporated. But the book scene in Dallas from the 1920s through the 1950s remains a golden era for the city's book collectors and readers. As the gap began to widen in the available sources for interesting books around his home town, Stanley Marcus turned in other directions. One of these was toward designing and publishing books of regional importance and interest, along the way establishing close friendships with Carl Hertzog and J. Frank Dobie.

Chapter Four

Mr. Stanley and Mr. Texas

Stanley Marcus and J. Frank Dobie were both committed to writing that clearly expressed the identity of their region. They had that in common from the start. What caused their friendship to grow and endure, however, was more than their shared interest in reading and making books. Outspoken, both respected the other's candor and wisdom. At times they disagreed frankly, but they never stopped seeking each other's help and advice.

Their friendship began in 1929. Marcus had the first title of the Book Club of Texas, *Memoir of Col. Ellis P. Bean,* in production. Dobie's *A Vaquero of the Brush Country* had recently been published by the Southwest Press in Dallas. Seeking ideas for future book club projects, Marcus wrote to Dobie and other club members attuned to the history and cultural developments of Texas. Dobie, having access to the archives and library of the University of Texas, responded with several suggestions as well as a request of his own:

> I have been casting around to see what I could suggest that might fulfill the requirements you laid down for our second publication. I am sending you two narratives from the Archives of the University of Texas. Personally, I think that the "Reminiscences of Rogers" is preferable. . . .
>
> We [also] have here a diary written by a trail boss of the X.I.T. outfit along in the '90's, perhaps early '90's. It is quite interesting, but as you can see, does not go so far back. I doubt, also, if it has as much humanity in it as either of these other manuscripts.
>
> One of the most interesting rare books in early Texana is an account by Nelson Lee of his capture by the Comanches. It is a small book, not a great deal longer than "The Bean Memoirs."
>
> This next semester, I am to give a course in "Life and Literature of the Southwest." I want very much for my people to read Peter Ellis Bean. Would it be possible for the University of Texas Library to procure a half a dozen copies of his autobiography? I believe that the rules of the club preclude printing more copies than there are members, but it seems to me that an exception might be made in this instance.[1]

Apparently nothing developed from these suggestions, but Dobie received the extra copies of the *Memoir of Col. Ellis P. Bean* for his students, because the book soon appeared on the reading list for his new course and in the list's subsequent and expanded publication in 1943 as *Guide to Life and Literature of the Southwest.* The entry read: "*Memoir,* published first in Vol. I of Yoakum's *History of Texas;* in 1930 printed as a small book by the Book Club of Texas, Dallas, now OP. A fascinating narrative."

By March, 1931, Marcus was writing to Dobie again. With his wide-ranging interests in books, Marcus was among the first to read Dobie's second book. His admiration for the author's work was growing. "I have just finished reading *Coronado's Children* and I must tell you how much I enjoyed it. I knew Texas had a great deal of historical background but I did not realize to what extent the folklore had grown. Please accept my heartiest congratulations for writing such a monumental book."[2]

Struggling to boost sales for the book club, Marcus applied some of his marketing skills in a 1933 letter to Dobie. Saying he had examined the ledgers of the club, he noted that Dobie had not purchased any of its publications recently. "We are extremely interested in finding out why you have not exercised this prerogative of membership, because the Club's primary purpose is to publish books that its members will want to own. Insofar as you are concerned, we have failed and it is greatly to our interest to know why we have failed." In the same letter Marcus called attention to the fact that the club was "doing a noteworthy piece of work in the Southwest by publishing books indigenous to the region." By this time he could list four titles: *Memoirs of Col. Ellis P. Bean* ($9), *Eneas Africanus* ($3.50), *Code Duello* ($3.50), and *Miss Zilphia Gant* ($3.50). Marcus ended his letter by saying, "We are very anxious to have an active membership, so that we may continue the work that we have embarked on. Won't you assist us?"[3]

A week later Marcus had Dobie's candid reply:

> Dear Mr. Stanley: Since you write and ask me why I have not bought the recent publications of the Book Club of Texas, I will tell you frankly that they have not interested me. I saw no point whatsoever in bringing out *Eneas Africanus* when good copies of it could be bought for four bits. I am not in the least interested in *Zilphia Gant,* although I am interested in anything that my friend Henry Smith writes, and I hope that the professor in Southern Methodist University who tried to get him fired for writing a preface to this book will roast in Hell. Furthermore, I think that the membership dues plus the prices of the books have amounted to too much. As I recall, the *Memoirs of Col. Ellis P. Bean* cost me $19.00.[4] That is the most costly book in my library;

> I mean by that not that it is the most money that I have paid for a book, but that the cost of the book exceeds its value inordinately. I believe in a book club, but I would much prefer to see the club pursue the policy of the Grabhorn Press, or some other such paper *[sic]* of limited editions. I should be glad to buy a copy of the Terrell book,[5] but if it is necessary for me to pay for membership and then pay also the regular price of the book, I shall, on account of stringent finances, have to do without the book.[6]

Marcus knew the effects of the Depression were felt in all quarters. Furthermore, such openness and directness appealed to one who had never been reluctant to make known his own stand on any issue. He continued to engage his friend in considerations about book club publications, and within a few years Dobie submitted a manuscript to the club's publication committee. After some delay in the review process, it met with enthusiastic response and soon went into production. Marcus wrote Dobie in August, 1935, that he had turned over the manuscript for *Tales of the Mustang* to the printer for design of the new book. He also sent, for Dobie's consideration and reaction, suggested changes to the manuscript from one of the officers of the club.

Dobie's response was no less candid than Marcus might have expected. "I think Mr. Bromberg's criticism of certain subtitles in my manuscript good, but his comments on certain phrases in the body of the book are impertinent. I would be the last person in the world to think my own style impeccable, but in the instances pointed out by Mr. Bromberg I have said accurately what I wanted to say and therefore do not wish to make the suggested changes."[7] Marcus knew he had a fine writer on his hands, and production went forward on Dobie's book without substantive changes.

Through mutual respect, their friendship was growing. After *Tales of the Mustang* was published, Dobie softened his stance about Book Club of Texas publications and placed orders for several titles, at the same time mentioning some of Carl Hertzog's work. Marcus was pleased and replied: "Dear Mr. Dobie, upon my return from New York I found your letter together with the order for some of the club's publications. I am very much interested in this fellow, 'Hertzog,' in El Paso and expect to use him on our next publication as soon as we definitely decide on our material."[8]

Unfortunately, Marcus was unable to follow out this intention. Though he was not aware of it at the time he wrote to Dobie, the Book Club of Texas had published what would be its last title until its revival in 1988. Nevertheless, his friendship with Frank Dobie continued to develop. When Marcus discovered a book he thought unusually important for its time, he bought multiple copies and sent them to friends and acquaintances in different walks of life. In 1943 he shared with Dobie his enthusiasm for Philip Wylie's *Generation of Vipers* by sending a copy and soliciting Dobie's opinion and his reactions to the book.

Dobie responded in his regular weekly column, "Out of the Books," in the *Dallas Morning News*. "It is tonic to see a man so moved by a book that he yearns to share it with others, especially if, being able, he buys copies to give away. His friends must read it. I am one of the friends of Stanley Marcus of Dallas, to whom he has sent Philip Wylie's iron and acid *Generation of Vipers*. Reading it makes me yell, 'Lay on Macduff!' At the same time I doubt if 'whaling the whey' out of a cow ever made her give sweeter or richer milk." Dobie followed with excerpts that revealed some of Wylie's ideas and style of presentation in arguments for better education, businessmen who can make the distinction between their own rhetorical promotion and discernible facts, and the need to strengthen personal ethics and social integrity.

Dobie also returned Stanley Marcus's kindness in other ways by paying special attention to Marcus's contributions toward better typography and design in Texas. In the summer of 1943 Marcus wrote Dobie: "Dear Frank, I have had a few days at home because of enforced illness, and have had the opportunity of reading through the recent publication of the Folklore Society. I am very appreciative of your kind words. I do want you to know that I think that the typography of all of the Folklore Society books is showing terrific improvement. I am very happy to feel that I have had some slight influence in this direction."[9] As early as 1935, Stanley Marcus was advising Dobie and the Texas Folklore Society on typographical matters. In *Puro Mexicano*, the society's twelfth annual, Dobie thanked Marcus in the printed acknowledgments for "designing the format of the book and advising the artisans who set the type for it and printed it."[10]

By 1945 Stanley Marcus's reputation as an enlightened benefactor of worthwhile cultural projects and developments was as well established as the friendship he shared with Frank Dobie. Thus, it was natural for Dobie to turn to his friend even with an unusual proposal because he thought it would measure up to the Marcus standards. On the eve of his departure for England, Dobie wrote the following letter. It helped bring about one of the most important books written by a Texas author:

> Dear Stanley: I wish I had thought about this business with you before I left Texas. I go aboard the Queen Elizabeth this evening and expect to be in England 7 or 8 months.
>
> Roy Bedichek has the most richly-stored mind that I know in Texas. He is the best naturalist that I know, and he has read more literature than most professors of English. He has read more literature of other countries than many professors of Comparative Literature. He is a liberal but not a radical and knows the stuff of social sciences. He is a wonderful conversationalist. He used to be a newspaper man and has written millions of words. For years he has been director of the Interscholastic League of Texas. His salary is, I think, $4,000 a year (12 month basis). His duties are a grind. Once in a while he gives a paper before Town and Gown that is supreme. He never publishes. His letters are literature.
>
> For years he has kept notes on nature and has the stuff all garnered for the best natural history book, especially on birds, that Texas has a chance to be partly civilized by, or will have the chance at for a long time. The only way he will ever write that book is for somebody to buy him some time through the University. Since I came up here I wrote to Walter Webb about the matter. Webb is a great admirer of Bedi's. He is in charge of some Rockefeller money advanced to Texas State Historical Association. Webb says he can make a grant of $1,875, for a year. Bedichek should have at least $5,000, I think. Money for the grant could be given to the University of Texas, ear-marked for Bedichek research, or writing. I thought you might be interested in this project, or know somebody who would be. Income tax deductions are allowed, you know, on grants to the University.
>
> Bedichek knows nothing at all about this plan. I spoke of it to Ireland Graves[11] at Austin, to Webb, now to you—to nobody else. Here is a chance to do something for civilization in Texas. I love Bedichek and admire him greatly, but I do not regard this matter as personal to him, but as personal to society. I will guarantee publication of the book. If you are interested, please write Walter P. Webb. With many good wishes and regards, I remain, Your friend, Frank Dobie.[12]

Precisely the kind of project that Marcus liked to support, the idea almost sold itself—a book by an unknown Texas naturalist, someone whose correspondence read like literature according to Dobie; a book endorsed by "Mr. Texas" himself; a book to be written only if the author could be freed for a year from a grinding job; a book with the promise of a major contribution to Texas letters. Within five days Stanley Marcus had written nine other prominent men in Dallas, including Tom Gooch at the *Dallas Times Herald,* noting Bedichek's qualifications and ideas for a book, and inviting them to join him in contributing $500 each toward support of the project. Within a few more days letters pledging funds began to arrive, including one from fellow book collector Everette Lee DeGolyer. Before the end of the year Marcus forwarded to Austin half of the funds he was raising, and shortly thereafter put out the call to collect the remaining pledges, as in this letter to DeGolyer:

> Last summer I wrote you relative to a fund that I was trying to raise to make it possible for Mr. Roy Bedichek to complete his book on Texas Nature Study. I told you at that time I was planning to raise five thousand dollars and you kindly advised me if I succeeded in raising the amount that I could count on you for a matter of five hundred dollars.
>
> I am happy to advise you that the fund has been completely raised and I am ready to send the amount to Mr. Walter Webb at the University of Texas so that the project can be undertaken.[13]

In the meantime, Walter Prescott Webb had been doing his part down in Austin by soliciting a proposal from Bedichek that would go before the Research Council at the University of Texas. In September of 1945 he wrote:

> Dear Bedi, I would suggest, and in fact I insist, that you prepare an application to be submitted to the Research Council for a grant of $2,200.00 or less for the preparation of your work as a *field naturalist.* There is no necessity for you to discuss other work you propose to do, except to state that you plan to take a full year's leave. . . . Since the application goes before a group of some dozen people, it is desirable that you be as specific as possible in reference to the material you have collected, the notes you have on hand, the place the study is supposed to fill in the educational vacuum, and the absolute impossibility of doing the job while looking after the routine of your present office. . . . I know the nature of the mill-run projects submitted and there is no doubt that a grant will be made, and made gladly. Please get up this application and let me see it before it is turned in. Please don't nerve me up by arguing. I'll try to see you within a week. Yours, Webb.[14]

By November the Research Council had met and approved Bedichek's proposal, and Stanley Marcus had communicated with Webb that the first half of the pledges by Dallas businessmen had been collected. Thus Webb was able to inform Bedichek of the good news. "Dear Bedi, You will find herein the formal statement, as formal as I can make it to one with whom I have rarely been formal. If I can believe the word of an individual who would not dare break his word, the $2,500.00 is in his hands and will be sent in as soon as he returns from a business trip. I have this word by telephone and also by letter. Yours, W.P.W."[15] This note was attached to the formal letter in which Webb outlined terms of the grant to Bedichek.

After *Adventures with a Texas Naturalist* was published to wide acclaim, Webb wrote Henry Allen Moe at the Guggenheim Foundation about the process. "I can tell you some amusing stories about his first book, how I would visit him in his hideout, read his chapters, and convince him for the time being, that he was doing good stuff. I was quite honest, and I am still convinced that Roy Bedichek has turned out the finest quality of literary production that has come out of Texas. Others share the opinion now."[16]

The concept of sharing resources to encourage new works of art was well established in both Marcus and Dobie. They also shared a passionate commitment as enlightened liberals who communicated their beliefs in a variety of ways. Both men articulated their stands in letters to newspaper editors, radio talks, and speeches to various groups and, in turn, were widely quoted by others interpreting the current political and social scene. In the end, this cost Dobie more than it did Marcus.

Marcus was able to maintain independence even while he catered to the socially elite in his tough field of retail marketing. Frank Dobie was equally independent. His friend Henry Nash Smith described Dobie as "two widely different personalities," the down-to-earth folklorist / storyteller of the Old West and an effective controversialist. In the latter role he was "a highly vocal enemy of reactionary demagogues and a defender of labor unions and of many unpopular causes."[17] In his newspaper column Dobie had made powerful enemies of the University of Texas regents when he wrote about their firing of university president Homer Rainey.[18] They took their petty revenge in due time. In 1947, when Dobie requested additional leave (for health reasons and to finish another book) after having been away from the university for four years, he was turned down. Neither side was willing to negotiate, so the regents dropped Frank Dobie from the faculty, a full professor since 1933 with more books to his credit than most academics write in a lifetime.[19]

News of Dobie's firing spread quickly, and when Stanley Marcus learned of it he was upset over what happened to his friend. Addressing Dobie as "My Dear Frank," he wrote, "It has been a long time since we've had a chance to chat together but I just want you to know that my thoughts have been with you during your troublesome period. I am sorry that the Regents made a goat out of you but it was to be expected. I shall look forward to seeing you on your next visit to Dallas."[20]

Dobie was out of the university, but he was not forgotten by Marcus and as time passed their friendship began to mellow. Having decided to publish a Neiman-Marcus cookbook, Marcus turned to Dobie for a contribution. In

February, 1948, Marcus wrote to Dobie explaining how the concept developed when one of his customers asked at the Epicure Bar why Neiman-Marcus did not publish a cookbook. After market research predicted favorable results, he had begun soliciting recipes and stories about their origins or incidents relating to them. The new book was not intended to teach people to cook, "but rather one for those who are already excellent cooks and gourmets. In addition, the book is going to make good reading. It will include recipes from interesting people all over the world, but will have a strong regional flavor."[21]

Sketching out the plan for the book, Marcus asked Dobie if he would contribute one of his favorite or most successful recipes, preferably one with a story attached that revealed something about its origin, how it was obtained, or some humorous or unusual situation in which it was served. The answer was vintage Dobie: "Dear Stanley, the only recipe I could give you would be for frijoles. The only liquids I know how to mix are coffee and whiskey. With good wishes to you on the cook book, I remain, Your friend, J. Frank Dobie."[22]

Undaunted, Marcus tried another approach. He wanted a contribution for his new cookbook from "Mr. Texas." Adopting his own folksy style and appealing to Dobie's intense commitment to his native region, Marcus wrote: "Dear Mr. J. Frank Dobie: Now, I ask you, what's wrong with Frijoles? Why not give out with how you put 'em together? We would be quite flattered if you would, y'know. The cook book is coming along beautifully and mouth-wateringly and, to date, we have not one recipe for the very regional recipe known as 'Frijoles' . . . which would make it even more mouth-watering."[23]

No longer reluctant, Dobie soon sent a long, single-spaced typed letter with his own recipe for making frijoles, starting with the chore of picking out "the little rocks that are frequently mixed in sacks of pinto beans." Dobie commends beans that have been reboiled on the second and third days for better taste, and he discourages the use of soda, chili powder, and too much salt pork. After discussing the fine points of chilipiquines, fresh onions, and honey, he ends his recipe with some comments on where he found frijoles at their best in Mexico (the Saenz Hotel in Saltillo) and how they were a staple food in the border country where he grew up.[24]

When Jane Trahey's *A Taste of Texas* was published later in the year, Dobie's contribution appeared near the beginning under the following heading: "J. Frank Dobie, Texas author, naturalist, professor, symbol and frijole-man sent us this one. It is reprinted here in its original letter because in Texas nobody rewrites Dobie." Stanley Marcus was clearly delighted and wrote Dobie, "Thanks to you the lowly frijole has come into its own. Your recipe is superb!"[25]

The book sold well for several years, particularly in Texas and especially in Neiman-Marcus. However, early in 1951 Stanley Marcus wrote his friend Bennett Cerf at Random House asking how it was doing and if there were anything they might devise to stimulate some additional sales throughout the country. While sales in The Store were still strong two and a half years after the book was published, Marcus's eye for the bottom line told him overall sales were down. Cerf reported sales in 1950 of 1,946 copies, but in the first two months of 1951, only 206 copies had sold nationwide. With the trend going down, he thought they had gotten about all they could expect from the book and advised against a promotion campaign. The publisher also admitted that Marcus was right about the dust jacket, which he had not liked for its lack of class.[26]

It is a curious note, however, that for all the collecting interest centered on Dobie's own books and his contributions to other books, this item has been overlooked by his bibliographers and many of his collectors.

A few years later Dobie wrote to say that his niece was working for Neiman-Marcus. After checking with the Personnel Director, Marcus wrote: "My Dear Frank . . . I was very pleased to learn that [Miss Catherine Dobie] joined our organization on February 13th and is currently selling glassware in our gift shop. If she sells a lot of highball glasses, it will undoubtedly be due to the interest in this line of merchandise which was transmitted to her by her uncle."

Both men understood the significance of a cocktail party, so in his last year as president of the Texas Institute of Letters, Dobie wrote Marcus seeking help one more time:

> Dear Stanley, Mark Twain said that an ax should be the symbol of the human race. I have one to grind. . . . A long time ago we had no party either before or after the evening dinner. Then Lon Tinkle inaugurated a midnight party, too late and too wearing for many people. A few years ago I tried to get some of the members of the Institute together for cocktails before the dinner. The gathering was too limited. The last year or two the Institute itself has been providing cocktails before the dinner, and we have run short on money.
>
> What do you think about a Stanley Marcus or a Neiman-Marcus sponsorship of a cocktail party for the Texas Institute of Letters preceding the annual dinner?. . . If you are interested you might agree to try this out for say three years. The Institute has more standing than it used to have, and a few cocktails will not impede its standing up a little stronger for free thought and civilization.[27]

Once again Marcus quickly agreed, asking Dobie to let him know when the event would take place so he could make the necessary arrangements. So Dobie wrote him again:

> Dear Stanley, you are always a gracious gentleman. Being generous to the Texas Institute of Letters does not diminish that state. I thank you. Many people will rise up and call you blessed. The Texas Institute of Letters is to meet in Dallas February 21. . . . Nearly always we have the dinner at the Down Town Club. The last time we had the cocktail party there also. . . . I don't think you'll have to make many arrangements. Lon Tinkle and Allen Maxwell are attending to everything in Dallas. I'm sending Lon a copy of your letter, . . . and no doubt he will communicate with you shortly.[28]

Marcus's support for the cocktail party before the annual banquet of the Texas Institute of Letters continued for several years and was only his first step in helping the organization. In the meantime, Dobie's increasing age and declining health prevented him from attending later meetings of the Institute. Perhaps sensing that time was growing short for his good friend who had helped make the Book Club of Texas a success, who had shared a passion for books and the freedom of speech, and who had enlisted aid in numerous worthwhile projects relating to Texas letters, Marcus sent the following telegram to J. Frank Dobie at the end of September in 1963. "We wish you the happiest of all birthdays and hope to see you sometime soon to convey our congratulations to you personally. Warmly, Billie and Stanley Marcus."[29] Before September came again, Frank Dobie died while taking his afternoon nap at his home near Waller Creek.

Chapter Five

The Printer at the Pass

As with J. Frank Dobie, Stanley Marcus developed a longtime professional and personal relationship with Carl Hertzog. In the printing business since the 1920s, Hertzog had the experience and reputation to open his own small shop in El Paso in 1934. He did not, however, make close connections with the Texas literary or historical scene until he met Tom Lea in 1937, the same year Stanley Marcus became aware of him. It was early in 1938 that Stanley Marcus first wrote Carl Hertzog: "I have been very much pleased with the various examples of your printing I have seen and feel sure the Book Club would like to use you for its next publication. At the present time we are being held up awaiting the discovery of a worth-while piece of material. Do you happen to know of anything relative to Texas or the Southwest that would be worthy of publication. If you do, we would be happy to consider it."[1]

The El Paso printer suggested "The Adventures of Big Foot Wallace," the same title he would later recommend to Everette Lee DeGolyer as a possible title for a series of books the oilman was publishing. While a book project on Big Foot Wallace did not emerge for the book club, Marcus furthered his contact with Hertzog early the following year with a telegram: "Am passing through El Paso tomorrow morning enroute to California. Arrive on Sunshine Special at 7 o'clock. Going out on Argonaut. Would like very much to talk to you and see further examples of your printing. Could you meet me at station and breakfast with me?"[2]

Before the year was out Hertzog designed and printed a book for Marcus, not for the Book Club of Texas but under an altogether new imprint—Neiman-Marcus. The project grew from Frank Dobie's suggestion that a Yale professor, Townsend Miller, approach Hertzog. Miller had just written a poem titled "A Letter from Texas," and Dobie thought Hertzog might work with it on a nonprofit basis, knowing well that poetry was an unlikely money-maker. Hertzog and Tom Lea, now good friends, both took up the Townsend Miller poem as something of an experiment. After discussing design alternatives for the book, Lea produced a drawing for the title page.

Having recently bought some 18-point Goudy Truesdell type for trial page proofs, Lea and Hertzog set a title page and one page of text in the new type. The proofs looked interesting, but the projected expense of the art-for-art's-sake project made it unfeasible. Remembering Marcus's interest in publishing a Texas item as a Christmas gift book, Hertzog sent him the two trial page proofs. He wrote Marcus that the "layout has possibilities that can be developed into a very striking small book."[3]

Vacations, buying trips, and final planning for the autumn season delayed approval of the project until the 23rd of September, when Marcus wrote that Neiman-Marcus had decided to go ahead and commission Hertzog to produce three hundred copies of *A Letter from Texas* with the store's imprint on the title page. The only condition was that Hertzog make satisfactory arrangements with the author for release of the work to N-M.[4] While this condition seemed like a reasonable request, it generated a set of complications that nearly killed the project, already on an extremely short time line, and ran the risk of straining several friendships. Though Hertzog did inform Marcus that Miller was "very finicky, wants copyright in his name, etc.," he did not tell him that the poet had already indicated that a release might be difficult to get.[5]

With Marcus in the picture, matters were growing more serious. Hertzog turned for help to Dobie, who had referred Townsend Miller in the first place. He told Dobie that Miller had "gone sour on me" after agreeing to pay $50 for cuts and for one hundred copies of the poem printed in a deluxe manner. Hertzog could sell two hundred to three hundred additional copies to cover expenses. When Miller learned that Marcus was Hertzog's client for the additional copies, he wanted to sell them himself. To further complicate the problem, as Hertzog tried to iron out details, Miller asked Donald Gallup, who was then teaching at SMU, to act as his agent. With the holiday season fast approaching, Hertzog saw little hope of producing *A Letter from Texas* before Christmas.

He asked Dobie to recommend a backup manuscript in case he had to tell Marcus that Miller was not going to keep his part of the original agreement. "As you know, Neiman-Marcus does not have a book department; they ordered the book as a gift item. If Marcus will take another manuscript for the same purpose it will give me the finances to do one of those jobs I like to do even though there is no profit. I know you are interested in assisting projects of this kind and will appreciate your suggestions. Of course we would make a number of copies for your personal use in addition to the copies for Marcus."[6]

Instead of recommending a substitute, Dobie fired off a letter to Townsend Miller, sending a copy to Hertzog, saying "it will probably make him mad and I don't care if it does. I hope it will make him mad enough to live up to his bargain with you."[7] In his letter to Miller, Dobie laid out the facts as he understood them and then turned up the heat:

> Carl says that you have refused to live up to your agreement and want to sell the copies to Marcus yourself. It was on my word that you wrote to Carl Hertzog and that he agreed to do your work. He runs a small business and makes no more than a living doing commercial work. He is the finest and most artistic printer in Texas, however, and he wanted to do your poem right for the sole reason that he loves beautiful work and loves to do it. You knew nothing of the Marcus possibility until Carl Hertzog told you of it. Marcus would not have the least interest in your book if it were not for the Hertzog printing.... I do not believe you can afford to break your agreement with Carl Hertzog and deprive him of just compensation for the work he has done for you.[8]

A month passed with no response from Miller. Discouraged to see time running out on the project for his new client, Hertzog wrote Marcus on November 7 that he could not go ahead because Miller had not sent the release. He also enclosed a copy of Dobie's letter to Miller to "give you an idea of how I became involved and was then unable to produce."[9] Unknown to Hertzog, Marcus was wrapping up details with Donald Gallup at SMU. Just as Hertzog's discouraging letter reached Marcus, good news was making its way to El Paso in the form of a signed release. Marcus had negotiated an arrangement wherein Miller would receive copies of the finished book in lieu of any other payment. He asked Hertzog to proceed "with all possible speed" on an edition of three hundred copies of *A Letter from Texas* using the Neiman-Marcus imprint, with another hundred copies for the author without the store's imprint.[10] Hertzog hastened to assure him that he could finish the job by the middle of December. No doubt watching the clock with nervous anticipation, Hertzog set to work on a project that would now be troubled further by the selection of a typeface.

When Hertzog and Lea had set a trial page of the Miller poem on a slow summer day earlier in 1939, they were experimenting with a small supply of Goudy Truesdell type which Hertzog had recently bought. Marcus and Miller both liked the result of the text set in Goudy's new typeface, and they did not want to see it changed. However, Hertzog did not have enough type to complete the book and could not purchase any more because the previous January a fire had destroyed the matrices for Truesdell. None remained in stock for sale at the foundry.[11] Thus, to complete the job, Hertzog had to handset and print three pages at a time, distribute the type, and then set the next three pages. This painstaking routine was followed until the book was finished.

Nevertheless, he was able to send Marcus a mock-up and two sample bindings by the 20th of November. Marcus, who had already served his apprenticeship as a book designer and had achieved national recognition for one of his early efforts with the Book Club of Texas, was a demanding client. He did not approve the nontraditional layout Hertzog had produced. Instead, he specified that the printer add a title page with the Neiman-Marcus imprint, "one blank page before your title page, and then the beginning of your copy. Your [printer's mark] should appear in the place which you have designated for our signature, and a final sheet should be plain on both sides."[12]

In the meantime, Hertzog was forced by circumstances to serve two clients on this project—one who was paying the bill and the other who had written the work being published. To meet the December deadline, he had to push ahead without sending proofs to Miller in New Haven. Since he was limited to setting three pages at a time, he had to split his presswork into five different lots. Exchanging proofs with someone in New England would have extended completion far beyond Christmas.

At first, Miller agreed to limit his involvement to one final editing so they would not have to exchange proofs. Hertzog would do the proofreading in El Paso to save time. Then, either forgetting about this agreement or becoming uneasy with it, Miller brought Gallup back into the picture. On December 12 Gallup wrote Hertzog and called Stanley Marcus to express alarm that neither the author nor his agent had seen a proof for the book. Marcus, ever expedient, followed up with a letter to El Paso asking Hertzog to send him a set of sheets he could pass along to Miller. "There is nothing that we can do now, but he may feel better about it. Do not delay, though, in the binding of the book."[13]

As production was completed, Marcus received the finished copies in batches from the bindery. By the 22nd of December he wrote enthusiastically to Hertzog that "the first group of the books arrived and sold out before we could even put in an advertisement on them. It looks like we have hit something good and that we will be able to run the year around." He noted that if sales on the remainder of the edition were good, Hertzog might be getting a new printing order by the first of the new year, and he asked for a quote on a second printing.[14] This good news along with accolades now reaching Hertzog undoubtedly raised his spirits.

Marcus proudly sent copies of *A Letter from Texas* to friends and associates who appreciated the art of book design and typography, especially those in California attuned to the work of John Henry Nash and the Grabhorns. Among recipients of the new book was James Ransahoff, who headed Ransahoff's, a specialty shop at 250 Post Street in San Francisco. Having just received a handsome piece of printing commissioned by Ransahoff from Grabhorn, Marcus wrote to thank his friend, saying, "It is a beautiful book, and I am delighted with it. Under separate cover I am sending you a copy of our publication, which is not anywhere near as pretentious, but at least it marks our debut in the field of publishing. It was printed in Texas by a Texas printer, and, although he is not a Grabhorn, I think that he has some future."[15]

Both publisher and printer received praise for the book. Donald Gallup wrote a review for the *Dallas Morning News* and many others wrote warm letters of thanks, but the most enthusiastic response came from Tom Lea, to whom Hertzog had sent a copy. "A real Christmas present came today from the best damned printer since Gutenberg! Both Sarah and I are delighted with our copy of *A Letter from Texas,* and very proud of you for having done such a really superb job. . . .To a loud BRAVO both of us wish to add, also from our hearts, MERRY CHRISTMAS and for 1940, SALUD Y PESETAS!"[16]

Early in January Hertzog worked up the estimate for a new edition of *A Letter from Texas*. Sales were still good. It had cost $300 to produce and was selling at $2 per copy. But before the end of the month, sales had slowed to the point where Marcus told Hertzog they would have to delay another printing until more were sold. Perhaps this news dampened Hertzog's assessment of the book. A short time later, he sent a copy to Frank Dobie and confessed he had not done as good a job as he hoped to do. The printer clearly wanted to linger over every letter and "do some delicate spacing and take enough time" to make it one of the "Fifty of 1939." After the "hemming and hawing" with Townsend Miller had delayed the start of the project, it had been thrown into the middle of the Christmas rush. As a result, Hertzog had been unable to ride herd on it the way he had wanted to for his new client.

Nevertheless, Marcus liked the book very much and in 1944 turned to Hertzog for a second edition, which sold for $1.25 per copy. In 1951 he initiated discussions about a third edition, but by that time Hertzog was feeling unsettled about some aspects of his work on the project and was growing weary of it. He recommended an offset edition, but Marcus, whose negative reaction to offset printing of fine books echoed Tom Lea's, was not interested. Discussion rocked along until 1955, when Hertzog indicated he could not undertake the job because he was in the midst of work on Tom Lea's history of the King Ranch. He suggested Marcus talk with W. L. Thompson of the Steck Company. Nothing materialized.

Then, in 1957 Marcus raised the subject again in conjunction with the fiftieth anniversary of Neiman-Marcus. At this point Hertzog suggested producing an especially attractive book in collaboration with his bookbinder friend in Denver, Edward McLean. Behind this suggestion, however, lay a desire to throw the job to somebody else, for by 1955 Hertzog was feeling pressed from all sides and talking more and more about leaving El Paso for a secluded spot in New Mexico. A recent campaign on the part of some of his Dallas friends who wanted him to come work for SMU may also have been weighing heavily on Hertzog's mind. Whatever the case, he would not produce a third edition of *A Letter from Texas*.

Whatever Hertzog may have ultimately thought about the project, Marcus was pleased with his work and obviously saw a bright future for the printer at the Pass of the North. As a regional vice-president of the American Institute of Graphic Arts, he extended an invitation for Hertzog to become a member of the organization, stating, "As an important member of the graphic arts industry in Texas, I feel that you would be interested in the work of the Association and that you will enjoy the privileges of membership."[17] Without hesitation Hertzog joined.

By early 1940, Marcus and Hertzog were involved in another project. This one would prove even more challenging than the first. It was a short book involving Stanley Marcus, Carl Hertzog, Walter Prescott Webb, the Texas State Historical Association, the Texas Memorial Museum, one of Webb's graduate students, and a set of high-powered lawyers threatening to sue all of the players! The idea for the book was relatively simple — a brief account of about five thousand words written about the oil discovery that made the University of Texas and Texas A & M University enormously wealthy. Complications arose out of the hard feelings which lingered in the wake of extensive litigation following the development of the Big Lake Oil Field, all of which was colored and shaded by the myths which naturally become attached to great moments in history.

The project started innocently enough in 1939 when Walter Prescott Webb assigned a thesis topic on the history of the University of Texas oil fields to Martin Schwettmann, a graduate student from Texon, a small west Texas town. The oil well that opened up one of the richest discoveries in Texas was named Santa Rita for the Saint of the Impossible. Having grown up nearby, Schwettmann knew that the derrick, still standing, was the only remaining wooden structure in a field of steel towers. Webb quickly envisioned the Santa Rita derrick as the "symbol for the greatest fortune which has ever befallen this institution," and he proposed it be dismantled and moved to the university campus in Austin.[18] After Schwettmann gathered a good amount of material for his master's thesis, Webb decided a brief account would make an attractive and interesting publication for members of the Texas State Historical Association attending the annual meeting in 1940. He contacted Marcus, seeking advice on a first-class publication. Webb was hopeful that Marcus would like the content of the book well enough to participate in its underwriting as a joint imprint of the Book Club of Texas and the Texas State Historical Association.

With the annual meeting of TSHA scheduled for 26 and 27 April, Webb wrote Marcus on the 6th of March, outlining the idea. "It seems to me that oil is the current topic about which much of the history of Texas will crystallize during the next century. All literature having to do with the beginning of this industry is sure to be sought after by collectors and some of them are already alive to the future importance of this category of Texana."[19] Webb's idea was to produce a short limited edition book illustrated with photographs of the well, the promoter, and the drillers. In addition to giving a copy to those members attending the forthcoming TSHA annual meeting, each chapter of the Junior Historians would receive a copy for its library, while ten copies would be offered in the auction and ten copies held in reserve.

Webb suggested that such a book would "create great interest in the Association and will attract to the meeting book collectors and Texana lovers. . . .If I may judge by results so far, this Historical Association has great possibilities for developing a broad interest among Texas people in the culture of this state, in books about the state and in all that pertains to good books."[20] No doubt, from discussions with Dobie, Webb knew that Marcus had broad-ranging interests in Texas history and in seeing Texas history presented in a printed form that reflected good taste in book production. He also knew that Marcus was still seeking shorter nonfiction for consideration by the Book Club of Texas. Thus, he asked Marcus for suggestions on type style, paper, binding, and printer.

With characteristic enthusiasm and efficiency, Marcus sent an inquiry to

Carl Hertzog via postal telegraph: "Could you print small book 5,000 words including some photographs approximately 200 copies guaranteed delivery in Austin by April 20? Please wire answer postal telegraph immediately. H. Stanley Marcus—Neiman Marcus."[21]

By asking for delivery only six days before the annual meeting of the Texas State Historical Association, Marcus was clearly building into the schedule as much time as possible for book production. Hertzog, pleased to have another project from Marcus, telegraphed his reply the same day: "I can deliver books April 20th if copy available this week. Time may restrict choice of paper and binding. Carl Hertzog."[22]

As soon as Hertzog's telegram arrived, Marcus sent another to Webb. The next day Webb modified his original concept to reflect a larger press run, reasoning that members not attending the annual meeting should have an opportunity to order the book. He guessed that there might be three hundred present at the dinner, with another two hundred members wanting to order copies. In the meantime, Webb still did not have a manuscript in hand and did not think it would be ready until the following week.[23]

In less than a week Schwettmann came through with a draft, which Webb sent immediately to Hertzog on March 18. Webb realized that production of a completed book, even a short one, was practically impossible. In a letter accompanying the manuscript, he asked for something "as near ready as possible"—perhaps a dummy for the meeting. He also told Hertzog that the number of finished copies might range between five hundred and one thousand.[24]

A few days later Hertzog presented his idea for the book to Stanley Marcus and Walter Webb. He thought the subject provided an opportunity to move away from the traditional "special" book on deckle-edge paper in old-style type. Instead, he offered a "strong, modern type with the 'black gold' color scheme." Along with the dummy, he suggested pen drawings by Tom Lea instead of the halftones from photographs which would create impossible typographic problems. "There may be objections to drawings as actual photographs would be considered more documentary, but you can see from the dummy how the drawings can harmonize with the type and keep a constant style throughout the book. I believe Tom can follow the photographs accurately so that his drawings will be documentary even though he adds an element of design."[25]

Shortly after Hertzog's letter and the dummy for *Santa Rita* reached Marcus, Webb came by to visit. After discussing the dummy with Webb, Marcus wrote the first of several letters critical of Hertzog's design.

> Quite frankly I was not pleased with the dummy at all, because it looked much too much like a commercial brochure that an oil company might send out. I think the book should have a stiff binding of paper covered boards, and I do not care at all for the running page heads in color.
>
> I had envisioned a title page that would have the bare outlines of a derrick in the background with the title superimposed. I do not care for the handling of the very black title as indicated.
>
> I think they would be willing to forego the photographs and would consider Mr. Lea's drawings, but I would prefer to see the drawings in the form of full page drawings in preference to marginal drawings.
>
> In other words, the book should look like a book, and not like a brochure.[26]

Hertzog tried to take the criticism in stride, but he could not mask all of his disappointment. He wrote that the title page might look like advertising from an oil company, "but it has originality and would be something new and striking for book composition. I am sorry to lose this point." He also clarified that he intended to use boards for the binding—"that the dummy was merely an idea for color and layout. If our dummy had been bound in boards perhaps you would have liked it better."[27] Along with his letter Hertzog attached a sheet of questions about typeface and paper, the color scheme (yellow ochre cover, cream paper, black ink), and the number of illustrations. A choice had to be made between a book costing $1.50 with eight illustrations, and one costing $1 with four illustrations. He also asked for a firm decision on the quantity, and pointed out the need for an immediate selection of photographs so Tom Lea could make the drawings the following week.

Only twenty-three days had passed since Webb first wrote Stanley Marcus with his proposal about the Santa Rita book and request for advice on its design and production. With the book concept agreed upon, a designer engaged, an illustrator prepared to produce drawings, a typescript in hand (but still needing some heavy editing), a design plan and dummy sent to a potential copublisher (or at least a prospective underwriter) and to the president of TSHA, the project had moved with amazing speed. But the possibility of a lawsuit now slowed the momentum.

The specter of litigation against the author and publishers emerged as Schwettmann tried to validate the apocryphal stories surrounding the drilling of the Santa Rita oil well and the opening of the Big Lake Oil Field. On one side was Frank T. Pickrell, the promoter and developer of the well, who wanted to tell the story himself, having taken serious offense at what he viewed as Schwettmann's inclination for historical fact at the expense of a good story. On another side was Clarence R. Wharton, a principal in the Houston law firm of Baker, Botts, Andrews & Wharton. Some of his clients had been key players in the litigation which erupted after the well was brought in. By one estimate, twenty lawsuits or sets of legal proceedings surrounded Santa Rita. They could be divided into three groups: the promotion of the company and discovery of the field (which Schwettmann ultimately discussed briefly in the book he wrote), the litigation between groups of stockholders involved in the property, and the litigation with the State of Texas wherein the attorney general sought to recover property from the lessees "on the theory that the constitution did not justify the character of the lease that was made."[28] In the spring of 1940 Wharton tried to get Schwettmann to drop the idea of even a short book, then some months later he offered to cooperate by making available all the pleadings, evidence, and briefs in all the cases. Nevertheless, the combination of Wharton on one side and Pickrell on the other suggested several complicated scenarios. Webb, wanting to avoid litigation, delayed the project. It was no longer possible to have a book ready for the upcoming annual meeting of the Texas State Historical Association.

Writing to Marcus, Webb explained about "temporary difficulty in the publication of this book because of the intense feeling developed during litigation over Santa Rita. The author needs more time to gather his facts and polish the final article and he may hesitate, in view of the circumstances, to publish at this time."[29] Despite the slowdown, Webb still saw the project as viable. He went on to answer some of Hertzog's recent questions and to say he wanted Marcus and Hertzog to do the designing and thus make decisions on the remaining questions relating to style and production. If it proved impossible to publish the book on Santa Rita, then Webb would begin an immediate search for another book project, since there was an abundance of good material. He assured Marcus that "the program of publication will be carried out in some form. I desire that our selection shall be acceptable to the Book Club of Texas as well as to the Historical Association."[30]

Hertzog prepared another dummy before the end of April and sent it to Austin in time for the TSHA meeting. Marcus and Webb met once more to discuss it. Although Marcus thought the design showed great improvement, he was still not completely satisfied, as his next letter to Hertzog indicated. "I do not care for the paper that you have chosen as your binding paper. I do not like mottled papers, nor am I completely pleased with the blackness of the title page. Do you get what I mean when I say that the thing gives an impression of an advertising brochure? Dr. Webb is going to send the dummy on up to me in the next day or so, and I shall give you further criticisms on it."[31]

While there is no record of "further criticisms" from Marcus, we know that Hertzog kept working with the title page, the binding, and a dust jacket. One element which Hertzog especially liked and which he mentioned in several of his letters was the image of the Saint of the Impossible on the top of the derrick Lea had drawn. When Marcus and Webb asked him to remove it from the title page, he moved it to a dust jacket. Even so, it did not survive. By the end of May, Marcus was growing more satisfied with the new design and thought a little more "importance" to the binding would make a dust jacket unnecessary. Hence, Hertzog's saint for whom the well was named ended up as a cutting on the floor.

Summer was approaching and Hertzog knew it would bring slack time for giving unusually close attention to typographic details. Such attention would enhance the book's chances of being selected for a design award. Thus, he pressed Webb and Marcus for approval to begin setting type. By the end of July he had photographs from Schwettmann, and both Marcus and Webb had signed off on having Lea create pen and ink drawings rendered from the photographic images. Coordinating a meeting with his two busiest clients, however, proved unusually difficult, and it was not until mid-August that Hertzog, Marcus, and Webb could meet to discuss what Hertzog hoped would be final typographic details. The printer's slack time was quickly disappearing.

Before the end of August, Marcus had decided not to include the Book Club of Texas in the Santa Rita project, so the quantity schedule was revised, the time frames extended, and Hertzog began to think once more about his original design concept.[32] When he received the revised manuscript from Schwettmann the following March, he posed the design question to him. "I have your ms. but I hardly know where to start. The numerous delays and criticisms have interrupted my thought about its design (the book). I liked the original layout I made although Dr. Webb seemed to favor a more conservative layout (old style type), but I think he was unduly influenced by Mr. Marcus. . . . Do you think I could convince Dr. Webb on this point, or should I just go ahead with the more conventional design?"[33] Schwettmann was no more enthusiastic for Hertzog's "bold, strong treatment" than were Marcus and Webb, and he answered with the suggestion that they proceed with the more conventional design.

The project dragged on for two more years before being completed. Several times in the interim, Hertzog indicated that Marcus's blunt criticism had disturbed him. He mentioned it in a conversation with Webb in 1941 and later wrote Webb that he did not mean to be "resentful about those old criticisms. All have had a constructive influence and perhaps we will have a better book because of the delays as well as the criticisms."[34] Later, he appeared a bit testy on learning that the book would be dedicated to Marcus. "Why the dedication to Stanley Marcus? Is he paying the bill? If so, maybe we don't need to do that extra work to show special half-finished copies."[35]

H. Bailey Carroll, by then head of the Texas State Historical Association, was quick to clarify his position regarding the dedication in *Santa Rita.* He wrote Hertzog, "In the early stages of the book, Stanley Marcus did have much to do with its ever getting started as a project on our part. Stanley was most emphatic in saying that you ought to do the printing. He is not at all paying the bill, but the Neiman-Marcus store will aid in the publicity and sale of the book."[36]

Carroll also wrote Stanley Marcus to be certain that he was comfortable with the dedication, even though he had thought at one time Marcus "might possibly relish the surprise angle" of the book's publication at long last "along with the dedication." He told Marcus that "in appreciation of your work in the very beginning and also of your services to good printing in Texas given through the Book Club of Texas, it has been decided to dedicate the *Santa Rita* book to you." The proposed statement would read:

> This book is dedicated to
> H. Stanley Marcus
> Patron of and authority on fine printing—
> Distinguished Texan—
> His services in the planning
> of this work have
> been invaluable[37]

Stanley Marcus was indeed pleased by the honor, so with improvements in line endings and spacing added by Carl Hertzog, the dedication appeared when the book was at long last published in November, 1943.

The response to publication of *Santa Rita* was enthusiastic, with press notices coming from as far away as New York, where Charles Messer Stow discussed the book in his column signed "The Quester" in the *New York Sun.* He wrote that "someone on the publication committee of the Texas State Historical Association might be adept in typography, or the association might patronize a printer who is an expert. . . .Like other books the association has issued, this is a clever piece of book-making, hand-made paper, wide margins, good type face and firm binding."[38] With the publication of *Santa Rita,* Marcus had now influenced the design and typography of the two most prominent learned societies in the state, the Texas Folklore Society and now the Texas State Historical Association.

Though the criticisms of the design of *Santa Rita* may have strained the relationship between Marcus and Hertzog, it was soon to ease, for Marcus was championing the printer's cause in other ways, including a campaign to entice Carl Hertzog to move to Dallas. Hertzog, for his part, was clearly pleased to undertake new projects for the Dallas executive.

During the Christmas holidays of 1943 H. Bailey Carroll visited with Stanley Marcus, who expressed much pleasure with the appearance of *Santa Rita.* On New Year's Day Carroll wrote of this to Hertzog, reinforcing his confidence and also telling him that Marcus noted "he would like to secure your services permanently but had made an attempt and failed."[39]

With his perseverance and persuasiveness, Marcus had been able to bring Hertzog to his way of thinking on a number of occasions. Getting the Printer at the Pass to move to Dallas would be the biggest challenge and one that would test his resolve over a period of five years. For the printer, the concept held an intriguing allure. Perhaps it tapped a dream, but it was more fulfilling in its process than in its realization.

Of all the cities in Texas with the right mix of publishing, bookselling, and collecting interests likely to lure Carl Hertzog away from El Paso, Dallas topped the list. Soon after he began establishing his reputation, Dallas clients turned to Carl Hertzog repeatedly for a variety of projects ranging from Christmas greetings and broadsides to full-scale books. Consequently, even before the end of World War II there was much discussion in Dallas about bringing Carl Hertzog to the center of book-related activity in Texas, and the Dallas resident mentioned most frequently in the process was Stanley Marcus.

Indeed, it was Stanley Marcus who first tried to lure Carl Hertzog to Dallas not long after *Santa Rita* was published. If Hertzog could design and print something as attractive and successful as *A Letter from Texas* followed by *Santa Rita,* what could he do as the head of graphic design for Neiman-Marcus? This was a question Stanley Marcus asked at the end of 1943. He laid the groundwork for the concept with his father and then picked up the telephone to call Carl Hertzog with the best offer he could imagine. Would Hertzog consider moving to Dallas to take charge of all the graphic design for Neiman-Marcus? Marcus adopted the time-honored strategy of all good salesmen—seeking to close the deal right away. Hertzog asked for a day to think about it. Later the same day he wrote to decline, saying that the call from Stanley Marcus was "highly complimentary and I appreciate your confidence." He explained that it was not possible to make a quick decision. "Although small, I have a well-established business with contracts and goodwill that are worth as much as the equipment. It would take several months to make a transfer as the business is highly personalized."[40]

This was a turndown, yet it lacked a note of finality. Looking for a new angle, Marcus realized that if he could not bring Hertzog to Dallas to work for "The Store," Southern Methodist University might attract him with its university press and highly regarded journal, the *Southwest Review*. He apparently mentioned his idea to John McGinnis after Hertzog declined the initial offer. It took two years, but the idea of Hertzog moving to Dallas next emerged from the editor's office at the *Southwest Review*. Donald Day, the journal's new editor, wrote to Carl Hertzog suggesting that a move could be good for both Hertzog and Dallas. Day recommended they approach Marcus for the underwriting that a move would require. Hertzog gave cause for hope and, at the same time, explained why he had not warmed to Marcus's original offer. He wrote Day that he was ready to quit job printing "any time I can figure out how to do it. I am no longer afraid to quit on account of making a living but the fine work requires facilities that must be financed and staffed. If it has to have high pressure deadlines, the 'fine' idea will get lost in the rush. That's the reason I'm afraid of Stanley as a backer. How about S.M.U. putting in a Laboratory Press?"[41]

As soon as Hertzog's letter arrived, Day composed his reply: "Your idea of the Laboratory Press interests me, and I think that I shall try to do something about it. Just as an exploratory matter—suppose this sort of a deal could be put over, and suppose you were put in charge of the publications of the University Press? What sort of an annual salary do you require? Also—what would such a laboratory demand in the way of equipment? Suppose we started doing something and planning on it? It's entirely possible that we can get someone to put up the money. If we could get the right sort of a deal, there would be no harm in letting Stanley back it, but it would have to be set up right."[42]

In response to Day 's enthusiasm, Hertzog turned cautious, weighing both sides of the question of leaving El Paso for Dallas. He told Day that the Laboratory Press was "perhaps an idle dream" and immediately projected equipment costs of $10,000 for "a handmade deluxe affair" or $40,000 for a shop that would include offset, linotype, and a cylinder press, but without bookbinding capacity. He thought a studio or laboratory shop might influence the trade shops to do better work and offered the example of Jaggars (the

Dallas printing company of Jaggars, Chiles & Stovall) doing the machine work with the lab handling the make-up for better spacing, initial letters, and title pages. He also suggested an SMU-owned studio shop offering a course "in what literary people should know about type. The average printer does not know design or historical background and cannot advise his customers. Consequently, many cultured (literature and history) people distribute printing in extremely bad taste. . . .Stanley would be a good understanding backer but I am afraid he would have me working for the store before long. I might have to supplement a salary with some outside chores. Would I have to have a Ph.D. to teach a course?" Hertzog ended his letter by musing that he could double his dollar income right where he sat by putting aside books and typography "in the category of culture" and concentrating on production. "Then in ten years I could be my own angel. What do you think?"[43]

Day replied that they could discuss the matter further at the forthcoming Southwest Book Fair in Dallas, if Hertzog would attend. When he was unable to leave El Paso for the book fair, Stanley Marcus sent him a copy of the complimentary column he had written on Hertzog for the Southwest Book Fair Supplement in the *Dallas Times Herald*. Hertzog thanked Marcus for the kind remarks and took the opportunity to introduce a new element in the equation—competition from Albuquerque. "I have been offered the University of New Mexico Press. This would reverse the proportion of how I spend my time—and cut my income in half—but still I am tempted. Something better might be done at S.M.U. or Austin. Do you think there is any chance?"[44]

He then turned for advice to Elizabeth Ann McMurray, someone on the Dallas scene whose judgment and impartiality he trusted. He wrote her a long, chatty letter. First he commented on the column Stanley Marcus had written, saying he did not know Marcus was such a good fan. "I criticized his Nash broadside when he asked for a 1945 suggestion, so he is probably mad at me now. I am going to be in bad all over Texas, as I also bawled out Fannie Ratchford recently." Other book chat was devoted to a trip he and Tom Lea had just made to New York, where they visited Tom Streeter and Charles P. Everitt. "When I see you, I'll have some book talk that'll keep you up all night." Then Hertzog ended on the topic of most current interest to McMurray and her closest book friends: "What would you think of a Laboratory Press at S.M.U.? Or a private press with Stanley Marcus?"[45]

There is no record of McMurray's response, but Hertzog did not accept the offer to become director of the University of New Mexico Press (although he did agree to design for them Ross Calvin's *River of the Sun,* which was chosen as one of the Best Western Books of 1946 by the Rounce and Coffin Club in Los Angeles). Thus, he left open the chance that he might consider the prospect of moving to Dallas.

As the war ended, Allen Maxwell returned from active duty in the navy to become Director of the University Press in Dallas (the precursor of SMU Press) following Donald Day's departure. Soon he took up the subject of Hertzog's moving to Dallas and began to champion the cause in discussions with Herbert Gambrell, Jerry Bywaters, President Umphrey Lee of SMU, and Stanley Marcus. By the spring of 1946 Hertzog was writing of the move at length to Maxwell. He warned that relocation would require "a lifetime guarantee." Though he praised "big advertising printing in Texas," he condemned most of the book printing as "abominable except in a few cases." He described typography as a fine art, just as were music and painting, and clinched the argument by declaring Texas far behind in the field. He expressed interest in teaching a course on the subject "in connection with literary or art subjects. A laboratory press would be an adjunct. The students would not become printers. I believe Stanley Marcus would endow this department but I don't know how the University would respond." He then suggested that Maxwell and Gambrell approach President Umphrey Lee.[46]

In response to Hertzog's evident interest, discussions at SMU expanded. By midsummer Maxwell wrote Hertzog to learn about his salary requirements if he were to come as "production manager and designer of University publications, and lecturer in the art of typography and book design," indicating salary possibilities of up to $6,000 per annum. He also sought Hertzog's advice on how they might best approach Marcus. Hertzog's reply is a masterful combination of restraint mixed with encouragement. "You have been more active than I expected in regard to our Laboratory Press. This will involve a terrific decision for me if it can be arranged." Hertzog said he could make $12,000 a year from his present setup. He also suggested that Maxwell approach Marcus.[47]

Hertzog's high salary expectations and his reservations dampened the mood, causing discussions to languish for a year. In August, 1946, he wrote Maxwell that "when the long dreamed-of laboratory press becomes a real possibility, I am scared. That's why I have delayed answering your last letter."[48] Then, in 1947, as Carl Hertzog was getting closer to selling his printing shop in El Paso, Marcus renewed the proposal to move. "I think you will receive a visit in a short time from Dr. John McGinnis of Southern Methodist University who is going to come out to see if he can inveigle you into giving part or all of your time to come to Dallas to be the typographical director of the University Press. It is a wonderful opportunity to do the kind of thing that you always wanted to and for which you have all of the necessary qualifications. I certainly hope you will be able to work out something with Dr. McGinnis."[49] Hertzog was ready to talk more about a move, especially since he had a buyer interested in his business, Hertzog & Resler. He told Marcus that he would be glad to talk with McGinnis, "although the last time I saw him he was awfully rambling and hard to understand."[50]

On 4 July 1947 Hertzog & Resler was sold, and Maxwell renewed his quest immediately. He asked Hertzog if he had further ideas about coming to SMU, teaching typographical design, working for the SMU Press, and doing some design free-lancing for clients like Stanley Marcus. In the same letter Maxwell added an incentive, asking if Hertzog were interested in redesigning the format of the *Southwest Review* "inside and out, from cover to cover?"[51] For Hertzog, the idea of working with SMU on typographic design, production, and teaching was appealing, but not the idea of leaving El Paso. He kept the discussions alive by telling Maxwell that he had not yet decided how or where he would locate, "but even if I stay here, I will be able to spend considerable time in Dallas and we can work together."[52] The distance of over five hundred miles separating Dallas from El Paso at a time when air travel was in its expensive infancy made this plan unworkable.

Instead of being deterred, the Dallas contingent made Carl Hertzog an offer. Maxwell wrote him a long letter after talking at length with Jerry Bywaters, Chairman of the Art Department, who was keen to have Hertzog teach typography for him. Since the University Press was not large enough to take on Hertzog full time, Maxwell outlined a plan whereby he would work part time at the Press, teach part time, and do free-lance design for discriminating clients: "I rather imagine that Dallas is the best spot in this whole region for free-lance designing—what with DeGolyer, Marcus, Moseley, *et al*, located here; and I have no doubt that your work in this direction would be purely a matter of embarrassment of choice."[53]

With the pressure building from most of his Dallas friends and a specific plan from Maxwell now on the table, Hertzog tried to clear his mind on a two-week visit with his good friend Evetts Haley. After pitching hay and branding for a week, they set off with Harold Bugbee on a trip to Santa Fe, Taos, and the ranch country in northeastern New Mexico. Haley was seeking out papers and recollections about branding from oldtimers, but they also visited noted artists in Taos, as well as Frieda Lawrence.

The break from typographical and printing routines did not solve Hertzog's dilemma, however, so he turned to the one friend in Dallas who could and would "talk straight"—Elizabeth Ann McMurray. He told her that after two weeks with Evetts Haley he was "more mixed up than ever" because on top of the offer from SMU he had now been offered a country printshop in New Mexico. "Everything is extremes with me."[54]

The thoughts which McMurray shared with Hertzog were as level-headed as ever, but rather than give him answers, she asked questions. McMurray knew the Dallas book scene very well as an insider, and she was also a close friend of Hertzog's. Knowing his love of hands-on work with type, his penchant to keep seeking new typographic solutions even as a project was moving into production, his love of El Paso (and his family's love of El Paso), the pressure of book production combined with teaching, and the demands that clients like Stanley Marcus and Everette L. DeGolyer would make if Hertzog lived in Dallas, Liz Ann knew precisely what to ask: "SMU seems to have several *notions*, including teaching veterans printing, to present to you. Can you answer a couple of questions to your own satisfaction—1. What type of work do you want to do most—& what sort of auspices are preferable to you? 2. Where do you think your family is going to be happiest—El Paso—or some place else? Savoie Lottinville feels that openings in printing & designing etc. will show up, but that it takes a little time to get the word around."[55]

Playing his last card shortly after Hertzog and McMurray corresponded about the Dallas prospects, Allen Maxwell made a firm offer of $5,000 per annum for him to become Production Manager of the University Press in Dallas. It was a figure which he had introduced and which had been approved for the press's 1948 budget. With a specific proposal and a salary offer pending, Hertzog reluctantly brought the discussions to a close, even though the idea still lingered rather fondly in the mind of everyone who had taken part in the great effort to transport the state's greatest typographer to Dallas.

It was Stanley Marcus who had introduced the idea in 1943, and it was he who raised the question for the last time three years after Hertzog had turned down Maxwell and SMU in 1948. In a letter to Umphrey Lee, President of SMU, Marcus tried once more to generate sufficient interest to bring about a move that would have established Dallas as the center of the typographic renaissance in Texas. Speaking warmly of Hertzog, Marcus wrote that he was "undoubtedly one of the most gifted book designers in America and could do a wonderful job for SMU, both in teaching and in typographical supervision of its publications. I know Mr. DeGolyer was very much interested in this idea and if the project has any apparent merit to you, I would be delighted to discuss this with you and Mr. DeGolyer together."[56] Lee asked Allen Maxwell and Publications Board chairman Herbert Gambrell to meet with him, but by this time their enthusiasm for the idea had waned. Without strong support the effort collapsed, so Texas had to wait for another city to supplant El Paso as the center of its typographic activity. That it would turn out to be Austin rather than Dallas was not the fault of Stanley Marcus, who tried to make it otherwise.

Following the publication of *Santa Rita* in 1943, Marcus had turned to other typographers and printers for the Christmas greetings he and his wife Billie sent to close friends. The style and fine press work of California printers continued to draw his attention, and in 1944 John Henry Nash produced *Bene Dicte* for the Marcuses. But in September, 1945, at the time Hertzog was considering SMU's job offer at the University Press, Marcus turned once again to the El Paso printer, seeking suggestions for a Christmas greeting.

Hertzog's suggestion of James Emmit McCauley's "A Stove-up Cowboy's Story" did not appeal to Marcus because it had only one reference to Christmas, and did not meet the criterion of "something that has a little bit more firmness attached to it."[57] Hertzog replied that he was sorry that he had not yet found what Marcus wanted for "a deluxe mailing piece." At the same time he reinforced the idea that Texas could hold its own with California: "A classical Texas quotation or an epochal event properly illustrated could be just as handsome and more appropriate than the Medieval piece by Nash."[58] The point was not lost on Marcus, for by the following September he was writing Hertzog again regarding a Christmas greeting for 1946.

This time Marcus knew exactly what he wanted. He referred Hertzog to *The Gourmets' Almanac* in which "A Recipe for the Newly Rich" appeared. The full title was "A Recipe for the Newly Rich wherein all the edible birds of the air and the fields are brought together to make the ONE SUPREME DISH in which there is the quintessence of the plains, of the marshes, and of the finest poultry yards." This piece of eighteenth-century satire appealed to Stanley and Billie Marcus, who dealt on a daily basis with the newly rich.

Hertzog rose to the occasion by producing a handsome folio piece printed in red and black, with small images of six birds spaced carefully within and around the text block, each illustrating a bird used in a particular recipe. As was usual during the Christmas season, the printer was pressed for time, but he delivered the finished job to Marcus as promised by the first of December. A letter to Hertzog from Marcus after the project was delivered suggests the printer may have taken a shortcut to save time. Marcus wrote that he had just received a card from his friend Bob Moseley and was surprised to

The Four Stumbling Blocks to Truth

by the Anglican Mage Brother Roger Bacon, O.F.M.*

I. *THE INFLUENCE OF FRAGILE OR UNWORTHY AUTHORITY.* II. *CUSTOM.* III. *THE IMPERFECTION OF UNDISCIPLINED SENSES.* IV. *CONCEALMENT OF IGNORANCE BY OSTENTATION OF SEEMING WISDOM.*

*Order of Friars Minor, founded 1209 by St. Francis of Assisi, first of Franciscan orders.

Broadside of *The Four Stumbling Blocks to Truth,* designed by Carl Hertzog, 1949.

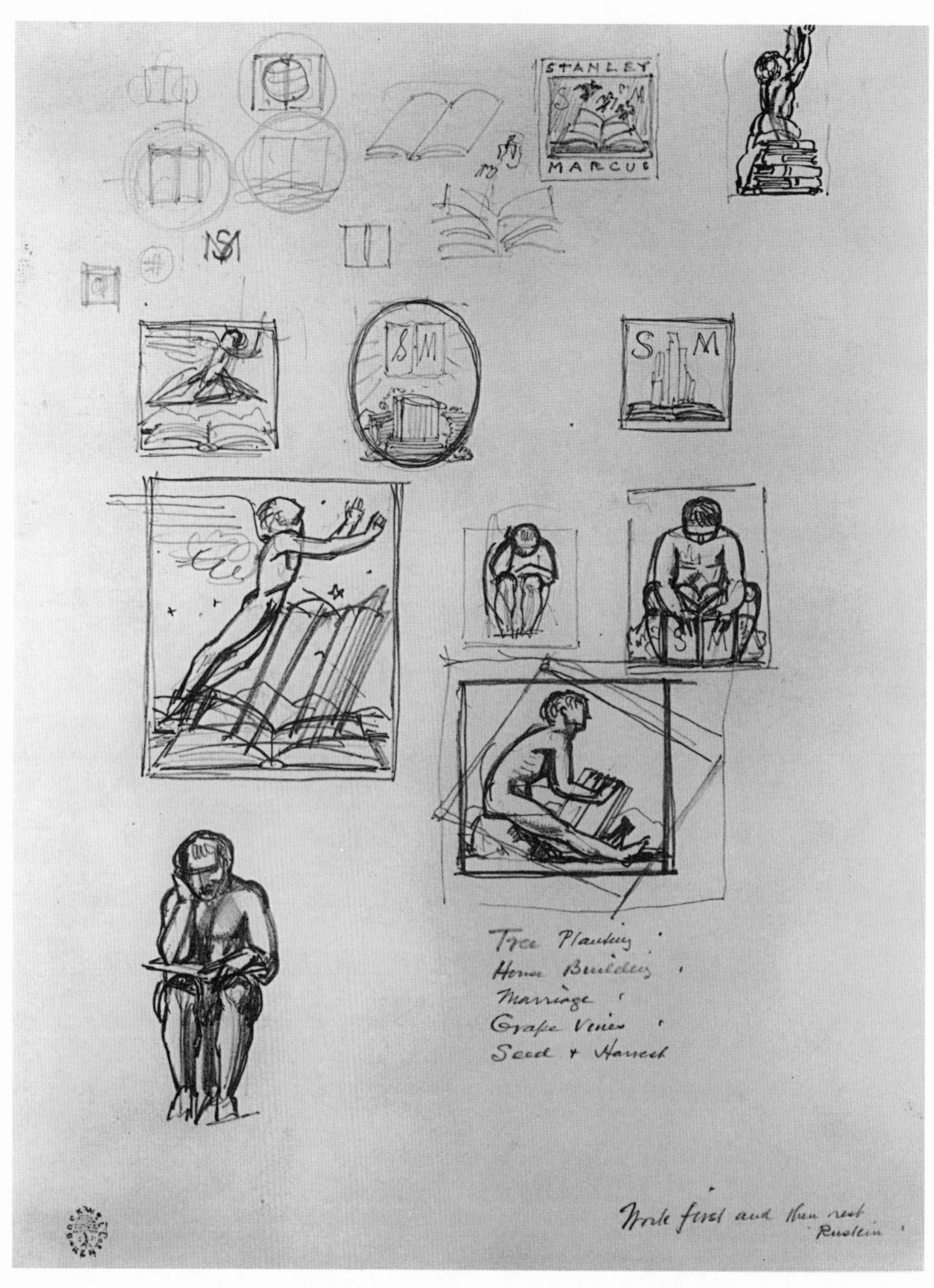

Sketches by Rockwell Kent for Stanley Marcus bookplate. Courtesy Stanley Marcus.

Four Marcus bookplates designed by (clockwise) William Kittredge, Carl Hertzog, Rockwell Kent, and Bruce Rogers. Courtesy Stanley Marcus.

"Was du ererbt von deinen Vätern hast, Erwirb es, um es zu besitzen." ("What you have inherited from your fathers you must earn in order to possess.") Quotation from Goethe etched in gold and set in red granite, a paperweight designed by Carl Hertzog for Billie Marcus as a birthday gift for her husband, 1955. Courtesy Stanley Marcus.

find that the envelope was identical to one Hertzog had prepared for him. "I think it might have been better judgment to have used a different typographical design," Marcus wrote.[59]

Hertzog was learning that no detail was too small to catch this client's attention, but Marcus's admiration and respect for Hertzog's typographic inventiveness was undiminished. Again in 1947 he turned to Hertzog with another idea for a Christmas greeting. It would be a broadside titled *The Four Stumbling Blocks to Truth* with a powerful message in the form of four very brief statements. When Marcus sent the copy to El Paso, Hertzog, thinking a booklet might be better than a broadside, prepared a mock-up of each format. Marcus liked the booklet concept, but not enough to abandon the broadside presentation. After all, he argued, the broadside has "greater impact value when the four principles are all printed on one page."[60] He also suggested that if the broadside turned out the way they were hoping, some people might want to frame it.

The Four Stumbling Blocks to Truth by Brother Roger Bacon turned out well, indeed. Set with a roman numeral printed in red and centered above each of the four elements, the messages could not be ignored:

I
The influence of fragile or unworthy authority.

II
Custom.

III
The imperfection of undisciplined senses.

IV
Concealment of ignorance by ostentation of
seeming wisdom.

It is probably true that every printing project since Gutenberg's first job has run into some problem, large or small, which forced a change in what was originally intended. On *The Four Stumbling Blocks to Truth* the size of the paper delivered to Hertzog forced the broadside to appear cropped at the top margin. Seeing the first copies of the finished piece, Marcus asked Hertzog what he thought about the margin. The printer explained that twenty-six-inch paper was delivered rather than the twenty-eight-inch which was ordered, and by the time the mistake was discovered it was too late to get more. "I am not so concerned over the margin as the type-setting. This was one of those pieces of copy that just won't work. I reset every line, spread and squeezed, doubled up, etc. I guess it was that short number II that made trouble. Finally I got the top in alignment, and then squared up the bottom." Hertzog offered to do the job over for later use, explaining that he not only wanted a satisfied customer but also that he did not like any problem to get him down.[61]

The printer had turned out good work, and the customer was growing increasingly more satisfied. In 1948 Stanley Marcus asked Hertzog if he would like to design a bookplate. "I am enclosing one that Bruce Rogers did for me several years ago which I have never been too pleased with. I think I would like to have a Hertzog mark to use henceforth."[62] Hertzog felt honored and thanked him for the compliment. He then set about the task, asking Marcus, "Could you give me any ideas? Do you want all type or a drawing? Modern or oldstyle? Texas history or scenery? Bookish or stylish?"[63] Marcus replied that he was thinking of something that had the same feeling as Hertzog's own colophon. After several exchanges of thumbnail sketches and some discussion of letter styles and borders, Marcus obviously felt the right approach was not emerging from these exchanges, so he suggested they let the matter rest for a while.

A year later Marcus came across the familiar woodcut of an early medieval bookman sitting at his desk wearing glasses that looked like goggles. He sent this to Hertzog and asked him to try another design for a bookplate based on the woodcut. At the same time, he asked for a reprint of *The Four Stumbling Blocks* just for his use at Neiman-Marcus. Hertzog took the opportunity to redesign the 1947 broadside completely, setting the text in all caps as one continuous paragraph, with the red numerals falling where they may. This was a happy solution and a fresh look which both agreed was most appropriate for the 1949 reprint.

With the job completed, Hertzog realized its production had brought together men with unusually diverse religious backgrounds. In sending a copy to a friend in Los Angeles, he observed that it was "a Christmas card for a Jew, written by a Catholic, printed by a Presbyterian, and I do my work in the Baptist Publishing House."[64] There is no evidence that he shared his observation with his client, but if he had it would have undoubtedly appealed to both Marcus's sense of humor and his commitment to ecumenism.

Before the year was out, Marcus had two bookplates that he liked very much from Hertzog. One had a modern, calligraphic appearance with the initials "SM" intertwined on a dark background with a simple border rule. The other used this same design in the lower left corner of the woodcut of the old-style medieval bookman. In reality, the latter bookplate was a collaboration between Hertzog and José Cisneros, who redrew the medieval bookman in pen and ink for the final art needed to make the printing plate. Marcus was especially enthusiastic about the contemporary bookplate, telling Hertzog that of all the bookplates he had commissioned, he liked the last one best of all. Hertzog would reprint it ten years later and again in 1962. It is still in use in Marcus's home library.

At the end of 1950, when Marcus asked Hertzog for some suggestions for a new printed piece the following year, the printer was caught without much new to offer. In desperation he turned to his old friend Frank Dobie for ideas. Hertzog told Dobie how he had tried to interest Marcus in Texas or Western items, but he had turned these aside in favor of "medieval quotations." Hertzog then mentioned an idea for a short book to be titled "Illustrated by the Author," featuring color prints and short biographies of six famous Western artists who had become successful authors—Frederic Remington, Charles Russell, Will James, John W. Thomason, Jr., Ross Santee, and Tom Lea. Dobie must have encouraged Hertzog in the idea, for he soon proposed it to Marcus. It failed, however, to "ring the bell" because it lacked the broad human appeal that would "make people who are not too interested in history per se want to buy the book as a Christmas gift."[65] Marcus was considering the appeal of traditional pieces like "The Gift of the Magi" by O. Henry or "A Christmas Carol" by Charles Dickens, hoping to find something comparable, while Hertzog was hoping to interest him in something that had not been done before. Since no prospects emerged, another year passed without Hertzog designing a book for Marcus.

Then, in 1952 one of Walter Lippmann's newspaper articles caught Marcus's eye. He made arrangements with the *New York Herald-Tribune* for permission to reprint the piece and turned Hertzog loose. Once the type was set, the printer noticed that some of the syntax was garbled, so he asked Marcus's secretary to approach the newspaper for authorization to adjust parts of the column in the interest of clarity. When Lippmann's answer came back an emphatic "no," Hertzog kept his peace and produced three hundred copies for delivery on the first of December.

His next Marcus project took him far afield from book printing. For Marcus's fiftieth birthday on April 20, 1955, his wife Billie asked Hertzog to help her create something which would have a special appeal for her husband. She wanted to work with the quote from Goethe which Marcus kept under the glass on top of his desk: "Was du ererbt von deinen Vätern hast, Erwirb es, um es zu besitzen." ("What you have inherited from your fathers you must earn in order to possess.") She knew, however, that he was not fond of framed pictures on his desk, so she ruled out a framed broadside. Much to her delight, Hertzog recommended a paperweight.

Deciding on the type of gift was only the first challenge. Meeting the time frame was an even bigger hurdle. Billie was leaving Dallas on March 22 to join her husband in Europe, where later they would celebrate his birthday. She needed to take the gift with her. Hertzog thought it could be finished in time and set out to have an etching made of the quote. Since he could not get a copper etching in El Paso, he tried zinc. When zinc would not take gold plating well, he ordered a copper etching from Fort Worth. Hertzog overcame the obstacles and sent the completed paperweight by air express. It arrived in New York only a few hours before Billie Marcus sailed for Europe.

The resulting gold-plated etching set into a small block of red granite and lettered on the underside, "To Stan from Billie—April 20, 1955," was precisely what Billie Marcus had hoped for. Hertzog also enclosed two prints of the quotation printed on seventeenth-century paper, just in case the couple wanted to frame them after all. Billie Marcus dictated a letter over the phone to the New York office of Neiman-Marcus before boarding the boat. "The paper weight just arrived, and I think it's simply marvelous," she wrote. "I know Stan will be thrilled to death. Thank you again for everything."[66]

As soon as they returned from Europe, Stanley Marcus also wrote and praised Hertzog: "My Dear Carl: By far the most exciting birthday gift I received was the wonderful paperweight that my wife had made for me with the Goethe quotation cast in bronze. I am deeply grateful to you for the wonderful assistance you gave her in helping to achieve this unusual gift. I am framing the proofs which you pulled on seventeenth-century paper for my own office and for my son's room. Thanks a lot for your invaluable cooperation. With warm regards, Stanley Marcus." Hertzog liked to tell friends the story of producing the paperweight for Marcus's fiftieth birthday present, saying, "Can you imagine the problem of giving Stanley Marcus something he didn't already have!"[67]

Every printing project is subject to error or change. In the case of the paperweight, the error either escaped Stanley Marcus's careful eye or he did not want to appear ungrateful in calling it to the printer's attention. Hertzog caught it, though, and wrote Stanley immediately: "Thank you for your letter of appreciation. The paperweight project was a challenge to do something different—which is always fun. But— — —. There is an error in your birthday Quotation! If you are going to frame the prints, they should be corrected. In our type we do not have the umlaut. To avoid cutting the type I intended to add the dots on *Vätern* with a pen but forgot. Before you frame the prints you can add the dots with India ink. Correcting the metal is not so easy. However, our silversmith says he can add gold dots—so if you will return the paperweight we will fix it. Sorry to make this error—I knew better but overlooked it in the excitement of etching in copper and gold—and didn't discover the error until you had already received the work."[68]

Marcus was away from the office when Hertzog's letter about the missing umlaut arrived, but his secretary replied and assured the printer that one of the graphic artists at Neiman-Marcus could fix the broadsides without any difficulty before they were framed. Marcus next asked Hertzog to design bookplates for his children. His oldest daughter, Jerrie, was grown and married and the twins, Wendy and Richard, had finished college and were beginning their own professional careers. He wanted two hundred bookplates for each of them.

Hertzog liked the idea of bookplates for one's children because he felt they would encourage an even deeper interest in books. "On the other hand," he wrote, "it is a frightening assignment because there are a thousand different ways of doing it and, since it is something to live with forever, it is like picking out a wife. Too much responsibility." He then asked Marcus if he would settle for bookplates centered around type designs rather than any that employed some kind of symbolism.[69] Marcus indicated his preference for a typographical design built around initials or names, and this was all that Hertzog needed to know before turning out some thumbnail sketches which met with quick approval.

Though there was, as always, give and take as proofs passed back and forth and details were resolved, the relationship between Marcus and Hertzog had by then clearly matured to one of great mutual respect and admiration. Hertzog enjoyed working for his discerning client and knew how to please him. He happily made changes suggested by Marcus, created several additional designs, and presented them all on a one-page color press proof to make the final choice as easy as possible. In addition, he printed a thousand bookplates rather than two hundred, all at no extra cost. As he explained to Marcus, "This can hardly be considered a commercial [job]—no telling how much dollar time I consumed in mixing inks and splitting hair spaces — so the invoice is problematical."[70]

Hertzog designed and printed because he loved the challenge of presenting on paper the results of a carefully conceived and beautifully executed job. Marcus understood and valued the printer's craft. In addition to the bookplates, he arranged with Hertzog to provide each child the designs, proofs, and blocks from which the plate was printed—a unique set of materials created especially for them. Shortly after Christmas 1959 he wrote

Hertzog that the gift "made a great hit" and that his children were as pleased as he was.

Hertzog's next job with Marcus would again involve something from the newspaper. The *Houston Chronicle* had printed views on academic freedom expressed by Dr. Phillip G. Hoffman, president of the University of Houston in the 1960s. Hoffman's remarks articulated a long-held belief of Marcus that any issue of substance is naturally controversial, and that one of the roles of the university is to explore issues. He sent Hoffman's statement to Hertzog in December, 1962, saying that he thought they should not be "overpowered by an oversized format" and asking for Hertzog's suggestions. Hertzog responded by asking for more detail: what was the event, where did it happen, who made the statement, and why. He also sent Marcus the text already set in type "to help visualization," with penciled suggestions for credits and what he called "connections" to aid the reader's understanding of the context of the piece. Marcus liked what he saw, and Hertzog printed six hundred copies of the single-fold pamphlet.

The "Controversial Issues" pamphlet came in 1963, the fateful year in which President John F. Kennedy was assassinated in Dallas. Marcus was one of the key figures in Dallas to take a public stand in an attempt to restore some feelings of community spirit and self-esteem after the assassination. On New Year's Day of 1964 he took out full-page advertisement space in the newspaper to articulate his viewpoint that Dallas was not to blame for what happened. Then when he read the text of Kennedy's undelivered Dallas speech in the *Dallas Morning News*, he immediately recognized its historical importance and the need to preserve it in a typographical form befitting its significance. Thus he commissioned Hertzog to do the job.

Marcus and Hertzog agreed that the presidential seal should appear on the cover or on the title page, so they set out to obtain a clear impression of the artwork. Hertzog tells the story best in his own unpublished summary of the project:

> On December 7, 1963 Stanley Marcus wrote, "How would you like to print the speech that President Kennedy was preparing to make in Dallas," and he enclosed the text of the speech as printed in the *Dallas Morning News*. After several exchanges of ideas regarding size, style and cost, we decided on the larger format and I began the typesetting. Since I wanted this to be elegant, and since I had a good supply of 16 point Centaur left over from *The King Ranch* book, I elected to set the type by hand!
>
> After 40 years in the machine age and now in the photo-computer era, I had forgotten how tedious hand-setting type can be, especially when I wanted to

respace every line for better sense breaks, and put copper hair spaces between letters that looked too close. Then I drafted an old-timer to come up to the college after work and on Saturday and Sunday to help me finish the composition. Little did we know that our careful work would have to be redone on account of the sloppy reporting of the *Dallas Morning News*.

In planning the front cover I thought the Presidential Seal would be appropriate, legal and make an attractive design. I went to the library, thinking it would be easy to find. But the only pictures of the seal that I could find were fuzzy or in color that could not be photographed. What I wanted was a simple black on white pen drawing. Then I phoned our Federal Judge, R. E. Thomason, and asked, "Do you have anything which includes a print of the Presidential seal?" He replied, "No, why should I?" Then I chided him, "Don't you have a diploma from Harry Truman?" Then the judge looked on his wall and said, "Yes, and it includes the Presidential seal." After my frustrations in the library, I thought to ask, "Is it in black ink or gold?" He replied, "It is gold embossed." Then I told him what I was working on and that I could not get a reproduction from a gold-embossed image. He was quick to cooperate and said, "Write Ralph Yarborough to get what you need and tell him I said to do it."

I wrote Ralph that I was printing the "Last Speech of John F. Kennedy" and needed a sharp copy of the Presidential seal for the design of the front cover. He crashed through with a pamphlet that showed the seal on flags, in color, and all the regulations about its use. And there was a simple black on white drawing which I needed. Eureka, we had it made!

No, we didn't "have it made" because Ralph wrote, "You cannot call this 'The Last Speech of John F. Kennedy' because he had already written another speech to be made in Austin on the day after his speech in Dallas." To prove his point, he sent me the *Congressional Record* which had both speeches in their entirety. This challenged me but in the middle of the night I woke up with a new title, *The Unspoken Speech of John F. Kennedy*—a much more dramatic title. Now, I thought, we had it made. But I had a hunch that we should compare our typeset proof with the *Congressional Record*. Alas, and thanks to the Lord, we escaped from committing the unpardonable sin of misquoting the words of a man who was trying to do the right thing. The *News* had garbled or left out significant words or phrases and we had to reset several paragraphs. Even so, with our diligence, we still had an error in the final printing: we had "million" when it should have said "billion." . . .

We printed 500 copies on Curtis Colophon paper but we did not have enough of the gray-blue handmade cover paper. Hence part of the first printing has a gray cover. At this time we printed 12 copies on Parson's Imitation Parchment. These were hand-sewed and inserted in double-fold covers. I suggested to Mr. Marcus that he send six of these to the Kennedy family, a good thought but we never got an answer.[71]

As might be expected, Mr. Marcus needed more copies and there was a second printing, different paper and all with gray cover, not the same as the original gray covers.[72]

The personal copy of the Kennedy speech which Carl Hertzog sent to his client was inscribed thus:

> To Stanley Marcus who encourages extra care* in the production of things worth while. Carl Hertzog
>
> *I used over 1000 copper hair spaces in adjusting the words in this document. CH

The personal letters from those to whom Stanley Marcus sent a copy of the Kennedy speech read like a who's who of the time—President Lyndon B. Johnson, Justice William J. Brennan, Jr., Governor John Connally, Judge Sarah T. Hughes, Chancellor Harry Ransom, Ronnie Dugger, O'Neil Ford, Alfred Knopf, and Isaac Stern, among others. Perhaps the letter from Paul Horgan best sums up the sentiment expressed by a number of others. He thanks Marcus for the "superbly printed" speech, which "is a splendid thing in every way." Then Horgan concludes: "I have greatly admired the full play you have given to your own fine qualities of public spirit, high conscience, courage, and style. Your example, given from the plateau of the high place you have earned for yourself in the world of affairs, has been of immense value."[73]

Soon after the Kennedy project another broadside was in the works, inspired by an antique clock which Marcus had at home and by his keen interest in quotes and *bon mots*. In September of 1965 he wrote Hertzog:

> How would you like to do a broadside for me that would have a large old fashioned clock at the top of the page with these quotations printed beneath it. I'm enclosing a rough drawing to show what I have in mind. . . ."You may ask me anything you like except time." Napoleon to one of his officers, 1803. "Time will reveal everything. It is a babble, and speaks even when not asked." Euripides. "O for an engine to keep back all clocks." Ben Jonson. "No clock is more regular than the Belly." Rabelais. "Time is a circus always packing up and moving away." Ben Hecht. [74]

Hertzog responded that the "clock picture" would certainly attract attention, and for it he suggested a 10" x 16" broadside. He sent a rough sketch, but asked if production could be delayed. Knowing the printer was not well, Marcus approved the sketch and readily agreed to make it a New Year's mailing piece, "or even a few weeks later, if necessary."[75] To cheer Hertzog up,

Marcus sent him some books relating to their old friend Alfred Knopf, including an unusual set of booklets honoring Knopf, produced by the Typophiles in New York City.

Finally, just before mid-January, 1966, Hertzog wrote again to say "your CLOCKS stopped while I was sick—don't feel so good yet—but I'll send you a proof Monday." He thanked Marcus for the books, especially the Typophiles set "that would not be seen here, except for your generosity."[76] A few weeks later, Hertzog wrote again in a reflective mood:

> Dear Stanley: Instead of sending you a proof of the Clock-Time broadside, I went to Tom Lea for his expert advice.[77] I had trouble getting a base for the clock and adjusting the proportion and balance of the type. I try too hard to manipulate the type—forgetting that Bruce Rogers said, "adopt a pattern, and let the type fall into place" (no artificial spacing).
>
> As usual, with all my cooperation with Tom Lea, Art becomes a "taking-away" process rather than the adding of ornaments, rules, and other foofaraw. We eliminated paragraph marks, red spots, and simplified the arrangement. A subtle touch will be that the bowl clock is in a brownish black ink, and the type will be solid black to create a base, no red. Instead of asking your OK of a proof I am going to go ahead and do it. You will like it—if I complete it next week, which is the plan. Best to you and Billie*
>
> *Remembering the delightful evening when Alfred wore a yellow shirt, and John Graves was there. Next day I traded Berte a King Ranch special edition for a pair of earrings—you should see them.[78]

After nearly thirty years of working together, Marcus and Hertzog were so comfortable with one another that Hertzog could print the broadside without sending his client a final proof. Marcus, pleased once more with the results, wrote Hertzog that he had done "a fine job as usual."

Hertzog's last job for Marcus came only a few years before the printer's death. Indeed, he came out of retirement to produce the only miniature book he ever created. Marcus approached Hertzog early in 1978, saying he had been "hankering to get back into the publishing business in one way or another, and it occurred to me that I might do a group of miniature books for which I've developed a great interest. These would be books on a variety of subjects printed in a height not to exceed three inches."[79]

Pleased to hear from his good friend, Hertzog responded that he would like to work on some "small" projects, especially if they involved creating something. He was finding that retirement involved too much time arranging his archives, work which was interesting but not productive. The height restriction of three inches made him uneasy, though. Saying he had begun to feel cramped, he asked, "Could we go four inches? I have some real miniatures as small as 7/8" which are excellent examples of craftsmanship but I consider them as novelties of no literary value. Can you tell me more? The subject matter. Greetings to Billie, and don't forget Goethe."[80] Hertzog signed his letter "Carlos ex impresor."

Marcus quickly wrote back, "Your answer was good news!" He told Hertzog that he was very excited about the prospect of working with him again, and over the next weeks sent him examples of attractive miniatures. By early March, Hertzog was still suffering from emphysema, and told Marcus with much regret that he would have to pass. "Sorry to be delinquent," he wrote, "but I enjoy remembering the good things we did together and I appreciate the support you gave me in those early years."[81] Marcus told his friend that he understood the decision, but he "received the news with a great sense of sadness. I had hoped to be the publisher of the one and only Carl Hertzog miniature."[82]

Five months passed before Marcus would try once more to persuade Carl Hertzog to create a miniature for the Somesuch Press, Marcus's publishing company, founded in 1975. An unusual book offered to him by Ray Walton, a notable antiquarian bookseller in Austin, gave him the opportunity. The book was *The Captive Boy* by Barbara Hofland, published in Boston as a miniature in 1831. Walton described it as possibly the first miniature book with Texas as the locale of the story. Marcus wrote to Hertzog: "Does this tempt you sufficiently to justify you in changing your mind? It ought to be printed by Carl Hertzog."[83]

Hertzog couldn't resist. "You do me honor," he wrote. "If I am elected to do *The Captive Boy* I would want to set the type and print from the type—no computerized photo-reduced offset printing."[84] Once Marcus sent him the book, he began to consider the possibilities of a photo facsimile, including the early illustrations, all designed to catch the flavor of its early publication. He also suggested a preface to set Hofland's work in its time and place. On Walton's recommendation, Marcus asked Archibald Hanna, curator of the Western Americana collection at Yale's Beinecke Library, to write the preface.

When Hertzog began working on *The Captive Boy*, he had not been as actively involved with printing and production matters as he was earlier in his career. Although he had actually worked on several other recent design jobs, he told Marcus he was shocked at printing-cost increases. Hertzog was probably trying to prepare his client for possible bad news, but learning that Marcus thought the finished book should be priced around $50 gave him some relief.

While waiting for Hanna's preface, Hertzog took time to rethink elements of the book's design and returned to the idea of printing it letterpress. He also began to discover how the production of miniatures differs from that of other types of books. First, his binder was "jittery" about the leather binding Marcus wanted because gold stamping has a tendency to spread. Then, Marcus wanted a deckle edge left on the paper in the book—another challenge. Next, in the small format the slightest variation while folding the paper could make the page appear crooked. Hertzog decided to fold the gatherings himself. Finally, the possibility that the sewing needle could push one signature higher or lower than the preceding one presented another hazard. "In a regular book this is not noticeable but in our miniature it becomes grievous."[85]

Hertzog found solutions to all of these problems but did not foresee other difficulties his binder would experience in working with so small a format. Marcus returned eighty-six books with binding defects. Hertzog fixed twenty-four of them himself, using a hot crimp on the hinges and applying a special treatment to improve the appearance of the leather. The balance were sent back to the bookbinder to remove the text block, straighten the headbands, and replace the cases and endpapers.

Two years elapsed between the time when Marcus approached Hertzog with the idea of producing a miniature book and when the last bindings were repaired, but Marcus found the results worth the delay. With his health continuing to decline, Hertzog must have known this would be the last time he and Stanley Marcus would work together. He documented his work on *The Captive Boy* with meticulous attention to detail. He also grew more reflective about his association with Marcus. Organizing his papers for the archives, he came across the telegram Marcus had sent in 1939 to arrange their first meeting as he traveled to California by train. Following his heart, Hertzog sat down and wrote his old friend:

> Dear Stanley: Do you remember how we operated before the airplane and long distance telephone became so common? The enclosed telegram was a landmark. It was preceded by a letter that started a 40-year friendship.
>
> My papers and files (now called Archives!) are in better condition than I thought. Finding the attached was easier than I expected. In the same file are the letters from Billie concerning the Goethe project. We had fun.
>
> This reminds me of the evening that you had Alfred [Knopf] and me to dinner. John Graves and his wife were there. Billie was so friendly that she made

me feel not only comfortable but important! She made me know you better. You should follow her suggestion and come this way again soon. . . . Sincerely yours, Carlos ex-impresor.[86]

Carl Hertzog died in his El Paso home on July 24, 1983, at the age of 82.

Chapter Six

The Business of Authorship

Stanley Marcus's association with designers, printers, and booksellers was not the full extent of his connections with the book world. He was also well acquainted with the world of authors, literary agents, and publishers. Through frequent book promotions at Neiman-Marcus and through his own publishing efforts, he became friends with publishers Alfred A. Knopf and Bennett Cerf; authors Roald Dahl, Art Buchwald, Max Beerbohm, S. N. Behrman, Irwin Shaw, and Ludwig Bemelmans; and literary agents and editors Aaron Priest and Ned Bradford. While some of these distinguished associates would influence his decision to write, other developments, such as the one which led to his first writing assignment, would come through chance encounters.

When Paris fell to the Germans on 14 June 1940, thereby closing American access to the great center of fashion, Marcus had left Dallas on an overnight sleeper flight bound for New York. At that time it was the only direct flight, even though the plane made a stopover in Philadelphia. It was there that he and other passengers bought newspapers and read about developments in the French capital. Fellow passengers asked Marcus what effect the fall of Paris would have on the fashion business. On hearing his reply, Charles C. V. Murphy, a senior editor of *Fortune* magazine asked, "How would you like to write that for *Fortune*?" Marcus agreed, and six months later his article, "America Is in Fashion," appeared. With the hallmark of someone who knows his own mind and has formed his opinions from experience, he launched the article, setting out his thoughts in an engaging and forthright manner.

> The American garment industry is now in a position to prove whether it can make a silk dress, or whether it will be a sow's ear. For decades our garment industry has depended for inspiration on a handful of Paris designers. The *Nor-*

mandie shuttled so many American buyers back and forth between Paris and New York that she was familiarly known as the Seventh Avenue Express; now she lies at anchor in the North River, and the American Garment industry is left to its own devices. How will it get along? For not only must it create designs for dresses, it must find its own inspiration for new materials and then weave them; it must devise its own buckles, invent new buttons, trimmings, and beads, and see them translated into actuality.[1]

He went on to discuss two fundamental factors upon which the creation of fashion depends—the audience to play to and the raw materials with which to work. "Paris was the ancient and beautiful backdrop against which played the leisured classes of all Europe, South America, India, and the U.S. These people had the money, time, and taste to absorb the creations of the couturiers and to experiment with their own new ideas."[2] He contrasted the American fashion business, which was geared more for mass production, with the couturier system in Paris, where famous name designers were actually superstylists working in conjunction with a number of *premieres*, each of whom had her own workroom and developed her own models. Supporting these creative people were craftsmen offering beads, buckles, and other accessories, and fabric manufacturers producing small quantities of experimental cloth on long-term credit to the designers.

He explored the "cordial entente" between the fashion designers and artists in other fields. Sets for the theater and ballet designed by Picasso and paintings by Dali and Dufy were inspirations for the creation of clothes, and kept Paris at the center of fashion design. With Paris now isolated by the war, the challenge for American designers was to overcome attitudes reinforced by *Vogue* and *Harper's Bazaar* that all fine designs must be imported from France.

The American designers of the time, whom Marcus identified for their innovative work, were Hattie Carnegie, Valentina, Nettie Rosenstein, Germaine Monteil, and those associated with Bergdorf Goodman, the largest custom-made dress business in the country. Now these designers were free to give full rein to their own imaginations. Fine specialty stores would also play important roles, Marcus predicted, because women would be impressed by a particular store sponsoring a fashion collection. Cities such as Chicago and St. Louis, growing centers of quality dress manufacturing, would no longer be regarded as centers of the "yokel" business in cheap and uninspired clothes. And New York should take heed, as other cities would provide what the customer wanted when they wanted it.

Marcus criticized the fashion industry for its poor timing, for presenting spring Paris collections in February and fall collections in late July. Even if the schedule worked for Europe, it was ill-suited to American manufacturers, who were responsible for turning Paris models into new ready-to-wear lines. "The dress industry is the only industry in the country that produces its goods with no regard for the demands of its customers," Marcus wrote, and he recommended that new lines be introduced a full month earlier throughout the year.

He also called for improvements in labor arrangements, for more innovation in the manufacture of American fabric, and for a new source of inspiration throughout the industry. Instead of trying to please the "public," the industry must concentrate on getting to know its customers as individuals who live in certain communities and whose lives reflect certain tastes. As a source of design inspiration, it must turn to historic design as reflected in the paintings and collections of great museums.[3]

With fourteen years' experience at Neiman-Marcus, the young vice-president had already established numerous contacts in and out of specialized retail merchandising, but the article in *Fortune* thrust him even more firmly into the public arena. Not only did the article carry a by-line, the first that the magazine granted to an unknown writer, but it also earned him $500, his first income from writing, and resulted in earlier scheduling when introducing new lines throughout the industry.

Another opportunity for Stanley Marcus to write for a well-known magazine came in 1948, when the *Atlantic Monthly* approached him for an article. "Fashion Is My Business" appeared in the December issue under an editorial lead-in entitled "Good Taste," which identified Neiman-Marcus as having as much influence in establishing new fashions as any of its rivals in New York City. Marcus, the executive vice-president, was praised "for promotion techniques which have made the store not only a powerful influence in the taste of the whole Southwest but also one of the foremost arbiters of the fashion world."[4]

The article opens with some background on how modern manufactured garments replaced those fashions once determined by court decree, then later by the custom-made clothes of Paris. Democratization of fashion was furthered even more by the introduction in the 1920s of rayon, which made possible the production of fashionable daytime dresses at a variety of prices. However, Marcus notes, "as fashion became democratized, the education of public taste did not keep pace with the production and distribution of merchandise in good fashion." Thus it was necessary to help some customers assemble various articles of a wardrobe into a tasteful ensemble. Other customers, those with an innate sense of fashion experimentation, did not require help. These customers were the "hard" ones to please. Because they knew more, they wanted more. Marcus learned to watch them for cues on which motifs would be popular each season.

Marcus also discussed other sources for Neiman-Marcus's new fashion ideas, one from two women in Oklahoma who used the dress of Native Americans as inspiration for wearable modern-day apparel. The colors in paintings by Paul Gauguin formed the basis for an entire collection of clothes. To promote the line, Marcus borrowed twenty original Gauguin paintings and hung them in special galleries. In the store's windows, he showed reproductions of other paintings by the artist. The five-hundredth anniversary of the invention of printing was commemorated with a collection of black-and-white dresses inspired by pages from the Gutenberg Bible.

Marcus concluded his article by pointing out that the development of Neiman-Marcus was tied closely to the rapid growth of the Texas economy, a result of the discovery of oil. The store, a recognized authority on matters of taste, guided and molded the tastes of the newly rich, making them hard to distinguish from "any 'old' monied group in America."

Marcus was beginning to gain a following among general readers around the country. In March, 1950, *Pageant Magazine* published "Why I Live in Dallas," his assessment of the community.[5] "I live in Dallas because I had no choice," he begins. "But now that I've seen most of the other cities of America and Europe, I think I would have chosen Dallas even if I hadn't been born here." He describes the industries that contribute to the city's growth and success, including cotton, insurance, banking, and oil. Of course, Neiman-Marcus is mentioned as "one of the most remarkable retail establishments in the land."

He also talks about the city's liabilities — congested downtown streets, inadequate parking, insufficient hotel accommodations, overcrowded schools, and a public library that did not "inspire pride." And finally, he recognized the city's civic improvements—expanded commercial transportation, and increased cultural offerings, such as the Dallas Symphony Orchestra, the Margo Jones Theatre, and spectator sports. In the end, he says that he prefers Dallas to other cities because "it has more homes than apartments, because you can eat out of doors a good portion of the year, because John Rosenfield, the amusement and music critic for the *Dallas Morning News*, edits one of the best pages in the country, because the Dallas Symphony Orchestra provides superb musical education for the school children of the community, because it is a nice place to come back to after traveling

THE HAPPY HYPOCRITE

Dear Mr. Stanley Marcus

Here is the book that you left with me. I have dared to amend, here and there, what seemed to me a lack of continuity in the narration.

Yours very sincerely
Max Beerbohm

Rapallo,
1955.

Inscription to Stanley Marcus by Max Beerbohm on the half-title page of *The Happy Hypocrite,* Rapallo, Italy, 1955. Courtesy Stanley Marcus.

Above: A selection of miniature books from Stanley Marcus's Somesuch Press. Photograph courtesy Padgett Printing Corp., Dallas. Top: Title page from the press's latest publication, 1993. Courtesy Stanley Marcus.

Stanley Marcus holding a tumbler full of miniature books from his collection. Courtesy *Dallas Morning News,* photograph by Phil Huber.

Stanley Marcus in his library at 1 Nonesuch Road, Dallas, 1992. Photograph by David Farmer.

all over the world."[6] *Pageant Magazine* had a wide readership, but distribution of the article was significantly expanded when *Reader's Digest* reprinted it. In addition, Marcus, always the marketer, sent reprints to customers and friends of the store, as well as to personal friends.

The article's popularity was not lost on the publishing world. In the spring of 1951 Edward C. Aswell, a McGraw-Hill vice-president who was on an extended trip through the South, called on Marcus, encouraging him to undertake a book for his company. Returning to New York, Aswell wrote that he had "thought a great deal about the book which I hope you will write which might be partly an autobiography and partly an expansion of your *Reader's Digest* article. . . . It could be a grand book and I hope you will continue to think about it and let it grow in your mind."[7] But Marcus was not ready to commit either to writing a book or to a publisher. "If I ever get around to the writing, which looks doubtful at this moment, I will be more than happy to keep you in mind," he replied.[8]

Knopf, too, had aspirations of publishing a book by Marcus. By the 1950s Marcus had become good friends with all three Knopfs—Alfred, Blanche, and their son, Pat. Both Stanley and Billie Marcus dined with them in New York, and reciprocated with dinner parties for them at 1 Nonesuch Road when they came to Dallas. On these occasions they regularly exchanged books and ideas for books. At one dinner hosted by the Marcuses, Stanley brought to Alfred Knopf's attention the work of a new writer who became one of the publisher's notable authors. Marcus knew of Knopf's great interest in wine and asked him if he had read the story by Roald Dahl on blind tasting in the latest *New Yorker*. As Knopf had not seen the story Marcus loaned him the magazine to take back to his hotel. The next morning his first call was from Knopf, who said, "I must meet this fellow. This story is terrific, and I want to publish him." Dahl had called on Marcus while traveling in Texas at the close of the war, and they had maintained contact. Thus, Marcus provided the address to Knopf, who immediately called Dahl and agreed to publish his first novel.

Providing the lead for a good new writer made the relationship between the Knopfs and the Marcuses all the more comfortable. Stanley Marcus corresponded regularly with Blanche, sending her occasional gifts from the store, such as a new perfume introduced in 1951. She responded warmly, saying the perfume "seems a very good one. I congratulate you on the packaging, which is very attractive, and wish you all success with it."[9] And he read and commented from time to time on books, such as Alexis Lichine's *Wines of France*, while they were still in galley proofs.

Formalizing Knopf's interest in a book by Marcus, Herbert Weinstock, executive editor at Alfred A. Knopf, Inc., visited Texas and called on Marcus. By the spring of 1953, they were exchanging letters on the direction the book should take. Marcus wrote Weinstock, "Do you feel that this book should be pitched to a general public, or to any specific part of the public? Do you think that the book should attempt to be a biography of Neiman-Marcus; a biography of Stanley Marcus; or a general resume of the field of retailing? Or should it be all three? I recognize that anecdotes and personal experience would play an important part in making the book readable and interesting."[10] He offered to develop an outline after receiving answers to his questions.

In the meantime, Alfred, Blanche, and Pat Knopf were also sending their own encouragements to Marcus. Along with Joseph Wechsberg's *Blue Trout and Black Truffles* Alfred enclosed a personal letter. Pat followed with a letter and a copy of John Mark's *To the Bullfight.* Meanwhile, Blanche sent two long and chatty letters in April about the Rouault show, happenings at the Museum of Modern Art, paintings she had just seen in Paris, and, of course, the book. "I still wish that you would think about that book for us and I still want you to do it," she concluded.[11] Marcus replied that he had been in correspondence with Weinstock "about the proposed book that I shall write, and I shall talk to both you and him about it further on my next visit to New York."[12]

Though the book piqued his interest, Marcus had little time to pursue it given the mounting pressures of business. Yet he did find time to write an occasional article and to give speeches. One address (later turned into an article) was delivered before a meeting of the Seagram Distillers in Houston, Texas, on 22 April 1953. In his talk entitled "Community Responsibilities of a Business Leadership," he pulled no punches in calling for businessmen to consider their roles as citizens in their communities. Against a background of national anticommunist intimidation and innuendo fed by Senator Joseph McCarthy, Marcus related his own experience with customers who had tried similar tactics to discourage his support of a political candidate they did not like.

> I received a visit from three men who vehemently expressed their dissatisfaction and threatened boycott. After listening to them, I said, "I'm quite surprised at you, for I surely thought you believed in the democratic way of life." They bristled and said, "Why, of course, we do. What do you mean?" I replied that the democratic procedure allowed differences of opinion without threat of economic sanctions, and that their tactics suggested the methods of the po-

> lice state rather than those of a democracy. I concluded by saying, "Gentlemen, if I were living in Russia, your visit wouldn't have surprised me, but I am truly amazed to have this happen here." I think they were amazed, too, for they had no more to say and departed. To my knowledge, not a single charge account was closed.[13]

Allen Maxwell, editor of the *Southwest Review*, published Marcus's speech in the "Points of View" section of the journal, a forum for guest writers expressing opinions on timely subjects. It appeared in the Autumn 1953 issue under the more hard-hitting title, "Are American Businessmen Moral Eunuchs?" In the principal intellectual forum published in Dallas, Marcus admonished and challenged the business community "to come to the defense of freedom in business, education, religion, law, and government, for wherever freedom is stifled by fear, it may next be strangled by hysteria."[14]

Meanwhile, another event was taking place at SMU which would result in a book with a foreword by Stanley Marcus. Following his own dictum emphasizing the importance of becoming involved in the civic affairs and intellectual and artistic life of his community, he enlisted the aid of eleven other men to underwrite the cost of the Institute on American Freedom to be held at Southern Methodist University. The Institute invited four speakers to talk about the way fear of freedom in some quarters was replacing the traditional devotion to basic American liberties. Paul G. Hoffman, Chairman of the board of the Studebaker Corporation; Gerald W. Johnson, respected newspaperman, professor, and author; Kenneth C. Royall, lawyer and former Secretary of War and Secretary of the Army; and Henry M. Wriston, President of Brown University, were the guest speakers, carefully selected for their conservative backgrounds as well as for their ability to articulate ideas about freedom of expression.

Upon completion of the program, SMU Press published the lectures in book form. Marcus's foreword set the stage for the book. He explained that the title, *The Present Danger: Four Essays on American Freedom*, "refers to the battle for men's minds which has been in progress since the end of World War II. This struggle, early christened 'the Cold War,' has in the past few years generated a heat that has become a serious divisive force in our national life."[15]

Ordering one hundred and fifty copies, Marcus sent the books to decision makers in the private sector, to government officials, and to people in education. For example, copies went to Arthur E. Sutherland at Harvard Law School; John Lord O'Brian, a senior partner at Covington & Burling in Washington, D.C.; Stuart Symington and Lyndon B. Johnson in the Senate; Clint

Pace of the National Citizens Commission for the Public Schools; Mrs. Nelson Rockefeller, Charles Van Doren, and Palmer Hoyt of the *Denver Post.* He even used the book as one of his Christmas gifts for 1953 and received enthusiastic responses from the recipients.

Ironically, Stanley Marcus created a dilemma for a number of his New York friends, who were unable to find copies at their local bookstores. Inquiring of SMU Press Director Allen Maxwell why they were unavailable, Marcus learned a valuable lesson that he would put to use when his own books were published. Maxwell replied, "We have found the stores up there on the whole rather provincial in their attitude toward books published West of the Hudson—they order titles from us repeatedly, one or two copies at a time as they receive requests, but they seem to lack the space necessary to stock our volumes in good quantity."[16]

Though Marcus seemed to have less and less time to pursue his writing, the Knopfs never lessened their expressions of interest in a potential book from him. He and Herbert Weinstock continued to discuss a book that would combine the history of Neiman-Marcus, autobiographical reflections of Marcus himself, and observations on retail merchandising. At the same time, Blanche extended another proposal. In 1955 she wrote, "You will remember my asking you years ago about a book on taste, and I think you still should do it. Why don't you? Lesser people than you have tried to and have failed. I think it is up to you."[17]

This suggestion unleashed a string of letters, telegrams, and transcontinental cablegrams that carried well into the summer while she and Marcus tried to resolve complicated travel schedules and meet once more to discuss a manuscript the Knopfs might publish. Nothing seemed to work. Schedules did not mesh and Blanche, who could be downright unpleasant, as Marcus later confided, began changing her concept for the book.[18] In spite of their perseverance, the Knopfs were not to land the book they so eagerly sought.

Instead, Little, Brown would eventually publish *Minding the Store*; and its editor-in-chief, Larned G. Bradford, would be responsible for securing the contract. His first meeting with Marcus was another chance encounter on an airplane. The two men sat next to each other on the way to El Paso for a testimonial dinner on 14 September 1957 for Tom Lea. The occasion was organized to celebrate the publication of Lea's new two-volume work, *The King Ranch*, designed and printed by Carl Hertzog. Bradford, Tom Lea's editor, began asking questions about the store. After hearing some of Marcus's anecdotes he said, "It sounds to me like you've got a book in you. Have you ever thought of writing?"[19] Marcus replied that he had thought of writing a book but the retail business left little time for such endeavors. Bradford expressed interest in publishing such a book and left the matter open, inviting Marcus to get back in touch any time he was ready to talk further about the project.

With McGraw-Hill, Knopf, and Little, Brown all expressing interest in a book, Stanley Marcus knew he had the publishing world's attention, but he would wait more than a decade before testing the market any further. By 1971 he had decided that a short version of his concept, suitable for a magazine with nationwide circulation, would help him gauge potential success. Thus, the *Saturday Evening Post* carried his personal reminiscence, "While We Were Watching the Store, the State of Texas Grew Up." With all the earmarks of an opening chapter for a new book, Marcus set the background by revealing his custom of welcoming new employees at a morning coffee where he explained how Neiman-Marcus was established. The founders, originally from Dallas, were highly successful sales promoters in Atlanta, he wrote. "They were so successful that at the end of two years they had two offers to sell out: one was for $25,000 in cash; the other the franchise for the State of Missouri for a brand-new product which had only recently come on the market—called Coca-Cola. They apparently were too sophisticated to be taken in by this unknown soft drink, so they took the $25,000 in cash instead and went back to Dallas to start a business of their own, to be run in a manner they had dreamed about."[20]

Marcus went on to relate the early history of the store, how it weathered the Great Depression and how the West Texas and later the East Texas oil discoveries introduced a new economic strength to the state, with Dallas, a growing metropolis, situated between the two great oil fields. The growth of the defense, banking, insurance, and computer industries in Texas all helped to raise the standard of living. Personalized service for customers seeking quality merchandise was the guiding principle on which the reputation of Neiman-Marcus was built, and Marcus included a generous share of stories to develop this theme.

Pat Knopf, then at Atheneum Publishers, wrote Marcus that he had just heard that the opening chapter of what might be a new book was published in a current magazine. He expressed hope that he stood somewhere near the head of the line as its publisher. But alas for Knopf, the last of Marcus's fateful chance encounters with Larned Bradford at Little, Brown was still to come. Marcus tells the story best:

> I was in New York, having just flown in from Dallas. Usually in those days when I came into town I'd take a walk down Fifth Avenue. It was a safe thing

> to do in those days, relatively speaking. But as I was walking, somebody put their hand on my shoulder and a voice came through and said, "It's later than you think. When in the hell are you going to write your book?" And I thought I was being mugged, and I spun around and here was the friendly hand of this man who was senior editor at Little, Brown. And he said, "You'd better get going on that. When are you going to do it?" And I said, "Well, I guess when some enterprising publisher gives me a contract and a suitable advance, I will feel obligated to do it." He said, "You'll have a check tomorrow morning *and* a contract." And I did. It was delivered early the next day to me at The Plaza. And having taken a check was the thing I needed to spur me on.[21]

As soon as he returned to Dallas, Marcus put his check in escrow so it could be easily returned to the publisher in the event he did not deliver the manuscript. Then he started the book, writing in the evening after dinner from eight until midnight after working twelve to sixteen hours in the store. His routine lasted for about nine months, except for weekends, and in less than a year he had completed the manuscript. He recalls very little "tinkering" with it before it was published by Little, Brown in 1974 as *Minding the Store: A Memoir*, the book that established his name as a household word for everyone who was interested in fashion, marketing, excellence in service, the history of American business, and Texas.

In the book he recalls, in general chronological order, his growing up in Dallas and his early schooling and university experience—an unhappy freshman year at Amherst where prejudice against Jews was rampant, followed by three years of culturally enriching experiences at Harvard. He moves quickly into the history and development of the store, the book's central narrative. Throughout he reiterates the philosophy which guided the founding of Neiman-Marcus and embellishes it with personal recollections and memorable anecdotes.

With the manuscript finished, Stanley Marcus turned his attention to marketing a new book. To the publisher he offered lists of people having previous contacts with the store—manufacturers, suppliers, customers, everybody he knew. The delighted publisher asked how he had conceived such a plan, and the answer was simple. It was just good retailing. Thus the techniques for marketing *Minding the Store* would be similar to those for selling hosiery, shoes, and other merchandise. Amazed, Little, Brown decided on a first printing of 50,000 copies, an unusually large number for an author's first book.

Little, Brown and Neiman-Marcus cooperated in sending out thousands of announcements for the book and invitations to autographing sessions. Marcus autographed enthusiastically, aware that once a book was personalized by an inscription, the risk of having it returned for credit was virtually eliminated. And who could attract more people to an autographing than the man who exemplified what Texas had become—a successful, thriving state with a history and a mystique that drew much attention from the media.

No place was better than the Neiman-Marcus stores for promoting *Minding the Store*. By the time of its publication Neiman-Marcus had become one of the five largest fashion institutions in the country. The book was displayed at every sales point throughout every Neiman-Marcus store in the nation, and Marcus made the rounds of all the stores. He also appeared at selected bookstores in Neiman-Marcus's market areas and backed up the autographings with radio and TV interviews. Just before he reached town, postcards were sent reminding people to secure their own autographed copy of *Minding the Store*. The advertising and promotion resulted in long signing sessions, one lasting for six hours. At one Dallas appearance Stanley Marcus signed two hundred copies in less than an hour, and while he was in San Francisco the store there sold a record twelve hundred copies of the book.

Yet Marcus did not relax. He found still more ways to draw attention to the book and, of course, the store. In 1975, Neiman-Marcus bought advertising space in papers for a letter he had written his friend Art Buchwald. The humorist's latest book, *I Am Not a Crook*, had just been published, and Marcus found a clever way to tie a mention of it to a discussion of the difficulties of marketing books in general.

> Dear Art: You forewarned me that writing a book was easy compared to getting it into the book stores and helping to sell it.
>
> With some 20,000 new titles being issued in the fall of the year, a writer doesn't have much of a chance (whose name isn't Michener or Mailer) unless he goes out and does the television circuit of talk shows across the country. That I did and drank endless cups of bad coffee offered me at each studio. Nowhere on the TV circuit did I find a good cup of coffee. Poor TV workers!
>
> Many of the booksellers and wholesalers were caught in the credit crunch and the publisher had to hold up deliveries until they paid up. National printed reviews were late in appearance, but personal appearances before all kinds of audiences and autographing parties have helped bolster the TV stimulation of sales. So, I can't complain. *Minding the Store* was well received by the public. . . .
>
> One book makes a *writer*; it takes a second to qualify as an *author*. Good luck to you with your latest, I AM NOT A CROOK.[22]

Late in 1975, New American Library announced a paperback edition of *Minding the Store*, selling for $1.95. It, too, was carried in all Neiman-Marcus stores, but airports and shopping malls also received an especially high distribution. Seizing the opportunity to piggyback on the book's success, Coca-Cola tied ads to the author's anecdote about his father, his Aunt Carrie Neiman, and her husband, Al, who turned down the offer to participate in the emerging soft drink company. Coca-Cola ads featured its world-famous bottle decorated with a chain on which the equally famous Neiman-Marcus logo appeared. The anecdote appeared in the ad copy along with the comment, "So now America has both a soft drink and a store that are the real thing."[23] Thus, Coca-Cola broke its tradition of never before allowing any company to advertise with it, and undoubtedly helped sell more copies of *Minding the Store* in the process. Stanley Marcus smiled when he was asked if Neiman-Marcus approached Coca-Cola. "No," he replied, "they came to us."

Minding the Store attracted major reviews in the *New York Times*, the *Wall Street Journal*, *Publishers Weekly*, and the *Christian Science Monitor*. The *Times* identified Stanley Marcus as "the personification of the Dallas specialty store" . . . who is "undoubtedly one of America's great merchants. In the 24 years that he has run the store and in the previous 24 years that he worked there, he has demonstrated how a superior talent for merchandising, promotion and salesmanship can build a profitable and world-renowned retail institution. Now Mr. Marcus has told the story of that institution in an anecdote-filled memoir [in which] the personality of opulence at the best-known store in Texas comes through with the clarity and insight that only an insider could muster."[24]

In the *Wall Street Journal* Helen R. Stephenson's review appeared under the headline "How to Be an Entrepreneur, Texas-Style,"which opened with a discussion of the 1974 Neiman-Marcus Christmas catalogue that featured his and her Hoverbugs. "However, the best bargain of all is a copy of *Minding the Store* for $10." She recounted notable "coups de publicity" as well as some of the legends that made the store known around the world. In addition, she suggested that the book might also be accurately titled "The Education of Stanley Marcus" for the way it traces "the formations of his personal and business philosophies and the involvement of his family and the store in the cultural and civic development of his hometown."[25]

It was not only the American success story of an immigrant Jewish clan that caught the attention of *Publishers Weekly*, it was also the parallel account of the changing pattern of Texas life from early oil days to "the reaching out to art and culture that followed," and the "rabid political conservatism that still haunts the region." All of this is "perceived by a liberal, intelligent humanitarian who risked a great deal to keep faith with his own integrity." The reviewer recommended *Minding the Store* to everyone connected with retailing, "including bookselling."[26]

At the end of the year Olin Chism, Book Editor of the *Dallas Times Herald*, included *Minding the Store* in his pick of the ten books for 1974 "that were important to me in some way, whether because of lasting merit for a wide audience or simple entertainment for one person."[27] Along with Stanley Marcus's book Chism included Alexander Solzhenitsyn's *The Gulag Archipelago*, Bob Woodward's and Carl Bernstein's *All the President's Men*, and James Herriot's *All Things Bright and Beautiful*.

With reviews like these, *Minding the Store* went into four printings in two years. Eighty-five thousand copies were sold. Before long, Marcus began work on another book in response to a question his audiences asked repeatedly as he traveled the lecture circuit, "What has happened to quality?" In *Quest for the Best* he defines quality based on his own worldwide search for goods that exemplified the highest standards. The first chapter, "The Death of Elegance," opens with an obituary to a bygone era:

> Funeral services for eighteenth-century ELEGANCE were held in the mid-twentieth century without fanfare or even any general cognizance of its occurrence by admirers. Death was attributed to a variety of causes, including the replacement of hand labor by machine production, the establishment of the minimum wage, high taxation, the overthrow of monarchical government, and inevitability. Most of the friends of ELEGANCE were unaware of the long illness that had preceded its death.
>
> So might an obituary have read, if the press took the same notice of the decease of eras as it does of people. I know, because I was there.[28]

Marcus moves on to define quality as "a summary word denoting the ultimate in beauty, craftsmanship, and quality—all put together with taste," and to discuss some of the historical forces that helped produce elegant, handmade goods from the Middle Ages through the Renaissance to the Industrial Revolution. He notes that the political and economic conditions "which made elegance possible were not consistent with the nineteenth-century's democratic concept of government." Throughout the discussion in this and subsequent chapters are examples and anecdotes drawn from fifty years of experience in specialty merchandising—stories that drive home the point with, yes, an elegant turn of phrase.

Later chapters address matters of taste, service, the search for the best in a myriad of venues: products for clothing, the building and preservation of a mystique, the famous Neiman-Marcus Christmas catalogue, hotels and food, travel abroad, and museums and the phenomena of collecting. The book closes with an epilogue of Stanley Marcus's picks for "The Best Things List" and his "Less Than the Best List." On the first list of forty items are linen bed sheets at Claridge's, Texas pink grapefruit, Château Petrus '53, Tarte Tatin at Maxim's in Paris, felt-tip pens, and London cabs and cabbies. The second list of twenty-six items includes Las Vegas, hotel art boutiques, fish and chips, instant coffee, plastic toys, teased hair, and political campaigns.

Though *Quest for the Best* would, in time, make the *New York Times* bestseller list, finding a publisher was not as easy as it had been the first time. While working on the manuscript, Marcus had become acquainted with Aaron Priest, a former Doubleday salesman in the Southwest, turned literary agent. Priest expressed interest in representing Marcus, and since no one else had offered, they struck a deal. When the manuscript was finished, Priest sent it to Harper's and later Simon & Schuster, but with little success. At S&S they met with Michael Corda, who struck Marcus as more interested in himself than in someone else's book manuscript. After this meeting they called on an editor at Alfred A. Knopf, Inc., but by this time Blanche had died, Alfred had retired, and Pat had left to start Atheneum. The old firm, which had encouraged Marcus to write his first book, showed no interest; nor did Little, Brown, which had a new editor-in-chief following Ned Bradford's death.

Viking, on the other hand, liked the book very much and offered a substantial advance. In addition, Priest negotiated for his client an additional degree of control over the book which few authors have the skill, the clout, or perhaps the interest, to demand—the right to select the type, paper, and book jacket for their new book. Marcus requested that the book be set in Bodoni Book, a traditional and elegant typeface. Facing each chapter opening is an illustration taken from Larmessin's *Costumes Grotesques*, splendid images of eighteenth-century French costumes before elegance died.

When Marcus again provided a detailed set of recommendations for marketing the new book, the people at Viking Press were as surprised and pleased as their counterparts at Little, Brown had been five years earlier. Once again a new book by Stanley Marcus was offered through the Neiman-Marcus stores around the country, as well as in every bookstore where Viking could place the title. Once again the author hit the road for signings, which were backed up with radio and TV appearances.

This time the *New Yorker* took notice, with a discussion of Stanley Marcus's two abiding enthusiasms—good quality and good taste. The editor observed that Marcus found them in decline, in part because people new to opulence "are unsure of their taste [and] mask their insecurity by purchasing articles with designer labels," and in part because cheap goods tend to drive out fine goods. *Publishers Weekly* called the book an "entertaining commentary on the changes in taste and standards brought about by mass production and the disappearance of cheap labor."[29] They identified Marcus as a connoisseur-businessman and noted how his appreciation of art enriched his quality of life and led him to the best.

The *Dallas Morning News*, on the other hand, took the opportunity to tweak the author. Having received an advance copy for review purposes which contained an errata slip, they ran a short item on 6 July 1979 under the headline "Marcus quest continues," quoting the slip: "Please note that pages 46 and 47 have been transposed in this copy. The error is being corrected for our first printing. In order not to delay advance review copies, we are sending you this uncorrected copy." The column ends thus: "And Stanley Marcus's quest for the best apparently continues."

The book also provided the basis for an unusual gift at the time Stanley Marcus and Linda Robinson were married. (His first wife, Billie, died in 1978.) Their architect friend Bill Booziotis designed a special sweater set just for the newlyweds. Five couples contributed to the cost of the sweaters, which were commissioned from a craftswoman in Santa Fe. On the sweater for Stanley Marcus is a repeated pattern of small open books, each titled "Quest." The bride's sweater has an identical design, except each little book is titled "Best."

When *Quest for the Best* made it to the *New York Times* bestseller list, along with an article about its author and his book in the *Times* column "Behind the Best Sellers," it did so without the thousands of copies sold at all the Neiman-Marcus stores. The list, based on computer-processed sales figures in every region of the United States, includes only bookstore sales. Had the calculation included Neiman-Marcus's sales, the book would have remained on the bestseller list at least half a year, and *Minding the Store* would have made the list as well five years earlier. But the oversight didn't seriously inhibit sales. The Neiman-Marcus stores sold well over a million and a quarter dollars' worth of Stanley Marcus's first two books.

Writing has become a way of life for Stanley Marcus, and he likes it that way. In addition to the articles and books previously discussed, he has written *His & Hers: The Fantasy World of the Neiman-Marcus Catalogue*, published by Viking Press in 1982, along with many introductions, forewords, and prefaces to a variety of books, including Kenneth Ragsdale's *The Year America Discovered Texas: Centennial '36*, Frank X. Tolbert's *Tolbert of Texas: The Man and His Work*, *The Helen Corbitt Collection* edited by Elizabeth Ann Johnson, Al Lowman's *Printing Arts in Texas*, Robert Flynn's and Susan Russell's *When I Was Just Your Age*, Sharon DeLano's *Texas Boots*, and Howard Garrett's *Landscape Design—Texas Style*. His introductory remarks for these books reveal once more his wide-ranging interests and his involvement in promoting Texas culture.

Of all his forewords, the one for *Printing Arts in Texas*, published in 1975, tells the most about his sustained interest in the art of the book. Opening with a quote from Walt Whitman—"Camerado, this is no book, who touches this touches a man"—Marcus discusses the circumstances under which fifteenth-century printing craftsmen produced books on sacred subjects for the culturally elite, comparing that era to the unsettled restlessness of 1836, when the Bordens printed the Texas Declaration of Independence in the face of an advancing Mexican army. Because pragmatic business affairs governed the kind of work done by Texas printers of the nineteenth century, Lowman was unable to find a single Texas printer before the 1920s who achieved typographical distinction. Marcus discusses the challenge of finding local printers for early productions of the Book Club of Texas in the 1930s, and pays tribute to the role of Carl Hertzog in establishing a tradition of quality bookmaking in Texas. He closes with a response to those who might regard the attention to fine printing as "effete and unnecessary," stating that "the maker of a fine book is in fact aspiring to create something quite uncommon: a work of art which, by the subtle and harmonious combination of a good text and pleasing format, can provide hours of pleasure in the appreciation of quiet beauty. For myself, I can only wish for more."[30]

And, indeed, there has been more pleasure for Marcus, as some of the recent printing-arts talent in Austin has been applied to his own on-going work. In 1989, Marcus delivered an illustrated lecture on the Book Club of Texas for the Friends of the Southern Methodist University Libraries and received the DeGolyer Medal for outstanding contributions to the world of books, their writing, publishing, and collecting.[31] His talk was then published as one of the DeGolyer Library keepsakes, set in Bembo type and printed on Mohawk Superfine paper by W. Thomas Taylor in an edition of eight hundred fifty copies, of which one hundred were specially bound and signed by the author.

Shortly afterwards, while touring the DeGolyer Library's 1990 exhibition on the development of railroad cars, Marcus mentioned that he would soon be speaking to a group of officials from the Société Nationale de Chemins de Fer Français (the SNCF, or French National Railroad). The SNCF was scheduled to meet in the greater Dallas area under the auspices of AMR Information Services, Inc. (AMRIS), the subsidiary of American Airlines responsible for the worldwide Sabre reservation system. Marcus noted that he would address the delegation at a luncheon meeting and would read his talk in French.

At his suggestion, DeGolyer Library extended an invitation to AMRIS President George Van Derven and the group to view the exhibition, and subsequently coordinated the bilingual publication of Marcus's talk. Once again Tom Taylor was the printer of choice, and he produced an attractive dos-à-dos (back-to-back)[32] entitled *Au Service du Client / Minding the Customer,* in which Marcus set out specific steps for building service quality. While the booklet was produced in paper wrappers, a handful of special copies was casebound by BookLab for distribution to the author and the individuals responsible for the visit of the French delegation.

All of Stanley Marcus's recent writing has not, however, been preserved in fine press editions. Since 1984, he has also written a weekly newspaper column for the *Dallas Morning News*. The opportunity arose as he ended a daily, two-minute commentary on any topic of his own choosing for a local radio station. When Burl Osborne, Publisher and Editor of the *Dallas Morning News,* asked Marcus to write a column for the newspaper, the retailer reminded Osborne that they had often found themselves on opposite sides of editorial issues. Marcus wanted an assurance that he would not be restricted or censored. The publisher agreed and asked him to produce a column three times a week, but settled for once a week when Marcus replied that anything more frequent was "too much like work."

On Tuesday, 21 February 1984, the first column with the by-line Stanley Marcus appeared in the editorial pages of the *Dallas Morning News*. Under the headline "A Sporting Proposition," the new columnist wrote about the "professional amateurism" which is found throughout sports and called for the U.S. government to finance the cost of competing in the Olympic Games against teams that are funded by other nations. To those opposed to government support, he suggested we could be "completely capitalistic by selling our participation outright to the highest commercial bidders. We are already half way there when the broadcast rights are auctioned for the highest price and the sponsorships command such figures only the largest corporations can afford them. To paraphrase the words of Dickens' Scrooge, 'Amateurism—Bah, humbug!' "[33] Following his commentary was the note:

"Stanley Marcus, who identifies himself as 'a marketing consultant, gadabout and gadfly,' is a new Viewpoints page contributor."

Subsequent columns have taken various forms. In addition to straight commentary, Marcus has included letters or examples from letters written by others and even observations of an occasional interplanetary visitor from Mars named Yupe, who finds aspects of human behavior most puzzling. One of the latter "reports" begins: "My occasional visitor from Mars, Yupe, has just completed one of his drop-in trips, and as usual he bestowed on us some of his pungent and penetrating observations. His frankness is occasionally discomforting, but as his prickly barbs heal, we always find he's left us with some ideas that we can put to work." On this particular visit Yupe responded enthusiastically to the IBM complex in Southlake designed by the great Mexican architect Ricardo Legorreta, the new GTE corporate headquarters in Las Colinas, and the Myerson Symphony Center in downtown Dallas. However, he noticed that other parts of Dallas were showing signs of laxness in enforcing the antilitter laws.[34]

On another occasion Stanley Marcus let his alter ego from another planet comment on the contradictions in American society, such as Yupe's saying that "guns kill, yet you permit their sale almost indiscriminately; you tolerate a bully pressure group to prevent you from demanding an immediate and nationwide, positive solution to the problem. Similarly, your society recognizes the damage by the misuse of TV's power and its visible consequences on the educational standards of your country; the only visible protest is a national wringing of the hands."[35] In an enlightened commentary on the lack of ethics on Wall Street, Yupe lands in New York, rents a "Diogenes outfit" complete with lantern, and searches for six days without success, especially around Salomon Bros., for an honest stockbroker. "I went to the Salomon Bros.' offices, first of all, to talk to Mr. Friendgood to see if he would qualify, but when I explained that to him, they called the local gendarmes, who arrested me on the grounds that I was impersonating a dead Greek. They took me before a magistrate, who happened to know about Diogenes. He dismissed the charge with the comment, 'Good luck, but you're going to have pretty tough pickings around here.'"[36]

Marcus searches constantly for column topics, all the while working with his consulting clients, travelling, reading, listening to the news, or entertaining. Headlines of some of the columns reveal the diversity of his sources: "Those efficient Swiss," "Santa Fe reveres the old," "Buried under junk mail," "Comic strips have become more cerebral," "You have to import to export," "Will collecting be a lost art?" and "Politicians still blame the press." His tolerance for nonconformity also prevails, as he writes about mavericks:

> We used to call them "characters," those who chose to be, or found themselves, different from their daily associates.
>
> Our current culture tends to encourage standardization of people and merchandise, with the result that there is less recognition of the value of those who dissent, who march to a different drummer.
>
> Mass production and distribution have been responsible to a great extent for the uniformity of consumer products.
>
> Mavericks are vital in every walk of life, be it politics, business or education.
>
> They're the people who ask questions, who take nothing for granted.
>
> And that makes us all think.[37]

And his appreciation for imagination is evident in his example of a waiters strike in Italy as a creative approach to problem solving.

> Diners were seated as usual, and their orders were courteously taken. Then they were served impeccably—except in reverse order. . . . My source didn't tell me how the diners reacted to this version of Alice-in-Wonderland dining, but if I had been management, I would have been so delighted with this different type of strike that I probably would have met the waiters' demands. . . . Perhaps more problems between labor and management could be solved without resorting to the same old predictable, unproductive strikes if both sides would demonstrate the same kind of creative thinking as the Italian waiters.[38]

"The Chicken Little gap"[39] was a column inspired when Marcus read the results of an education study showing a decline in the number of students who could identify Rip Van Winkle, Cain and Abel, Robin Hood, Sir Galahad, Tom Sawyer, and Chicken Little. Marcus retells the story of how Chicken Little "sounded a false alarm, which the other animals accepted as real without investigating for themselves. Even worse, they didn't consider that the source of information was a dumb cluck just hatched. Finally, they didn't question the credentials or the motives of their self-annointed savior, a fatal mistake," since Foxy Loxy trapped them and ate them. Marcus suggests Chicken Little would have benefited from the wisdom of Friar Roger Bacon, who enunciated The Four Stumbling Blocks to Truth (which Stanley Marcus liked so much forty-four years earlier he commissioned Carl Hertzog to print as a broadside).

One of the best examples of his response to correspondence was his 1990 letter to a nine-year-old girl in England who had written of her interest in studying watercolor painting in America. Her letter and his response were as follows:

> My Dear Mr. Stanley Marcus: When I'm older I'm going to be a very famous painter and then I will live in America like you and it says in my Who's Who book that you collect famous paintings and I want to know please if I send to you one of my best watercolour paintings and you love it very much will you put it on your wall with all the famous paintings Please and I'm saving up to go to New York where all the famous painters live and I hope you are very happy seeing the famous paintings all the time.
>
> Love Rebecca XXX

> Dear Rebecca: I very much like 9-year-old girls, having had a lot of experience with my two daughters who were 9 once upon a time and six granddaughters who also were 9. I find that a very nice age, for girls are just then beginning to realize how big this world is in which they were born and are starting to discover some of the tremendously interesting things in it. . . .
>
> I must tell you that I'm very much flattered that you picked my name from all the others to write about your watercolors. I will be honored to receive one from you, and if it is as good as you say it is, I shall hang it with pride.
>
> You must have a good teacher who is helping you to understand the techniques of watercolor painting. I know that there are excellent art schools in England that have been attended by numerous British artists. The Slade is one with which I'm particularly familiar. Then there is your Royal College of Art which offers fine education in the arts and crafts as well.
>
> We do have a number of famous artists in America, but you have your full share of great painters whom we, in the United States, admire greatly. I hope you have seen the wonderful watercolors of Turner that are now in the Tate Gallery as well as those by Constable, William Blake and Sisley, which are hung variously in the National Gallery and the Tate. We hold all of them in high esteem in this country.
>
> I mention these names for your letter suggests that you may be a little over awe-struck by the Americans and not sufficiently impressed by your own great painters. . . . I'm looking forward to receiving your painting, and I promise that I shall be very honest with you in appraising it. Your generous offer deserves more than just a flattering reception.
>
> Most of all, I shall look forward to meeting you someday in England.[40]
>
> Sincerely,
> Stanley Marcus, age 85

On another occasion one of the Marcus Viewpoints columns was built around a letter he received from Tom Taylor about changing telephone answering routines. Marcus observed that "different businesses have differing problems. A solution that works for one may or may not satisfy the needs of another. A friend, Tom Taylor of Austin, is a fine, creative printer. He found that his productive ability was affected by frequent telephone interruptions. He solved his problem by sending out this letter to his customers:

> Dear Friends and Clients: It is said that when the telephone was first introduced in London, a salesman for the new device called on Oscar Wilde. "How does it work?" asked Wilde. "Well," the salesman said, "when someone wants you, the bell rings, and you pick up the receiver to answer." "Ah," Wilde replied. "Just like a servant."
>
> Almost everyone, with the exception of teen-age girls, complains about being a servant—or more precisely a slave—to the telephone. Our entire office is enslaved—people darting to and fro to answer three lines, losing concentration on whatever they are doing, trying to answer questions on the spot that in fact require time and energy to deal with properly, finally getting off the phone and trying to remember what it was they were doing before it rang.

The letter goes on to explain a new routine whereby messages left on an answering machine will be responded to twice daily, in the hour just before noon, the last hour of the work day, "or at another time you specify if needed. . . . We're going to restore the phone to its rightful role, so that we can do a better job of our real work—making and selling fine books, and giving unexcelled service to our clients."

This letter from Taylor gave Marcus the idea for another column, but he waited sixty days before calling to see how the new routine was working. The report from Austin was that customers were pleased and productivity had increased. Only then did the column appear.[41]

In his Viewpoints column Stanley Marcus has called attention to the needs of charitable organizations like United Way and the Visiting Nurse Association, pointing out, for example, the cost of feeding one of the homebound ill, elderly, or disabled people they serve. Addresses and phone numbers for directing donations and pledges are also given.

Stanley Marcus is proud of his weekly columns, which he has been writing for nearly a decade. He has several columns under way at any one time and maintains a current file of about a half-dozen finished pieces so as not to feel the pressure of a deadline. This explains why Marcus has never missed a week since February, 1984, even with regular and at times extended business travel.

"I am a firm believer that writing as a discipline for thinking is very, very important," Marcus observes. "It is one thing to get up and make a speech, but it is another thing to put it down in black and white and face your critics." Neither has Marcus found it difficult keeping the columns within prescribed limits. He attributes this to the discipline from the earlier writing of his own radio commentaries, which ran a precise one hundred twenty seconds.

Response to his column has been favorable, but it has never generated as much mail as one might expect. Apparently, his experience is not unique. In talking with *New York Times* columnist Anthony Lewis last year Marcus learned that the regular writers on Lewis's paper get much less mail than they once did. While people do not write often, they do respond in force on some occasions. His observations on the decline of manners several years ago touched a responsive note with close to a hundred readers who wrote to say so. But it was his column on the disappearance of biscuits that brought the most surprising results—over seventy-five packages of flour, dough, biscuits, recipes, and letters.

Following the dictum that two books are required for a writer to become an author, Marcus has undoubtedly won his place in the annals of American authorship, especially when you add to his major books—*Minding the Store, Quest for the Best*, and *His & Hers: The Fantasy World of the Neiman-Marcus Catalogue*—his articles in national magazines, his introductions to other books, his speeches turned into articles, and his newspaper column running weekly without interruption for more than nine years. And he is not finished yet. His latest book in progress explores concepts of customer service and their application to customer satisfaction in American businesses. Marcus is interested in measuring how American businesses, including retailing, airlines, and hotels, have scored. Considering his demonstrated ability as an author to satisfy the reading public, it is not surprising that three major publishers are standing in line to consider Stanley Marcus's forthcoming book.

Chapter Seven

The Quest for Books

Stanley Marcus's deep interest in books was nourished and encouraged at Harvard, but one of the first lessons he learned as an undergraduate was that his allowance was not going to support his quest for books. Remembering his experience as a boy selling neighborhood subscriptions to the *Saturday Evening Post*, he soon determined how he could put his growing knowledge of books to use. With a marketing twist that carried a little snob appeal, he launched "The Book Collector's Service Bureau" from his college residence, sending out an initial solicitation addressed "To the One Hundred People Who Will Receive Copies of This Letter."

> Do BOOKS mean anything to you? If not, then throw this letter into your basket without further perusal. If they do, then read carefully, for it will inform you of a new and valuable service which has been opened for book lovers and collectors.
>
> Being in the heart of the book market, in Boston and New York, I naturally have the advantage of being in closer touch with unusual books than are those who live in other parts of the country. Many fine old libraries go on auction every week in Boston, and I am able to secure handsome sets and rarities at exceedingly low figures.
>
> It is my purpose to offer my patrons a service which will be of inestimable value to them in locating scarce books at the lowest possible prices. I have a thorough knowledge of the stock of the leading book stores and second-hand shops, and I am well acquainted with bindings, first editions, pirated editions, out of print books, and their prices. Here is your chance to get the books you have long sought. . . . I can find them for you.
>
> I shall undertake to locate any book and quote prices to you. Please specify (where possible) the edition, binding, and approximate price you wish to pay. Any favors you can confer upon me by notifying your friends of this unusual service will be appreciated.
>
> Yours very sincerely,
> H. Stanley Marcus[1]

Before long the young entrepreneur was clearing from fifty to two hundred dollars a month, a significant sum for an undergraduate in the 1920s. Marcus applied profits from the new venture to the purchase of books for his own library. One of his earliest customers was his own father, who was self-educated and who read widely in European philosophy and literature. For some of his own early collecting interests Stanley Marcus took his cue from "Dr. Eliot's Five-Foot Shelf of Books," the Harvard Classics, and from George Parker Winship's course in the history of books and printing, where he learned about Bruce Rogers.

Bruce Rogers, one of the finest typographers America has produced, had been a close friend of Winship from the time they first met at Brown University. He and Rogers (also known to his admirers as B.R.) would occasionally arrange summer vacations at Nantucket, and at other times they corresponded regularly about book people, especially printers and their work. Rogers also sent Winship examples of his own work, which the students of printing history at Harvard examined closely.

Marcus was soon collecting books designed by Rogers. Having solved the problem of supporting his penchant for book collecting, he now had a new challenge—how to collect the work of a famous book designer whose name often did not appear on the books he designed. Rogers had begun designing books for the Riverside Press in Cambridge in 1901, but he had also designed for other U.S. publishers and presses who were erratic about giving him credit for his designs. Furthermore, he had designed pamphlets, keepsakes, and Christmas greetings for discriminating clients who sent them only to their personal friends. Then, there were books from the time Rogers had lived in England, working for Cambridge University Press and private printers.

To seek out these elusive items by B.R., Marcus developed a network of antiquarian booksellers who were knowledgeable in the book arts. After he graduated from Harvard the list grew to include Jake Zeitlin, George Goodspeed, Warren Howell, Philip and Fanny Duschnes, Dawson's, Franklin Gilliam, Lawrence Kunetka at J&S Graphics, Philip Kaplan, and S. R. Shapiro, as well as booksellers abroad.

Shapiro, who for years dealt in "New, Old, and Rare Books" from 505 Fifth Avenue, shared Marcus's deep interest in Bruce Rogers. He had an uncanny way of turning up some unusual and even ephemeral examples of printing designed by Rogers, and once he discovered someone new who shared his interest, he or she became a candidate for announced (and unannounced) visits when Shapiro set off on his long drives across the country.

Shapiro also knew Bruce Rogers and lived within easy driving distance of his home in Connecticut. It was often after visiting B. R. that Shapiro would write Marcus with a list of new offerings. As Marcus's collection grew, he would order a number of titles at one time only to find later that he already owned some of them. Shapiro cheerfully accepted Marcus's return of duplicates, knowing the businessman was a serious and seasoned collector who did not have as much time to spend with his books as he would have liked.

Marcus was especially pleased when he could find association copies of books designed by Rogers. Among these were *A Study of Prose Fiction* (1902) and *The Amateur Spirit* (1904), both by Bliss Perry, who taught Marcus literature at Harvard. Another unusual find was the *Catalogue of an Exhibition of the Private Papers of James Boswell from Malahide Castle* held at the Grolier Club late in 1930. The exhibition was prepared with the assistance of Frederick A. Pottle of Yale University, who was editing the Boswell correspondence, only recently discovered in an ebony cabinet at Malahide Castle near Dublin. Marcus's copy includes a series of original letters written by Pottle in 1932-33 regarding the production of "aquatone" illustrations of other letters by Boswell for a book on an even more remarkable discovery of papers at Fettercairn House in Scotland.

Several other association copies concerned Elmer Adler, whom Marcus knew quite well and entertained in Dallas. One of these was John Rothwell Slater's *Printing and the Renaissance,* produced by William Edwin Rudge in 1921. Designed by Bruce Rogers, it is one of fifty copies on handmade paper made for Adler, with a laid-in letter from Adler presenting the book to George Parker Winship (and with G.P.W.'s signature on the flyleaf). In addition, Marcus also prized *The Colophon,* which Adler produced, and some of Adler's other work issued by the Pynson Printers in New York.

Another extraordinary association copy Marcus acquired was Siegfried Sassoon's *Picture Show,* privately printed in England and issued in 1919. Sassoon and B.R. developed a close friendship while working on this book, and the Marcus copy was Sassoon's presentation copy to Thomas Hardy, whom he counted as a close and cherished friend. The inscription to Hardy and Hardy's bookplate from Max Gate (Hardy's home) put it in a class by itself.

A Most Friendly Farewell to Sir Francis Drake by Henry Robarts, which Harvard University Press issued in 1924, has a more subtle association. This copy is from the library of Alfred W. Pollard, whose bookplate it contains—the same A. W. Pollard who lectured enthusiastically to the Bibliographical Society in London about a little-known but brilliant typographer in America by the name of Bruce Rogers. It was only after this lecture that Rogers began to be studied and collected.

Nevertheless, the Bruce Rogers item that has given Stanley Marcus the most pleasure (and some degree of anxiety) was one offered to him by S. R. Shapiro in the 1950s. There is little doubt that Marcus found Shapiro's description appealing:

> From the standpoint of rarity and interest, the book which I shall now describe is undoubtedly in first place.
>
> In 1952 BR designed the plans for an edition of Max Beerbohm's THE HAPPY HYPOCRITE. This was to be published by William E. Rudge's Sons and was to be the 85th book which BR had done for Rudge, since the beginning of the association in 1919.
>
> Unfortunately the project did not come to fruition. I have available a *trial copy* of the book, as it was designed in mauve and black by BR, bound in mauve boards with a most charming all-over design by him of fauns.
>
> 75.00
>
> This book ranks as a presque-unique example of Mr. Rogers work. Perhaps six copies of the trial issue were made. To the best of my knowledge, no copies have ever come into the market. I am keenly desirous of this copy coming in a major permanent collection such as the HSM collection. I would gladly send you the Beerbohm . . . on approval, with no obligation on your part. I believe that I am correct in assuming that you are particularly interested in such material as this.[2]

As soon as Marcus saw it, he knew it must join his collection. He had long admired Beerbohm's criticism of literary mannerisms and social pretenses and had thought from time to time how much he would like to meet this master of wit, irony, and satire. It was intriguing to find this example of his work, incomplete though it was, in a trial copy designed by Bruce Rogers.

Within a few years he would have the opportunity to meet Beerbohm and ask him to sign the unique volume. In 1955 he visited his friend S. N. Behrman, an American playwright, in Portofino, Italy, where Behrman was working on a new book, *Portrait of Max: An Intimate Memoir of Sir Max Beerbohm*. Behrman arranged the meeting.

The next day Stanley Marcus, his wife Billie, and their daughter Jerrie drove to Rapallo to Beerbohm's villa and were welcomed by Miss Jungmann, Beerbohm's companion, whom he married shortly before his death. They were shown to the sitting room where Max was then brought in, frail and thin. "He wore a little skull cap to protect his head against draft and had a shawl wrapped around him," Marcus recalls. "He acknowledged the introduction, but said he hadn't slept well the night before and so he wasn't feeling too well."[3] Marcus showed Beerbohm the book and told him about Bruce Rogers, whose work was unfamiliar to him. He also explained that since it was a trial proof, it contained incomplete examples of the text. At the end of the visit Marcus asked the famous satirist if he would sign the book. As Marcus remembers: "Beerbohm replied, 'Well, I'm not feeling very well. You leave it and I'll sign it. I said, 'I'm leaving tomorrow.' 'Well, I'll mail it to you,' came the reply." Marcus remembers his feeling of helplessness: "There wasn't anything I could do. I couldn't say, 'Give me back my book.' So I left it, and nothing happened for four months. Then one day in the mail came a brown envelope with this book in it."[4]

When Marcus opened the package he found his treasured book with the following inscription: "Dear Mr. Stanley Marcus, here is the book that you left with me. I have dared to amend here and there what seemed to me a lack of continuity in the narration. Yours very sincerely, Max Beerbohm." But there was more. As he turned the pages, he discovered what Max meant when he "dared to amend" the "lack of continuity." He had cleverly added phrases and sentences that linked the sample text of one page with the next, creating a delightful surprise. Behrman remembered these emendations at the end of *Portrait of Max*:

> Max's careful labor on these random pages was the last literary task that he ever undertook. The task he set himself was to make the sense carry over from one page to the next as if he had originally written them that way, and it required great ingenuity. For example, one page ended, "And in the middle of this vain galaxy hung the pre-." The next page, since it was far away, gave you no idea of what it was that hung in the middle of the vain galaxy. At the bottom of the first of these pages, Max added, in his strong and beautiful handwriting, "*sent writer's eviscerated book.*"
>
> One page ended, "Presently he heard a footstep in the hall beyond, and a pair of." The next page began, "soon forgot him." Max caused these disparities to coalesce: "Presently he heard a footstep in the hall beyond, and a pair of *boots appeared with nobody in them, and at sight of them he uttered a piercing scream. But he soon forgot them—and they, it appears,* soon forgot him."
>
> Max was to work for weeks on this. . . . When, long before [his] self-imposed task was completed, I came back to Rapallo, it turned out to be for only one day. I found that I had to leave immediately for New York. That afternoon, I went to the Villa to bid Max goodbye. Miss Jungmann, without saying much, took me to the terrace. We stood in the middle of it.
>
> "Look," said Miss Jungmann, pointing to the open door of Max's blue-walled study.
>
> I looked. Max, completely unaware of us, was bent over his worktable, writing. He was wearing glasses; he looked very tiny. He was using pen and ink, and the pen kept dipping into the inkpot. He was working with the avidity and the concentration of a writer slaving to meet a deadline at the end of which glitters a pot of gold. Again, and for the last time, he was working to amuse one reader.[5]

Having successfully acquired Beerbohm's inscription and additions to *The Happy Hypocrite,* Marcus then wanted something from Bruce Rogers. He had dictated a letter from Paris telling Shapiro about his success in getting an inscription and emendations from Max Beerbohm, and the bookseller offered to take it to Bruce Rogers for him to sign. Early in September, 1955, Marcus accepted Shapiro's offer and sent the book to New York. "I am forwarding to you by registered mail the 'Happy Hypocrite' which has been annotated by Sir Max Beerbohm. Would you be kind enough now to get Mr. Rogers to make some sort of inscription in the book so that it will become doubly unique. Please return it to me at your earliest convenience."[6] Once again Marcus trusted the mail and someone else to care for his most prized Bruce Rogers item, hoping all the while that it would receive the same care and attention he had given it.

The following week Marcus wrote Shapiro again, ordering another book and asking him to return the Beerbohm as soon as he had a chance to have it inscribed. As the end of September approached, there was still no word from the bookseller. Marcus wrote again: "I haven't heard from you acknowledging the Beerbohm annotated copy of the HAPPY HYPOCRITE. Will you please let me know at once if you received it and when I may expect it back."[7] The following week while he was in New York, he tried to call Shapiro about the book but got no answer, so he wrote again, saying, "Do let me know when you expect to be able to return it to me."[8]

The fall passed without Shapiro's taking the book to Rogers to sign, but the bookseller and the collector kept up a lively correspondence. Marcus replied to Shapiro's frequent quotes for other B.R. items. By the end of the year, Marcus, responding to a new offer, queried, "Incidentally, when oh when are we going to get my 'Happy Hypocrite' back? I have a meeting coming up very shortly, and I should like very much to show this item at that time."[9]

On the 16th of January Shapiro sent still another list of ephemera designed by Bruce Rogers, but no word on the Beerbohm book. Marcus's patience was wearing thin. For five months Shapiro had had the book without getting it inscribed, all the while offering Marcus a steady stream of other B.R. material. Finally, Marcus demanded, "If you can't get up to Connecticut, why don't you just mail it up to him or send it up by messenger, whom I will gladly pay. I am anxious to get this book back within the next few weeks."[10] Marcus's letter crossed in the mail with one from Shapiro saying that the Beerbohm book was "duly signed by BR" on Sunday when he visited Rogers.[11] It was being returned by Air Express. At last the ordeal was over.

At the time Shapiro returned his book, Marcus may have felt that he would never let it out of his sight again, but in subsequent years he loaned it to at least two exhibitions. The first loan was to the Arts Club of Chicago in 1971 for an exhibition of drawings and paintings by writers, a show for which Max Beerbohm was high on the curator's list of multitalented writers.[12] Three years later it was included in an exhibition of the works of Max Beerbohm at Stanford University, featuring the collections of Mr. and Mrs. Stanley Marcus, David Magee, Franklin Gilliam, and Mr. and Mrs. James D. Hart, among others. The exhibit was staged in the Albert M. Bender Room, named for the great California collector whom Stanley Marcus still regards as an early mentor.

Everyone who follows the work of a fine typographer dreams of commissioning him for a special work—a book, a broadside, or perhaps a bookplate. By the 1940s Stanley Marcus and Bruce Rogers were well acquainted, and Marcus wanted his B.R.-designed books to bear a bookplate also designed by the master typographer.

Marcus's first bookplate, designed in the 1930s by William Kittredge at the Lakeside Press in Chicago, provided one of the starting points for something new by Rogers. In a small oval, Kittredge had placed a barrel cactus, around the top and sides of which was a band containing "Ex libris H. Stanley Marcus." Rockwell Kent had also created a bookplate for him featuring a young boy reaching for a star. Rogers, judging both of the earlier bookplates a little small, suggested something larger but still discreet. He produced some thumbnail sketches, with a different kind of cactus, a jackrabbit (for its association with Texas), and a six-pointed star. He wrote Marcus that he had argued often with Rockwell Kent, pointing out that his five-pointed stars were impossible since the rays of a star are in the observer's eyes.

Rogers and Marcus exchanged ideas on the number of points for the star and on the addition of birds and finally agreed to one star, two birds, and one rabbit. Rogers, however, forgot to put his initials on the final art from which the bookplate was printed in 1944. He apologized for the oversight and agreed to sign some twenty-five to fifty of the prints Marcus sent back for signatures. Part of his problem, Rogers confessed, was being 74, working with no assistant, and having projects scattered all over the house so that he could work in the warm rooms that were available. Nevertheless, Marcus was pleased with the bookplate and used it proudly not only in his Bruce Rogers collection but in the many other books that were forcing the expansion of his home at 1 Nonesuch Road.

Rogers's income was minimal, since he chose to work alone and maintain his independence by taking on only those projects which intrigued him. In the late spring of 1956, after a visit to Rogers at his home, October House, Marcus grew concerned about the elderly designer's finances. By this time Bruce Rogers was 86 and had the help of a Mrs. Pearson, who looked after the house and meals. The typographer and his collector friend from Dallas had enjoyed each other's company, talking about current projects and ideas for new ones. Rogers outlined his concept for the "October House Classics," important works of Old English literature in uniform editions that he would design. They also discussed the prospect of having a group of supporters to be known as the "B. R. Associates," who would underwrite the cost of the new series. Stanley Marcus offered to participate.

Afterwards, Marcus sent some photographs of Rogers and Mrs. Pearson taken with his new miniature camera, and reiterated his offer to send a dictating machine "for experimental purposes. Then if you feel that you can use it, we will arrange for a semi-permanent loan to you."[13] He also wrote a mutual friend, Frank Leslie, in Minneapolis:

> My Dear Frank: About two weeks ago I paid a visit to Bruce Rogers in Connecticut and had lunch with him and Mrs. Pearson. He gave no indication of being in difficult financial condition, although he did refer to one set of books by saying that some day he might want to convert them into cash. He showed me some of his water colors, and I tested him out by asking if any of them were for sale. He told me that he had never put any of them up for sale and closed the subject.
>
> I imagine that he has enough to live on but probably just enough with little to spare. I told him that I would be happy to participate in the financing of the books that he has undoubtedly described to you.
>
> With best regards,
> Stanley Marcus[14]

A few weeks later, Philip Duschnes, another antiquarian bookseller in New York who specialized in books designed by Bruce Rogers, sent out the announcement for the series. Rogers had not approached Marcus for the help he had offered. The funding had come from another source. Then later the same year the typographer offered the collector a set of books cataloging the Henry Clay Frick collection of art in New York City for $2,000. Because production of the catalogue was severely limited by Mrs. Frick, this particular Bruce Rogers work has turned into a legendary twentieth-century rarity, but for 1956 it was already carrying a premium that would deter most collectors. Marcus declined.

By the mid-1970s Stanley Marcus had been acquiring books and ephemera designed by Bruce Rogers for half a century and had amassed one of the premier collections in private hands. He had pursued obscure titles assiduously and had turned up significant association copies, even taking great pains to gain the appropriate signatures on *The Happy Hypocrite* and coming out of the transcontinental exchange with a copy enhanced beyond all expectations by the last piece of writing by Max Beerbohm. But S. R. Shapiro was not the only rare book dealer with whom he did business regularly, nor was the work of Bruce Rogers his only collecting interest.

Marcus received catalogues and lists from booksellers throughout England and the United States, and he regularly circled items for his secretary to order. A retailer by trade, he was a comparison shopper, watching the rare-book market for signs of strength or weakness and always seeking the best buys he could find. When he had several copies of a title, he would sometimes offer the duplicates for sale or trade. And when booksellers did not meet the prices he expected, he would politely but firmly decline. He could, on occasion, have a significant difference of opinion with booksellers over price, and cling tenaciously to his own viewpoint; yet these differences did not seem to damage his relationships with them. During the summer of 1974, for example, Marcus purchased for $225 a copy of *The Book of Genesis,* printed by the Allen Press, from Warren Howell's bookshop in San Francisco. Shortly afterward he received a new catalogue from Dawson's offering another copy of the book for $175. He wrote John Windle at Howell's, saying, "There is such a high difference in the price that I felt confident that you would wish to be competitive. I'm enclosing a clipping from their catalogue herewith."[15]

Windle's prompt reply was not all that Marcus expected. He thanked Marcus for the clipping, told him that he had already seen Dawson's catalogue, and had bought the Dawson copy to fill a second order that he had received subsequent to Marcus's purchase. Then he signed off. Marcus was not so easily dissuaded. "I have your letter of explanation but quite frankly I don't consider it completely satisfactory. It is our policy when we are under priced on occasion to meet competitive market. Obviously any company can be undersold on occasion, but when prices aren't met it does create a sense of distrust of the pricing policy of the company."[16]

Windle responded, "What is the issue here, for me, is that I have sold copies of *The Book of Genesis* at $225, and I have multiple back orders at my prices for all of the Allen Press books. Having sold at these prices, with requests for further copies, it would not be fair, I believe, to my customers to supply another copy at a lower price. In fact, at the moment, I am not so concerned with selling them as I am about buying them. I was very happy to acquire the Dawson's copy. I hope that this acquisition will not leave you with a feeling of distrust, to which you alluded, regarding my prices. I feel quite sure that our prices are competitive, in view of the multiple orders generated."[17] Windle then closed with the offer to accept the book back for credit to Marcus's account.

For Stanley Marcus, this might have been the final offer from the bookseller at Howell's, but it was not the last word. He replied, "If you are satisfied with the pricing on the *The Book of Genesis* then I shall have to accept your decision, but I shall feel obligated to shop all of your prices in advance of purchase. I appreciate your willingness to take it back for credit."[18] Windle knew who the customer was and ultimately acquiesced. He wrote Stanley Marcus, saying that he was "truly disturbed" by the feelings he expressed. Howell's always attempted to be competitive *and* fair, and to that end he enclosed a credit memo to Marcus's account in the amount of $50.

Pricing differences aside, Warren Howell and Marcus had a long and warm relationship. Marcus had first bought books as early as the 1950s from "John Howell — Books," founded by Warren's father in 1912. Located at 434 Post Street across from the St. Francis Hotel and, in time, only two blocks from Neiman-Marcus's San Francisco store, Howell's was widely regarded as one of the major antiquarian book firms in the nation. Both men shared a commitment to serving a discriminating clientele interested in quality goods.

Among other materials, the Howell firm provided Stanley Marcus with Christmas books, which he collected for many years. The tradition of publishing books that would serve as gifts at Christmastime began in mid-nineteenth-century England. Many have been the subject of considerable typographic attention, with some showing innovation and excellence even though they were produced by amateur printers. This is one aspect of the genre that appealed to Stanley Marcus, but he also found them intriguing for their contents, selected to help observe the season. Some did not carry a Christmas theme, yet because they were created especially for presentation as gifts at the end of the year, they were considered Christmas books.

Among the seven hundred Christmas books which Marcus collected over twenty-five years, there is a remarkable variety to be found. Some were printed in editions as small as twenty copies, such as *The Gospel of St. Luke,* printed by hand by John S. Fass at the Harbour Press in 1926. *A Yuletide Toast or the Fairfield Wassail* (1971) provides a recipe calling for six large apples, a pint of ale, brown sugar, and other ingredients. The printer of the book's colophon suggests there would have been more than 120 copies issued had there been but fewer wassails! There is also work by one of the printers Marcus engaged for the Book Club of Texas, Hal Marchbanks, who emanated from nearby Ennis, Texas. For the *Golden Garland of Verse and Family Keepsake* of 1929, Marchbanks used bright floral patterned paper boards with a label on the cover, a striking contrast to his design for the Book Club's *Eneas Africanus,* published in Dallas the following year.

The collection includes the Christmas book printed at the Stinehour Press in 1969, sent by Marcus's friend Philip C. Duschnes. The book contains two chapters from an unfinished autobiography and is entitled *It's Better Than Working: Confessions of a Dealer in Rare Books.* California printers—the Grabhorns, Helen Gentry, and John Henry Nash—are also represented in the collection, as are Marcus's friends from the publishing world, Alfred and Blanche Knopf, who sent *Christmas Eve* by Alistair Cooke in 1952. *Christmas Eve* is made up of three stories Cooke broadcast in England on successive Christmas Eves as a part of his series of weekly talks called "Letter from America."

During the British Fortnight of 1967, when Chancellor Harry Ransom was in Dallas to help open the British Heritage exhibition on loan from the University of Texas at Austin, he learned about Marcus's Christmas books and began considering the possibility of exhibiting them at the university. When the Ransoms and the Marcuses were together for dinner in Washington shortly thereafter, the subject of a loan exhibition came up again, and early in 1968 Ransom wrote Marcus:

> Dear Stanley: Indeed we *would* be "interested" in the exhibition of the books for Christmas and the modern printing!
>
> Next semester we're having a small, knowledgeable group of bookmen in and out of Austin to look at unusual collections. Could we mount and catalogue the exhibits for a continuing show during those times? [Our exhibit catalogues are proving the really educative value of *collection* as historic fact.]
>
> You say when.
>
> Hazel and I start 1968 deeply grateful to you two, especially for the heartlifting night in Washington.
>
> Sincerely yours,
> Harry
> 2.i.68 [19]

While the modern-printing items were not included, the Humanities Research Center exhibited the Christmas books and produced an illustrated catalogue written by Mary Hirth, then the Academic Center Librarian. A decade later, after Marcus gave his collection of Christmas books to the Dallas Public Library, selections were exhibited at the library along with an attractive french-fold brochure featuring twenty-nine books, with commentary on each. The exhibition of the Marcus Christmas books was prepared by Linda Robinson, a staff member at the Dallas Public Library who also worked part time as Stanley Marcus's personal librarian.[20]

The idea of hiring a personal librarian occurred to Stanley Marcus in the 1950s, as the collections at home grew beyond his capacity to manage them. Assistance was clearly needed to help keep track of the books arriving nearly every day at 1 Nonesuch Road and the corporate office at Neiman-Marcus. Books were coming from a variety of sources, ranging from trade and antiquarian booksellers to authors and publishers. Many were bought for the library at home, while others were intended as gifts for friends, colleagues, and organizations. Still others came unsolicited from publishers seeking a tie-in with one of the many innovative displays and promotions taking place all the time at the store. After one of Marcus's many buying trips to Europe, it was not unusual for oversized books to be included in the huge shipping crates arriving from Paris, London, or elsewhere containing foreign goods for the store.

Even with books coming at such a rate that a librarian was needed to help track, inventory, and organize them, Stanley Marcus never entirely turned over the process to anyone else. Indeed, he was critically aware of the books he was acquiring. For example, at the end of 1955 he wrote Alfred Knopf a revealing letter:

> My Dear Alfred: I have just been reviewing the contemporary books that I have purchased during the past year, and it was interesting for me to note that a large portion of them bore the Borzoi imprint. While I have always liked your list, I was tremendously impressed with it during the past fall. I not only bought a large number of your fiction titles but about three-quarters of your non-fiction as well. I just thought you might like to have this little note as this year passes on to a new one.
>
> With warm regards to Blanche and to Pat, I am
>
> Most sincerely yours,
> Stanley Marcus[21]

In the 1950s and again in the 1960s the Marcuses' house at 1 Nonesuch Road had undergone multiple changes and additions to accommodate collections of books, art, sculpture, textiles, and masks. When it was first built in the 1930s, the Marcus home had a reasonably sized study lined with bookshelves, beyond which was a downstairs bedroom. In time the books spilled out of the study, forcing the conversion of the adjacent bedroom to another library room. This served for a few more years, but when a third expansion of the library was needed, Stanley and Billie Marcus added an even larger room. Measuring approximately thirty-by-fifty feet, with alcoves near the entrance for African masks and sculpture, this largest of the three libraries comfortably houses most of the books on art, with one exception — *Jazz* by Matisse. The walls and ceiling of the bathroom nearest the library are decorated with the plates from *Jazz*, one of the greatest *livres de artiste* productions of all times. Marcus enjoyed the book so much when he acquired it that he wanted to see as many of its plates as possible at one time, and at least once a day!

After the large library room was added, the new shelves quite naturally began to fill with books. Then, as Billie Marcus watched the available space systematically disappear, she finally drew the line. She reminded her husband that they lived in a home, not a museum or a library that could be continuously expanded. Yet Marcus knew he could not shut off his instinct for collecting altogether, even if he could curb some of his inclinations to buy art and other objects, so he cleverly found a way to pursue his interest in books by collecting them in a size that he could bring home undetected in his coat pocket. Thus he turned to miniature books. Of course, even this new interest could not be hidden for long, and Billie soon knew what was happening.

At first, the collection of miniature books did not require much space because it was easy to triple- or quadruple-bank them on existing shelves, or even to house them in special cases on window sills. By 1968 the collection numbered over 250 titles, according to an inventory prepared near the end of the year. This included eighteenth- and nineteenth-century books, as well as miniatures printed throughout the twentieth century. The subjects are legion, ranging from the Bible to *Ali Baba and the Forty Thieves*, from *Pig Latin Grammar, Pilgrim's Progress*, and *Poems D'Amours* to John Muir, Voltaire, and Bonnie and Clyde. For one interested in the American West there were books on Crazy Horse, Fort Union, Sebastian Vizcayno, Geronimo, and Mission cattle brands. In the categories of heads of state and prominent political figures, Thomas Jefferson, John Kennedy, Winston Churchill, and Abraham

Lincoln were well represented. As for literary figures, Walt Whitman, Henry David Thoreau, Charles Lamb, Cervantes, and Lafcadio Hearn were Marcus's choice.

The quest for miniature books put Stanley Marcus in touch with a new group of booksellers, among them Miss Alla T. Ford in Florida, Walter Schatzki in New York City, the Bromers in Boston, Doris Frohnsdorff in Maryland, Bennett & Marshall in Los Angeles, and Louis W. Bondy in London. Dawson's, Duschnes, Philip Kaplan, and J&S Graphics also sold miniatures.

By 1971 the Marcus collection of miniature books had become widely known, but this should not be surprising. After all, the world of serious collecting is a relatively small one in which word travels quickly about individuals who have been successful in forming their own strong collections. Thus in planning an exhibition of miniature books, the Hallmark Gallery on New York City's Fifth Avenue approached Stanley Marcus, who, once terms were settled, sent one hundred books from his collection for the exhibit.

Late in 1978 another exhibition was based on Marcus's collection, this one at the Dallas Public Library, co-curated by Linda Robinson. The following year, Stanley Marcus spoke at the Library of Congress at a program devoted to miniature books. In 1980 another exhibition of his miniatures was held at the Chicago Public Library Cultural Center. By this time Marcus's library of small books had grown to 2,500, including a good number from the golden age of miniature printing, from 1775 to 1825.

Fortunately for the libraries of Dallas, Stanley Marcus has been a generous donor of his collections. For nearly half of the time that Marcus was collecting Bruce Rogers, Decherd Turner had been guiding the development of the Bridwell Library at Southern Methodist University, acquiring strong holdings in the book arts. Turner looked to Stanley Marcus for help with some of the Bridwell acquisitions and shared with him a personal interest in the design and typography of books.

Thus, as Marcus began thinking of an appropriate repository for his Bruce Rogers collection, he talked with Turner about giving it to Bridwell Library. Early in 1975 Marcus had a visit from Simon Hornby, whose family still held the finest collection of the Ashendene Press, which had achieved a pinnacle of fine typography and design in England. Since Bruce Rogers held a similar reputation in American typography, the idea of preserving the two collections some day at the Bridwell Library soon emerged.

Meanwhile, Turner told Marcus that he had accepted the huge task of being the host and on-site planner for another of the Grolier Club's legendary trips. This time the members were coming to Texas in May, 1976 for a tour which would begin in Dallas and take them to Fort Worth, Austin, San Antonio, and Houston, where they would visit the best private libraries and the most notable rare book collections at universities in the state. Turner proposed that Marcus give his Bruce Rogers collection to the Bridwell Library in time to offer Grolier Club members a special preview of a major exhibition planned by the library. Both Marcus and Turner were also Grolier Club members, so the idea carried a certain logic and appeal.

Seeking to sway the pending decision in England about the Ashendene books, Turner suggested that Marcus make a stipulation regarding his Rogers collection—that it would go to SMU on the condition that the Bridwell Library acquire the Hornby Ashendene Collection as its British counterpart. The negotiations for the Ashendene Collection had been painfully slow, and Turner sought this additional leverage to close the deal. The idea made sense to Marcus, who enjoys to this day the strategy required to close a complicated deal.

In January, 1976 he wrote Turner that "on the theory that you are going to get the Ashendene Collection sooner or later, I will be glad to give you the Bruce Rogers Collection, so that you can exhibit it at the time of The Grolier Club's visit to Texas."[22] He went on to reiterate the conditions of the gift intended to help land the Ashendene Collection for SMU, and to insure that his own collection remained intact. Several days later Turner replied, revealing how closely linked the acquisition of the two great collections had been:

> Dear Mr. Marcus: As indicated in our conversation last evening, there has been something wonderfully psychic about this matter of the relationship of yourself, the Ashendene Collection, and Bridwell Library.
>
> 1. A year ago, February 24, 1975, when you first called that Mr. Simon Hornby was in your office, I was at that exact moment typing the first draft of a brief article which is to appear in the Festschrift honoring Levi Olan—and the subject of the article was/is—The Ashendene Press!
>
> It seems that almost every time since then that we have had occasion to exchange notes as to the progress of the negotiations—that such an exchange occasioned one more development in getting the collection.
>
> 2. However, as a result of the long silent periods from the Hornby family, and particularly following the last exchange of offers and counter-offers, I had grown rather discouraged. And so I asked you to insert in the terms of the Marcus Rogers gift a stipulation that a complete collection of Ashendenes which we would put together would satisfy that particular stipulation in the Marcus

gift. And, within thirty minutes of sealing the envelope, I had a telephone call from Mr. Simon Hornby which indicated at that time . . . some bending toward our last offer. And then, last evening, the final telephone call closed the deal. All within the same period of time in which we were having an exchange of letters![23]

The Stanley Marcus Collection of Bruce Rogers did not arrive in time for the Bridwell Library to prepare a large exhibit for the Grolier Club, but the touring members saw portions of it included in highlights of the Bridwell Library. Marcus, abroad on business at the time of the club's tour, missed the festivities; nevertheless, news of his gift to the Bridwell added to the Grolier Club members' appreciation of the riches of Texas libraries.

Once he had donated his collection to the Bridwell, Marcus continued to acquire the works of B.R. and to support the collection, which he knew lacked certain titles. He indicated to Turner that he would be glad to fill the gaps as opportunities arose. Both the collector and the librarian were well acquainted with Warren Howell, the San Francisco bookseller regarded as one of the most eminent in the country and well positioned to identify and locate the most elusive Bruce Rogers items. Howell, in turn, was thoroughly familiar with the Marcus collection, having conducted the gift appraisal before its transfer of ownership to SMU. Howell was made aware of Marcus's interest in continuing to add to the collection, and sent him quotes of B.R. items. Marcus purchased those needed to fill out the collection. Such ongoing support by donors after they have contributed their collections is not unheard of, but it is rare, especially in Texas and the Southwest. It is a great boon to any library committed to the continued enhancement of its holdings.

In the late 1970s Stanley and Billie Marcus gave their collection of Christmas books to the Dallas Public Library. In time, the miniature books reached a point where he felt he had explored practically all acquisition possibilities and had fashioned a discriminating collection. Half of them he gave to the Bridwell Library in 1986 and the other half he offered for sale through a series of catalogues issued by the Bromers in Boston.

Gifts of books from Marcus extended to other libraries and institutions as well. He has regularly sent boxes of art books to the Meadows School of the Arts at SMU. Other boxes have gone to the annual book sales held by Smith College alumnae, as well as to the Dallas Public Library and the Dallas Historical Society. When he discovered a new book he considered of sufficient importance to schools and art organizations, Marcus would buy multiple copies to send around the state. One example in 1953 was *Films on Art*, published by the American Federation of Arts. A source guide to all the known films dealing with art, the book was a welcome gift, as evidenced in the letters of thanks Marcus received from the one hundred school districts, museums, and college libraries receiving it. The use of books as personalized gifts has included an unusually rare history of Parker County, which Marcus sought from Texana dealers for his friend Mary Martin, who had grown up in Weatherford. While traveling abroad he found an unusual book on the history of barbering and sent it to his favorite barber at the Waldorf-Astoria.

Now, even with the absence of the Bruce Rogers collection, the Christmas books, and the miniatures, there are at least 12,000 books and pamphlets in the library rooms at 1 Nonesuch Road. The largest room still holds the books on art (mainly primitive and modern), along with other large-format volumes on the subjects of fabric, design, and nineteenth-century manufacturing. Elsewhere one finds a substantial section of books about books, other sections devoted to books by and about close friends like Carl Hertzog, Tom Lea, and J. Frank Dobie, and a large collection of books devoted to the great department stores and their founders. In the first library room are general books in the various categories of fiction, history, current opinion, wit, philosophy, cartoons, advertising, and, yes, the Harvard Classics.

By 1975 Stanley Marcus's quest for books took on another dimension, that of the publisher seeking good manuscript material. Because of his deep interest in miniature books, Billie wanted to give him a miniature edition of *Minding the Store* for his seventieth birthday. As she began to explore the processes for producing such a book, she realized that she would have to engage someone with more experience. At that point she revealed her plan to her husband, asking if he would like to help. Marcus discussed the idea with Padgett Printing Company in Dallas, which was able to prepare offset plates from a regular edition of the book.

Before the book was printed, Stanley Marcus needed a name for the new publishing venture he was about to launch. His first inclination was to use the name of the street where he lives—Nonesuch Road. That would have been confusing, however, since the name had already been adopted by a well-known press in England. With a whimsical turn of language, he came up with Somesuch Press and was soon in the publishing business. Yet he was not altogether pleased with the way the miniature edition of *Minding the Store* turned out. The reduced text block of each page is quite difficult to read. All Somesuch Press miniatures would thereafter be designed in an appropriate format and printed in a typeface readable with the naked eye.

The second Somesuch title was John Houghton Allen's *That Was Randado,* printed by David Holman in 1978. Holman was getting started as a printer at the time and soon discovered some of the difficulties in printing miniature books. Yet the book he produced, bound in marbled paper boards with a spine label in an edition of 295 copies, sold out before long. Somesuch Press had a busy year in 1978. *Randado* was followed by three more titles—*Yes, Virginia* (the famous letter about Santa Claus to the editor of the *New York Sun* and the editor's reply), *A Christmas Tree* by A. C. Greene, and *The Gift of the Magi* by O. Henry.

Each of the three books with a Christmas theme sold out quickly, but for different reasons. With *Yes, Virginia* it was partly because Stanley Marcus slashed the announced price in half when he saw the finished book produced by Hampshire Typothetae. He discovered that some of the text blocks were not square with the outside trim of their pages and complained to the printer, who in turn grew angry and denied anything was wrong. "I felt strongly enough that the book was not absolutely perfect that I reduced the price to half for everybody who had already ordered it," Marcus recalls. That put it at $22.50, and it sold out immediately. The stories by O. Henry and A. C. Greene were highly popular and sold out even at full price. However, when Andrew Hoyem finished printing *The Gift of the Magi* he told Stanley Marcus that he would never produce another miniature book. The small format was troublesome indeed. Nevertheless, it was the fastest selling book Somesuch Press has ever published.

The next year Marcus turned to another noted printer, Carl Hertzog, for *The Captive Boy* by Barbara Hofland. When the job was finished, Hertzog, too, swore he would never do another miniature. Before long Marcus learned about the Feathered Serpent Press in San Rafael, California, whose proprietors enjoyed the challenge of designing and printing miniature books. The first book that Susan Acker and the late Don Greame Kelly did for Somesuch Press was *The War of the Words* by Willard R. Espy in 1980, followed the same year by Daniel J. Boorstin's *Knowledge or Information?*

In 1981 Stanley Marcus turned once again to the Feathered Serpent Press for the first of a number of elegant miniature books illustrated with postage stamps. The idea had been suggested by Billie Marcus, and the result was *A Christmas Album: Twenty Years of Yuletide Stamps,* with an introduction by Belmont Faries, night editor of the *Washington Star.* The book called for a considerable amount of hand work in the printing as well as the proper mounting of the stamps in each copy. This drove the price up to $135, whereas most previous titles were in the $30 to $50 range. Nevertheless, the

Yuletide stamp book sold out quickly. With such success and with so many other recent Christmas stamps to select from, Marcus tried to repeat his success. In 1982 the size of the edition of *Christmas Stamps from Around the World* was increased to eight hundred and the price to $150. The edition is still in print, and after this experience Marcus has decided there are not enough collectors of miniature books to justify large editions. Thus, the more recent Somesuch Press miniature books are published in editions of around two hundred, and it takes about two years to sell out each edition.

The Feathered Serpent Press also produced *Pueblo Art: Southwestern Indian Pottery* by Francis H. Harlow, with an informative and amusing introduction by Ford Ruthling. Harlow, an authority on Pueblo pottery, whose 1974 book on the subject was published by the New York Graphic Society, provided an essay on the subject, while Ruthling wrote about his paintings and the process of designing the Pueblo Art series of four United States postage stamps issued in 1977. The book is illustrated with the actual stamps, which show to great advantage in the format of a miniature book.

The Somesuch Press sells its books throughout the United States as well as in Finland, Japan, England, and Hungary. "Hungary produces more miniature books than the rest of the world put together," Marcus observes. He attributes this to the fact that before World War II Hungary had very strong printing trade schools, and says that much of the printing for the Balkans was produced there. When the war ended the schools reopened only to find limited supplies of paper. They still needed to train students, so to provide them practical experience requiring the least amount of paper, miniature books were the answer. An entire generation of printers were thus trained, and their well-designed and printed trial efforts soon began showing up in bookstores.[24]

Following his interest in miniature books, Stanley Marcus traveled to Hungary to learn more about the phenomenon. There he found the bookstores featuring miniature books, not on the shelves but placed in little baskets at the sales counters. It was there that one could still purchase with spare change miniature books attractively printed in the trade schools. This had encouraged the collecting of miniatures to the point where a decade ago there were some eighteen thousand collectors of miniature books in Hungary alone.

In the United States most of the miniature books are produced in New England or on the West Coast. Closer to home, Stanley Marcus has made a happy discovery of some young printers in Austin. Having seen some of the work of Carol Kent, Marcus asked her if she would undertake the printing of a new miniature book for Somesuch Press. Occupied with other projects at the time, she suggested a solution—that her daughter, Susanna, print it. The publisher asked for samples, which arrived with a note informing him that the printer was ten years old. "Can she truly print?" Marcus asked. "Yes, she can, and I will supervise the process," Carol Kent replied. "And her brother Zachary who is eight years old will help her."

Marcus decided to take a gamble and asked the Kents to suggest a title for a new miniature. *The Golden Chain* by Rockwell Kent was their first choice, based on a copy they found at the Harry Ransom Humanities Research Center in Austin. During Rockwell Kent's lifetime only five copies of this short, imaginative piece had been printed. Marcus secured permission from Decherd Turner, who was in 1985 the director of the Harry Ransom Humanities Research Center, to reproduce the original in a new Somesuch Press edition.

The first quote for the cost of the new book did not meet with the publisher's approval—he thought it too low. He countered with another figure, which was agreed upon, and then advanced the money, since the young printer did not have sufficient capital to launch the project. Work progressed slowly, and it was difficult to stay in touch with the Kents, as they had no phone. Finally Marcus sent a registered letter inquiring about his books. The Kents replied, saying the books were finished and would be delivered the following Friday afternoon via Greyhound bus from Austin. At four-thirty that afternoon mother and daughter arrived as promised, looking to Marcus as if they had just stepped out of one of Tenniel's illustrations for *Alice in Wonderland.* His delight with the quality of the work on *The Golden Chain* (1986) has led to two more Somesuch Press titles printed by the Kents—*The Perfect Blind* by Decherd Turner (1989) and *Helen Corbitt: The Balenciaga of Food* by Elizabeth Ann Johnson (1992).

Twenty-eight books have been published by the Somesuch Press since its founding eighteen years ago. A new title, *No Calamity Equals a Bad Neighbor,* appeared in May, 1993, an old folktale about San Ysidro told again by New Mexico artist and writer Frank Applegate. Susan Acker and Mary McDermott at Feathered Serpent Press were the printers.

Now eighty-eight, Stanley Marcus is continuing to line up new titles for the Somesuch Press, write his weekly column for the *Dallas Morning News,* and proceed with writing another book. He still adds to his library new books he finds interesting and those given to him by writers and friends. He has never been persuaded to stop tucking reviews and letters inside the covers of his books, despite protestations from the Marcus librarian of longest tenure, Mrs. Linda Robinson Marcus, whom he married in 1979, after Billie's death. There is no telling what surprises await the visitor to Stanley Marcus's library, with its books and related clippings and correspondence revealing the collector's life of associations with notable people.

Founder of the Book Club of Texas, collector, author, publisher, newspaper columnist, arbiter of good taste—"Citizen of the World"—Stanley Marcus has brought his keen sense of quality to the realm of books, enriching his own life and contributing immensely to the literary culture of the Southwest.

Notes

Chapter One: The Harvard Experience

1. Stanley Marcus, *Minding the Store* (Boston: Little, Brown, 1974), p. 27.

2. *Ibid.*, pp. 28-29.

3. *Ibid.*, p. 34.

4. *Ibid.*, pp. 34-35.

5. *Official Register of Harvard University*, 21, no. 24 (May 14, 1924): 15.

6. Richard Norton Smith, *The Harvard Century* (New York: Simon & Schuster, 1986), p. 75.

7. Roger E. Stoddard, "Teaching the History of Books at Harvard, 1910-1987/88," paper delivered at the American Antiquarian Society for a conference in 1987 on Teaching the History of the Book.

8. Stephen Winship to author, 22 December 1991.

9. George Parker Winship to Stanley Marcus, 13 January 1939, Stanley Marcus Collection of Bruce Rogers, Bridwell Library, Southern Methodist University (hereafter cited as SMU).

10. Carl Bode, ed., *The Editor, the Bluenose, and the Prostitute: H. L. Mencken's History of the "Hatrack" Censorship Case* (Boulder: Roberts Rinehart, 1988), p. 22.

11. *Ibid.*, p. 21.

12. *Ibid.*, pp. 51-72.

13. "Mencken Raps Watch and Ward at Union," *Harvard Crimson*, 8 April 1926.

14. Stanley Marcus, "Are American Businessmen Moral Eunuchs?" *Southwest Review* 38 (Autumn 1953): 335.

Chapter Two: The Book Club of Texas

1. Stanley Marcus, *Minding the Store* (Boston: Little, Brown, 1974), p. 49.

2. Rick Stewart, *Lone Star Regionalism: The Dallas Nine and Their Circle, 1928-1945* (Austin: Texas Monthly Press and Dallas Museum of Art, 1985), p. 20.

3. Muriel Q. McCarthy, *David R. Williams: Pioneer Architect* (Dallas: SMU Press, 1984), p. 31.

4. Stewart, *Lone Star Regionalism*, p. 20.

5. Henry Nash Smith, "Culture," *Southwest Review* 13 (January 1928): 253.

6. Alexandre Hogue, "With Southwestern Artists: Victor Higgins," *Southwest Review* 14 (January 1929): 260.

7. *Southwest Review* 14 (July 1929): 475.

8. *Ibid.*

9. Marcus to McGinnis, 13 June 1928, DeGolyer Library, SMU.

10. Stanley Marcus, *The Book Club of Texas* (Dallas: DeGolyer Library, 1989), p. [2].

11. *Ibid.*

12. Lomax to Payne, 1 December 1928, Texas Folklore Society files, Stephen F. Austin State University, Nacogdoches.

13. Harry Hertzberg was a retired circus performer whose extensive circus collection was given to the San Antonio Public Library.

14. Maury Maverick would go on to distinguish himself in the U.S. Congress and as mayor of San Antonio.

15. Lomax to Woodhull, 18 September 1928, McFarlin Library Special Collections, University of Tulsa.

16. Prospectus, author's files.

17. *See* John H. Jenkins, *Basic Texas Books* (Austin: Texas State Historical Association, 1988), pp. 590-92.

18. Al Lowman, *Printing Arts in Texas* (Austin: Roger Beacham Press, 1975), p. 24.

19. Prospectus, author's files.

20. Faulkner to Marcus, n.d., private collection.

21. Henry Nash Smith, interview with Toni Terry, ca. 1979, private collection.

22. Marcus to McGinnis, 7 May 1932, DeGolyer Library, SMU.

23. *Ibid.*, 4 July [1932].

24. Copy in the McGinnis Collection, *ibid.*

25. Marcus to Selecman, 3 November 1932, *ibid.*

26. Beaty to pastors (mimeographed letter), n.d., *ibid.*

27. Cooke to Beaty, undated transcription, *ibid.*

28. SMU faculty to Selecman, 9 December 1932, *ibid.*

29. John William Rogers, "Frank Lloyd Wright Voices Eloquent Plea for Organic Architecture in U. S. Building," *Dallas Morning News*, 1 March 1933, p. 5.

30. Mary Carolyn Hollers George, *O'Neil Ford, Architect* (College Station: Texas A & M University Press, 1992), p. 38.

31. Marcus to Williams, 15 November 1934, Williams Collection, Dupre Library, University of Southwestern Louisiana.

32. Williams to Marcus, 19 December 1934, *ibid.*

33. David Farmer, "The Texas Printmakers, 1940-1965," in *The Texas Printmakers*, ed. Paul Rogers Harris (Dallas: Meadows Museum, 1990), p. [7].

34. Walter Prescott Webb, ed., *The Handbook of Texas*, vol. II (Austin: Texas State Historical Association, 1952), p. 725.

35. *A Catalogue of the Publications of Six American Book Clubs*, 1934, photocopy in author's files.

36. Lowman, *Printing Arts in Texas*, p. 25.

37. This inscription is reproduced in "A Keepsake on the Occasion of John Henry Faulk's Lecture, 'J. Frank Dobie—Freedom of Speech' " (Dallas: DeGolyer Library, 1988), 250 copies printed by W. Thomas Taylor.

38. Irvin Haas, *Bibliography of Modern American Presses* (Chicago: Black Cat Press, 1935), pp. 87-89. For further information on the Rydal Press, *see* "The Rydal Press of Santa Fe, New Mexico: A Brief Account of Its History and Its Purpose," *The Annual of Bookmaking* (New York: The Colophon, 1938).

39. Carl Hertzog, "Calendar of Twelve Travelers through the Pass of the North" (typescript about the making of the book), Hertzog Papers, University of Texas at El Paso (hereafter cited as UTEP).

40. *Ibid.*

41. Horgan to Hertzog, 26 May 1940, *ibid.*

42. Louise W. Kahn to Hertzog, 9 July 1940, *ibid.*

43. Hertzog to Kahn, 25 July 1940, *ibid.*

44. Hertzog to Horgan, 21 August 1940, *ibid.*

45. *Ibid.*, 23 October 1940.

46. Horgan to Lea and Hertzog, 11 November 1940, *ibid.*

47. Hertzog to Marcus, 27 November 1940, *ibid.*

48. Marcus to Dobie, 18 April 1941, Texas Folklore Society files, Stephen F. Austin State University, Nacogdoches.

49. Dobie to Marcus, 10 May 1941, *ibid.*

50. Lowman, *Printing Arts in Texas*, p. 25.

51. Marcus had just been awarded the newly struck DeGolyer Medal for significant contributions to the writing, making, and collecting of books.

Chapter Three: The Dallas Book Scene

1. Adolph L. Schmalzried began his own book business around 1923, before which he was vice-president of Walton Book & Stationery Co. and working out of his home at 5453 Goodwin Ave. His location at 911 Main was in a basement-level shop. In 1939 Schmalzried moved to 1023 Main, where he remained until moving to 1801 Greenville Ave. in 1947. *Dallas City Directory*, 1923-1947.

2. Jeff Dykes, "A Personal Memoir about Edward Eberstadt," *AB Bookman's Weekly* (7 October 1985): 2512.

3. Jeff Dykes, *I Had All the Fun* (College Station: Texas A & M University Library, 1978), p. 9.

4. *Ibid.*, p. 52.

5. Franklin Gilliam, interview with author, 2 March 1993. Gilliam, a native Texan, moved the Brick Row Book Shop from New York City to Austin in 1954 after buying it from the estate of its founder, E. Byrne Hackett. Its first Texas location was above Renfro's Drugstore on Guadalupe St. In 1961 the shop moved to 1913 Rio Grande where it operated until 1968, when Gilliam consolidated it in Houston with a branch opened in 1963. In 1971 the Brick Row relocated to San Francisco where Gilliam sold it to John Crichton in 1983.

6. *Dallas City Directory*, 1923-24.

7. Elizabeth Ann McMurray Johnson, interview with author, 22 October 1990.

8. Wirt Davis, Jr., telephone interview with author, 2 December 1991.

9. Dykes, *I Had All the Fun*, pp. 39-40.

10. DeGolyer to Lobdell, 18 January 1947, DeGolyer Papers, DeGolyer Library, SMU.

11. John William Rogers, *The Lusty Texans of Dallas* (New York: E. P. Dutton, 1951), p. 262. For a fascinating account of an early-twentieth-century Methodist preacher who traveled widely on church business and collected books, *see* Elijah L. Shettles, *Recollections of a Long Life*. Shettles sold Southern Methodist University a core collection which became its first library. He also established the longest unbroken succession of bookselling in Texas, his ward, Mrs. Bessie L. Wright, continuing in the business until she passed it along to her son, Hugh Wright, a present-day bookseller in Waxahachie.

12. Rogers, *Lusty Texans of Dallas*, p. 263.

13. Melrich V. Rosenberg, "Cokesbury 'Handsomest Book Store in the World'," *New York Herald Tribune Book News*, 3 December 1937, p. 1.

14. Rogers, *Lusty Texans of Dallas*, p. 262.

15. *Ibid.*, p. 263.

16. *Dallas Morning News*, 14 November 1956.

17. Dykes, *I Had All the Fun*, pp. 37-39.

18. *New York Herald Tribune Book News*, 3 December 1937.

19. *Dallas Morning News*, 25 April 1983.

20. The title page differs from the cover title, which reads: *Texas Book List: Bibliography of Books on and about Texas and the Southwest.* Sam Ratcliffe of SMU brought this item to my attention, for which I am most grateful.

21. *Publishers Weekly* (March 28, 1936): 1335.

22. *Ibid.* (April 25, 1936): 1690.

23. Allen Maxwell, interview with author, 10 December 1991.

24. *Publishers Weekly* (April 23, 1938): 1683.

25. Dykes, *I Had All the Fun*, p. 53.

26. Leon Harris, interview with author, 12 December 1991.

27. Elizabeth Ann Johnson, "Recalling the Good Old Days at a Legendary Book Store," *Dallas Morning News*, 13 July 1980.

28. *Ibid.*

29. *Ibid.*

30. *Ibid.*

31. *Ibid.*

32. *Ibid.*

33. *Ibid.*

34. McMurray to Hertzog, 5 June 1951, Hertzog Collection, UTEP.

35. J. B. Priestley and Jacquetta Hawkes, *Journey Down a Rainbow* (New York: Harper & Brothers, 1955), pp. 28-29.

36. Leon Harris, interview with author, 12 December 1991.

37. *Dallas Morning News*, 26 December 1954.

38. Leon Harris, interview with author; Rogers, *Lusty Texans of Dallas*, pp. 260-62; Marvin Steakley, interview with author, 5 December 1991. It was not until after the 1950s that the Dallas Public Library began to gain the support needed to meet the book-borrowing needs of a fast-growing community. See the discussion by John William Rogers in his chapter, "A Romance of Books," *Lusty Texans of Dallas*.

39. Evelyn Oppenheimer, interview with author, 10 November 1991.

40. Planning files, Southwest Book Fair, Southern Methodist University Archives (hereafter cited as SMU Archives).

41. B. F. McLain to James Albright, 18 July 1945, *ibid.*

42. *Dallas Times Herald*, 7 October 1945.

43. *Ibid.* Although he was invited, Hertzog was unable to attend the Southwest Book Fair. Had he done so, he would have no doubt been pleased to see the enthusiastic response to an event highlighting the importance of books in the lives of Dallas people, even if he would have found little to praise in the typographical artistry of trade book publication.

44. Mildred C. Smith to Lon Tinkle, 24 June 1948, Southwest Book Fair files, SMU Archives.

45. Marcus to Crossman, 30 October 1954, *ibid.* A blind carbon of this letter was directed to Lon Tinkle, suggesting that he and Marcus had recently explored ways to renew efforts for staging another fair and that the expression of encouragement to the Chamber of Commerce would best come from a major businessman and civic participant in the Dallas community like Stanley Marcus.

46. Crossman to Lon Tinkle and J. F. Albright, 3 December 1954, *ibid.*

Chapter Four: Mr. Stanley and Mr. Texas

1. Dobie to Marcus, 28 December 1929, Harry Ransom Humanities Research Center, University of Texas, Austin (hereafter cited as HRHRC, UT, Austin).

2. Marcus to Dobie, 26 March 1931, *ibid.*

3. *Ibid.*, 13 October 1933.

4. Dobie was mistaken; the book was published at $9, not $19.

5. A forthcoming Book Club of Texas publication, *From Texas to Mexico and the Court of Maximilian in 1865* by Alexander Watkins Terrell.

6. Dobie to Marcus, 21 October 1933, HRHRC, UT, Austin.

7. *Ibid.*, 6 August 1935.

8. Marcus to Dobie, 10 December 1937, *ibid.*

9. *Ibid.*, 1 July 1943.

10. J. Frank Dobie, ed., *Puro Mexicano* (Austin: Texas Folklore Society, 1935).

11. Ireland Graves (1885-1969) served as district judge of the 26th Judicial District and was the founder of the prominent Austin law firm of Graves, Dougherty, Gee, Hearon, Moody, and Garwood.

12. Dobie to Marcus, 25 July 1945, HRHRC, UT, Austin.

13. Marcus to DeGolyer, 5 January 1946, DeGolyer Library, SMU.

14. Webb to Bedichek, 19 September 1945, Bedichek papers, Barker Texas History Center, University of Texas, Austin (hereafter cited as BTHC, UT, Austin).

15. *Ibid.* [before 20 November 1945]

16. Webb to Moe, 21 September 1948, Webb papers, BTHC, UT, Austin.

17. Ronnie Dugger, ed., *Three Men in Texas* (Austin: University of Texas Press, 1967), 201-203.

18. Ronnie Dugger, *Our Invaded Universities* (New York: Norton, 1974), p. 49.

19. Lon Tinkle, *An American Original: The Life of J. Frank Dobie* (Boston: Little, Brown, 1978), pp. 197-204.

20. Marcus to Dobie, 21 October 1947, HRHRC, UT, Austin.

21. *Ibid.*, 20 February 1948.

22. Dobie to Marcus, 2 March 1948, *ibid.*

23. Marcus to Dobie, 5 March 1948, *ibid.*

24. Dobie to Marcus, 22 March 1948, *ibid.*

25. Marcus to Dobie, 25 March 1948, *ibid.*

26. Cerf to Marcus, 14 March 1951, Marcus papers, DeGolyer Library, SMU.

27. Dobie to Marcus, 1 January 1958, Dobie papers, HRHRC, UT, Austin.

28. *Ibid.*, 11 January 1958.

29. Marcus to Dobie, Western Union Telefax, 26 September 1963, *ibid.*

Chapter Five: The Printer at the Pass

1. Marcus to Hertzog, 17 January 1938, Hertzog Collection, UTEP.

2. *Ibid.*, 28 January 1939.

3. Hertzog to Marcus, 18 May 1939, *ibid.*

4. Marcus to Hertzog, 23 September 1939, *ibid.*

5. Hertzog to Marcus, 25 September 1939, *ibid.*

6. Hertzog to Dobie, 6 October 1939, *ibid.*

7. Dobie to Hertzog, 11 October 1939, *ibid.*

8. Dobie to Miller, 11 October 1939, *ibid.*

9. Hertzog to Marcus, 7 November 1939, *ibid.*

10. Marcus to Hertzog, 8 November 1939, *ibid.*

11. Frederick W. Goudy to Hertzog, 8 July 1941, *ibid.*

12. Marcus to Hertzog, 22 November 1939, *ibid.*

13. *Ibid.*, 12 December 1939.

14. *Ibid.*, 22 December 1939.

15. Marcus to Ransahoff, 21 December 1939, Marcus papers, DeGolyer Library, SMU.

16. Lea to Hertzog, 21 December 1939, Hertzog Collection, UTEP.

17. Marcus to Hertzog, 16 March 1940, *ibid.*

18. Webb to E. H. Sellards, 20 July 1939, Texas State Historical Association (hereafter cited as TSHA), Barker Texas History Center (hereafter cited as BTHC), UT, Austin.

19. Webb to Marcus, 6 March 1940, *ibid.*

20. *Ibid.*

21. Marcus to Hertzog, 13 March 1940, Hertzog Collection, UTEP.

22. Hertzog to Marcus, 13 March 1940, *ibid.*

23. Webb to Marcus, 14 March 1940, Webb papers, BTHC, UT, Austin.

24. Webb to Hertzog, 18 March 1940, Hertzog Collection, UTEP.

25. Hertzog to Marcus, 24 March 1940, *ibid.*

26. Marcus to Hertzog, 27 March 1940, *ibid.*

27. Hertzog to Marcus, 29 March 1940, TSHA, BTHC, UT, Austin.

28. Wharton to Webb, 22 May 1940, *ibid.*

29. Webb to Marcus, 1 April 1940, *ibid.*

30. *Ibid.*

31. Marcus to Hertzog, 29 April 1940, Hertzog Collection, UTEP.

32. Hertzog to Webb, 21 August 1940, TSHA, BTHC, UT, Austin.

33. Hertzog to Schwettmann, 22 March 1941, *ibid.*

34. Hertzog to Webb, 1 October 1941, *ibid.*

35. Hertzog to Carroll, 4 March 1943, Hertzog Collection, UTEP.

36. Carroll to Hertzog, 12 March 1943, *ibid.*

37. Carroll to Marcus, 1 April 1943, TSHA, BTHC, UT, Austin.

38. *New York Sun*, 25 February 1944.

39. Carroll to Hertzog, 1 January 1944, Hertzog Collection, UTEP.

40. Hertzog to Marcus, 10 November 1943, *ibid.*

41. Hertzog to Day, 6 August 1945, DeGolyer Library, SMU.

42. Day to Hertzog, 8 August 1945, *ibid.*

43. Hertzog to Day, 13 August 1945, *ibid.*

44. Hertzog to Marcus, 5 November 1945, Hertzog Collection, UTEP.

45. Hertzog to McMurray, 26 November 1945, *ibid.*

46. Hertzog to Maxwell, 5 April 1946, DeGolyer Library, SMU.

47. *Ibid.*, 3 July 1946.

48. *Ibid.*, 10 August 1946.

49. Marcus to Hertzog, 11 March 1947, Hertzog Collection, UTEP.

50. Hertzog to Marcus, 19 March 1947, *ibid.*

51. Maxwell to Hertzog, 7 August 1947, *ibid.*

52. Hertzog to Maxwell, 9 August 1947, *ibid.*

53. Maxwell to Hertzog, 27 August 1947, *ibid.*

54. Hertzog to McMurray, 8 September 1947, *ibid.*

55. McMurray to Hertzog, [?] October 1947, *ibid.*

56. Marcus to Lee, 24 March 1951, DeGolyer Library, SMU. Marcus did not give up the idea of bringing an expert in typography to Dallas. In 1953, he entertained Elmer Adler, founder of the Pynson Printers and publisher of *The Colophon*, and discussed with him the idea of splitting his time between Dallas and the University of Texas, Austin.

57. Marcus to Hertzog, 6 October 1945, Hertzog Collection, UTEP.

58. Hertzog to Marcus, 5 November 1945, *ibid.*

59. Marcus to Hertzog, 20 December 1946, *ibid.*

60. *Ibid.*, 21 October 1947.

61. Hertzog to Marcus, 17 December 1947, *ibid.*

62. Marcus to Hertzog, 31 March 1948, *ibid.*

63. Hertzog to Marcus, 11 April 1948, *ibid.*

64. Hertzog to H. Richard Archer, 6 August 1949, *ibid.* I am grateful to Al Lowman for calling this letter to my attention.

65. Marcus to Hertzog, 9 March 1951, *ibid.*

66. Billie Marcus to Hertzog, 23 March 1955, *ibid.*

67. Hertzog to Morris Cook, n.d., *ibid.*

68. Hertzog to Marcus, 26 June 1955, *ibid.*

69. *Ibid.*, 1 September 1959.

70. *Ibid.*, 1 December 1959.

71. Unknown to Hertzog, Marcus did get a response from Jacqueline Kennedy, whose office asked for a copy to be placed in the Kennedy Library.

72. Carl Hertzog, "Episodes in Printing: John F. Kennedy, Stanley Marcus, Ralph Yarborough: The Printing of a Speech," undated manuscript, personal collection of Al Lowman.

73. Horgan to Marcus, 26 May 1964, Marcus Collection, DeGolyer Library, SMU.

74. Marcus to Hertzog, 14 September 1965, Hertzog Collection, UTEP.

75. Marcus to Hertzog, 18 December 1965, *ibid.*

76. Hertzog to Marcus, 13 January 1966, *ibid.*

77. After they met in October, 1937, Tom Lea influenced Hertzog's work exten-

sively, especially in his early years as a printer in El Paso. This aspect of Lea's contribution to Hertzog's development merits further examination.

78. Hertzog to Marcus, 20 January 1966, Hertzog Collection, UTEP.

79. Marcus to Hertzog, 13 January 1978, *ibid.*

80. Hertzog to Marcus, 25 January 1978, *ibid.*

81. *Ibid.*, 7 March 1978.

82. Marcus to Hertzog, 13 March 1978, *ibid.*

83. *Ibid.*, 14 August 1978.

84. Hertzog to Marcus, 22 August 1978, *ibid.*

85. *Ibid.*, 25 March 1979.

86. Hertzog to Marcus, 13 April 1978, Marcus files.

Chapter Six: The Business of Authorship

1. H. Stanley Marcus, "America Is in Fashion," *Fortune* (November 1940): 81-84, 140-48.

2. *Ibid.*

3. *Ibid.*

4. Stanley Marcus, "Fashion Is My Business," *Atlantic Monthly* (December 1948): 43-47.

5. *Dallas Morning News* also ran an excerpt of the article on 17 February 1950.

6. Stanley Marcus, "Why I Live in Dallas," *Pageant* (March 1950).

7. Edward C. Aswell to Marcus, 28 May 1951, Marcus papers, DeGolyer Library, SMU.

8. Marcus to Aswell, 1 June 1951, *ibid.*

9. Blanche Knopf to Marcus, 22 October 1951, *ibid.*

10. Marcus to Herbert Weinstock, 20 April 1953, *ibid.*

11. Blanche Knopf to Marcus, 10 April 1953, *ibid.*

12. Marcus to Blanche Knopf, 2 May 1953, *ibid.*

13. Stanley Marcus, "Community Responsibilities of a Business Leadership," mimeographed typescript, 6 pp., *ibid.*

14. Stanley Marcus, "Are American Businessmen Moral Eunuchs?" *Southwest Review* 38 (Autumn 1953): 333-36.

15. Allen Maxwell, ed., *The Present Danger: Four Essays on American Freedom* (Dallas: SMU Press, 1953).

16. Maxwell to Marcus, 13 January 1954, Marcus papers, DeGolyer Library, SMU.

17. Blanche Knopf to Marcus, 27 April 1955, *ibid.*

18. Stanley Marcus, interview with author, 8 November 1990.

19. *Ibid.*

20. Stanley Marcus, "While We Were Watching the Store, the State of Texas Grew Up," *Saturday Evening Post* (Winter 1971): 46-49.

21. Stanley Marcus, interview with author, 8 November 1990.

22. *Fort Worth Star Telegram.*

23. *Dallas Morning News*, 12 November 1974.

24. *New York Times*, 22 November 1974.

25. *Wall Street Journal*, 31 December 1974.

26. *Publishers Weekly*, 19 August 1974.

27. Olin Chism, "World of Books: Choices of 1974," *Dallas Times Herald*, 22 December 1974.

28. Stanley Marcus, *Quest for the Best* (New York: Viking, 1979), p. 1.

29. *Publishers Weekly*, 18 June 1979.

30. Al Lowman, *Printing Arts in Texas* (Austin: Roger Beacham Press, 1975), pp. 7-8.

31. It was after this program that several individuals spontaneously offered contributions to help re-establish the Book Club of Texas, which was accomplished shortly thereafter.

32. Dos-à-dos is a term describing two books bound together but facing in opposite directions.

33. Stanley Marcus, "A Sporting Proposition," *Dallas Morning News*, 21 February 1984.

34. Marcus, *Dallas Morning News*, 29 September 1992.

35. *Ibid.*, 4 June 1991.

36. *Ibid.*, 27 August 1991.

37. *Ibid.*, 7 January 1992.

38. *Ibid.*, 4 August 1992.

39. *Ibid.*, 8 October 1991.

40. *Ibid.*, 8 May 1990.

41. *Ibid.*, 24 December 1991.

Chapter Seven: The Quest for Books

1. Stanley Marcus, *Minding the Store* (Boston: Little, Brown, 1974), pp. 36-37.

2. S. R. Shapiro to Marcus, n.d., private collection.

3. Stanley Marcus, interview with author, 14 June 1991.

4. *Ibid.*

5. S. N. Behrman, *Portrait of Max: An Intimate Memoir of Sir Max Beerbohm* (New York: Random House, 1960), pp. 297-98.

6. Marcus to Shapiro, 7 September 1955, Marcus Collection, DeGolyer Library, SMU.

7. *Ibid.*, 24 September 1955.

8. *Ibid.*, 7 November 1955.

9. *Ibid.*, 28 December 1955.

10. *Ibid*, 30 January 1956.

11. After all the buildup about his close association with Bruce Rogers, Shapiro could not persuade the typographer to write anything more than his signature in the book.

12. It was at this exhibit that I first saw the Marcus copy of *The Happy Hypocrite*.

13. Marcus to Rogers, 29 May 1956, Marcus Collection, DeGolyer Library, SMU.

14. Marcus to Frank Leslie, 11 June 1956, *ibid.*

15. Marcus to John Windle, 1 June 1974, Howell Collection, Stanford University Library.

16. *Ibid.*, 8 June 1974.

17. Windle to Marcus, 12 June 1974, *ibid.*

18. Marcus to Windle, 18 June 1974, *ibid.*

19. Harry Ransom to Marcus, 2 January 1968, Marcus Collection, DeGolyer Library, SMU.

20. Linda Robinson worked with the Marcus library for ten years before she and Stanley Marcus were married in 1979, a year after the death of his first wife, Billie. Marriage to Linda, however, did not gain Marcus a permanent librarian. While she held an undergraduate degree in comparative literature from SMU, she returned to her alma mater and earned a Ph.D. in anthropology in 1991.

21. Marcus to Alfred Knopf, 20 December 1955, HRHRC, UT, Austin.

22. Marcus to Decherd Turner, 30 January 1976, Bridwell Library, SMU.

23. Turner to Marcus, 5 February 1976, *ibid.*

24. Stanley Marcus, interview with author, 21 April 1993.

Index

BUSINESS
SUTRA

BUSINESS SUTRA

A VERY INDIAN APPROACH TO MANAGEMENT

DEVDUTT
PATTANAIK

Illustrated by the author

ALEPH BOOK COMPANY
An independent publishing firm
promoted by ***Rupa Publications India***

This edition published by
Aleph Book Company
7/16 Ansari Road, Daryaganj
New Delhi 110 002

ISBN: 978-81-92328-07-2

7 9 10 8

For sale in the Indian subcontinent only.

Page layout and typesetting: Special Effects, Mumbai

Printed and bound in India by
Gopsons Papers Ltd.

For Kishore Biyani

Acknowledgements

Sanjay Jog, who was Chief People Officer of the Future Group, and earlier with the RPG group, DHL Worldwide, and Taj Hotels, and is currently with Reliance Industries. Long conversations on his vast experience with corporations and human resource practices helped reaffirm many of the frameworks that constitute this book. Every day a new dot would appear, redefining old patterns, filling us both with wonder and awe, confirming that the world described by the rishis is indeed ananta and sukshma, full of infinite forms, layered with infinite meanings. Few joined in these deliberations. Some found it tedious and repetitive, others disturbing. Many resented this timepass on official time, reminding us once again what the rishis kept pointing out: observers create observations! I can safely say that this yagna changed us both forever. We finally understood what the rishis meant when they said: in wisdom, the daughter turns into the mother.

Contents

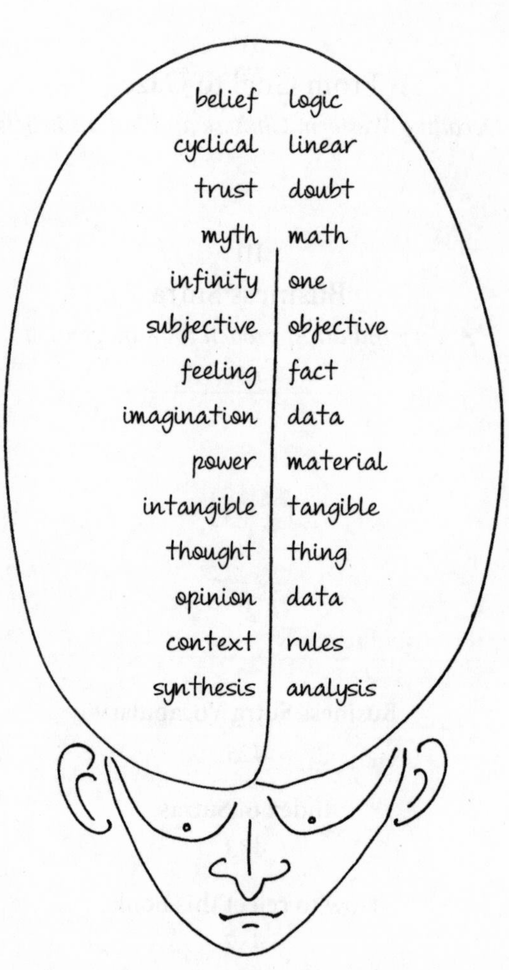
belief logic
cyclical linear
trust doubt
myth math
infinity one
subjective objective
feeling fact
imagination data
power material
intangible tangible
thought thing
opinion data
context rules
synthesis analysis

I
Introduction
Connecting Belief to Business

In the monsoon of 2008, I was made Chief Belief Officer of the Future Group. The idea behind this unusual designation was deliberate and simple: to startle people and make them see the critical role of belief in business.

There was the risk of being mistaken for a pastor, a guru or a priest, for many equate belief with religion and spirituality. Some were even convinced that my role was that of an evangelist or a propagandist: to help the organization manipulate the beliefs of employees and customers until they were more enterprise-friendly.

My job, however, was to neither judge nor change beliefs; it was simply to articulate them. The intention was to expand the mind of those involved in business so that they could see the misalignment between business practices (that they blindly followed) and the beliefs of people (that they remained oblivious to). When the mind is expanded, we are able to see more frameworks, understand the world better, take better decisions, ones that ensure a viable, sustainable and happy business.

The 3B Framework

Belief is subjective truth, my truth and your truth, the lens through which we make sense of the world.

Animals do not have beliefs. Animals want to know if the other is food, a mate or a threat. Humans, however, are consumed with notions of what is true (satyam, in Sanskrit), good (shivam) and beautiful (sundaram). Belief establishes these. Belief enables us to qualify people as heroes, villains and victims. Everyone believes their subjective truth to be the objective truth, and clings to it firmly, as it determines their self-image and their self-worth.

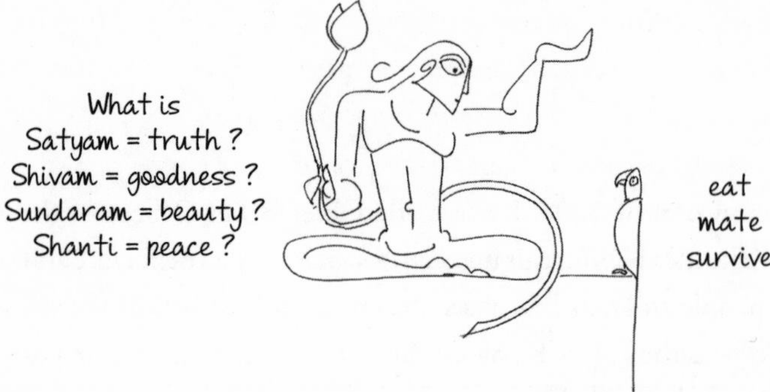

Belief plays a key role in business: it determines choices and propels the decisions of buyers and sellers, regulators and shareholders, investors and entrepreneurs, employers and employees, vendors and customers. It determines how we do business, and what ultimately gets done.

As is belief, so is behaviour, so is business. This is Business Sutra. We can call it the 3B framework. Sutra is a string that connects the dots; here the string connects belief with business.

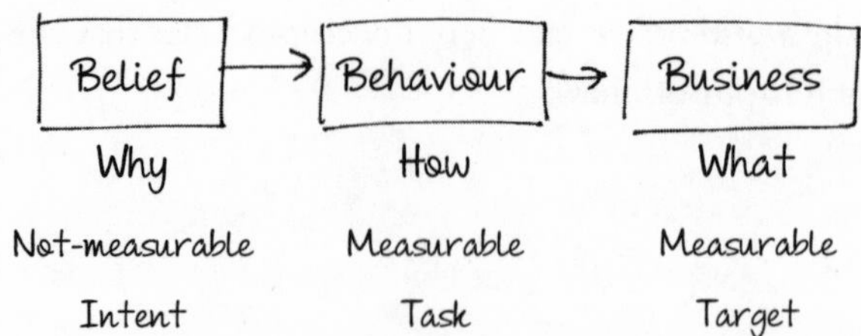

Management science, however, steers clear of belief. A child of the scientific revolution and the industrial era, it shuns the intangible, subjective and non-measurable. It pays greater value to objectivity. Hence, greater attention is paid to institutional values, arrived at by a team through consensus following a logical process. These belong to no one but every constituent member of the institution is contractually obliged to adhere to them, even at the cost of personal beliefs, at least during office hours. Organizational values are mapped to particular behaviours: the assumption is that certain behaviours reflect certain beliefs. This assumption allows the pretender to thrive in corporations, for as long as you are polite or mindful of protocol and respectful of rules, no one really cares what you feel or think. Belief may express itself in behaviour, but the reverse may not be true. Respect (intangible belief) may manifest in politeness (tangible behaviour), but politeness may not always reflect respect.

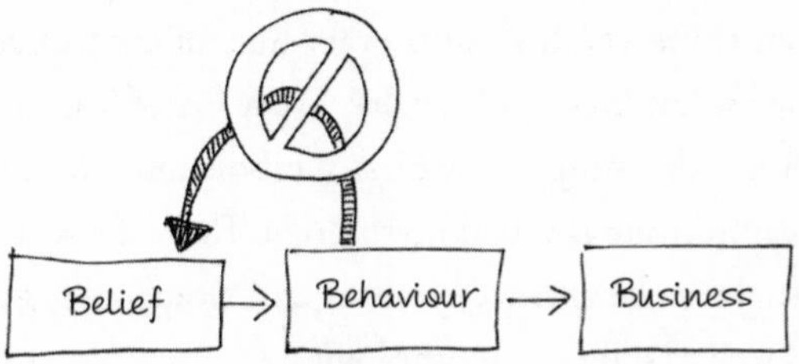

When corporations speak of growth, they speak of institutional growth not individual growth. And growth is always seen in terms of accumulation of wealth or equity or skills, never in terms of emotion or intellect. By doing so the corporation invalidates the personal, celebrates the professional, and creates the divide between work and life. This is what dehumanizes corporations, and is the root cause of many of the problems facing organizations today: from lack of initiative and lack of ownership to the lack of ethics. Failure to recognize this is the greatest shortcoming of modern management studies.

Despite the veneer of objectivity and logic, management science is itself firmly rooted in a cultural truth, the subjective truth of the West, indicated by its obsession with goals. Targets come first, then tasks, then people. The value

placed on vision, mission, objectives, milestones, targets and tasks in modern business practice resonates with the Greek quest for Elysium, the heaven of heroes, and the biblical quest for the Promised Land, paradise of the faithful.

This is not surprising as the purveyors of management science are mostly engineers, bankers and soldiers from twentieth century North America, which is deeply entrenched in the Protestant work ethic, a unique blend of Greek and biblical beliefs. And like all believers, they are convinced that goal-orientation is logical, hence the universal solution to all business problems. But it is not so. In fact, there are cultures, like India, where this goal-orientation is seen as a problem, not a solution.

This is obvious to any student of mythology. But who studies mythology in a world where most managers are engineers?

Belief, Myth and Mythology

Belief is the seed from which sprouts every human enterprise, every culture, every act of human kindness and cruelty. Every belief is irrational and hence a myth. Therefore, the study of stories, symbols and rituals to decode the beliefs they communicate is called mythology. There are secular mythologies in the world, such as the stories, symbols and rituals of a nation state, or a corporation, as well as religious mythologies.

For the believer, his belief is objective truth; he therefore rejects the notion of myth, and shuns the subject of mythology, a key reason why belief remains an invisible unacknowledged lever in modern business practices. We convince ourselves that our beliefs are rational hence right, while those of others are irrational, hence wrong.

To have beliefs, we need imagination. Imagination springs from the neo-frontal cortex, or the enlarged part of the brain that is located behind the forehead. This exists only in human beings. Some animals, like the dolphin and the chimpanzee, may imagine, but nothing on the scale that humans can.

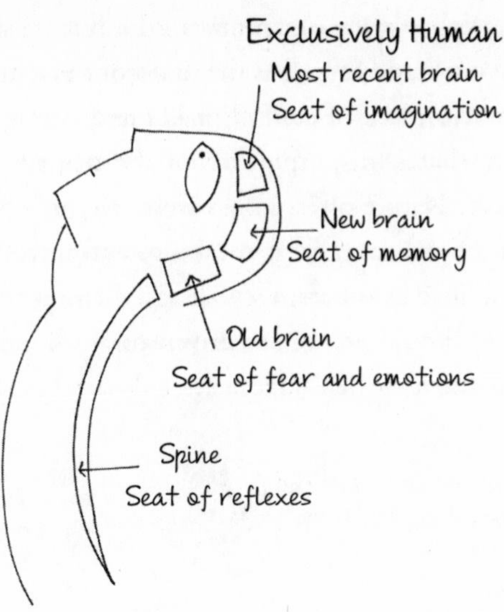

It comes as a surprise to most people that the imagination is a neurobiological function specific to the human species, not a universal phenomenon. It means accepting that every human being inhabits his own customized personalized subjective version of reality that no one else has access to.

Every animal looks at the world differently but the human gaze is especially different because the reality of nature is being constantly compared and contrasted with imaginary reality inside the head. We can control the subjective world in our head but not the objective one outside. This leads to conflict as the imagination seeks a world that is much more controllable, hence delightful.

Conflict is further amplified because every other human we encounter has their own version of imagined reality and each person is convinced that their imagined reality is the 'correct' version of reality. What is true then? This brings about awareness of the self (my view versus the view of others), and the need for language, creativity and reason (to communicate my view and convince others of my view).

Humans have the ability to control fire, water, plants as well as animals,

something that no other living organism can do. But we struggle to control the human mind: our mind as well as the mind of those around us. Control makes us feel powerful; lack of control makes us feel powerless. And so we are left to wonder: what is the purpose of our abilities, who are we, and what happens after death? Nature offers no answers. We only have our beliefs to guide us, structure our lives, give it meaning, and direction. Most people follow beliefs prescribed by others; a few design their own. As we agree upon what life can be or should be, we are driven to work, establish businesses, create civilizations and leave behind legacies.

Decoding Culture

There was once a priest who was very poor, there were constant quarrels in his house between his unhappy wife, his hungry children and his helpless parents. He begged the deity of his temple to help. So the deity gave him a pot of gold. The happy priest sold the gold and used the money to repay his debts, bought all the things money could buy, and even made investments to secure his future. But soon after the quarrels started again: between his greedy wife, his ambitious children and his neglected parents. Each one wanted a greater share of the treasure. Annoyed, the priest went to the deity and demanded a solution. Once again the deity gave him a pot of gold. "No, I don't want

another pot of gold. Give me something that solves the problem truly," cried the priest. "Pot of gold!" exclaimed the deity, "But I never gave you a pot of gold. I gave you the nectar of wisdom. Did you not drink it? Or were you too distracted by the container?"

Stories, symbols and rituals that define a culture, even business practices that shape an organization, make up the pot of gold that we all engage with; contained within it is belief in the culture that makes us see the world in a particular way. It is often overlooked.

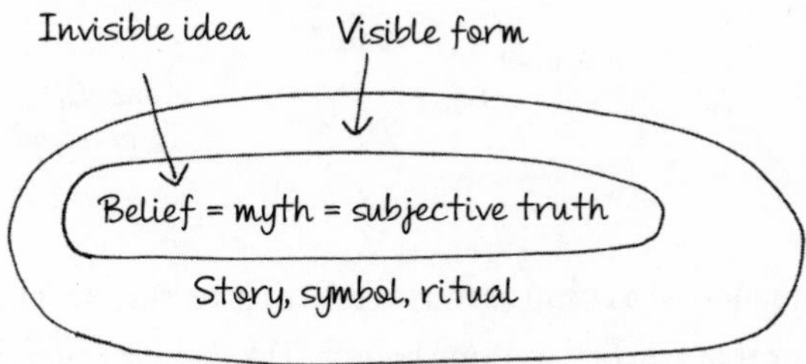

Every belief expresses itself in the stories we tell, the symbols we create, and the rituals we follow. Stories, symbols and rituals create culture. Culture in turn shapes the beliefs of those who inhabit it. Thus, from nature comes imagination, from imagination comes subjectivity and from subjectivity comes belief, from belief comes culture and from culture springs forth humanity.

American stories, symbols and rituals reveal American beliefs. Indian stories, symbols and rituals reveal Indian beliefs. Modern stories, symbols and rituals reveal modern beliefs. Tribal stories, symbols and rituals reveal tribal beliefs. Organizational stories, symbols and rituals reveal organizational beliefs. Religious stories, symbols and rituals reveal religious beliefs. Secular stories, symbols and rituals reveal secular beliefs.

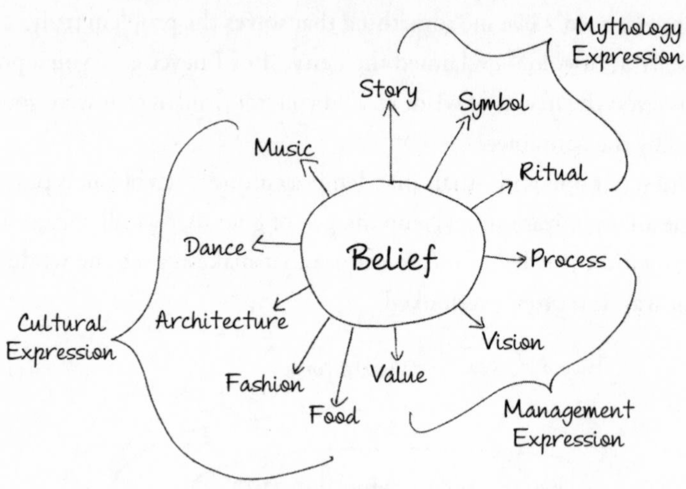

The uniqueness of a culture's music, art, architecture, food and fashion is an expression of that culture's unique beliefs. The diversity of cultures around the world indicates diversity of beliefs, hence plurality of human thought. Mythology involves studying these stories, symbols and rituals (the codes) and decoding the underlying patterns of thought. It reveals that different communities think differently and so approach life very differently. It reveals that management science is rooted in Western beliefs and indifferent to Indian or Chinese beliefs.

Myth got a bad name, and rationality got a good name, because of the scientific revolution of the sixteenth century, according to which only that which is rational is real and relevant. The word was used to dismiss ideas of every culture other than European. European ideas were assumed to be rational, hence not mythic. This has naturally put other cultures on the defensive. Nobody wants to be associated with myth, hence falsehood.

Myth has since been positioned as being the opposite of the truth. Unfortunately, in the West, truth is claimed on one hand by scientists and on the other hand by religious authorities. There is much debate even today between the theists and atheists. Academicians and scientists have legitimized this fight by joining in. This fight has been appropriated by most societies in the world that seek to be modern.

But the divide between myth and truth, between religious truth and scientific truth, this rabid quest for the absolute and perfect truth is a purely Western phenomenon. It would not have bothered the intellectuals of ancient China who saw such activities as speculative indulgence. Ancient Indian sages would have been wary of it for they looked upon the quest for the objective and absolute as the root cause of intolerance and violence.

The 'modern era' that flourished after the scientific revolution of Europe mocked the 'pre-modern era' that did not challenge irrational ideas propagated by religious and royal authorities.

In the second half of the twentieth century, people started observing that rational ideas propagated by modern scientists, especially social scientists, in the realm of economics, politics, sociology, anthropology, philosophy, arts, religious and cultural studies, were also steeped in prejudice. The language used to express ideas harboured cultural ideas: innocuous words like 'evolution' and 'development' revealed a belief that the world had, or should have, a purpose, a direction, and a movement towards betterment. Capitalism and Communism were deconstructed to reveal roots in the Greek epics or the Bible as they spoke of individualistic heroes and martyrdom for the greater social good. This discovery gave birth to the 'postmodern era'. Modern ideas may not be religious, but that did not make them universal truths; they were as rooted in cultural beliefs as the superstitions of yore.

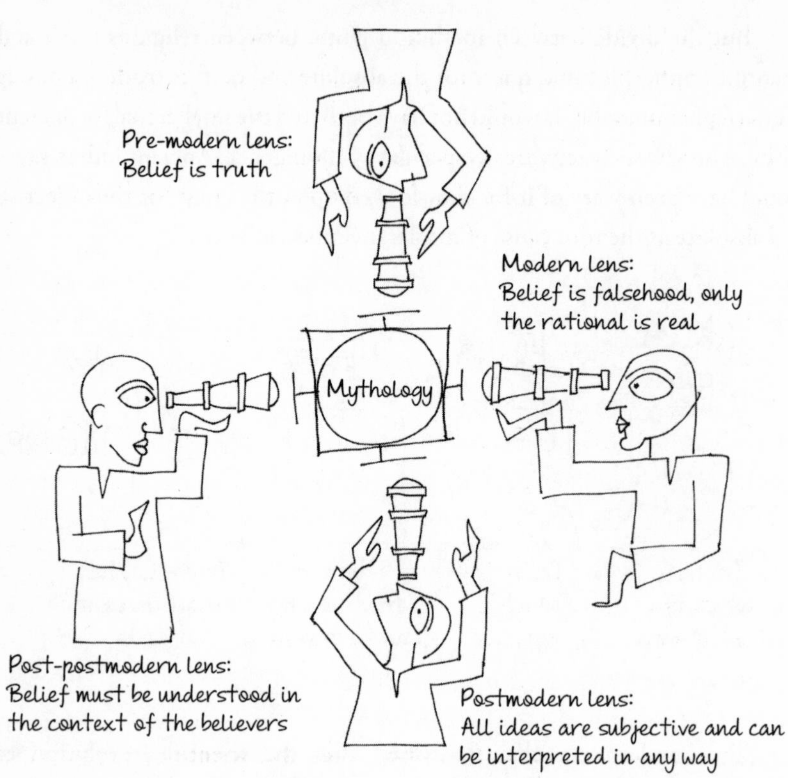

But there was a problem with the postmodern revolution. It implicitly suggested that everything was up for interpretation, there was no correct decoding, and no view could be criticized, as everything was subjective. Judgment of any kind was bad; any form of evaluation was prejudice. The era of remixes was born. Ravan could be worshipped and Ram reviled, invalidating the traditional adoration of Ram in hundreds of temples over hundreds of years. Images of Santa on a crucifix could be used to evoke the Christmas spirit.

Another problem with the postmodern lens is that the authors are typically critical of the authoritarian and manipulative gaze but are indifferent to their own gaze, which is often equally authoritarian and manipulative. Deconstruction of the Other is rarely accompanied by deconstruction of the self.

Today people speak of 'post-postmodernism'. It means looking at beliefs from the point of view of the believer. It demands empathy and less judgment, something that is in short supply in academia today, as it is designed to argue and dismiss ideas in its quest for the objective truth.

Connecting Mythology and Management

I discovered my love for mythology while studying in Grand Medical College, Mumbai. After my graduation, I chose to work in the medical industry, rather than take up clinical practice, to give myself the time and funds for my passion. So I lived in two worlds: weekdays in the pharmaceutical and healthcare industry and weekends with mythologies from all over the world.

In my professional capacity, I was first a content vendor, then a manager at Goodhealthnyou.com, Apollo Health Street and Sanofi Aventis, and finally, a business adviser at Ernst & Young. In a personal capacity, I conducted workshops as part of Sabrang, an organization dedicated to demystifying the arts, started by the late Parag Trivedi. Conversations with him, and other members of the Sabrang gang, revealed a gap between Hindustani melody and Western harmony, the value of facial expressions in Indian classical dance and the relative absence of the same in Japanese theatre, ballet and modern American dance, the intense arguments of European philosophers on the nature of the truth and the reason why Indian, or Chinese, philosophers were excluded from these arguments. Shifts in patterns I had seen in stories, symbols and rituals, were now apparent in music, dance, architecture, and philosophy.

I never studied management formally though I grew up listening to stories of sales and marketing from my father who did his MBA from New York University in 1960, long before it became fashionable in India (IIM itself was founded in 1961). One of his teachers was the famous Peter Drucker. My father returned to work in the private sector in India at the height of the licence raj. He always spoke of trust, relationships and respect, rather than processes and control.

I did do a formal postgraduate diploma course in comparative mythology from Mumbai University, but it was too rudimentary for my

liking. I delved into the literature written around the subject (*Myth* by Lawrence Coupe, for example) and realized that mythology demanded forging links with literature, language, semiotics, the occult, mysticism, anthropology, sociology, philosophy, religion, history, geography, business, economics, politics, psychology, physics, biology, natural history, archaeology, botany, zoology, critical thinking, and the arts. Courses offered by universities abroad, on the other hand, were not inter-disciplinary enough. Self-study was the only recourse.

The more I explored mythology, the more I felt like Aladdin in a cave of undiscovered treasures. Every day I learned something that took me by surprise. I realized how mythology tends to be read literally, causing it to be seen through a sociological and historical lens (did Ram exist?) when, in fact, its greatest value comes when it is read symbolically and seen in psychological terms (what aspect of our personality does Ram represent?).

As my mind exploded with new ideas, I wondered if they were true. And this lead to the unearthing of various theories on truth that helped me understand myth even better. It exposed the gap between neuroscience and psychoanalysis and the discomfort of scientists with the idea of imagination. It also revealed how the truth of the East is always studied in Western terms, rarely has the truth of the West been studied in Eastern terms. If it has, it has been dismissed as exotic, even quaint.

For a long time, management and mythology were parallel rivers in my life, unconnected with each other. Things began to change when I became increasingly sensitive to the problems plaguing corporations: the power play between sales and marketing, the need as well as threat of unions, the burden of templates, the cultural insensitivity of multinational advertising, the lack of inter-departmental empathy, the pretence of teamwork, the tyranny of technology, the feudal mindset beneath institutional veneers, the horrors of mergers and acquisitions, the deceptiveness of valuations, and the harsh reality of balance sheets.

I was fortunate that early in my career I interacted with Dr. Giri Shankar and his wife, Shailaja, who came from a strong behavioural science background, which is the cornerstone of many human resource practices in the business world. The frameworks they provided explained and helped resolve many of the issues I saw and faced. But our intense and illuminating conversations kept telling me that something was missing. I found the subject too rational, too linear and too neat. Then it dawned on me that both management science and behavioural science have originated in American and European universities and are based on a Western template. Practitioners of behavioural science use questionnaires to map the mind in objective mathematical terms but the subject itself springs from Jungian psychoanalysis and the notion of archetypes, which is eager to be 'universal' despite being highly subjective, and skewed towards mythologies of Western origin.

The problems of the corporate world made more sense when I abandoned the objective, and saw things using a subjective or mythic lens. It revealed the gap in worldviews as the root of conflict, frustration and demotivation. Modern management systems were more focused on an objective institutional truth, or the owner's truth, rather than individual truths. People were seen as resources, to be managed through compensation and motivation. They were like switches in a circuit board. But humans cannot be treated as mere instruments. They have a neo-frontal cortex. They imagine. They have beliefs that demand acknowledgment. They imagine themselves as heroes, villains and martyrs. They yearn for power and identity. Their needs will not go away simply by being dismissed as irrational, unscientific or unnecessary. Knowledge

of mythology, I realized, could help managers and leaders appreciate better the behaviour of their investors and regulators, employers and employees and competitors and customers. Mythology is, after all, the map of the human mind.

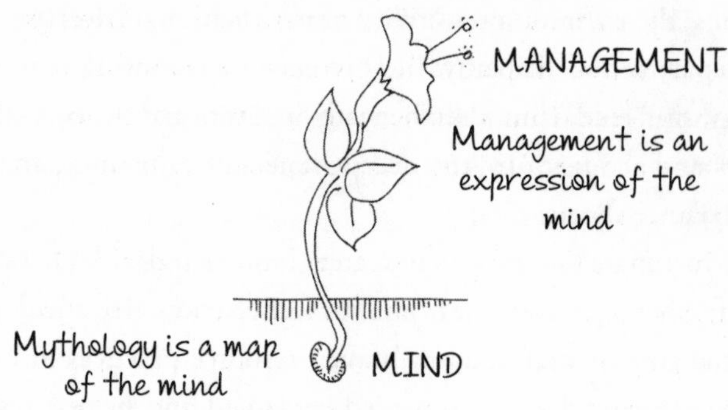

The management framework is rooted in Greek and biblical mythologies. The Indian economic, political and education systems are also rooted in Western beliefs, but Indians themselves are not. What would be a very Indian approach to management, I wondered. Since the most popular mode of expression, in India, was the mythic, I chose to glean business wisdom from the grand jigsaw puzzle of stories, symbols and rituals that originated and thrived in the Indian subcontinent, especially in the Hindu, Jain, Buddhist and Sikh faiths.

The patterns I found revealed something very subtle and startling very early on. Belief itself, as conventionally approached in modern times, is very different from the traditional Indian approach:

- The desire to evangelize and sell one idea and dismiss others reveals the belief that one belief is better, or right. Missionaries evangelize, social activists evangelize, and politicians evangelize; management gurus also evangelize. Everyone wants to debate and win. There is celebration of competition and revolution. In other words; only one belief is allowed to exist, weeding out other beliefs. This explains the yearning for a globally applicable morality and ethics, ignoring local contexts. At

best, allowances are made for the professional and personal space. This value placed on a single belief, religious or secular, naturally makes a society highly efficient. Since changing beliefs is difficult, perhaps even impossible, the attention shifts to behavioural modification through rationality, righteousness, rules, reward and reproach. In fact, great value is given to 'habits', which is essentially conditioning and a lack of mindfulness. Thus value is given to changing the world, as people cannot be changed. This is typical of beliefs rooted in one life, religions that value only one God.

- The notion of conversion is alien to Indian faiths. Greater value is given to changing oneself, than the world. Belief in India is not something you have; it is what makes you who you are. It shapes your personality. Different people have different personalities because they believe in different things. Every belief, every personality, is valid. Energy has to be invested in accommodating people rather than judging their beliefs. That is why there is so much diversity. We may not want to change our beliefs, but we can always expand our mind to accommodate other people's beliefs. Doing so, not only benefits the other, it benefits us too, for it makes us wiser, reveals the patterns of the universe. But we struggle to expand our mind as growth is change, and change is frightening. Our belief, our personality, marks the farthest frontier of our comfort zone, beyond which we are afraid to go. Such ideas thrive in beliefs rooted in many lives, and religions that value many gods.

The idea I came up with finally, which I later called Business Sutra, was unique in the value it paid to belief, imagination and subjectivity.

Mythologies of Indian origin value the nirguna (intangible and immeasurable) over the saguna (tangible and measurable), in other words the subjective over the objective. Subjectivity tends to be more appreciative of the irrational. Subjectivity draws attention to other subjects and their subjectivity. Respect for other people's worldviews allows diversity.

What emerged was a management model that valued gaze over goal, accommodation over alignment. This is what, I believe, the global village needs. Its absence is why there is so much strife and conflict.

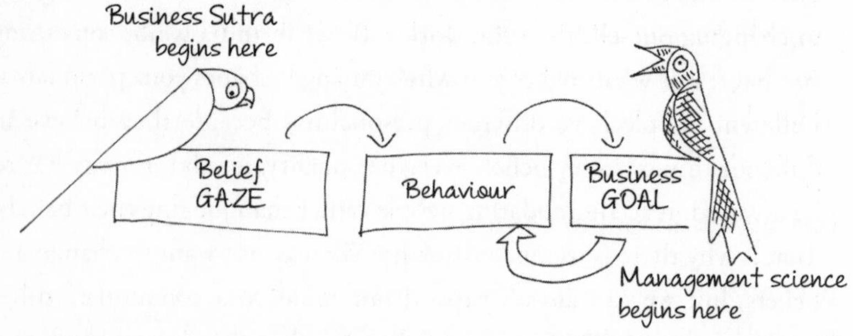

My initial observations were met with wry amusement. Modern society had bought into the 'myth of mythlessness' created by the scientific discourse that locates humans outside subjectivity. Most people seem to be convinced myth and mythology belonged 'then and there' and not 'here and now'. No one wanted to believe that businesses were anything but rational and scientific. Moreover, for most people, mythology is religion and religion is a 'bad' word, hence mythology is a bad word. To be secular is to dismiss both religion and mythology, and treat those who speak of it as heretics, which did not bode well for me.

Susheel Umesh of Sanofi Aventis was the first to value my ideas on management principles derived from Indian mythology; the illustration of the yagna I drew for him several years ago still hangs in his office. I got an opportunity to present my views through *Corporate Dossier*, the weekly management supplement of the *Economic Times,* thanks to the

encouragement of Vinod Mahanta, Dibyendu Ganguly and Vikram Doctor. This was a personal enterprise; professionally, no one took notice. The column, however, was widely appreciated, perhaps because of cultural chauvinism, some may argue. But gradually it caught the eye of business leaders, academicians and practitioners. They felt it articulated what many had intuitively sensed.

Santosh Desai, author of *Mother Pious Lady,* who came from the world of advertising and branding, reaffirmed my understanding of humans as mythmakers and meaning-seekers, constantly giving and receiving codes through the most innocuous of cultural practices. Rama Bijapurkar, author of *We Are Like That Only,* who came from the world of market research and consumer insights, encouraged me to find original ideas in Indian mythology that had escaped academicians and scholars who were entrenched in Western thought.

Becoming Chief Belief Officer

The tipping point came when Kishore Biyani asked me to join the Future Group. He had set up the unique retail chain, Big Bazaar, based on Indian beliefs, and had long recognized the role that culture and storytelling play in business. He was looking for someone to articulate these thoughts to his investors, to the world at large, and also to the many sceptics within his team, who were all hitherto spellbound by Western discourse. My initial conversations with him, his daughter, Ashni, as well as Damodar Mall and Tejaswini Adhikari of Future Ideas on the possibilities of mythology changed the course of my life forever.

Within the group, tea started being served in the peculiar 'cutting chai' glass that is found in railway stations across India to symbolically communicate the group's determination to be grounded in simplicity and community reality. The karta ritual was initiated wherein the store manager is blindfolded in the presence of his team and his family before being given keys to the store along with his target sheet by his boss; the aim was to draw attention to the eyes, symbolically provoke a mind-shift along with the job-

shift, encourage a wider, longer, deeper and more mature line-of-sight to accompany the increase in responsibilities. An abbreviated version of the gaze-based leadership model was displayed visually, using symbols, and used in leadership workshops and appraisals for senior team members so that all aspects were approached simultaneously rather than sequentially. Suddenly, the corporation seemed more rooted in culture, and not burdened by an alien imposition.

Outside the group, the designation did the trick. It opened many doors and led to many fine conversations with senior leaders and consultants of the industry that helped flesh out my idea into a full-blown theory. My interactions revealed how divorced modern business practices are from all things cultural. Very few managers saw culture as a lever; most seemed to be embarrassed by all things traditionally Indian, except Bollywood and cricket. It explained why industry is increasingly at odds with society. It became clear that professionalism and processes are aimed at domesticating people, and so could never inspire entrepreneurship, ethics, inclusiveness or social responsibility. I also realized how ideas that I found in Indian mythology helped many to join the dots in businesses very differently.

The most difficult thing about this designation has been to see how people receive new ideas. After over a century of gazing upon Indian ideas through orientalist, colonial, socialist and capitalist lenses, we are today far removed from most Indian ideas presented in this book. While many are thrilled by the rediscovery, many are eager to dismiss it: we may not be happy with what we already know, but we are terrified of exploring anything new.

The success of my *TED India* talk in Mysore 2009 and the *Business Sutra* series on CNBC in 2010 with Menaka Doshi and the viral spread of these videos through social networking sites allayed my self-doubt. The *Shastraarth* series on CNBC-Awaaz with Sanjay Pugalia in Hindi highlighted the gap between Indian beliefs and beliefs embedded in management science. It convinced me to write this book.

Design of the Book

The word 'sutra' in the title of the book has two very particular meanings.

- A sutra is a string meant to join dots that create a pattern. The book strings together myriad ideas from Jain, Hindu and Buddhist traditions to create a synthesized whole, for the sake of understanding the India way. Likewise, it strings Greek and biblical ideas separately to understand the Western way and Confucian and Taoist ideas to understand the Chinese way. Each of these garlands is man-made and reveals my truth, not the Truth.

- Sutra also means an aphorism, a terse statement. The book is full of these. They are like seeds which, when planted in the mind, germinate into a plant. The nature of the plant depends on the quality of the mind. Indian sages avoided the written word as they realized that ideas were never definitive; they transformed depending on the intellectual and emotional abilities of the giver as well as the receiver. Thus, an idea is organic. Many sages chose symbols rather than sutras to communicate the idea. What appears like a naked man to one person, will reveal the nature of the mind to another. Both are right from the point of view of each individual. There is no standard answer. There is no correct answer. The point is to keep expanding the mind to accommodate more views and string them into a single whole. This approach can be disconcerting to the modern mind seeking the truth.

I call this book a very Indian approach to business for a very specific reason.

- An Indian approach traces Western ideas to Indian vocabulary. Here, dharma becomes ethics and yajaman becomes the leader. It assumes the existence of an objective truth in human affairs.

- A *very* Indian approach to business reveals the gap in the fundamental assumptions that defines management science taught in B-schools today. It celebrates my truth and your truth, and the human capability to expand the mind, thanks to imagination.

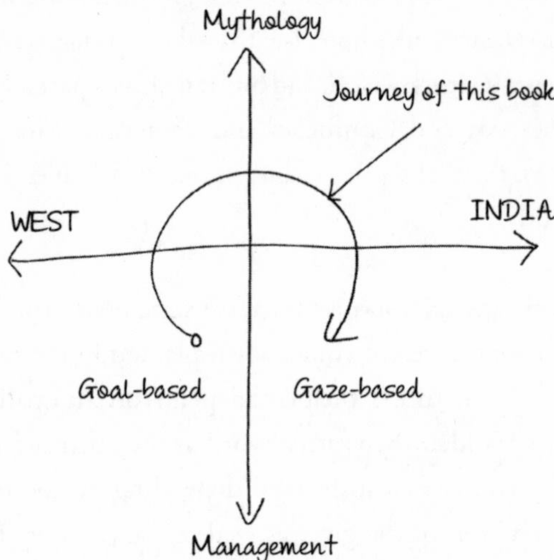

Not all will agree with the decoding of some of the popular mythological characters in this book. It may even be contrary to religious and scholarly views. This is not simply because of differences in perspective; it is also because of differences in methodology. More often than not each character in mythology is seen in isolation. But a mythologist has to look at each one relative to the rest, which helps us create the entire mythic ecosystem, where every element is unique and there are few overlaps, just like a jigsaw puzzle. The point is not so much to explain mythology as it is to derive frameworks from it.

Business is ultimately about decisions. When we take decisions, we use frameworks, either consciously or unconsciously. This book is full of frameworks, woven into each other. While frameworks of management science seek to be objective, the frameworks of Business Sutra are primarily subjective.

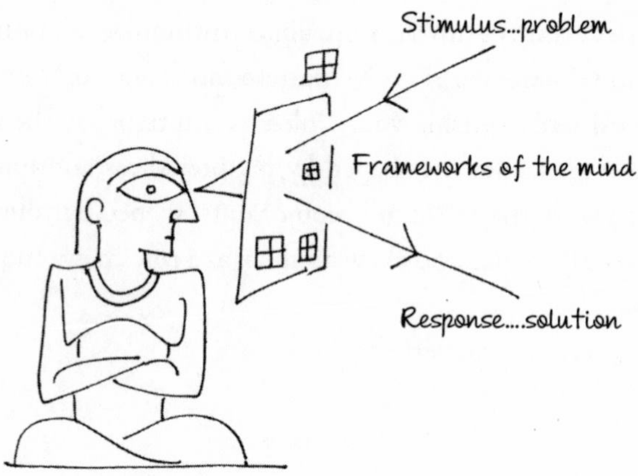

The book does not seek to sell these frameworks, or justify them as the truth. They are meant to be reflective, not prescriptive. They are not substitutes; they are supplements, ghee to help digest a savoury meal. The aim is to expose the reader to more frameworks to facilitate better decision-making. Apply it only if it makes sense to your logic, not because someone else 'won' when he applied it.

You will find no references, no testimonies or evidence, not even a bibliography. Even the 'case studies' are imagined tales. The aim is not to derive knowledge from the past, or to seek the consensus of other thinkers, but discover invisible levers that play a key role in business success or failure.

The number of non-English words may be mind-boggling but English words are insufficient to convey all Indian ideas. New ideas need new vehicles, hence new words. There are layers of meanings in each word, crisscrossing between sections and chapters.

A book by its very nature creates the delusion of linearity, but the subject being presented is itself not linear. Think of Business Sutra as a rangoli or kolam, patterns created by joining a grid of dots, drawn for centuries every morning by Hindu women using rice flour outside the threshold of their house. The practice is now more prevalent in the south than the north of the

country. Every idea in this book is a dot that the reader can join to create a pattern. Every pattern is beautiful so long as it includes all the dots. And no pattern is perfect. Every pattern is usually an incomplete section of a larger pattern known to someone else. No pattern, no framework, no dot has an independent existence outside you. Unless you internalize them, they will not work. Currently, they are shaped by my prejudices and limited by my experiences; to work they have to become yours, shaped by your prejudices, limited by your experiences. So chew on them as a cow chews cud; eventually milk will flow.

If it does not, it is still perfectly fine.

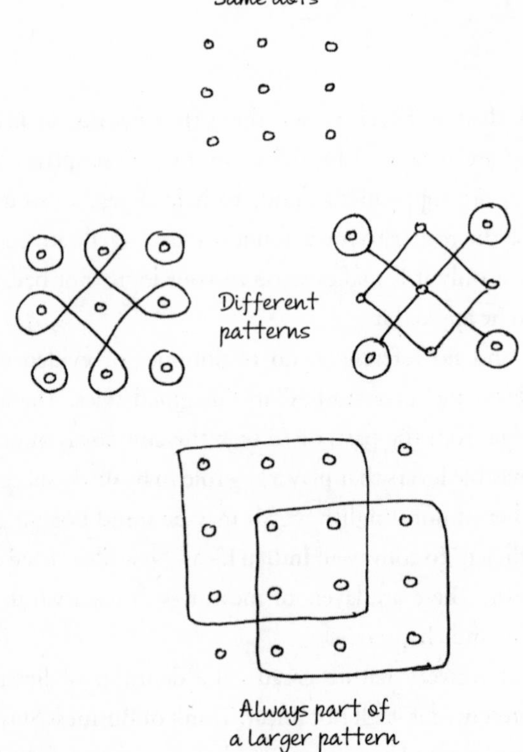

As the sages remind us: thoughts exist on shifting sands and flowing waters. Ideas presented can always change, or be further elaborated, or explained differently, by different people in different times and different places faced with different challenges. For now, every time you disagree, and wish to argue, and are driven by the belief that there must be one truth and only one truth, find peace by reminding yourself:

Within infinite myths lies an eternal truth
Who sees it all?
Varuna has but a thousand eyes
Indra, a hundred
You and I, only two.

Peace
Why?
They are obsessed with things
I am focussed on thoughts

Order
How?
They are speculative
I am pragmatic

Truth
What?
They are exotic
I am objective

II

From Goal to Gaze

Decoding Western, Chinese and Indian Beliefs

Elephant-headed Ganesha and his brother, the six-headed Kartikeya, decide to race three times around the world. Kartikeya being athletic jumps on his peacock and flies around the mountains, oceans and continents. Ganesha simply goes around his parents. In some versions, Ganesha simply twirls around and declares himself winner. When asked for an explanation for this audacious declaration, Ganesha tells Kartikeya, "You went around your world: the objective world of things. I went around my world: a subjective world of thoughts. What matters more?" With a typical Indian headshake, head bobbing from side to side, Kartikeya smiles and replies, "Depends!"

Everything depends on our beliefs: the lens of subjective truth that helps us make sense of the world.

- The Western lens clubs India and China as the exotic, where the symbolic is preferred over the literal. It seeks the truth and believes there is only one life with one goal. It is most concerned with the what of business.

- The Chinese lens clubs India and the West as Indo-European, for being overly speculative rather than pragmatic. It seeks order and believes in keeping out chaos. It is most concerned with the how of business.

- The Indian lens clubs China and the West as materialistic for valuing things rather than thoughts. It seeks peace as the mind is very aware of different goals of different people in different contexts or different lifetimes. It is most concerned with the why of business.

In this chapter, we shall gaze upon these beliefs and learn to appreciate the diversity of human thought. Only when the horizon is broadened can we begin our journey into the gaze-based approach to management.

The ideas presented here are neither politically correct nor academically certified, as sweeping generalizations need to be made to ascertain a pattern, which is buried under layers of forms. This book will also not answer questions as to what actually defines the 'West', 'India' and 'China': are these historical, geographical, political, religious or cultural terms? Any attempt to answer these questions will burn the ship at the port before any exploration can begin.

The approach may not please those who seek validation of their religious, scientific or secular beliefs. For the rest, this book will open a new world of seeing. It will reveal that people today, stripped of modern technology and language, continue to see the world exactly as their ancestors did a thousand years ago. We are still seeking the heaven of heroes, the paradise of the faithful, the nectar of immortality and the order of celestials.

You see the world with six pairs of human eyes. I see the world with two elephant eyes. We see the same thing differently.

Western Beliefs

Two mythic streams feed the river of what we call Western thought today: the Greek and the biblical. The latter is also sometimes referred to as Abrahamic or Semitic. Greek beliefs thrived in the Greek city-states and the Roman Empire. Abrahamic belief, expressed formally in Judaism, Christianity and Islam, has many tributaries from across many ancient civilizations of the Levant (the Near East), Mesopotamia, Persia, Arabia and even Egypt.

What separates the two belief systems is the value they place on the individual over the collective, on defiance over compliance. What unites these two belief systems is belief in one life, and hence the sense of urgency to do the great thing, or the right thing, in this—our one and only—life. Hence, the goal!

The goal for the Greeks was Elysium, meant for individuals who lived extraordinary lives. It was the final destination of mythic heroes such as Achilles, Odysseus, Theseus, Jason and Perseus. Those who lived ordinary unremarkable lives were sent to the Asphodel Fields after death. Those who angered the gods were thrown into Tartarus, condemned to do monotonous tasks, like Sisyphus who was condemned to roll a rock up a mountain all day, only to find it rolling back down at night. This was hell: doing monotonous mundane chores endlessly. The gods lived on Mount Olympus,

controlling everything. These Olympians achieved their exalted position after overthrowing older gods, the Titans, and so constantly feared overthrow at the hands of humans, who they kept in check through the Fates. To be extraordinary, and win a place in Elysium, humans had to defy the gods.

Greek beliefs inspired Alexander of Macedonia in the fourth century BCE to conquer the world. They also inspired the very efficient and rather ruthless Roman Empire that saw itself as the harbinger of civilization and held sway over much of the Mediterranean for centuries. Both the Greeks and Romans were wary of all authority, be it at home (dictators) or outside (the Persian Emperor and the Egyptian Pharaoh). Authority was equated with the capricious Olympian gods, who had to be resisted.

When the Roman Empire collapsed around the fifth century, Christianity became the dominant force across Europe. Christians believed in one all-powerful God, who created humanity, and rules, for the betterment of humanity. The goal now was compliance, not defiance, which led to a place in the Promised Land on earth and Heaven in the afterlife. Unfortunately, humans kept breaking these rules. The Bible is full of stories of prophets and kings struggling to follow the Commandments laid down by God. There is constant reference to the martyrdom of the faithful who stand up for the faith.

- This was the belief of Jewish tribes who roamed the deserts around the Levant and Mesopotamia since 2000 BCE. Their holy books, the Tanakh, are full of laws and negotiations of the prophets with God seeking to ensure humans lived the right way. This came to be known as Judaism.

- This became the belief of Roman slaves, later Roman nobility, and finally the Roman royalty, but with one crucial difference: they believed Jesus to be Christ, the anointed one, the Son of God, who sacrificed himself out of love to save prodigal humanity. This was Christianity.

- This belief also rose in Arabia in the seventh century where Jesus came to be seen as just one of many prophets, the last being Muhammad who

transmitted the word of God through the book known as the Koran. This was Islam.

It is important at this juncture to clarify that from the Indian point of view Western thought stretches beyond Europe and America to include the Islamic world, for the quest for objectivity shapes Islam too. Just as Europe was torn between the Greek way and the biblical way and later the Protestant way and the Catholic way, the Islamic world was torn between the Sunni way, with its roots in Arabic tribal egalitarianism and the Shia way, with its roots in Persian dynastic culture. Every denomination is convinced the other is wrong and that they are right. Everyone harbours a worldview that accommodates only one truth.

Divinity in the Abrahamic faiths is always articulated as the Word of God and divine laws are always presented in written form (such as the Ten Commandments) that need to be read, indicating the objectivity of these laws.

The covenant is valued greatly. The bond with God is not assumed; it has to be ritually enacted through circumcision or baptism. This reveals the deep-rooted need for documentation and written memorandums of understanding.

Every time Josephine concludes a conversation with Mukul, her counterpart in India, she sends an email summarizing the contents of her call. When Mukul does not do the same, Josephine finds it annoying. She reminds him of company policy, compelling him to comply.

Despite many shared beliefs, Christians persecuted the Jewish people across Europe and fought Muslims over four centuries, from the tenth century onwards, in what came to be known as the Crusades. Within Christianity itself there were many schisms, with the Churches of Rome in the West and Byzantium in the East vying for supremacy. Every side believed in one God, one life, one way of living life, but they differed violently over who had the patent over the right way.

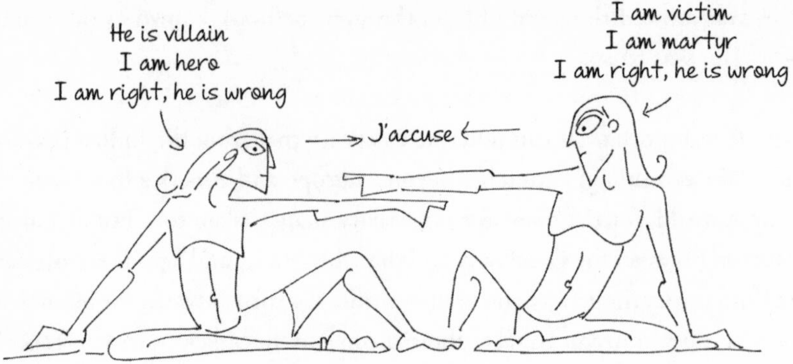

The end of the Crusades saw the start of the scientific revolution in Europe, inspired by the rediscovery of Greek beliefs. Truth imposed by authority was rejected; truth churned by reason was sought. The scientist was the Greek hero on a lone quest, those who opposed him were the Olympian gods. The scientific spirit inspired discoveries, inventions, and industrialization. It laid the foundation for colonization and imperialism.

Scientists did not find any rational explanation for the existence of inequality and social unfairness. They blamed it on irrational ideas like God whose existence could not be measured or proved. With the scientific revolution, society no longer needed anchors of faith. Knowledge mattered, not belief. Everything had to be explained in tangible material terms. The goal had to be here and now, not in the hereafter. The goal had to be measurable, even in matters related to society. Thus rose economic theories that saw all the problems of society as a consequence of faulty wealth generation (Capitalism) and faulty wealth distribution (Communism). Both promised a heaven, one through development and the other through revolution.

But not everyone was willing to give up religion altogether. Those who were firm in their belief in God attributed social wrongs to temporal religious authority, clergymen in particular, for legitimizing the feudal order of kings. The Church became the new Olympus to be defied. Scientific evidence was demanded for their dogmas and their claim of divine rights. Failure to present it led to the Protestant Revolution, spearheaded by the newly emerging class

of merchants, industrialists, and bankers. They valued autonomy over all else, and sought equal if not higher status than landed gentry, who for centuries had been inheriting both fortune and status, without any personal effort.

The Protestant Revolution was marked by great violence, especially the Thirty Years' War that devastated Europe in the seventeenth century. It marked the end of feudal orders and the rise of nation states. Many Protestants made the newly discovered continent of America their home: this was the New World, the Promised Land. Here there were no kings, no clergy. Everyone was equal; everyone had a right to personal faith in the privacy of their homes; work was worship, and wealth born of effort was seen as God's reward for the righteous. This was the Protestant work ethic, a unique combination of biblical value for compliance and Greek disdain for authority.

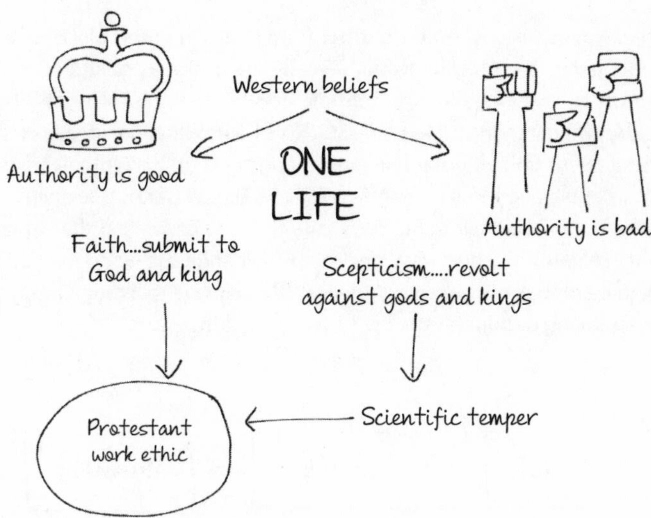

Much of the political system of the United States came to be modelled along the lines of the pre-Christian Roman republic, complete with a senate in times of peace and a dictator in times of war. The American system ensured the victory of democracy, secularism, and most importantly Capitalism. It is from this context that management science arose.

Not surprisingly, the recommendations of management science resonate with not just a scientific obsession with evidence and quantification but also biblical and Greek beliefs. The vision statement is the Promised Land; the contract is the Covenant; systems and processes are the Commandments; the 'fifth' level leader who is professionally ambitious and personally humble is the prophet; the invisible shareholder is the de-facto God. The innovator is the Greek hero, standing proud atop Maslow's hierarchy of needs, self-actualized, and secure in Elysium. Every advocate of any idea from greed to good governance is convinced they know the truth, hence the moral burden to evangelize and sell.

All this makes management science a secular expression of beliefs that have always existed in the West.

Kshitij always smiles when his partner from a very reputed global strategic firm meets him in the club. Kshitij reveals, "He is always selling something or the other. Two years ago he told me about the importance of a matrix structure where no one is too powerful. Now he is selling the idea of creating a special talent pool of potential gamechangers. Then he kept talking about getting people aligned to a single goal. Now he talks about flexibility. They can never make up their mind. Each time they are convinced that whatever they are selling is the best idea, one that will change the world forever. They claim to be global, but are so evangelical. But we have to indulge them; their way of thinking dominates the world. It comforts investors."

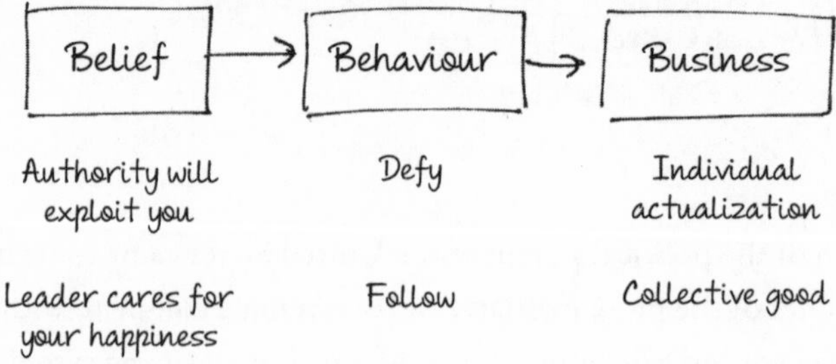

Chinese Beliefs

The West, with its preference for the historical, would like to view current-day China as an outcome of its recent Communist past. But the mythological lens reveals that China functions today just as it did in the times of the Xia and Shang dynasties, over five thousand years ago, with great faith in central authority to take away disorder and bring in order.

A pragmatic culture, the Chinese have never invested too much energy in the religious or the mythic. What distinguishes Chinese thought from Western thought is the value placed on nature. In the West, nature is chaos that needs to be controlled. In China, nature is always in harmony; chaos is social disorganization where barbarians thrive.

The mythologies of China are highly functional and often take the form of parables, travelogues, war stories and ballads. The word commonly used for God is Shangdi, meaning one who is above the ruler of earth. The word for heaven is Tian. But God in Chinese thought is not the God of biblical thought. Rather than being theistic (faith in a divine being who intervenes in the affairs of men in moral and ethical matters), the Chinese school of thought is deistic (faith in an impersonal greater force within whose framework humanity has to function). The words Shangdi and Tian are often used synonymously, representing morality, virtue, order and harmony. There are gods in heaven and earth, overseen by the Jade Emperor, who has his own celestial bureaucracy. They are invoked during divination and during fortune telling to improve life on earth. More importantly, they represent perfection. So, perfection does not need to be discovered; it simply needs to be emulated on earth. The responsibility to make this happen rests with the Emperor of the Middle Kingdom. This is called the Mandate of Heaven. It explains the preference for a top-down authoritarian approach to order that has always shaped Chinese civilization. The Chinese respect ancestors greatly. They are believed to be watching over the living; the least they expect is not to be shamed.

In the Axis Age (roughly 500 BCE) when classical Greek philosophers were drawing attention to the rational way in the West, and the way of the Buddha was challenging ritualism in Vedic India, China saw the consolidation

of two mythic roots: the more sensory, individualistic, natural way of Tao proposed by Laozi and the more sensible social way proposed by Confucius. Taoism became more popular in rural areas amongst peasants while Confucianism appealed more to the elite in urban centres. These two schools shaped China for over a thousand years, before a third school of thought emerged. This was Buddhism, which came from India via the trade routes of Central Asia in the early centuries of the Common Era.

- Taoism is about harmonizing the body and mind by balancing nature's two forces, the phoenix and the dragon, the feminine Yin and the masculine Yang. It speaks of diet, exercise, invocations and chants, which bring about longevity, health and harmony. It is highly personal and speaks of the way (Tao) through riddles and verses, valuing experience over instruction, flow of energy over rigid structure, and control without domination. It speaks of various gods who wander between heaven and earth, who can be appeased to attract health and fortune. The division of the pure soul and impure flesh seen in Western traditions does not exist. There is talk of immortality, but not rebirth as in Indian traditions.

- Confucianism values relationships over all else: especially between parent and child, man and woman, senior and junior, and finally the ruler and the subjects. Great value is placed on virtue, ethics, benevolence and nobility. This is established more by ritual and protocol, rather than by rules, as in the West, or by emotions, as in India. Thus, the Chinese (and Japanese) obsession with hierarchy, how the visiting card should be given and where it should be placed, and what colours should be worn at office, and what items can or cannot be given as gifts. The gwanji system of business relationships that this gives rise to is very unlike the caste system, as it is not based on birth, or bloodline, or even geography, but can be cultivated over time based on capability and connections.

- Buddhism met fierce resistance as it is highly speculative and monastic. It denied society, which followers of Confucianism celebrated. It denied

the body, which followers of Taoism valued. It spoke of rebirth, which made no pragmatic sense. It was seen as foreign until it adapted to the Chinese context. The Buddhism that thrived in China leaned more towards the altruistic Mahayana school than the older, more introspective Theravada line that spread to Myanmar and Sri Lanka. In keeping with Confucian ideals, greater value was given to petitioning the compassionate Bodhisattva, visualized as the gentle and gracious lady Kwan-yin, who is more interested in alleviating rather than understanding human suffering. In line with the Taoist way, the minimalist Zen Buddhism also emerged, but it was less about health and longevity and more about outgrowing self-centredness to genuinely help others.

The famous Chinese novel, *Journey to the West,* describes the tale of a Chinese monk travelling to India assisted by a pig (the Chinese symbol of fertility) and a monkey (inspired by Hanuman?) and indicates the gradual assimilation of Buddhism into the Chinese way of life.

Tangibility plays a key role in Chinese thought. Central to it is the idea of China, the geographical entity. It is the Middle Kingdom, the navel of civilization, connecting heaven and earth, bringing the order of the celestials to humanity. "The general trend under the celestial sphere," the Chinese say, "is that there is bound to be unification after prolonged division and division after prolonged unification." Tales about the struggle of kings and warlords to

unify China form the main theme of epics and ballads. Over two thousand years ago, the first emperor to unite the land burned books and killed scholars for the sake of stability; this has happened repeatedly in history ever since.

Nothing discomforts the Chinese more than chaos, confusion, and disorderliness, what is generally termed 'luan'. To maintain a calm exterior even in the face of the most severe crisis is indicative of moral courage and inner strength. Any breakdown, social or emotional, is indicative of luan; to break down is to lose face. To lose face is to dishonour the ancestors, most revered in a Chinese household. Disharmony is disease in the Taoist scheme of things. Even when there is health and order, Confucius advises people to think about and feel for forces that could threaten the state of comfort in the future.

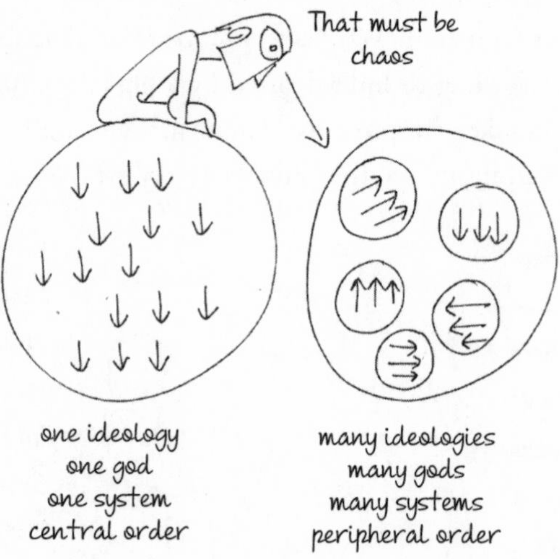

Order for the Chinese waxes towards the centre of power where the emperor resides. In the social hierarchy, the 'white' aristocrat was envied as he lived in orderly cities, closer to the king, away from the blazing sun of the countryside, which is home to the 'black' (tanned) peasant. In the periphery, there is chaos, hence the need to build the Great Wall and consolidate military forces to keep the barbarians in check by force and domination.

Order in China has always been enforced with ruthlessness, albeit with grace and subtlety, focusing on 'pressure points' for maximum result. The

following tale from Sun Tzu's seminal military treatise *The Art of War,* popular in management circles today, reveals this. Sun Tzu believed in winning wars without fighting, and this demanded not overt acts of heroism but outwitting the opponent with patience, sensitivity and discipline. He claimed he could turn anyone into a soldier. To humour him, the king took him to his harem and asked him to make soldiers of his concubines. Sun Tzu took up the challenge and asked the women to stand in a straight line. The concubines giggled in response and did nothing. Sun Tzu repeated his order, this time with a warning that those who failed to do so would be executed. The women giggled again. The third time, he made the command and the women giggled, Sun Tzu ordered the execution of the king's favourite concubine. Everyone was horrified by this. But what followed was far more remarkable: when the order was repeated again, the women did as told. The king was grudgingly impressed and he appointed Sun Tzu as his general.

When asked his views about the world, Saud who had worked in various branches of a multinational company made the following comment, "In China, roads are built before cities. In India, cities are built before roads. In China, people submit to the wisdom of the state. In India, people do not believe the state has their interests at heart. I find China more organized but am unnerved by its ambitions and lack of transparency. I find Indians exasperating as they have an opinion for everything but decide on nothing. In China, the state controls everything, while in India there is much more freedom of expression."

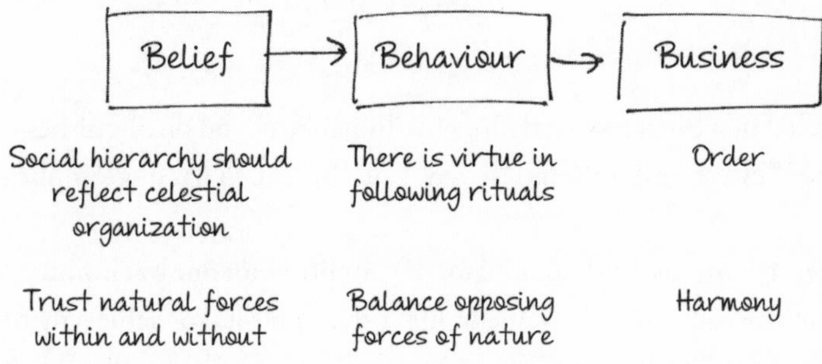

Indian Beliefs

Over two thousand years ago, Alexander, the young Macedonian, after having conquered the Persian Empire, reached the banks of the river Indus. There he found a person whom he later identified as a gymnosophist: a naked thinker, sitting on a rock staring into space. Alexander asked him what he was doing. The gymnosophist replied, "Experiencing nothingness. What about you?" Alexander said he was conquering the world. Both laughed. Each one thought the other was a fool.

But while the gymnosophist would have allowed Alexander to stay the fool and discover wisdom eventually, at his own pace, on his own terms, Alexander would have wanted the gymnosophist to change, not waste his life without a goal, for the gymnosophist believed that we live infinite lives while Alexander believed we live only one.

Belief in rebirth is what defines the Indian way, and distinguishes it from both the Western and the Chinese way. Faith in rebirth has huge implications.

- Rebirth means the denominator of your life is not one but infinity. When you live only once the value of life is the sum total of achievements, but when you live infinite lives, no matter what we achieve, its value is zero.

The point then is not to control life but to understand it, not achieve but introspect.

- Rebirth means that birth is not the beginning and death is not the end. The events of past lives impact the present while the events of the present life will impact the future. A child is born with karmic baggage, and not in innocence with a clean slate. Every experience, good or bad, is a reaction to past conduct either of this or a previous life. It means we alone are responsible for all that has happened to us, is happening to us and will happen to us; blaming others is not an option, nor is complacency.

- Rebirth demands we accept the existence of infinitely diverse, even paradoxical, contexts existing simultaneously as well as sequentially. Everyone sees the world differently. Everyone's perspectives are bound to change over time. It means allowing for intellectual, emotional and material variety, for depending on karmic baggage, different people will have different fortunes, opportunities, capacities and capabilities.

Belief in multiple lives establishes a worldview that is comfortable with the absence of binary logic, where there are no fixed goals, continuously changing plans, dependence on relationships, celebration of trust and loyalty, uneasiness with rules, actions dependent on crisis, preference for short-term results over long-term vision, and a reliance on resourcefulness that gives rise to contextual, non-replicable improvizations: the jugaad. This is the Indian way.

A European food company that had made high-end cuisine accessible to the common man entered India, determined to provide the same service and product to customers in a new market. But then they realized most Indians do not eat beef and pork. And what was a common man's budget in Europe was a rich man's budget in India, especially since the restaurants could be housed only in the more affluent quarters of major Indian cities. What was food for the commoner in Europe became food for the elite in India.

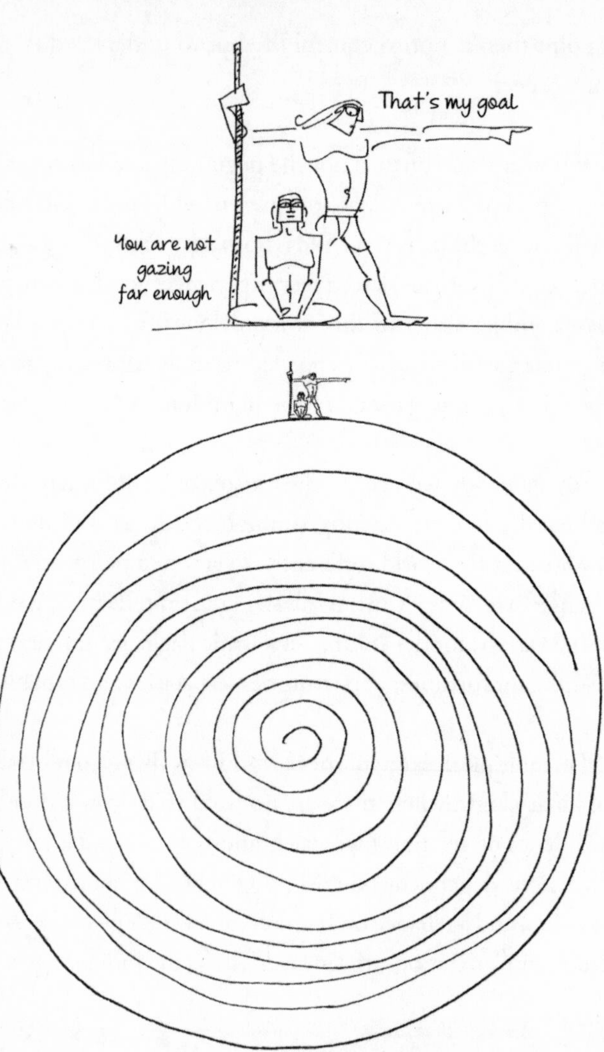

Western ideas, be they Greek or biblical, had their origin in cities such as Athens, Babylon, Jerusalem and later, Paris, Berlin and London. Chinese ideas reveal a preference for cities such as the Forbidden City of the Dragon Emperor that offers the promise of greater order. Indian thought springs from villages on the fertile riverbanks of the Indian subcontinent where change takes time, like lentils boiling over a slow fire fuelled by cowdung cakes.

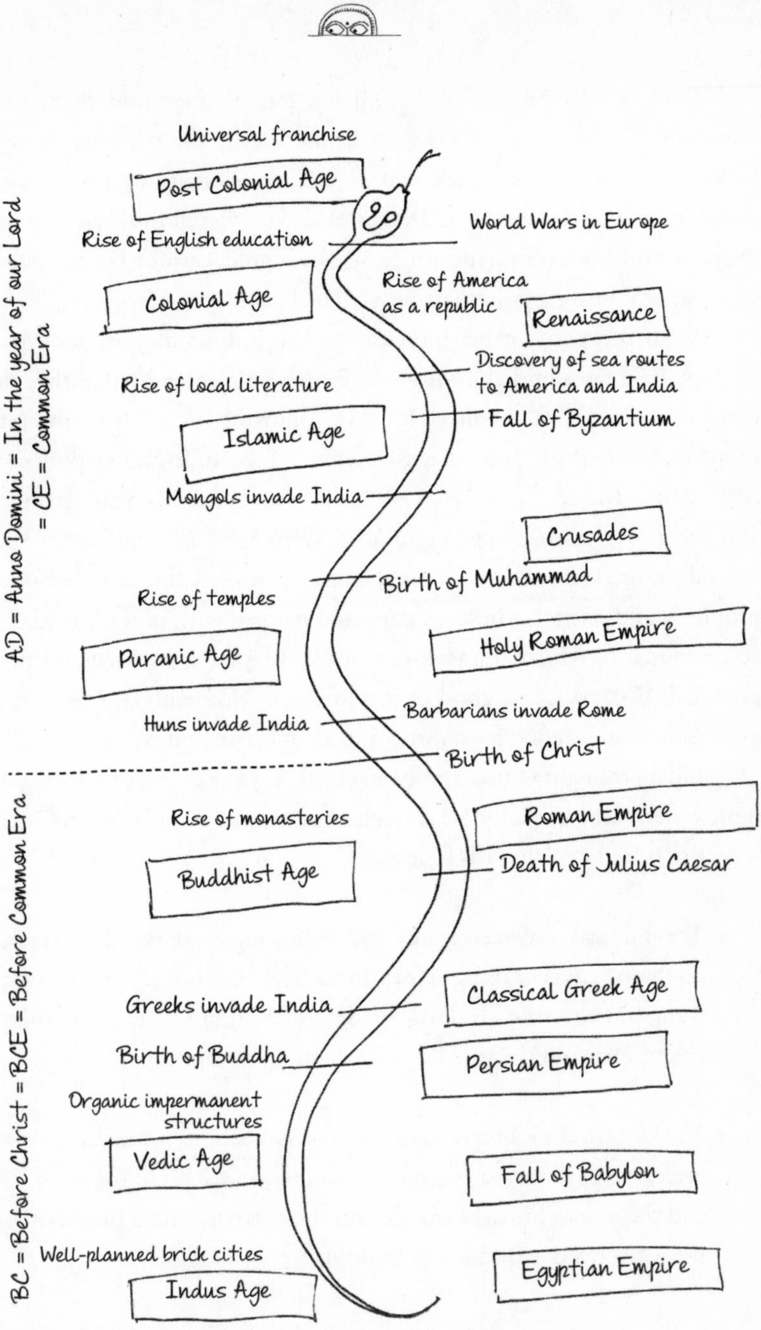

AD = Anno Domini = In the year of our Lord = CE = Common Era

Universal franchise

Post Colonial Age

World Wars in Europe

Rise of English education

Rise of America as a republic

Colonial Age

Renaissance

Discovery of sea routes to America and India

Rise of local literature

Fall of Byzantium

Islamic Age

Mongols invade India

Crusades

Birth of Muhammad

Rise of temples

Holy Roman Empire

Puranic Age

Barbarians invade Rome

Huns invade India

Birth of Christ

BC = Before Christ = BCE = Before Common Era

Roman Empire

Rise of monasteries

Death of Julius Caesar

Buddhist Age

Classical Greek Age

Greeks invade India

Birth of Buddha

Persian Empire

Organic impermanent structures

Vedic Age

Fall of Babylon

Well-planned brick cities

Egyptian Empire

Indus Age

Indicative history (not drawn to scale)

India is relatively isolated from the rest of the world thanks to the mountains in the north and the sea in the south. These barriers have been penetrated primarily by trade routes and occasionally by invaders. More people came in than went out. The spices and textiles of India were sought all over the world; what Indians sought was only gold, earning the reputation of being the gold-eating gold sparrow, or sone ki chidiya.

With prosperity came the cities of the Indus valley, of the Mauryas, Guptas, Bahmanis and the Mughals. But these rose and fell, either due to climatic changes (Indus valley cities) or following invasions by the Greeks, Huns and Mongols. The villages offered refuge to escaping philosophers and artists. There, the wisdom of India was nurtured, assimilating ideas and technologies that kept coming in from time to time, ideas such as centralization, imperialism, writing, coinage, stone sculptures, monotheism, prophecy and science. These mingled and merged with prevailing ideas. The accommodating rebirth framework ensured everything was included, nothing excluded. What was not good in this life, or in this context, was allowed to exist as it could be good for another life, or another context.

Indian thought yearns not for an efficient way like Western thought, or a more orderly way like Chinese thought, but an accommodative and inclusive way. This is best explained as follows:

- The biblical way celebrates rule-following leaders. The Greek way celebrates rule-breaking heroes. India celebrates both: the rule-following Ram and the rule-breaking Krishna of Hinduism; the rule-following chakravarti and the rule-breaking Vasudev of Jainism.

- The Confucian way celebrates social responsibility while the Taoist way prefers individualistic harmony. India celebrates both: the royal Vishnu and the ascetic Shiva of Hinduism; the compassionate Bodhisattva and the introspective Buddha of Buddhism.

- In Western thought, nature is danger: Greek tales speak of wild nymphs and satyrs who create pandemonium and need to be tamed, while biblical

tales repeatedly refer to women and serpents who embody sexuality and temptation and need to be overpowered. In Chinese thought, nature is power, the regenerating phoenix or yin that needs to be channelized by, or harmonized with, the Emperor, who is the dragon or yang. In India, nature is both: danger and power. Embodied as the Goddess, she is wild as Kali and demure as Gauri. For Ram, she is Sita. For Krishna, she is Radha. For Vishnu she is Lakshmi, for Shiva she is Shakti. This idea of the Goddess in Hinduism is very different from the Goddess of modern Western literature that reimagines divinity along feminist lines.

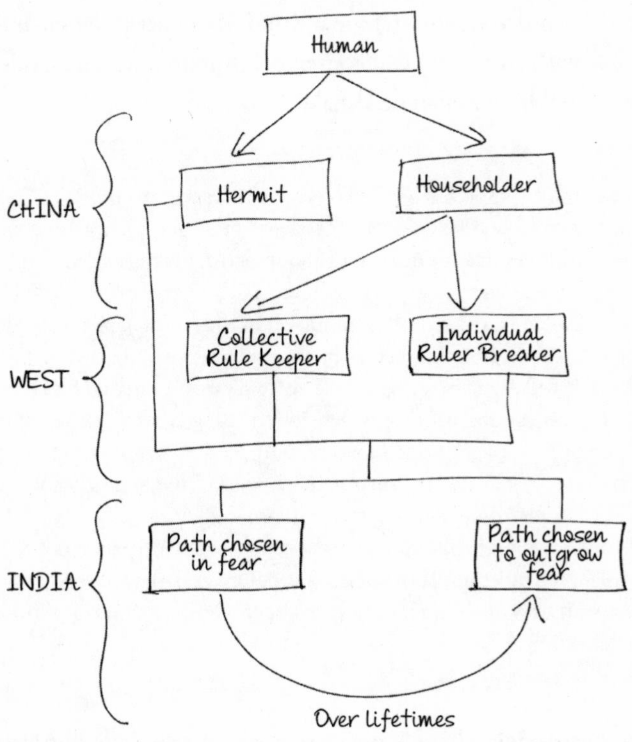

"Who is better," the West will ask, "the rule-following Ram or the rule-breaking Krishna?"

The Indian will answer, "Both are Vishnu."

"Who is better, the hermit Shiva, or the householder Vishnu?" the Chinese will ask.

The Indian will answer, "Both are God."

"So you don't have one God?"

To this the Indian will respond, "We have one God. We also have many gods, who are manifestations of that same one God. But our God is distinct from Goddess. Depending on the context, God can be an external agency, a historical figure, or even inner human potential awaiting realization. What God do you refer to?"

Such answers will naturally exasperate the goal-focused Western mind and the order-seeking Chinese mind. They seek clarity. Indians are comfortable with ambiguity and contextual thinking, which manifests most visibly in the bobbing Indian headshake.

Steve wanted to enter into a joint venture with an Indian company. So Rahul decided to take him out to lunch. They went to a very famous hotel in New York, which served a four-course meal: soup, salad, the main course, followed by dessert. There was cutlery on the table, such as spoons, forks, knives, to eat each dish. In the evening, Rahul took him to an Indian restaurant where a thali was served. All items were served simultaneously, the sweet, the sour, the rice, the roti, the crispy papad, the spicy pickles. Everyone had to eat by hand, though spoons were provided for those who were embarrassed to do so or not too adventurous. Rahul then told Steve, "Lunch is like the West, organized and controlled by the chef. Dinner is like India, totally customized by the customer. You can mix and match and eat whatever you wish in any order you like. The joint venture will be a union of two very different cultures. They will never be equal. They will always be unique. Are you ready for it? Or do you want to wait till one changes his beliefs and customs for the benefit of the other?"

Not surprisingly, there is not one single clearly defined holy book in India. The Ramayan of the rule-following Ram complements the Mahabharat of the rule-breaking Krishna, both of which are subsets of the Vishnu Puran that tells the story of Vishnu. The Vishnu Puran speaks of the householder's way of life, and complements the Shiva Puran, which speaks of the hermit's

way of life. Both make sense under the larger umbrella of the Brahma Puran, which speaks of human desire and dissatisfaction with nature that is described as the Goddess in the complementary text, the Devi Puran. All these fall in the category of Agama or Tantra where thoughts are personified as characters and made 'saguna'. These complement Nigama or Veda where thoughts remain abstract, hence stay 'nirguna'.

Vedic texts came to be known as astika because they expressed themselves using theistic vocabulary. But many chose to explain similar ideas without using theistic vocabulary. These were the nastikas, also known as shramanas, or the strivers, who believed more in austerity, meditation, contemplation and experience rather than transmitted rituals and prayers favoured by priests known as brahmins. The astikas and nastikas differed on the idea of God, but agreed on the idea of rebirth and karma, which forms the cornerstone of mythologies of Indian origin.

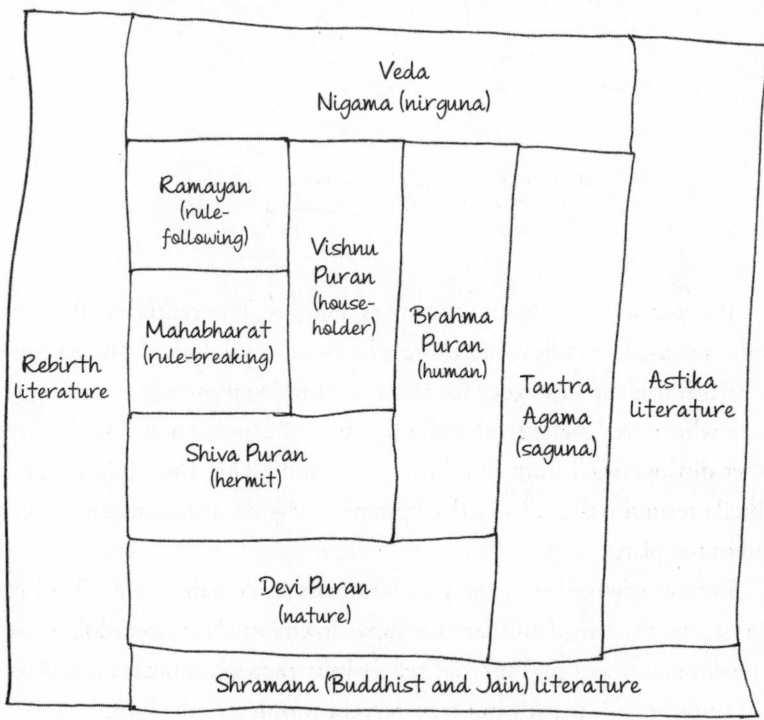

Over two thousand years ago, the nastikas distanced themselves from the ritualistic brahmins as well as their language, Sanskrit, and chose the language of the masses, Prakrit. They did not speak so much about God as they did about a state of mind: kaivalya, when all thoughts are realized, or nirvana when all forms dissolve. The one to achieve this state was Jina or tirthankar according to the Jains, and Buddha according to the Buddhists. The shramanas also believed that there have always existed Jinas and Buddhas in the cosmos.

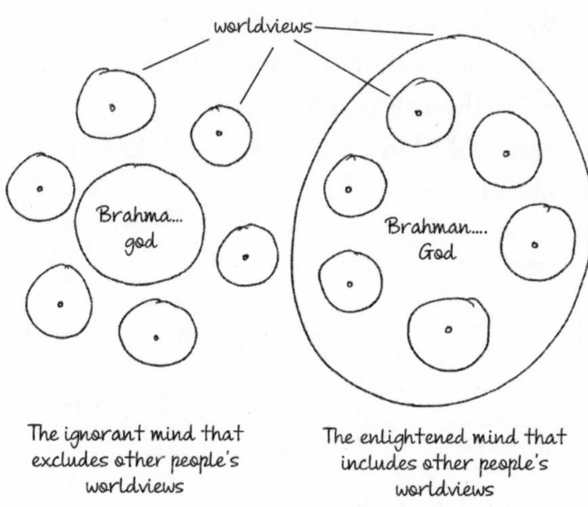

The astikas came to be known as Hindus. For centuries, the word Hindu was used to indicate all those who lived in the Indian subcontinent. The British made it a category for administrative convenience to distinguish people who were residents of India but not Muslims. Later, Hindus were further distinguished from Buddhists, Jains and Sikhs. Thus, Hinduism, an umbrella term for all astika faiths, became a religion, fitting neatly into the Western template.

Sikhism emerged over the past 500 years in Punjab, as a result of two major forces: the arrival of Islam that came down heavily against idolatry, and the bhakti movement that approached divinity through emotion, not rituals. Like Hinduism it is theistic but it prefers the formless to the form.

	God as external agency	God as internal potential	Goddess as external resources	Pantheon of gods and goddesses embodying natural and cultural forces
Greek	✗	✗	✗	✓
Abrahamic	✓	✗	✗	✗
Science	✗	✗	✗	✗
Hindu	✓	✓	✓	✓
Jain / Buddhist	✗	✗	✗	✓
Sikh	✓	✓	✗	✗

These religions that value rebirth can be seen as fruits of the same tree or different trees in the same forest. All of them value thought over things, the timeless over the time-bound, the infinite over the finite, the limitless over the limited. They differentiate between truth that is bound by space, time and imagination (maya) from truth that has no such fetters (satya). They can be grouped under a single umbrella called 'sanatan'. Right-wing fundamentalists tend to appropriate this word more out of chauvinism than curiosity.

Sanatan means timeless. It refers to wisdom that has no founder and is best described as open-source freeware. Every idea is accepted but only that which survives the test of time, space and situation eventually matters. Unfettered by history and geography, sanatan is like a flowing river with many tributaries. At different times, at different places, different teachers have presented different aspects of sanatan in different ways, using different words, resulting in many overlaps yet many distinguishing features.

- Sanatan is rooted in the belief that nothing is permanent, not even death. What exists will wither away and what has withered away will always come back. This is the nature of nature. This is prakriti, which is visualized as the Goddess (feminine gender). The law of karma, according to which every event has a cause and consequence, governs prakriti.

- The human mind observes nature, yearns for permanence, and seeks to appreciate its own position in the grand scheme of things. The human mind can do this because it can imagine and separate itself from the rest of nature, as a purush. As man realizes the potential of a purush, he walks on the path of his dharma.

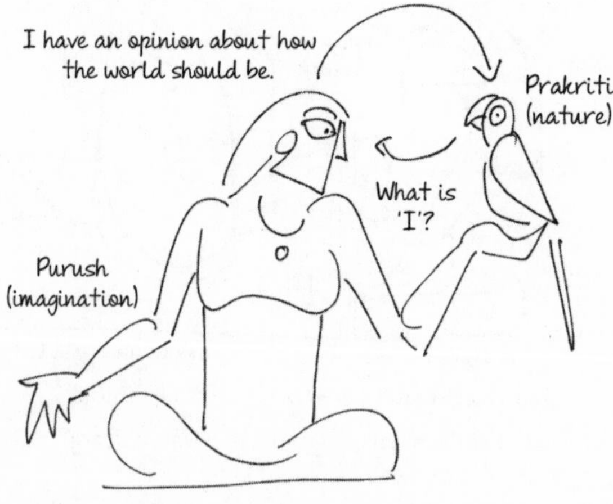

This is the Indian differentiator: the value given to imagination, to the human mind, to subjectivity. While truth in the West exists outside human imagination, in India, it exists within the imagination. In the West, imagination makes us irrational. In India, imagination reveals our potential, makes us both kind and cruel.

In sanatan, fear of death separates the animate (sajiva) from the inanimate (nirjiva). The animate respond to death in different ways: plants grow, animals run, while humans imagine and create subjective realities.

Of all living creatures, humans are special as they alone have the ability to outgrow the fear of death and change, and thus experience immortality. He who does so is God or bhagavan, worthy of worship. Those who have yet to achieve this state are gods or devatas.

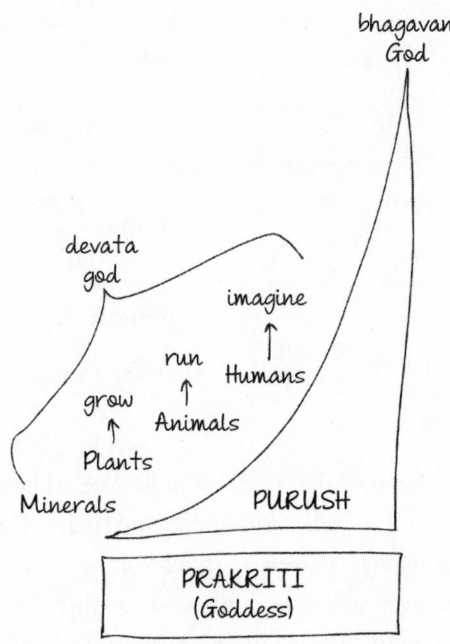

Since every human is potentially God—hence god—every subjective truth is valid. Respect for all subjective realities gave rise to the doctrine of doubt (syad-vada) and pluralism (anekanta-vada) in Jainism, the doctrine of nothingness (shunya-vaad) in Buddhism and the doctrines of monism (advaita-vaad) as well as dualism (dvaita-vaad) in Hinduism.

With diversity came arguments, but these were not born out of scepticism but out of faith. The argumentative Indian did not want to win an argument, or reach a consensus; he kept seeing alternatives and possibilities. The wise amongst them sought to clarify thoughts, understand why other gods, who also contained the spark of divinity, did not see the world the same way. The root of the difference was always traced to a different belief that shaped a different view of the world in the mind.

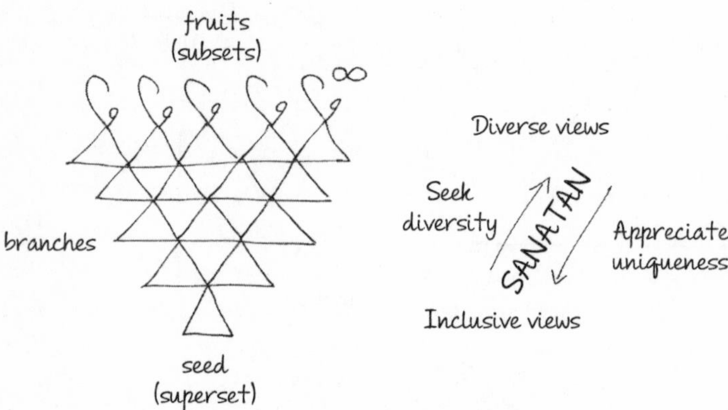

As one goes through the epics of India one notices there are rule-following heroes (Ram) as well as rule-following villains (Duryodhan), rule-breaking heroes (Krishna) as well as rule-breaking villains (Ravan). Thus, goodness or righteousness has nothing to do with rules; they are at best functional, depending on the context they can be upheld or broken. What matters is the reason why rules are being followed or broken. This explains why Indians do not value rules and systems in their own country as much as their counterparts in Singapore or Switzerland, but they do adhere to rules and systems when they go abroad.

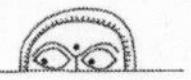

Between 2002 and 2012, international observers noticed that when cases of fraud and corruption were raised in the UK and US, they were dealt with severely and a decision was arrived at in a short span of time. During the same period, the Indian legal system pulled up many Indian politicians, bureaucrats and industrialists for similar charges. Their cases are still pending, moving from one court to another. The Indian legal system is primarily equipped only to catch rule-breaking Ravans, not rule-upholding Duryodhans.

That Ram and Krishna (avatars of Vishnu) are worthy of worship and Ravan and Duryodhan (sons of Brahma) are not has nothing to with behaviour. It has to do with belief. Why are they following or breaking the rule? The answer to this question is more critical than whether they are following or breaking the rule.

Belief is forged as imagination responds to the challenges of nature: death and change. Fear contracts the mind and wisdom expands it. From the roots brah, meaning growing or widening, and manas, meaning mind endowed with imagination, rise three very important concepts in India that sound very similar: the brahman (pronounced by laying stress on neither vowel), Brahma (pronounced by laying stress on the last vowel only) and brahmana (pronounced by laying stress on the first vowel and the last consonant).

- The brahman means an infinitely expanded mind that has outgrown fear. In early Nigamic scriptures, the brahman is but an idea that eventually becomes a formless being. By the time of the Agamic scriptures, the brahman is given form as Shiva or Vishnu. The brahman is swayambhu, meaning it is independent, self-reliant and self-contained, and not dependent on fear for its existence.

- Brahma is a character in the Agamic literature. He depends on fear for his existence. From fear comes his identity. Fear provokes him to create a subjective truth, and be territorial about it. The sons of Brahma represent mindsets born of fear: devas who enjoy wealth, asuras who

fight to retrieve wealth, yakshas who hoard wealth, rakshasas who grab wealth, prajapatis who seek to enforce rules and tapasvis who seek to renounce rules. Brahma and his sons are either not worshipped or rarely worshipped, but are essential constituents of the world. They may not be Gods, but they are gods. Asuras and rakshasas started being visualized as 'evil beings' by Persian painters of the Mughal kings and being referred to as 'demons' by European translators of the epics.

- Brahmana, more commonly written as brahmin, commonly refers to the brahmana 'jati', or the community of priests who traditionally transmitted Vedic rituals and stories. It also refers to brahmana 'varna', representing a mindset that is seeking the brahman.

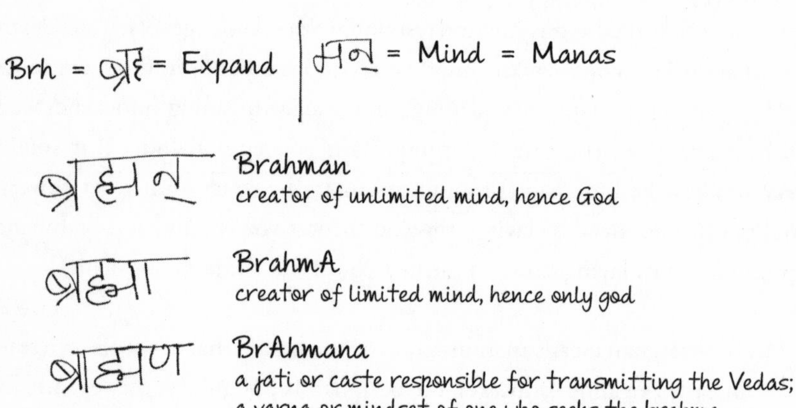

Ravan and Duryodhan descend from Brahma, unlike Ram and Krishna who are avatars of Vishnu; though born of mortal flesh, Ram and Krishna embody the brahman. Fear makes Ravan defy other people's rules. Fear makes Duryodhan pretend to follow rules. Both are always insecure, angry and bitter, always at war, and trapped in the wheel of rebirth, yearning for immortality. This is rana-bhoomi, the battleground of life, where everyone believes that grabbing Lakshmi, goddess of wealth, is the answer to all problems.

Ravan and Duryodhan are never dismissed or dehumanized. Effigies of Ravan may be burned in North India during Dassera celebrations and sand sculptures of Duryodhan may be smashed in Tamil Nadu during Therukuttu performances, but tales of the nobility of these villains, their charity, their past deeds that may account for their villainy still persist. The Ramayan repeatedly reminds us of how intelligent and talented Ravan is. At the end of the Mahabharat, Duryodhan is given a place in swarga or paradise. The point is not to punish the villains, or exclude them, but first to understand them and then to uplift them. They may be killed, but they will eventually be reborn, hopefully with less fear, less rage and less bitterness.

Vishnu descends (avatarana, in Sanskrit) as Ram and Krishna to do uddhar (thought upliftment), to turn god into God, to nudge the sons of Brahma towards the brahman. At no point does he seek to defeat, dominate, or domesticate. He offers them the promise of ranga-bhoomi, the playground, where one can smile even in fortune and misfortune, in the middle of a garden or the battlefield. Liberation from the fear of death and change transforms Brahma and his sons into swayambhu, self-contained, self-reliant beings like Shiva and Vishnu, who include everyone and desire to dominate no one. The swayambhu is so dependable that he serves as a beacon, attracting the frightened. Those who come to him bring Lakshmi along with them. That is why it is said Lakshmi follows Vishnu wherever he goes.

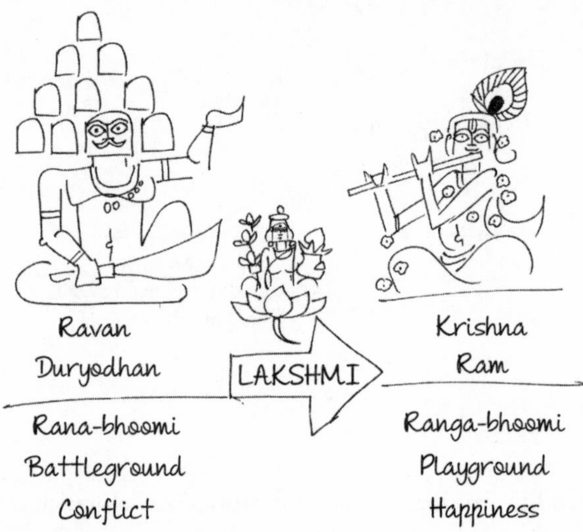

Amrit, the nectar of immortality, takes away the fear of death. The quest for amrit makes Brahma pray to Shiva and Vishnu in Hindu stories. In Buddhist stories, Brahma beseeches the Buddha to share his wisdom with the world. In Jain stories, Brahma oversees the birth of the tirthankar. Both the brahmanas and the shramanas knew that amrit is not a substance, but a timeless idea. This idea cannot be forced down anyone's throat; like a pond in the forest, it awaits the thirsty beast that will find its way to it, on its own terms, at its own pace.

The head of the people department, Murlidhar, suggested that they do personality tests to identify and nurture talent in the company. The owner of the company, Mr. Walia, did not like the idea. "The personality of people keeps changing depending on who they are dealing with, depending on what they are going through in life." Murlidhar pointed to scientific evidence that personality can be accurately mapped and how core personality never changes. "I do not believe it," said Mr. Walia. "How can you not," said Murlidhar, "It is science!" Murlidhar believes there is only one objective truth outside human imagination that science can help us discover; he does not care much for the subjective. Mr. Walia believes that everyone believes in different things, and these beliefs forged in the imagination are true to the believer, hence must be respected, no matter what objective tests reveal. Mr. Walia values perspective and context; he is more aligned to the sanatan than Murlidhar.

Indians never had to articulate their way of life to anyone else; the gymnosophist never felt the need to justify his viewpoint or proselytize it. Then, some five hundred years ago, Europeans started coming to India from across the sea, first to trade, then to convert, and eventually to exploit. What was a source of luxury goods until the seventeenth century became the land of raw materials by the nineteenth century, and a market by the twentieth century, as the industrial revolution in Europe destroyed indigenous industry and changed the world.

Indians became exposed to Western ideas for the first time as they studied in missionary schools to serve as clerks in the East India Company, the world's first corporation. Sanatan had to be suddenly defended against Western ideas, using Western language and Western templates. Indians were ill-equipped to do so. So the Europeans started articulating it themselves on their terms for their benefit, judging it with their way of life. After the eighteenth century fascination with all things Indian, Orientalists spent the nineteenth century disparaging the new colony. Every time a local tried to explain the best of their faith, the European pointed to the worst of Indian society: caste, the burning of widows, and idol worship.

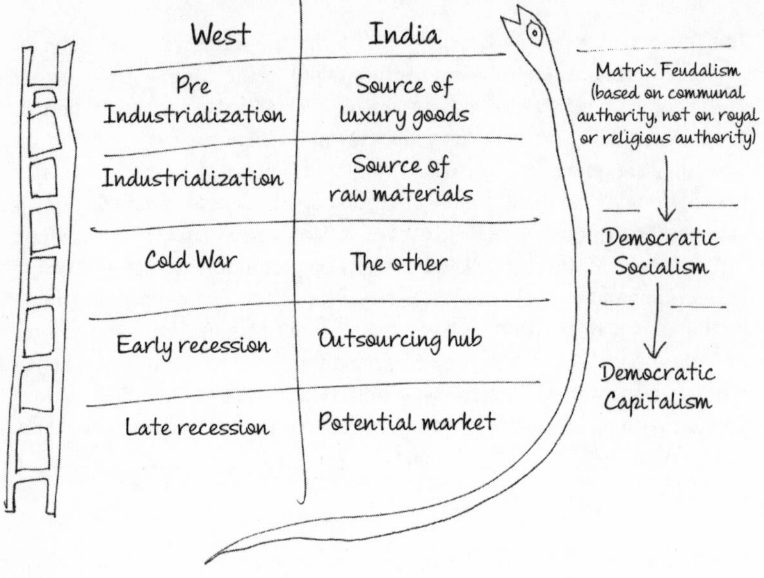

Indians became increasingly defensive and apologetic, as they had to constantly match Indian ways to Western benchmarks. Attempts were even made to redefine Hinduism in Christian terms, a Hindu Reformation, complete with an assembly hall where priests did not perform rituals, only gave sermons. Hindu goal-based 'missions' came into being, as did Hindu 'fundamentalists' determined to organize, standardize and sanitize customs and beliefs. This was when increasingly the idea of dharma started being equated with rules, ethics and morality, the Ramayan and the Mahabharat were rewritten as Greek tragedies, and everything had a nationalistic fervour.

Salvation for Indian thought came when Gandhi used non-violence and moral uprightness to challenge Western might. The non-violent doctrine of Jainism, the pacifism of Buddhism and the intellectual fervour of the Bhagavad Gita inspired him. That being said, Gandhi's writings, and his quest for the truth, do show a leaning towards the objective rather than the subjective. Gandhi's satyagraha was about compelling (agraha) on moral and ethical grounds; it called for submitting to what he was convinced was the

truth (satya). This may have had something to do with the fact that he trained as a lawyer in London, and learnt of Buddha and the Gita through the English translations of Orientalists such as Edwin Arnold and Charles Wilkins.

When India secured political freedom, the founding fathers of the nation state, mostly educated in Europe, shied away from all things religious and mythological as the partition of India on religious grounds had made these volatile issues. The pursuit of secular, scientific and vocational goals meant that all things sanatan were sidelined.

Most understanding of Indian thought today is derived from the works of nineteenth century European Orientalists, twentieth century American academicians, and the writings of Indians that tend to be reactionary, defensive and apologetic. In other words, Indianness today is understood within the Western template, with the Western lens and the Western gaze. These are so widespread that conclusions that emerge from them are assumed to be correct, as no one knows any better. Thus India, especially Hinduism, finds itself increasingly force-fitted into a Western religious framework complete with a definitive holy book (Bhagavad Gita), a trinity (Brahma, Vishnu and Shiva), a set of commandments (Manu Smriti), its own Latin (Sanskrit), a Protestant revolution (Buddhism versus Hinduism), a heretical tradition (Tantra), a class struggle (caste hierarchy), a race theory (Aryans and Dravidians), a forgotten pre-history (the Indus valley cities), a disputed Jerusalem-like geography (Ayodhya), a authoritarian clergy who need to be overthrown (brahmins), a pagan side that needs to be outgrown (worship of trees) and even a goal that needs to be pursued (liberation from materialism). Any attempt to join the dots differently, and reveal a different pattern is met with fierce resistance and is dismissed as cultural chauvinism. This academic tsunami is only now withdrawing.

Words such as 'gaze', 'construct', 'code' and 'design' that are more suited to explaining the Indian way entered the English language only after the 1970s with the rise of postmodern studies and the works of Foucault, Derrida, Barthes and Berger. These were not available to early writers who sought to express Indian thoughts in Indian terms, like Raja Ram Mohan Roy, Vivekananda, Jyotibha Phule, Rabindranath Tagore, Sarvepalli Radhakrishnan,

C. Rajagopalachari and Iravati Karve. Only in recent times have a few Indian scholars started taking up the challenge to re-evaluate ancient Indian ideas on Indian terms.

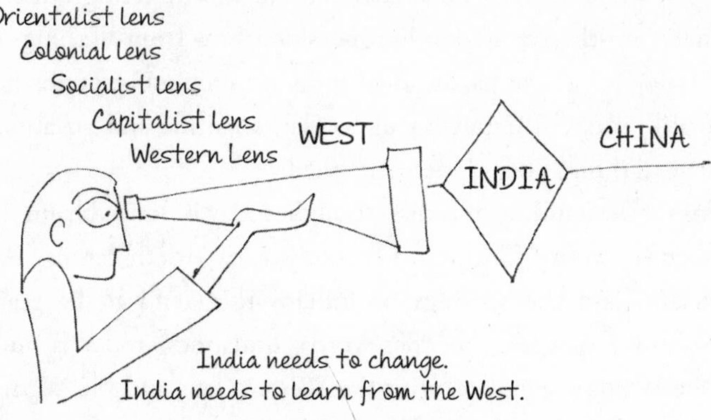

Indian universities dare not touch mythology for fear of angering traditionalists and fundamentalists who still suffer from the colonial hangover of seeking literal, rational, historical and scientific interpretations for sacred stories, symbols and rituals. Western universities continue to approach Indian mythology with extreme Western prejudice, without any empathy for its followers, angering many Indians, especially Hindus. As a result of this, an entire generation of Indians has been alienated from its vast mythic inheritance.

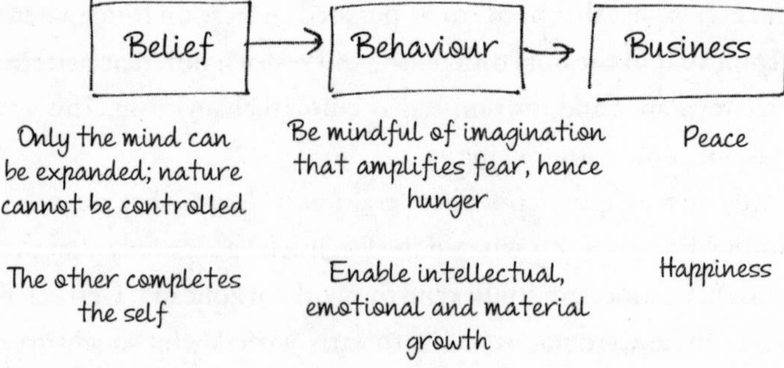

Caution!

There is vast difference between what we claim to believe in and what we actually believe in. Often, we are not even aware of what we actually believe in, which is why there is a huge gap between what we say and what we actually do.

- A corporation may believe that it is taking people towards the Promised Land, when, in fact, it may actually be compelling people to build its own pyramid.

- An entrepreneur may believe he is making his way to Elysium, when, in fact, he is one of the Olympian gods casting the rest into the monotony of Tartarus.

- Every 'jugadu' following the Indian way may believe that he is Ram or Krishna, creating ranga-bhoomi to attract Lakshmi, when, in fact, he may be the very opposite, Ravan and Duryodhan, establishing rana-bhoomi to capture Lakshmi.

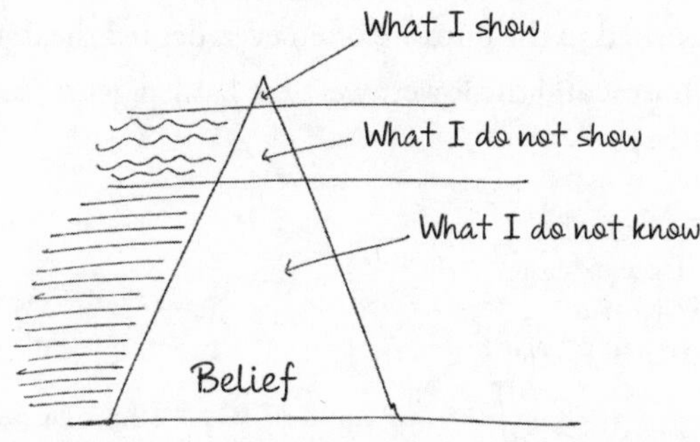

A hospitable home in India prides itself on providing every visitor to the house at least a glass of water on arrival; yet it is in this very same India that large portions of the population have been denied water from the village well, a dehumanizing act that costs India its moral standing. No discussion of India can be complete without referring to the plight of the dalits, a term meaning

downtrodden that was chosen by the members of communities who face caste discrimination.

It is another matter that the problem of caste is used by the West to make Indians constantly defensive. Every time someone tries to say anything good about India, they are shouted down by pointing to this social injustice. With a typical Western sense of urgency, one expects a problem that established itself over the millennia to be solved in a single lifetime.

Caste is not so much a religious directive as it is an unwritten social practice, seen in non-Hindu communities of India as well, amplified by a scarcity of resources. So the attempt to wipe it out by standard Western prescriptions, such as changing laws and demanding behavioral modification, is not as effective as one would like it to be. A systemic, rather than cosmetic, change demands a greater line of sight, more empathy rather than judgment, something that seems rather counter-intuitive for the impatient social reformer.

The colloquial word for caste in India is jati; it traditionally referred to the family profession that one was obliged to follow. Jobs were classified as higher and lower depending on the level of ritual pollution. The priest and the teacher rose to the top of the pyramid while sweepers, undertakers, butchers, cobblers, were pushed to the bottom, often even denied the dignity of touch. In between the purest and the lowest were the landed gentry and the traders.

A person's jati was his identity and his support system, beyond the family. It determined social station. Whether a person belonged to a higher or lower jati, he avoided eating with, or marrying, members of other jatis.

This institutionalized the jati system very organically over centuries. When members of one jati became economically more prosperous or politically more powerful, they did not seek to break the caste system; they sought to rise up the social ladder by emulating the behaviour of the more dominant caste of the village, which was not always the priest but often the landed gentry. This peculiar behaviour was termed Sanskritization by sociologists. Thus, the jati system was not as rigid as one is given to believe. At the same time it was not as open to individual choice as one would have liked it to be.

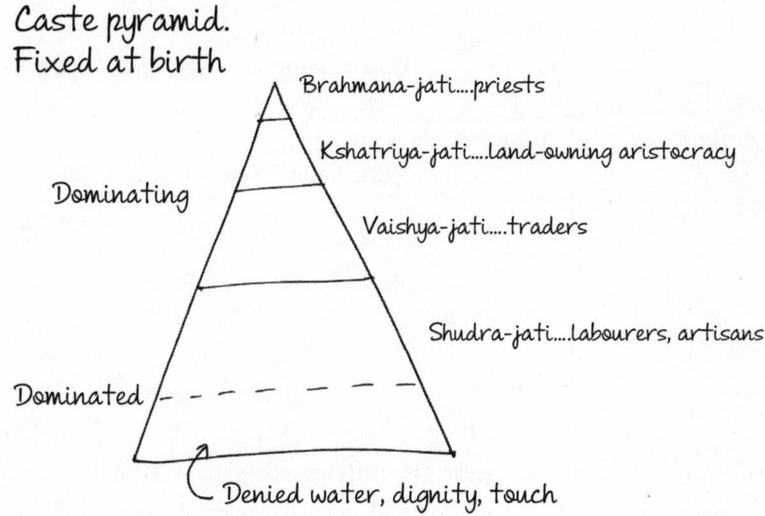

In the Mahabharat, the sage Markandeya tells the Pandavs the story of a butcher who reveals to a hermit that what matters is not what we do but why we do what we do. In other words, varna matters more than jati.

Varna, a word found even in the Vedic Samhitas, the earliest of Hindu scriptures, means 'colour'. Orientalists of the nineteenth century, predictably, took it literally and saw the varna-based division of society in racial terms. Symbolically, it refers to the 'colour of thought', or mindset, a meaning that is promptly dismissed as defensive.

The sages of India did not value jati as much as they valued varna. Jati is tangible or saguna, a product of human customs. Varna is intangible, or nirguna, a product of the human imagination. Jati is fixed by virtue of birth but varna can flow and rise, or fall. A mind that expands in wisdom will see jati in functional terms, while a mind that is contracted in fear will turn jati into a tool for domination and exploitation.

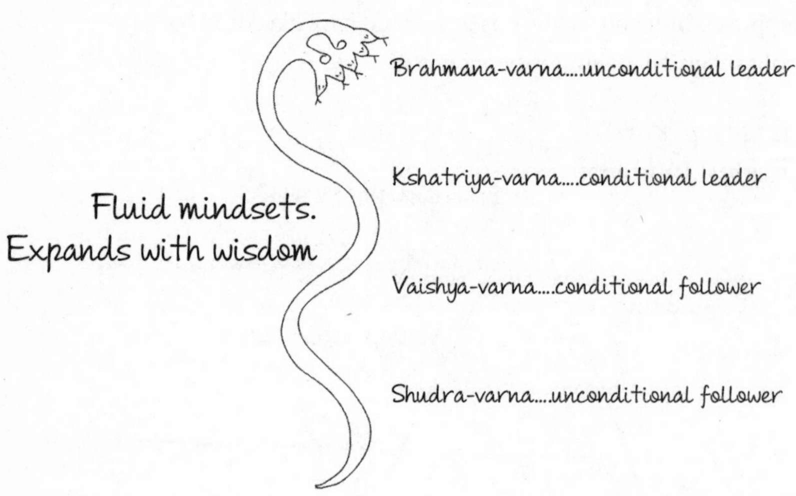

Once, a teacher gave a great discourse on the value of thoughts over things. As he was leaving, a chandala blocked his path. A chandala is the keeper of the crematorium, hence belongs to the shudra jati. The teacher and his students tried to shoo him away. "What do you want me to move?" chuckled the chandala, "My mind has wandered away long ago, but my body is still here." The teacher had no reply. The chandala had truly understood what the teacher only preached. The chandala clearly belonged to the brahmana varna. But because he belonged to the shudra jati, he was shunned by society. Society chose to revere the teacher instead, valuing his caste, more than his mind. Observing this, the teacher realized society was heading for collapse, for when the mind values the fixed over the flexible, it cannot adapt, change or grow.

In medieval times, many brahmins wrote several dharma-shastras giving their views on how society should be organized. One of the dharma-shastras known as Atreya Smriti stated that every child is born in the shudra-varna and can rise to the brahman-varna through learning. Another dharma-shastra known as Manu Smriti, however, saw varna and jati as synonyms, assuming that people of a particular profession have, or should have, a particular mindset. Atri was proposing the path of wisdom while Manu was proposing the path of domination.

It did not help that in the nineteenth century the British used Manu's treatise, choosing it from amongst all the dharma-shastras, to create the law of the land, perhaps because European scholars mistakenly equated Manu with the biblical Adam. With that, the Manu Smriti, once an obscure text known only to Sanskrit-speaking brahmins of North India, became the definitive Hindu law book in the eyes of the world.

The global order is drifting in the same direction. People are being valued not for who they are (varna) but for the lifestyle they lead (jati). A neo-caste system is being organized. The rich nation, like the rich man, is assumed to be smart. The literate nation, like the educated man, is assumed to be good.

The modern passport functions just like caste, granting people identity and resources, legitimizing the exclusion of 'polluted' economic migrants and

political refugees from rich nation states. Everyone knows how difficult it is to change one's passport. Everyone is, however, convinced it needs to exist.

The rational arguments of the West do not seem to be making people ethical or moral. Greed is qualitatively similar in all nations, rich or poor, with the lion's share of every nation's income being enjoyed by less than 10 per cent of the population. Rules are being designed, and rights are being enforced, to establish diversity, eco-friendliness, and corporate social responsibility. But these are never at the cost of shareholder value, revealing the cosmetic nature of these changes meant to satisfy the auditors and charm buyers and voters. Outrage, consequently, seethes beneath the surface. With reward and reprimand failing, panic is setting in. Once again, in typical Western style, there is talk of revolution.

But the shift being proposed is once again behavioural. No attempt is made to expand the mind. Everyone is convinced personality is hardcoded, with room only for one truth. Everyone speaks of the truth, rarely your truth or my truth. Unable to get belief alignment, more and more leaders are convinced that people have to be led like sheep, forced to be good.

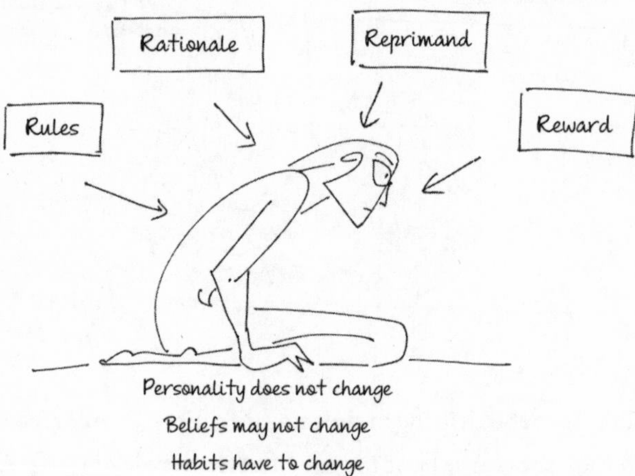

Determined to be fair and just, management science strives to make organizations more and more objective. Therefore, institutions are valued over individuals, data over opinions, rules over relationships, instruction over

understanding, contracts over trust, and processes over people. Professionalism, which involves the removal of emotions in the pursuit of tasks and targets, is seen as a virtue. Incredibly, scholars and academicians actually expect corporations designed on dehumanization to be responsible for society!

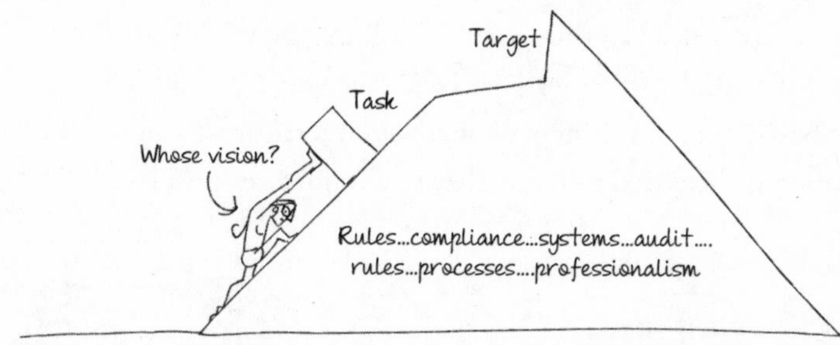

Sameer who works in the corporate communications division has to make a report on corporate social responsibility. The lady who heads the department, Rita, who majored in social service at a reputed university says, "Here, it is not about helping people but about meeting a target so that the company can tell its shareholders and the media that they have changed the world and contributed to the well-being of society. They hope this will help improve their brand image. Nobody will say this as they are trained to be politically correct in public by their media team. There is no feeling, no empathy, just excel sheets. But at least something is happening at the ground level where the situation is rather dismal, that is why I am sticking around." Sameer also participated in a meeting where there was a discussion as to what would be more impactful: providing latrines in villages, or laptops? The majority voted in favour of laptops.

But before we judge humanity harshly, we must remind ourselves that humans are 99 per cent animals (technically it is 96 per cent, but 99 per cent sounds more dramatic). Only a tiny percentage of our genes are exclusively human. In the evolutionary scale, fear is thus a far more familiar emotion than ideas that spring from the imagination. Fear has enabled us to survive for three billion years; imagination has been around for less than a million. In doubt, we naturally regress towards older, more familiar emotions. Further,

the body physiology resists thinking and introspecting and analyzing, as brain activity needs glucose, a precious fuel that the body would rather conserve in the muscles in anticipation of a crisis. That is why the human mind prefers the tangible to the intangible, behaviour to belief, simpler ideas to complex ones, predictable models to models that thrive on uncertainty, the jati construct to the varna construct. Even though every culture and every organization bases itself on lofty ideals, when crisis strikes, everyone regresses, relying on age-old fear-based animal instincts of aggression, territoriality and domination. Imagination is then used to rationalize one's choice, ex post facto.

Perhaps, the time has come to realize our evolutionary potential, open our eyes once again, and do darshan. Darshan means looking beyond the measurable: if imagination has the power to make us value profit over people, it also has the power to make business growth an outcome of people growth, not regardless of it.

Trusting human potential is not easy. Including other truths is not easy. But to rise in grace, we must outgrow gravity.

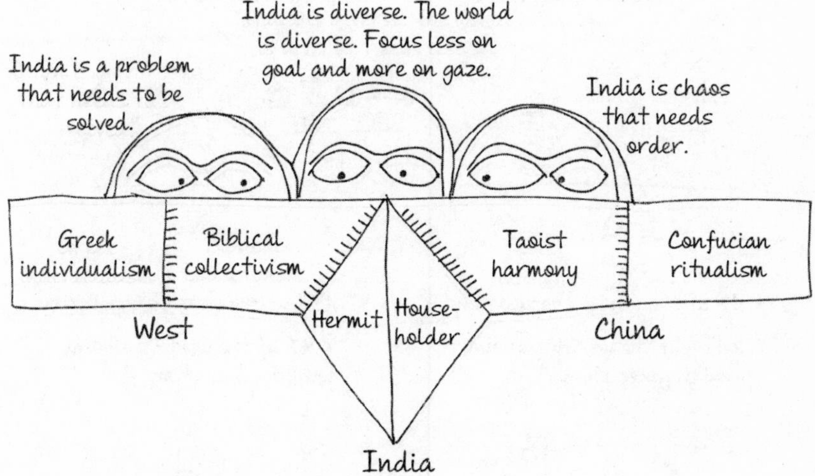
India is a problem that needs to be solved.
India is diverse. The world is diverse. Focus less on goal and more on gaze.
India is chaos that needs order.
Greek individualism
Biblical collectivism
Hermit
House-holder
Taoist harmony
Confucian ritualism
West
China
India

Crude comparison of two very different contexts that are often expected to have the same goals.

USA

1 Language on currency note

4% of the world's population

> 17% of the world's annual wealth generation

90% of the total wealth is controlled by 10% of the population

INDIA

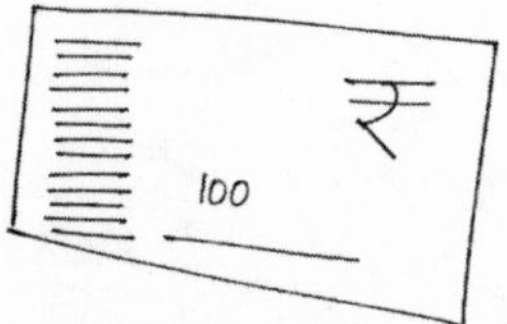

17 Languages on currency note

17% of the world's population

< 4% of the world's annual wealth generation

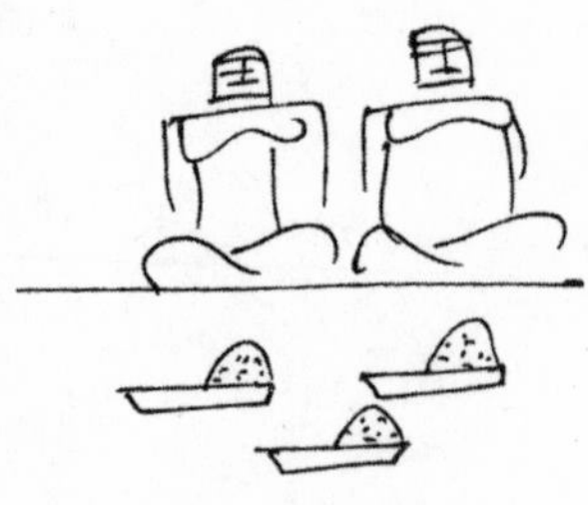

90% of the total wealth is controlled by 10% of the population

III

Business Sutra

A Very Indian Approach to Management

Business is yagna, the ritual described in the oldest and most revered of Hindu scriptures, the Rig Veda.

The yajaman initiates this ritual, makes offerings into agni, fire burning in the altar, exclaiming, "svaha"—this of me I offer, hoping to please his chosen deity or devata who will then give him whatever he desires, exclaiming, "tathastu"—so it shall be.

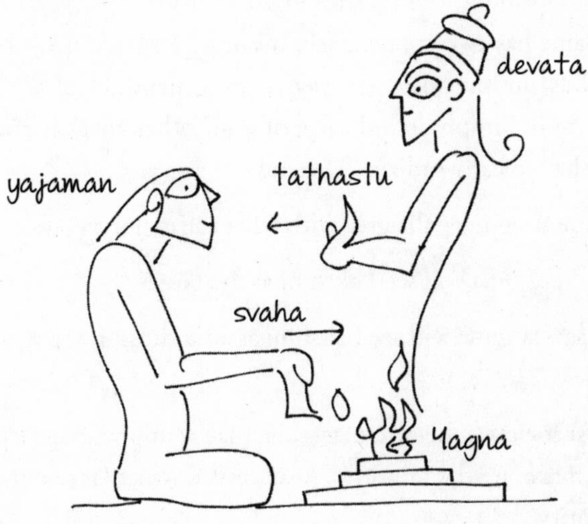

Svaha is what the yajaman invests: goods, services and ideas. Tathastu is the return on investment: revenue in the marketplace or salary paid by the employer, or even the services offered by the employee. It all depends on who plays the role of the yajaman, who initiates the yagna. The yagna can operate both downstream, as well as upstream, so the devata can either be the buyer or the seller, the investor or the entrepreneur, the employer or employee, director or doorman.

Paresh believes that because he pays a good salary, his cook prepares his meals just the way he likes them. He is the yajaman and the cook is the devata. The cook, however, believe that it is his skill at preparing good meals which gets him a good salary from Paresh. In the cook's imagination, he is the yajaman and Paresh the devata. Both do svaha, which gives them a satisfactory tathastu.

A yagna is declared a success only if it ushers in wealth and prosperity. Everyone agrees then that Lakshmi has arrived. Lakshmi is the goddess of wealth. She is also goddess of auspiciousness; her image adorns not only Hindu homes but also Jain temples and Buddhist stupas, indicating her popularity even amongst those who shunned ritual.

Her name has two roots: laksh, meaning target and lakshan, meaning indicator. Was the purpose of a yagna the generation of wealth? Or was wealth generation simply an indicator of some other goal? The answer to this question is the typically Indian, "Depends!"

- He of tamas-guna will agree with what the majority says.
- He of rajas-guna will see Lakshmi as the target.
- He of sattva-guna will see Lakshmi as an indicator of personal growth.

In most societies, he of tamas-guna makes up the majority while he of sattva-guna makes up the minority. A successful society is one that is directed by this minority.

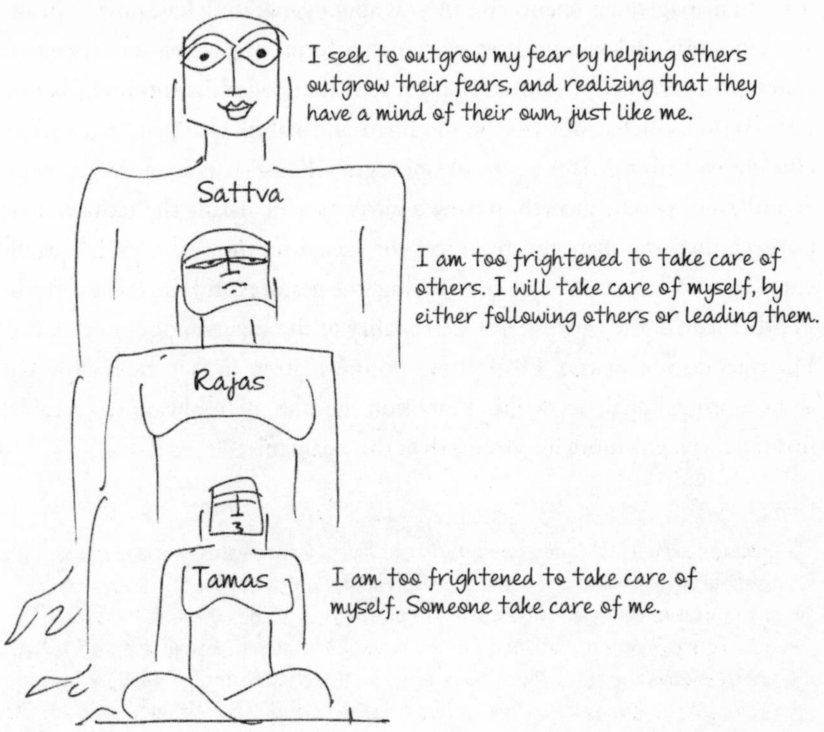

Guna means personality. It indicates how we think and feel. It depends on how we imagine the world and ourselves in it. It is an outcome of fear.

- He of tamas-guna is too frightened to have an opinion of his own; he is dependent on the opinions of others.

- He of rajas-guna, is too frightened to trust the opinions of others; so he clings to only his opinion and those of others that favours him..

- He of sattva-guna, trusts other people's opinions as well as his own and wonders why different people have different opinions of the same thing. Sensitivity, introspection and analysis help him discover and outgrow his fears.

In management science, business is about generating Lakshmi, ethically and efficiently. Behavioural science, which informs human resource practice, states that personality cannot change; it is hardcoded in the brain before puberty; only behaviour can be modified and habits changed, made more efficient and ethical. This is why business growth is seen as economic growth, regardless of people growth. Business starts by articulating the tathastu first (target), then the plan and resources for executing the svaha (tasks). Skills come later. What matters are the offering, the gestures and the exclamations; in other words, the process. The personality of the yajaman does not matter. His fears do not matter. His feelings do not matter. In fact, he is expected to be a professional, act without emotion. Besides, he is always replaceable, making the yagna more important than the yajaman.

Suhasini serves fast food at an international fast food centre. She is expected to speak in English and is trained on how to greet the guests. She knows that the customer can speak Marathi or Hindi, both languages that she is fluent in but her supervisor is watching her, as is the CCTV, and she can lose points for not following the rules. Rules have ensured the chain is highly efficient and profitable. So she puts on her artificial smile, continues to speak in English and does nothing to comfort the customer, even though she feels miserable about the whole situation. Neither her views nor the annoyance of a single customer really matter.

But according to Vedic scriptures the yagna had no independent existence outside the yajaman. Business is always about people: of people, by people, for people. Everything hinges on the bhaav of the yajaman towards the devata, the feeling with which he offers the svaha and receives the tathastu. Bhaav also means value. The feeling of the yajaman determines the value he grants to the devata.

- He of tamas-guna, will look upon the devata with the bhaav of an unconditional follower (shudra-varna), who is totally dependent on the devata.

- He of rajas-guna, will look upon the devata with the bhaav of a conditional follower (vaishya-varna) or a conditional leader (kshatriya-varna). He will always value the devata for his possessions and not for who he is. He will blame the devata for all his problems and resent his own dependence on the devata.

- He of sattva-guna, will look upon the devata with the bhaav of a dependable, independent, unconditional leader (brahmana-varna). He values the devata, includes the devata, protects and provides for him, provokes him to grow, knowing that the devata may be too frightened to reciprocate.

Feelings change when mindset changes; the mindset changes when fear is outgrown. For that we have to pay attention to fear and what it does to us. Every human being may have different physical and mental capabilities and capacities, different fortunes and social stations, but everyone has the same ability to gaze upon fear.

Gaze is under voluntary control; it is not something we inherit. Gaze can be long-term or short-term. Gaze can be narrow or wide. Gaze can be superficial or deep. But everyone can gaze. Gaze allows us to expand or control our mind by being mindful of fear—our fear and the fears of others, how it shapes our mind, hence our feelings, which impacts how we engage with the world and

what kind of relationships we end up having. Meditation, contemplation and introspection are all about becoming more aware of our gaze.

- Everyone sees objective reality, all that is tangible and measurable, or saguna. This is drishti, or sight.

- Everyone can 'see' subjective reality, thoughts and feelings, the fears underlying actions that are neither tangible nor measurable, or nirguna. This is divya-drishti, or insight.

- Everyone can also let the subjective truth reveal the subject: the varna of the one who is observed as well as the varna of one who is observing. This is darshan.

Those who did darshan first were known as the rishis, or the sages of India, often identified as 'seers', those who saw what others would not see.

Fear

Wisdom

Guna	Varna	Gaze	Belief	Goal	Focus
Tamas	Shudra	*	*	*	*
Rajas	Vaishya	drishti	Objective truth	Wealth	Jati
	Kshatriya	divya-drishti	Subjective truth	Power	Jati
Sattva	Brahman	darshan	Subject	Wisdom	Varna

* follows dominant trend

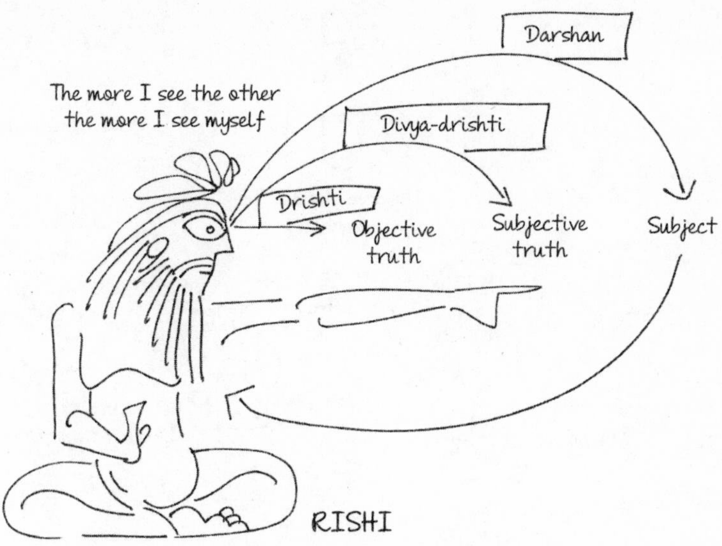

Darshan is also a Sanskrit word which means philosophy or worldview. It is also a common religious practice among Hindus: devotees are encouraged to look at the image of the deity, which looks back at the devotee with large, unblinking eyes. Placed atop the temple doorway is a head with protruding eyes watching the act of observation.

The rishis realized that humans are not only capable of seeing varna, but can also rise up the varna ladder by outgrowing fear. However, this can only happen when we help others outgrow their fear. That is why they designed the yagna, as a tool that compels us to pay attention to others.

Using the yagna, the yajaman can become less dependent and more dependable, and hence be a refuge for the frightened, those who seek Lakshmi as a child seeks a comforter.

The more dependable a yajaman is, the more able he is to attract the devatas, as bees to nectar. The devatas in turn will churn out Lakshmi for him from the ocean of milk that is the marketplace. Thus will Lakshmi walk his way.

Economic growth does not lead to intellectual and emotional growth; if anything it can amplify fear. The rishis saw economic growth without personal growth as a recipe for disaster for then Lakshmi would come along with her sister, Alakshmi, goddess of conflict, and create enough quarrels to ensure Lakshmi could slip away from the grasp of the yajaman who was unworthy of her.

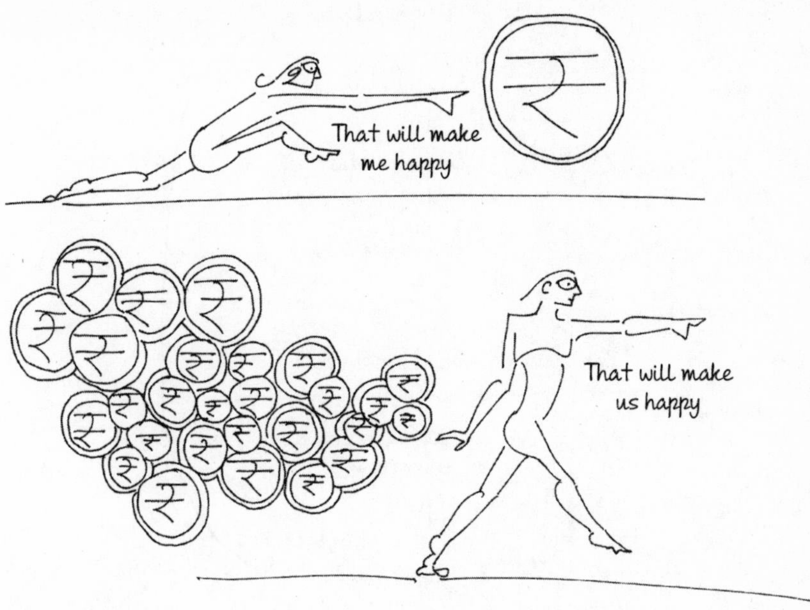

They were convinced that economic growth has to be an outcome of intellectual and emotional growth. For the workplace to be a happy playground (ranga-bhoomi) rather than a fierce battleground (rana-boomi), Lakshmi had to be an indicator and darshan, the lever.

As is darshan, so is guna; as is guna so is varna; as is varna, so is bhaav; as is bhaav, so is svaha; as is svaha, so is tathastu. In other words, as is belief, so is behaviour, so is business. This is Business Sutra, a very Indian approach to management.

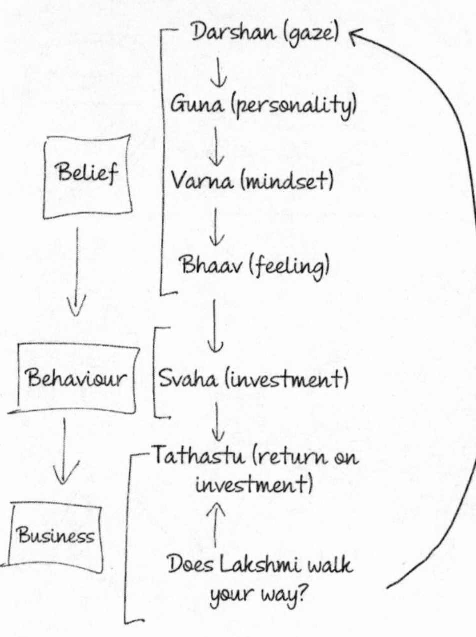

- We shall begin by exploring how imagination transforms every human into Brahma, the creator of the yagna.
- In the following three chapters, we shall explore drishti, divya-drishti and darshan, which determine the quality of the yagna.
- In the final chapter, we shall explore the impact of the yagna on the yajaman.

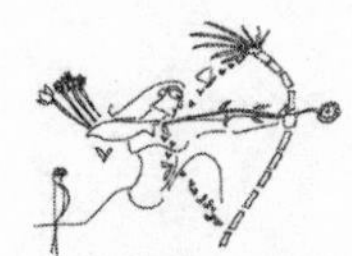

Kama's Vision Statement

Drishti, observing objective reality

Divya-drishti, observing subjective reality

Darshan, observing the subject

Yama's Balance Sheet

Kama's Vision Statement

Drishti, observing objective reality

Divya-drishti, observing subjective reality

Darshan, observing the subject

Yama's Balance Sheet

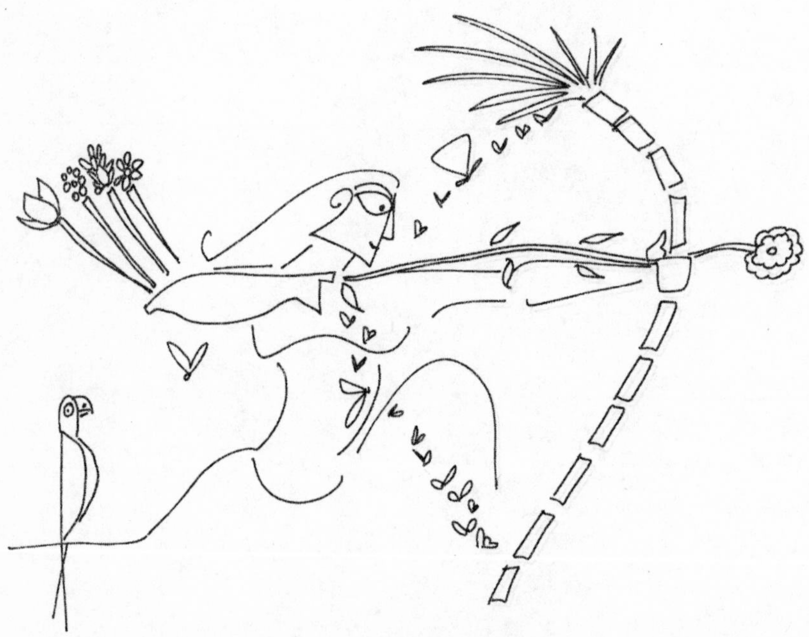

If there was no desire there would be no dream, no aspiration, no ambition, no vision, no enterprise.

Human hunger is unique

It all starts with hunger. Hunger distinguishes the living from the non-living. Jain scriptures identify beings that do not feed as nirjiva and those that feed as sajiva. It is hunger that makes plants grow, and animals seek pastures and prey. But human hunger is unique:

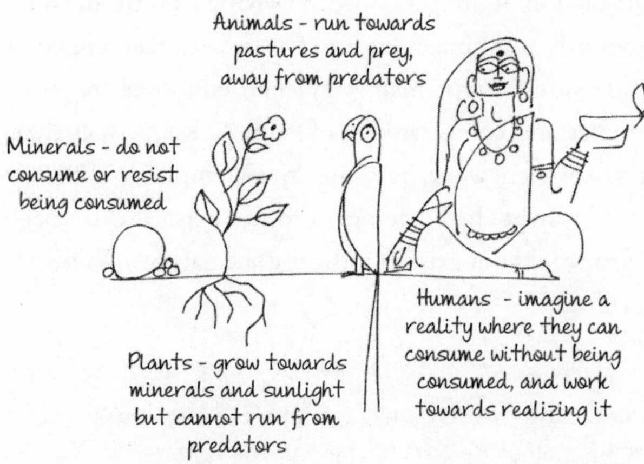

- Humans can visualize future hunger—tomorrow's hunger, next year's drought, and even next decade's recession, which fuels great anxiety.

- Humans can visualize food coming towards them despite the fact that every plant and every animal around them seeks out food.

- Humans can visualize consuming without getting consumed, even though every living organism in nature consumes as well as gets consumed.

This is because, according to mythologies of Indian origin, Kama, the god of desire, has raised his sugarcane bow and struck our five senses with his five flowery arrows. In neurobiological terms, it is because humans possess imagination. Animals get frightened when they see, smell or hear a predator; humans get frightened because they can always imagine a predator. Animals

get excited when they see, smell or hear a prey; humans get excited because they can always imagine a prey.

Imagination allows humans to break free from the fetters of time and place; sitting in one place we can travel to the past and the future, we can travel to other lands, we can concoct memories, propel ourselves with fabricated hunger, make ourselves miserable by imposing expectations on ourselves.

The satisfaction of hunger constitutes happiness for most people while the failure to satisfy this hunger leads to frustration, rage and conflict.

Every investor, entrepreneur, employer, employee, regulator, auditor, vendor, customer and competitor is a victim of Kama. It is their insatiable hunger that makes them work, innovate, invest, employ, compete, marry, start a family and a business. If this hunger did not exist, if this imagination did not exist, yagna would not exist. It is the unique nature of human hunger that gives rise to culture.

> Abhirup was born into a rich family and inherited huge wealth from both his father and his mother. He does not have to work a day in his life. He can live a life of absolute luxury. Yet, he is determined to start a business of his own. It is not about the money or power; it is something else. He cannot explain this drive. He expects support from his wife and his family and gets annoyed when they find his ambitions unnecessary, even silly. This is human hunger, very different from other hungers.

Imagination expands human hunger

Humans have full power over their imagination. We can expand, contract and crumple it at will. This makes each individual a Brahma, creator of his/her own subjective reality, the brahmanda, which literally means the 'egg of Brahma'.

We can choose what we want to see. We can choose what we want to value. Animals and plants do not have this luxury. They are fettered by their biology. They cannot be punished for hurting humans (though we often do); but humans can be punished for hurting other humans. Imagination liberates us from submitting to our instincts. We are, whether we like it or not, whether we are aware of it or not, responsible for our actions.

Prakriti or nature does not care much for human imagination, and expects humans to fend for themselves just like other animals. As far as nature is concerned, humans deserve no special treatment, much to Brahma's irritation. They, too, must struggle to survive.

In his imagination, Brahma sees the whole world revolving around him. So Brahma works towards establishing sanskriti or culture where the rules of nature are kept at bay, and rules from his brahmanda are realized. Sanskriti is all about creating a world where might is not right, where even the unfit can survive.

In sanskriti, Brahma encounters the brahmanda of other Brahmas, and he either battles them to enforce his rules, or bears the burden of their rules.

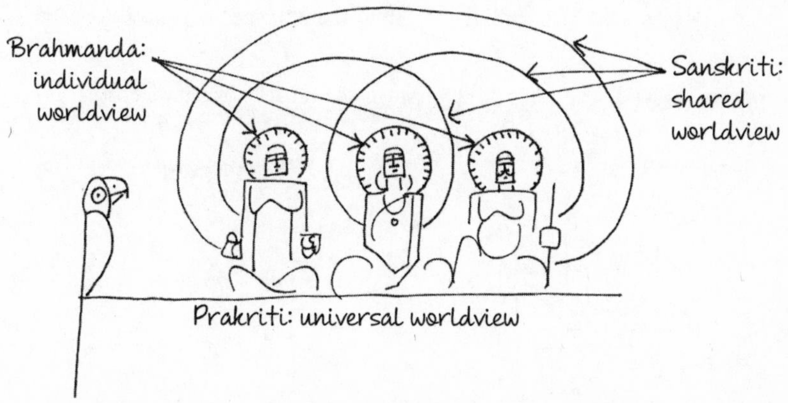

Brahma, thus, inhabits three worlds or tri-loka:

1. Nature or prakriti
2. Imagination or brahmanda
3. Culture or sanskriti

There are as many brahmandas as there are people, as many sanskritis as there are organizations and communities; but only one prakriti. Each of these worlds grant Brahma a body:

1. Physical body or sthula-sharira, granted by prakriti.
2. Mental body or sukshma-sharira, designed by brahmanda
3. Social body or karana-sharira, created by sanskriti.

A good illustration of the three bodies is the character of Ravan from the Ramayan. He is born with ten heads and twenty arms, which constitute his sthula-sharira. Society recognizes him as a devotee of Shiva and king of Lanka, which constitute his karana-sharira. His desire to dominate, be feared and respected by everyone constitutes his sukshma-sharira.

In contrast to him is Hanuman, a monkey of immense strength (sthula-sharira) who is content to be seen as the servant of Ram (karana-sharira), who does not seek to dominate and would rather seek meaning by helping the helpless Ram without seeking anything in return (sukshma-sharira).

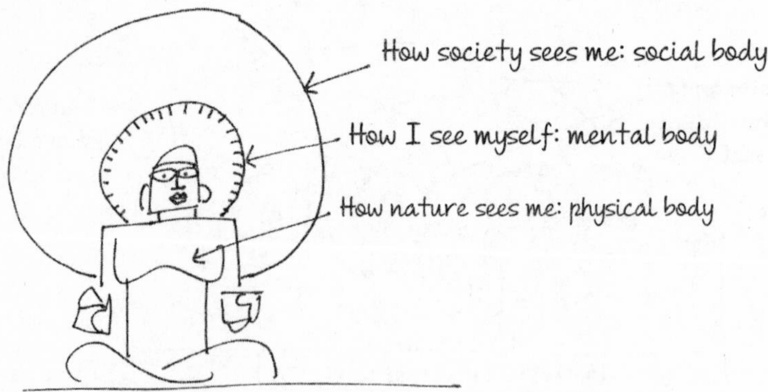

While animals need food to nourish only their physical body, humans also need sustenance for their mental and social bodies. Animal movements are governed by feeding and grazing, human choices are governed by desire for wealth, power, fame, status and recognition. The purpose of yagna is to satisfy every human hunger. Failure to satisfy these hungers transforms the workplace into a rana-bhoomi.

Balwant is a tall man who has always been good with numbers. But his father could not send him to school beyond the fourth standard and he was forced to work in a field. Balwant imagines himself as a leader of men and so he migrated to the city looking for opportunities to prove his worth. Currently he works as a doorman in a building society, a job he got because of his commanding height. Everyone notices his height and uniform. Thus, they are able to identify his role and his status in society. A few observe how good he is with numbers. Hardly anyone notices that he loves to dominate those around him. As a result no one understands why he gets irritated when members of the building society order him around. They feel he is lazy and arrogant. They see his physical body and his social body, not his mental body.

Only humans can exchange

There is always more hunger than food. The Upanishads tell the story of how Brahma invites his children to a meal. Brahma's children are a metaphor for people who feel they have no control over their imagined reality. They expect to be fed. After the food has been served, he lays down a condition, no one can bend their elbows while getting to the food. The food as a result, cannot be picked up and carried to the mouth. Some children complain, as they cannot feed themselves. Others innovate: they pick up the food, swing their arms and start serving the person next to them. Others feed them in reciprocation.

This is the first exchange, which leads to its codification as a yagna in the Rig Veda. Brahma's children who complain and ignore the value of the exchange came to be known as the asuras; while the children who appreciate its value came to be known as the devas.

Every interaction in business is a yagna, be it between investor and entrepreneur, employer and employee, manager and executive, professional and vendor, seller and buyer. The yagna is the fundamental unit of business, where everything that can satisfy hunger is exchanged. He who oversees the yagna and makes up its rules is Daksha, or the chief prajapati.

Animals cannot exchange (though some trading and accounting behaviours have been seen in a few species of bats). Exchange is a human

innovation that reduces the effort of finding food. It increases the chances of getting fed. It improves the variety of food we get access to. Exchange creates the marketplace, the workplace, even the family. It is the cornerstone of society. He who oversees sanskriti and makes up its rules is called Manu, another prajapati.

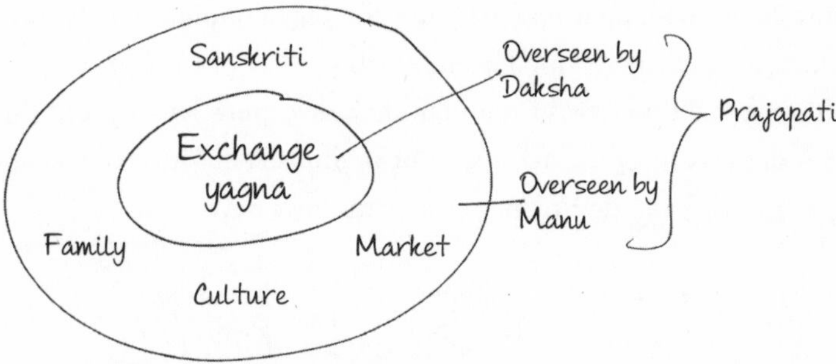

Svaha is food for the devata. Tathastu is food for the yajaman. Unless svaha is given, tathastu cannot be expected. As is svaha, so is tathastu.

Ideally, the yajaman wants the devata to give tathastu voluntarily, joyfully, responsibly and unconditionally. When this happens, it is said Lakshmi walks his way. In the Purans, only Vishnu achieves this. He is identified as bhagavan, he who always feeds others even though he is never hungry.

> Madhav has a pan shop near the railway station. He sells betel leaves, betel nuts, sweets and cigarettes. He even has a stash of condoms. He knows that as long as there is a crowd in the station, there will be people with the need to satisfy cravings and pass the time. He offers them pleasures that are legally permitted (though the temptation to offer illegal products is very high). In exchange, they pay money that helps him feed his family. If he did not have a family, he would have, perhaps, stayed back in his village. But he has six mouths to feed, which has brought him to the city where he has had to learn this new trade to earn his livelihood. The day people stop craving betel or nicotine or sweets or sex, his business will grind to a halt. The day his family can fend for itself, he will end this yagna and close down his shop.

Every devata seeks a high return on investment

The yajaman who initiates the yagna is Brahma. So is the devata who participates in the yagna. Both know the value of exchange. Both can also imagine a yagna where both can get tathastu without giving svaha, or get svaha without being obliged to give a tathastu in return. This is a yagna where there is infinite return with no investment. It is the yagna of Brahma's favourite son, Indra, king of devas, performed in Amravati.

Though the two terms sound familiar, deva and devata mean different things. A deva is one of the many sons of Brahma. A devata is the recipient of the yajaman's svaha. A devata may or may not be a deva.

	Svaha Investment	Tathastu Returns
Exploitation	+++	+
Fairness	+++	+++
Success	+	+++

Located beyond the stars, Indra's Amravati houses the wish-fulfilling cow Kamadhenu, wish-fulfilling tree Kalpataru, and the wish-fulfilling jewel Chintamani. Here, the Apsaras are always dancing, the Gandharvas are always singing and the wine, Sura, is always flowing. It's always a party! All hungers are satisfied in Amravati because Lakshmi here is the queen, identified as Sachi. Some would say Sachi is Indra's mistress for while she is obliged to pleasure him, he feels in no way responsible to take care of her.

Amarvati is the land of bhog, of consumption, where all expectations are satisfied without any obligations. For humans, Amravati is swarga, or paradise. Every yajaman yearns for the idle pleasures there. Every son of Brahma—be it deva, asura, yaksha or rakshasa, from Ravan to Duryodhan—wants to be Indra.

It is to attain swarga that a yajaman initiates a yagna and a devata agrees to participate in it. The desire for swarga goads both the yajaman and the

devata to be creative and innovative all the time. Both constantly crave more returns, to keep pace with their ever-increasing hunger. Simultaneously, the willingness to put effort in keeps decreasing. Both feel cheated or exploited every time more is asked of them and when growth slows down. Both are happiest when they get a deal or a discount, when they get a bonus or a lottery or a subsidy. The improvement of returns and reduction of investment are the two main aims of every stakeholder in business as humans inch their way towards paradise.

> Renjit noticed something peculiar in his town. Young men would gather in the fields in the middle of the day to drink toddy and eat fish. They would not work in the fields. "Work is for the labourers," they said disdainfully. The area has a shortage of workers. People are being called from neighbouring states to work in the fields. The local young men prefer doing deals with high returns like real estate and even gambling. Some are contractors. But when they get contracts from government, they subcontract it to others, so that they can spend the afternoon, like Indra, having a good time.

Conflict is inherent in exchange

The exercise of exchange is fraught with misunderstandings and problems. The first problem is the burden of expectations and obligations. The yajaman has expectations once he gives svaha, and the devata has obligations once he receives svaha. Exchange creates debt, or rin. With debt come borrowers and lenders. We get entrapped in a maze of give and take, called samsara. We yearn to break free from samsara. We do not want to receive, or give. This is liberation, or mukti. Overseeing the yagna—ensuring that the rules of the yagna are fair to all and respected by all—are the prajapatis, led by Daksha, a son of Brahma.

The second problem is the differing imaginations of both devata and yajaman that often leads to a mismatch between svaha and tathastu. What the devata receives may not be to his satisfaction and what the yajaman receives may not be to his satisfaction. Indra deems his enemies as asuras, or demons, who wish to snatch what he has. The asuras accuse the devas of theft and trickery, of denying them their fair share. This leads to conflict where the devas are constantly at war with the asuras. Sometimes, the devas behave like yakshas, refusing to share what they have, hoarding everything that they possess. Then the asuras transform into rakshasas, who reject every rule of the yagna and simply grab what they want.

The third problem is the anxiety that one day the devata will not want the svaha being offered. He may accept the invitation of another yajaman. Worse, he may seek to outgrow hunger, not expect svaha or give tathastu. Indra especially fears tapasvis—those who engage in tapasya, or introspection. They could turn out to be asuras seeking power to conquer Amravati and take Indra's place. He dispatches his legion of nymphs, the apsaras, to seduce them, and distract them from their goals.

Businesses are always answerable to regulators and tax collectors who accuse them of trying to bypass the system. They have to face the wrath of workers and vendors who feel they are being unfair and exploitative. They are constantly threatened by customers who reject what they have to offer and seek satisfaction elsewhere. There is always a battle to fight: shrinking

sales, shrinking margins, labour disputes, attrition, auditors, lawyers, regulators. Plagued by the demands of shareholders, regulators, customers and employees, the yajaman is unable to enjoy Amravati. There is prosperity but no peace. Indra finds his paradise forever under siege.

Gayatri is irritated. She is having problems with her investors who are delaying the next instalment of desperately needed funds. Her uncle, and business partner, is demanding a greater role in the management. Her chief operating officer has quit because he felt there was too much interference from the management. A competitor has poached two of her most prized engineers. The employees are threatening to go on strike if their wages are not increased. And her husband is not giving her the support he'd promised when she started her own business. She feels like Indra with the prajapatis, asuras and tapasvis ganging up against her.

Imagination can help humans outgrow hunger

Both the yajaman and the devata seek peace, a place without conflicts. This is only possible in a world where there is no exchange, and no hunger. This is the world of Shiva.

Shiva's abode, Kailas, is a snow-covered mountain where he lives with his wife, Durga, and their children, Ganesh and Kartikeya. There is no grass or any other kind of vegetation on Kailas and yet, Shiva's bull, Nandi, does not seem to mind. Nor does Nandi fear the tigers and lions that serve as Durga's mount. Kartikeya's peacock does not eat Shiva's serpent who, in turn, does not eat Ganesha's rat.

In Kailas there is no anxiety about food; there is no predator or prey. This is because Shiva is the greatest of tapasvis, who has outgrown hunger by performing tapasya, that is, introspection, contemplation and meditation. By churning his imagination, he has found the wisdom that enables him to set Kama aflame with inner mental fire, or tapa. Shiva is ishwar, he who is never hungry. Indra's apsaras have no effect on him. His abode is the land of yoga, not bhog.

Because Shiva neither seeks tathastu, nor feels the need to give svaha, he invalidates the yagna. Naturally, Daksha dislikes him and deems him the destroyer.

Eshwaran is a rank holder in the university. A scientist, he has the opportunity to work with many international agencies, but he chooses to work in India and teach at a local college. His work is published around the world and he is a recipient of many grants, all of which he has refused, much to the annoyance of his wife. "With grants come obligations," he explains. He values his freedom and his simple life in his ancestral home more than anything else. He nurses no ambition and has no desire to live a lavish lifestyle. His wife argues that he is missing out on many a golden opportunity. "But I do not feel deprived. I am content with what I have. Must supply always generate demand?" His wife has no answer. She never sees her husband complain or fret or fume about the life he has chosen. He feels no envy for those scientists living a more glamorous lifestyle. She feels he could win the Nobel Prize, to which his reply is, "Like it matters to me. I enjoy physics, not the fame that comes with it." Mrs. Eshwaran calls her husband Shiva in her irritation, as his contentment makes her insecure.

Human hunger for the intangible is often overlooked

Every Brahma wants the prosperity of Amravati with the peace of Kailas. This exists only in Vaikuntha, where Lakshmi voluntarily sits at Vishnu's feet. This is ranga-bhoomi, the playground, where everyone feels happy and fulfilled. This is the realm of great affluence and abundance, where milk flows and everyone is showered with gold.

Vishnu is an affectionate god. Like Daksha, he values the role of the yagna in feeding the hungry. He understands that every Indra wants to be fed rather than feed. He knows that true happiness can only come from the wisdom of Shiva, that enables one to outgrow hunger. Vishnu is sensitive to the fact that Brahma and his sons do not see the world as he does. Not that they cannot. They will not. They are afraid.

Vishnu focuses on giving svaha. Still he does not feel exploited because he receives intangible returns for tangible investments. His yagna is always successful. He attracts talent, investors and customers like cows to the pasture known as Goloka and helps Brahma and his sons cope with their fears. In exchange, they voluntarily bring with them Lakshmi. Thus does he manage to attract the goddess of wealth his way.

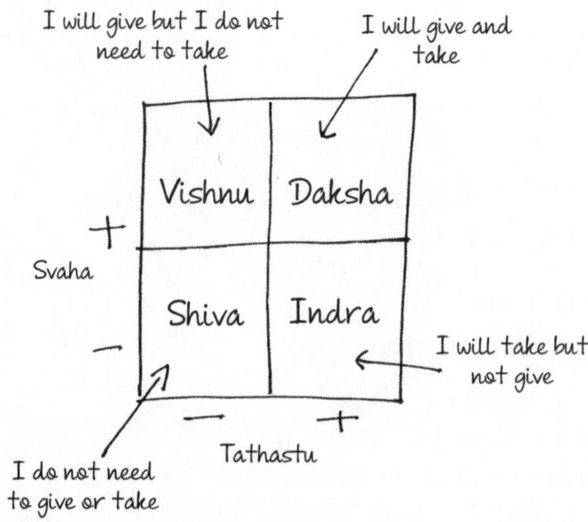

After passing out from a reputed business school, Mahesh, a truly gifted young man, opted not to work in a large multinational and chose to work in a mid-sized Indian ownership firm instead. When asked why by his friends he said, "The multinational firm will hire me for my brilliance and spend years forcing me to fit into a template. Here, I have the freedom to create a template on my own to realize a vision that is my own." Mahesh's new boss, Mr. Naidu, knows that to get the most out of Mahesh, he has to give Mahesh svaha of not just money but also freedom and patience. These are intangible investments that cannot be measured, but they give Mahesh joy and ensure that he works doubly hard. Mr. Naidu does not calculate the returns: a long-term investment demands trust in his assessment of Mahesh.

There are three types of food that can be exchanged during a yagna

Vishnu recognizes that human hunger is not just quantitatively but also qualitatively different. We seek more food. We see different kinds of food. Food is not only tangible; it is also intangible. Power and identity, for instance, are intangible 'foods' that nourish our social and mental bodies.

- We hunger for Lakshmi, or resources, to nourish our physical body (sthula-sharira). So we organize ourselves, create workplaces to extract value from nature, not stopping even when our stomachs are full.

- We hunger for Durga, or power, to make us feel secure. Animals fend for themselves but humans expect to be granted status, dignity and respect through tools, technology, property and rules. Durga nourishes our social body (karana-sharira). In fact, Lakshmi is a surrogate marker for Durga in most cases: we feel safer when we have money.

- We hunger for Saraswati, or identity, to nourish our mental body (sukshma-sharira). This is an exclusively human need that makes us curious about nature as well as imagination. We study it, understand it, control it, determined to locate ourselves in this limitless impermanent world that seems to relentlessly invalidate us. In fact, Lakshmi and Durga are compensations when the hunger for Saraswati is not satisfied.

While Indra sees the yagna only as an exchange of Lakshmi, Vishnu sees the yagna as an exchange of Lakshmi, Durga and Saraswati. These three goddesses are for him three forms of Narayani, the goddess of resources. Narayani is prakriti seen through human eyes. The more we see, the more she reveals herself.

Drishti reveals Lakshmi; divya-drishti reveals Durga; darshan reveals Saraswati. This is the Narayani potential. As long as the gaze is limited and the mind contracted, Brahma will either behave like Daksha, focusing on the

yagna more than the yajaman, or he will give birth to a son who aspires to be Indra, focused on his self-actualization, indifferent to the needs of others. But when the gaze widens and the mind expands, when varna rises and the sattva-guna blooms, he makes his journey towards the independent Shiva and the dependable Vishnu.

The Jain classification of worthy beings suggests a similar pattern. Vasudev is witness to the movement of Lakshmi, the chakravarti is witness to Durga while the tirthankar sees Saraswati. Vasudev sees the world in economic terms, the chakravarti sees the world in political terms. Only the tirthankar understands that philosophy is the seed of all economic and political decisions; only he understands that every each human being has a different philosophy and only the wise are able to accommodate everyone's philosophy.

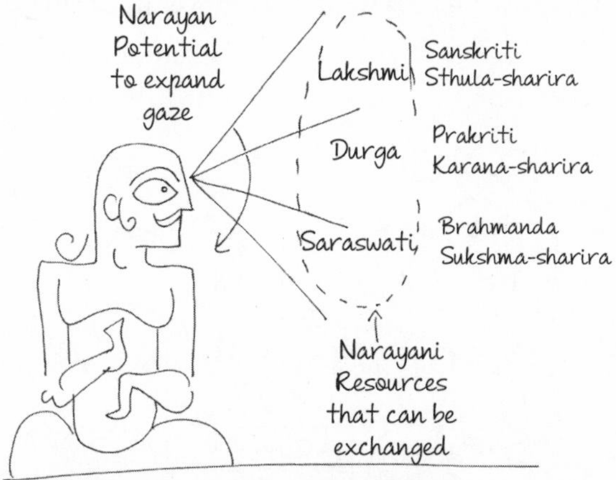

Nick is rich but he does not believe in charity. He does believe in investing though. He keeps investing in high-risk businesses and low-return businesses and is constantly creating opportunities where people can earn and, learn and grow. He does not need to do this. But he does it for fun, and to appreciate his own insecurities and anxieties that reveal themselves with each transaction. The more Nick learns about the world and himself, the more his business skills improve and he attracts more wealth. Even when an investment fails, he smiles, for with it comes more wisdom.

We have to make room for the Other

Animals focus on their hunger alone. They do not pay attention to each other's hunger, except when parenting because they do not have the wherewithal to do so. But humans do; this is also the Narayan potential.

By paying attention to other people's hunger, we get a glimpse of who they are. In other words, realizing the Narayan potential helps us do darshan. When we do darshan of others, we do darshan of ourselves. This makes us realize how much more Narayan potential there is to realize.

Initially, as children following parents, we are all unconditional followers (shudra varna). Gradually, we grow up, are able to shift focus from getting to giving, from being dependent to being dependable. Thus our varna changes. We become aware of our own needs and those of others. We rise from tamas-guna to rajas-guna, from shudra varna to vaishya or kshatriya varna.

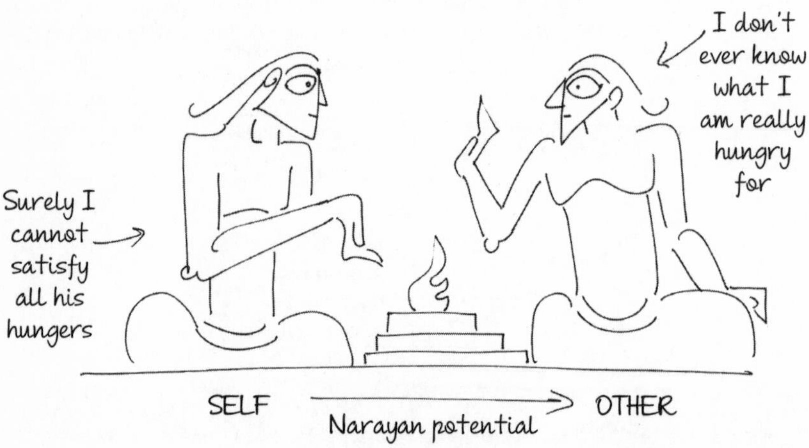

Changing varna is difficult; changing guna seems impossible. We prefer social growth to mental growth. We prefer things to thoughts. We do not trust Narayan's ability to attract Narayani. We would rather grab resources than invest in the potential. This is because at least some resources (Lakshmi) are tangible; potential (Narayan) is totally intangible. The quest for sattva-

guna and brahmana varna is always difficult as along the way we get distracted by what we have or do (jati) and less by who we are and can be.

The Jain vasudev blames the exploitative and tyrannical prati-vasudev for the problems of society; the chakravarti believes upholding the law is the solution to all social problems. In the absence of wisdom, we tend to blame the Other, or seek solutions using external structures like law and wealth. Only the wisdom of the tirthankar reveals how expanding the imagination to include, enable and encourage the Other, brings peace and joy to everyone around.

Ravindra has a Rs. 7,000 crore company that makes spare parts for cars, planes and ships. That is why his peers adore him. But wealth and public adoration is not Ravindra's motivation. All his life he has sought to create an ecosystem that enables people to be entrepreneurs. For those who cannot be entrepreneurs he strives to create jobs. The turnover and profit are just outcomes of this ambition. But when he says this in forums people do not believe him. They would rather believe that greed is his motivation, especially since he prefers investing in businesses rather than engaging in charitable activities. They find all talk of mental growth exotic and all talk of resource growth pragmatic. Discussions on actions and rules excite them; discussions on thought, on the other hand, bore them.

Yagna can be a tool for personal growth, if we allow it to be

Fire's dharma is to burn because that is what it is capable of doing; water's dharma is to flow because that is what it is capable of doing; a plant's dharma is to survive by growing because that is what it is capable of doing; an animal's dharma is to survive by running after food and away from a predator, because that what it capable of doing; humanity's dharma is outgrowing fear by expanding the imagination because that is what it is capable of doing.

By expanding the mind, Brahma can outgrow hunger and fear, and realize the brahman. Humans do not have to compete for resources like plants or dominate the weak like animals; for them to do so is, in fact, adharma.

In mythological terms it means moving from being Daksha ("We must be right") and Indra ("I am right") towards Shiva ("Nobody is right") and Vishnu ("Everyone is right from their point of view but everyone has to face the consequences of their choices.")

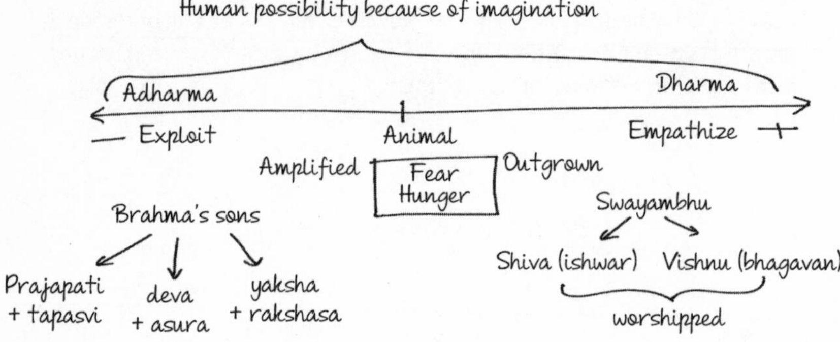

Daksha and Indra are sons of Brahma who get increasingly dependent on the yagna for their identity, while Shiva and Vishnu are swayambhu, increasingly self-reliant and having an identity which is independent of the yagna.

To become swayambhu—dependable, responsible yet autonomous—is dharma for humans. It is the realization of our potential. The alternative is

to keep controlling nature; with control comes conflict—this is adharma. Adharma entraps us in hunger and fear; dharma grants us moksha, or liberation from conflict.

Shiva is called ishwar because his independence is accompanied by indifference for the Other; Vishnu is called bhagavan because although independent, he remains dependable. When Shiva opens his eyes and becomes a householder, he is called Shankar, and he is more like Vishnu. When Vishnu shuts his eyes, and goes to sleep and dreams the dreamless slumber as Narayan, he is more like Shiva.

Most humans are like Indra, seeking returns without investment. Indra needs help and Shiva can help, but neither looks at the Other. Daksha pays more attention to the yagna, than to the yajaman or the devata. Observing this, Vishnu smiles.

In most humans Narayan is asleep, which is why humans are called nara. Only nara can awaken the Narayan within him; no one else can do it for him. At best, the yajaman can provoke through the yagna. This is sanatan, or the timeless truth everyone can see if, like the rishis, we expand our gaze.

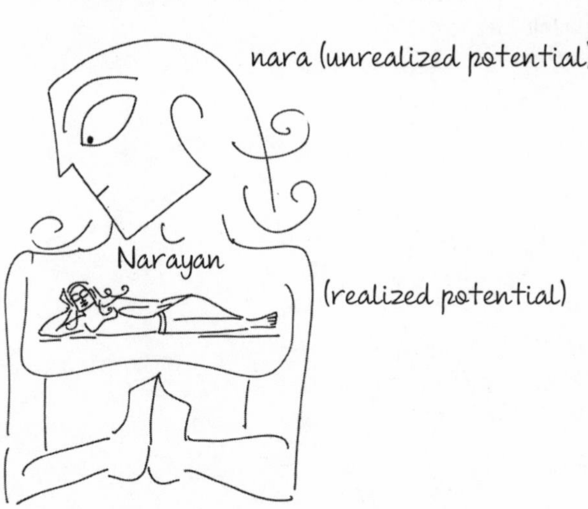

In Buddhist mythology, this idea is expressed as discovering the jewel (mani) by letting the lotus-mind (padma) bloom. In Jain mythology, it is expressed as discovering the tirtha just like the tirthankar. While inquiry into the nature of suffering establishes a Buddha, caring for the other transforms Buddha into Bodhisattva. The idea of the Buddha is celebrated in Theravada, the older school of Buddhism, while the idea of the Bodhisattva is celebrated in Mahayana, the later school of Buddhism.

When Priya reflects on her life, she realizes that with time she has changed. She used to be impatient and demanding, very rigid with her rules. But with time she has allowed herself to be more forgiving of others as well as herself. She is patient with other people's opinions. She does not convince anyone but instead slowly builds a consensus, not because it is the right thing to do but because she believes everyone is right from their point of view and it is a struggle to accommodate another's point of view. How can she expect others to do what took her a long time? Priya has risen in the corporate ladder and is a much sought-after professional; but that social achievement she knows is an outcome of mental maturity. She was once self-absorbed like Indra, then process-driven like Daksha, then withdrawn and wise like Shiva, but now she feels like Vishnu—focused on talent growth. It demanded the awakening of Narayan within her.

Kama's Vision Statement

Drishti, observing objective reality

Decisions *Violence* *Seduction* *Churning*

Divya-drishti, observing subjective reality

Darshan, observing the subject

Yama's Balance Sheet

Pot
Cultural wealth
Shridevi
Help the helpless
Lotus
Natural wealth
Bhudevi
Might is right

The ability to see the human quest for wealth is drishti. Plants grow seeking sunlight and water. Animals run seeking pastures and prey. The fear of starvation makes food the ultimate target or 'laksh'. From laksh comes Lakshmi, the goddess of food, the embodiment of bhog or consumption. Lakshmi is the most primal of hungers; she sustains the physical body, or sthula-sharira.

It is the fear of starvation and the quest for food that makes animals mark territories and organize themselves into pecking orders where the strongest animal in the pack, the alpha, dominates and so gets the most food, increasing his chances of survival, while the weakest, the omega, survives on the leftovers, often turning into food for another predator. It is hunger that makes animals compete.

Humans reject the way of the jungle. Imagination allows Brahma to seek maximum food even if he is weak and powerless. From imagination comes the vision of a world where the helpless are helped and even the unfit can thrive. And so he creates the pot.

While animals have to go to a water body to quench their thirst, humans can drink water whenever and wherever they wish, and give it to whomever they want, thanks to the pot. The pot represents the human capability to innovate. It enables humanity to break free from the constraints of nature.

Lakshmi holds a lotus in one hand and a pot in the other. The lotus represents natural wealth or Bhudevi while the pot represents cultural wealth or Shridevi. The nectar of the lotus is available to whichever bee gets to it first. The contents of the pot, however, are available only to the owner of the pot and to whomsoever the pot is bequeathed. This can never happen in nature. This can only happen in sanskriti.

In Jain mythology, a yajaman who makes pots to convert Bhudevi to Shridevi walks the path of the vasudev, which literally translates to mean 'master of the earth and the elements'. Vasudev is shalaka-purush, a worthy being, an action-driven hero who fights on behalf of his pacifist brother—the baladev—a victim of the prati-vasudev, or the villain.

- Vasudev takes decisions and makes things happen, taking full responsibility for the consequences.
- He knows that without violence the wealth of the earth cannot be drawn out.
- He knows that things need not be done nastily; there is always a nice way to do things.
- He knows how to churn, pull and push, adapt, transform the rigid organization into a nimble organism.

In this chapter, we shall explore decisions, violence, seduction and churning and by doing so appreciate the vasudev's gaze. A yajaman who possesses drishti and seeks Lakshmi, walks the path of the vasudev. A vasudev's gaze is that of the passionate entrepreneur who appreciates the elusive nature of wealth.

Mandeep can see an opportunity. The new bus stop will attract a lot of people. And people need tea and snacks. Opening a tea stall next to the bus stop will allow him to be independent. He has slaved at a tea stall in the station for years and knows what it takes to run such an enterprise. All he needs is some money and the support of local authorities. He will need to charm a few people for capital, seek favours from others and force his way to realize his dream. His boss will not be supportive but if he gets the backing of the local don, no one can stop him. The police may harass him, but even they need tea. Mandeep is a vasudev, unafraid of a fight, determined to create the pot that will harness Lakshmi.

Decisions

Key to the yagna is the decision: the willingness to pour svaha into the fire. Once poured, it cannot be pulled back. Not everyone takes decisions. Few want to be responsible for the escalating cost and the unpredictable consequences of an investment. Humans are the only living creatures who can, and do, outsource decision-making.

He who takes a call is a karta

In the epic Ramayan, Sita finds herself in a predicament. She is alone in the middle of the forest. Her husband, Ram, and brother-in-law, Lakshman, are away on a hunt. A line has been drawn around her hut. She has been told very clearly that only within the line do the laws of culture apply; here she is Ram's wife. Outside is nature, where the rules of marriage make no sense; she is just a woman for the taking.

A hermit standing outside the line asks for some food. She invites him in but he refuses explaining that as she is alone it would be inappropriate for him to enter. She stretches her hand over the line and offers him food. This annoys the hermit. He demands she step outside and feed him properly.

Must she or must she not? If she does step out, she brings her family honour by being a good host, but she takes a huge risk as she makes herself vulnerable. If she does not, she protects herself but condemns a hermit to hunger. What matters more: hospitality or security?

Sita steps out.

Had she obeyed her husband without any thought, she would have been the karya-karta, or the obedient follower, and he the karta, or the responsible leader. But the instructions were given to her in a context very different from the one she encountered; there was no hungry hermit then. Now a hungry hermit stood outside the hut; would Ram have allowed a hermit to starve to secure his wife?

Sita chooses to take a call. She is not obliged to, yet she takes the responsibility upon herself. That proactivity transforms her into a karta, a doer, regardless of the fact that her decision did not serve her well. The hermit turns out to be the rakshasa-king, Ravan, who abducts her.

To build a business, we need decision-makers and decision-followers. He who takes decisions is the karta. He who follows decisions is called a karya-karta.

After the interview, Mahmood asks Rajiv, the head of his human resource department, to stay back. They are about to select the Chief Operating Officer for the telecom division of the business. Mahmood is anxious. It is a huge risk, hiring a foreigner with no experience of India. To retain him, they have to assure him a golden parachute: compensation should the company terminate the contract before the stipulated three years. But Hugh, who has been selected, has knowledge the company desperately needs. "Will it work?" Mahmood asks. Rajiv keeps quiet. There are no guarantees. Only time will tell. Ultimately, the boss has to decide. Rajiv will diligently obey. Mahmood is the karta and Rajiv is the karya-karta.

Every one is a potential karta

The mind of every human being can be compared to the mythic serpent Adi-Ananta-Sesha whose name translated literally means One-Infinity-Zero. Narayan sleeps in the coils of this serpent. Vishnu sits on it. Sesha, the coiled hoodless state, is like a dormant mind that does not think or take a decision. Ananta, the state with infinite unfurled hoods, is like a mind full of ideas. Adi, the state with a single hood, is like a focused mind, ready to strike; this is the mind of the karta.

Animals take decisions all the time. Only humans have the option not to take decisions. We can outsource decision-making to the karta and stay a karya-karta. We may even choose not to follow the decisions of a karta, like an impudent devata who needs to be cajoled or forced into action. When we choose to help others take decisions, we transform into yajamans. A yajaman is a karta too; but all kartas are not yajamans.

Thus humans have a choice to be proactive like a decision-making karta or a decision-enabling yajaman. We also have a choice to be reactive like a decision-following karya-karta or a reluctant devata.

We can let the serpent of the mind stay coiled or spring out its many hoods. Only we can make it strike.

Yajaman encourages others to decide
↑
Karta decides
↑
Karya-karta obeys
↑
Devata can obey

Proactive (Yajaman, Karta)
Reactive (Karya-karta, Devata)
Brahma (all)

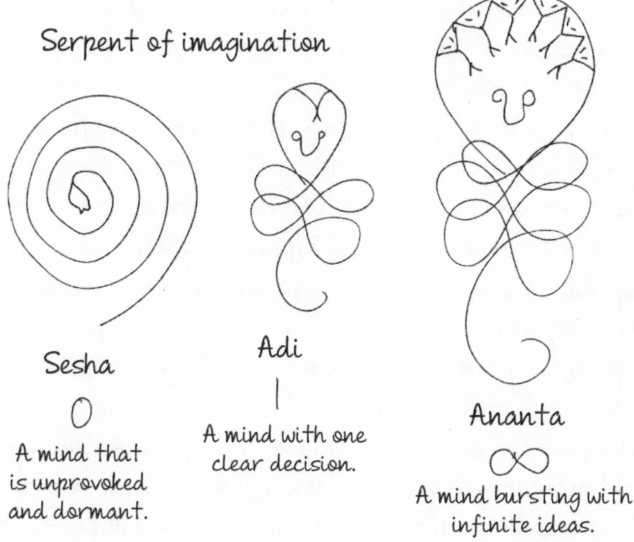

When the customer walks into the shop and Babulal does not engage with him, it is the Sesha state of slumber when no exchange take place. When the customer makes a request and Babulal reacts immediately; thus does Sesha turn into Adi. Babulal can return to the Sesha state or stir Ananta in the customer by a simple question, "Anything else you wish to buy?" This one question provokes thoughts and ideas in the customers' mind, infinite ideas are unfurled, and there is a possibility of more business.

A karta who allows and enables others to take a call is a yajaman

One day, the sage Narad asks Vishnu, with a bit of hesitation, "Why do you insist that the image of Garud be placed before you in your temples? Why not me? Am I not your greatest devotee?"

Before Vishnu can reply a crash is heard outside the main gate of Vaikuntha. "What was that?" asks Vishnu. Garud, Vishnu's eagle and vehicle, who usually investigates such events, is nowhere to be seen. "I have sent Garud on an errand. Can you find out what happened, Narad?" asks Vishnu. Eager to please Vishnu, Narad runs out to investigate. "A milkmaid tripped and fell," he says when he returns.

"What was her name?" asks Vishnu. Narad runs out, speaks to the maid and returns with the answer, "Sharda."

"Where was she going?" asks Vishnu. Narad runs out once again, speaks to the maid and returned with the answer, "She was on her way to the market."

"What caused her to trip?" asks Vishnu. "Why did you not ask this question the last time I went?" mumbles Narad irritably. He then runs out, speaks to the maid once again. "She was startled by a serpent that crossed her path," he says on his return. "Anything else?" he asks.

"Are all her pots broken?" asks Vishnu. "I don't know," snaps Narad. "Find out," insists Vishnu. "Why?" asks Narad. "Find out, Narad. Maybe I would like to buy some milk," says Vishnu patiently. With great reluctance, Narad steps out of Vaikuntha and meets the milkmaid. He returns looking rather pleased, "She broke one pot. But there is another one intact. And she is willing to sell the milk but at double price."

"So how much should I pay her?" asks Vishnu. "Oh, I forgot to ask. I am so sorry," says Narad running out once again. "Do not bother. Let me send someone else," says Vishnu.

Just then, Garud flies in. He has no idea of what has transpired between Vishnu and Narad. Vishnu tells Garud, "I heard a crashing sound outside the main gate. Can you find out what happened?" As Garud leaves, Vishnu whispers, "Let us see how he fares."

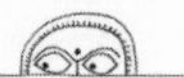

Garud returns and says, "It is a milkmaid called Sharda. She was on her way to the market. On the way, a snake crossed her path. Startled she fell down and broke one of the two pots of milk she was carrying. Now she wonders how she will make enough money to pay for the broken pot and the spilt milk. I suggested she sell the milk to you. After all, you are married to Lakshmi, the goddess of wealth."

"And the price of the milk?" asks Vishnu. Pat comes Garud's reply, "Four copper coins. One actually but I think she hopes to make a handsome profit when dealing with God." Vishnu starts to laugh. Garud always anticipates situations and takes calls accordingly without checking with his boss or master. In that micro-context, he behaves as karta.

Vishnu's eye caught Narad's and Narad understood in that instant why Garud's statue, and not his was always placed before the image of Vishnu in Vishnu temples.

Despite being given the freedom to take decisions, Narad chooses to stay karya-karta, follow decisions rather than take them, as he is too afraid of the consequences. Garud, on the other hand, anticipates the needs of Vishnu, decides to enquire voluntarily and is thus a karta. Vishnu who allows Garud to be a karta is a yajaman.

Arindam realizes the value of Meena as a team member over Ralph. Both are good workers. But when Arindam has to go for a meeting with Meena, she gives him a file with all relevant details about the client so that he can prepare well. Ralph will do no such thing. When Arindam points this out, Ralph says, "Is that the process? Do you want me to do that? I will do that, no problem." Arindam realizes that Ralph is no Garud.

A yajaman has the power to take and give life

The sage Vishwamitra storms into the kingdom of Ayodhya and demands that the crown prince Ram accompany him to the forest and defend his hermitage from rakshasas. King Dashrath offers his army instead, as he feels Ram is too young, but Vishwamitra insists on taking Ram. With great reluctance, Dashrath lets Ram go.

In the forest, Vishwamitra points to Tataka, the female leader of the rakshasas, and asks that she be killed. When Ram hesitates because he has been taught never to raise his hand against a woman, Vishwamitra argues that a criminal has no gender. Ram accordingly raises his bow and shoots Tataka dead.

Later, Vishwamitra shows Ram a stone that was once Ahalya, the wife of Gautama, cursed to become so after her husband caught her in an intimate embrace with Indra. Vishwamitra asks Ram to step on the stone and liberate the adulteress. When Ram hesitates because he has been taught the rules of marriage should always be respected, Vishwamitra argues that forgiveness is as much a part of marriage as fidelity. Ram accordingly places his feet on the stone and sets Ahalya free from her curse.

Ram, well-versed in theory, is thus given practical lessons about being a yajaman: he will be asked to take life as well as give life. At times, he will be expected to be ruthless. At other times, he will be expected to be kind.

In business, the yajaman has the power to give a person a livelihood, grant him a promotion, sideline him or even fire him. These decisions have a huge impact on the lives of the devatas who depend on the business.

One day, Jake is asked by his boss to fire an incompetent employee. While the reasons are justified, Jake finds it the toughest thing to do. He has several nights of anxiety before he can actually do it. Then, a few weeks later, Jake is asked to mentor a junior employee who has been rejected by the head of another department. This is even tougher as the junior employee is rude and lazy and impossible to work with. Jake struggles and finally succeeds in getting work done through the junior employee. Jake does not realize it but his boss is being a Vishwamitra mentoring a future king.

The size of the contribution does not matter

To rescue Sita, Ram raises an army of animals and gets them to build a bridge across the sea to the island-kingdom of Lanka where Sita is being held captive by the rakshasa-king Ravan.

Vultures survey the location. Bears serve as the architects. Monkeys work on implementing the construction, carrying huge boulders and throwing them into the sea. The work is tedious. The monkeys are jumping and screeching everywhere to ensure everything is being done efficiently and effectively. Suddenly, there appears amongst them a tiny squirrel carrying a pebble.

This little creature also wants to contribute to the bridge-building exercise. The monkeys who see him laugh. One even shoves the squirrel aside considering him an overenthusiastic nuisance.

But when Ram glances at the squirrel, he is overwhelmed with gratitude. He thanks the tiny creature for his immense contribution. He brushes his fingers over the squirrel's back to comfort him, giving rise to the stripes that can be seen even today, a sign of Ram's acknowledgment of his contribution.

In terms of proportion, the squirrel's contribution to the bridge is insignificant. But it is the squirrel's 100 per cent. The squirrel is under no obligation to help Ram, but he does, proactively, responsibly, expecting nothing in return. Ram values the squirrel not for his percentage of contribution to the overall project but because he recognizes a yajaman. A squirrel today, can be a Ram tomorrow.

Proportions or matra play a key role in Indian philosophy. The scale of a problem has nothing to with the potential of the decision-maker. A kupamanduka, or frog in a well, and a chakravarti, or emperor of the world, are no different from each other, except in terms of scale. Both their visions are limited by the frontier of the land they live in. In case of the frog, it is the wall of the well. In case of the king, it is the borders of his kingdom. Both can be, in their respective contexts, generous or prejudiced. To expand scale, both have to rise.

> Whenever Mr. Lal goes to his factory, he makes sure he speaks to people at all levels, from workers to supervisors to managers to accountants to security people. He is not interested in finding out who did the job well or who did not. That, he feels, is the job of managers. He is only interested in identifying people in the factory who take proactive steps to solve a problem. He consciously seeks decision-makers, like the executive who prepared a report on waste management without being asked to, or the supervisor who voluntarily motivated his team to clean the toilets when the housekeeping staff went on strike. For Mr. Lal these 'squirrels' who take responsibility are talents to be nurtured.

All calls are subjective

The *Kathasaritsagar* tells the story of a sorcerer who requests Vikramaditya, king of Ujjain, to fetch him a vetal or ghost that hangs upside down like a bat from a tree standing in the middle of a crematorium. "Make sure you do not talk to the vetal; if you speak, he will slip away from your grasp," warns the sorcerer.

Vikramaditya enters the crematorium, finds the tree, and the vetal hanging upside down from its branches. He catches the ghost, pulls it down and begins make his way back to the city when the ghost starts chatting with him, telling him all kinds of things, annoying him, yelling into his years, cursing him, praising him, anything to make him speak but Vikramaditya refuses to succumb to these tricks.

Finally, the vetal tells Vikramaditya a story (a case study?), and at the end of it asks the king a question. "If you answer this question, then you are indeed Vikramaditya, a king, a yajaman who thinks and takes decisions. But if you stay quiet, and simply follow orders, you are no Vikramaditya. You are a pretender, a mere karya-karta, who simply follows orders."

Vikramaditya cannot bear being called a pretender or a karya-karta. So he speaks and answers the question with a brilliant answer. The vetal gasps in admiration.

However, almost immediately after that the wily ghost slips away, cackling without pause and goes back to hanging upside down from the tree in the crematorium.

The next night, Vikramaditya walks back to the tree and once again pulls the vetal down. The vetal tells him another story with a question at the end. Once again the vetal tells the king, "If you are indeed the wise Vikramaditya, as you claim to be, you should be able to judge this case. So answer my question. And if you choose to stay silent, I am free to assume I have been caught by a commoner, a pretender, a mimic!" Once again the proud king gives the answer to which the vetal gasps in admiration. And once again he slips away with a cackle.

This happens twenty-four times. The twenty-fifth time, a tired and exasperated Vikramaditya, sighs in relief. He has succeeded.

"Have you really?" asks the vetal, "How do you know the answers you gave the previous times were right? All answers are right or wrong only in hindsight. You made decisions because you thought they were right. The answer would have been subjective this time, too. Only now, you are not sure of the answer, you hesitate, and so remain silent. This silence will cost you dear. You will succeed in taking me to the sorcerer who will use his magic to make me his genie and do his bidding. His first order for me will be to kill you. So you see, Vikramaditya, as long as you were karta, taking calls, you were doing yourself a favour. As soon as you stop making your own decisions, stop being a karta, you are at the mercy of others and you are sure to end up dead."

Everyone looks at the karta for a decision despite data being unreliable, the future being uncertain, and outcomes that are unpredictable. Not everyone can do it. He who is able to make decisions independently is the karta. He who allows others to do so is the yajaman.

The investors are chasing Deepak. He built an online coaching class of engineering students that was bought by a large educational portal for a phenomenal amount. Now the investors expect Deepak to repeat this success. Deepak is filled with self-doubt. He is not sure what it was about the website he built that made it so valuable in the eyes of the buyers. Was it just luck? Since he does not know what made him successful, how can he repeat the success. There was nothing objective about his creation. Must he follow his gut instincts again? But the investors will not allow him to do so; their auditors will keep asking him for explanations and reasons, assuming his calls are rational. And the media, which celebrated the sale, is watching his every move continuously. He is a victim of success. How he wishes he never became an entrepreneur. How he wishes he could roll back the clock, be a simple engineer working in a factory, diligently doing what the boss tells him to do.

All decisions are contextual

Amongst the twenty-five stories that the vetal told Vikramaditya, this is one: a king killed a merchant and laid claim to all his property. The merchant's widow fled the kingdom swearing revenge. She seduced a priest and was impregnated by him. She abandoned the son thus born at the door of a childless king who adopted the foundling and raised him as his own. "Who is the father of this child: the merchant who was married to his mother, the priest who made his mother pregnant or the king who adopted him?"

Vikramaditya replies with the caveat that the answer would depend on the culture to which the king belongs. In some cultures only biological fathers matter, in some, legal fathers matter and in others, foster fathers matter more. There is no objective answer in matters related to humans.

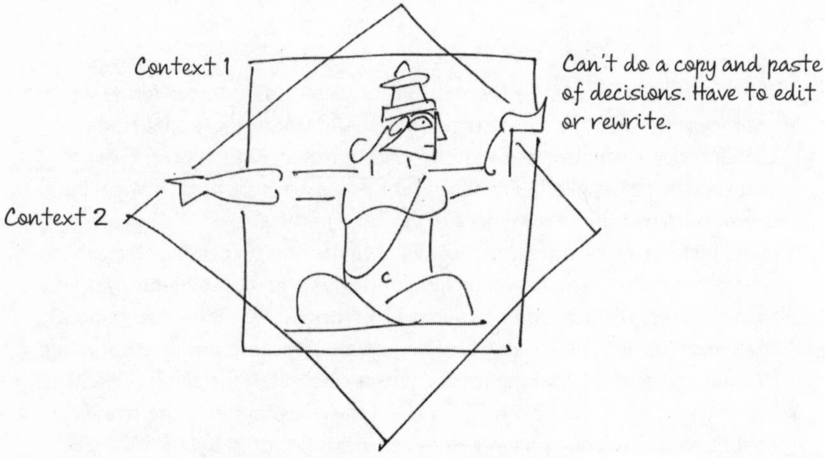

In the Mahabharat, Pandu is called the father of the Pandavs even though he is not their actual biological father. The law of the land states that a man is the father of his wife's children. The Pandavs demand a share of Pandu's kingdom on the basis of this law. Is this law the right law? At Kurukshetra, the Pandavs kill Bhisma, the man who raised them as a foster father would, because he fights on the opposing side. Is that ethical? In the Ramayan, Ram

is celebrated for being faithful to one wife, yet in the Mahabharat, men have many wives and the Pandavs even share a common wife. What is appropriate conduct?

Laws by their very nature are arbitrary and depend on context. What one community considers fair, another may not consider to be fair. What is considered fair by one generation is not considered fair by the next. Rules always change in times of war and in times of peace, as they do in times of fortune and misfortune.

Thus, no decision is right or wrong. Decisions can be beneficial or harmful, in the short-term or long-term, to oneself or to others. Essentially, every decision has a consequence, no matter which rule is upheld and which one is ignored. This law of consequence is known as karma.

Mr. Gupta has to choose a successor. Should it be his eldest son who is not very shrewd? Should it be the second son who is smart but not interested in the business? Must it be his daughter, who feels gender should not be a criterion, but who fails to realize she is not really that smart? Should it be his brilliant son-in-law, who does not belong to the community which will annoy a lot of shareholders? Must the decision be based on emotion, equality, fairness, loyalty, or the growth of the business and shareholder value? Each and every answer will have opponents. Must he simply divide the business before he dies for the sake of peace or let his two sons and daughter fight it out in court after his death? There is no right answer, he realizes. Traditionally, in the community, the eldest son inherited everything. That was convenient but often disastrous. Mr. Gupta does not want to impress the community; he wants his legacy to outlive him. He also wants all his children to be happy. His desires impact the decision as much as the context.

Not everyone can handle the burden of uncertainty

One day, Bhartrihari receives a jewel from a traveller who is visiting his kingdom. "Only a king such as you is worthy of possessing it," says the traveller.

That night, the king gives the jewel to his beloved queen because he feels she is more worthy of it.

The next day, to his great surprise, he finds the same jewel in a basket full of dung being carried by the lady who cleans the stables.

On being questioned, the cleaning lady says it has been given to her by her lover, the man who grooms the royal horses. When the groom is accused of theft, he reveals it is a gift from a nymph who visits him every night in the stables. The king decides to investigate.

The following night, Bhartrihari hides in the stables and realizes that the 'nymph' is none other than his beloved queen! Blinded by love, he does not see that his wife loves another man and she does not see that the man she finds attractive cares for another woman.

After this incident, the king is unable to take any decisions. He doubts everything he sees. Uncertainty paralyzes him. He trusts no one. In despair, he decides to become a hermit and give up his throne to his younger brother, Vikramaditya.

Bhartrihari has to confront the horror of human existence. We can never know everything and we can never be sure. All information is incomplete, and all readings distorted by personal prejudice. And yet we have to take decisions all the time and hope the results favour us. Bhartrihari feels powerless. He is unable to conduct the yagna and passes on the reins of his kingdom to his younger brother, Vikramaditya.

While everyone has the potential of being a karta or a yajaman, not everyone is willing to take decisions and be responsible for the outcome. We would rather be devata (reactive) than yajaman (proactive).

Madhukar, head of marketing, recommends that Arshiya be made the head of corporate communications. Soon after her promotion, Arshiya begins to behave very differently. She becomes more arrogant and imperious. She is no longer as gentle or as kind. Madhukar realizes that as long as Arshiya reported to him, she behaved very nicely. Now that she reports directly to the managing director, she is not obliged to be nice. Madhukar realizes that the data on the basis of which he made the recommendation was false. He decides to never again recommend anyone for a job or promotion. Ergo, he will never be a yajaman again.

Does she really love me?
Does she pretend to love me?
Does she love her idea of me?
Does he love what I have?

Every decision has a consequence

In the Ramayan, Dashrath shoots an arrow in the direction of a sound that he believes to be the sound of deer drinking water. It turns out to be the sound of water being collected in a pot. The arrow fatally injures the young man who was fetching the water. The young man is Shravan. His old and blind parents do not see this event as an accident. They see it as murder. They curse Dashrath to, like them, die of heartbreak following separation from his son.

In the Mahabharat, Pandu shoots an arrow at a deer, not realizing that it is copulating with a doe, and that it is, in fact, no deer but a sage called Kindama who has taken the form of a deer, along with his wife, in order to mate in the open air. Kindama curses Pandu that should he touch a woman and try to have sex with her, he will die instantly. As a result, Pandu cannot father children. He feels he is unfit to be king as he will never father an heir. So he renounces the throne and stays in the jungle, choosing to be a hermit, a decision that takes everyone in the palace by surprise.

The notion of karma is unique to Indian thought. No action exists in isolation. Every decision impacts the ecosystem. Karma is often mistaken for the adage, "As you sow, so shall you reap." The assumption then is that if we sow good deeds, we will reap good rewards. But who decides what action is good or bad? The desire to qualify an action, and its consequence, as good or bad, right or wrong, is a peculiarly human trait. Nature does not do so.

Action impacts the self, the people around and the environment at large. Every person is impacted at three levels: the physical level, the mental level and the social level. Thus, a tiny ripple can result in a storm, and the ripple-causer needs to take responsibility for it.

An arrow that has been released from the bow is a metaphor for a decision that cannot be withdrawn. It has consequences that a yajaman has to face. There is no escape. This is a heavy burden to bear.

For years, they manufactured automobile parts. But when Ritwik decides they should open service centres for luxury cars, the whole family opposes him. "Do it with your own money!" his brother says. So Ritwik uses his own money and investments. If he succeeds, the profits are his alone. He will prove once and for all that he is smarter than the rest of his family. If he fails, he will have to face the double humiliation of being a business failure and being told by his family, "We told you so." If Ritwik chooses to listen to his family, he will have to spend the rest of his life wondering about all the things that could have happened if only he had had the guts to take a risk. There is no escape from consequences.

Decisions are good or bad only in hindsight

Garud, the eagle, is enjoying the song of a sparrow atop Mount Kailas when he observes Yama, the god of death, also looking at the bird. But Yama is frowning. Maybe he does not like the song. Fearing for the welfare of the little bird, Garud, with compassion in his heart, decides to take the bird away from Yama's line of sight.

Garud takes the bird in the palm of his hand and flies to a forest far away, beyond the seven mountains and seven rivers. There, he leaves the sparrow on a tree full of succulent fruits. When he returns to Mount Kailas, he finds Yama smiling. Yama explains, "My account books are balanced. I saw a sparrow here singing a song. It is supposed to die today but not here. It is supposed to die in a forest far beyond the seven mountains and seven rivers, eaten by a python that lives under a tree full of succulent fruits. This has happened, thanks to you, Garud."

Garud realizes in hindsight that what he thought was an act of kindness turned out to be an act of cruelty for the sparrow.

When strategies are made it is in the hope that they will minimize surprises. Huge amounts of time are taken to ensure the data and, the analysis is right so that the results are predictable. As organizations grow larger, the cost of mistakes is higher, and so much more time and energy is taken while taking decisions. And yet, despite all precautions, things can and do go wrong, often because assumptions are incorrect. A yajaman needs to take this in his stride.

A yajaman needs to be defined not by the outcome, achievement, goal or performance, but by his ability to take decisions proactively and responsibly.

It seemed like the right thing to do at the time: leaving the job and starting out on his own. Parul thought that the clients would love to have the same work done at a lower cost by a freelance consultant. But when she started visiting clients she realized there were more freelance consultants than she had anticipated. The competition was fierce. So she started offering outsourcing services. And suddenly, she found herself much in demand and the owner of a thriving business. Her husband said that resigning from the consulting firm was the best thing she had done. But Parul knows that she left to be a consultant and had never dreamed she would become an entrepreneur. This was not a future she had planned or anyone had predicted. She is not sure if what has happened is good or bad.

Decisions are often rationalized in hindsight

In the battlefield of Kurukshetra, when Bhisma sees Shikhandi standing on Krishna's chariot, he lowers his bow. Taking advantage of this, Arjun who is standing behind Shikhandi lets loose a volley of arrows that pins Bhisma to the ground. Even though the great general of the Kaurav army cannot be killed, Arjun has managed to incapacitate him, increasing the chances of Pandav victory.

The Kauravs protest: the rules were breached, Shikhandi was a woman and no woman is allowed on the battlefield.

The Pandavs insist Shikhandi is a man: he was born with a female body but later in life, due to the intervention of a yaksha called Sthuna, had obtained male genitalia. Does that make Shikhandi a man or a woman? Is Bhisma wrong to assume Shikhandi is a woman? Is Arjun right to assume Shikhandi is a man? Since the outcome benefits the Pandavs, we can say Arjun's call is right, but the answer is anything but objective.

At the time of action, our decision is based on a set of assumptions. The assumptions may be wrong. Leaders have to constantly deal with uncertainty, give hope to the people even when nothing is clear. Decisions become good or bad in hindsight. We would like to believe that a decision is rational. More often than not, decisions are rationalized.

Often in business we take decisions based on how we interpret the situation, not being sure of whether the call we have taken will work or not. When it works, we are often taken by surprise. But the world at large demands an explanation. We are expected to prove that our decisions were strategic, not simply a fluke. To say that a certain victory was a fluke makes us nervous. Corporations reject this. Once the numbers come, the manager has to spend hours creating a story rationalizing his action so that everything looks as if it were part of a pre-conceived plan.

As the head of research and development, Dr. Sulabha prepares various types of snacks that the company then promotes in the market. Some succeed, some do not. Some become very successful. Each time the management asks Dr. Sulabha to give reasons why she feels a particular snack will be very successful and why they should invest in that product's development. She feels there is no one, except maybe a fortune-teller, who could actually give the right answer, but she is compelled to come up with satisfactory logic to comfort the management and ensure she gets funds, and keeps her job. At conferences she is often called to speak about her successful creations and the audience loves it when she tells them how she observed customer behaviour and strategized a product that eventually became a winner. The lectures would not be a hit if she were thanking providence or intuition for her best-selling snacks.

If the decision is bad, the yajaman alone is responsible

A sage once asks a thief, "Why are you stealing?"

The thief replies, "I am poor. I need to feed my family. There is no other employment. I am desperate."

"Will your family bear the burden of your crime?"

"Of course, they will," Suddenly, not so sure of his own response, the thief decides to check. He asks his wife and son if they would bear the burden of his crimes and they reply, "Why? It is your duty to feed us. How you feed us is your problem not ours."

The thief feels shattered and alone. The sage then tells the thief, who is Valmiki, the story of Ram, as told in the Ramayan and compares and constrasts it with the story of the Pandavs from the Mahabharat.

Ram is exiled from Ayodhya for no fault of his, following the palace intrigues of his stepmother Kaikeyi. In the Mahabharat, the five Pandav brothers are exiled because they gamble away their kingdom, Indraprastha. In the Ramayan, Ram's exile lasts fourteen years. In the Mahabharat, it is an exile of thirteen years. In the Ramayan, there is no guarantee that at the end of the exile, Ram will be crowned king. In the Mahabharat, however, the Kauravs promise to return the Pandav lands on completion of the latter's exile.

While it is his father's request that he go to the forest, it is ultimately Ram's decision whether to obey his father or not. He decides to obey. He is no karya-karta to his father. He is a yajaman. He is never shown complaining or blaming Kaikeyi but is rather visualized as being stoic and calm throughout. In contrast, the Pandavs blame the Kauravs and their uncle Shakuni and are visualized as angry and miserable, even though they agree to the terms of their exile. They are compelled to obey the rules. Yudhishtir cannot bear the burden of being a yajaman, and agrees to play a game of dice, which costs him his kingdom, while his brothers assume the role of reluctant karya-kartas.

For Ram, Kaikeyi is no villain; he is no victim and certainly not a hero. A hero is provoked into action. A yajaman needs no provocation to act. Provocation makes action a reaction, turns a yajaman into a devata and a karta into a karya-karta. A yajaman takes his own decision. Ram has chosen to accept

his exile. He could have defied the wishes of his father, and taken control of the throne, but he chose to obey. He takes ownership of his exile. The Pandavs constantly see their exile as an unfair punishment, a burden they are forced to bear. Perhaps that is why Ram (and not the Pandavs) is enshrined in temples.

A yajaman is one who does not blame anyone for any situation. He knows that his fortune and misfortune are dependent on many forces. Besides his knowledge, skills, experience and his power of anticipation, a lot depends on the talent of people around him—the market conditions and regulatory environment. He simply takes charge of whatever situation he is in, focusing on what he can do, never letting the anxiety of failure pull him back, or the confidence of success make him smug.

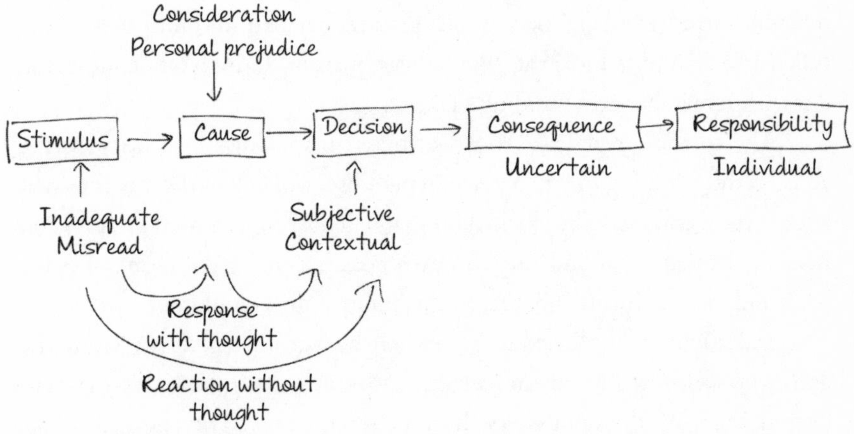

Upon the completion of their course in college, there is placement week. Jaideep gets two offers: one from an investment banking firm in New York and one from a leading trading firm in India. Jaideep chooses the job in New York, but the moment he lands there, news of recession fills Wall Street. Companies are forced to shut down or downsize. Jaideep finds himself without a job. As he flies back to Mumbai, he is angry and anxious. But he keeps reminding himself: it is his decision; no one forced him into the choice he made. He realizes that being a yajaman is tough.

If the decision is good, the yajaman is the beneficiary

There is a king called Indradyumna, who after death goes to paradise to enjoy the rewards of his good deeds on earth. But, one day, he is told by the gods to leave paradise. He can come back only if he finds at least one person on earth who recounts his great deeds.

When Indradyumna reaches earth, he realizes that centuries have passed since his reign. The trees are different, the people are different, even his kingdom looks different. The city and temple he built no longer stand. No one remembers him. He visits the oldest man on earth, and goes to the oldest bird, but neither of them recall him. Finally, he goes to the tortoise, who is older than the oldest man and the oldest bird and the tortoise says he remembers Indradyumna because his grandfather had told him that a king called Indradyumna built the lake he was born in. Indradyumna, however, does not remember ever building a lake.

The tortoise explains, "You distributed many cows in charity during your lifetime, hoping to win a place in paradise, which you did. As the cows left the royal cowshed, they kicked up so much dust they created a depression which collected water and turned into a lake, becoming the home of many birds and, fishes, worms and, finally, the home of my grandfather."

Indradyumna is pleased to hear what the tortoise has to say. So are the gods who welcome Indradyumna back to paradise. As Indradyumna rises to heaven, the irony does not escape him: he is remembered on earth for a lake that was unconsciously created, and not for the cows that were consciously given. He benefits not from his decisions but from the unknown consequences of his decisions.

Making decisions is not all gloom. It also yields positive results, sometimes even unexpected windfalls. Just as the yajaman is responsible for negative consequences, he has a right over positive consequences. It is this hope of unexpected positive consequences that often drives a yajaman.

Harish-saheb's factory provided a livelihood to Suresh who was able to give a decent education to his two sons, one of whom went on to become a doctor. Suresh was always grateful to Harish-saheb because before the factory was set up in the small town where he lived, he had been unemployed for over a year. When his son builds a hospital, Suresh insists that it be named after that 'giver of cows'—Harish-saheb. The Harish Nursing Home that serves the local community is, in this allegory, Indradyumna's lake. Harish-saheb's factory is long gone, replaced by a shopping mall.

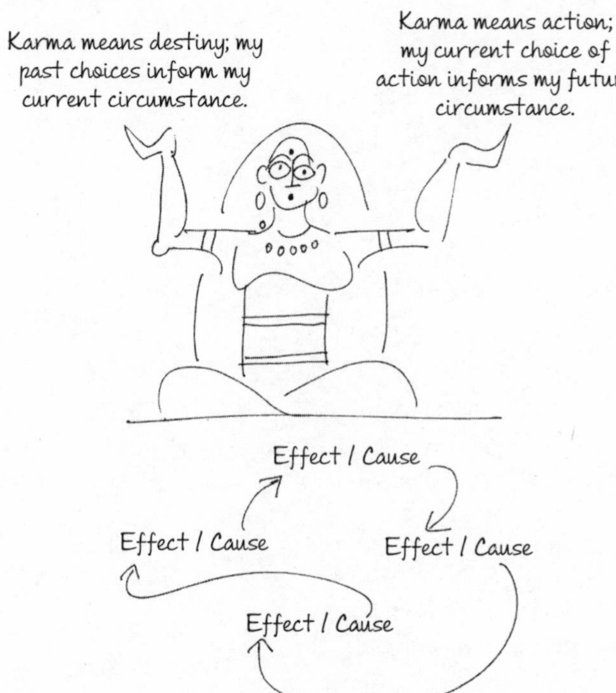

Violence

Without violence, there is no nourishment. Unless the mineral is consumed, the plant cannot grow. Unless the plant is consumed, the animal cannot grow. Physical growth demands the consumption of another. Only mental growth is possible without consuming another; but it is a choice humans rarely make.

Business is violent

In the Mahabharat, the Pandav brothers inherit a forest, Khandavprastha, and want to build on it a great city, named Indraprastha, the city of Indra. So Krishna says, "Burn the forest. Set aflame every plant, every animal, every bird and every bee." When the Pandavs express their horror at the suggestion, Krishna says, "Then do not dream of a city."

Humans have the choice of outgrowing hunger like Shiva, or indulging hunger like Brahma. When we choose the latter, forests have to be cleared to make way for fields, and mountains have to be bored into to get to the minerals. The bull has to be castrated and turned into an ox, to serve as a beast of burden. The spirit of the wild horse has to be broken if it has to be ridden. Each of these actions has a consequence. This is violence and like all actions, even violence has consequences.

Culture is essentially domesticated nature. Different groups of humans have domesticated nature differently.

In Hindu mythology, the wild, naked and bloodthirsty goddess Kali and the gentle, demure and domestic goddess Gauri are one and the same. The former embodies the forest. The latter embodies the field. The former embodies prakriti. The latter embodies sanskriti. In between stands Brahma, performing the yagna that tames the wild and lays down the rules of man. Kali is the mother who existed before Brahma and his yagna. Gauri is the daughter, a consequence of Brahma's desire, forged by his yagna. Kali creates Brahma; Brahma creates and controls Gauri. He wants her to be obedient.

Humans have been constantly finding new and innovative ways of controlling nature. First it was the agricultural revolution. Then it was the industrial revolution. All these are violent attempts to gain more and more resources to satisfy the ever-increasing demands of humanity.

With each economic revolution, something has been sacrificed. The agricultural revolution had a negative impact on the lives of tribals who lived in forests and nomads who wandered freely over land. The industrial revolution displaced farmers, made them landless workers in factories and cities. The knowledge revolution means that jobs are being outsourced to foreign lands, benefitting the rich in the homeland, at the cost of the poor.

Violence is an intrinsic part of nature. In nature, animals kill plants and animals in order to survive. Animals compete with each other to survive. Humans have the ability to create a culture that can survive and thrive without needing to kill or compete. But this is not the path that is taken. Using force and fire, we tame nature. We expect Kali to turn into Gauri without resistance, but when she demands that Brahma turn into Vishnu, we mock her. In other words, we want to change the outer world (nature and society) rather than the inner world (mind). So long as we are not the victims of violence, we do not mind being the perpetrators of that violence. This is the human condition.

When Raymond bought a house in the suburbs ten years ago, he had a clear view of the sea and the mountains. But today his view is blocked by huge buildings, malls, roads and office complexes. He hates it. But then his wife pointed out, "Before our housing society was built I am sure there was a beautiful meadow here full of birds and butterflies. Someone would have been upset that a house was built here. But thanks to that decision by the builder, you and I have a home. Are you willing to sacrifice your house for the environment? Just as you wanted a house, other people also want a house and a job and so for them new houses, offices and roads have to be built. As long as society wants development, we have to be willing to sacrifice the environment. Everything has a price."

Violence is not always apparent

Manu gives a tiny fish shelter in his pot, determined to save it from the big fish. As the days pass, the fish in Manu's pot keeps growing bigger and so Manu builds bigger pots to accommodate it. A point comes when the fish is so big that it has to be put in a pond, then a lake, then a river, and finally, the sea. The fish keeps growing and so to expand the sea, Manu asks the rain to fall. The rising sea causes flooding. The earth starts getting submerged beneath the waters. This is Pralay, the end of culture, the end of humanity, the end of all organic life.

Manu does not see the inherent violence in the creation of the pot. By saving the small fish he was denying the big fish their food. Another small fish was killed in place of the one rescued. The small fish does not stay small forever. It keeps growing. By seeking resources to provide for the ever-growing fish, he was destroying nature. At no point does Manu think the big fish can fend for itself. In trying to expand the pot to satisfy the demands of the fish, Manu ends up destroying the world.

Human society is built on the principle that the strong shall provide for the weak. The alternative is called jungle law and frowned upon. We also speak in terms of permanence: no aging but eternal existence, a growth curve that never wanes. The alternative is called being defeatist and philosophical. But in trying to provide everything for everyone, all the time, much is destroyed: cultures are destroyed, more of nature is destroyed, often for the noblest of intentions.

When the factory was built, the government insisted that schools and jobs be created to support the local tribal community. The factory owners did so diligently. Members of the tribal community were encouraged to study and learn new skills. They got menial jobs and they encouraged their children to study harder so that they could get more senior positions. Two generations down the line, the old tribal ways have been all forgotten. The stories are no longer told. The rituals are no longer practiced. A whole way of life has ceased to exist. Only anthropologists and museums have any memory of it. But the factory does not see itself as the destroyer of a culture; it simply sees itself as the harbinger of economic growth.

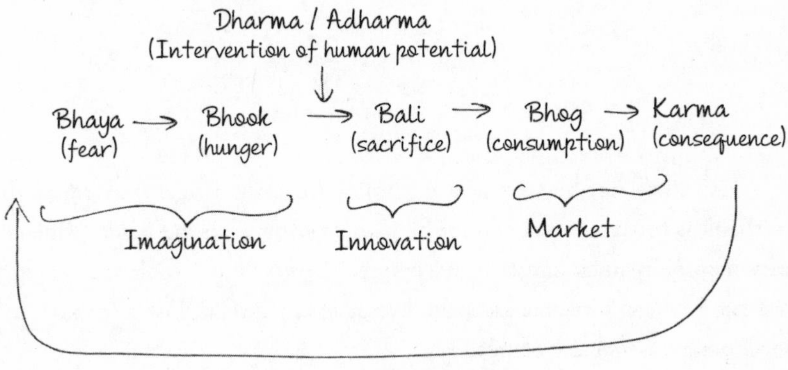

Mental violence is also violence

The Bhagavat Puran tells the story of the river Yamuna that flowed past Vrindavan, the forest that was the favourite haunt of Krishna and his companions. One day, Krishna's elder brother, wanted to take a bath and he asked Yamuna to come to him. Yamuna said, "But I cannot break the riverbanks. You must come to me." Balaram did not heed her words. He simply swung his plough and hooked it on the riverbank and dragged Yamuna, by the hair, to come towards him.

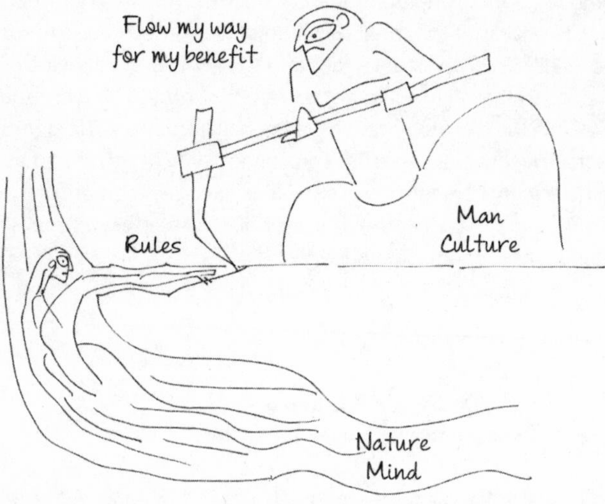

This story can be seen as a metaphor for canal irrigation. Unless the riverbank is broken, water cannot be made to flow into the fields. Violence helps man reorganize nature to his benefit. This is saguna violence, violence that can be seen. Violence associated with agriculture, industrialization and development is visible violence.

This story can also be seen as a metaphor for domesticating the mind. Our imagination flows in different ways as determined by our whim. Society, however, demands we control our imagination and function in a particular way, guided by rituals and rules. This is also violence: mental violence or

nirguna violence, violence that cannot be seen. Every human wants to live by his rules but laws, values, systems, processes, regulations compel them to live by organizational rules. This results in invisible violence. Through mental violence, the human-animal is compelled to behave in a civilized way. At first there is resistance, but later it becomes a habit.

Radhakrishna loves Sundays when he wakes up at 10 a.m. and spends the day playing with his daughters, not shaving, not bathing, eating a late lunch, ending the day watching a movie with his wife on their home theatre system. Mondays he hates, as he has to get up at 6 a.m. and drive to work to be in office by 8 a.m., following up with team members, cajoling them or compelling them to finish their tasks so that he can give a favourable report to the client located in another time zone. It is a thankless job as he has to hear complaints from everyone around. But it pays well. On Sunday, Radhakrishna's Yamuna flows as per her will. On the rest of the days, it flows along the canals dug by others.

Violence creates winners and losers

Harvest festivals are typically associated with the death of asuras: Diwali is associated with the death of Narak-asura, Onam and Diwali with the death of Bali-asura, and Dassera is associated with the death of Mahish-asura.

The Purans states that asuras live in Pa-tala, the realm under the ground. All wealth in its most elemental form, be it plant wealth or mineral wealth, exists under the earth. Asuras will not let Lakshmi leave their realm; so the devas have to use force.

The sun (Surya) and the rain (Indra) pull out plant wealth, while fire (Agni) in the furnace and wind (Vayu) through bellows melts rocks and gets metal out of ore. Activities such as farming and mining are thus described as war waged by devas against asuras. Unless the asura is killed, Lakshmi cannot be obtained.

Lakshmi is called Pulomi, daughter of the asura-king, Puloman, and Bhargavi, daughter of the asura-guru, Bhrigu. Shukra, the other asura-guru, is her brother. In victory, the daughter of the asuras ends up as Sachi, wife of Indra, showering devas with pleasure, creating paradise with her arrival.

This story of the devas defeating the asuras is a narrative acknowledgment of the violence inherent in creating wealth. It refers to the visible violence of agriculture, mining, industrialization and every other extraction process.

It also reveals that with violence, there is bound to be a winner and a loser. Someone gains from the violence, and from that comes conflict. We adore those who pull wealth towards us rather than those who push wealth away from us. For humans, devas are gods, as their activities bring forth hidden wealth while asuras are demons, as they hide wealth in their subterranean realms.

The new road connecting the two major cities was going to pass through their farms. Twenty families would be displaced. The government promised them adequate compensation. For Mita-tai, this meant the end of all the things she had grown up with. The pond would go, as would the orchard. She would have to move to a new house maybe in the city with her son. She wanted to protest, but who would listen to an old lady. They would see her as an obstacle to progress. She cursed the government and all those who would ride on the road that took away her farm. But these were hollow curses of an unknown woman. According to the collector, the land belonged not just to her but also her two sisters and four brothers. All their names were on the deed, attested by her father's thumb impression. Only she had stayed in the village, with her husband, and taken care of the farm. Suddenly, all the relatives descended to take a share of the compensation. The deed was prepared thirty years ago before anyone had migrated and before the family quarrels began. Everyone had forgotten about the deed, until now. The government refused to pay any money until a consensus was reached. It took two years for that to happen. Mita-tai got only a fraction of what she felt she deserved. She went to her son's house, heartbroken. She died soon after. The road connecting the two cities brought livelihood to thousands of families. Indra had won his Sachi.

Violence is culturally unacceptable if taking is not accompanied by giving

King Harishchandra had once promised to sacrifice his son, Rohit, if the gods cured him of a terrible ailment. The gods kept their end of the bargain, but Harishchandra hesitated about keeping his. He sought a way out, so his courtiers suggested he adopt a son. "The gods will not mind so long as you sacrifice a son," they said. So the king offered a reward of a hundred cows in exchange for a son he could adopt.

No one offered their sons; even orphans were not willing to be adopted, as they knew what was in store for them. But one priest, by the name of Ajigarta, agreed to sell his son, for he was very poor and he had three sons. "The eldest is dear to me. The youngest is dear to my wife. The middle one, we can spare." And so, the king adopted Ajigarta's middle son, whose name was Sunahshepa.

The time came to sacrifice Sunahshepa, but the royal priests refused to carry out the sacrifice of a human being. No one was willing to commit such a heinous act. "I will do it," said the boy's father, "if I am given another hundred cows."

This story fills us with horror, as the yajaman does not behave as a yajaman ought to. Rather than taking care of his subject, the king wants to sacrifice him for his own benefit. Rather than taking care of his son, the father wants to sell him for his own benefit. Both king and father are thinking only of their hunger. Both are indifferent to the needs of Sunahshepa.

In nature, it is acceptable that animals think only about themselves. But in culture, such selfishness is condemned.

We demand a fair exchange from people who have more wealth and more power. Unfortunately, those who have more wealth and power are often in those positions because they have denied others any share of wealth and power. This is the root cause of rage and revolution. But things get complicated in defining what is fair. Is it fair for a king to kill another man's son to save his own? Is it fair for a father to sell one child to feed the others? Animals do not resent the predator who catches the prey, but humans do resent humans who exploit other humans.

The story of Sunahshepa draws attention to greed too. Ajigarta can plead poverty when he sells his son. But when the king offers to sacrifice his son, his motivation is not poverty anymore. What is acceptable when we are poor is not acceptable when we are not hungry. But then who decides who is poor and who is not. Certainly not a king who changes the definition of who his son is depending on convenience.

When Kanta could not pay back her dues, she gave her son Raghu away to a man called Pal who, in exchange, cleared her loan with the local moneylender. Raghu would work at Pal's house and be provided with food and shelter, but no salary. That was all right as Kanta could barely feed her six children. For Pal, transactions such as this enabled him to get labour at so low a cost that he was able to offer goods at prices that interested many foreign buyers. Kanta and Raghu are not even aware that there are laws against bonded labour and child labour. They are simply trying to survive, and Pal is taking advantage of the situation. Raghu, like Sunahshepa, lies in the twilight zone where neither parent nor state are able to take care of him.

Violence becomes culturally acceptable when we take because no one gives

Indra, king of devas, once forbade the sage, Dadichi, from sharing the secret of the yagna with anyone. "If you do reveal the secret, your head will burst into a thousand pieces." But the twin sons of Surya, the Ashwini, were eager to learn this secret. When informed about the curse, the twins found a way out.

The Ashwini used their knowledge of medicine to cut off the head of Dadichi and replace it with a horse's head. Through the horse's head, Dadichi revealed the secret of the yagna. As soon as the revelation was complete, the horse head burst into a thousand pieces thus fulfilling Indra's curse. The Ashwini twins then attached the sage's original head and Dadichi came back to life.

Thus, the secret was transmitted. But a price had to be paid. The horse had to die. This could have been avoided, had Indra allowed the free sharing of knowledge. But if knowledge was freely shared, would Indra be Indra, the king of devas and ruler of Amravati?

The devas believe that they have a right to what they have, that they are not obliged to give, like the inventor of an intellectual patent or the inheritor of a large conglomerate. This is disputed by those who believe wealth and knowledge need to be shared freely, that locking in wealth and building walls is the root of wars, deprivation and suffering.

For the devas, the asuras are barbarians, who have to be killed for trying to steal the wealth that they have created. For the asuras, the devas are thieves who exploited resources that they never knew they had. Therefore, the battle between them is never-ending; both are convinced the other is unworthy and wrong.

Violence often happens when we take what others will not give. In Hindu mythology, the devas are often shown withholding treasures that other creatures want. This results in violence. The devas never lead a peaceful existence. Amravati is always besieged.

Kulapathi is an adviser to the government. He has advised the government against signing international patent laws. He believes that the creator does have the moral right to benefit from his creation. However, if he respects the creator's right, millions in his country will not get life-saving medicines. These will have to be imported at high cost and the government will be forced to provide subsidies and grants to make them available, which will ruin an already weak economy. Against immense international pressure, Kulapathi argues passionately about ignoring the rights of the creator. He feels he may be ethically wrong, but he is morally right. The rest of the world disagrees. Kulapathi is Dadichi who will ensure knowledge passes to the Ashwini, whether Indra allows it or not.

Exploitation is violence

Once, Lakshmi disappears from Swarga as the excesses of Indra disgust her. She dissolves herself in an ocean of milk. The devas decide to churn the ocean of milk to get Lakshmi back. They use Mount Mandara as the churning spindle and the serpent-king, Vasuki, as the churning rope. But they realize they alone cannot churn the ocean; they need a counterforce. So they call upon their half-brothers, the asuras. The asuras agree as they are assured a share of the treasures that will emerge: the share is not clarified; no one knows what they will receive.

Many treasures emerge from the ocean: symbols of prosperity such as the wish-fulfilling tree, the wish-fulfilling cow, the wish-fulfilling gem; symbols of kingship such as the horse and the elephant; and symbols of pleasure such as wine, musicians and nymphs. The greatest treasure to emerge is amrit, the nectar of immortality.

The devas consume the amrit, and do not share it with the asuras, arguing that there was no agreement on what share would go to the asuras.

Rendered immortal, the devas now have an unfair advantage. They claim all the treasures of the sea and rise to the sky. The asuras are angry and they return to their realm under the earth. Never will they forgive the devas for their trickery. They will fight to repossess what was originally theirs, again and again for time immortal.

This story has confounded many Hindus, as conventionally, the devas are seen as gods, and are hence morally upright, while the asuras are demons, hence morally fallen. How can the gods trick and cheat?

The root of this confusion lies with the English words 'gods' and 'demons', used first by European orientalists, and the attribution of morality to devas. This distinction does not exist in the ancient Sanskrit texts, the Purans. In the Purans, both the devas and asuras are sons of Brahma, and represent different aspects of human personality.

The asuras sit over raw material, which unless extracted has no value. The devas bring value. If the devas did not come along, Lakshmi would stay dissolved in the ocean of milk. Because of the devas, Lakshmi becomes Sachi.

Once she becomes Sachi, the asuras seek her back.

Often in a yagna, the tathastu is far greater than the svaha. The yajaman claims it as his right, since the yagna was his idea. But that does not stop the asuras from feeling they have been tricked or cheated. This sparks resentment and changes the mood of the yagna.

The asuras can be seen as the workers who work in industries which have been built using the money and knowledge of the devas. Who should be the beneficiaries of the fruit of their labour? Those who invested in the machinery and raw material, or those who laboured over it? The shareholders or the employees? The line of sight of the investor is different from that of the entrepreneur. What would construe a fair share? One party feels exploited and the other party feels fettered. Even the prajapatis disagree: Brihaspati sides with the devas and Shukra with the asuras.

The rishi saw the event from both points of view and realized there was no objective answer to the conundrum. The narrative of the battle between devas and asuras draws our attention to the violence inherent in a culture where both the haves and have-nots co-exist. At the same time, if there are no have-nots, there can be no haves.

When Hemadri returned home after completing his education, he spent hours looking at the financial statements of the family business. He realized that the family could easily pay the workers more wages and provide them with better facilities. His father and grandfather had a very different view altogether. "Before we came here, this place was a jungle with no employment opportunities. Now many have a job. If we overpay them, they will use that money to drink and beat their wives, which they do anyway with the meagre salaries we pay them. It will get worse. They will not turn up for work. They will become arrogant and demanding. Immigrant labour is no solution, as the locals will beat outsiders and drive them away. We have to control them and the best way to control them is by keeping them on a tight leash financially." Hemadri disagrees but as long as he is not in charge he has to keep his views on social justice to himself.

Hoarding is violence

Like the never-ending conflict between devas and asuras, there is another conflict that is ceaseless: that between yakshas and rakshasas; also sons of Brahma who represent different aspects of human personality.

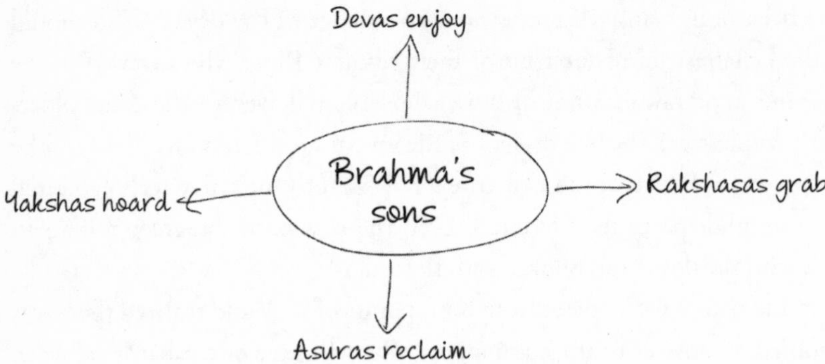

While devas do not share, the yakshas simply hoard. The latter are guardians of earth's treasures. They built the golden city of Lanka. The rakshasas led by their king, Ravan, drive the yakshas out of Lanka and lay claim to the city. The yakshas then seek refuge on the slopes of Kailas and build another city, called Alanka, more popularly known as Alaka. In Shiva's shadow, they feel safe.

The rakshasas are often mistaken for the asuras. They are two very different sons of Brahma. Asuras fight the devas to reclaim what they believe has been stolen from them. Rakshasas, on the other hand, do not believe in exchange; they simply take what they want.

The yakshas do not see hoarding as excess consumption even though by hoarding, they deprive someone of wealth. The deprivation of wealth leads to starvation which, in turn, fuels violence.

It is ironical that both the yakshas and rakshasas worship Shiva who yearns for nothing. Yakshas keep hoarding because they are anxious to create enough wealth to satisfy future starvation. The rakshasas keep stealing because that is the only way they know to gather food. The yakshas accuse rakshasas of

laziness; the rakshasas accuse yakshas of greed. Each see the other as villains and themselves as victims. Neither sees the fear, fuelled by imagination that makes them, and the other, behave the way they do.

The number of robberies in the neighbourhood have risen especially affecting senior citizens. Naturally, Mrs. Nagarkatti is scared. Her two sons are in America and her daughter is in Singapore. They call her every day and send her money by wire transfer. But in the house she is alone with one servant during the day and one at night. In the city there are many unemployed and underemployed young men and women who envy those who drive around in fancy cars, eat in fancy restaurants, and live in fancy homes. Every time they switch on the television they are enticed by advertising and lifestyles they cannot afford. One of them is Girish who visited Mrs. Nagarkatti's house to solve a small electrical problem. He noticed the diamonds in her ears and the gold bangle she was wearing. He asked her for 500 rupees. She called him an overcharging cheat, paid him only 200 rupees and complained to his boss. He wants to teach her a lesson. Or is that simply an excuse to justify his desire for the earrings and bangle that will allow him to experience all those fancy things he only dreams about. A lonely Mrs. Nagarkatti wants to move to an Alaka of her own, where she will feel safe in Shiva's shadow. Girish is on the verge of breaking the law and getting the diamonds and gold by force to his Lanka.

Hunger is insatiable

Kubera, king of yakshas, once paid a visit to Kailas. There he saw Shiva's elephant-headed son, the corpulent Ganesha seated next to his father, and thought to himself, "Ganesha clearly loves food but Shiva cannot afford to feed him to his heart's content." So as a favour to Shiva, Kubera invited Ganesha to a meal. Ganesha accepted the invitation and entered Kubera's kitchen.

When the food was served, Kubera said, "Eat to your heart's content." Kubera regretted these words soon after, for Ganesha kept eating and eating. He ate everything that was in the kitchen and asked for more. Food had to be bought from the larder and then from the market. But Ganesha was still hungry. "More please," he said, raising his trunk. Kubera saw his treasures dwindling but there was no sign of Ganesha stopping. Finally, Kubera fell at Ganesha's feet realizing he was being taught a lesson.

Ganesha raised his trunk and said, "You really think food will satisfy hunger! Food fires the imagination, imagination enhances hunger. You seek to create more food, but food is finite and hunger infinite. My father seeks to destroy hunger. That is why I sit in his house, and not in your kitchen."

Sharda is thrilled when she learns that her contractor has to pay her more. She has a right to minimum wages. But now it has been two years, and the minimum wages she has been regularly paid is just not enough. With a regular income, she has been able to create a simple and secure lifestyle for her children. Unlike her, they have not spent a childhood going to bed hungry. Now they have dreams. They want things that she cannot afford to buy. Suddenly, what seemed like a lot of money two years ago seems paltry now. Unknown to Sharda, her contractor's son, Digvijay, was most happy when he got a salary that allowed him to buy a car; no more bus, train, or rickshaw rides to get to work. But now, two years later, he too is unhappy. He wishes he had a better salary so he could afford to hire a driver. Both Sharda and Digvijay are experiencing their hunger expanding because of imagination. Only introspection or tapasya will curtail it.

Indra's Amravati satisfies hunger. But Indra's name suggests that hunger is not physical—indriya, the term which gives rise to the name Indra, means the senses. Human hunger is not just the physical hunger of the stomach, but also the hunger of the senses. We yearn to pleasure the mind. We want entertainment otherwise we are plagued by boredom, loneliness and angst. The hunger of the mind is far greater than the hunger of the body. That is why Indra needs not just the wish-fulfilling triad of Kalpataru, Kamadhenu and Chintamani but also needs the dance of the apsaras and the song of the gandharvas. So, no amount of wealth can satisfy him. That is why the rich aspire to be richer.

Civilized society speaks of generating and distributing enough wealth to satisfy the basic needs of people. We imagine that when these needs are met, there will be peace. But when basic needs are met, the mind craves the next level of needs. When that craving is not satisfied, there is conflict. Conflict will therefore never end, unless we address the root issue: craving itself. We can fill the stomach, but we can never satisfy the mind.

As long as the wound of Kama festers, there will be kalah, or conflict. Alakshmi, the goddess of kalah, is said to be Lakshmi's sister. There is conflict with and/or without wealth; only wisdom can rid us of kalah.

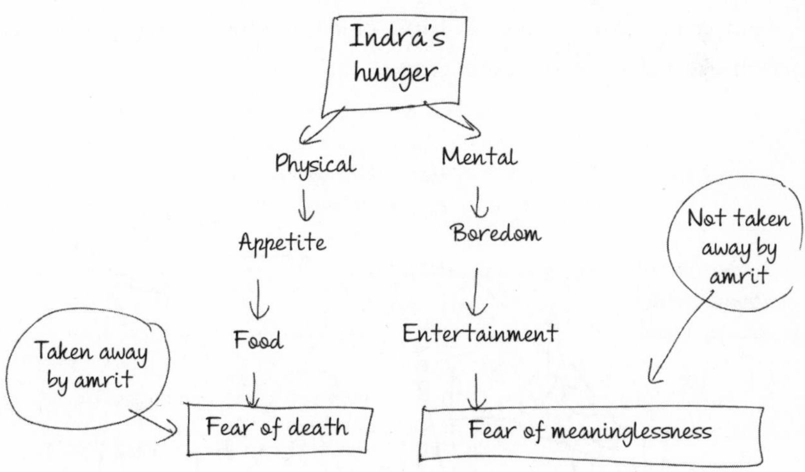

Regeneration ensures sustainable wealth

Vishnu's most popular avatar is Krishna and Krishna's abode is called Goloka, the pastureland, which is full of cows that gather around Krishna who enthralls them with the music of his flute. These cows are not tethered and do not need to be. They give their milk to Krishna joyously, continuously and voluntarily.

Cows feed on grass which when eaten grows back, making grass a renewable raw material. The story goes that a pot containing amrit was placed on the grass a long time ago, enabling it to regenerate itself. With an assured and sustainable source of food, the cow is able to give a sustained supply of milk. This makes the cow and grass symbols of sustainable and regenerating resources, which makes them sacred and an integral part of Hindu and Jain rituals.

It is very easy to see this story literally: as an appeal for a vegetarian lifestyle, or as an endorsement for protecting cows. But the message is more symbolic: it reaffirms the need to secure a sustainable livelihood. This is why the gift of the cow, go-daan, is the greatest of gifts. It makes a man autonomous; he depends on no one for food (milk) or fuel (dung).

People are advised to give so many cows that the depression left behind as a result of the dust kicked up by the gifted cows turns into a lake which sustains more life. Go-daan is an appeal to create more means of livelihood that sustain more households. Go-hatya, or killing a cow thereby destroying a man's livelihood, is the greatest of crimes.

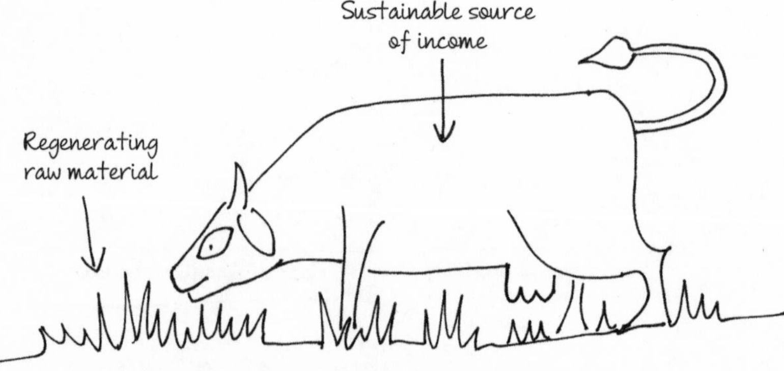

In Vishnu temples, Vishnu's mount, the eagle Garud, is shown holding a naga, or serpent, in his talons. It is an acknowledgement of the violence inherent in feeding. But the devotee is repeatedly told that the naga is immortal. The nagas slithered over the grass on which the amrit was kept and so they, too, possess the power to regenerate themselves like grass.

Vishnu is, thus, associated with the cow and the eagle, both of which consume what is in the mythological world considered renewable food sources. Regeneration is the key to sustainability. Words like regeneration and renewal are thus intrinsic to the yagna. They compensate for the harm done by violence.

Paresh-bhai noticed his son, Raghu, negotiating a price with the tempo owner. He saw the sense of triumph Raghu felt when he managed to bring down the price by another 10 per cent. Paresh-bhai, instead of congratulating Raghu, warned him, "If he runs out of business, we will lose a very good and honest transporter for our goods. In trying to improve your margin, you are destroying his very livelihood. He is already in debt. We need our vendors to survive and thrive so that they can support our business. If we grow at the cost of our vendors, we will do well for a short time, but then collapse. They will either shut down their business or rush to aid the competition as soon as it arrives." Paresh-bhai knows the value of regenerating serpents and regenerating grass.

Restraint ensures regeneration

After harvest, for the land to restore its fertility, the farmer has to leave the land fallow. During spawning season, the fisherman must not go fishing so that he has enough fish to catch the rest of the year. Restraint is the key to regeneration and hence, also, sustainability.

Shiva is the god of restraint. He knows the secret of outgrowing hunger. Unlike Indra who only wants amrit, Shiva has the power to consume halahal, or the poison that accompanies amrit when the devas churn the ocean of milk. This is a metaphor for industrial waste that is a natural outcome of industrial activities. Indra does not care about the waste. But Shiva pays full attention to it; finding ways of containing, and even consuming, it so that the poison does not end up destroying the world. Without Shiva, the devas would not have access to amrit.

The devas, however, do not know the value Shiva brings to their lives, they remain wary of tapasvis. They prefer entertainment to introspection any day.

While the devas kill asuras, the asuras have the power to be reborn, thanks to Shiva. He gives them sanjivani vidya, the power to come back to life. The farmer may clear the forest, but sooner than later the weeds and floods come back. These weeds and floods play a key role in the regeneration of soil. Like the farmer who resents the weeds and floods, Indra resents the asuras who keep attacking Amravati at periodic intervals. He does not like Shiva helping them with sanjivani vidya. He imagines a world where every plant is a crop, existing solely for the satisfaction of his own hunger.

The asuras do tapasya to become more powerful, not wiser. They worship Shiva as a source of power, and pay scant regard to his wisdom.

Only Vishnu knows the value of Shiva. He realizes that while performing a yagna externally to generate Narayani, the yajaman has to simultaneously perform tapasya internally and invoke Narayan if he wishes to have regenerating resources and a sustainable business.

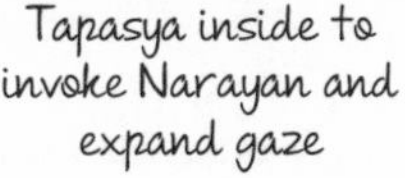

That is why the Veda keeps referring to the yagna-purush that has to be sacrificed during the yagna. While agni, the fire in the altar, burns resources externally, tapa, the fire in the mind, needs to burn the yajaman's ignorance. This needs to occur simultaneously with the ritual. Only then, can there be intellectual growth along with emotional and material growth. If the yagna does not provoke intellectual and emotional growth in the yajaman, material growth will be indiscriminate and that will herald the floods of pralay.

Pranita was always careful about money. She wanted to ensure that her children got a good education and lived a comfortable life. When she was forty, her fortunes changed. Her business started to boom. She began earning much more than her husband. "Now you can buy the jewellery that you never bought," her husband said jokingly. Pranita smiled. She never bought jewellery not because she could not afford it but because she never desired it. Why should the availability of money change that about her? Why should extra resources make her change her comfortable lifestyle? Money for her was simply a tool of comfort. She did not value people, including herself, for the money they had. This mindset allowed Pranita to use her money to invest in more businesses, both high-risk and low-return ones. Before she knew it, she had become a small investment banker partnering with an NGO, giving out micro-loans, helping women in the slums near her house, all the while maintaining a comfortable lifestyle and ensuring her children were well educated and happy. Pranita's tapasya had enabled her not to be swayed by wealth, which enabled her to perform a better yagna than others.

Restraint is violent

Rather than be encouraged to outgrow hunger through tapasya, humans typically seek to control hunger using external forces like rules and values. The path of Shiva is sidelined, as it is too mentally demanding, unpredictable, and uncontrollable. The more tangible path of Daksha and Manu is preferred.

Humans are the only living creatures with the power to contain fire in an altar, water in a pot, plants in a field, and animals in a barn. Likewise, we seek to restrain human behaviour by first defining what is acceptable behaviour and then taming the mind through force.

In nature, the strongest or most beautiful animal gets the mate. In culture, marriage laws are created to ensure everyone gets a spouse. In nature, the strongest and smartest gets the best and most food. In culture, property laws are created so that everyone, not just the strongest and smartest, can own things. The king is expected to enforce these laws; those who disobey risk punishment, exile and even death.

The Vishnu Puran tells the story of how Renuka, wife of the sage Jamadagni, is sexually attracted to the handsome king, Kartaviryarjuna, and how Kartaviryarjuna is fascinated by the magical cow, Nandini, that belongs to Jamadagni. Rules state that both wife and cow belong to the sage and everyone should respect the laws of marriage and property. Yet, neither Renuka nor Kartaviryarjuna is able to contain their respective desires. Renuka continues to dream of the handsome king while doing household chores and Kartaviryarjuna uses his military might to take Nandini by force despite Jamadagni's protests. Finally, Jamadagni orders his son Parashuram to pick up the axe, behead his mother and hack the greedy king to death.

Through rules and values, unacceptable desires and ambitions are contained and the imagination is encouraged to flow in a certain way. If the imagination resists, the axe falls. Modern society does not condone physical abuse, but considers it perfectly fine to terminate employment, or deny sustenance to a person caught cheating or stealing.

Vighnesh was very annoyed at the amount of paper work and bureaucratic demands involved every time he took a loan. His father explained, "As long as you do business with your money, the authorities do not care so much. But once you take someone else's money, you have laws and regulations, and auditors and independent directors to ensure the money is not being misused. You have to continuously reassure the regulators that you are being honest and not rash." Vighnesh found this rather amusing. He realized the assumption was that a strict teacher would compel their students to have integrity. Since when did laws make people good? Rules and punishment would only encourage the greedy to be more cunning and manipulative to get around the system. Could the rules of society stop the craving to succeed at any cost?

Seduction

No one is obliged to receive what we give. No one is obliged to participate in the exchange. Not everyone needs to be compelled into desirable behaviour; customers and employees can also be charmed. Our enchantments can be a trick, a trap, a manipulation, or an expression of genuine affection that benefits all.

Business is seduction

When King Dashrath's wives bear him no children and Lompad's kingdom suffers drought, both are advised to get Rishyashring to perform a yagna. Rishyashring cannot perform a yagna unless he is married and he will not get married because his father, Vibhandak, has raised him without any knowledge of women. In fact, his celibacy is suspected to be the cause of the childlessness and drought that plagues Dashrath and Lompad.

So Lompad's daughter, Shanta, is sent to the forest to seduce the young celibate sage. She spends hours with him, first pretending to be a sage herself, then gradually introducing him to the idea of gender, and finally by stirring sensual urges in him. Eventually, Rishyashring succumbs. He becomes Shanta's husband and she brings him to Lompad's city where he is welcomed with open arms. As a married sage, he conducts yagnas, one that brings rains to his father-in-law's drought-ridden kingdom, and another that grants Dashrath four sons, including Ram.

Business is about seduction. To increase market size, we have to seduce customers who have never used our product or service. To increase market share, we have to seduce customers away from the competition. Unless Rishyashring is seduced, neither Dashrath nor Lompad can have what they want.

For generations, Indian kitchens did not have pressure cookers. When they were first introduced in India, no one bought them. Although it cooked food faster and gave the cook more time to do other chores, people saw no value in a pressure cooker. They wondered what the cook would do with that extra time. Besides, experts were convinced that food did not taste as good. To change this mindset, a marketing campaign was created, which showed that a husband who loved his wife would buy her a pressure cooker, thereby making her life a little less stressful. And so went the seduction. Wives began to see pressure cookers as proof of their husbands' love. The sale of pressure cookers rose phenomenally. Today, pressure cookers are considered a necessity, hardly a luxury. Rishyashring had been seduced.

He who satisfies hunger becomes desirable

This story comes from the Buddhist Jatakas. A young lad overheard a merchant say that a good entrepreneur would find opportunity even in a dead rat. The lad picked up a dead rat and wondered what opportunity there could be in it. While he was lost in thought, a cat approached him and began trying to catch the dead rat in his hand. "Give my cat that rat and I will give you a copper coin," said the owner of the cat. The lad pocketed the coin, and realized where there is hunger there is opportunity.

He thought of the grass-cutters who had to walk deep into the forest and got very thirsty on their way back, walking as they were in the afternoon sun carrying huge bundles of grass. So he greeted them midway, and offered them water from a pot he had bought with the copper coin he earned for the rat. In exchange for quenching their thirst, he asked each grass-cutter for a bundle of grass. Consequently, every day he got a bundle of grass without actually having to cut it. This he sold in the horse market, which earned him a copper coin every day.

Days later, he went to the merchant who had got him started by commenting about opportunities being present even in dead rats. He thanked the merchant for his wisdom. Hearing his tale of success, the merchant thought, "This young man is really smart and enterprising. An opportunity that I must not lose." He made the lad his son-in-law and before long, the lad was the most prosperous merchant in town, earning great wealth by satisfying the many hungers of the marketplace.

In the jungle, all animals, both predator and prey, come to the pond to quench their thirst. Business is about becoming the water body that attracts talent, investors and customers towards us.

When the new mall opened in Poonam Colony, Jayesh, the owner of the local kirana shop that sold provisions, became very nervous. He felt he would never be able to compete with the prices in the mall. Then, he realized, that his customers had small needs: a biscuit, bottle of soda, or a packet of snacks. It was too much to make the journey to the mall for such small items. Jayesh promised home delivery, however small the order. Before he knew it, he was flooded with calls. And invariably, the orders were large. The convenience of home delivery was something everyone had got used to in Poonam Colony and the mall could not break that habit despite great pricing. Jayesh's business was safe, at least for now.

Many devatas need to be seduced

Every year, for the past six hundred years or so, in the temple of Jagannath in Puri, Orissa, a chariot of wood is made for the great chariot festival. A whole series of ceremonies precedes the building of the chariot. Worship is offered to the logs of wood, the instruments that will be used to carve it, and the carpenter who will turn the wood into the chariot. Before the satisfaction of the presiding deity, the wood, the carpenter and his instruments have to be pleased.

This behaviour is not an isolated practice. In household rituals, before the deity is worshipped, prayers and offerings are made to the implements of worship like the bell, the pot, the conch-shell and the lamp. In traditional dance performances, the dancers worship the stage, musicians, instruments and even the audience, before beginning their performance. Every link in the chain is worshipped; each one is sacred and significant.

In business, too, the yajaman depends on many devatas for his success. Each one needs to be acknowledged and paid obeisance to.

- There is the customer/consumer/client from whom the organization earns revenue.
- There is the employee through whom we get our work done.
- There is the employer who we report to, directly or indirectly, or via a dotted line.
- There are colleagues and co-workers without whose support we cannot do our task or achieve our target.
- There is the driver, doorman, office assistant and support staff who make life more comfortable.

There are devatas downstream and upstream and in lateral spaces. This presence of many devatas means that business is not merely a single yagna but a series of yagnas, or sattra. In fact, it is a maze of yagnas, each exchange interlocked with other exchanges, where the yajaman of one yagna serves as

devata in another. We have to feed many devatas and many yajamans have to feed us.

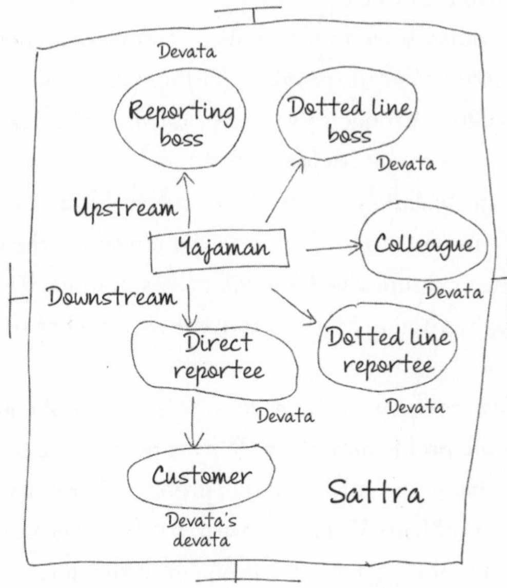

If the yajaman sees the business as a single yagna, he will frown upon personal goals if they are not aligned to the organizational goal. If he sees business as a sattra, he endeavours to make the organizational goal an outcome of everyone's personal goals.

As the manager of a pharma company, Manish knows that his success depends on many people. He knows that each of these devatas has separate needs. His team members, for example, work for their salaries and their bonuses. He makes sure that their appraisals are done on time. In fact, he is one of the few area managers who does appraisals proactively and does not have to be chased by the HR department for timely submission, indicating the value he places on that process. He knows that his boss needs the target plans and achievement sheets every Monday morning; he ensures these are emailed by Sunday evening. He regularly calls the HR and finance executives, even if he has no work, as he wants to build a relationship with them. This ensures that his work gets done smoothly and usually faster than others.

Every devata has a devata of his own

In the Purans, when the devas are in trouble they turn to their father Brahma. When Brahma cannot solve their problem, he takes the devas to Vishnu. When Vishnu cannot solve the problem, Vishnu takes Brahma and the devas to Shiva. When Shiva cannot solve the problem, Shiva takes Vishnu and Brahma and the devas to the Goddess.

This is like an escalation matrix. When the problem cannot be solved at a particular level, one goes to the higher level. However, if the Goddess solves their problem, the next time the devas will bypass Brahma, Vishnu and Shiva and go directly to her. Yet, in every narrative there is no bypass. The structure is respected.

The Goddess does not really have to solve the problem of the devas. She has to solve the problem of Shiva. Why is he not able to solve Vishnu's problem? And Shiva has to solve Vishnu's problem. Why is Vishnu not able to solve Brahma's problem? Vishnu, in turn, has to solve Brahma's problem. Why is Brahma not able to solve the problem of the devas? Brahma has to figure out how to make the devas independent, so they can solve their own problems.

Every yajaman has a devata and every devata, in his capacity as yajaman, has a devata of his own. The yajaman has to solve not just the devata's issues but also figure out how to make him a better yajaman. Otherwise, there will be upward delegation and the gaze of the organization will be towards the boss, not the customer.

Felix has six people reporting to him. Each of them have ten people under them who, in turn, manage teams of about a dozen people who are client facing. Felix realized that while the tathastu of the company (revenue) came from the market, the tathastu of the employee (salary) came from the head office via the boss. Hence the gaze was typically upstream not downstream. People were more interested in boss management than customer management. To change this orientation, when he became head, Felix put the names of his six team members on a notice board in front of his desk. "You are the people who will help me succeed if I help you succeed," he told them in a team meeting. Next to each one's name he put down their individual short-term goals, first personal and then professional. Every week he would take time out to discuss these goals. As the months passed, he noticed each of his team members had similar sheets of papers on their notice boards, with the names of their respective team members. They were mimicking downstream what they were experiencing upstream. Were they being sincere or strategic? Felix did not know, but at least he ensured that his people focused a little more of their attention downstream than upstream.

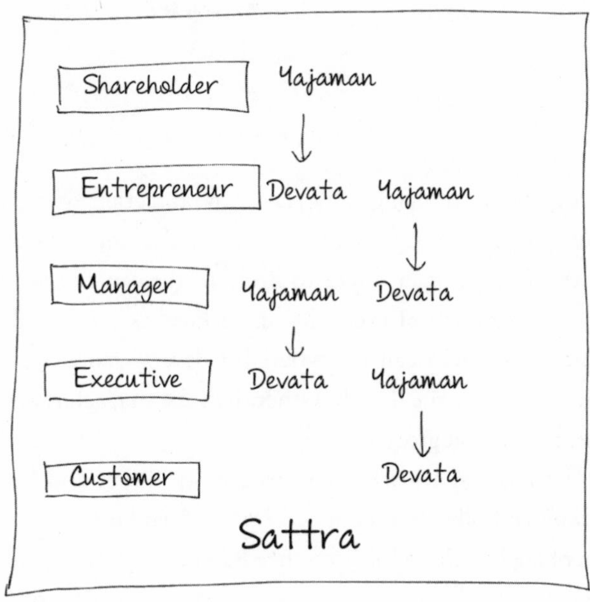

Every devata's hunger is unique

All devatas are placed in a puja room. The puja room is typically located in the northeast corner of the house. Just as the rising sun of the east indicates growth, the Pole Star of the north indicates permanence or stability. Accordingly, the puja room is grounded on the paradoxical and universal desire for growth on the one hand and stability on the other.

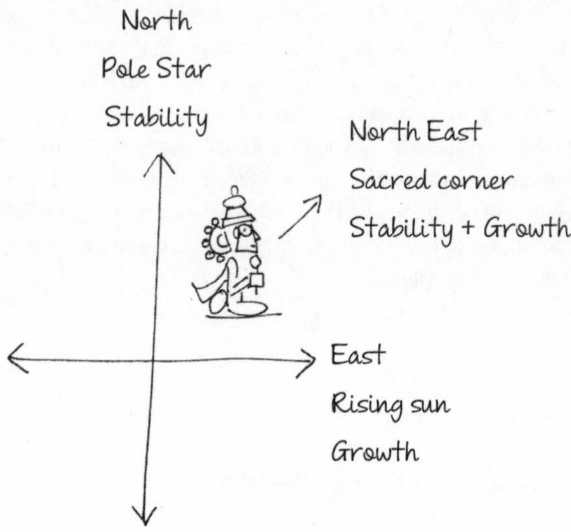

Each deity is kept facing the east, or the direction of the rising sun, a symbol of growth. The yajaman stands where the sun is supposed to be, suggesting that the yajaman hopes to bring in the same value as the sun, contribute to the growth of every devata he invokes. Also implicit in this arrangement is that the yajaman favours his devatas more than the rising sun. He chooses to face the devatas rather than the sun, acknowledging that without them he cannot grow.

Each deity is given his/her favourite food, flower and leaf. Shiva is given raw milk and bilva leaf while Krishna is given butter and tulsi leaf—recognition of the fact that while some needs like growth and stability may be common, every devata's tastes are unique. The more we customize the svaha,

the more likely we are to delight the gods.

The puja room forces the yajaman to look at each devata as an individual, not as part of a collective. Often people look at organizations and forget they are sets of people. And we have to deal with people, not sets. Each person has his own strength and weakness, and he would like them to be at the very least acknowledged. A company with five thousand employees actually has five thousand individual vision statements. But typically, we focus only on one, that of the impersonal institution. This may be efficient, but it does dehumanize the organization.

At the annual internal conference, Inderjit is busy networking with the many partners of the consulting firm. When he meets Sorabh, he talks about the latest gadgets. When he meets Rathor, he talks about cricket. When he meets Satyendra, he talks about philosophy. When he meets Yamini, he talks about films. He never talks business with any of them. He knows that they are all tired of work and want to relax at parties. He also knows that they are bored and need entertainment. What better way to get entertained than talk on their favourite subject. Inderjit thus ensures every devata gets his favourite bhog. His performance is above average but not great. But his ability to make every partner smile has contributed to his being on the fast career track in the firm. The senior partner, Jagdish, who observes Inderjit make his moves, comments to Yamini, "If he can do the same with clients, we can be sure business will flow."

Every devata matters depending on the context

In the nineteenth century, when European orientalists first translated Vedic hymns, they noticed that each hymn evoked different gods. Naturally, they assumed Hindus were polytheists like the Greeks. Then they noticed that each time a deity was being invoked he was treated as the supreme god, suggesting Hindus were monotheists like the Christians. This confused them. Were Hindus polytheistic or monotheistic? Monotheism was seen as superior back then and the British did not lose a single opportunity to embarrass Indians about their many gods.

Some suggested Hindus were henotheistic; they worshipped only one god but acknowledged the existence of others. Max Mueller came up with the term kathenotheistic, which means every god is treated as the supreme god turn-by-turn at the time of invocation. In other words, context determined the status of the god. In drought, Indra who brought rains was valued. In winter, Surya, the sun god was admired. In summer, Vayu, god of the winds was worshipped. And so it is in business. Everybody we deal with in business is important. But their importance soars as our dependence on them increases. Importance is a function of context, which makes all businessmen followers of kathenotheism.

In the puja ghar, the gods are classified under various categories; personal gods are called ishta-devata; household gods are griha-devata; family gods are kula-devata; village gods are grama-devata, and forest gods are known as vana-devata. Thus, there are different gods for different contexts: the personal, departmental, regional and the market. Each deity is of value only in a particular season or at a particular place. No one is of value everywhere and at all times. Each one plays a role in our life. Individually or collectively, they bring fulfilment to our existence.

Everybody in the Delhi office resents John. He has been hired by Sethji for a very good salary but does hardly any work. He spends all day surfing the net, leaves office early and spends his evenings out in clubs, partying with the rich and famous. When questioned by his rather conservative head of accounts, Sethji says, "When I have work with government agencies, I ask John to make the calls. Because he is a foreigner, doors open for him. I get appointments. He starts the meeting and I finish it. And because of his clubbing, he invariably knows the sons and daughters of ministers and other influential people. The officers try to impress him by ensuring the work gets done without too much hassle. So you see, John is like my umbrella. Not useful everyday but certainly of great value on a rainy day. He is worth every penny I pay him."

Not all devatas are equal

Once, a child defeated Taraka, a great asura. The child had six heads, rode a peacock, had the symbol of a rooster on his banner and a lance in his hand. As the bearer of such potent symbols of virility, he was clearly no ordinary child. Who was he?

"He is my son," said Gauri, "I merged six babies into one to create this divine warlord." "He is our son," said the six Krittika stars, "Each one of us nursed those six babies since their birth." "He is my son," said the Saravana, the marsh of reeds, "I provided the fuel for the fire that transformed six seeds in a river into six babies on a lotus." "He is my son," said the river-goddess, Ganga, "My flow turned a single seed into six." "He is my son," said Vayu, the wind god, "I reduced the heat of the single seed otherwise it would have scorched dry the rivers of earth." "He is my son," said Agni, the fire god, "Only I had the power to catch that fiery seed that Vayu cooled and Ganga turned to six." "And who caused the seed to be released from the body of Shiva? It was me! I am the mother of this warrior," said Gauri again.

Gauri, Krittika, Saravan, Ganga, Vayu and Agni, six deities claimed to be the mother of the child-warlord, and each was right from their own point of view. To stop the bickering, the contribution of each of these 'mothers' was acknowledged by giving the child many names: Kumara for Gauri, Kartikeya for the star-goddesses, Saravana for the reed marsh, Gangeya for the river-goddess, Guha for the wind-god and Agneya for the fire-god. This made everyone happy. A special prayer was reserved for the father, Shiva, from whose body came the seed of which the child was a fruit.

We depend on the entire team for its outputs. Every member of the team is a devata. But in teams there are always idea generators and idea implementers. It makes good sense for the yajaman to distinguish between the two. While idea implementers are essential, the idea-generator is critical.

When their advertising campaign won a prestigious global award, Rima threw a huge party where she personally thanked everyone from the planning team to the creative team and media team. Without their contribution, this would never have happened. When the crowds were gone, Rima walked up to Milind, the quiet creative head. She knew it was he who had sold the bold concept to the client. He was the cornerstone of the project. Everyone was essential; but Milind was critical, the idea-generator, the Shiva whose seed was incubated in many wombs to create Kartikeya.

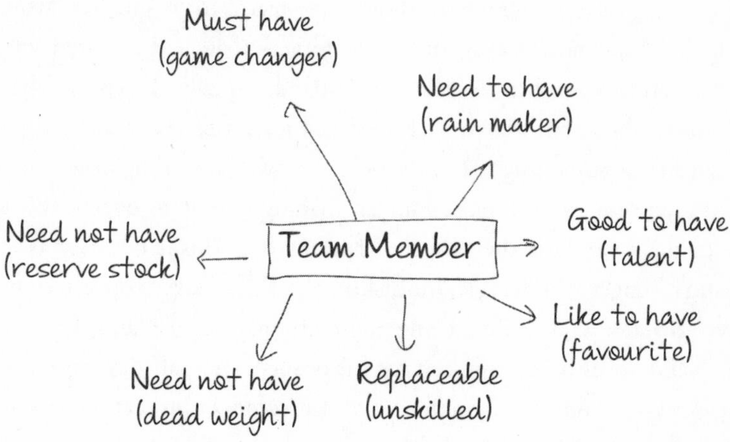

Seducing multiple devatas is very demanding

Dealing with many devatas is not easy. Chandra, the moon god, was a failure. Draupadi, the heroine of the epic Mahabharat, was a partial success, but Krishna was the most successful of all.

Though Chandra marries the twenty-seven daughters of Daksha, he prefers only one—Rohini. Only a threat from Daksha makes Chandra pay attention to his other wives. But he gives his svaha reluctantly, waning as he moves away from Rohini and waxing when he comes close to her.

By contrast, Draupadi treats all her five husbands equally and constantly tries to satisfy each of them. Even though she yearns for Arjun, her favourite, and finds Bhim most useful, she never forgets that as the shared wife of the five Pandavs she has to treat all husbands equally. To ensure there is no jealousy, she is faithful to each husband for a full year and then passes through fire, regenerating her body, before moving on to the next. She pays careful attention to everyone's hunger, making herself so dependable that none of them can bear the thought of losing her. This is not easy as every husband's hunger is different: Yudhishtir, the eldest, loves conversations on matters of state; Arjun enjoys being praised for his archery skills; Bhim loves food; Nakul loves being admired for his beauty; and Sahadev enjoys being silent. And yet, despite all her efforts, when it comes to protecting her, all the brothers fail—both individually and collectively—when they do nothing as she is being publicly abused by the Kauravs.

In the Bhagavata, Krishna dances with many milkmaids or gopikas in the forest of Madhuvan. Every gopika thinks he dances exclusively for her, so well does he meet all their demands. For that reason, the dance of Krishna and the gopikas forms a perfect circle, with each one equidistant from him despite their varied personalities. This circle is called the rasa-mandala. Here, no gopika resents the other. Just as Krishna treats them as devatas, they give due respect to him, their yajaman and strive to make him happy by being ensuring the rasa-mandala includes everyone. Krishna focuses on the personal goals of the gopikas, and the gopikas—by focusing on the personal goal of Krishna—end up meeting the organizational goal.

	Gives svaha to all	Gets tathastu from all
Chandra	✗	✗
Draupadi	✓	✗
Krishna	✓	✓

Seduction is truly successful only when the devatas strive to satisfy the hunger of the yajaman. The point is for the employer to get the employee to give his best voluntarily, and vice versa. When we rely on rules, regulations, reward and reprimand to get our work done, it means we want to domesticate our devatas, rather than seduce them. It means they are doing work reluctantly not joyfully.

Ever since Rehman took over as the manager of the restaurant, there has been a marked change in the energy of the place. The sweeper does not need to be supervised, the waiters do not need to be ordered around, and the cook does not need to be instructed. Everyone is taking ownership of their duties and giving their best. This is because Rehman never talks about tasks and targets, except on Saturdays. The rest of the week, he checks if everyone is happy doing their job, satisfied with what they have achieved. He nudges them gently when they slack, never admonishing or shaming them. With Rehman around, they feel less like servants and more like owners. Rehman does not see work as a fulfilment of contract; he has linked their work with their self-esteem and their self-worth. The workplace energizes everyone and so they contribute beyond the call of duty.

Seduction needs to satisfy both parties

Seduction is an essential component of the yagna. Who does the seduction benefit: only the yajaman or also the devata? When the seduction benefits only the yajaman and leads to material growth for him, the yajaman is Menaka. When the seduction benefits both yajaman and devata and also generates intellectual and emotional growth, the yajaman is Mohini.

Menaka is an apsara sent by Indra to distract the tapasvi Kaushik from his austerities. Menaka dances in front of the aspiring hermit and compels him to open his eyes. Menaka thereby successfully seduces Kaushik much to Indra's delight. On Kaushik's failure rests Indra's success.

Mohini is the form that Vishnu takes when the devas and asuras fight over the distribution of amrit they have churned out of the ocean of milk. She offers to distribute the nectar fairly, and spellbound by her charms, everyone is eager to believe she will be fair. But she is not. It is some time before the asuras realize that Mohini pours the amrit selectively down the throat of only the devas. By then it is too late. The devas become so powerful that they drive the asuras back to the nether regions and rise to the sky laying claim over every treasure that has risen from the ocean of milk.

On the face of it, it seems a simple story where Vishnu as Mohini tricks the asuras and favours the devas. What is left unsaid, though, is more interesting. By giving amrit to the devas, Mohini liberates them from physical death but condemns them to mental boredom. For life has no purpose, and the devas end up chasing thrills and excitement to fill their waking hours.

By denying amrit to the asuras, Mohini grants the asuras a sense of purpose. They feel like victims and are determined to get back what the devas stole from them. The devas can kill the asuras but sanjivani vidya resurrects them, so they keep coming back, again and again, denying the gods the pleasure of peace.

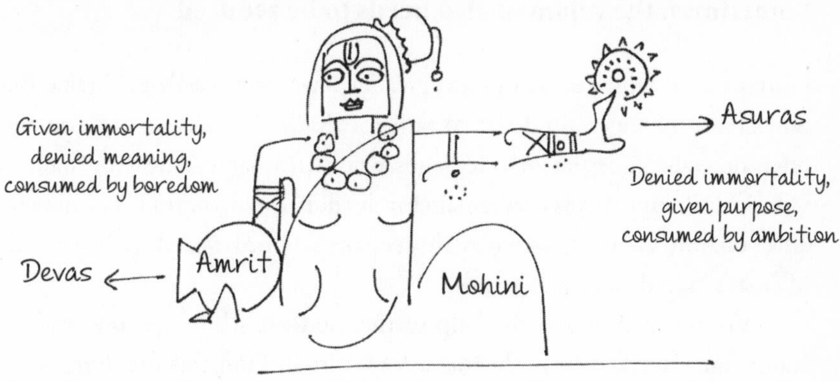

The asuras do tapasya for power; the devas do yagna for pleasure. Asuras crave justice only for themselves. Indra craves only his own happiness. Neither sees the other, or anyone else. Vishnu seeks to provoke thought in the sons of Brahma. For only when they stop fighting and are at peace can he go back to sleep.

> The promotion was given to Radha and not to Maithili. Maithili was very angry and accused Devesh of favouritism. Or was it a sexual favour? Devesh was annoyed by the accusation but did not get upset. He was well aware that both ladies were extremely competitive besides being competent. Neither liked losing which made them star performers. Unfortunately, he could not promote both of them. It was clear that Maithili would resign and join a competitor. In Devesh's view, both girls won. Radha got her promotion and Maithili got a chance to expand her experience by working with new colleagues. Radha would have to learn how to deal with old colleagues who would resist reporting to her. Maithili would have to learn how to deal with new colleagues who would see her as an outsider. Like the devas, Radha would gradually stop feeling obliged to Devesh, and like the asuras, Maithili would never stop resenting him.

Sometimes, the yajaman also needs to be seduced

Only a son of Shiva can kill Indra's great enemy, the asura-king, Taraka. But Shiva has no hunger, no desire to father a child. He seeks no tathastu and offers no svaha. A desperate Indra sends legions of apsaras along with Kama to seduce Shiva. But Shiva's eyes remain firmly shut. The arrows of Kama have no effect on him. In fact, an irritated Shiva opens his third eye, releasing a missile of tapas that reduces Kama to ash.

Vishnu then enlists the help of the Goddess who takes the form of Kamakshi. Kamakshi is another name for Gauri. In Tamil folk literature Gauri is often called the sister of Vishnu. She approaches Shiva not as a damsel but as a devotee, determined to marry him and have his offspring. Impressed by her devotion, Shiva marries her and together, they produce Kartikeya who becomes the commander of the devas and goes on to kill Taraka.

In lesser-known versions, Vishnu as Mohini makes Shiva father a son known variously as Manikantha, Sastha or Aiyanar, the great celibate warlord who defeats many asuras and is much revered as a folk god in South India. Shiva rejects Indra's overtures but accepts those of Kamakshi and Mohini. Why so? Indra wants Shiva to be seduced for his own pleasure. Kamakshi and Mohini want Shiva to be seduced for the benefit of the world.

Mohini and Kamakshi transform Shiva, the hermit, to Shankar, the householder and lead him from the icy peaks of Kailas to the riverbank city of Kashi, the great marketplace.

But Shiva has no need for the marketplace. He is described as digambar, the naked one. He wears nothing. At best, he is wrapped in animal hide and smeared with ash. Vishnu, on the other hand, is draped in silks, anointed with sandal paste, and bedecked with garlands of fragrant flowers and leaves, and necklaces of gold and pearls. Implicit in Vishnu's costume is the existence of different communities: farmers, spinners, weavers, dyers, miners, smelters, smiths, jewellers and traders. In other words, Vishnu's form symbolizes the idea of sanskriti. Vishnu sees the market as a great place to engage with humans. Every yagna is a great opportunity to pay attention to other people's hunger.

Indra does not care for the hunger of others. For him, the yagna exists only for his pleasure. Daksha looks at the yagna merely as a process, a duty, or burden to be borne. To make Indra and Daksha widen their gaze, Shiva's intervention is needed. Only he can teach them the futility of seeking happiness through Lakshmi alone. Happiness will come only when material growth is accompanied by intellectual and emotional growth. And this can only happen when they start paying attention to the hunger of the devata, expand their brahmanda to include that of others and make themselves dependable. And so, Kamakshi appeals to Shiva's grace. Shiva may not need the marketplace, but the marketplace needs him.

Business is not merely an instrument to generate wealth for shareholders or provide services to customers; it builds an ecosystem that provides opportunities to entrepreneurs and creates markets that benefit society at large. Indra sees industry as an end in itself. Vishnu sees industry as an essential ingredient of society at large. For the perfect marriage between industry and society, a perfect balance needs to be maintained between consumption and restraint. While the devata's hunger needs to be indulged, the yajaman needs to work on outgrowing his hunger. That is why Shiva needs to descend from Kailas and be in Kashi.

A similar transformation can be found in Buddhist literature when the wise Buddha of Thervada Buddhism (original school; popular in Sri Lanka and Southeast Asia) is gradually transformed into the form of the compassionate Bodhisattva of Mahayana (later school; popular in China). Buddha is serene and distant with eyes shut, while the Bodhisattva is more engaging and participative with his eyes open and his many hands reaching out to comfort people. Often Bodhisattva is visualized as the female Tara, or accompanied by her. In Vajrayana Buddhism (latest school; popular in Tibet and Bhutan), the two are often in passionate embrace indicating the union of intellect and emotion. In many ways, Tara performs the function of Kamakshi and Mohini. She is the glue of sensitivity and compassion that binds the hermit and the marketplace.

It is no accident that Shiva, who outgrows hunger, gets a wife who is also known as Annapoorna, the provider of food. He embodies the human potential and she embodies nature's resources. Both need to be realized.

Radhakant loves manipulating people, making them feel wanted, and getting them to do exactly what he wants. Many people fall for it, until one day they realize they have been used and leave the organization with a broken heart. Radhakant is Indra who hires Kama and Menaka to get his job done. He does not care for others. His brother Lakshmikant watches this and wonders where Radhakant's desire to manipulate people comes from. All his life Radhakant tricks people and gets his way. He calls this "winning". He is convinced he is right and everyone else is wrong. He wonders why his wife and son constantly fight with him; they refuse to be manipulated by him and get angry when he tries. So many times, Lakshmikant has thought of leaving the firm and working on his own, away from Radhakant's pettiness. But that would be like going to Kailas and finding peace in isolation. He feels he has to stay in Kashi, and help his brother find happiness. The more he watches people get manipulated by Radhakant the more he realizes how desperate people are for affection and love. They let themselves get entrapped and hunted by wily predators, and then feel like victims and martyrs. This realization makes him occasionally smile.

Churning

An organization is made up of various forces: production, marketing, sales, audit, legal, finance, logistics and so on. There are times when each force has to dominate and times when each has to submit. In a churn, one needs to know when to let go otherwise the act of churning turns into a tug-of-war where the organization becomes a battleground.

The organization is ultimately a set of people

Organizations are like the sky; it does not really exist. It is a visual illusion. What really exists are the taras or stars and the grahas or planets (celestial bodies, actually), and the relationships between them as perceived by observers. Sky-gazers are actually stargazers. Taras and grahas are people who make up the organization. The taras are the nameless workers while the grahas are the talent who determine the fate of the organization.

No one knows the names of individual taras; they are identified through the constellation they belong to such as the twelve solar houses (rashi) or the twenty-seven lunar houses (nakshatra). Stars are natural, constellations are not, yet it is constellations that enable us to map the sky and make sense of it. Likewise, in an organization, less value is given to individual workers and more to the group they belong to. An individual worker is not as important as the group he belongs to, as he is viewed as a replaceable set of skills. Teams, regions and departments are artificial divides, yet they are critical for the organization's efficiency and effectiveness. Replacing a team is not easy.

Every graha matters. Each one has a name and a detailed personality. Using information available in Jyositha-shastra or Vedic astrology, people who make a difference to an organization can be classified as:

- Ravi, the sun, who is radiant and attracts attention wherever he goes
- Soma, the moon, who is emotional and moody
- Mangal, or Mars, who is an aggressive go-getter
- Budh, or Mercury, who is an excellent communicator, slippery and silver-tongued
- Brihaspati, or Jupiter, who is rational and relies on data
- Shukra, or Venus, who is intuitive and relies on gut feeling
- Shani, or Saturn, who procrastinates and obstructs
- Rahu, or the eclipse-causer, who is secretive and hates being transparent
- Ketu, or the comet, who is restless and spreads anxiety

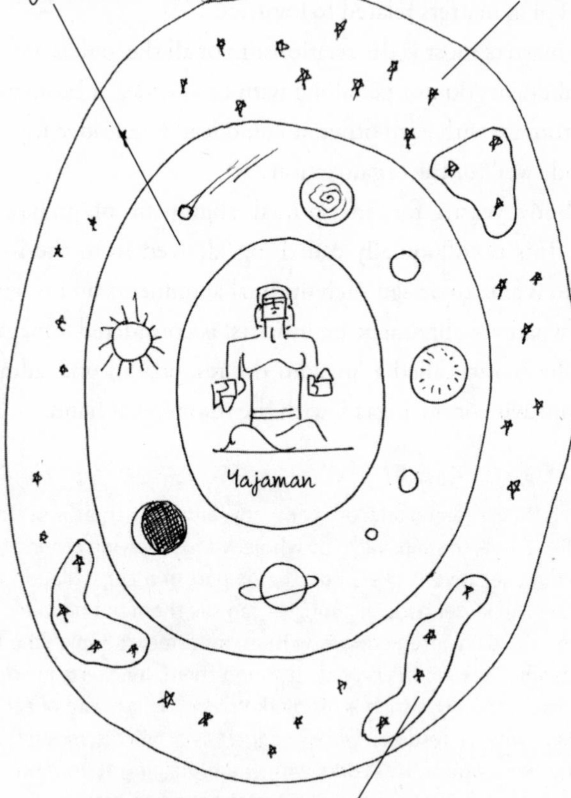
Grahas = planets = Talent whose individual personalities impact an organization
Tara = stars = Talent whose individual personalities do not impact the organization
Yajaman
Rashi/Nakshatra = constellation = groups or departments or teams, where collective performance matters not individual personality

A graha is a talented devata demanding his place in the grand pantheon of the organization. In conjunction with some groups, a celestial body has a favourable impact; in others, the relationship can be disastrous. Likewise, some talents do well in a particular group and not so well in another. A manager may do well in the audit team but not in the business development team. A manager may do well as long as he is dealing with marketing matters but he may fail in matters related to logistics.

What matters most is the relationship of all the grahas with each other. If individual talents do not get along with each other, if business unit heads do not collaborate with each other, it could lead to a leadership crisis, which does not bode well for the organization.

Everybody yearns for an optimal alignment of grahas, rashis and nakshatras. This is colloquially called jog, derived from the word yoga. A yajaman who is able to design such optimal alignments on his own, or makes the best of whatever alignment he inherits, is considered a magician, a jogi. Sometimes he is also called a 'jogadu', the resourceful one, admired for his ability to improvise or do 'jugaad' with the resources at hand.

Prithviraj is the head of a telecom company with forty thousand employees. He feels like Surya, the sun, with the whole world revolving around him. Each client-facing executive is like a star that is part of a constellation which, in turn, is part of a larger constellation. He can see them but he rarely engages with them. His daily interaction is with about fifteen people who make up his core team. They are his grahas. Through them, he exerts influence over all stars, across the sky, which is his marketplace. He is aware of each graha's personality; who is restless, who is aggressive, who is moody and who gets along with whom. He works with them, helping them enhance their positives and work on their negatives, to get the fine balance that will give him the success he so desperately wants. He wants a finance head who is firm yet gentle, a marketing head who is flamboyant yet level-headed, and an operations head who is both people and numbers driven. He is getting there.

Are these talents aligned well with reference to each other?
Is the talent team aligned well to the market?
Are the talents aligned well to respective departments?

Every organization is a churn

When the devas wish to churn the ocean of milk, Vishnu suggests they take the help of the asuras, for a churn cannot work without an equal and opposite counterforce. In business, the organization is the churn while the market is the ocean of milk in which Lakshmi is dissolved. The various departments of the organization and members of the leadership team serve as force and counterforce, respectively.

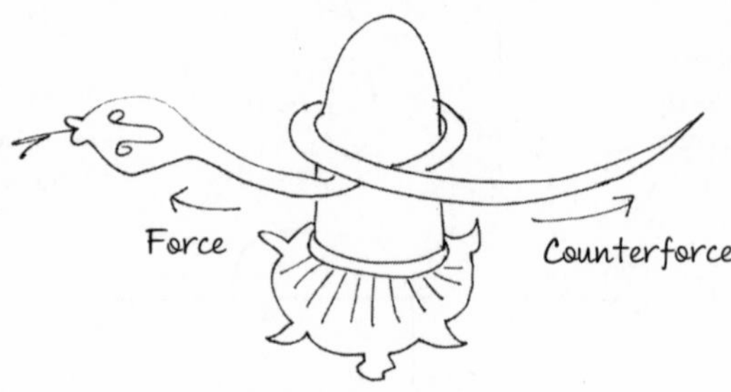

Vishnu alone knows when to pull and when to let go, how much to pull and how much to let go, who should pull and who should let go. To ensure that the churning is happening correctly, he holds four tools in his four arms. This is why he is also called Chaturbhuj, the one with four arms. Each tool symbolizes one of the four things to keep in mind when supervising any project.

- The conch-shell trumpet stands for clear communication. The yajaman needs to clearly communicate his expectations to his team.
- The wheel stands for repetition and review. The yajaman needs to appreciate that all tasks are repetitive and need to be reviewed periodically.
- The lotus is about appreciation and praise. It complements the club.
- The club stands for reprimand and disciplinary actions. It complements the lotus.

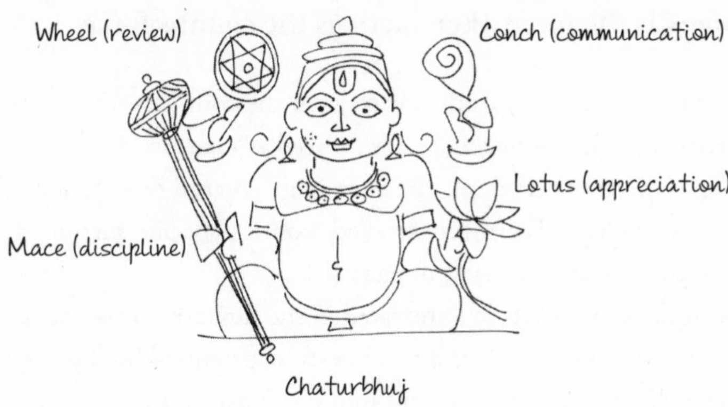

The conch-shell and lotus are instruments of seduction. The wheel and the club are instruments of violence. The yajaman needs to know when to be nice and when to be nasty, depending on the context, so that ultimately, work gets done.

When Lakshmi is not forthcoming, Vishnu knows that the churn has been damaged: either someone is pulling when they are not supposed to or someone is refusing to let go. It is then that he uses the four tools in the right proportion, as the situation demands.

> Arvind has a peculiar style of management that few in his team have deciphered. When everyone is together, he enjoys visioning and planning and ideating. He publicly announces individual and team successes and takes people on celebratory lunches. When he is reviewing his team members, or pulling them up for indiscipline or lack of integrity, he only does it in private. By doing the positive things in public, he amplifies the positivity in the team. By doing the negative but necessary things in private, he avoids spreading negativity.

If strategy is the force, then tactic is the counterforce

Vishnu rides an eagle or garud, and rests on the coils of a serpent or sarpa, which is to say he has both a wide view, as well as a narrow view. His vision is both long-term and short-term. The big picture is garud-drishti, or the bird's-eye view or strategy. The more detailed, context-specific picture is sarpa-drishti, or the serpent's eye-view or tactic.

Both these views are demonstrated in the Ramayan. Dashrath's second queen, Kaikeyi, asks him for the two boons he promised her long ago: that Ram, the eldest son and heir, be sent into forest exile for fourteen years, and that her son, Bharat, be made king instead. When Dashrath informs his sons about this, Ram immediately agrees to go into exile but Bharat does not agree to be king.

Ram agrees because he knows the immediate impact of his decision: the people of Ayodhya will be reassured that the royal family always keeps its promises, however unpleasant. Bharat disagrees because he knows the long-term impact of his decision: no one will be able to point to the royal family as being opportunists and thereby justify future wrongdoing. By demonstrating sarpa-drishti and garud-drishti, Ram and Bharat ensure the glory of the Raghu clan.

In contrast, neither view is demonstrated in the Mahabharat. Satyavati refuses to marry the old king Shantanu of the Kuru clan unless she is assured that only her children become kings of Hastinapur. Shantanu hesitates, but his son, the crown prince, Devavrata, takes a vow of celibacy, demonstrating neither sarpa-drishti nor garud-drishti.

In the immediate-term, both Shantanu and Satyavati are happy. But in the short-term, the kingdom is deprived of a young, powerful king. The old king dies and for a long time the throne lies vacant, waiting for Satyavati's children to come of age. In the long-term, this decision impacts succession planning. The Kuru clan gets divided into the Kauravs and the Pandavs, which culminates in a terrible fratricidal war.

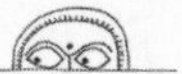

When asked why he needed a chief operating officer, Aniruddh told the chief executive officer that he needed someone downstairs to pay attention to quarterly targets and someone upstairs to pay attention to the long-term prospects of the company. "I want the CEO to think of the five-year plans, product development and talent management, not waste his time thinking of how to achieve today's sales." Aniruddh knows that there will be tension between the CEO and COO, as the COO will have more control over the present yet will have to report to someone whose gaze is on the future. This tension between the sarpa and the garud was necessary if Lakshmi had to keep walking into the company for a sustained time.

If creativity is the force, then process is the counterforce

Kama is the charming god of desire and creativity. He rides a parrot and shoots arrows of flowers rather indiscriminately, not bothering where they strike. Yama is the serious god of death and destiny, associated with the left-brain. He keeps a record of everything and ensures all actions are accounted for.

If Kama is about innovation and ideas, Yama is about implementation and documentation. Kama hates structure. Yama insists on structure. Kama is about play. Yama is about work. Human beings are a combination of the two.

Vishnu is a combination of both Kama and Yama. His conch-shell and lotus represent his Kama side, as everyone loves communication and appreciation, while his wheel and mace represent his Yama side, as everyone avoids reviews and discipline.

In folklore, there is reference to one Shekchilli who dreams all the time and never does anything. He is only Kama with not a trace of Yama. Then there is one Gangu Teli, who spends all day doing nothing but going around the oil press, crushing oilseeds. He is only Yama with not a trace of Kama. Then there are Mitti ka Madhav and Gobar ka Ganesh, characters who neither dream nor work, and are neither Kama or Yama. They do what they are told and have neither desire nor motivation. Finally, there is Bhoj, the balanced one, who knows the value of both Kama and Yama, and depending on the context, leans one way or the other. Bhoj is Vishnu.

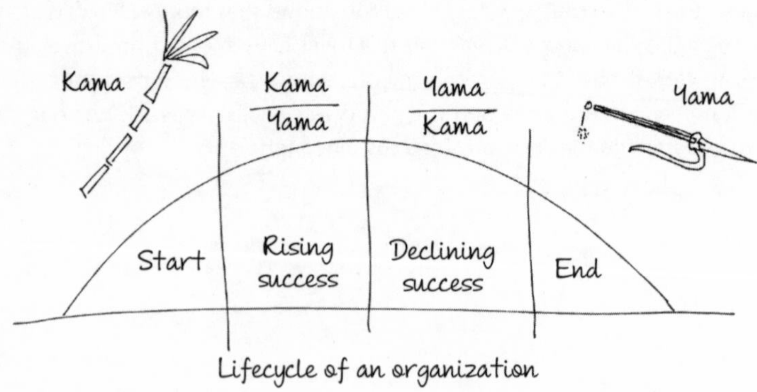

Lifecycle of an organization

In the early phases of an organization, when ideas matter, Kama plays a key role as the vision of the yajaman excites and attracts investors and talent to join the team. In the latter stages of an organization, when implementation is the key to maximize output, Yama starts playing an important role; more than dreams, tasks and targets come to the fore. When creativity and ideas cease to matter, and only Gangu Teli is in control, the organization lacks inspiration and is on its path to ruin. Thus, the proportion of Kama and Yama plays a key role in the different phases of a company.

When the team met to brainstorm, Partho always came across as a wet blanket. As soon as an idea was presented, he would shoot it down by citing very clear financial or operational reasons. His boss, Wilfred, would tell him to keep implementation thoughts for later, but Partho felt that was silly as the most brilliant projects failed either because of inadequate funding or improper planning of resources. He felt ideation should always be done with the resources in mind. Partho comes across as a Yama who always looks at numbers and milestones, especially when compared with his very popular boss, Wilfred, who is clearly a Kama. But he is actually a Bhoj, highly creative, but lets the reality of resource availability determine the limits of creativity.

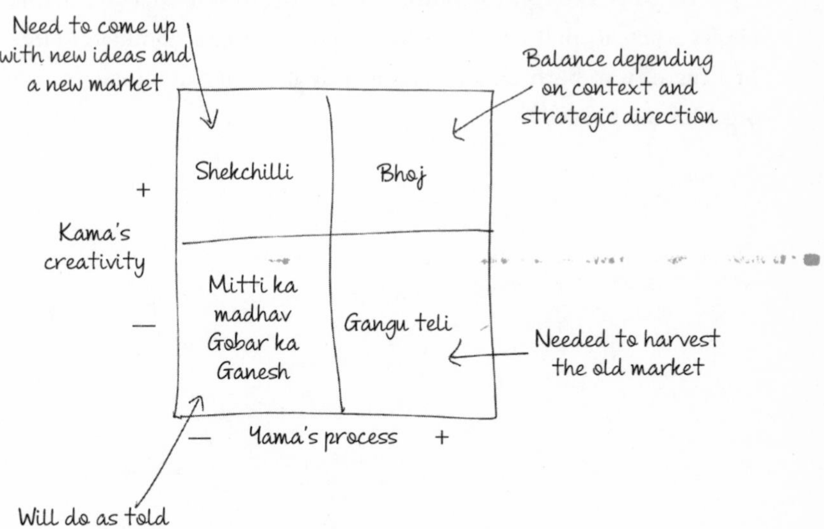

If ambition is the force, then contentment is the counterforce

Growth drives most organizations. Along with growth comes change, and change is frightening. In the pursuit of growth, one must not lose sight of the stability of things already achieved.

The most common example of force and counterforce in mythology are the devas and asuras. The devas are not afraid of death but they are afraid of losing everything they possess. On the other hand, the asuras are afraid of death but have nothing to lose, as they possess nothing. This makes devas insecure and the asuras ambitious.

The devas want to maintain the status quo whereas the asuras are unhappy with the way things are. The devas want stability, the asuras want growth. The devas fear change and do not have an appetite for risk while the asuras crave change and have a great appetite for risk. The devas enjoy yagna, where agni transforms the world around them; the asuras practice tapasya where tapa transforms them, making them more skilled, more powerful, more capable. The devas enjoy Lakshmi, spend Lakshmi, which means they are wealth-distributors, but they cannot create her; the asuras are wealth-generators hence her 'fathers'. An organization needs both devas and asuras.

They need to form a churn, not play tug of war. In a churn, one party knows when to pull and when to let go. Each one dominates alternately. In a tug of war, both pull simultaneously until one dominates or until the organization breaks.

When Sandeep's factory was facing high attrition and severe market pressures, he ensured that old loyalists were put in senior positions. They were not particularly skilled at work. They were, in fact, yes-men and not go-getters, who yearned for stability. By placing them in senior positions, Sandeep made sure a sense of stability spread across the organization in volatile times. They were his devas who anchored the ship in rough seas. When things stabilized and the market started looking up, Sandeep hired ambitious and hungry people. These were asuras, wanting more and more. They were transactional and ambitious and full of drive and energy. Now the old managers hate the new managers and block them at every turn. Sandeep is upset. He wants the old guard to change, or get out of the way, but they will not change and refuse to budge. Sandeep is feeling exasperated and frustrated. He needs to appreciate the difference between devas and asuras. Each one has a value at different times. They cannot combine well on the same team but are very good as force and counterforce during different phases of the organization. Sandeep must not expect either to change. All he needs to do is place them in positions where they can deliver their best.

If hindsight is the force, then foresight is the counterforce

Brihaspati is the guru of the cautious and insecure stability-seeking devas. Bhrigu-Shukra is the guru of the ambitious and focused, growth-seeking asuras. Sadly, neither do the devas listen to Brishaspti nor do the asuras listen to Shukra.

Watching Indra immersed in the pleasures of Swarga, Brishaspati cautioned him about an imminent attack by the asuras. "They always regroup and attack with renewed vigour. This has happened before, it will happen again. You must be ready," said Brishaspati. Indra only chuckled, ignored his guru and continued to enjoy himself, drinking sura, watching the apsaras dance and listening to the gandharvas' music. This angered Brihaspati, who walked away in disgust. Shortly thereafter, Indra learned that the asuras had attacked Amravati, but he was too drunk to push them away.

After Bali, the asura-king, had driven Indra out of Swarga, and declared himself master of sky, the earth and the nether regions, he distributed gifts freely, offering those who visited him anything they desired. Vaman, a young boy of short stature, asked for three paces of land. Shukra foresaw that Vaman was no ordinary boy, but Vishnu incarnate and this simple request for three paces of land was a trick. He begged Bali not to give the land to the boy, but Bali sneered; he felt his guru was being paranoid. As part of the ritual to grant the land, Bali had to pour water through the spout of a pot. Shukra reduced himself in size, entered the pot and blocked the spout, determined to save his king. When the water did not pour out, Vaman offered to dislodge the blockage in the spout with a blade of grass. This blade of grass transformed into a spear and pierced Shukra's eyes. He jumped out of the pot yelling in agony. The spout was cleared for the water to pour out and Vaman got his three paces of land. As soon as he was granted his request, Vaman turned into a giant: with two steps, he claimed Bali's entire kingdom. With the third step, he shoved Bali to the subterranean regions, where the asura belonged.

Brihaspati stands for hindsight and Shukra stands for foresight. Brihaspati is associated with the planet Jupiter, known in astrology for enhancing rationality, while Shukra is associated with the planet Venus, known for

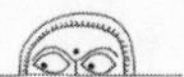

enhancing intuition. Brihaspati has two eyes and so, is very balanced. Shukra is one-eyed and so, rather imbalanced. Brihaspati is logical, cautious and backward looking while Shukra is spontaneous, bold and forward-thinking. Brihaspati relies on tradition and past history, or case studies. Shukra believes in futuristic, creative visualization and scenario planning; his father Bhrigu is associated with the science of forecasting. Brihaspati relies on memory while Shukra prefers imagination. Both are needed for an organization to run smoothly.

When Rajiv was presenting his vision and business plan to his investors, he realized they were making fun of him. His ideas seemed too strange and bizarre. They said, "Give us proof of your concept." And, "Tell us exactly how much the return on investment will be." Rajiv tried his best to answer these questions, but his idea was radical and had never been attempted before. It was a new product, like the iPad had been at its inception. He would have to create a market for it. He had sensed people's need for it though this need was not explicit. It was a hidden need, waiting to be tapped. Rajiv is a Shukra—he can see what no one else has yet seen. The investors before him are Brihaspati—they trust only what has already been seen.

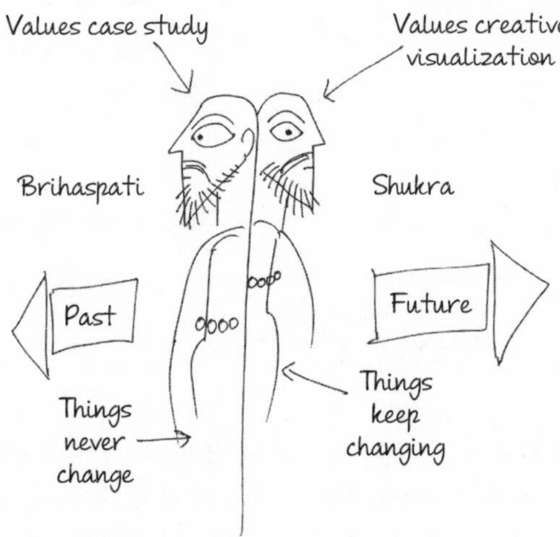

Upstream forces need to be balanced by downstream forces

The Purans state that Shiva resides in two places in two forms: he resides on the mountain in Kailas, and down by the riverbank in Kashi. In Kailas he is Adinath, the primal teacher, who offers cosmic wisdom. In Kashi, he is Vishwanath, the worldly god, who offers solutions to daily problems.

Every person is trapped between the god at Kailas who sits upstream and the god at Kashi, who sits downstream. Upstream are the bosses who sit in the central office. Downstream are the employees who face the client. Those upstream are concerned with revenue and profit, while those downstream are concerned with concessions, discounts and holidays. The yajaman needs to balance upstream hunger as well as downstream hunger.

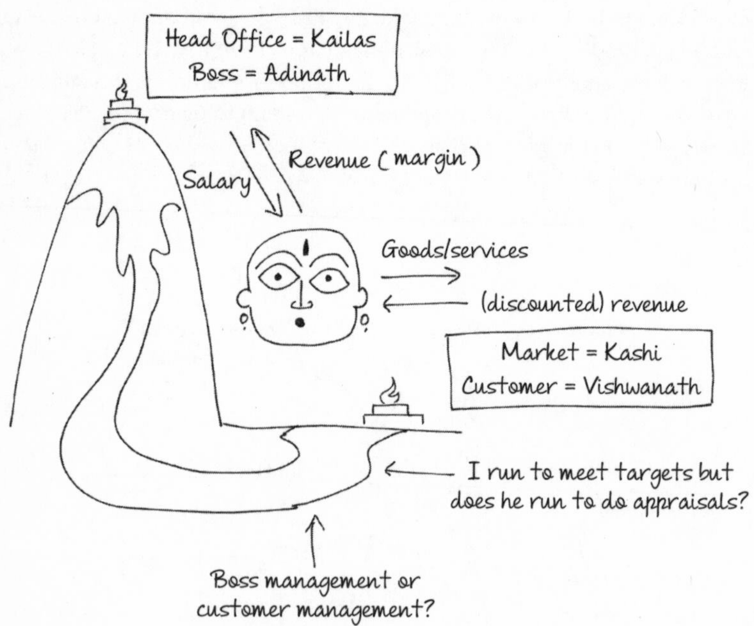

We hope that just as we see the devatas upstream and downstream, those around us do the same. When we are not treated as devatas by other yajamans, we too refuse to treat our devatas with affection. Only when we see each other

as the source of our tathastu will we genuinely collaborate and connect with each other.

At the annual meeting of branch managers, there was much heated discussion. The shareholders were clear that they wanted an improved bottom line. The bank had grown very well in the last three years in terms of revenue, but it was time to ensure profitability as well. However, the customers had gotten used to discounts and were unwilling to go along with the new strict policies that were being rolled out. General Manager Waghmare is in a fix. Kashi wants discounts while Kailas wants profit. Kashi is willing to push the top line but Kailas wants a better bottom line. He is not sure he can make both shareholder and customer happy.

Balance is the key to avoid tug of war

Vishnu has two wives, Shridevi and Bhudevi. Shridevi is the goddess of intangible wealth and Bhudevi, the earth-goddess, is goddess of tangible wealth. In some temples, they are represented as Saraswati and Lakshmi, the former being moksha-patni, offering intellectual pleasures, and the latter being bhoga-patni, offering material pleasures. Shiva also has two wives—Gauri and Ganga—one who sits on his lap and the other who sits on his head; one who is patient as the mountains and the other who is restless as a river. Krishna has two wives, Rukmini and Satyabhama, one who is poor (having eloped from her father's house) and demure, and the other who is rich (having come with her father's blessing and dowry) and demanding. Kartikeya, known as Murugan in South India, has two wives—the celestial Devasena, daughter of the gods, and Valli, the daughter of forest tribals. Ganesha has two wives, Riddhi and Siddhi, one representing wealth and the other representing wisdom. The pattern that emerges is that the two wives represent two opposing ideas balanced by the 'husband'. Amusing stories describe how the husbands struggle to make both parties happy.

The Goddess has never been shown with two husbands (patriarchy, perhaps?). However, as Subhadra in Puri, Orissa, she is shown flanked by her two brothers—Krishna, the wily cowherd and Balabhadra, the simple farmer. In Uttaranchal and Himachal, Sheravali, or the tiger-riding goddess, is flanked on one side by Bir Hanuman, who is wise and obedient, and on the other by Batuk Bhairava, who is volatile and ferocious. In Gujarat, the Goddess is flanked by Kala-Bhairo and Gora-Bhairo, the former who is ferocious and smokes narcotic hemp and the latter who is gullible and drinks only milk. In South India, Draupadi Amman, the mother goddess, has two guards, one Hindu foot soldier and the other a Muslim cavalryman; not surprising for a land that expresses tolerance and inclusion in the most unusual ways. Once again, the pattern is one of opposite forces balanced by the sister or mother.

Balance is also crucial to business. The marketing team needs to balance the sales team. The finance team needs to balance the human resources team. The back-ends need to balance front-ends. Marketing ensures demand

generation but its success cannot be quantified as its thinking is more abstract and long-term. Sales gives immediate results and is tangible, but cannot guarantee or generate future demand. The finance team focuses on processes, returns on investment and audit trails, or the impersonal facets of the company. The human resource team has to compensate this by bringing back the human touch. Back-end systems can ensure inventory and supply, but it is the front-end that has to ensure sales and service with a smile. A leader has to be the husband, sister and mother who balances the opposing wife, brother and son.

Navin started his career as a sales representative in a consumer goods company. He resented the marketing guys who sat in air-conditioned rooms all day poring over quantitative and qualitative market research data. He resented the fact that they were paid more while it was he who got in the revenue. He carries this resentment till date. Now he is the CEO of a retail chain. He spends all his time with his sales team and the guys on the frontline. He is impatient with his marketing team, tells them repeatedly to go and spend time in shops with the customers. As a result, the marketing team has become tactical about today's sales and this quarter's targets. No one in the company is thinking strategically. The CEO is meeting today's numbers and is not prepared for tomorrow's challenges. This does not bode well for the organization as a whole, or for Navin's career, because he has no one thinking ahead. This is what happens when one wife/brother/son gets more value than the opposing but balancing force.

The impact of an organizational decision is different depending on the source

In the scriptures, different beings live in different spheres. At the lowermost level are the humans. Above them are the devas or gods, led by Indra. Above Indra is Brahma and above him is Vishnu. Shiva is above Vishnu and the Goddess is above Shiva. It is said that when Indra blinks a human dies; every time Brahma blinks, an Indra dies; every time a Vishnu blinks, a Brahma dies; every time a Shiva blinks, a Vishnu dies; and every time the Goddess blinks, a Shiva dies. Thus, the notion of time differs at different levels. And the impact of blinking varies depending on who is blinking.

Organizations, too, have a similar hierarchy in place. At the top sits the CEO, below him sit many unit heads under whom are many managers who have many executives under them. Each one's 'blink' has a different impact on the market.

A leader has to realize two things with regard to this blinking. The first is related to the time-impact of his blink: it takes time for his decision to reach the periphery of his organization, that is, the frontline where people engage with the marketplace. This demands patience. The second is the space-impact of the blink: what seems like a simple decision for the leader has to manifest itself multiple times in the rest of the team. In other words, it has to be understood by many Brahmas. The impact of any error is huge. This makes the cost of an error huge. Large organizations are uncomfortable with such impacts. This is why they control the rate of decisions made upstream in the management chain. Unfortunately, this prevents large organizations from being nimble.

Further, in many organizations it is not clear who is the head. For example, in the Shiva Puran, Kailas is above Vaikuntha whereas in the Vishnu Puran, Vaikuntha is above Kailas. And not everyone agrees that the abode of the Goddess is supreme. And so, people get confused as to who is blinking and who is staring.

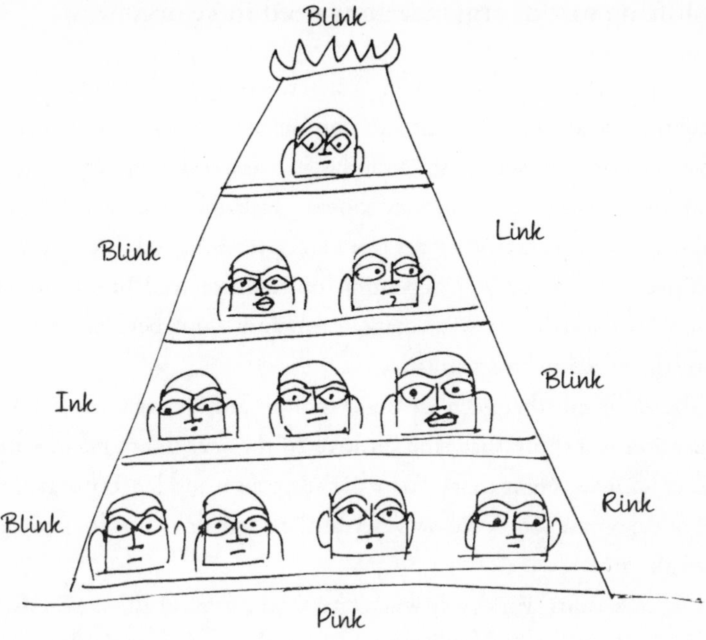

Gyanesh has still not realized the power of blinking. He is currently the head of a 800-strong sales force. Fifteen years ago, he was a salesman renowned for getting things done rapidly. He would take quick decisions and get things done. Owing to this ability, he was very popular in the market and a successful salesman. Fifteen years later, he is still restless and continues to make decisions on the spur of the moment. What he does not realize is that the decisions he makes impact the lives of 800 sales people located across the country. The impact is huge though the time taken for it to show is much longer. By the time everyone in the field understands a decision two months have passed. And by the time they implement the decision, they learn that Gyanesh has changed his mind once again.

In a shifting world, organizations need to be organisms

In the Rig Veda, the organization is described as purush, an outpouring of imagination, an organism. In Jain chronicles, the world is seen as being constantly volatile. It is never stable and is seen as a slithering serpent or sarpa that alternates between an upward boom (sushama) and bust (dushama). Our mind, too, constantly wavers from an optimistic gaze (utasarpini) to a pessimistic gaze (avasarpini), depending on resource availability and market response. With such a view of markets, organizations perforce need to be nimble; they need to be organisms.

The difference between an organization and an organism is that the organization is a thing that is insensitive to the world around it, while an organism is a living being that is aware of the world around it. The organization is a set of rules that people follow whereas the organism is a set of people who follow rules.

Organizations work well when the world around them is stable and predictable. But when the world is unstable, or the market is volatile because of political, economic and regulatory reasons, or because of the changing tastes of the consumer, the organization has to be super-sensitive and adaptable. It needs to be like an organism.

Organizations are of value when one deals with a single market. Organisms are needed when one has to deal with multiple markets. It may be a good time in one market but a bad time in another. In such cases, a global strategy does not help. One needs local strategies. That is why most Indian villages have a local village-god or grama-devata who is linked to the grand, cosmic distant and abstract bhagavan, who oversees everything. The grama-devata knows how to translate the global view to local conditions. Crisis in a particular village may not affect the whole organization, but it does matter to that particular village. The bhagavan may not give the village as much time and attention as the grama-devata would.

Most villages even have matrix structures in that there is the grama-devata who looks at problems within the context of the village, and the kula-devata who looks at the problem within the context of a particular community that is

spread across many villages. Since both the grama-devata and kula-devata are the local communities' manifestations of the global bhagavan, there is enough trust and understanding not to lead to conflict or demands for consensus.

It was a crazy idea but it worked. When Lalwani became the head of the firm, he observed that every department was a silo working in isolation. His leadership team was hardly a team but a bunch of people in the room with no connection to each other. Each of them was focusing on their individual key result area and ignoring the impact on others. So Lalwani came up with an idea. Every six months, the head of a department would make a presentation on the performance of another department and answer questions as if s/he were the head of that department. For instance, Randhir, who headed finance, would make the marketing presentation and Piyush who headed sales would make the human resource presentation. Departments were chosen by lots and to make the exercise serious, it was given a weightage of 20 per cent in the appraisal. Suddenly, everyone was talking to each other. Randhir had to understand marketing, Piyush had to understand human resources. The silos were ruthlessly broken. After much initial discomfort, people started empathizing with each other. The organization became an organism.

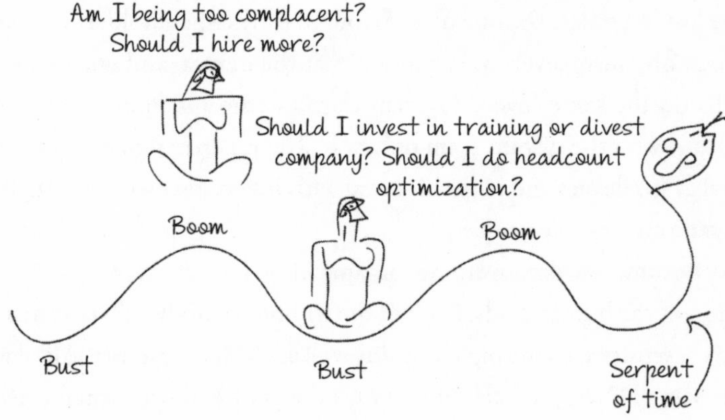

In an organism, individual potential and context are taken into consideration

In an organization, the centre takes decisions and those at the periphery follow. In an organism, people downstream (at the periphery) are as sensitive, proactive and responsible as the people upstream (at the centre). For an organization to become an organism, people need to understand both the universal as well as the particular. Everyone needs to see the big picture along with their context specific roles.

Inherent in the word 'leader' is that one who is so decides which direction everyone should go and the rest follow. Yet the leader is located in Kailas, far from the marketplace. His vision is wider, but lacks the local insight that comes from Kashi. Should his garud-drishti take precedence over sarpa-drishti?

To complement the leader's view, everyone else ought to look at the marketplace and then reach a consensus. This is teamwork preventing the autocracy of the leader. However, the people at different rungs of the organizational hierarchy do not have the same gaze, motivations, drive, or even the same line of sight. They will see different things. The eagle will end up fighting the snake and neither will win, except the most powerful, the one with the loudest voice, the one most favoured by the shareholder.

In an organism, every yajaman looks at the devata, and encourages the devata to do the same. Every yajaman clarifies who his immediate team of graha is and who the distant team of tara is. The yajaman works to evoke the potential of his devata and helps him deal with his context so that he delivers. The cascade creates an organism.

To become an organism, an organization has to try to emulate the perfection of the human body. Each of the trillions of body cells that make up our body is sensitive to the big picture as well as the local picture. All of them have the same DNA, but each of them produces only those proteins needed in their location. The eye cell has the same DNA as the skin cell, yet both are structurally and functionally very different, as demanded by their local roles. Every cell is sensitive to the world around itself. Each cell knows that the

excessive growth of one at the cost of another is cancer, which will destroy the whole organism, while suboptimal growth is degeneration and death.

Akhilesh's call centre appeared from nowhere and became a major competitor in the industry. What was the reason behind its success? Akhilesh said, "We have strict rules and systems that have to be followed by every manager. But we also have a bypass system that allows the local manager to take quick local decisions without consulting the central business unit head. The centre can in no way predict what will happen in different markets at different points of time. Every client's needs are unique and so we need to have flexible systems, which is rather ironical, as systems are meant to standardize and minimize deviations. The bypass routes make us nimble and also build trust. We do not treat those in the periphery as answerable to the centre; they are answerable to their own balance sheets. For me every employee is a manager and a leader from the first day itself. Only their contexts are small."

Organisms thrive when the yajaman is flexible

In an organization with Kamas and Yamas, devas and asuras, Brihaspatis and Shukras, garuds and sarpas, Kailas and Kashi, various constellations and planets, there is a need for liminal beings.

Liminal beings are creatures that belong in-between, neither here nor there, but on the threshold. A liminal being is a translator, an intermediary. They enable smooth transactions between different categories, as they are able to see each problem from everyone's point of view and the impact of each decision on various sections of the organization.

Ganesha is one such liminal being. He has the head of an elephant and body of a human, thus he stands at the threshold of the animal and human world. He understands animal fears which ensure survival over millions of years. At the same time, he also understands human imagination that can help us outgrow our fears, take risks, explore unfamiliar realms and create new possibilities.

He can easily move from the role of a manager to the role of a leader.

- As a manager, he has to simplify complex problems. So he yields the axe with the noose.

- As a leader, he has to direct people towards change. So he yields the sugarcane with the elephant goad.

Ganesha's axe is used to slice things apart and his noose to bind loose things together neatly. The axe represents analysis and the noose, synthesis. For the sake of administrative convenience, we can break an organization into departments. But the leader must constantly strive to bind things together so that every part also represents the whole. Unless the parts have knowledge of the whole, every individual yagna of the organizational sattra will not have the right svahas or tathastus.

To direct people towards change, the leader shares the sweetness of his vision and balances it with the sharpness of his determination. A mahout uses the ikshu or sugarcane to draw the elephant in a particular direction.

He also uses the ankush or elephant goad to make sure the elephant goes in the desired direction and does not stray from the path. The ankush has two parts attached to the tip of a short iron bar: a sharp tip and a hook. The sharp tip is used to goad the elephant forward. The hook is used to hold him back. The sharp tip pushes and the hook pulls. If the yajaman has to use an ankush repeatedly, it means that his team depends on orders and is not proactive and responsible. It is full of dependent devatas and no dependable yajamans. It means the leader is a karta and everyone else is a karya-karta. Everyone's gaze is towards the leader and not towards the market. In other words, the organization is not yet an organism.

Lalit was selected by the head of human resources to serve as the executive assistant to the managing director because he has the ability to understand the managing director's abstract ideas and articulate them in a very concrete, implementable form. Lalit is a liminal being who can easily explain the same problem to different teams in a way that each is be able understand. He can easily divide the problem into constituent units and see how each unit can contribute to the whole solution. He is easily able to see the manifold repercussions of a single event. When the company received a legal notice that forced them to recall a product from the market due to trademark issues, he immediately knew how to manage the crisis from a legal, logistical, marketing, sales, financial and people point of view. He knows which branches of the organization to push or pull, coax or threaten. Like Ganesha, he removes all obstacles and ensures the job gets done. And he manages and leads, doing what is appropriate whenever it is needed without throwing his weight around, never once stealing the limelight from the managing director.

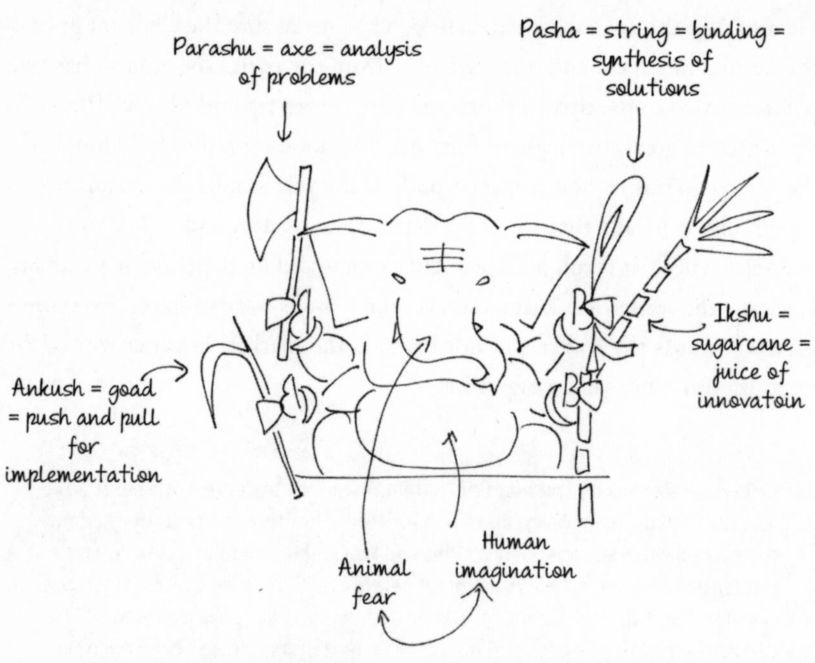
Parashu = axe = analysis of problems
Pasha = string = binding = synthesis of solutions
Ikshu = sugarcane = juice of innovatoin
Ankush = goad = push and pull for implementation
Human imagination
Animal fear
Liminal (moving seamlessly between categories and departments)

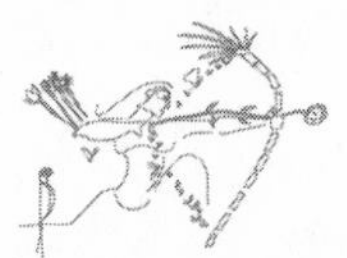

Kama's Vision Statement

Drishti, observing objective reality

Divya-drishti, observing subjective reality

Significance *Property* *Rules* *Stability*

Darshan, observing the subject

Yama's Balance Sheet

Animal instinct
to dominate, be
territorial and
aggressive.
Tools that
domesticate
nature

The human ability to see the quest for power is called divya-drishti. Plants cannot run from animals that feed on them, but animals can run from animals that prey on them. The prey lives in fear of the predator, never knowing when it will be ambushed. But it never thinks about asking for external help. Humans, on the other hand, constantly seek external help with a sense of entitlement. Fearful of exploitation, humans seek protection: a fence, a fort, or 'durg'. From durg comes Durga, the goddess of power.

Durga needs to be distinguished from Shakti, who is the inner power—physical and mental prowess—every living creature is born with. Durga represents external power, embedded in tools, technology, laws, titles and property that grants humans their social status, a location in the organizational hierarchy where they feel secure, physical and mental prowess notwithstanding.

This is made explicit in the following story: the gods one day sought protection from the asura, Mahisha. They were advised to release their inner Shaktis. These goddesses, embodying inner strength, emerged and merged into a blazing light that created a new, external goddess, Durga, who held in her many arms various weapons and rode a lion. Durga killed Mahisha and became the goddess of kings. Her weapons represent technological innovations and social structures that grant power to man. The lion represents the animal instinct within us, our desire to dominate, be aggressive and territorial.

Shakti cannot be given or taken; it can only be invoked by tapasya. Durga can be given or taken during a yagna: using social structures a person can be empowered or disempowered. A craving for Durga is indicative of a lack of Shakti. Durga compensates for a lack of Shakti. When Shakti is invoked, the hunger for Durga wanes. What is being protected here is not the physical body, but rather the mental body via the social body or karana-sharira.

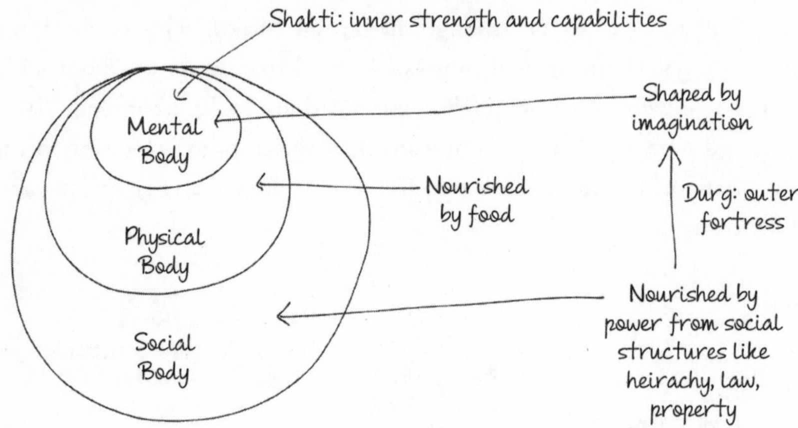

In Jain mythology, besides vasudev there is another shalaka-purush: the king or chakravarti. Chakra in the title means wheel or circle and refers to the horizon, which is circular in shape. The chakravarti is master of all that he surveys.

- The chakravarti knows that all subjects in his kingdom want to feel significant and seek status, a role and responsibility.
- He knows that the value of people comes from what they possess (property, talent, skills) which is tangible and measurable.
- He values rules as without rules the world is no different from the jungle where might is right
- He seeks stability, a world where there is certainty and predictability.

In this chapter, we shall explore significance, property, rules and stability, and by doing so, appreciate a chakravarti's gaze. A yajaman who possesses divya-drishti and values Durga walks the path of a chakravarti. A chakravarti's gaze is that of a leader determined to stabilize an already established organization and shape the destiny of his people.

Ramesh did not want to hire Shaila because she was a girl and she belonged to a lower caste. But the head of human resources, Mr. Sengupta, pointed out that company policy was very clear about not discriminating on the grounds of gender or caste. Whether Ramesh liked it or not, Shaila had to be hired because she had all the qualifications for the job. In time, Shaila gained a reputation for being a very good manager. She was promoted to the position of junior manager in less than three years. Shaila's gender and her intelligence constitute her Shakti. Her educational qualification constitutes her Durga, something she has obtained from the outside. The rules of the company that ensure she is treated with respect also grant her Durga. Over time, her social being that was being disempowered by her caste came to be empowered by her promotion at the workplace. Mr. Sengupta behaved like a chakravarti using rules to ensure she got the power she was due.

Significance

Every human being wants to feel they matter. Social structures grant this value through rules and property. This value allows us to indulge our animal instinct to dominate, hence feel powerful and secure. Unfortunately, social structures are not permanent. Any change can render us powerless; that is why we seek stability.

Every devata imagines himself differently from natural reality

Shiva, with ash-smeared face, was deep in thought. When he opened his eyes he saw a mirror in front of him held by Gauri who had anointed herself with turmeric in order to look radiant. "What do you see?" she asked.

"I see mortal flesh," he said.

"But I see a beautiful body," she said.

"That is your imagination," he argued.

"What is humanity without imagination?" she replied.

Shiva smiled. For this was true.

When animals look into a mirror they do not recognize themselves. They wonder if the reflected beast is a threat or an opportunity. If it is neither, they move away and continue with their lives. A few apes and dolphins seem to show curiosity about reflected images but they do not actively seek reflections as humans do, so scientists are not fully sure if they recognize themselves. We, on the other hand, are able to see ourselves in mirrors. Or do we?

Is it ourselves we see, or what we imagine of ourselves? This imagination of ourselves is our mental image of ourselves. The strong can imagine themselves as weak, the beautiful can imagine themselves as strong, a villain

can imagine himself as a hero. No one stops a Brahma from imagining himself in any way.

Nature does not care for this mental image. In the Ramayan, when Hanuman is flying over the sea on his mission to find Sita, the monster Surasa blocks his path, intent on eating him. Hanuman says, "I am on a mission for Ram. Let me complete it and then I promise I will return so you can eat me." Surasa retorts, "I do not understand the meaning of mission or Ram or promise. All I know is that I am hungry and you are potential food."

Nature only recognizes predators and prey, alpha on top of the pecking order and omega at the bottom. These are functional roles that facilitate survival; they are not permanent roles. They cannot be inherited.

Human structures make no sense to animals or plants. That is why all animals and plants treat all humans equally. Water will quench the thirst of both saint and sinner; the tree will give shade to the rich as well as the poor; the dog will adore its master, even if the world considers the master to be a criminal.

As the eldest son in his family, Virendra has always been the recipient of much love and respect. His siblings and cousins look up to him. He manages family funds and is sought when major decisions need to be taken. However, when Virendra goes to office, he feels miserable. For everything he does, he has to ask permission: fill forms, get approvals, and seek clearances. He does not feel he is trusted or respected. The workplace does not endorse the mental image of him that his family has helped create.

Only another human being can endorse the mental image

Two men approach each other on a bridge. Each expects the other to make way for him, but neither does. One identifies himself as a learned sage. The other identifies himself as a powerful king. The sage proves his learnedness by spewing chants and hymns. The king proves his power by flexing his muscles, but still neither of them yields to the other. The learned sage thinks learning is superior to power. The powerful king thinks power is superior to learning. Finally, the angry sage puts a curse on the king and turns him into a demon. The first act of this newly transformed demon is to eat the sage in front of him. Two lives are thus ruined by mutual stubbornness.

Every human being wants to be identified by those around them. With identification comes evaluation. The sage is not happy simply being identified as a sage; he wants to be valued for it and this value is demonstrated by receiving the right to first passage. Likewise, the king seeks right of first passage as a sign that he, too, has been identified and valued.

When we are recognized we feel powerful. When we are not recognized we feel powerless. When we are valued we receive Durga. When we are not valued we do not receive Durga. We want to feel significant. We want to be located in a social hierarchy. In other words, we seek aukaat, which means status and prestige. The purpose of social structures is to grant us a social position and power, which makes us feel powerful and secure. We seek izzat or respect, and acknowledgment of what we believe is our aukaat.

Only humans can endorse the mental image of other humans. This is why we feel nervous around strangers. We feel insecure until the other is able to identify us. So we exchange visiting cards and introduce ourselves. But identification alone is not enough, we want to feel seen and valued. And so following introductions we speak of our achievements and refer to mutual friends and contacts, especially those who are socially significant, so as to feel increasingly powerful when others are able to recognize us and locate us in a cultural hierarchy.

When Siddhu saw Abhays's visiting card, he was startled to find it detailing the latter's degrees, affiliations, titles, numerous charitable activities and business roles. Siddhu realized that Abhay wanted to be recognized for all his achievements. He wanted to feel he mattered for all that he had done. Abhay's promotion of his social roles through his visiting card drew attention to his mental image, his yearning for validation. When people looked at the card and showed amazement and admiration, Abhay got his Durga.

We defend our mental image at any cost

Kahoda suddenly hears a voice correcting him. It is his unborn child, speaking from within his wife's womb! "Perhaps," the child says, "the same hymn can be interpreted another way, father."

Rather than appreciate his son, Kahoda is annoyed. "May this over-smart child of mine be born deformed with eight twists in his body," he snarls. That is how the child gets his name—Ashtavakra, he who is bent in eight places.

While Ashtavakra is still an infant, his father goes to the court of King Janak to participate in a public debate. The condition of the debate is that the loser has to become the slave of the winner. Kahoda, who thinks highly of his wisdom, participates, but loses the debate to a sage called Bandi. He is stripped of his freedom, not allowed to go home and forced to serve his new master.

When Ashtavakra grows up and learns about the fate of his father, he decides to participate in the same public debate in Janak's court. Though barely eight years old, he manages to defeat Bandi. By the rules of the competition, Bandi now has to serve as Ashtavakra's slave. "Free my father instead," says the young genius.

When Kahoda enters Janaka's court he recognizes his saviour as his son by his deformity and breaks down. Ashtavakra's deformity springs from Kahoda's own insecurity.

Kahoda's aukaat is threatened by Ashtavakra's brilliance, which is why Kahoda curses his own son, behaving like a cornered beast. Later, his social body takes a beating anyway at the hand of Bandi who reduces him to a slave. Had Kahoda allowed his son's brilliance to nourish his mental body, enhance his Shakti, this would have perhaps not happened. In insecurity, we often keep away things that can benefit us in the long run, contribute to our sustainability. We choose comforting Durga over discomforting Shakti. We banish Ashtavakras from our own life and makes ourselves vulnerable to Bandis.

As soon as it was announced that the new CEO wanted a matrix organization, Vandana smiled. This was the CEO's way of ensuring no one threatened his position. There would be business unit verticals and functional horizontals. For every job, each team member would have to report to two bosses. The official reason for this was to create push and pull—tension to maximum output. The underlying motive, however, was to ensure there was tension between business heads and functional heads. They would be too busy fighting each other to threaten the new CEO. Moreover, by getting a management firm to propose the matrix structure, the CEO had ensured that the board of directors did not suspect he was playing politics to ensure the survival of his social image.

We are terrified of how strangers will evaluate us

We imagine those around us to be predators and ourselves as the prey. We fear we will be reduced to an omega in a group when we would rather be alpha, the centre of attention. Every devata has the desire to, at the very least, feel secure, recognized and valued, not sidelined and forgotten. The offering of haldi (turmeric), kumkum (red powder) and chaval (grains of rice) to deities, in that order, is a ritual acknowledgment of this human anxiety.

- The yellow of turmeric is a virile color, the colour of the sun, spreading across the sky and reaching out to the earth. The intent behind sprinkling it over the deity is to evoke the deity's grace and power. Turmeric is antiseptic, destroying germs as the gods destroy demons. It is meant to remove negative energy, the feeling of prevailing threat.

- Red is the colour of potential energy; virgin-goddesses are draped in a red sari. Red evokes a sense of the fertile red earth before the rains, holding the promise of crops. It is meant to usher in positive energy, a highlighting of our strengths.

- Rice is food, sustaining life, the final output that rises out of the earth and is warmed by the sun. It is meant to draw attention to the opportunity created by the relationship that can follow.

Often in meetings, for want of time, people get straight down to business, focusing on tasks and targets. Quick introductions are followed by a clarification of the agenda and the meeting is begun immediately. Meetings then, become a process and not a meeting of hearts and minds. There is no Durga exchanged in such a meeting and so it lacks energy, engagement and joy.

Whenever Herbert goes for a meeting, he always smiles and admits he is nervous, enough to want to visit the restroom several times. This relieves the tension in the meeting room and even makes people chuckle. This is his haldi. He then compliments the person he is meeting: sometimes about the company they work for, or the shirt they are wearing. Sometimes he starts a conversation about the country they're from, or the mobile phone they are using. There is always something nice to say about a person if one looks for it. This is kumkum. Only after easing the tension with a casual conversation, does Herbert get to the main body of the meeting—the chaval—drawing attention to the agenda. Over the years he has learned that when people feel relaxed and positive, the meeting gives better results. He also knows that haldi and kumkum offered mechanically and not genuinely yield nothing.

Praise empowers us

Aarti is the ritual of beholding the deity. Lamps are waved around the deity so that light falls on the image of the god or goddess. This is often accompanied by the singing of bhajans, the lyrics of which draw attention to the deity's great accomplishments: the killing of demons, the rescue of devotees, the admiration of all beings. It is an exercise that acknowledges the deity's deeds and achievements.

The ritual draws attention to the value of praise. Everyone likes to hear good things about themselves and their work. Our self-image thrives on it. Praise reaffirms our faith in ourselves. It makes us feel validated. It makes us feel acknowledged. It makes us feel alive.

The aarti ritual is conducted daily, for every day we need validation of who we are. And to ensure it does not become monotonous or thoughtless, festivals are organized where the same offering is made rather lavishly to the sound of music and the smell of incense. At the end of the ritual, the devotee asks the deity for a favour.

In temples, the aarti is not restricted to the presiding deity. Aartis are done to all the subsidiary and satellite shrines, even the doorkeepers of the shrine, the consorts and the vehicle or vahana. Everyone is acknowledged and praised, no one is invalidated. This increases the chance of divine intervention.

Is an aarti and bhajan strategic or sincere? Is praise by bosses strategic or sincere? We will never know. What matters is that it makes a difference to the subject being admired. No one ever complained when occasionally they found themselves being praised.

Farokh, the team leader of a media company, knows the value of praise. He introduces each member of his team as 'an expert', 'stalwart' or 'key member'. He remembers every little achievement of theirs. When Sanjay walks into a meeting, he beams when Farokh says, "Here comes the guy who stayed back late last week to get the files downloaded for client presentation." Shaila, the trainee, is thrilled to hear Farokh declare, "The way Shaila maintains records of client meetings is laudable." Through these words, Farokh empowers his team, makes them feel valued and important. It reveals they are not invisible performers of tasks. They are people who matter. His praise fuels them and they go that extra mile at work. But just as bhajans do not work without bhakti, praise does not work unless it is genuine. Whatever Farokh says is true. None of it is a charade. He constantly looks at what to admire in every person he meets. No person is perfect, but everyone has something of value to offer. It may seem insignificant to others but it becomes significant when noticed. That Ali always calls his wife at lunchtime has no corporate significance. But Farokh turns it into office fuel when he remarks in front of everyone, "I wish my daughter gets a husband as caring as Ali." It makes Ali blush. He feels happy. And in happiness, he delivers more.

Insults disempower us

In many Hindu temples, at least once annually, the devotee does ninda-stuti and ritually abuses the deity for failing him. This is a cathartic exercise, a safety valve. It is a reminder that the deity has no mental-image; it needs no Durga to sustain it. It is also a reminder that the devotee has a mental-image that feels deprived or denied when the deity does not satisfy a desire.

An animal in the forest does not resent or begrudge anyone. The predator does not complain when it fails to catch its prey, or when the rival drives it out of its territory. The prey does not jeer at the predator after outrunning it. Animals simply move on with life. Humans often consider their desire to be their due and expect life to provide them with whatever they yearn for.

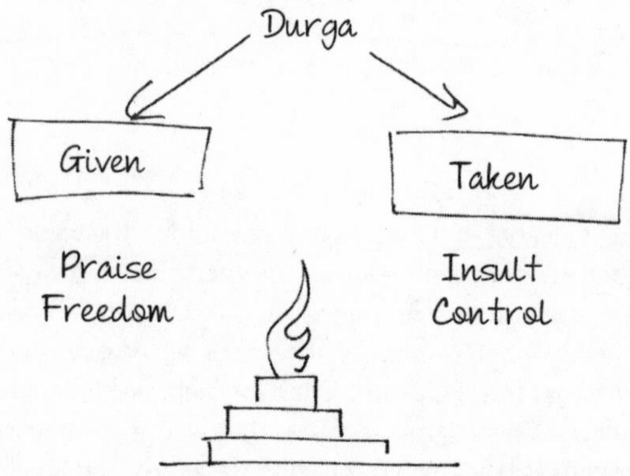

Ninda-stuti is the equivalent of office mockery or 'backbiting' or complaining (colloquially called bitching) about the boss. A yajaman understands its source and allows it to thrive as it relieves tension, helps the employee experience the delusion of power. Gossip serves the same purpose. By pulling down or mocking someone else, by imagining the Other to be inferior, we empower our mental-image. Jokes come from the same place—a narrative that grants superiority to the person hearing the joke over the person who is the subject of the joke.

During her coffee break, Reshma goes to the cafeteria and sits with the other office girls. After initial pleasantries, the topic shifts to the team supervisor: how she dresses, how she speaks, how she curries favours with the bosses, how she got promoted, how she travels. No one has a kind word for her. They see her as a monster. Sometimes, the girls talk about their experiences with callers: the accents, the demands, the time spent on inane matters. At the end of these short but spicy conversations, Reshma feels fresh and invigorated, full of Durga, strong enough to handle the monotony of her daily job. She looks forward to these meetings with the girls.

Enter to feel good about yourself

Comparison grants us value

The Mahabharat tells the story of Kadru and Vinata, the two wives of Kashyapa. Kashypa was one of the many sons of Brahma. Kadru asks to be the mother of many sons. Vinata asks for mighty sons. Kashyapa blesses them both. Kadru lays a thousand eggs while Vinata lays only two. Why does Kadru seek many sons? Why does Vinata seek mighty offspring?

The answer lies in mental image. It is not enough being the wife of Kashyapa. What matters more is knowing who is the preferred wife. Kadru feels many sons will get her more attention. Vinata feels mightier sons will get her more attention. Each wife wants to be envied by the other, and thus be in a dominant position. We yearn to be mental alphas of an imaginary pack. When we are envied we feel superior and powerful.

Kadru becomes the mother of serpents. Vinata becomes the mother of eagles. Serpents eat the eggs of eagles and the eagles feed on serpents. This eternal enmity is traced to the desire of the mothers to measure, hence evaluate ergo dominate.

Venu was happy he went to the business school that was ranked fifth while Raghav went to a business school that ranked seventh. He was happy that he got a placement before Raghav. He was happy that his first salary was more than Raghav's. He was happy that he got a promotion earlier than Raghav, but then Raghav started his own business and it was a success. Suddenly, Raghav is his own boss; he may not make as much money but he is answerable to no one. Venu now hates his life. He has fallen in the measuring scale. He is unable to see himself without comparing himself to Raghav. He lives in the world of measurement: the matrix called maya.

Comparison is a powerful tool to identify ourselves and locate ourselves in a hierarchy. Comparison means measurement. In Sanskrit, the word maya or delusion is rooted in the sound 'ma' meaning 'to measure'. For a world seen through measurement is delusion.

Maya and satya are opposites of each other. Both are truths, but maya

is truth based on comparison while satya is truth not based on comparison. Maya allows for judgment, as there is a reference scale; satya does not.

	Maya (delusion, value)	Satya (truth, identity)
Measure	✓	✗
Compare	✓	✗
Reference	✓	✗
Denominator	✓	✗

In nature, everything is perfect at every moment. Everything has a place and purpose. Nothing is better or worse. A bigger animal is not better; it simply has a higher chance of survival. But in culture, measuring scales are geared not towards survival of the species but towards the validation of our mental image. Measuring scales are designed to include and exclude, create a hierarchy. Measuring scales can grant us Durga if they favour us, and strip us of power when they do not. In nature, nothing is good or bad, right or wrong, higher or lower. Everything matters. Everything is satya.

On the other hand, marketing and business is all about maya. In interviews we rank candidates using measuring scales. In markets, we rank products using measuring scales. We give compensation and bonuses and perks based on measuring scales. The world of sanskriti is all about maya. The social body feeds on maya. Maya has the power to make us feel powerful and powerless. In culture, some things always matter more than others.

We seek hierarchies that favour us

When he is made chakravarti of the world, Bharat, the eldest son of Rishabh, expects all his brothers to bow before him. Rather than bow, most renounce the world and become Jain monks. One brother, however, refuses to bow or to renounce. His name is Bahubali, the second son of Rishabh. Bharat declares war on Bahubali. To avoid unnecessary bloodshed, the elders recommend that the brothers engage in a series of duels to prove who is stronger. Bahubali turns out to be stronger than Bharat, but a point comes when Bahubali has to raise his hand and strike Bharat on the head. The idea of striking his elder brother disgusts Bahubali. Instead, he uses his raised hand to pluck hair from his own head, thus declaring his intention to be a Jain monk like his younger brothers.

Since Bahubali has renounced the world after his younger brothers, he is a junior monk and is now expected to bow to the senior monks, his younger brothers included. Bahubali finds this unacceptable. Surely it is the other way around, and younger brothers should bow to their elder brothers? However, in the monastic order the rules of seniority are different.

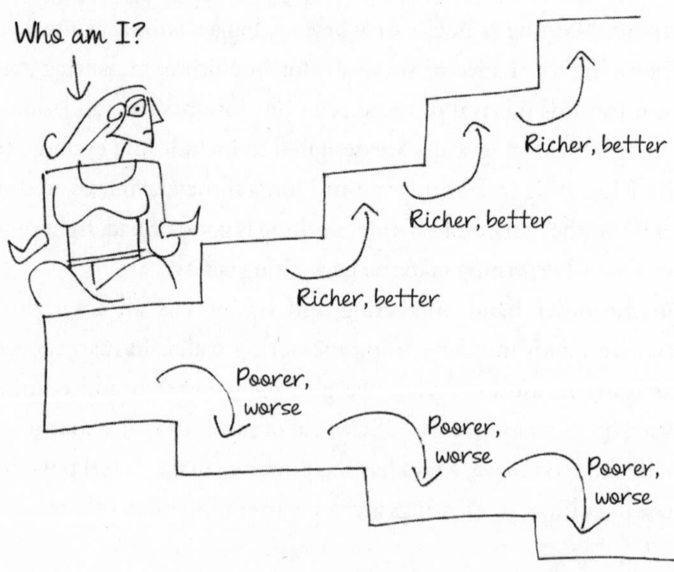

Every organization has a structure; every structure has a hierarchy. In some organizations this is determined by the duration of employment, or merit, or closeness to the owners, and in yet others, it is determined on the basis of the community, gender or institution one belongs to. The conflict comes when the hierarchy of the organization does not match the hierarchy of the mind.

Bahubali struggles. He became a monk to avoid bowing to his elder brother and ended up having to bow to his younger brothers. And yet, being a monk is not only about renouncing the social body but also renouncing the mental body. It is easier to give up material things and one's status in society, far harder to give up the thought of domination.

When Rahul joined as the assistant manager of a shipping firm, he was told that two people, Jaydev and Cyrus, would report to him. Jaydev and Cyrus were senior by many years and they found the idea of Rahul signing their appraisal forms unacceptable. Rahul did not see what the problem was, surely the system had to be respected. Like Bahubali, he realized the problem when he was asked to report to the owner's son, Pinaki, who, though senior in years, was neither as qualified or as smart as him. Jaydev and Cyrus could not handle reporting to a younger man. Rahul could not handle reporting to a man he thought to be less smart than him. Both had to struggle between the desire to dominate and the rules of domestication.

We would rather be unique than equal

There was a kingdom called Andher Nagari, literally meaning the dark land, where everything cost just one rupee. A measure of vegetables cost a rupee, the same measure of sweets also cost a rupee. A young man thought this place was paradise. "No, it is not," said his teacher, "A country where there is no differentiation between vegetables and sweets is a dangerous place. Just run from here." But the young man insists on staying back, enjoying the delights of the market.

It so happened that in this kingdom a murderer had to be hanged for his crime. Unfortunately, the rope was too short and the noose too wide to hang the short, thin criminal. So Chaupat Raja, the insane king of Andher Nagari, said, "Find a tall and fat man who can be hanged instead. Someone has to be hanged for the crime." The soldiers catch the young man in the market. He protested that he is no murderer. "But you are tall and fat enough to be hanged," said the king. It is then the young man realized what his teacher had been trying to tell him: that the people who could not differentiate between vegetables and sweets, where everything was valued equally and cost the same, in their eyes there was no difference between a criminal and an innocent man.

This folk story speaks of a land where everyone is treated equally. No value is placed on differences. Only humans can imagine such a world. In nature, physical differences matter. This difference results in food chains and pecking orders. Humans can, if they so will, create a world where no differences are seen. Such a utopia is frightening as it means in this world nothing is special, no one matters, no one is significant.

The head office prepared a design and insisted that every office of the company around the world be designed accordingly. They were essentially open offices, with no cabins for individuals, but with rooms for meetings and teleconferences. The point was to express the organizational value of transparency and equality. Instead of energizing the workplace, the new design demotivated many. Shridhar suddenly found himself without a cabin. All his life he had worked to become worthy of a cabin and now the policy had changed. He felt angry and humiliated. He felt he had been denied his Durga. He did not matter. He was a nobody like everyone else. As soon as he got a job in a rival firm, with the assurance of a cabin, he left. At the exit interview, the human resource manager felt that he was being immature: how did a cabin matter? Clearly what mattered to the manager was very different from what mattered to Shridhar, who did not want to be part of Andher Nagari.

Culture provides only a temporary framework for our social body

In the Ramayan, as Dashrath, king of Ayodhya, is dying, he panics and calls his wife and says, "I am dying. My eldest son, Ram, has been exiled to the forest. My other son, Bharat, has not yet returned from his uncle's house. I cannot afford to die. What will happen to Ayodhya if I am not there." To this, his wife says, "Nothing will happen. The sun will rise, and set. The moon will wax and wane. People will go about their business. Ayodhya will survive, perhaps not even noticing the absence of its king."

It is Ayodhya that makes Dasharath feel he matters. If there were no Ayodhya, he would not be king and his death would have no grave significance. Organizations grant us value. They position us both within the organization as well as outside. What we fail to realize is that while we need the organization, the organization does not need us. Brahma needs sanskriti to escape the indifference of prakriti but sanskriti does not need Brahma.

Every day, organizations hire new people and old people leave the company—either angrily, or happily, or because they have no choice. This is the 'birth' of a new employee and the 'death' of an old one. Both events are filled with insecurity. The arrival of a new employee threatens the old discourse, and so there is need to induct the new into the old ways of the company. The departure of the old employee also threatens the old discourse hence the desperate need for a talent pool and pipeline. Very rarely does an individual become indispensable to a degree that determines the fate of an institution. There is always someone who can take his place. The denial of this truism leads to panic. Acceptance leads to peace.

Pathakji had served the company as an accountant for over thirty-eight years. He was so good at managing the accounts that the owner felt he was indispensable. So did Pathakji, until one day, the owner died and his nephew took over. The nephew did not think much of Pathakji. He was given a nice salary and a nice cabin but no real work. Pathakji was furious and soon after submitted his resignation in a huff; this was accepted without even the pretence of resistance. "Let me see how they solve the accounts," he said as he left the building for the last time. Five years have since passed. Pathakji is still waiting for the new management to call him back. They are managing without him. It's a feeling he does not like. The management did suffer for a while without Pathakji, but his absence created a vacuum and new talent emerged. That was a good thing. But now that apparently indispensable Pathakji has been replaced, those left behind in the company feel they, too, are dispensable. It is a feeling no one likes. Suddenly, they all feel like 'full time equivalents' or FTEs, numbers on an excel sheet that can be deleted at any moment. Insecurity seeps into the organization. And in insecurity, everybody clings to their respective roles and responsibilities with tenacity. New talent is not allowed to come in and if they do come in they are not allowed to thrive. Everyone wants to make themselves indispensible. They will all die trying.

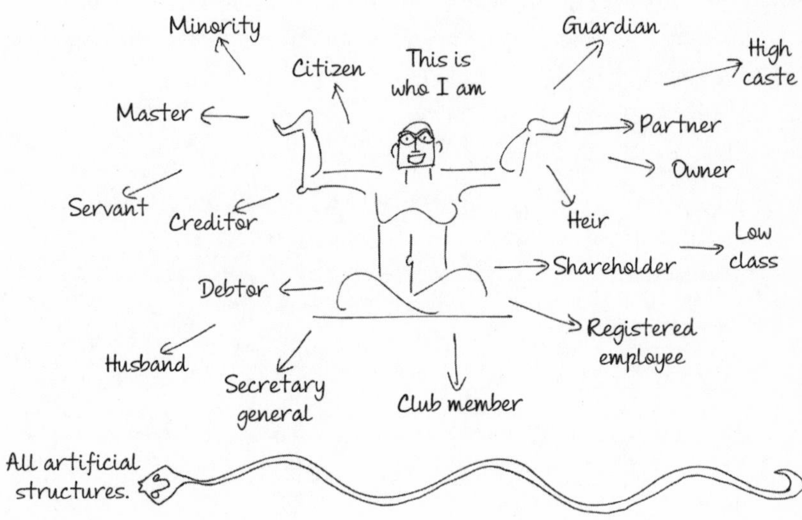

Property

Property is an idea of man, by man, and for man. Property gives a man value, for most people assume we are what we have because what we have is tangible, not who we are. We may die, but what we have can outlive us. Thus property gives us the delusion of immortality.

We see things not thoughts

When they decided to go to war, both the Kauravs and the Pandavs approached Krishna for help. "I love you both equally so will divide myself into two halves. Take whichever half you want."

Krishna offered one side the Narayani Sena, his fully-armed army. To the other, he offered Narayan, that is, himself unarmed. The Kauravs chose Narayani Sena. The Pandavs chose Narayan. The Kauravs chose Krishna's resources that are saguna: visible, tangible and measurable while the Pandavs chose Krishna's potential or nirguna: invisible, intangible and not measurable.

Narayan is who-we-are. Narayani is what-we-have. Narayan is expressed through Narayani. Most people rely on measuring Narayani to determine what is Narayan.

That is how the value of a person is determined by his possessions: his university degrees, income, bank balance, clothes, car, and so on.

Possessions are resources. They are tangible and measurable. Potential is not tangible and measurable. In the world of management where measurement matters, Narayan is ignored and Narayani preferred. We check what a person brings to the table during interviews. We value a customer's wallet, more than the customer. A employee is valued for his skills only. His vision, his fears, his feelings do not matter. The latter cannot be measured. Their value cannot be determined. Nobody knows how to leverage who we are. But we have many ways of leveraging what-we-have. In other words, we welcome Kauravs into the organization, not Pandavs, which does not bode well for anyone.

Every leader wonders if the person speaking to him speaks to his person or the authority he wields by virtue of his position. The king wonders if he matters or his sword: this is the curse of kingship.

To motivate his team, Bipin asked his guru to give them a speech. The guru quoted verses from the Bhagavad Gita about staying calm in success and in failure. While it felt good to hear the discourse, one of Bipin's sales managers was heard commenting, "I may be calm but my failure will certainly get Bipin agitated. He does not care for us. He only cares for our performance. We are a performance-driven organization after all." The sales manager knew that if his sales numbers dipped, he could bid his bonus goodbye. The company only cared for the Narayani, not the Narayan.

Things help us position ourselves

When Hanuman, a monkey, entered Lanka and identified himself as Ram's messenger and asked for a seat as protocol demanded, he was spurned by the rakshasa-king, Ravan, who insulted him by denying him one. Hanuman retaliated by announcing that he would create a seat for himself: he extended his tale, coiled it around and created a seat higher than Ravan's throne. Instead of being amused or impressed, Ravan was infuriated. His power was threatened. In a rage, he ordered Hanuman's tail be set aflame.

The story reveals how a thing (a seat) is used to communicate a thought (pecking order). Hanuman does not care for power or for thrones but he realizes things mean a lot to Ravan. By the dramatic use of his tail, he breaches the fortress of Ravan's mind and shatters his mental image in an instant.

What is interesting is that Hanuman does not need an external thing to position himself; he expands what he already has—his tail. In other words, he finds strength within and does not need the help of an object or a salutation. He has enough Shakti to compensate for the Durga that Ravan refuses to give him.

We constantly use material things to position ourselves: our cabins, our houses, our cars, our mobile phones, and so on. When these are taken away from us, or damaged, we feel hurt. When our possessions are damaged, when our car gets scratched, or our watch gets stolen, or our seat is given to someone else, our social body gets damaged and this causes pain to the mental body; even though the physical body is perfectly fine.

When it was time to buy a new mobile phone, Pervez had a simple rule. He checked what models his clients and his bosses were using. He then bought an inferior model. He did not want to intimidate any of them or make them feel insecure. In fact, he wanted them to criticize his choice and mock him for buying a poor-quality phone. "I want them to put me down. I want them to feel superior. It helps me in my relationship with them." Pervez has understood the power of using things to generate Durga.

Things are surrogate markers of our value

Indra calls Vishwakarma, his architect, and orders him to build a palace worthy of his stature. Vishwakarma builds a palace of gold but Indra feels it is not good enough. So Vishwakarma builds him a palace of diamonds; Indra is not satisfied with that either. So Vishwkarma builds him a palace using that most elusive of elements, ether; even this does not please Indra.

Why does Indra want to build a larger palace? Is not being king of the devas enough? Clearly not; he needs his mental status to have a tangible manifestation in the form of a palace. But no palace matches his mental expectation, as his mental body is much greater than all the things he can possess. That leaves him dissatisfied.

In the world Indra lives in, people are measured by the amount of things they have. Since he wants to be bigger and better than everyone else, he wants his palace to be bigger and better than others'.

Property is a physical manifestation of our mental body. It contributes to our social body. What we have determines who we are. We cannot see the mental body, but we do see the social body. Our possessions become an extension of who we are. We equate ourselves with what we have. When we die, what we have outlives us, thus possessions have the power to grant us immortality. That is why property is so dear to humans.

Raju hated driving. Since he could not afford a driver, he did not buy a car. He travelled every day to office by auto. This annoyed his boss. "Your team members will not respect you unless you have a car." Raju did not understand this: surely they respected him for his work and managerial skills. Nevertheless, he finally succumbed to the pressure and bought a car. His son was very annoyed, "But daddy, all my friends have bigger cars." Raju realized the car was not only a mode of conveyance; it was about grabbing a place in the social hierarchy.

Thoughts can be coded into things

Narad asked the wives of Krishna to give him something that they felt was equal in value to their husband. He gets a weighing scale into the courtyard and makes Krishna sit on one of the pans. On the other, each of the wives put what they feel equals Krishna's worth. Satyabhama puts all her gold, utensils and jewels, but the scale still weighs less than Krishna. Rukmini, on the other hand, places a sprig of tulsi on the pan and declares it to be a symbol of her love for Krishna. Instantly, the scales shift.

Both Satyabhama and Rukmini value Krishna for the impact he has had on them. How does one quantify this transformation? How do they give form to their mental image of him? Satyabhama expresses her thoughts through things while Rukmini uses a symbol, a metaphor. When people recognize this code, the tulsi becomes more valuable than gold. Everyone values gold. Only those who appreciate the language of symbols will appreciate tulsi.

The same principle applies to brands. Brands are thoughts embodied by things. When people buy a brand, they are buying a thought or a philosophy that makes them feel powerful, which raises their stature in the eyes of those who matter to them. Naturally, people are willing to pay a lot of money for such codes. The cost of making a product is much less than the cost at which brands are sold. In order to charge a premium, great effort has to be made through advertising and marketing to establish the brand's philosophy in a cultural landscape. Unless people are able to decode what the brand stands for, it will have no value.

Zafar has a small shop that sells fake brands at about a quarter of the real price. He has never understood why people pay so much for brand names. The actual cost of production is much lower. His uncle explained, "The customer is not buying a tool that tells the time. He is buying aukaat: status, dignity, respect, admiration and envy. For that the customer is ready to pay anything." Zafar thus understood the difference between the literal and symbolic value of Rukmini's tulsi.

We assume we are what we have

Paundraka, king of Karusha, wears a crown with a peacock feather. He holds a lotus flower in one hand and a conch-shell in the other. Around his neck he wears a garland of forest flowers, the Vanamali. From his ears hang earrings that are shaped like dolphins, the Makara-kundala. He is draped in a bright yellow silk dhoti or the Pitambara. He even has hairdressers curl his hair. He insists on eating rich creamy butter with every meal. He plays the flute in flowery meadows on moonlit nights surrounded by his queens and concubines who dance around him. "I look like Krishna. I do everything Krishna does. I must be Krishna," he says to himself. His subjects, some gullible, some confused and others frightened, worship him with flowers, incense, sweets and lamps. Everyone wonders who the true Krishna is since both look so similar?

Then a few courtiers point out that Krishna of Dwaraka has a wheel-shaped weapon that no other man has called the Sudarshan Chakra. "Oh that," Paundraka explains, "He borrowed it from me. I must get it back from the impostor." So a messenger is sent to inform Krishna to return the Sudarshan Chakra or face stern consequences. To this, Krishna replies, "Sure, let him come and get it."

Irritated that Krishna does not come to return the Sudarshan Chakra, Paundraka sets out for Dwaraka on his chariot, decorated with a banner that has the image of Garud on it, reinforcing his identity. When he reaches the gates of Dwaraka, he shouts, "False Krishna, return the Sudarshan Chakra to the true Krishna." Krishna says, "Here it is." The Sudarshan Chakra that whirrs around Krishna's index finger flies towards Paundraka. Paundraka stretches out his hand to receive it. As the wheel alights on his finger, he realizes it is heavier than it looks. So heavy, in fact, that before he can call for help he is crushed to pulp under the great whirring wheel. That is the end of the man who pretended to be Krishna.

The corporate world is teeming with pretenders and mimics. They think they know how to walk the walk and talk the talk but they simply don't know what the talk is all about. They know how to dress, how to carry their laptops and smart phones, what car to drive, where to be seen, with whom, how to use words like 'value enhancement' and 'on the same page' and 'synergy' and 'win-win'. In other words, they know the behaviour that projects them as corporate leaders, but are nowhere close to knowing what true leadership actually means.

At a fast-growing firm, Vijaychandra selects a young man who shows all the signs of having the talent and drive of a leader. The young man's name is Jaipal. His CV indicates he's from the right universities, has the right credentials and impressive testimonies. Besides which, he's also nattily dressed and articulate. He even plays golf! He is fit to head the new e-business division. Two years down the line, however, despite all the magnificent PowerPoint presentations and Excel sheets, which impressed quite a few investors, the e-division's revenue is way below the mark. The market has just not responded. Jaipal knows how to talk business, but evidently he does not know how to do business. Vijaychandra decides to investigate what Jaipal has done in the past two years. It emerges that while Jaipal has stayed in the right hotels and driven the right cars, he has never gone to personally meet the vendors or customers. He has not made the effort to immerse himself in market research; on the contrary, he has hired people to do it for him. He focuses on 'strategy' but not on 'tactics'. He loves boardroom brainstorming but not shop-floor sweat. His organization structure is designed such that it keeps him isolated from the frontline. He simply assumes that his team will know what to do in the marketplace. He has never picked up the phone and addressed client grievances—he prefers the summary of conclusions provided by reputed analysts. He does not get to hear his sales people whine and groan and prefers the echoes of the market presented by strategy consultants. Vijaychandra realizes he has a Paundraka on his hands—all imitation, no inspiration.

We expect things to transform us

One day, as King Bhoj and his soldiers approach a field, a farmer is heard screaming, "Stay away, stay away, you and your horses will destroy the crops. Have some pity on us poor people!" Bhoj immediately moves away. As soon as he turns his back, the farmer begins to sing a different tune altogether and says, "Where are you going, my king? Please come to my field, let me water your horses and feed your soldiers. Surely you will not refuse the hospitality of a humble farmer?" Not wanting to hurt the farmer, though amused by his turnaround, Bhoj once again moves towards the field. Again, the farmer shouts, "Hey, go away. Your horses and your soldiers are damaging what is left of my crop. You wicked king, go away." No sooner has Bhoj begun to turn away than the farmer cries, "Hey, why are you turning away? Come back. You are my guests. Let me have the honour of serving you."

The king is now exceedingly confused and wonders what is conspiring. This happens a few more times before Bhoj observes the farmer carefully. He notices that whenever the farmer is rude, he is standing on the ground, but whenever he is hospitable, he is standing atop a mound in the middle of the field. Bhoj realizes that the farmer's split personality has something to do with the mound. He immediately orders his soldiers to dig up the mound in the centre of the field. The farmer protests but Bhoj is determined to solve the mystery.

Beneath the mound, the soldiers find a wonderful golden throne. As Bhoj is about to sit on it, the throne speaks up, "This is the throne of Vikramaditya, the great. Sit on it only if you are as generous and wise as he. If not, you will meet your death on the throne." The throne then proceeds to tell Bhoj thirty-two stories of Vikramaditya, each extolling a virtue of kingship, the most important being generosity. It is through these stories that Bhoj learns what it takes to be a good king.

The story is peculiar. In the first part of the story, the throne transforms the stingy farmer into a generous host. In the latter half, the throne demands the king be generous before he takes a seat.

In organizations, we expect a man in a particular position to behave in

a particular manner. We assume that he has gained this position because he has those qualities. But what comes first: gaining the qualities or acquiring the position. Can a king be royal before he has a kingdom, or does the possession of a kingdom make him royal?

Can a person who seeks Durga from the outside world give out Durga? Or should a king have enough Shakti within him to be an unending supply of Durga to others?

Sunder was great friends with his team before he became the boss. The moment he was promoted, he started behaving differently, became arrogant, obnoxious and extremely demanding. Was it the role that had changed him or had it allowed him to reveal his true colours? Sunder blames the burden of new responsibilities and the over-familiarity of his colleagues as the cause of friction. That is when, Kalyansingh, the owner of the company, decides to have a chat with him. "Do you know why you have been given a higher salary, a car, a secretary, a cabin?" Sunder retorts that these are the perks of his job. Kalyansingh then asks, "And what is your job?" Sunder rattles off his job description and his key result areas. "And how do you plan to get promoted to the next level?" Sunder replies that it will happen if he does his work diligently and reaches his targets. "No," says Kalyansingh, "Absolutely not." Sunder does not understand. Kalyansingh explains, "If you do your job well, why would I move you? I will keep you exactly where you are." Looking at the bewildered expression on Sunder's face, Kalyansingh continues, "If you nurture someone to take your place, then yes, I may consider promoting you, but you seem to be nurturing no one. You are too busy trying to be boss, trying to dominate people, being rude and obnoxious. That is because you are insecure. So long as you are insecure, you will not let others grow. And as long as those under you do not grow, you will not grow yourself. Or at least, I will not give you another responsibility. You will end up doing the same job forever. Is that what you really want?" That is the moment Sunder understands the meaning of Vikramaditya's throne. After all, it is not about behaving royally, but rather about nurturing one's kingdom. He must not take Durga, he has to give Durga.

The loss of possessions reveals who we really are

Do kingdoms make us kings? Or can we be kings even without kingdoms? Is our value dependent on what we possess? These are questions raised in the Ramayan and Mahabharat. In both epics the protagonists have to deal with the loss of fortune and exile. It is the manner in which Ram deals with it and the Pandavs deal with it that reveals everything.

The loss of his kingdom does not affect Ram. He is king with or without the kingdom. Aranya-Ram (Ram of the forest) and Ayodhya-Ram (Ram of the city) have the same mental image. His mental body is powered by Shakti from within and does not need an external Durga to validate his social body. Contrarily, the loss of their kingdom shatters the Pandavs. They panic. They feel like victims. Their mental image takes a beating as their social body is battered. They feel deprived, denied and cheated because their mental image depends on the kingdom.

In Ram, Narayan is completely awake and so he does not need Ayodhya to make him feel secure. When his wife, Sita, is abducted he is determined to rescue her, finding resources along the way. He has no army with him, yet he creates an army in the jungle, transforming a troop of monkeys into fierce

warriors who do the unimaginable: build a bridge across the sea, tear down the citadel of Lanka, and defeat an army of fierce rakshasas.

The same is not the case with the Pandavs. They need Indraprastha to make them feel validated. Krishna helps them outgrow their dependence on Narayani and start discovering the Narayan within.

Often, a job has more to do with securing our social body, hence our mental image, than about the task at hand. And so, the loss of a job leads to the loss of self-worth and self-esteem. It is through things we get Durga, but like Ram we have to invoke the Shakti within us so that the vicissitudes of fortune and misfortune do not shake our faith in ourselves, and the world around us.

As the vice president (VP) of marketing, Birendra is highly regarded by his boss. He is a very good teacher, spending time explaining the principles of marketing to his team. Everyone sees him as generous and a gentleman. Until the merger takes place and the company is bought by a much larger firm. In the new organizational design, Birendra is no longer VP of marketing but made VP of market research and analytics instead. Birendra feels this is a step down. He sulks and becomes miserable. He refuses to talk to his former colleagues. He is angry and bitter unlike his former generous and gentle self. The loss of Narayani reveals the true Narayan within him. Birendra is no Vishnu; he is Indra, happy as long as things go his way, unable to take adversity in his stride.

Like things, talent and loyalty can also make us feel secure

A dog is very good for our self-image. As a pet, it adores us unconditionally, wagging its tail when it gets attention, whining when it does not, possessively barking when someone threatens us or lays claim over us. The dog upholds our mental image of ourselves at all costs. The world may or may not appreciate us, but the dog always will. It is the symbol of loyalty, nourishing our mental image.

By contrast, the cow gives us milk. It does nothing for our self-image, giving milk to whosoever milks it. The cow does not wag its tail when we appreciate it or whine when we do not. If one feeds a cow well, takes care of it, the cow produces milk generously. The cow provides for our physical body.

A cow gives us Lakshmi while a dog gives us Durga. The tathastu of talent makes the yajaman rich. The tathastu of loyalty makes the yajaman feel secure. At work what do we seek: cows or dogs? Do we seek talent that will help us achieve our goals or loyalty that will make us feel secure? What if the goal is to be secure?

Often, wealth exists not to nourish us but to make us feel secure. The idea of having more money makes us feel powerful. In fact, money is used to mark our position in society. The car it buys, the house it affords enables us to rise higher in the social hierarchy. Wealth, thus, is also a source of allaying insecurities. Lakshmi can be a functional Durga.

However, while people can be loyal to us, money and talent can never owe allegiance to anyone. That is why we need to surround ourselves with loyal people who stand by us in tough times, providing us emotional support more than anything else. Only the extremely independent or impersonal can survive in a world without loyalty.

When Santosh retired from his post as commissioner, even the peon stopped standing up to salute him. All his 'friends' stopped calling him to their parties. He suddenly realized he was a nobody. He realized that everyone had a relationship with his position and power, not with him. They cared not for him but for what he could do for them. He suddenly became aware of his hunger for loyalty and friendship. Life is, after all, not just about money and power.

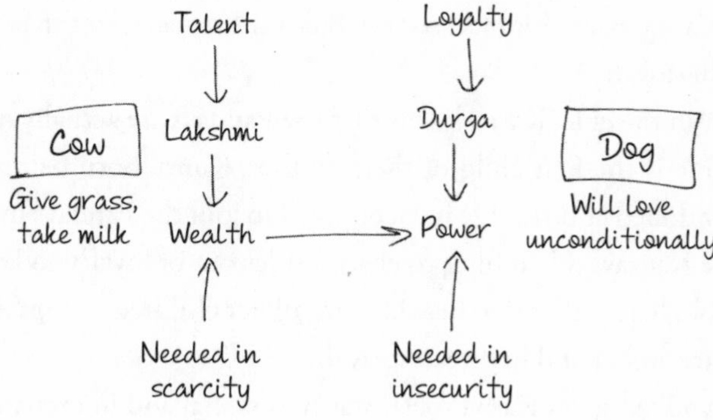

A transaction is about things, not thoughts

In the Mahabharat, Karna is a talented archer who is raised in a family of charioteers. He is identified as a charioteer's son and not as an archer. In the social hierarchy, the archer has a higher status than a charioteer. In other words, he has Shakti but not Durga.

Karna longs for social status and gets it from Duryodhan, the eldest of the Kauravs, who makes him king of Anga. In exchange, Durydohan seeks Karna's talent as an archer. He hopes to use Karna's archery skills against his arch enemies, the Pandavs some day. Duryodhan is insecure about the Pandavs. Karna makes him feel secure. But is it Karna's talent that makes him secure or his loyalty?

Later in the epic, Karna learns that the Pandavs are actually his younger brothers. He is the first child of their mother, Kunti, born before marriage hence abandoned at birth. He is encouraged to join the Pandavs in their fight against the Kauravs. He refuses to change sides out of loyalty to Duryodhan, but promises his mother that he will spare all her children, except Arjun, who is also an ace archer and his greatest rival.

Duryodhan gives Karna social status as svaha, and in exchange expects his talent as an archer to kill the Pandavs. In return, Karna gives him his loyalty. In trying to be loyal to both Duryodhan and his mother, Karna ends up sparing the Pandavs and failing his benefactor.

In the friendship of Karna and Duryodhan, Narayani is being exchanged but Narayan is not invoked. Both remain insecure and needy. Neither grows in wisdom.

Rudraprakash was unhappy. He had two managers handling two of his health clubs. Mehul had worked with him for years and was loyal. Amitabh was a brilliant manager, who did what he was told, but was clearly transactional. Mehul did not deliver results but could be relied on to stay on through bad times. Amitabh delivered results but would leave when things got rough. Each one is insecure in their own way. Mehul's insecurity makes him cling to Rudraprakash. Amitabh's insecurity makes him strive to be emotionally detached from Rudraprakash. Neither is trying to change, or outgrow their fear. They rely more on Narayani that comes from the outside than Narayan that comes from inside.

A relationship is about thoughts, not things

In the Ramayan, when Ram and Lakshman encounter Hanuman for the first time, Lakshman suspects he is a demon, until Hanuman speaks in Sanskrit, the language of the educated elite.

Later, when Ram learns how Hanuman serves Sugriv who has been kicked out of his kingdom by his elder brother Vali, Ram offers to help. But Sugriv is not sure if Ram is capable. Ram demonstrates his skill by shooting an arrow through seven palm trees and his strength by kicking the carcass of a dead buffalo so hard that it flies and lands in the court of Vali.

Lakshman and Sugriv need tangible proof of extraordinariness. They focus on the resources that the other possesses. Ram and Hanuman recognize each other's worth even before proof is provided. They focus on the Narayan potential within each of them.

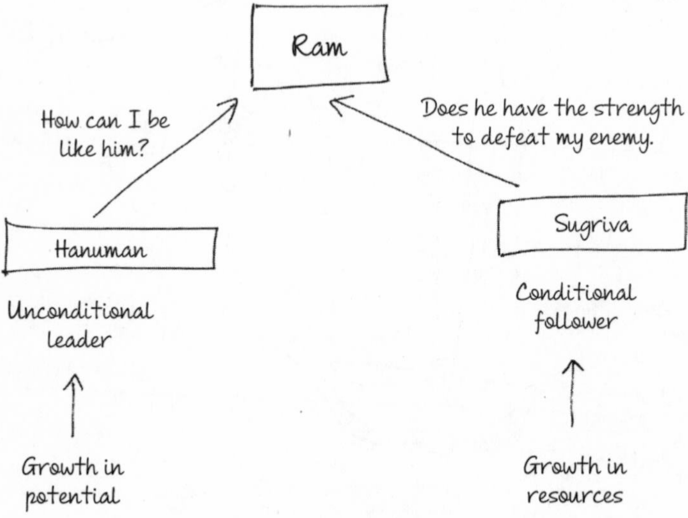

When two people meet, there are four things on the table: you and yours, me and mine. When yours is exchanged for mine, it is a transaction. When who-I-am impacts who-you-are, it is a relationship. Sugriv and Ram have a transaction: Ram helps Sugriv become king while Sugriv helps Ram

find his wife. Hanuman and Ram have a relationship: neither expects anything from the other yet both help each other. Hanuman helps Ram find Sita and, in doing so, discovers his full potential. He transforms from being a vanar, a mere monkey, to a deity in his own right.

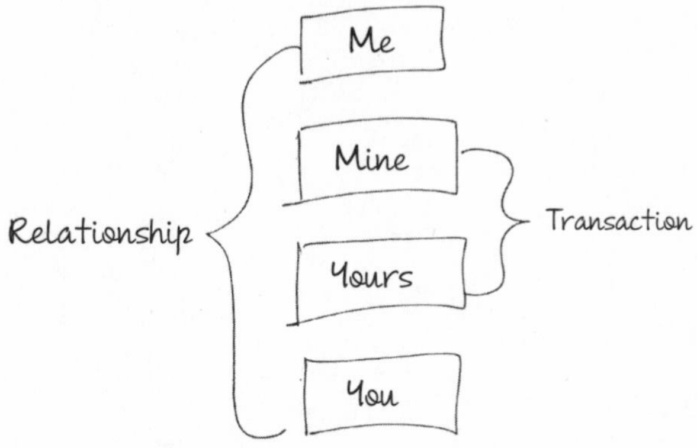

> Manish tells his wife, Gitika, to wear a new diamond necklace to the wedding and not the one she has worn earlier. "People will notice and I do not want people to think that my business is not doing well." Gitika feels like a billboard. In the circles she and her husband move in, what matters is what clothes you wear, what car you drive and where you go on holiday. Everything is constantly measured and keeping up appearances creates huge stress. But she enjoys spending time with Rafiq and Reshma who are her friends from college. They still met in the same canteen where they hung out, never bothering with each one's professional successes or failures. As Rafiq often tells Manish, "I want to spend time with you, not your car or your cash."

Rules

Any organization is essentially a set of rules. Rules help humanity overpower the law of the jungle that might is right. Rules domesticate the human-animal. But the human-animal can use rules to dominate and reinforce his position as the alpha. The human-animal can also pretend to follow rules, be subversive, or revolt when opportunity strikes. There is much more happening with rules. For life becomes work when we have to live by another's rules.

There are no thieves in the jungle

Once Uttanka was travelling through the forest carrying a pair of jewelled earrings secured from a king called Saudasa. These earrings were the tuition fees he had promised his guru's wife. On the way, serpents stole the earrings. Uttanka was so angry that he invoked Agni, the fire-god, and filled Bhogavati, the land of serpents with so much smoke that it blinded them all. The torture continued until Vasuki, the king of serpents, returned the earrings to Uttanka.

Uttanka saw the serpents as criminals; the earrings 'belonged' to him. The serpents saw Uttanka as the dominant beast who had defeated all rivals and claimed its prey. The human gaze is different from the animal gaze, as it assumes the existence of cultural structures like rights, rules and responsibilities. In nature, there is no concept of possession or property hence there is no thief, police, or court of law.

In the jungle there is territory not property. You cannot steal territory. You cannot bequeath it to children and loved ones. You have to fight for it. Winner takes it all.

In the jungle there is no law, no criminal, no rights, no duties, no judge, no jury. Everyone is on their own.

Brahma rejects this world. He wants a place where his possessions are protected and respected. This is the world of rules; this is sanskriti. In the world of rules there are rule-breakers, the criminal, the corrupt. There is need for a police force, an auditor, and a regulator. They ensure that the rights of the weak are respected by the strong.

Shabbir smiled. One day, a man seated in a bus spat on the car he was driving and his boss got very angry. He rolled down the window and abused the man, calling him ill-mannered and low-class. The very same day a bird flying over the car relieved itself on the window screen. The boss was upset but he could not shout at the bird. The bird would not understand what manners or class meant.

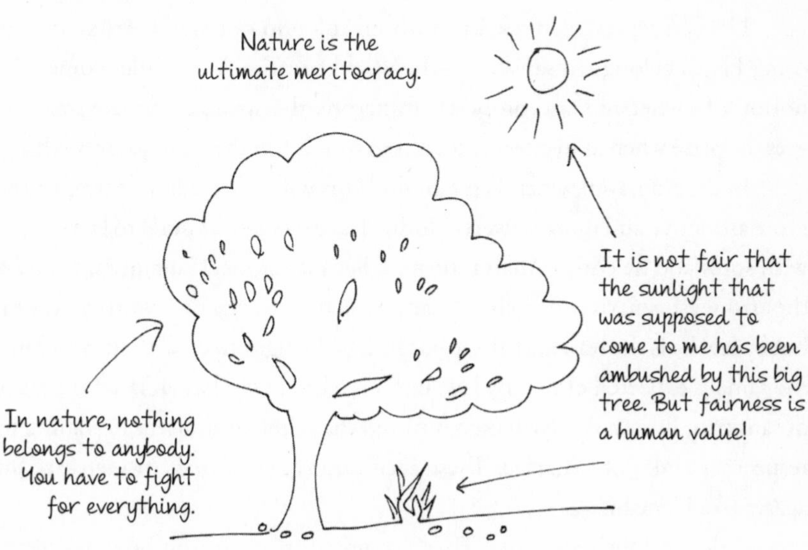

Without rules there is territory, not property

Apsaras, the nymphs who live in Indra's land, do not follow any rules. They subscribe to no law. They live in absolute freedom. In the Mahabharat, when Urvashi, an apsara, tries to seduce Arjun, he withdraws from her stating that she is like a mother to him for she had seduced and stayed with his ancestor, Pururava. She argues that she is ancestor to no one; she belongs to all. The rules of man do not apply to her, a nymph, she says. "But they apply to me," says Arjun.

Urvashi represents prakriti to whom rules do not apply. Arjun, on the other hand, belongs to sanskriti—the world of rules. With rules comes the notion of ownership and property. In nature, the strongest or the smartest gets the prize whereas in culture, thanks to rules, even the weak get something.

In the Ramayan, when Gautam finds his wife Ahalya in the arms of the more attractive and more powerful Indra, he curses Indra's body to be covered with sores and he curses Ahalya, turning her into stone. Gautam may not be the strongest, smartest or richest man; he may not even be a worthy groom, but by law he is the husband, none but he has the right to be with his wife, and the same is expected of her. By law, Indra is a thief who has violated the rules of sanskriti. By law, Ahalya has committed the crime of adultery for failing to respect the rules of marriage. These accusations would make no sense to an apsara like Urvashi.

Rules establish sanskriti. They are put in place in the hope to create a world where even the weak can thrive and the helpless have rights. Unfortunately, rules end up creating a new form of hierarchy, one that is not based on force, or cunning, but rather based on the whims of man.

Thus, in some organizations one gender is favoured over another, or a certain community or nationality is favoured over another. All these decisions are rationalized using complex arguments. We strive for meritocracy until we realize that it comes at a price that humans are unwilling to pay.

Initially, the parking lot outside the temple was free for all. Dozens of cars could be seen parked outside as hordes of families visited, especially on the auspicious Fridays and Saturdays. Soon, the number of cars increased so much so there were fights in the parking lot between people vying for the same space. Finally, to keep the peace, rules had to be introduced: it was first come first served. Those who came late had to park outside on the road and risk having their cars towed away. This inconvenienced many powerful and rich people in the area who complained to the temple committee and even subtly threatened to withdraw their financial support. The temple authorities decided to reserve a portion of the parking lot for VIPs. This only created more trouble: who was a VIP and who wasn't? The founding family of the temple, who were of modest means, demanded more rights than the rich donors. Politicians began to assert themselves and also demanded special rights. When these were denied, the temple suddenly found itself being questioned by the local municipality about the legality of its reserved parking. The inquiry stopped when the local legislative council member was given a VIP pass. In the absence of rules, there is chaos. In the presence of rules, there is order. But the order is constantly threatened if it fails to cater to the dominant alpha. With order comes hierarchy.

Rules domesticate the human-animal

Domestication is a violent process. In the Ramayan, Surpanaka is a free spirit who seeks intimacy with Ram. When he introduces her to Sita, Surpanaka sees her as a rival. She is unable to fathom the meaning of marriage and fidelity. These rules make no sense in the jungle. In the jungle, the strongest and the most beautiful gets the mate. So Surpanaka tries to take what she wants by force. She decides to attack Sita hoping that with the wife out of the picture, Ram will succumb to her.

To protect Sita from harm, Lakshman intervenes and pulls Surpanaka back. He then cuts off her nose, disfiguring her, making her less worthy of anyone's affection. With this act, the threat to the laws of the marriage is wiped away. The wild beast is domesticated. Order is restored.

From Lakshman's point of view, one informed by culture, he has done the right thing. From Surpanaka's point of view, she has been humiliated and invalidated. She may behave like an animal but that she feels anger indicates she is not an animal. She is human. Her mental image has taken a severe beating. Lakshman may think he is a hero for upholding the rules of culture, but he has only fuelled Surpanaka's fury. On her part, she feels like a victim, not a villain.

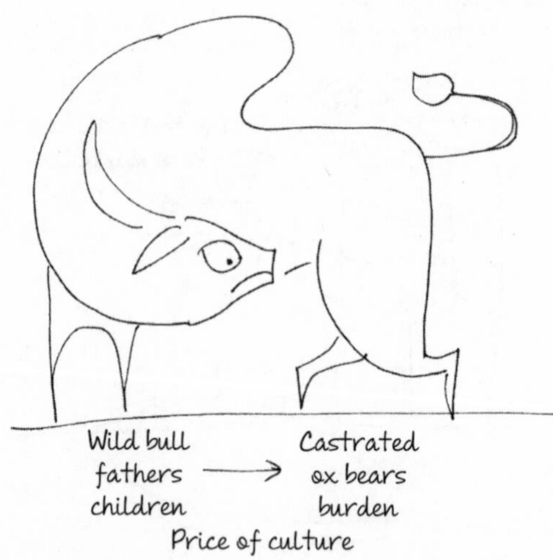

Those who make the rules and enforce them always feel powerful and righteous. Those who are obliged to follow the rules do not feel so. They comply willingly only if they feel good about the rules, else they quietly submit. Then there are some who disagree with the rules, rightly or wrongly, and they feel powerful by breaking them.

The hospitality firm and the builder had a joint venture. The hotel had been built by the builder but he did not know how to run the hotel. So the management was outsourced to the hospitality firm. Vikrant was the hotel manager and he soon had a problem. Sanjay, the son of the builder, would come to the bar every evening and simply grab cash from the counter. When the cashier tried to resist, he would say, "Don't you know who I am? I own this building." This had to be stopped. So Vikrant called his bosses in the head office and apprised them of the situation. "I can stop the bully but only if you give me full support." The bosses assured him full support. The next time Sanjay tried to grab cash, Vikrant and two of his managers intervened and stopped him. Sanjay threatened them with dire consequences. Vikrant pulled out his mobile and called Sanjay's father and said, "Sir, I have been told by the management to withdraw operations if Sanjay continues to misbehave with the staff and interfere with processes. Please advise on what needs to be done." The reply made Vikrant smile. Sanjay left the bar shamefaced and never returned again. Surpanaka had been controlled by rules. But Vikrant knew that this would come at a price. The builder's prestige had been dented and it could sour the relationship with the hospitality firm, create trouble in the future. Vikrant's bosses knew it too. He was transferred to another hotel and secretly given a cash bonus not to speak of the incident. And because Vikrant displayed immense maturity, his bosses marked him out as talent.

Domestication can be voluntary and involuntary

Garud was born a slave. His mother, Vinata, had lost a wager with her sister, Kadru, as a result of which she and her offspring were obliged to serve Kadru and her children, the nagas. "If you want to be free," say the nagas to Garud, "fetch amrit for us."

Garud immediately flies to Amravati and finds the pot of amrit there, guarded by the devas. He spreads his mighty wings, extends his sharp talons and swoops down on them. Indra and the devas are no match for Garud. He shoves them aside and claims the pot with the nectar of immortality.

On the way back, he encounters Vishnu. Vishnu says, "There is a way by which you can get your freedom without giving the nagas the amrit. If I tell you how, what will you give me in exchange?" Garud swears to serve him for the rest of his life.

Vishnu then says, "After you give the pot of nectar and secure your freedom, tell the nagas they must bathe before drinking it. They will leave the pot with you, assuming you will safeguard it until their return. Allow Indra to reclaim the pot while the nagas are away. When the nagas question your actions, remind them that you stopped being their slave as soon as you gave them the pot of nectar and were thus under no obligation to stop Indra from stealing what anyway belongs to the devas." Garud does as he is told: he gets his freedom, Indra gets back the amrit and the nagas get nothing. Indra is so pleased with Garud that he makes nagas the natural food for Garud. Garud then goes to Vaikuntha and serves Vishnu.

In this story, Garud resents serving the nagas while he willingly serves Vishnu. The former is involuntary domestication. The latter is voluntary domestication. In involuntary domestication, we are compelled to work according to other people's rules. In voluntary domestication, we choose to work according to other people's rules.

We voluntarily give up our rules and agree to follow other people's rules, if they grant unto us something that we value. The contract we sign when joining an organization is voluntary domestication.

Srikanth always comes to office on time. He likes coming early and setting up his desk before others. Then, one day, the company introduces the swipe-card system to ensure everyone comes on time. Suddenly, Srikanth does not feel like coming early. He hates his integrity being watched and measured. So he comes to office exactly on time and leaves on the dot too, never giving that extra time that he did before the company made domestication so involuntary. Srikanth would be servant to a trusting Vishnu, not to an exploitative naga.

We dislike those who are indifferent to rules

Sati was the daughter of Daksha Prajapati, the supreme patron of the yagna. When she met Shiva, she asked him, "Where is your home?" "Home? What does that mean?" he said. "Where do you stay when it gets very hot?" "Atop Mount Kailas," he replied. "Where do you stay when it gets very cold?" "In a crematorium, next to funeral pyres that are always burning," he said. "Where do you stay when it rains?" "In a cave," he said, "or even above the clouds!"

Sati laughed as she realized he did not understand the meaning of a home. She called him Bholenath, the innocent one, and fell in love with him. She even decided to marry him, to which her father agreed with great reluctance.

At the wedding, sons-in-law are supposed to bow to their fathers-in-law. When Shiva refused to do so, Sati's father Daksha took this as a great insult. At the feast that followed, Shiva fed his companions, ghosts and dogs, with his own hands. Daksha considered these creatures foul and inauspicious. His protests made no sense to Shiva.

Sati realized that Shiva had no mental image of himself, and so had no need for a social body. He was indifferent to property as well as rules that are needed to endorse and affirm one's self-image. Daksha, on the other hand, saw Shiva very differently. He saw him as the destroyer, a threat to social order. Shiva was comfortable with prakriti as Kali—wild and untamed, unbound by any rules. Daksha insisted on looking upon prakriti as Gauri, bound by his rules, under his control.

Daksha insists on rules being followed for the larger good. He demands domestication. But in enforcing the rules, his self-image gets inflated and he starts behaving as the dominant alpha. So much so that he starts seeing Shiva as an adversary, and not as one who cannot be domesticated.

Shiva is a bull. If a bull is castrated, it turns into an ox, a beast of burden. It can no longer impregnate a cow. It is important to allow Shiva to stay outside the purview of rules. Daksha fails to realize this and takes Shiva's intransigence as a personal insult. At no point is Shiva defying Daksha; he is just being himself.

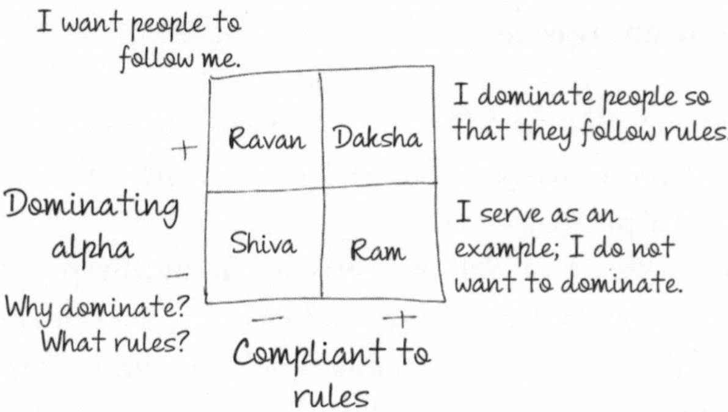

Ravan, king of Lanka, defies the rules, and Ram, prince of Ayodhya, follows them, but Ravan is no Shiva and Ram is no Daksha. Unlike Shiva, Ravan wants to control people; he defies authority because he wants to be authority. Shiva is a hermit with no desire to dominate or domesticate anyone. Unlike Daksha, Ram does not want to control people; he respects the rules, not authority. He knows the value of rules and their place in life. He also knows the price one pays to uphold the rules. Thus, he is quite comfortable sacrificing personal happiness in the process of upholding the law.

Mirchandani demands that every member of his accounting firm come to office on time. They lose half-a-day of salary if they are even a minute late, but Mirchandani always comes in late. He believes that as the owner it is his privilege and he rationalizes it by saying he works late into the night unlike other staff members who leave at 6 p.m. sharp. By this, he establishes his domination in the organizational hierarchy like Ravan. Vishal, a senior accountant, just cannot come to office on time. He likes starting work only by 11 a.m., and he does not mind staying back late till all the work is done. Cutting his salary, admonishing him, has had no effect on Vishal. Mirchandani calls him arrogant and insubordinate but Vishal has no desire to defy the system. He simply functions best later in the day and finds it very difficult to wake up early. The tension between Vishal and Mirchandani reaches a point where Vishal is asked to leave. Mirchandani loses a talented worker because, like Daksha, he is more interested in Vishal's obedience and adherence to rules than in Vishal's intelligence.

Rules can be oppressive

Ram's obsession with rules dehumanizes him and makes him detached and dispassionate. The structure he creates does not benefit all: certainly not Shambuka and Sita.

The rules state that only members of the priestly professions can renounce society and become tapasvis, not members of servant professions. So when Shambuka, a servant, becomes a tapsavi, Ram beheads him.

The rules state that the king shall not have a woman who is the subject of gossip as his queen. The abduction of Sita and her stay in Ravan's palace is the subject of gossip and so Ram abandons Sita in the forest when she is heavy with child despite knowing that she has never been unfaithful in letter or spirit.

Often in organizations, people are told to leave jobs on grounds that they have broken a rule. Even though the leader has the power to forgive or overlook such transgressions he does not, for fear of the repercussions to the company as a whole. Forgiveness may be seen as a favour. It may bring ethics into question.

The rules were very clear that bonuses had to be paid as per the bell curve. Some would get more than others, and at least one person would be denied a bonus. Uday argued that all his team members had done satisfactory work and no one person's work stood out as spectacular. Those upstream did not care: the rule had to be applied every time. The team had to be graded differently. No exceptions could be made. Uday felt disgust but he could do nothing about it. Shambuka had to be beheaded and Sita had to be exiled, if he wished to be Ram.

Rules create underdogs and outsiders

In the Mahabharat, there are three great archers: Arjun, Karna and Eklavya.

Rules state that as a member of the royal family, Arjun has the right to hold the bow. The same right is not given to Karna and Eklavya because Karna belongs to a family of charioteers who are servants, while Eklavya is a tribal who lives in the forest. Karna has to learn secretly, denying his identity to his teacher. Eklavya has to learn on his own as the royal tutor, Drona, refuses to teach him. The social structure of the land is anything but fair.

Rules that are meant to subvert the law of the jungle end up creating a culture that is unfair and oppressive. Hence, the god in Hinduism is not just a rule-follower like Ram but also a rule-breaker as in the instance of Krishna. Krishna is leela purushottam who is best at playing games. He is always visualized as a cowherd and charioteer, members of the servant class, even though he is born into a royal family. He seems to be mocking social status.

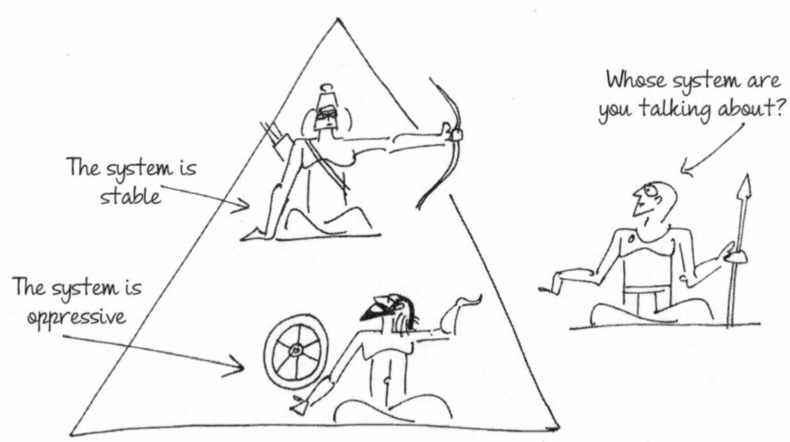

The point is not the rules, or the following or breaking of them, but the reason behind the rules. Are they helping the helpless as they are supposed to, or are they simply granting more power to the powerful? Rules were created to keep the jungle out of society but more often than not they become tools to make society worse than any jungle.

Mathias knows that because he is the eldest son of the family, his taking over as CEO of his departmental store will always be seen as a function of his bloodline rather than a result of his talent. No matter how hard he works, no matter what his performance is when compared with other professionals in the company, he will always be his father's son. He is the modern-day Arjun, found in almost every family business. In contrast, Mathur knows that despite years of proving himself, he will never become the CEO; he is not part of the family bloodline and the family will never give the mantle to a professional. He is our modern-day Karna, who leaves the family business and joins a professional company, only to realize that even a multinational company has a glass ceiling. He is not an alumnus of any known business-school hence he will never be good enough. He will always be the outsider. Bakshi works as a manager in the very same departmental store. He would have been a part of the strategic team but he will never be, because he is not a business-school graduate either. No school accepted him because in the group discussions he would only express himself in Hindi. His thoughts were outstanding but those who judged him heard only his language and felt he would not fit in because he did not know English. Bakshi did not learn English since the government schools he studied in taught only the local language, because the political parties insisted on supporting the regional language over a 'foreign' language, never mind the fact that the children of these very politicians went to English-medium schools. Bakshi is the modern-day Eklavya; not quite sure why well-meaning politicians and well-meaning academicians denied him his thumb.

Rules create mimics and pretenders

In the Mahabharat, Duryodhan breaks no rules. He simply invites Yudhishtir to play a game of dice for a wager. It is Yudhishtir who gambles away his kingdom and his wife, not Duryodhan. When Draupadi, the common wife of the Pandavs, is dragged by the hair from the inner chambers to the royal court, humiliated and publicly disrobed, no one comes to her rescue, neither Bhisma, Drona, nor Karna, even though she begs them for help. Rules and laws are quoted to justify her treatment.

Later, when the Pandavs return from their thirteen-year exile in the forest, Duryodhan refuses to return their lands. He argues that according to his calendar, the Pandavs were seen before the end of the thirteenth year and so as per the agreement, they have to return to the forest for another thirteen years. Krishna offers the counter-argument that the Kaurav calendar does not take into account the concept of leap years. In fact, the Pandavs have lived in exile longer than stipulated. Duryodhan disagrees with this. So Krishna offers a compromise, "Just give five villages to the five brothers for the sake of peace." Thus cornered, Duryodhan reveals the true intention behind his pretence of rational arguments and says, "I will not give them a needle point of land under any circumstances."

Duryodhan is the pretender, the mimic, who follows the rules but does not care for the purpose they serve. He uses rules to control the world around him and get his way.

In a world where processes and systems matter more than feelings, it is clear that the overwhelming culture promotes Duryodhans. We assume that the obedient person is the committed person. Yet, we can sense that the team is disconnected and detached emotionally. They become professional because they have stopped caring about people; all they care about is tasks and targets and go about accomplishing these ruthlessly and heartlessly. In fact, when we celebrate professionalism, we celebrate Duryodhan who values the letter of the law, not the spirit. Behaviour can be proven and measured, not belief.

During the breakout sessions at the international conference of a large cosmetics company, everyone was asked to voice their issues with the new positioning of the old product. Yasmin had many objections arising from the local realities of India. Before she could voice these, her boss, Gajendra, tapped her on the shoulder and said, "This is a charade. They have already printed the brochures and the leaflets and agencies have already filmed the ad-campaign that we have rolled out. So do not bother protesting or being honest. This meeting is just a formality to tell the board of directors that local markets were consulted before the launch. Nobody will believe it but everyone will applaud their efforts. So just smile and tell them how wonderful the new positioning is. That is what they want to hear. And if you tell them what they want to hear, they will reward you by calling you to the next international conference." With this dialogue, Gajendra encouraged Yasmin to become a Duryodhan and work with the system, her personal views notwithstanding.

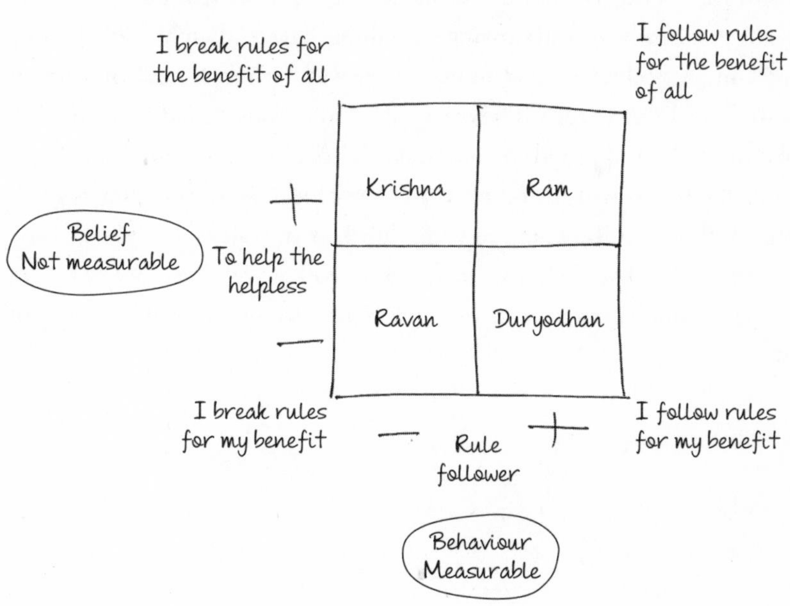

We want to live by our own rules

Ravan is the most charismatic and enchanting villain of Hindu mythology. With ten heads, twenty arms, a flying chariot and a city of gold in the middle of the sea, he stands out in the epic Ramayan. He drives his brother Kuber out of the city of Lanka and declares himself king. When Ram and his brother humiliate his sister, Surpanaka, he decides to teach them a lesson by abducting Ram's wife, Sita. Ravan is much admired as he lives by his own rules. What is overlooked is that he is the dominant alpha male, who does not care for anyone except those who please him. He kicks his brother Vibhishan out of the house because he refuses to align with him. He wakes up his other brother, Kumbhakarn, even though it has been foretold that if he is disturbed before it is his time to wake up he will meet certain death. He lets his city Lanka burn and his sons and brothers die, but refuses to give Sita up.

In the Mahabharat, the Pandav Bhim also displays this trait of living by his own rules. He is in the habit of walking straight towards his destination, refusing to take any turn, destroying everything that stands in his path. Fearing Bhim's might, rocks, trees and animals make way for him. Once, while on his way to fetch a flower for his beloved wife, Bhim finds an old monkey lying across his path. Too proud to go around this old creature, Bhim introduces himself and insists that the monkey make way for him. The old monkey tells Bhim, "I cannot move, I am too weak. Just kick my tail aside and go forth," Bhim tries to do that, but fails. The tail is just too heavy! The monkey reveals he is Hanuman, representing nature that refuses to submit to the excesses of man.

We admire people who do things their way, who stand up to governments, change policies and make their mark in industry and society. These defiant heroes represent raw power that shapes the world around them by grit and determination. Upon closer observation, we realize they use rules to dominate and control the world around them. Their rules only serve them.

Prakash wants to be an entrepreneur. Not because he has any great idea or a great service to offer, he simply wants to be his own boss. He is tired of obeying others, submitting to the whims and fancies of his superiors who he feels are much less talented than him. He refuses to be a cog in the wheel; he wants to be the owner of the wheel. He wants to be an alpha. He wants everyone to listen to him and live life on his own terms.

Innovation is not possible unless rules are broken

As a child, Krishna defies rules when he steals the butter of milkmaids as well as their hearts earning the titles of makhan-chor and chit-chor. Yet, he is forgiven, for his actions bring joy and compel people to be more generous with their resources and affection.

As a grown man, Krishna defies rules several times in the battlefield. He does it when he get the patriarch Bhisma to lower his bow, by getting the androgynous Shikhandi to ride on his chariot in front of Arjun. To get Drona to lower his weapons, Krishna spreads the rumour that Drona's son, Ashwatthama, is dead. He is referring to an elephant, but he knows Drona will assume it is his son and lower his weapons, giving Dhristadhyumna the chance to behead the old teacher. Krishna goads Arjun to strike Karna even though Karna is unarmed, helpless and busy trying to release the wheel of his chariot from the ground. He goads Bhim to strike Duryodhan with a fatal blow below the navel on his thigh, which is expressly forbidden by the rules of war.

Krishna can be described as an innovator, one who creates better rules by breaking and bending old rules that do not serve their purpose. But he does so gently, with a smile, taking people into confidence. The shift is subtle, taking one by surprise. And the change is aimed to create a society where jungle laws do not exist.

Every person is an innovator, a pretender—compliant and defiant in different contexts. Every team has someone who is such a person. This is the world of sanskriti, where all is not as it seems. It lacks the transparency of nature. As long as there is imagination, such transparency of feelings will not exist.

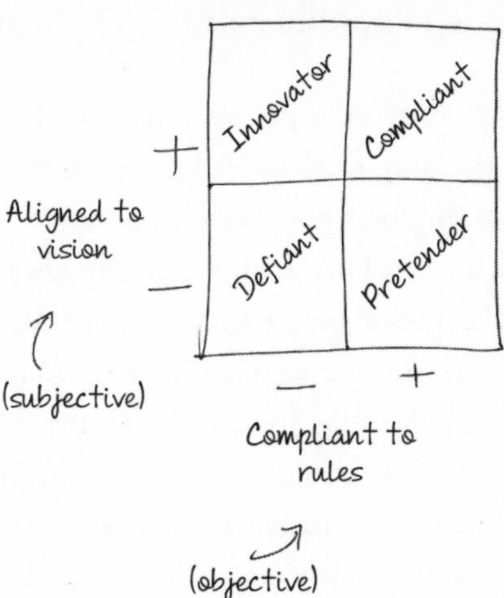

Mohit took a huge risk. Breaking all company policies, he told his team to talk to the client directly rather go through official intermediaries. This led to a huge furore and Mohit was summoned to the CEO's office. The client-facing team was there with proof of Mohit's audacity. Mohit did not deny the charges. He simply presented a slide show that proved the difference in turnaround time in the six months before he broke and after he broke the rule. The turnaround time had shortened and the number of customer complaints had dramatically gone down. Bypassing the client-serving team, the delivery team had reduced affairs getting lost in translation thereby improving the equity of the firm. The client trusted the firm more. Mohit was a Krishna breaking the rules not out of spite or indifference, but because they were doing more harm than good. The CEO agreed and Mohit was allowed to continue his initiative.

We respect those who uphold rules

Ram is maryada purushottam, supreme upholder of laws that make up the social order. He is the only form of Vishnu to be worshipped as king. He upholds rules even at the cost of personal happiness.

The rules state that the king shall always keep his word. When Dashrath tells Ram about Kaikeyi's demands, Ram leaves for exile immediately without a word of protest. This is not the act of an obedient son; this is an act of a law-abiding prince who upholds rules to ensure the integrity of the royal family.

The rules state that a man shall always be faithful to his wife. Ram never looks at another woman or remarries when separated from Sita. This, too, is an act of upholding the law rather than an act borne out of love. Ram does not make rules—he follows them. He is supremely compliant. And the kingdom he fosters is described as a world where nothing is unpredictable and everything is organized.

> When the branch office is established in Ahmedabad, Sunil is clear he wants Alok as the branch head. Alok is straightforward and trustworthy. He will follow the rules meticulously and ensure all processes are implemented and followed. He will create a culture of compliance. As the branch office is primarily a delivery centre and not a client-facing arm, Sunil is looking for a Ram to create a predictable and controllable environment. Alok is perfect for the job.

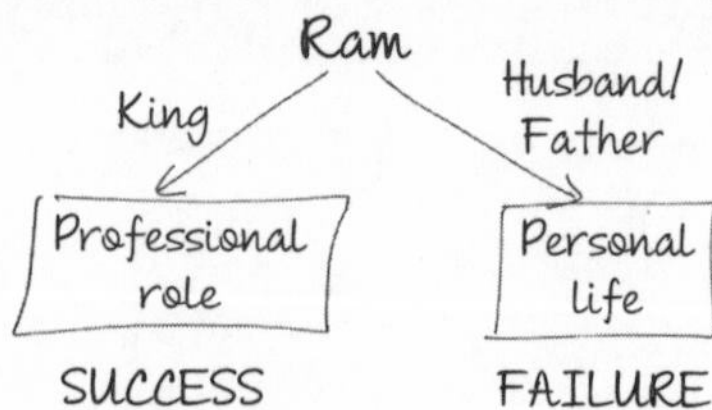

Rules need not determine our value

Sita goes into forest exile twice in the Ramayan. The first time, it is voluntary; she follows Ram as a dutiful wife. The second time, it is involuntary; she is abandoned in the forest on Ram's instruction following street gossip about her reputation. Ram does not see Sita. His gaze is only on the rules.

Despite this Sita never begrudges Ram. Though abandoned and alone in the forest, she knows that his role as a king compels him to take this drastic step. She knows where he is coming from, his commitment to the rules, his obligation as scion of a royal clan and his responsibility to his people. While she knows the consequences of his decisions, she also knows that he will always be true to her. When her sons are old enough, she sends them to their father. Ram asks her to come back, but she refuses. As a resident of the forest, she is no longer bound by the rules of the city. In the forest she is not obliged to obey. She asks the earth-goddess, her mother, to take her back. The earth opens up and takes her in.

Sita no longer needs the Durga offered by social rules. She has enough Shakti within her to live without them. She does not need a social body; she does not need to be wife or queen. Her mental body no longer seeks external validation.

Prathamesh was accused of sexual misconduct and asked to leave the firm as long as the inquiry was pending. Keeping him around would affect the image of the company negatively. It would speak volumes about the company's moral stand in such matters. Prathamesh was furious. He knew that it was impossible to prove what actually transpired behind closed doors. It was his word against the lady who had accused him. His conscience was clear but he kept reliving the day in his mind: had he said, or done something that could have been misunderstood? Three months later, Prathamesh was asked to rejoin the firm. There was insufficient evidence against him. It was a case of cultural misunderstanding. Prathamesh declined the offer. He had learned that there was life beyond the wealth and privilege offered by the firm.

Stability

Nature is changing. Markets are changing. Human needs are changing. New tools and technologies are appearing and old ones disappearing. Some seek stability, certainty and predictability: the status quo. Others seek change, revolution, and transformation: a change in their status. With stability comes peace, monotony and stagnation. With change comes stress, excitement and growth.

When the world changes, our social body dies

Markandeya has the boon of immortality, yet he feels great fear. One day, he sees the rains fall and the oceans rise until the whole world, every mountain, continent and person he knew, every village and city he'd visited, get dissolved. The sun disappears from the sky along with the moon, the stars and every cloud. Markandeya finds himself surrounded by vast, limitless water. Alone in the midst of nothingness, Markandeya experiences great dread. There is no one to see him or call him by his name. Without the world, who is he? He has no identity. Does he even exist?

As these thoughts cross his mind, he sees a banyan leaf floating on the waves. A child is sitting on the leaf and gurgling happily, sucking his big toe joyfully. The child breathes in and Markandeya finds himself being sucked into the child's body. Inside, he can see the entire universe—the sky, the earth and the underworld. He sees the realms of devas, asuras, yakshas, rakshasas, nagas, and manavas, some of whom recognize him and call him by name. Markandeya feels secure, his identity and value restored. All the fear that Markandeya experienced now disappears, thanks to the intervention of the child, who is undoubtedly Vishnu. Then the child breathes Markandeya out. He is back in the realm of the waters, of nothingness, where his fears return.

Markandeya's physical body may be immortal, but when the world around him collapses, his social body dies. He is stripped of all relationships, titles and status. He belongs to no hierarchy; is a nobody. That is why we cling to social structures around us: hierarchy, the rules of an organization, these grant us our identity and meaning. Sanskriti exists to make humans feel secure. That is why any change in society frightens us.

Our social structures depend on the organization. The organization depends on industry, which in turn depends on the market. The market depends on society, which in turn relies on the environment. All these are susceptible to change, and so are constant threats to our physical, social and mental body. We are only comfortable with change that nourishes our social body and reinforces our mental image. This constant, looming threat to our social beings is an eternal source of stress.

For ten years, Rupen handled the accounts of the jewellery factory where he worked. He did his job well and loved the routine of his life. Everything was familiar and in order. His boss, Motwani, loved him and his job was assured. Then Motwani died and his wife, unable to handle the business, sold it to a large conglomerate. Suddenly, all certainty disappears from Rupen's life. He has a boss to report to and is now seen as an old-school accountant who does not fit into the new way of thinking. With the end of one sanskriti and the rise of another, the social body also needs to die and be reborn, locate itself in the new structure.

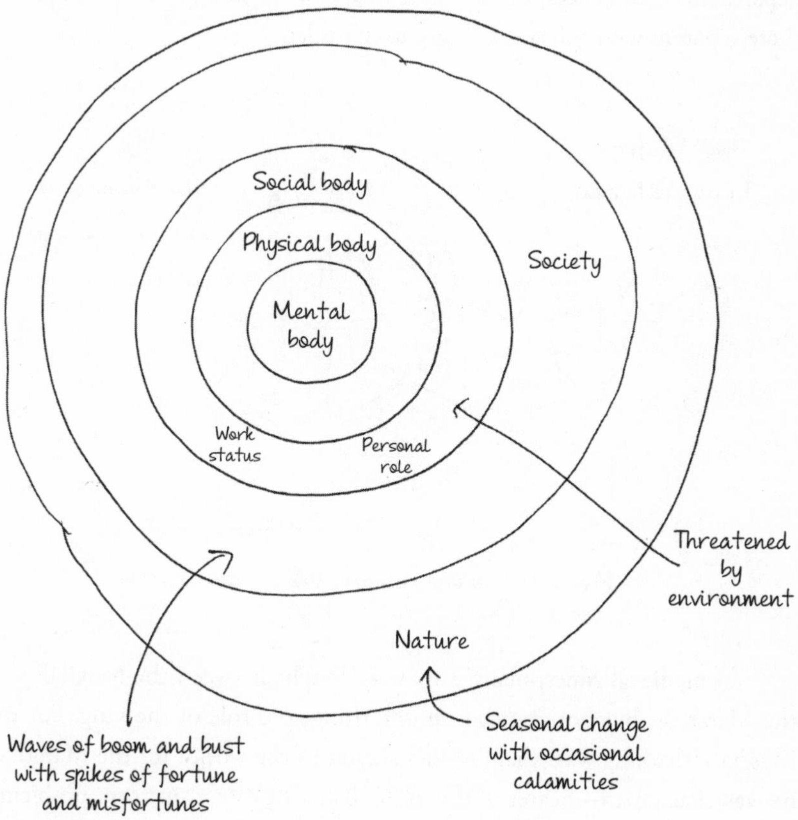

We want organizations to secure our social body

A little boy called Dhruva is pulled down from his father's lap by his stepmother. Feeling deprived and denied, he seeks a father from whose lap he will never be pulled down. He prays fervently until Vishnu picks him up and places him in his lap. There he sits in the sky, on Vishnu's lap, as the steadfast Pole Star. No one can pull him down.

We yearn for permanence in structures, systems and rules, as it reassures us about the permanence of who we are. When bosses change, organizations get restructured, when new teams are formed, when we are moved to another department, fear envelopes us. Like Dhruva, we hope there is a Vishnu out there, a parent who will always keeps us in his lap.

Please let no one pull me down from your lap

In medieval times, many wars were fought between the Mughals and the Marathas, but both agreed on one thing: the role of the king. For the Mughals, the king was jahanpanah—shelter of the world; for the Marathas, he was chattrapati—bearer of the umbrella that protects us from problems. The king was seen as one who grants security, not just physical but also social security that assures us of our meaning.

People are often loyal to bosses or to an organization because it guarantees them both livelihood and social status. Many see this as a fair bargain, a social contract. Some people believe that a leader should provide security actively like a cat that carries her kittens by the scruff of their neck to safety. Others believe a leader is there to provide security passively in the way baby monkeys cling to their mothers to feel secure.

Underlying this belief is the assumption that we are dependent and we need not be dependable. Most devatas want to remain Dhruvas, few want to grow up and be Vishnu for others. We do not wish to rise in the varna ladder. We are comfortable being karya-kartas and not becoming yajamans.

All his life, Sudha wanted a permanent job like her brother, Sai, who worked for the government, but it never happened. First the company she worked for got shut down. The next company shifted office three times. Then her boss changed, after which the company was reorganized and she was given various roles over a span of two years. She was never able to settle down, feel a sense of stability or order. When she complained and told her brother how lucky he was, he moaned, "Not quite. I have been transferred to three cities in the past ten years and now I have to use all my influence to avoid the next transfer." Both siblings are like Dhruva yearning for a lap from where no one can pull them down.

We resist anything that is new

This story comes from the Oriya Mahabharat. One day, Arjun sees a strange creature in the forest, one he has never seen before. At first, Arjun thinks it is a monster and raises his bow to kill it. All of a sudden, he notices a human hand and realizes the creature is not as unfamiliar as he thinks. On closer observation, he finds Navagunjara, the creature with the head of a rooster, neck of a peacock, back of a bull, waist of a lion, tail of a serpent and the four limbs of a human, deer, tiger and elephant. Every part is familiar but not the whole. Why did he assume the creature was a monster simply because it was not something he had encountered?

Often, we see the world full of predators and rivals threatening our business and us. We condemn unfamiliar markets as being chaotic and unethical. We want to dominate, domesticate or destroy the unfamiliar, rather than understand it. We assume what we know is the objective truth and everything else is threatening. Yet, it is the unfamiliar that offers us the opportunity to grow. We need to seek the familiar in the unfamiliar and allow ourselves to embrace the new. Rather than seek control of the union it is important to include and assimilate the unknown.

When Christopher first came to Mumbai, he was frightened. The roads were bad, traffic was all over the place, there were crowds of people everywhere, slums poured out of every corner, there was construction work wherever he turned; so different from back home where there were hardly any people on the road, where streets were neatly arranged, everyone drove cars, and poverty was practically non-existent. For Christopher, Mumbai felt like a monster that needed to be killed or tamed, until he noticed that the people he dealt with were no different from the people in his native land, kind as well as complex. They argued, negotiated and offered solutions. In Mumbai, he discovered a market for his company, a much-needed lifeline. This was different. It had to be different. In the difference lay new ideas, new thoughts and new challenges. Slowly the fear dissipated. Navagunjara need not be feared; it has to be admired and understood.

We want to control change

In the *Kathsaritsagar*, Vikramaditya hopes to rule forever by asking that he die only at the hands of a child borne by a girl who is only two-and-a-half years old. The impossible happens. One day he encounters Shalivahan whose mother is barely two-and-a-half years older than him. His father is Vasuki, the king of serpents. In a duel that follows, Vikramaditya is killed and his glorious reign comes to an end.

Hindu mythology is replete with stories where the impossible happens. Asuras demand boons that make killing them near impossible, and yet someone finds a chink in the perfect armour and they end up dead.

We create structures, systems and rules that we are convinced are perfect and will last forever, but they never do. Eventually, inevitably, they do collapse. Ultimately sanskriti is no match for prakriti.

Buddhism keeps describing the world as impermanent. Hindus saw time as cyclical, each cycle a kalpa composed of four yugas, marking childhood (Krita), youth (Treta), maturity (Dvapar) and old age (Kali) before death (pralay), which is followed by rebirth. And yet, Indra craves amrit and the asuras do tapasya, seeking immortality.

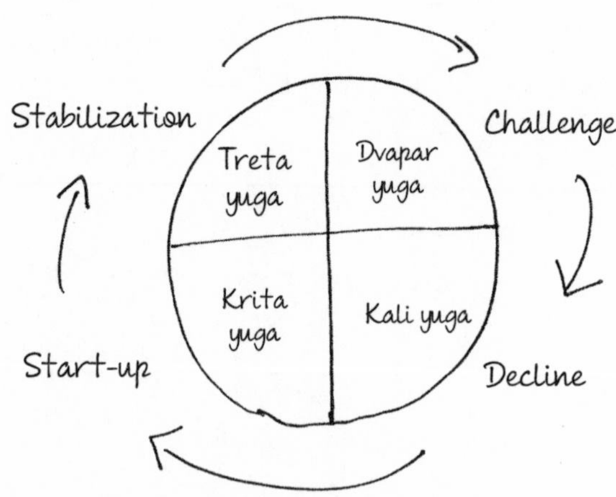

Organizations go through cycles and restructuring repeatedly. Change in market conditions, a new boss, target, merger, acquisition, etc. happens constantly, changing everything around us. Change can be upstream (bosses, investors, regulators) or downstream (employees, customers). Change can be central (strategy) or peripheral (market conditions). We ourselves can change, struck by boredom or desire. Still, everyone hopes to secure their position like Vikramaditya, getting upset when Shalivahan invariably appears.

Shekhar likes people who are organized and compliant. Organized and obedient people get ahead in his organization. Now the market is changing, and old familiarities are going out the window. He needs people who can think in the absence of structures, who can be proactive and take on-the-spot decisions. He needs kartas. But over the years he has groomed only karya-kartas. They ensured his success for a long time, but in the new market he needs kartas and there is no one around.

Insecurity turns us into villains

In the Bhagavad Gita, Kansa is foretold that his sister's eighth child will be responsible for his death. So he goes about killing all her children as soon as they are born in the hope of defying fate. In the Ramayan, as Ram's army nears Lanka, Ravan gets increasingly intolerant and demanding. When his brother, Vibhishan, pleads with him to let Sita go to save Lanka, Ravan views this as an attack on his mental image and kicks Vibhishan out. On the other hand, Ravan starts to increasingly rely on Kumbhakarn who does not challenge his mental image and keeps agreeing with him.

In the Mahabharat, Duryodhan tries to poison Bhim and sets fire to the palace in which the Pandavs are sleeping. He believes that with the Pandavs gone, his claim on the throne of Hastinapur will be secure. He wants to be king. He needs that social body and will do anything to destroy those who threaten it. Kansa fears for his physical body, Ravan for his mental body, and Duryodhan for his social body. In their own eyes, they are victims, fighting for survival. None accepts that death is inevitable.

Here, death is a metaphor for change. We do not want to accept the inevitable—that one day we will be replaced. We go about ensuring there is no rival, or threat to our existence. We create structures and systems that secure our roles, hence our self-image. But in securing ourselves, we end up hurting others. We become villains.

Rakesh thinks he is very smart. He can compute better than others and can organize things better than anybody else. If anybody challenges his system, he gets furious. He does not appreciate criticism, viewing it as opposition and a challenge. Smart people leave his team or sit there resenting everything he says, allowing him to make stupid mistakes, because they know he will not listen. Rakesh is a bully, he needs to be aggressive and dominating because this enables him to get Durga forcibly from people and feed his own sense of inadequacy. In doing so, he destroys all relationships. He remains alone and vulnerable, with no one around to help him when he really needs support.

Our stability prevents other people's growth

When Jarasandha, king of Magadha, learns that Krishna has killed his son-in-law Kansa, the dictator of Mathura and that the people of Mathura rejoiced at his death, he is furious. He orders his army to kill Krishna and set aflame the city. Krishna and the people of Mathura are forced to take refuge in the faraway island of Dwaraka.

Years later, after the Pandavs build the city of Indraprastha with the help of Krishna, Yudhishtir, the eldest of the Pandav brothers, declares their desire to be kings. Krishna says, "As long as Jarasandha is alive that is not possible. Jarasandha has subdued all the kings of the land. Until those kings are liberated, until they are free to attend your coronation and recognize your sovereignty, you cannot be king."

Jarasandha is a chakravarti, an emperor of all the lands he surveys. In Jain chronicles he is prati-vasudev, the enemy of vasudev (Krishna) and his pacifist brother baladev. Jarasandha's control and systems do not let other kings thrive. He may have established stability and order but the stability and order serve him, not Krishna or the Pandavs. Naturally, the vasudev considers the chakravarti as the prati-vasudev.

Without realizing it, our structures end up curtailing innovation. Innovators hate institutions and yet institutions are built on the principles of fairness and equality. In an equal world, no one can be special. An innovator, though, sees himself as different. From his different point of view come new ideas and innovation that will change the old order of things.

We call the innovator a rebel because he does not align with authority. We call the innovator a prophet because he challenges authority. But eventually, every innovator becomes a chakravarti and institutionalizes his rules. And with that he becomes a prati-vasudev or enemy to young entrepreneurs and other innovators.

Revant liked the licence raj era when business was assured from the government. Now, with liberalization he has to give tenders every year, deal with officers and prove his capability time and again, as the officers keep changing. They say this competitive environment is good for the country. But weren't the services he provided of top quality? What Revant does not realize is that because of the old system, many talented businessmen were denied opportunities to grow. They, in turn, resented the likes of Revant whose family had benefitted from British rule and subsequently, under the socialist governments. Revant saw himself as a chakravarti who creates order and stability around him. But ambitious men like Bilvamangal saw him as old money that does not like new money: a prati-vasudev, who uses his power to create rules that block others from rising.

We would rather change the world than ourselves

Shishupala was born deformed with extra limbs and eyes. The oracles revealed that he would become normal the day he was picked up by a man who was destined to kill him. That man turned out to be Krishna. Shishupala's mother begged Krishna to forgive a hundred crimes of her son. Krishna promised to do so.

At the coronation of Yudhishtir, Shishupala insulted Krishna several times. Krishna did not say anything and kept forgiving him, but eventually, after the hundredth insult, Krishna was under no obligation to forgive the lout. He hurled his Sudarshan chakra and killed Shishupala.

While Shishupala's mother got an assurance from Krishna, at no point did Shishupala's mother tell her son never to upset Krishna. Shishupala's mother gains Durga from Krishna but does not invoke Shakti in her own son. She relies on external powers for protection and has no faith in internal power. The burden of invoking inner power is too great. It demands too much effort. Like Indra, Shishupala's mother seeks external intervention to save her during crisis.

In the Puran, Indra never changes. Despite crisis after crisis and the repeated attacks of asuras, he does not change. He keeps asking for help from his father Brahma who asks Vishnu for help. When Vishnu solves the problem, Indra returns to his indulgent ways. We want problems to be solved, but we refuse to develop divya-drishti or realize that we want to change only the objective world and are convinced the subjective world needs no improvement.

When Atul resigned and moved to another firm, Derek was furious. He raved and ranted about Atul's lack of loyalty and his betrayal. "We should never hire professionals," he told his son. In his rage, he gave more powers to those who were loyal to him, not realizing that it was precisely this behaviour that had alienated the very-talented Atul. Derek's insecurity meant he was always suspicious of people who did not demonstrate loyalty. He wanted to hedge his bets and so gave equal value to those loyal as well as those who were talented. He wanted the world to be loyal to him, but did nothing to evoke loyalty in men like Atul by giving them the freedom and space they needed to perform. He believed, like Shishupala's mother, that the problem was with the world.

When the context changes, we have to change

Vishnu is at once mortal and immortal. Each of his avatars goes through birth and death, yet he never dies. The avatar adapts to the age. Jaisa yug, vaisa avatar (as is the context, so is the action). With each avatar his social body undergoes a change. He is at first animal (fish, turtle, boar, half-lion) and then human (priest, warrior, prince, cowherd, charioteer).

When Hiranayaksha dragged the earth under the sea, Vishnu took the form of the boar Varaha, plunged into the waters and gored the asura to death, placing the earth on his own snout, raising it back to the surface. This confrontation was highly physical.

Hiranakashipu was a different kind of asura. He obtained a boon that made him near invincible: he could not be killed either by a man or an animal, either in the day or in the night, neither inside a dwelling nor outside, nor on the ground or off it, and not with a weapon or tool. To kill this asura, Vishnu transformed himself into Narasimha, a creature that was half-lion and half-human, neither man nor completely animal. He dragged the asura at twilight, which is neither day nor night, to the threshold, which is neither inside a house nor outside, and placing him on his thigh, which is neither on the ground nor off, and disembowelled him with his sharp claws, which were neither weapons nor tools. This complex confrontation was highly intellectual, a battle of wits if you will.

Then came Bali, an asura who was so noble and so generous that his realm expanded beyond the subterranean realms to include the earth and sky. To put him back in his place , Vishnu took the form of the dwarf Vaman and asked him for three paces of land. When Bali granted this wish, the dwarf turned into a giant and with two steps claimed the earth and sky, shoving Bali back to the nether regions with the third step. This battle involved not so much defeating the opponent as it did transforming oneself.

A study of these avatars of Vishnu indicates a discernible shift in tactics. From Varaha to Narasimha to Vamana there is a shift from brute force, to brain over brawn and, finally, an exercise in outgrowing rather than outwitting. The demons become increasingly complex—Hiranayaksha is violent,

Hiranakashipu is cunning and Bali is good but fails to see the big picture. Each one forces Vishnu to change, adapt and evolve. There is no standard approach, each approach is customized as per the context determined by the other. At all times, Vishnu's intention does not change.

Narsi knew that some problems could only be solved by force. So he hired a security firm known for strong-arm tactics. He also had a team of powerful lawyers because he knew many problems could be prevented by watertight contracts and fear of litigation. When the head of his marketing department was being too impudent, Narsi decided to change the proportions of the business relationship. He appointed a senior group marketing head to oversee the marketing operations of all his businesses. Suddenly, the marketing head, once a big fish in a small pond, found that he had become the small fish in a big pond, and stopped being an upstart and creating too much trouble. Some people think Narsi has multiple-personality disorder. Sometimes he gives people complete freedom. Sometimes he controls every aspect of the project. Sometimes he is kind and understanding. Sometime he shouts and screams. Narsi told his nephew, Vishal, that he changes his management style depending on the situation and the person in front of him. "Some situations demand creativity and others demand control. Some people need to be instructed while others can be inspired. We need to change as per the situation and the people around us in order to succeed." Narsi is Vishnu who knows every context is a yuga and every yuga has its own appropriate avatar.

WHEN THE OPPONENT IS...	USE THE FOLLOWING TACTIC
strong	force
cunning	cleverness
good-intentioned but short-sighted	change the scale of engagement

Unless we change, we cannot grow

There was once a serpent called Kaliya who poisoned a bend of the river Yamuna. No cow, cowherd or milkmaid could come near the stretch of water inhabited by Kaliya. Krishna jumped into the water and challenged Kaliya to a duel. After a fierce fight, Krishna succeeded in overpowering the serpent; he danced on Kaliya's hood until the serpent, very reluctantly, agreed to move.

"What is the problem?" asked Krishna, out of concern for Kaliya. Kaliya explained that the eagle, Garud, wanted to eat him and because of a spell cast by a sage on that particular bend of the river Yamuna, he could not follow him there. "This is the only place where I am safe from Garud. That is why I do not venture out of this place." Fear had made Kaliya cling to a location. This location was his Durga. His refusal to move made the waters poisonous and deemed him a villain in everyone's eyes, though he felt he was a victim only trying to save himself.

Kaliya feels like an abandoned child. He seeks a yajaman who will protect him. Finding none, he has to protect himself. He is the animal in the forest with no one to turn to. The bend in the river Yamuna symbolizes the organization, the role and rules that guarantee his self-image. He refuses to move on. He refuses to grow. Growth demands changing himself and the world around him. That frightens him unless it is on his own terms. He feels safe in the old familiar way and resists any attempt to make him cross over to the new unfamiliar way.

But the world is constantly changing. Things will never remain constant. If we focus only on the coming and going of fortune, we will always be anxious and frustrated. On the other hand, if we focus on learning with every rise and fall, we will keep growing and generating internal Shakti rather than depending on external Durga for our survival.

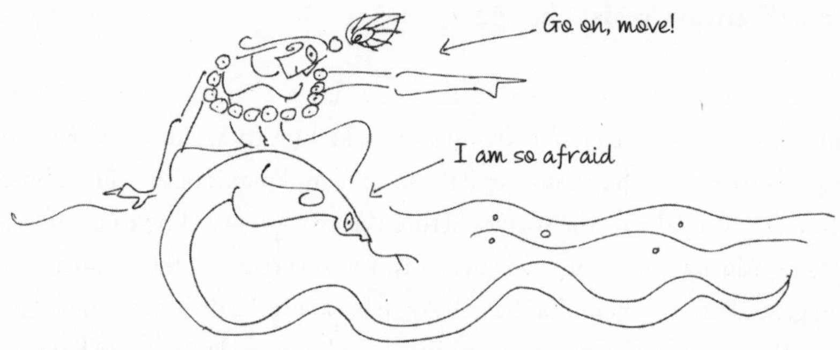

Shivkumar got transfer orders a week ago and he is upset. For years he has served the company loyally, taken not a single day's leave. He made it to office even when he had fever. All his life he stayed in Lucknow, in his family house. He walked to work and enjoyed the neighbourhood. Now this! How could they do this to him? How could they transfer him to Allahabad? Yes, the new office needed setting up, but why him? He had not taken a promotion so that he could stay here. He was even willing to take a pay cut to stay. He just did not want to go to Allahabad. But his new boss who has come from Delhi is a scoundrel and refuses to listen to reason. "You must go to Allahabad, Shivkumarji. The company needs you to do this. And I need you to do this. And it is for your own good." How can it be for his good? Moving to a new place, a new neighbourhood, a new house, the headache of school admissions, the pain of shifting furniture. And who would look after his family house while he was away? And his parents? Would they also have to move? His mother would never agree. Shivkumar believes his boss from Delhi is Kaliya who needs to be kicked back by Krishna. But in fact, he is the Kaliya himself. His boss has recognized his potential—his ability to contribute, not just to the organization but also to himself. Shivakumar sells himself short. He hides behind apparent contentment. Deep down, he is envious of the young ones in the company who have been promoted and given better bonuses and incentives. He gets upset when bosses accept transfers, when the houses in the neighbourhood are broken down to make way for new structures. Things are changing every day around Shivkumar, but he is refusing to adapt. Before him is an opportunity to experience something new, but he is afraid. Garud lurks beyond the bend of his river. He is angry with Krishna. He does not want to go. But Krishna's dance will not stop; the transfer order will not be revoked.

We will always resist change

In the Bhagavat Puran, it is said that one day a charioteer called Akrura comes to Vrindavan to fetch Krishna and take him to Mathura. As Krishna prepares to leave with his brother Balaram, the milkmaids of the village break into tears. They throw themselves before the chariot and cling to its wheels, begging Akrura not to take Krishna away. Krishna requests the women to let him go and assures them that he will come back, but he does not return.

This event marks the end of the Bhagavat Puran and the start of Krishna's role in the Mahabharat. The ranga-bhoomi of Vrindavan, full of song and dance, in the middle of the forest, is replaced by the rana-bhoomi of Mathura, Dwarka, Indraprastha, Hastinapur and Kurukshetra.

Every year, the chariot festival at Puri, Orissa, is a festive expression of the desire of devotees for Krishna to return. He does so for a brief period and then returns to his temples once again. For ultimately, the gopikas have to let go.

The gopikas had found great security in the company of Krishna. They had grown to depend on the Durga he gave them. But by leaving, Krishna compels them to grow, find Shakti within themselves. It is time for them to become Krishna for others. It is time for them to be less dependent and more dependable, move away from tamas-guna towards sattva-guna.

Krishna leaves his beloved Radha behind because duty beckons him in Mathura. By letting him go, she grows by being more independent. By letting her go, he grows by being able to bear more responsibility. But the change has consequences. Never again will Krishna play the flute as he did in Radha's presence.

We cannot stay dependent forever. We have to learn to be independent. Like Hanuman who found Ram in his heart, the gopikas have to find Krishna inside them and create the rasa-mandala, the circle of joy and security around them.

During a conference of entrepreneuers, Kalra spoke on the value of letting go, allowing people to grow up and take responsibility. "When I had fifty people working for me, I interfered in every aspect of business. When I had five hundred, I had to change and they, too, had to change. I had to let managers think for themselves, transform from being karya-kartas to kartas. And the only way to do this is by becoming a yajaman, allowing others to take the decision. Unless we let go, the dependent will never become dependable, and neither they nor we will ever grow."

Adapting to change is not growth

Animals adapt to circumstances. Some hibernate, some migrate. Humans can change with circumstances, too. Organizations have to change to keep up with the new realities of the market and the industry, and that compels people to change, learn new skills, adapt to new organizational structures. But such a change is adaptability, not growth.

Adaptability is the ability to change with the context to achieve the same end-result. Growth is change in mindset, when the same context can be seen differently. Adaptability enables the conversion of Bhudevi (natural wealth) to Shridevi (personal wealth) no matter what the context. Growth is turning Durga (dependence on external power) to Shakti (dependability by invoking internal power).

In the Treta yuga, the enemy is Ravan. In the Dvapar yuga, the enemy is Duryodhan. From a subjective point of view, neither is different from the other. Both are frightened. They differ from an objective point of view. Ravan is strong while Duryodhan is cunning. So Ravan openly confronts Ram while Duryodhan uses guile to overpower the Pandavs.

Likewise, Vishnu changes his tactics when dealing with Ravan and Duryodhan. For the rule-breaking villain, he chooses to be the rule-following Ram and for the rule-following villain, he chooses to be the rule-breaking Krishna. These tactical changes indicate adaptability, not growth.

Growth happens when Brahma's sons (Daksha, Indra, Ravan and Duryodhan) make the journey to Vishnu, when intention shifts from self-preservation, self-propagation and self-actualization to a greater concern for the Other, a greater inclusiveness. This can only happen by invoking Shakti and outgrowing fear. Such growth can never be collective; it is always individual. But the yajaman can create an ecosystem where such growth is encouraged and enabled.

A manager is expected to adapt to changes in the organization. A leader is expected to change the circumstances, have greater vision. A follower does as told.

In Jain mythology, a vasudev thinks in terms of growth and a chakravarti

thinks in terms of adaptability; the tirthankar takes both into consideration for he understands the value of both adaptability to context, and growth.

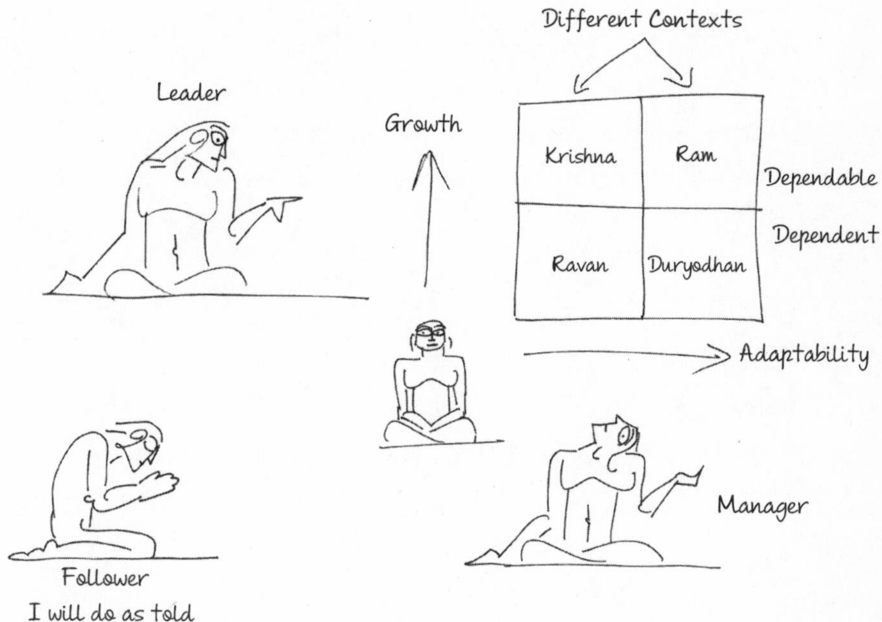

Following the merger, the company's focus changed from commodity-selling to brand-creating. This meant that the sales force now had to sell concepts, not products. Everyone was expected to change. Many people who could not adapt to the change left the organization. Rajiv adapted to the situation and continued to serve as manager. Rohit, on the other hand, was curious to know why the organization had changed its strategy. He wanted to know what change in the market had prompted such a change in the company. His curiosity enabled him to expand his mind, appreciate the thought process of the company. His shift was not just behavioural. Rajiv is merely a manager, but Rohit has the potential of a leader.

Kama's Vision Statement

Drishti, observing objective reality

Divya-drishti, observing subjective reality

Darshan, observing the subject

Isolation *Reflection* *Expansion* *Inclusion*

Yama's Balance Sheet

Ik-tara or
one stringed lute
symbolizing shruti,
the inner voice
of the mind
Book symbolizing smriti,
the outer voice for
exchange of ideas
Goose is a symbol of
analysis because it
can supposedly
separate out milk
from water in a
mixture of the two

The ability to see the human quest for identity is darshan. The identity of a person or sukshma-sharira is how he imagines himself. And this identity depends on brahmanda, how he imagines the world. Identity and worldview are thus manas putra, the children of Brahma's imagination.

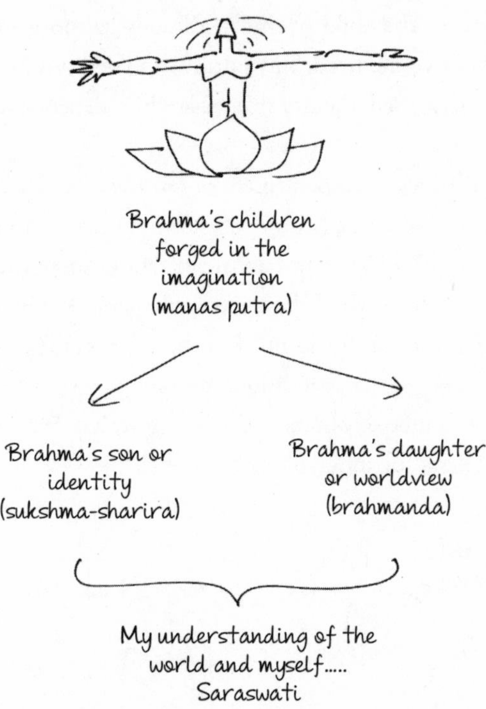

Imagination is fluid, or saras. Our imagination of the world, hence ourselves, keeps changing all the time. It will change with context or with better observation. If in one context, we may see ourselves as heroes, in another, we may see ourselves as victims or martyrs. Initially, we may see the employer as a saviour; but over time, with more information, on closer inspection, we may see the employer as the oppressor and ourselves as the oppressed. From saras comes Saraswati, goddess of knowledge. Knowledge is fluid; springing from imagination, constantly shape shifting, with the potential to expand towards infinity.

In the Brahma Puran, brahmanda is referred to as Brahma's daughter, his creation. She is Shatarupa, she of many forms, a reminder of her fluid nature. In the Shiva Puran, Brahma is accused of having incestuous affection for his daughter. This must not be taken literally (as it often is). It is a metaphor for how every human being clings to his creation, his subjective reality, convinced it is objective reality. The child of this incestuous liaison is our identity, also assumed to be objective and fixed. Shiva attacks and beheads Brahma, hoping he will abandon this imagined identity that makes him dependent and needy, but Brahma resists.

We constantly seek an endorsement of our identity. We adore those who see us as we imagine ourselves. Nature refuses to do that. Nature does not care if one is a doorman or director, but an organization does. The social identity, however, ceases to matter when the context changes. A military general may be valued during a war but not so much in peace. A culture's endorsement of our identity is thus occasional, conditional and temporary. This fills us with the fear of invalidation, a uniquely human fear, the greatest of fears that makes every human being feel dreadful, miserable and invisible.

Some react to this invalidation by seeking escape: either in work, entertainment or alcohol. Others seek an adrenaline rush to feel alive, anything from extreme sports to gambling. Still others turn to gluttony and greed, perversions and pettiness, grabbing more wealth and power in a bid to

punish nature or culture itself. These may be condemned in society as vices, but they are in fact the cry of victims of imagination, desperately seeking meaning.

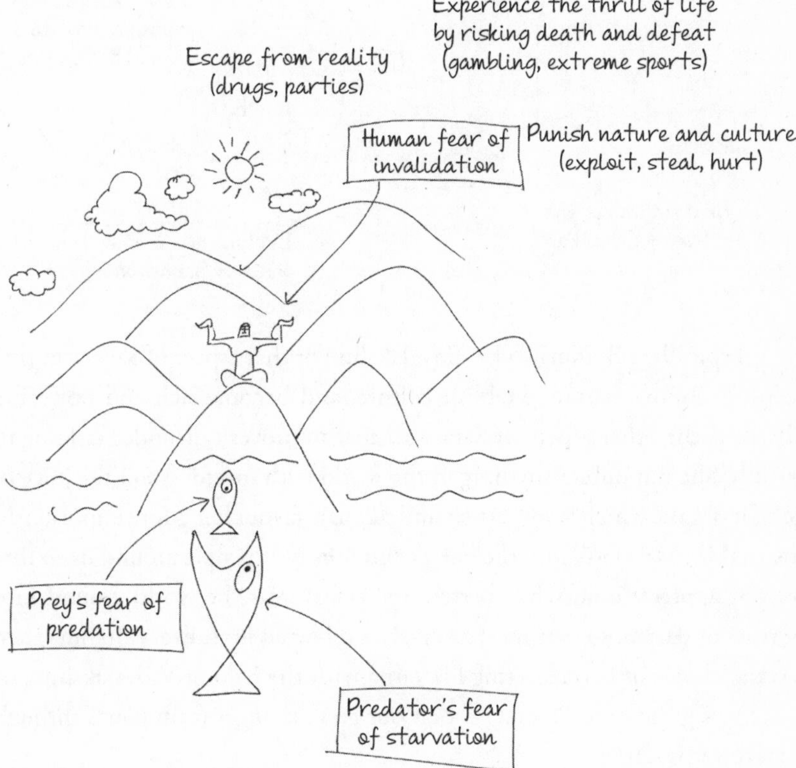

Shatarupa—imagination that amplifies our fears—can also liberate us from fear, for she is also Saraswati. In order to transform we need to stop clinging to and controlling imagination, but allow her to flow. If Brahma allows Shatarupa to be Saraswati, the trap will turn into a teacher. Saraswati will enable Brahma to outgrow fear and become the self-reliant swayambhu, like the independent Shiva and the dependable Vishnu. This can happen only if the 'father' wills it so, that is, Brahma allows himself to become the 'child'.

Typically, a Brahma seeks Vidyalakshmi or that aspect of Saraswati that helps us control nature, establish culture, and become rich and powerful. Sharda is the other aspect of Saraswati that improves our understanding of purush. She can imbue anything in the world with meaning and the juice of delight or rasa, which is why artists and scholars favour her. More importantly, she enables us to look into the hearts and minds of people around us so that we can appreciate ourselves better. She transforms the world around into mirrors or darpan so that we see ourselves reflected in it. Every Brahma then has the choice of consolidating his varna with the help of Vidyalakshmi, or outgrowing fear with Sharda, so that our guna changes from tamas through rajas towards sattva.

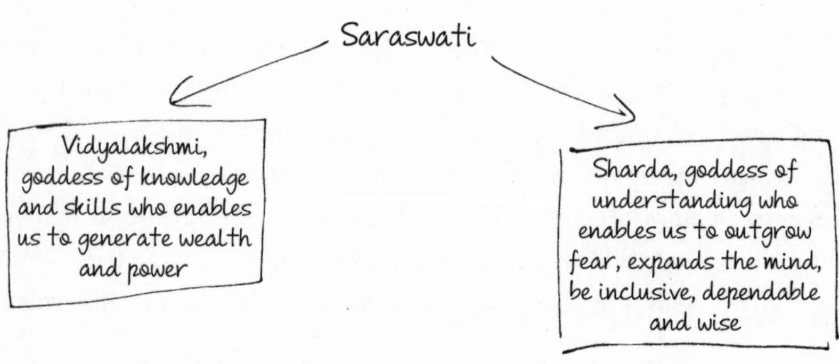

For this to happen, smriti must become shruti through tapasya. Smriti means the external voice through which information can be exchanged during the yagna. Shruti means the inner voice of our thoughts that cannot be exchanged. We communicate through smriti but we listen only to shruti. Smriti may inspire us but only shruti can transform us. Tapasya or introspection and contemplation play a key role in transforming smriti into shruti. When smriti becomes shruti, what I have becomes what I am. We no longer have power; we become powerful. We no longer have knowledge; we become wise. We do not need Durga from the outside world as we invoke Shakti within. We discover our potential within and hence find resources everywhere. We move from dependence towards dependability.

Smriti is represented by the book in Saraswati's hand while shruti by the one-stringed lute, the ik-tara that she plucks as she waits for realization to strike. Saraswati's goose or hamsa represents the human ability to analyse and introspect as it has the power to separate milk and water. In Buddhist mythology, Saraswati is Tara. The lotus (padma) in her hand represents our mind. As the imagination expands, these petals unfold to reveal the jewel (mani) of Buddha's wisdom. In Jain mythology, the third worthy being, besides vasudev and chakravarti, is the tirthankar, the supremely sensitive and caring sage.

- Tirthankar is the non-violent one, with no desire to be aggressive, dominating or territorial, for he can see how imagination can amplify fear and isolate humans from the rest of the world.

- He draws attention to the tirtha or ford, existing in the river of imagination, waiting to be discovered, that allows us to connect with

worlds that seem otherwise separated and reflect on them.

- It is tough for a yajaman to walk across the tirtha and see the world from the devata's point of view. This demands expansion of the mind.

- It is tougher still to get the devata to walk across to the yajaman's side. Instruction is of no use. Inclusion demands we make room for even those who refuse to make room for us.

In this chapter we shall explore isolation, connection, expansion and inclusion and by doing so, appreciate the tirthankar's gaze. A yajaman who does darshan and seeks Saraswati, walks the path of the tirthankar. He knows that business is neither a burden to bear nor a battle to win, but a chance to outgrow fear by helping others outgrow theirs. This opportunity is available only to humans. To realize it is humanity's dharma.

All her life, Bela believed in an open-door policy for managers, but people rarely entered her cabin. She concluded that they were fools never to take advantage of her charitable nature. She saw herself as a misunderstood hero, until someone pointed out that everyone was intimidated by her. She was such a hard taskmaster and so demanding that people feared entering her cabin for it would invariably lead to her pulling them up for something or the other. She was the villain according to all the people who ever worked with her. Bela now had a choice: shrug her shoulders and accept the situation, as she wasn't about to change, or take responsibility for the world of fear she had unintentionally created around her. Bela chose to take responsibility and began watching how she engaged with people. She started looking at her team as a set of people, not task-completers or target-achievers. She started seeing the world from their point of view. Saraswati began to flow in Bela's head, widening her gaze, making her pay attention to the imagined realities around her and how they clashed with her own imagined reality. The more she walked the path of the tirthankar, the more she felt in charge; more of a swayambhu and less of a helpless offspring of circumstances. As Brahma, she replaced the old world of fear with a new world of encouragement much to the delight of her team.

Isolation

We want to be seen by others, but more often than not are unable to see others ourselves. We focus on making ourselves attractive. Focused on self-preservation, self-propagation and self-actualization, everyone gets isolated and wonders why they feel so lonely.

The gaze can be cruel or caring

In the Mahabharat, Duryodhan denies the Pandavs their throne while Krishna helps them reclaim it. Duryodhan abuses Draupadi, the wife of the Pandavs and Krishna rescues her. It is easy to see Duryodhan as the villain and Krishna as the hero if we restrict our gaze to these actions. If we seek the seed of the fruit, on the other hand, we can look beyond. We can wonder: what makes one man a villain and another man a hero? The epics provide some answers.

Duryodhan's father is denied the throne because he is born blind. Duryodhan's mother Gandhari blindfolds herself, as she wants to share her husband's suffering. She refuses to remove the blindfold even to look at her son because she refuses to break the vow taken during marriage. Thus, Duryodhan ends up with one parent who cannot see him and the other parent who will not see him. Unseen, Duryodhan feels uncared for. He has to fend for himself, as an animal fends for itself in the forest. Naturally, he displays animal traits: aggression, territoriality and domination. He sees the Pandavs as predators.

Krishna, on the other hand, has a childhood full of love and affection. When he broke pots, stole butter and played pranks, his mother, Yashoda,

punished him but simultaneously she wept, indicating how much it pained her to punish him. In punishment, she never let him lose sight of her affection for him. That she was disciplining him did not mean he was wrong; it simply meant he had not expanded his mind to accommodate others' point of view. A child is allowed to not consider the feelings of others but an adult does not have that luxury. Krishna never felt isolated and alone. He did not see the world of humans as being full of predators and prey, as Duryodhan did.

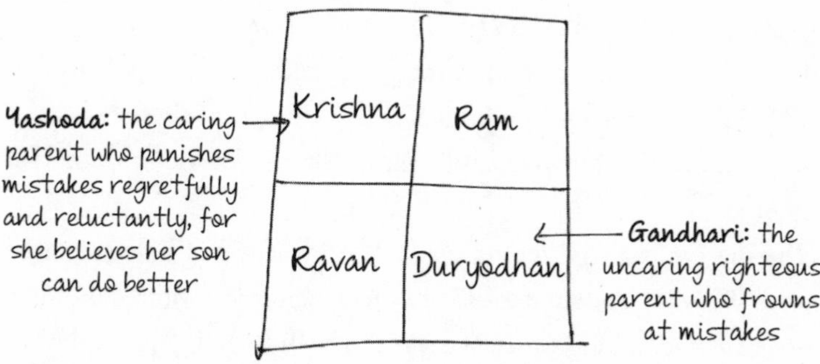

Tariq heard a great motivational speech at the annual sales conference. Charged, he spent the year going beyond the call of duty, developing clients who he knew would give the company business a few years down the line. When the time for the appraisal and bonus came, these efforts were not even considered. The software that was developed to capture the work done in the previous year had no columns for 'going beyond the call of duty'. It only measured results against organizational expectations and plans. Then the bell curve of organizational performance, achieved through a series of complex algorithms, graded Tariq far below his expectations, even below his manager's rating of him. Tariq's manager protested but to no avail. The technology for determining compensation was world-class, recommended by the best consultants in the world and implemented by the best software company in India. Its results could not be challenged. Tariq felt like a fool. Worse, he felt invisible. He realized that the shareholders of his company valued the technology more than his manager or even his manager's manager. The organization was his Gandhari who saw only his measurable deeds not his disappointment.

Everyone seeks a caring gaze

For humans, the forest is a place of fear as is the time of night. Yet, according to the Bhagavat Puran, the rasa-lila always takes place outside the village in the forest at night. Krishna plays the flute and the women leave the security of their homes to secretly be with him, dancing around him in a perfect circle. He is no brother, father, son or lover, bound by neither law nor custom and yet the women seek his company. Krishna multiplies himself for each of them, giving each one his complete and exclusive attention.

Later, Krishna moves to Dwarka, and ends up having 16,108 wives. When Narad visits the city, he finds Krishna in each of these houses, giving his full attention to all his wives and their children. He has multiplied himself once again.

The market is a frightening place. We are afraid of being cheated and exploited. We want someone to make us feel secure and wanted. Someone to validate us instead of judging us. We want to be indulged. The employee seeks individual attention from the employer; the buyer seeks individual attention from the seller. We seek Krishna in the forest, who does not use the collective as an excuse to forget the individual.

Everyone in Sanjog's team hates him. In brainstorming meetings only Sanjog speaks, not letting anyone get a word in. If the meeting lasts for an hour, he speaks for 55 minutes. When someone interrupts, they are promptly silenced. If someone disagrees, they are told they do not have the experience to understand. Sanjog is blind to his team. He is blind to himself. He does not realize that he is drawing power from his team, making them powerless. He is no Krishna. The team is far from experiencing rasa-lila.

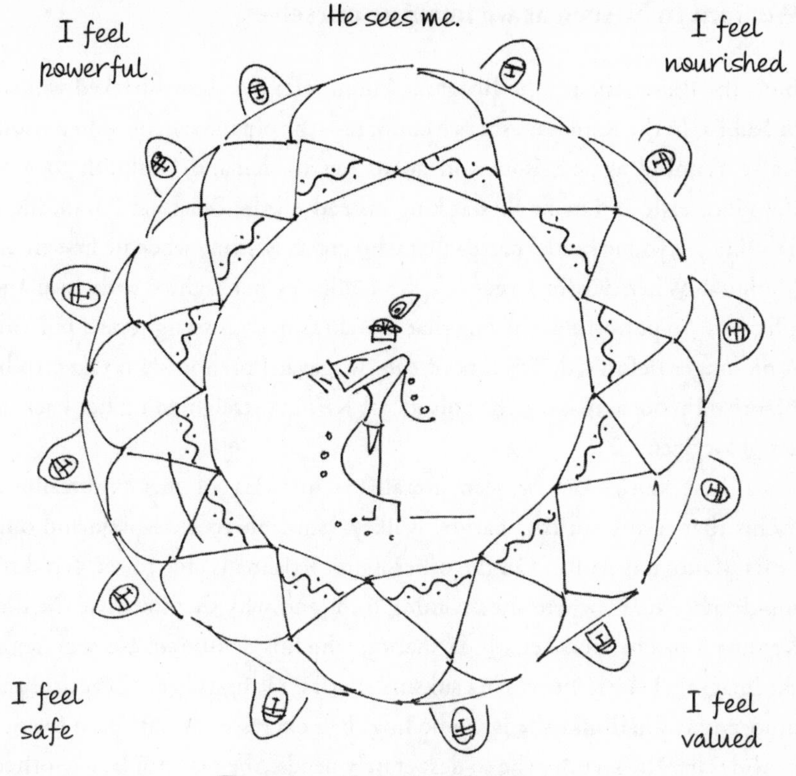
He sees me.
I feel powerful
I feel nourished
I feel safe
I feel valued
They do not distract him.

We want to be seen as we imagine ourselves

Both the Ramayan and the Bhagavat Puran refer to a hunchbacked woman or Kubija. In the Ramayan, she is Manthara—the old nursemaid who poisons Kaikeyi's mind against Ram and goads her to demand Dashrath to send Ram into exile and make Bharat king instead. In the Bhagavat Puran, she is Trivakra—a young sandal paste seller who greets Krishna when he first enters Mathura. When Krishna sees her, he embraces her tightly with love and affection. So powerful is the hug that Trivakra's body is straightened out. She is no longer deformed. Trivakra of the Bhagavat Puran is often taken to be Manthara reborn, making the episode of Krishna straightening her back an act of forgiveness.

These stories can be seen literally as miracles, or metaphorically, as events that reveal our true nature. Kaikeyi is unable to see Kubija and only hears Manthara's words. On the other hand, Krishna is able to see Trivakra's mind: who she is, where she's coming from and why she did what she did. Krishna looks beyond her sthula-sharira, which is deformed. He sees her as she imagines herself; he sees her suksma-sharira. He finds her as beautiful and innocent as she thinks she is. So he hugs her, expresses his affection for her, provides her the security she so desperately needs. She may not be like others but that does not mean she needs any less validation. Having got it from Krishna, she no longer feels like an outsider or an ugly person who can only get the master's attention and affection through manipulation.

The workplace is full of Kubijas. In a world where only performance seems to matter, they are mediocre, at the wrong end of the bell-curve, people who can be justifiably kicked out. And this makes them insecure. The only way then to secure their job is to have a relationship with people in power, display loyalty by poisoning their ears against others, making the yajaman feel there is someone looking out for them.

Every year, the Clark Travel Company selects two management trainees. This year they have selected Meghna and Rose. Meghna comes from an affluent family and this job is a way for her to pass her time before she gets married. She, therefore, resents it when her manager piles work on her and makes her stay late on weekends. Rose comes from a very poor family and has been able to go to college thanks to the kindness of relatives. She is deeply in debt. She is very grateful for the job, anxious about losing it and eager to please. Her boss keeps finding fault with her work and that frightens her further. Both Meghna and Rose feel unloved like Kubija and yearn for a Krishna who will see them for who they truly are.

A cruel gaze focuses on our compliance rather than our capability

Hanuman plays a crucial role in the Ramayan. He is asked to discover Sita's whereabouts, build a bridge across the sea with the aid of the monkeys, fetch the lifesaving herbs that save Lakshman's life—all of which he accomplishes. Throughout the epic, he proves his capability time and again. He is strong enough to carry mountains and smart enough to trick sea-monsters like Surasa and Simhika.

Yet in the epic, he does not hold any great position. He is just one of the many monkeys Ram encounters in the forest. He is not Sugriva, leader of the monkey troop. He is not Angad, son of Vali, who is told to lead the band of monkeys searching for Sita. He is not Jambavan, the bear, or Nila, the monkey, who are given the responsibility of building the bridge. At no point does Hanuman make any attempt to steal anyone's glory; while in his own temple he stands powerful with a mountain in his hand and his feet on a demon, in Ram's temple he is most content sitting at the feet of his master, hands in supplication.

Who would not want a Hanuman on his team? The perfect karya-karta, one who is very good at his work, one who will do whatever he is told without ever seeking either reward or recognition; one who finds validation in obeying his master.

Years after the events in the Ramayan took place, Hanuman narrates the entire tale to his mother, Anjani. After hearing everything that's transpired, she wonders aloud, "Why did they go through the trouble of raising an army and building a bridge to defeat Ravan? Why did you not simply flick your tail and sweep the rakshasa-king and his army away?"

Hanuman replies, "Because no one asked me to."

And suddenly we wonder if this was a lost opportunity. Everyone saw Hanuman's obedience, but no one saw his true potential. Everyone saw Hanuman on their terms, not on his terms. In a world that celebrates alignment and compliance to the vision, systems and processes of an organization, is the individual increasingly getting invisible?

Unless the yajaman pays attention to the potential of the devata, the yagna achieves only a portion of what it could potentially achieve. The tathastu stays limited by the yajaman's gaze.

At Raju's auto-repair shop, all the work is done by his Hanuman: Amol, a young boy, who has been working with Raju for three years. Amol is a natural, able to fix the most complex of problems. Raju knows he can totally rely on Amol. No job is too big or too small for Amol. He is as happy changing a tyre as he is fixing the brakes. He does not boss over the juniors and does not feel slighted if the seniors ask him to fetch tea. If there is a problem that eludes a standard solution, everyone knows to leave it to Amol. He will, like Hanuman crossing the sea, find a way. Yes, Raju loves Amol's work. Yes, Raju admires Amol's work. But is Raju harnessing Amol's full potential?

Unseen, we are compelled to fend for ourselves

A fisherman catches a river fish, inside which he finds, miraculously, a pair of twins: a boy and a girl. The fisherman takes the children to Ushinara, the childless king of the land. The king adopts the boy, not the girl. She is named Satyavati and raised among the fishermen.

When Satyavati grows up she ferries people across the river. Shantanu, the old king of Hastinapur, falls in love with her and wants to marry her, but the leader of the fishermen says, "Only if her sons inherit your throne."

Shantanu has a son called Devavrat from an earlier marriage. To make his father happy, Devavrat gives up his claim to the throne, paving the way for Satyavati to marry his father. "But what if your children fight my children?" says Satyavati.

The roots of Satyavati's ambitions lay in her rejection by Ushinara who preferred the male child to the female child. She, who was not allowed to be princess, now wants to be queen and mother of kings. She wants to be seen as she imagines herself.

Our desire to achieve does not happen in isolation. We seek an audience. When the audience refuses to cheer for us, we work hard until they admire us. We validate ourselves, like Satyavati, through the Other. The Other is the parent whose attention we crave.

Nandita's dream has come true. She is a successful television actress. She has the best role she could have ever imagined and she is paid very well. The days of struggle are over. The audiences love her, as indicated by the ratings of her show. Still, every day she throws tantrums on the sets. She arrives late, refuses to come out of her trailer until the director begs her to, demands audiences with the television channel head, and insists on changing dialogues at the last minute. Unless she does this, she feels she is not being given her due. She is worth so much more. She was happiest when a trade journal revealed that she was the highest paid television star in history. She felt she had finally been seen.

We refuse to see ourselves as villains

Naraka, the asura, attacks Amravati and drives Indra out, laying claim to the treasures of paradise. Indra seeks the help of Vishnu and gets anxious when there is no sign of him in Vaikuntha. He is directed to Krishna, who lives on earth, and is considered to be Vishnu incarnate.

Indra doubts Krishna's divinity but desperate, seeks his help anyway. To his surprise, Krishna summons and mounts the eagle Garud and, with his wife Satyabhama by his side, rises to the sky bearing his resplendent weapons to battle with Naraka. After an intense battle, Krishna manages to vanquish Naraka and Indra regains his kingdom.

Naraka is no ordinary asura. He is the son of the earth-goddess, Bhudevi, and Varaha, the boar avatar of Vishnu who had rescued Bhudevi from the bottom of the sea after she had been dragged there by the asura, Hiranayaksha. When Krishna kills Naraka, Vishnu effectively kills his own son, but Indra is not even aware of this.

While leaving, Satyabhama expresses her desire for the parijata tree that grows in Indra's courtyard. Indra, however, refuses to part with it. Indra's refusal shocks Satyabhama who now becomes adamant about taking the tree back with her to earth. So Krishna takes it by force. When Indra tries to stop Krishna, another battle follows, this time with the devas, in which Indra is predictably defeated.

The story reveals the character of Indra. He is desperate to get help from Krishna but is unwilling to share even a tree with his saviour. He wants things, but never gives things. The king of the devas is not known for his generosity. He clings to his paradise but cannot enjoy it as he continuously fears losing it. His clinginess creates circumstances that contribute to his losing control over Amravati. When he manages to get it back with a little help from Vishnu, he returns to his clingy ways. Misfortune makes him miserable but fortune does not make him gracious. Circumstances teach him nothing as he is convinced he has nothing to learn. When this is pointed out, people like Indra simply shrug their shoulders, become defensive and say: we are like this only.

And so at the workplace, Indra comes to your workstation only because

he wants something. He expects you to do it because that is your job. But when you ask him for something, he refuses to help as he feels you are asking for a favour.

When Murli calls John, John knows that there is trouble in the family. Murli is one of the star directors of a family business and John is the head of accounts. Whenever the family members have a fight Murli calls John and spends hours saying nasty things about the family, claiming they are ganging up against him. John knows never to take these things seriously. Once the family dispute is settled, Murli will stop calling John and start maligning John lest John reveal what was said in those earlier phone calls. Everybody thinks that John is close to the family but John knows that no matter how loyal he is, how well he performs, he will never ever be a member of the family, never a shareholder of the company, regardless of the many promises made by Murli. John's wife says he should ask for his rights. "Rights?" John replies with amusement, "I only have a salary that I get paid every month. Everything else is just wishful thinking." John knows that Indra will not part with his parijata tree. John also knows he is no Krishna capable of overpowering his Indra.

We use work as a beacon to get attention

After Valmiki writes the Ramayan, he learns that Hanuman has also written a Ramayan. Curious about Hanuman's version, he goes to the distant plantain forest in the warm valleys cradled by the Himalayas where Hanuman lives.

There he finds the banana leaf on which Hanuman has etched his version of Ram's tale. The vocabulary, grammar, melody and metre are so perfect that Valmiki starts to cry, "After reading Hanuman's Ramayan, nobody will read Valmiki Ramayan." On hearing this, Hanuman tears the banana leaf with the epic on it, crushes it into a ball, pops it into his mouth and swallows it. "Why did you do that?" asks a surprised Valmiki.

Hanuman replies, "You need your Ramayan more than I need my Ramayan. You wrote your Ramayan because you want the world to remember you. I wrote my Ramayan because I wanted to remember Ram."

Ram embodies Narayan, human potential. Valmiki is nara, the human being. Hanuman is vanar, a monkey and an animal—less than human because he is not blessed with the power of imagination. Still, it is Hanuman who sees his work as an exercise to discover what he is capable of becoming while Valmiki sees his work as a beacon to gather fame, attention and validation. Hanuman seeks Narayan while Valmiki seeks Narayani. Narayan helps us see others. Narayani gets others to see us.

It is important to remind ourselves of who it is we work for. While the official purpose of work is to satisfy customers, employers, employees, shareholders and family, the unofficial purpose of work is to satisfy ourselves, feel noticed and alive.

Our work can become the tool that helps us grow not just materially but also emotionally and intellectually. It can widen our gaze. Valmiki, without realizing it, focuses only on material growth; Hanuman focuses on emotional and intellectual growth. When we widen our gaze, material growth follows. But the reverse is not true.

Lakotiaji has established some of the finest educational institutions in areas that did not have, until twenty years ago, even a decent primary school. Because of him many children have been educated and many adults have got jobs. The business has made him very rich, a much-respected member of the community. But Lakotiaji is upset. "The government has not recognized me. I deserve a Padma Shri." He is currently lobbying local politicians and the media hoping someone will recommend his name.

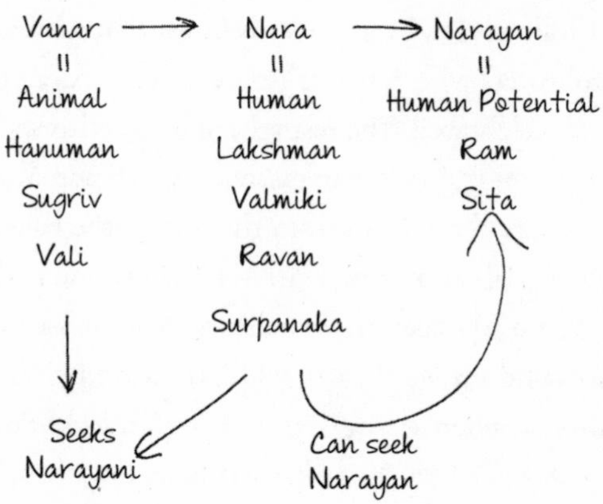

Our goals justify our lack of a caring gaze

In the Mahabharat, every character is invisible. Nobody sees anybody. Everyone is too busy gazing at ideals and institutions until Krishna arrives.

Bhisma sacrifices property and conjugal rights so that his old father, Shantanu, can marry Satyavati. Before long, the celibate and childless Bhisma finds himself responsible for Satyavati's children, grandchildren and her great-grandchildren. Since he sacrificed everything to please his father, he expects the children of the household to display similar selflessness and nobility. Fears and insecurities of individual family members are dismissed as being self-indulgent. So fixed is his gaze on family name that the family members feel small and invalidated.

Before long, the gaze of his great grandchildren shrinks. The Pandavs and Kauravs start seeing the kingdom as their property more than responsibility. They start valuing the kingdom more than each other. This marks the downfall of the household. But at no point does anyone see the venerable ancestor's sacrifice as contributing to the downward spiral. Even Bhisma blames external influences for family problems, never once gazing upon his own gaze.

Often leaders are so consumed by their personal values and agendas that they expect their followers to be as excited about what matters to them. They get angry with followers who resist or refuse to keep pace. Those who align with their goals are celebrated. The rest are condemned as selfish.

For many, the whole purpose of existence is self-actualization and thus, they voluntarily isolate themselves from the rest of the ecosystem. Nothing matters except their goals and ambitions. Achieving them makes them heroes while the failure to do so makes them martyrs. No one looks at the string of disappointed faces and broken hearts that they leave behind in their wake. Feelings don't matter when we do business, we are told. We are taught to believe that if it is not personal, it is okay to hurt.

At the open house session, the staff of an organization that sold mobile toilets complained that they were being forced to work overtime. They were promised a half-day on Saturday, but they ended up working late. The owner, Purab, shouted, "I work much more than you do, twice as much, so I expect you to give more. Isn't this work noble? We are liberating people from the humiliation of open toilets. How can you ask for holidays when there are people who do not have even basic amenities?" The staff immediately kept quiet. No one pointed out that they were not shareholders, they were not going to get a share of the profit and that their salaries would not rise proportionately if the business grew. They did not care for Purab's ideals or vision. They felt embarrassed telling their families about their jobs. The staff felt that Purab would see such candid views as subversive and threatening so they kept quiet, submitting to what each one imagined to be exploitation. Purab kept grumbling about the absence of ownership amongst the staff for the noble vision of his organization. Purab is Bhisma, so blinded by his vision that he does not see his staff is made of Indras seeking higher returns with low investment. He refuses to see how, for centuries, Indians have always looked down upon those who clean toilets.

Reflection

When we genuinely see others, we realize that they are often responding to their perception of us. How they see us is very different from how we see ourselves. As we contemplate this, we understand the world and appreciate ourselves better.

Fear isolates us while imagination connects us

The Garud Puran refers to a river called Vaitarni, which separates the living from the dead. This is the metaphorical river of fear that surrounds every brahmanda separating it from the other brahmanda.

The word 'tirtha' refers to a ford, a shallow part of the river that allows one to cross over to the other side. Unlike a bridge that needs to be built, a ford exists naturally and has to be discovered. Imagination is the ford that enables a yajaman to explore the devata's brahmanda and even reflect on how his own brahmanda appears from the other side. Tirtha transforms Vaitarni, the river of fear that separates, into Saraswati, the river of knowledge that connects. The yajaman who discovers the tirtha and walks on it is the tirthankar. In Jain scriptures, all worthy beings are classified as:

- Those who are action-driven like the vasudev who fights the prati-vasudev since his pacifist brother, the baladev, refuses to.
- Those who are rule-driven or the chakravartis.
- Those who are thought-driven or the tirthankars.

The tirthankar can see that while the vasudev feels like a hero and views the prati-vasudev as villain, the prati-vasudev sees himself as a leader, the chakravarti or keeper of the universal order. For the chakravarti, the vasudev is no hero; he is a rule-breaker, a threat to order. Neither sees the other. Vaitarni isolates each one. Unless they walk over the tirtha, there will always be conflict and violence in their relationship.

For the tirthankar, the other serves as a mirror or darpan. In them, he sees reflected aspects of his own personality and his own fears. If he judges these feelings, and choices, he will deny them, indulge them, justify them, fight them, but never outgrow them. To outgrow them, he has to accept their existence and be at peace. This is non-violence.

We often see the world through our own prejudices. The realization that everyone does the same thing should prompt us to observe other people's prejudices and wonder why they feel the way they do, rather than simply dismissing them. The chakravarti is too busy finding fault in vasudev, and the vasudev too busy fighting the prati-vasudev. Should the chakravarti invest more time in wondering why vasudev looks upon him as prati-vasudev, and should the vasudev invest more time in wondering why not everyone looks at the king as the villain, both would walk the path of the tirthankar.

Urvashi started a toy business. She could see huge potential both locally and internationally, but she could not scale up her business as government policies saw it as a cottage industry. These laws were instituted to protect and encourage small players. But these laws were shortsighted and they did not stop international players from supporting their toy industry and enabling them to create products at low rates and exporting them to other markets. As cheap foreign toys flooded the market, Urvashi lost her competitive edge in the market. Urvashi begged the government to intervene and the banks to reconsider their policies. But like stern chakravartis the bureaucrats and ministers refused to budge. Urvashi sees the government as prati-vasudev, the obstacle to her chance of being a successful entrepreneur. She had to close down her business and take up a job once again.

We often forget that others see the world differently

After the war at Kurukshetra, where the Pandavs defeat the Kauravs, there is an argument as to who is responsible for the victory. Is it Arjun who killed the mighty Kaurav commanders Bhisma, Jayadhrata and Karna? Or is it Bhim who killed the hundred Kaurav brothers? No one can decide, so they turn to the talking head on top of the hill overlooking the battlefield.

This is the head of a warrior who was decapitated before he entered the battlefield. He so longed to see the war that, taking pity on him, Krishna had his head put atop a hill. From this vantage point, he could see everything that happened in the battle over eighteen days.

When asked who was the greater warrior, the talking head said, "I did not see Bhim or Arjun. I did not see the Pandavs or Kauravs. I only saw Vishnu's discus severing the neck of corrupt kings and the earth-goddess stretching out her tongue to drink their blood."

In our yearning to be seen, we assume our own importance, until someone comes along and reminds us that we are but part of the big picture. Our roles in our departments sometimes become so important that we forget that we are part of a bigger picture. Our transaction that causes us great joy or pain is merely one of the thousands of transactions that are part of our enterprise.

People who have been in line-functions or customer-facing functions resist doing desk jobs in special projects or corporate offices. This is usually a good thing in one's career, at least for a short duration. But by working for some time in the HR department or finance department or CEO's office, they get a wider view of the organization and are able to contextualize the roles of those in the frontline. Somehow, from the dizzy heights of Kailas, the frenzy in Kashi seems insignificant.

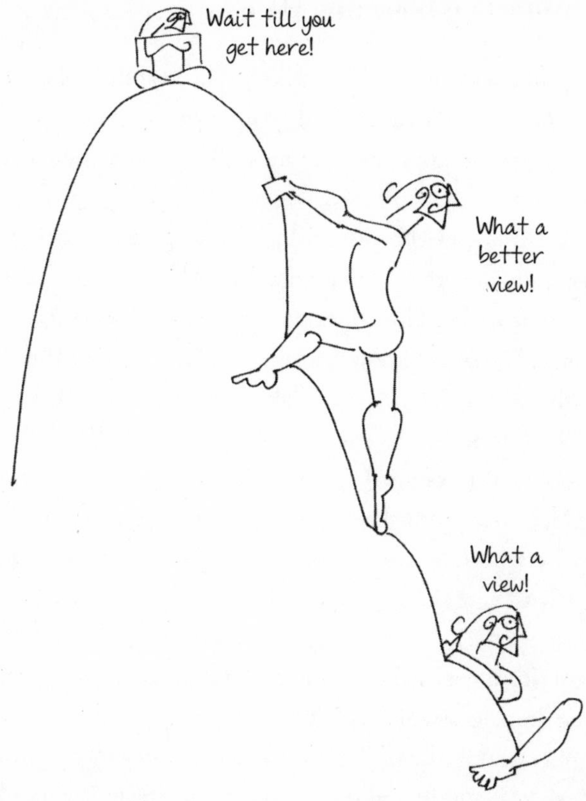

When Utpal's company made 40 per cent profits, the workers expected a 40 per cent bonus. But they received only a 10 per cent bonus, barely enough to account for inflation. The workers protested. Utpal explained he needed the profits to build another factory that would allow him to increase capacity and lower the cost of goods produced, which would enable him to stay competitive in the markets. But the workers felt this was an elaborate argument to deny them their dues. And how would they benefit from a larger factory? Utpal was thinking long-term while the workers were thinking short-term. This led to many arguments and threats of a strike. Utpal saw the workers as obstacles to his vision. He was determined to have his way and create more automation so that he would never have to deal with such labour issues.

How we see others reveals who we are

In the forest, while searching for Sita who had been abducted by Ravan, Ram and Lakshman meet an old lady called Shabari who invites them to a meal in her house. She offers them her frugal meal: berries she has collected in the forest.

Lakshman is horrified to see Shabari taking a bite of each berry before passing it on to his brother. Sometimes, she does not even pass the berry and just throws it away. "How dare you give leftover food to my brother?" Lakshman snarls. "Do you know who he is? He is Ram of the Raghu clan, king of Ayodhya!" An embarrassed Shabari throws herself at Ram's feet and apologizes for her mistake.

Ram looks at Lakshman with amazement, "What are you seeing, Lakshman? Here is a woman who is sharing the best of the food she has gathered for herself with two complete strangers, armed men at that. And you are angry with her? Look at her: she lives in the forest, and you expect her to know palace etiquette. She is biting the berries to make sure she feeds us the sweetest, most succulent ones. And instead of appreciating her generosity and kindness, you are angry with her! What does that say about you? Ayodhya and the Raghu clan may be important to you but they mean nothing to her. You expect her to see me as you see me. But do you really see me? Do you see anything except the way you imagine the world?"

The way Lakshman sees Shabari says nothing about Shabari; it reveals everything about Lakshman. The decisions, instructions and attitude of a yajaman reveal how he sees the yagna and the devata, and his own role. More often than not, a workplace is full of Lakshmans, ready to judge and instruct the Other, unlike Ram who appreciates people for who they are.

Many leaders insist that their assistant leave a small note about the background of the person they are about to meet before the meeting takes place. This ensures they do not make any blunders during the conversation and they are able to give the person they are meeting the impression that they matter, that they have been seen.

Excludes by refusing to let Saraswati flow and imagine the world from other people's point of view.

Includes by expanding mind

Shabari

Ram

Lakshman

At a team meeting, the junior-most trainee proposed an idea. "That is ridiculous," snapped the chief operating officer, Qureishi. Later, during a coffee break, the chief executive officer, Ansari, took Qureishi aside and said, "By ridiculing that trainee's proposal you have frightened everyone in the team. Now they will not be free with their ideas. They will be wary of what you may say. No one wants to look foolish. Imagine the trainee was brave enough to open up in front of the top management. Instead of appreciating him, you have mocked him. Made him feel even smaller than the junior status he currently occupies in the organization. You saw his proposal objectively, I understand. I wish you had seen it subjectively. Then you would not have demotivated him." Like Lakshman, Qureishi had failed to see the courage of the trainee. Now he realized why Ansari was such a favourite with everyone in the organization. It was not just the position he held. Ansari never ridiculed anyone; he never made anyone feel small. He genuinely valued everyone's ideas and helped each one see why it could, or could not be, implemented.

How others see us reveals who we are

Surya, the sun-god, was horrified when he noticed that the woman in his house was not his wife, Saranya, but her shadow, Chhaya. He stormed to the house of his father-in-law for an explanation, only to learn that she had run away because she could not bear his celestial radiance.

Surya realized that while in his story he was the victim, according to his wife he was the villain. That she had slipped away in secret and left a duplicate behind in her place was an indicator of the extent of her fear. Had he seen the world from her point of view, he would have realized beforehand what had frightened his wife before she had taken the drastic step of running away.

Surya then sought out his wife, and discovered she had taken the form of a mare. Instead of asking her to change back to human form, he turned into a horse and followed her to the pasture.

Yes, he could expect his wife to accept him as he was, or compel her to change for him, but that would mean he was incapable of growth. Reflecting on the other person's viewpoint prompts Surya to discover his ability to adapt, accommodate and grow. From god, he becomes animal and leads a happy life in the pasture until Saranya is able once more return to the sky by his side as his goddess.

This story reveals how the behaviour of people around us is a reaction to how they perceive us. If they fear us, they behave in a certain way. If they trust us, they behave differently. All behaviour depends on how other people perceive us. We can demand of others that they change their perceptions of us or we can decide to change ourselves and work on being more trustworthy. In the latter choice lies growth.

People often wonder why they are treated with respect in office and not the same way at home. It is usually an indicator of the power structures in the family and workplace. If we are feared in the family, everyone obeys us. If we are feared in the office, everyone tiptoes around us. If we are cruel to family members, it usually indicates that we feel they do not see us as we would wish to be seen or listen to us. The Other is always the mirror, the darpan, in which we can have a darshan of ourselves.

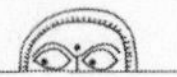

	I am...	He is...		
1.	Tiger	Tiger	________	Conflict
2.	Tiger	Goat	________	I dominate him
3.	Goat	Tiger	________	He dominates me
4.	Goat	Goat	________	We graze together
5.	Human	Whatever	_____	I can include him even if he does not include me

For two years, Sandesh had headed the operations department and put in place a whole set of systems and processes. With great difficulty, he had managed to get his team to align with the new environment and the results had been spectacular. Then Sandesh decided to spend more time on strategic thinking and appointed Ketan to handle the operations role. He just had to ensure the systems and processes set up over two years were being followed. But no sooner had Sandesh handed over the reins of the company than everything went awry. No one followed processes or systems and all reports came in late. Sandesh was angry with Ketan and his team for failing to do their jobs. Then he realized, the event revealed something about him. He had instituted the new processes by force of his personality. Alignment happened because people followed him, not the process. So when Ketan replaced him, everything collapsed. Ketan did not have the same force of personality as he did. No matter how much he blamed Ketan and his team, he was the source of the problem. Now, he had to go back to focusing on operations. But this time, like Surya, he had to change himself. Coach people to do the tasks not because he told them to, but because it was work that had to be done; in other words, take ownership. He also had to work with Ketan so that Ketan could take on the huge responsibility without feeling abandoned. By this singular shift in thinking, Sandesh had created a growth opportunity for himself.

The Other reveals the power of our gaze

Rishabh is a highly revered king who is invited by Indra to Amravati to attend a dance recital. It turns out to be an outstanding performance. Rishabh is enthralled by the skill of the dancer, but suddenly, in the middle of the performance, the dancer dies. Indra uses his magic power to make the dead dancer disappear and replaces her with another. It happens so fast that no one notices except Rishabh. It makes him wonder.

Why does Indra do what he does? Where does the need to hide the truth come from? Rishabh realizes that for all his outward pomp and glory, Indra imagines himself as prey. He needs to secure himself with this magic trick. Who does Indra imagine as his predator? Rishabh realizes that in Indra's eyes he is the tiger. This takes Rishabh by surprise, as he thinks of himself as a benevolent king. Is Rishabh's imagination of himself truer than Indra's imagination of him?

Indra's image of Rishabh is born out of fear. Maybe Rishabh, without realizing it, is contributing to Indra's fear. Rishabh comes across as self-righteous and noble, with clearly a higher level of ethics and morality than Indra, and this makes Indra insecure. Rishabh sees how imagination creates the jungle even when there is none. In the mind's eye, predators appear to be seeking prey, and alphas appear to be seeking domination.

This event transforms Rishabh into a tirthankar, for he sees clearly the violence of thoughts. He decides to renounce this violence and outgrow every underlying fear. He decides to spend his time observing the realm of thoughts so that he can understand and accommodate everyone he meets rather than trying to combat them. It is important to note that the event has no impact on Indra who stays the same.

Our presence impacts those around us. We may see them in one way. They see us in another. We may think we are helping while they think we are being patronizing. In each one's brahmanda, the Brahma is always right.

Ipsita notices that the way her secretary, Siddharth, speaks to her is very different from the way he speaks to the peons in office. In front of her, Siddharth is deferential and gentle whereas with the peons he is rude and imperious. Ipsita realizes that he sees her as alpha and respects her power. But he wants to position himself as alpha in front of the peons thus establishing a pecking order in the office. Ipsita has no desire to dominate Siddharth; she wants a transparent and professional relationship. But she cannot control Siddharth's worldview. Siddharth can turn the most professional workplace into a feudal order in no time. Upon introspection, Ipsita realizes that she does enjoy his deference to a degree. And by enjoying it she is contributing to the power equation. Now she realizes how expats who praise the equality in workplaces abroad, enjoy the servility of their team when they are posted to India. Unlike Rishabh, Ipsita enjoys being feared. It makes her feel powerful.

The Other reveals our insensitivity

In the Mahabharat, news reached King Virata of Matsya that his son, Uttar, had singlehandedly defeated the Kaurav army, pushing back great warriors like Karna and Duryodhan. The city prepared to welcome the young prince—the streets were watered, the buildings decorated with flowers, lamps and fluttering flags. King Virata's heart was filled with pride. His son had done the impossible. He ordered the poets to compose songs in Uttar's honour.

"But sir," said a priest standing next to Virata, "Does it not seem odd that a slip of a boy was able to defeat such mighty warriors? Surely he had help. Maybe that of his charioteer, Brihanalla, the eunuch, who once served Arjun, the great archer." The king ignored what the priest had to say and continued praising his son. Once again the priest said, "Surely sir, you do not believe he did it all alone. He must have had the support of another, perhaps Brihanalla, the eunuch, who once served Arjun, the great archer." Again the king ignored him and continued praising his son. When the priest suggested that the prince may have been helped by the eunuch-charioteer one more time, the king reacted violently. "Shut up!" he shouted, and slapped the priest so hard that his nose started to bleed.

The priest had been speaking the truth. Uttar was indeed helped by the eunuch-charioteer, Brihanalla, who was actually Arjun in disguise. But the king was not ready to hear the truth. He wanted to enjoy the alleged success of his son but the priest, in his relentless pursuit of correctness, did not appreciate a father's desire. The priest's truth was cold and insensitive. The king wanted compassion, at the cost of the truth, for some time at least.

The priest was Yudhishtir in disguise. This event takes place in the final year of exile of the Pandavs when they have to lose their identity and live incognito. The humiliation revealed to Yudhishtir the human desire for delusions and the importance of being gentle with the harsh truth. Yudhishtir was so caught up with his honesty that he did not realize the other's inability to receive it.

The ability to communicate with a king with deference and dexterity is known in Sanskrit as sabha-chaturya, which translated literally means

'tactfulness in court'. It is a trait that ministers and courtiers had to possess if they wished to survive in court and get their jobs done. It is a trait that people who work with leaders must possess. It is a trait that even leaders need to possess if they wish to lead.

The foundation for this skill lies in the observation that people are uncomfortable with the truth, especially when it shows them in a bad light or has consequences that could affect them adversely. When confronted with it, they react negatively—with rage or denial. They may get defensive or simply reject the submission. So the work does not get done. One needs strategic communication, also known as diplomacy. One needs sabha-chaturya.

Rathodji mastered the art of sabha-chaturya long ago. He knew his boss, Mr. Khilachand, was a brilliant man with a rags-to-riches story. He also knew his boss had an ego the size of a mountain. He refused to accept or admit a mistake. In fact, if a mistake was pointed out, he would do everything in his power to justify it. Mr. Khilachand was very fond of a distant cousin of his. So when a candidate presented himself before Mr. Khilachand with a recommendation from this cousin, he was, without much consideration, appointed manager in one of the many oil depots he owned. The candidate was a good-for-nothing layabout. He did no work and impeded the smooth running of operations. But no one dared complain to Mr. Khilachand. To do so would imply that Mr. Khilachand was a fool for having appointed a candidate purely on a recommendation, without checking credentials. And Mr. Khilachand did not appreciate being taken for a fool. In a rage, just to prove he was right—and everyone else who thought he was a fool was wrong—he could simply sack the person who had complained and give the incompetent candidate he had hired a raise or promotion. It was irrational, but that's the way he was. Rathodji knew this and so when the problem was presented to him, he pondered long and hard on how to give Mr. Khilachand the message without upsetting him and making matters worse.

The Other reveals our inadequacy

As Ravan lies mortally wounded on the battlefield and the monkeys are celebrating their victory, Ram turns to his brother, Lakshman, and tells him to learn whatever he can from the rakshasa-king who is a renowned scholar. Lakshman obeys but returns soon after saying the arrogant Ravan turned his face away when asked to share his knowledge.

Ram looks at his brother and asks him, "Where did you stand while asking him for knowledge?" Lakshman replies, "Next to his head so that I could hear what he had to say clearly." Ram smiles, places his bow on the ground and walks over to where Ravan lies and, to Lakshman's astonishment, kneels at Ravan's feet.

With palms joined in extreme humility, Ram says, "Lord of Lanka, you abducted my wife, a terrible crime for which I have been forced to punish you. Now, you are no more my enemy. I bow to you and request you to share your knowledge with me."

To Lakshman's greater astonishment, Ravan opens his eyes and raises his arms to salute Ram. "If only I had more time as your teacher than as your enemy. Standing at my feet as a student, unlike your rude younger brother, you are a worthy recipient of my knowledge." Ravan then shared his vast knowledge and died.

Despite having fought against Ravan for as long as Ram did, Lakshman never saw Ravan for who he was. He did not see Ravan's desire to dominate everyone around him. He did not see what made Ravan cling to Sita even when the army of monkeys killed his brothers, his sons, his subjects, and threatened his city. Would such a man share his knowledge freely? Ram can see Ravan's need to dominate even as he is dying. That is what stops Ravan from being unconditionally generous with his knowledge. So Ram indulges the rakshasa-king, grants him the power he so desperate needs in svaha and receives Ravan's knowledge as tathastu.

Yes, in an ideal world, we should not encourage delusions. Everything should be factual. Ravan should be told that he is being mean and petty on his death bed. But this is not an ideal world and delusions enable us to cope with the harshness of reality. Fear makes us crave delusions. Delusions grant value. Without delusions there would be no want, no market for luxury goods, no need for brands, no room for advertising.

The attendant at the ticket counter was being very rude, but Manish said nothing. He kept smiling even though he wanted to shout back. He realized that the attendant had no other place to get Durga from and so was trying to be overly imperious. If he behaved deferentially, he would get his ticket changed quickly and not be subjected to a bout of unnecessary harassment. No, this was not right. He could complain to the station manager. But that would be a waste of time. He was not here to change the world. He just wanted to get his work done and move on. So he gave the attendant a good dose of Durga and got his Lakshmi in exchange. The attendant felt like Indra in Amravati: his job gave him more than his salary; it gave him the respect that he did not get at home or from his superiors.

The Other reveals our blindness

Karna's mother, Kunti, a princess, abandons him at birth. He is raised in a charioteer's family but he learns archery and becomes a warrior of great repute by his own merit. All the kings and warriors of the land taunt him about his lowly origins. But Duryodhan, the eldest Kaurav, makes him commander of his armies on the battlefield of Kurukshetra and even compels Shalya, king of Madra, to serve as charioteer. "You who have been called a charioteer's son all your life, shall ride into battle, bow in hand, with a king serving as your charioteer," says Duryodhan to Karna.

Blinded by his victimhood, overwhelmed by Kaurav generosity, Karna does not realize the folly of this decision. For Shalya is the uncle of the Pandavs, tricked by Duryodhan into serving the Kauravs. While Shalya is legally bound to serve Duryodhan, in spirit he favours his enemies. So as they ride into battle, Shalya keeps praising Arjun and demotivating Karna.

Then, when the chariot wheel gets stuck in the ground, Shalya says, "I am no charioteer. I am a king. I do not know how to pull out wheels stuck in the ground. Only charioteers like you know what to do." So Karna is forced to abandon his bow, get down from the chariot and pull the chariot wheel out. While Karna is thus unarmed and vulnerable, Krishna directs Arjun to take advantage of the situation and shoot Karna dead. As the arrow rips through his heart, Karna sees something that was always before him but he had never really seen: Krishna!

Born in a royal family, taunted for being raised by cowherds, Krishna was comfortable serving as a 'lowly' charioteer. Social status made no dent on his mental body. Karna finally realized what really matters in life is Narayan, not Narayani, what a person is, not what a person has.

Our imagination binds us and blinds us. We get trapped in brahmanda and do not see how limited our gaze us. It makes us heroic in our eyes, but villainous to others. Karna can be celebrated as a victim and a hero. Yet, Krishna has him killed. Not because he is a villain but because defeat is the final way to open his eyes and expand his gaze. This is 'uddhar', upliftment of thought.

When Mark came to India, he noticed that most of his friends had servants: someone to clean the house, a cook, a driver, and someone to even take the children to school. "This is so feudal," he commented. Sridhar did not take the remark kindly. "Why is it not feudal when you outsource work you do not want to do to India? Are we not the cleaning ladies of the developed world? Why is hiring a servant bad but encouraging the service-industry good? When I employ a servant I am creating employment in my country. But when you outsource, you are creating unemployment in yours." Mark merely chuckled at this defensive retort but wondered later if there was a measure of truth to what Sridhar had said.

Expansion

Growth happens when we make the journey from being dependent to being dependable. This happens when we focus on who we are rather than what we have: how much we can accommodate the Other, even if the Other does not accommodate us.

Growth happens when the mind expands

Humans are called manavas because they possess manas, a mind that can imagine, hence expand. A non-expanding limited mind is identified as Brahma. An infinitely expanded limitless mind is identified as the brahman. As Brahma makes the journey towards the brahman, the mind acquires four colours or varna:

- Shudra-varna: the obedient gaze of unconditional followership, like a dog who adores his master and is eager to please him, wagging his tail when acknowledged and whining when ignored. Shudra-varna is also associated with the eternally anxious deer, seeking a herd. This is tamas-guna, as it indicates the absence of thought and a preference for mimicry. It is the varna of a newborn child. Everyone is born in this varna.

- Vaishya-varna: the merchant's calculating gaze of conditional followership like an elephant that follows the oldest matriarch in the herd as she has lived through the most droughts and therefore has more knowledge of waterholes than the others. This is rajas-guna, as the merchant thinks only for himself.

- Kshatriya-varna: the warrior's dominating gaze of conditional leadership, like a lion who leads his pride so that the lionesses can hunt and bear his children. This is also rajas-guna, as the warrior thinks only for himself.

- Brahmana-varna: the sage's gaze of unconditional leadership, like a cow who provides milk, meant for her calf, generously to the cowherd. She is dependable so the cowherd can always rely on her but she is also independent so while the cowherd needs her, she does not need the cowherd. This is sattva-guna, as the sage thinks of himself as simply a part of a wider ecosystem, and encourages others to do the same.

As Bhairava, Shiva is shown giving shelter to a dog. As Pashupati, Shiva is shown comforting a doe in the palm of his hands. He is also described as wrapped in the hide of an elephant and a lion that he flayed alive. Vishnu is Gopal, associated with the cow.

A yajaman is encouraged to be like Shiva, give shelter to those who are too frightened to think for themselves. He must also be like Vishnu, encouraging those who are too frightened to think for others to expand their gaze, become more dependable. This is growth.

Every month, Wadhwa would call the heads of his various coaching classes and check how much fees had been collected. But ten years down the road, Wadhwa only checks how many of his students have passed with distinction. The old method meant that the most important department of his company was the sales department; the coaching and quality control department did not matter. With the new method, the passing of students was an indicator of how good the institute was. This demanded coaches and quality control to be very high and this made the selling of seats much easier. The shift happened because Wadhwa's gaze shifted from Narayani (share of student's wallet) to Narayan (growth of students). When students began to matter to him genuinely, he made more money than before; but it did not matter. Lakshmi for him was no longer the goal; she was but an indicator. Wadhwa thus moved from vaishya-varna towards brahmana-varna. His leadership is still conditional, but he is moving in the right direction.

Growth is about pursuing thoughts not things

In Hindu mythology, God means what we can become, that is, the acme of human potential. God is visualized either as Shiva, who can give up everything and so is the supreme hermit; and as Vishnu, who can engage with all situations in life with a gentle smile and so is the supreme householder. To be a devotee of God means to try and be like him, in other words invoke the human potential within us.

But Ravan, the rakshasa-king, devotee of Shiva, wants to possess Shiva, rather than be like Shiva. He tries carrying Mount Kailas to his island-kingdom of Lanka and gets crushed under its weight. When pulled out from underneath, he returns home shamefaced, accepting Shiva's superiority, not realizing that the hermit does not seek to be superior. Ravan may be Shiva's devotee but he does not want to see the world as Shiva does. In fact, he assumes like him Shiva also values pecking orders.

By contrast, when Sita offers Hanuman pearls, he bites the pearls to check if Ram is within them. Everyone laughs at this comment: how can Ram who sits on the throne be inside a pearl? "Just as he can be in my heart," says Hanuman, ripping open his chest, revealing Ram within. Hanuman does not care what Ram has, or can give him; he seeks to invoke Ram within him.

Hanuman seeks to realize his potential, not increase his resources. Ravan, on the other hand, does not believe there is any potential he needs to realize; he is perfect and all he needs is more resources.

Hanuman begins by serving Sugriv out of gratitude to his teacher, the sun-god, Surya, Sugriv's father. He then serves Ram without any expectation or obligation. He moves from vaishya-varna (conditional follower of Sugriv) to brahmana-varna (unconditional leader like Ram). Ravan, on the other hand, slips from being kshatriya-varna (conditional leader of Lanka) to vaishya-varna (conditional follower of Shiva).

It is important to note that Ravan is often called a brahmin, which means he belongs to brahamana-jati. He belongs to a family of priests but chooses to be a king. This does not mean he is of brahmana-varna. In the work place, we often mistake educational qualifications and institutional pedigree,

which is jati, for attitude and potential, which is varna. We may not be able to change our jati, but we can always change our varna.

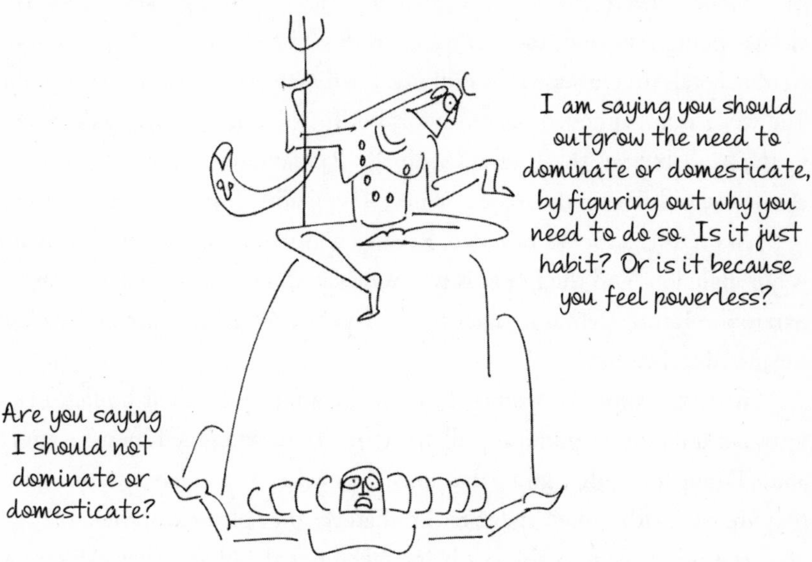

When asked why many public projects fail, this is the answer a retired civil servant gave, "If two tenders come, the officer will always pass the one at the lower cost. Why? Because then he will not be asked too many questions by his superiors. He knows that the price will be inflated midway through the project when it is impossible to change contractors. But he will keep quiet. Should he choose a better candidate, on qualitative rather than quantitative grounds, he will be pulled up by the audit committee and be forced to answer a lot of questions. So to save himself the trouble, he just accepts the lowest quote, ignoring all qualitative aspects." What the civil servant is saying is that the system encourages rajas-guna (lead or follow so long as it serves you) or tamas-guna (mindlessly follow), not sattva-guna. "Naturally, things are going awry." The servants of the system are turning into Ravans not Hanumans, because upstream and downstream, everyone is only paying attention to things not thoughts, evidence not intent, resources not gaze.

Growth is indicated when we prefer giving than taking

In the story of Krishna, there are two episodes of vastra haran, of women's clothes being removed. In one, which is described in the Bhagavat Puran, Krishna steals the clothes of the milkmaids while they are bathing in the pond. The women are annoyed but not violated. In the other, which is described in the Mahabharat, the Kauravs strip the Pandav queen, Draupadi, of her clothes, in full view of the royal assembly. Draupadi is humiliated and abused.

In the Bhagavat vastra-haran, Krishna is violating the law but the intent is not malicious and the mood is full of mischief. In the Mahabharat vastra-haran, the Kauravs are not violating the law but the intent is malicious and the mood full of rage.

Krishna wants the women to know he appreciates their bodies, in its most natural state, wrinkles and all, without adornment. The Kauravs want to abuse Draupadi while arguing that since she has been gambled away as a slave, they are well within their rights to do whatever they please with her.

In both cases something is being taken but the bhaav is very different. Krishna takes to enable the Other to outgrow the fear that causes embarrassment. The Kauravs take to instil and amplify fear. Krishna seeks to generate trust. The Kauravs seek to establish authority. Krishna grants Saraswati while the Kauravs take Durga.

The yajaman who takes with the desire to dominate and domesticate is not on the path to becoming Vishnu. He will only create rana-bhoomi, not ranga-bhoomi, as he does not include the devata in his world. He wants to control the world of the devata rather than understand it.

Duryodhan dominates Draupadi because he feels she has hurt him. He wants to punish her. In his eyes, he is meting out justice. But he is capable of outgrowing his anger towards her by understanding her reasons for hurting him. The reason is invariably rooted in fear; when this is understood every villain, evokes karuna, compassion.

The idea of karuna is an essential thought in Buddhism. When we realize that people do what we consider villainous deeds out of fear, we do not condemn them, or patronize them, but find out in our heart what it is about us

that makes them fear us too. Only when we recognize that perhaps we are the cruel parent, or we are perceived as the cruel parent, will we empathize with the Other. The story of Buddha's life is filled with instances where he meets angry beings: from a mad elephant to a murderous serial killer, Angulimala. They calm down before the Buddha because he 'sees' them and understands where they are coming from. They are not condemned for their behaviour; that their belief springs from fear is understood.

Karuna demands the expanding of the mind. This is visualized as the lotus. Hence Buddha is often shown holding a lotus, a gesture known as Padmapani, he who held the lotus. Sometimes the goddess Tara, embodiment of pragna, or wisdom, holds the lotus.

> In every conversation, Sunil wants to dominate. He wants to come across as the alpha. He must know more than the Other. He must know things before the Other. He is constantly seeking Durga every time he dismisses those before him. The day he starts to listen, allows people to express themselves, appreciates their point of view, feels comfortable giving rather than receiving Durga, he will have grown. He will be more Vishnu, fountainhead of security, and more people will be attracted to him.

Growth happens when more people can depend on us

In the Ramayan, Lakshman is the obedient and loyal younger brother of Ram, following him wherever he goes, doing whatever he is told to do. One day, Ram tells Lakshman, "I want solitude so I am shutting the door of my chambers. Do not let anyone in. Kill anyone who tries to open it." Lakshman swears to do so.

No sooner is the door shut than Rishi Durvasa, renowned for his temper, demands a meeting with Ram. Lakshman tries to explain the situation. "I don't care," says an impatient and enraged Durvasa, "If I don't see the king of Ayodhya this very minute I shall curse his kingdom with drought and misfortune." At that moment Lakshmana wonders what matters more: his promise to his brother, or the safety of Ayodhya? What decision must he take? Must he be karya-karta or yajaman?

Lakshman concludes that Ayodhya is more important and so opens the door to announce Durvasa. But when he turns around there is no sign of Durvasa. And Ram says, "I am glad you finally disobeyed me and decided Ayodhya matters more than Ram."

The tryst with Durvasa makes Lakshman ask the fundamental question, "For whom are you doing what you are doing?" Lakshman realizes in his yagna, all his life, Ram was the only devata. But with this decision, he has made all of Ayodhya his devata. His gaze has expanded. Until then only Ram could depend on him. Now all of Ayodhya can depend on him.

Lakshman realizes that obedience is neither good nor bad. What matters is the reason behind the obedience, the belief behind behaviour. Is it rooted in fear or is it rooted in wisdom? Does he obey to ensure self-preservation, self-propagation and self-actualization or because he cares for the Other? A yagna is truly successful when the svaha helps both devata and the yajaman outgrow dependence.

When Shailesh moves, he takes his team with him. So everyone knows when Shailesh resigns from a company, six more people will go. Shailesh thinks of this as his great strength. He has a power team that can change the fortunes of a company. He does not realize this is also his weakness. He does not see new talent and new capabilities and capacities. His team is his comfort zone and he is assuming they will be strong and smart enough for any situation. Will they be as successful in a new situation, in a new market, when economic realities change, when resources are scarce, when clients demand different things? Shailesh will grow only when he is able to expand his team, include new people, allow people to move out, work on their own. He is growing too dependent on his team and they are too dependent on him. It is time for him to become more independent, to become dependable to others.

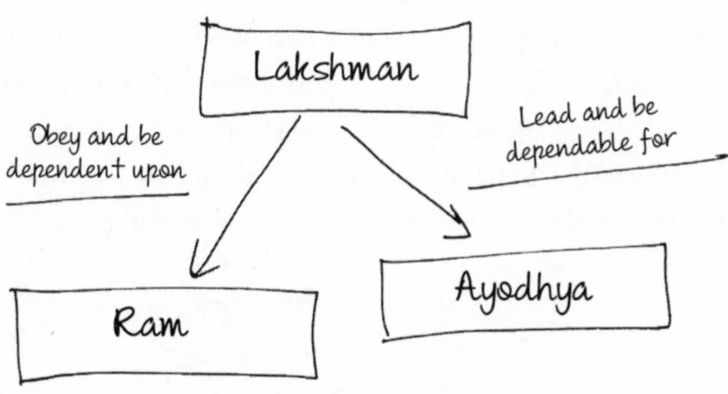

Growth happens when even the insignificant become significant

For eighteen days, the Kauravs and the Pandavs fight on the plains of Kurukshetra. Hundreds of soldiers are killed on either side. In the middle of the war, Krishna tells Arjun, "We have to stop. The horses are tired. They need to rest and be refreshed. Shoot your arrow into the ground and bring out some water so that I can bathe and water the horses. Keep the enemy at bay with a volley of arrows while I do so." Arjun does as instructed. Refreshed, the horses pull the chariot with renewed vigour.

The horses pulling Arjun's chariot did not ask to be refreshed. Krishna sensed their exhaustion and made resources available so that they could be comforted. Often, we forget the 'horses' that help us navigate through our daily lives. Horses are a crude metaphor for those who make our lives comfortable but who do not have much of a voice when it comes to their own comfort. In every office, especially in India, there are a host of people who keep the office running—the office boy, canteen boy, security guard, drivers, peons, and so on. This is the silent support staff. They take care of the 'little things' that enable us to achieve the 'big things'. A simple study of how organizations treat this silent support staff is an indicator of leadership empathy.

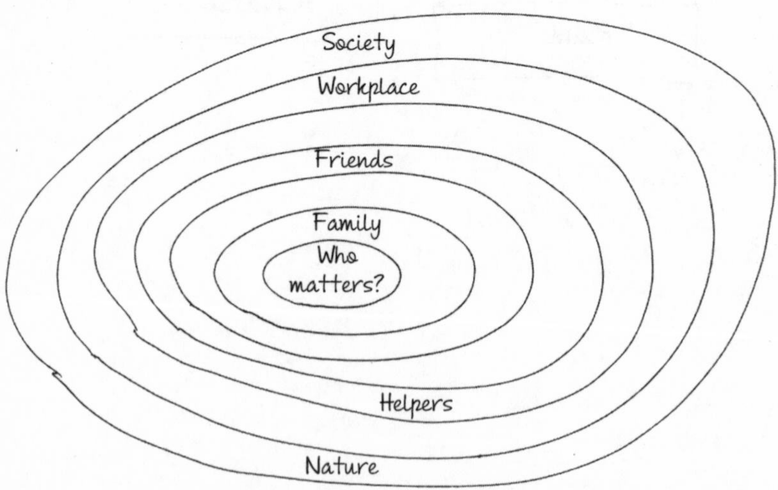

Randhir drives his boss to work every day negotiating heavy highway traffic for over two hours to and fro. His boss, Mr. Chaudhary, is a partner in a large consulting firm that is responsible for over fifty high net-worth clients. This means a lot of travel both in the city and outside, which means many trips to the airport early in the morning and late at night. This also means travelling from meetings from one end of the city to another and short trips to satellite cities. Randhir is frustrated. His boss does not know that he lives in a shantytown an hour away from Mr. Chaudhary's swanky apartment block. To travel to his place of work, he needs to take a bus or an auto. These are not easily available early in the morning or late at night. His travel allowance is insufficient to take care of this. When he raised this issue with Mr. Chaudhary, he was told, "This is what the company policy says you should be paid." Randhir does not understand policy. He serves Mr. Chaudhary, not the company. But Mr. Chaudhary does not see it that way. And then there are Sundays when Mr. Chaudhary visits his farmhouse with his wife and children. No holidays for Randhir. "His family is in the village so why does he need a holiday?" Often there is no parking space at places where Mr. Chaudhary has meetings. At times, there are parking spaces but no amenities for drivers—no place to rest and no bathrooms. "You cannot eat in the car; I do not like the smell," says Mr. Chaudhary, who also disables the music system when he leaves the car "so that he does not waste the battery." And when Mr. Chaudhary got a huge 40 per cent bonus over and above his two crore rupee CTC, he very generously gave Randhir a 500 rupee hike. "I am being fair. That's more than the drivers of others got. I don't want to disrupt the driver market."

Growth happens when we include those whom we once excluded

In the Mahabharat, during the game of dice, Yudhishtir gambles away his kingdom and then starts wagering his brothers. He begins with the twins, Nakul and Sahadev, and then gambles away Bhim and Arjun, then himself and finally, their common wife, Draupadi.

Later, during his forest exile, his brothers drink water from a forbidden pond and all die. The guardian of the pond, a stork, offers to resurrect to life one of the four brothers. Yudhishtir asks for Nakul to be resurrected. "Why not mighty Bhim or the archer Arjun?" asks the stork. To this Yudhishtir replies, "Because Nakul is the son of Madri, my father's second wife. If I, son of Kunti, first wife of my father, Pandu, am alive, surely a son of Madri needs to survive too. When Madri died, Kunti promised to take care of her children. I have to uphold my mother's promise."

Thus, we see a transformation in Yudhishtir. The stepbrother who is the first to be gambled away is also the first to be resurrected. He, who was excluded before, and hence dispensable, has been included. The king who sacrificed the least fit person now helps the most helpless. Yudhishtir's gaze has thus expanded from taking care of himself to taking care of others. His mind has expanded and he has risen in varna. He has become more dependable. He has grown.

At a party, Karan met Mansoor, who had unceremoniously fired him years ago. He found himself caught up in a dilemma. Should he speak to Mansoor, relive those ugly memories? Should he discreetly avoid eye-contact? Suddenly, Mansoor waved to him with a smile and asked him to join the group he was with. "This is Karan," he said, "We worked together a long time ago." He did not mentioning the firing or the unpleasantness of the past. He had moved on in his mind, and made no attempt to justify his action or apologize. Karan, who was once excluded, suddenly felt included. It felt good.

Growth happens when we stop seeing people as villains

In the final chapter of the Mahabharat, Yudhishtir renounces his kingdom and passes on his crown to his grandson Parikshit and sets out for the forest. His wife and brothers follow him. As they are climbing the mountains, they start falling into the deep ravine below, one by one. Yudhishtir does not turn around to help them, "Because," he says, "I have renounced everything."

When he is alone, with no one but a dog for company, Indra opens the gates of Amravati and lets him in. "Dogs are inauspicious," says Indra, "This dog cannot come in." Yudhishtir refuses to enter Amravati without the dog because the dog has been his one true companion. Indra relents.

Inside Amravati, Yudhishtir finds the Kauravs enjoying the joys of paradise. "How can that be?" asks Yudhishtir angrily, "If these warmongering villains can be allowed here, surely my brothers should be allowed here too. Where are they?"

At this point Indra says, "You demand that your unconditional follower enter paradise with you, but you are unwilling to share paradise unconditionally with those who have already been punished for their crimes. When will you forgive them, Yudhishtir? How long will you hold on to your anger? Can Swarga be yours unless you lead unconditionally?"

Inclusion means not just allowing those who follow you into paradise, but also making room for those who reject and oppose you. This is brahmana-varna.

> Vimla is happy with herself. There was a time she would find disorganized people very irritating. She would try to correct them. And punish them if they resisted. Over the years, as she rose to head the audit department, she realized that different people function differently. That it was perfectly fine to not be as organized as she herself was, or be differently organized. She no longer mocks those who are different. She includes them. She has grown.

Growth happens when we seek to uplift the Other

The word dharma has often been translated as ethics, morality, righteousness and goodness. These English words are rooted in the notion of objectivity. But dharma is not an objective concept. It is a subjective concept based on gaze.

Depending on our varna, we will see dharma differently. For the shudra, it is doing what the master tells him to do. For the vaishya, it is doing what he feels is right. For the kshatriya, it is doing what he feels is right for all. For the brahman, it is realizing that everyone is right in his own way, but every one can be more right, by expanding his gaze. As our gaze expands, our varna changes and so does dharma.

Dharma is about realizing our potential. While all other creatures grow at the cost of others (plants feed on minerals, animals feed on plants and other animals), humans can grow by helping others grow. This is not sacrifice. This is not selflessness. This is making the yajaman's growth an outcome of the devata's growth. This is best demonstrated in the ritual that takes place during Nanda Utsav.

Every year, during the festival of Nanda Utsav, pots of butter are hung from great heights and human pyramids are formed to climb to the pot, commemorating how Krishna would steal butter from the milkmaids of Gokul and Vrindavan that was kept out of his reach when he was a child. In this exercise, the most crucial stage is the one in which people in the lowermost tier, who sit while the pyramid is being set up, have to stand up. Only when they stand, balancing the entire pyramid on their shoulders does Krishna get the butter. In their growth lies Krishna's success.

True expansion happens when I grow because you grow. When only I grow, it is selfish. When only you grow, it is selfless. Only plants and animals are allowed to be selfish, as they do not have the capacity to imagine, hence empathize. Only minerals and inanimate objects can be truly selfless.

In sanatan, only the digambar shramana, or the naked, wise sage can be truly selfless. Only he has no fear and can walk around without food, shelter or clothing, comfortable as he is. That is why monks were associated with forests, not social organizations, never allowed to stay or settle in a single place. Around Shiva, there are only snow-capped mountains where no life can thrive. It is good for the individual but not for those who are dependent on him.

For society, we need neither selfishness nor selflessness. We need a connection with the ecosystem. We need a method of mutual exchange and growth, one that includes more and more people. This is uddhar, the uplift

of thought, which leads to an uplift in action, and intellectual and emotional growth, eventually leading to economic and political growth. The point is to invest in other people's growth such that the return is our growth. This is the path of Vishnu, the path of Shankar, the path of the Bodhisattva.

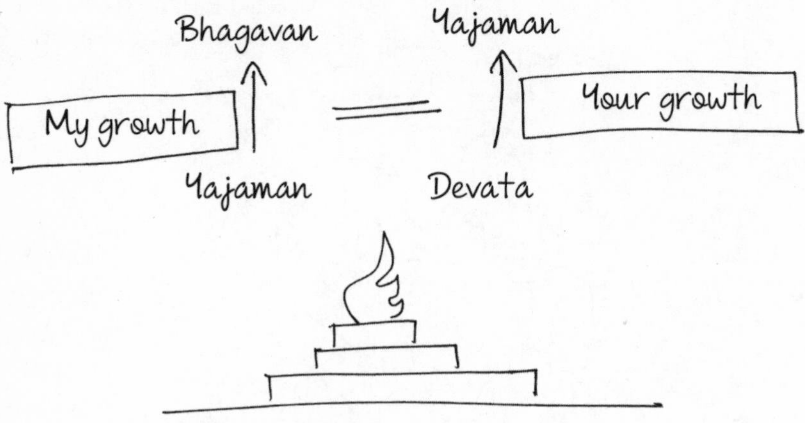

When Vikram took over as the CEO, he called the head of his human resource department and said he wanted to redesign job descriptions. He wanted financial goals to be the primary objective of executives. He wanted customer satisfaction and employee engagement to be the primary objective of junior managers. He wanted talent management to be the primary objective of senior managers. "As you climb the ladder, you cannot be paying attention to the same thing the same way," states Vikram.

Inclusion

It is easier to teach than to learn. It is easier to instruct than to let people be. It is easier to focus on things than thoughts. It is easier to expand our mind than get others to expand their mind. Wisdom is having the faith and patience to create an ecosystem where the mind-lotus can bloom at its own pace, on its own terms.

More yajamans are needed as an organization grows

At first, the yagna is small and simple. As the yagna progresses into a sattra and more fires are lit, specializations arise. Those who chant hymns and make offerings sit close to the fire. Those who protect the enclosure stand a little beyond. Those who get the firewood, mould the bricks, bake the pots, weave the cloth, tend to the cows and grow the crops, visit the enclosure only occasionally. Those who clean the enclosure are never seen as they emerge only when everyone has left.

Over time, those closest to the fire get the most attention and receive the most value while those who are further away and rarely seen, get the least attention and least value. This is because, often, though the yagna grows in size, the yajaman's gaze does not. This gives rise to the caste system where people are classified for the value placed on their measurable contribution (jati). Sanskriti becomes no different from prakriti where the dictum of survival of the fittest applies—the powerful thrive on resources and the less valued perish.

But humans are not animals. When Brahma at the top behaves like Gandhari, those at the bottom transform into Duryodhan, or even Ravan; at first subversive, but eventually defiant. When those at the top of the pyramid behave like devas and yakshas, those at the bottom will turn into asuras and rakshasas. Conflict rages. The sea rises. Pralay is imminent. All because Brahma was being stubborn and refused to see.

That is why in India the divine gaze is scattered and distributed through a variety of deities: gods who look after individuals (ishta-devata); gods who look after the household (griha-devata); gods who look after the village (grama-devata); gods who look after the city (nagar-devata); gods who look after the forest (vana-devata); and gods who look after communities (kula-devata).

These are not diminutive replicas of the distant bhagavan. Rather, each of these deities has an individual personality, a local flavour. The deities help in expanding and extending the gaze of the common bhagavan. Despite different roles, responsibilities and contributions, none of them feels inferior or superior; everyone feels revered.

Similarly, to create an organization where everyone feels they matter, it is important to extend the central gaze to the periphery, much like the hub-and-spoke model of supply chains which decentralized decision making so that every local market got attention from a local office, and did not rely on the gaze of the central office. However, this can only work when the head of the local office is as much of a deity in his or her own right and not subordinate to the deity in the central office.

Every deity takes ownership and acts locally keeping in mind global needs, sensitive to the internal organizational ecosystem as well as external market conditions. It is the yajaman's responsibility to create more Vishnus who know how to descend (avatarana) and to uplift (uddhar) those around them. Otherwise he will end up creating frightened sons of Brahma who think only of themselves and forget that a yagna is an exchange.

When he had only one office and thirty people serving clients, Sandeep could make everyone in his team feel included. Now that he's been promoted, he is a distant god; no one connects with him. They rarely see him except at the annual town-hall meetings where he speaks, but never listens. Sandeep's managers feel they are merely his handmaidens and his messengers, with no power or say in local matters. Naturally, the energy that once buzzed around Sandeep is restricted to the corporate office. In zonal, regional and local offices, there is just process, tasks and targets, very little proactivity or enthusiasm.

The yajaman has to turn devatas into yajamans

The sage Agastya performed tapasya and wanted to have nothing to do with society. But he was tormented all night by dreams of his ancestors who begged him to father a child. "Just as we gave you life, you have to give someone else life." This is Pitr-rin, one's debt to one's ancestors: one is not allowed to die unless one leaves behind a life on earth.

Thus every yajaman is obliged to create another yajaman to replace him. This makes talent creation an obligation. Talent management is not merely the passing on of knowledge and skills; it is the expanding of the gaze of the next generation of managers. It is the responsibility of those upstream to help those downstream see the world as they do.

A new manager can be equated to the many images of gods and goddesses sold in the market; they are not worshipped until the ritual of prana-prathistha or the giving of life. This involves chakshu-daan, the granting of eyes, whereby the image becomes sentient and sensitive to the human condition, hence a deity. The yajaman thus gives eyes to the devata, helps the Other see what he can see. This is the essence of talent management.

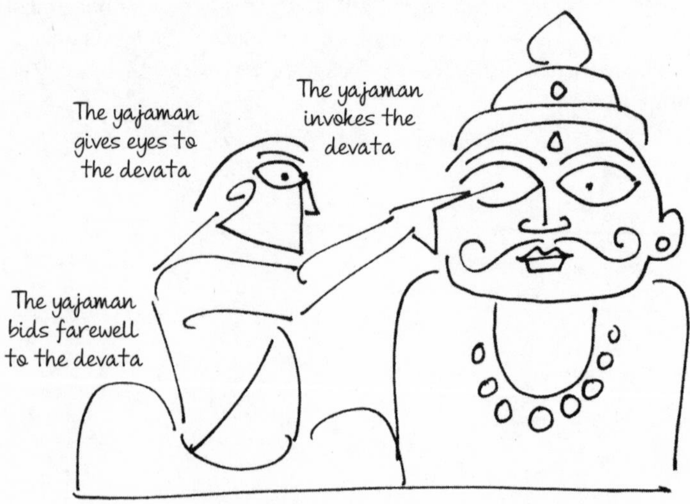

A yajaman can be self-created, self-motivated, swayambhu. Or he may be created by another yajaman. Daksha sees talent development as an obligation and converts it into a process, a series of ritual steps. Indra sees talent management as a burden; he is even threatened by the talent. Vishnu sees talent management as an opportunity to help himself: for by helping someone else grow, we grow ourselves. By making another person dependable, the yajaman liberates himself from current responsibilities so that he can take on new responsibilities.

Raghu is a consultant in a large auditing firm. He has been made a manager with client-facing responsibilities. And he has been asked to attend a training programme designed to equip him to face the challenges of his new role. Raghu has been an executive for seven years; he does what he is told to do. Now they are instructing him to take initiative and ownership. Nice words, but how? And why? There is no discussion on that. At the end of the training programme he has been taught many skills on how to engage with clients, but there has been no change of gaze. He feels the only difference between his previous role and the current one is scale: now he has to do more of the same work for more clients through more people. He certainly does not see the world as the founding partner of the firm did. And he probably never will.

Creating talent enables us to grow

Vedic scriptures divide life into four phases: in the first phase we are students (brahmachari); in the second, we are householders (grihasthi); in the third, we retire (vanaprasthi); in the fourth, we renounce the world and retreat to the forest (sanyasi). The person who retires educates the student before he is allowed to renounce the world for the householder is too busy earning a livelihood for his family. Thus, while grihasthi is focused on wealth generation, the vanaprasthi and the brahmachari are involved in knowledge transmission.

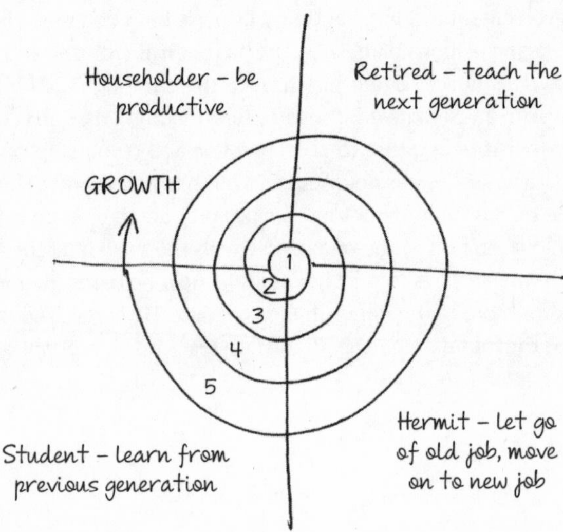

Our time in a particular job, or in a role, can be seen as a lifetime. We are born when we get a job and we die when we leave that job. In every job, there is a learning phase and a productive phase, and eventually a time to move on. In between there is boredom and frustration. The monotony of the job gets to us. The executive wants to be manager and the manager wants to be director.

This is when it is time to retire. We seek new opportunities, different opportunities or greater responsibilities, either in the same organization or another. We seek the death of our current job and rebirth in another. In other words, we seek growth.

But to grow into the next job, we have to create talent from someone downstream who will replace us and make ourselves available to someone upstream, who by helping us grow enables us to move on to the next phase of the career.

When Akhilesh became the head of a cooperative bank, he made it a rule that no one would get promoted until they spent a year as trainers developing future talent. His reason for this is two-fold: to ensure new talent is developed and to ensure the experienced executive's practical knowledge is updated with the latest academic theories. His training department exists primarily for administrative and supportive roles with the course content and direction being determined by those who are market-facing. Initially, people resisted the change because in their view a posting in training was akin to being sidelined. Now they see it as a route to higher and more powerful responsibilities. By being vanaprasthis to the next generation, they free themselves from being brahmacharis to the previous generation. By helping those downstream grow they grow in the upstream direction. Akhilesh's plan has been so successful that other banks are asking him to help them set up a similar system. It is not about creating a system: it is about giving attention to what matters.

We seek to inherit things, not thoughts

At the end of the war at Kurukshetra, as the victorious Pandavs are about to assume control of Hastinapur after vanquishing the Kauravs, Krishna advises them to talk to Bhisma, their grand uncle, who lies mortally wounded on the battlefield. As the result of a blessing, death will elude him for some time. "Make him talk until his last breath. Ask him questions. He has a lot to tell and you have a lot to learn," says Krishna.

Sure enough, when prompted, the dying Bhisma spends hours discussing various topics: history, geography, politics, economics, management, war, ethics, morality, sex, astronomy, metaphysics and philosophy. Bhisma's discourse is captured in the Shanti Parva (discussions of peace) and Anushasan Parva (discussions on discipline) that make up a quarter of the Mahabharat. After listening to their grandsire, the Pandavs have a better understanding of the world, and this makes them better kings.

The Pandavs need Krishna's prompting to seek knowledge from Bhisma. They do not need this prompting to sit on the throne or wear the crown. Like plants and animals, we are naturally drawn to Lakshmi and not Saraswati. We have not yet got used to what it means to be human. Tapping our human potential is not our top priority. We are convinced we have already realized it. Hence the focus on growing what we have rather than who we are.

Gyansingh watches in dismay as his children fight over the property and business. For years, he insisted they work with him. He wanted them to learn the tricks of the business, but they sat with him only out of a sense of duty. He sensed they did not think they had much to learn. They had their degrees from great colleges and so assumed they knew everything. All they wanted from Gyansingh was power and control. They see him as the source of Lakshmi and Durga not Saraswati.

Being a yajaman is about gaze, not skills

When Vishnu descends as Parashuram, he has three students: Bhisma, Drona and Karna. When he descends as Krishna, he gets all three killed on the battlefield of Kurukshetra, for they had failed him as students.

All three learnt the art of warfare from Parashuram and became great warriors. The purpose of all Vishnu's avatars is to establish dharma. Dharma is not about skill; it is about gaze. None of these students expanded their gaze; their gaze was focused on their own desires and anxieties and fears and hence they ended up leading the Kaurav army, much to Vishnu's dismay.

Every Brahma focuses on understanding prakriti so that he can control the outer world. Few focus on understanding purush so that they can develop their inner world. Sharda does not matter as much as Vidyalakshmi.

Since every Brahma is convinced that his gaze is perfect, he focuses on domesticating the world around him with rules. But for humans, dharma is about expanding the gaze. When the gaze expands the futility of trying to dominate those around us or domesticating them with rules is revealed.

Parmesh, the head of the training department in a public sector company, has come to the conclusion that most people see promotions as a chance to wield authority and dominate those around them. They see being bossy as a perk. They do not see promotions as enabling them to see the organization, the market and themselves differently. This belief stops them from acquiring new knowledge and skills, or paying attention to the gaze of seniors. They see training simply as a way by which the organization domesticates talent. That is why, while they court promotions, they resist coming to training programmes; they already know what they need to know. What they do not know they expect their juniors to know.

Questions teach us, not answers

Students can be classified as the five Pandavs: Yudhishtir, Bhim, Arjun, Nakul and Sahadev.

- Yudhishtir, as king, expects others to know the answers.
- Bhim, a man of strength, prefers to do rather than think.
- Arjun, as an archer, sees questions as arrows shot at him and deflects them by asking counter questions. He is not interested in the answer.
- Nakul, the handsome one, is not capable of thought.
- Sahadev is the wise one who never speaks but is constantly thinking and analyzing. When asked a question, he is provoked into thought and comes up with an intelligent answer. If not asked a question, he stays silent.

A teacher who wants to invoke Narayan in his students follows the Sahadev-method of teaching: he asks questions and does not give answers. The teacher is not obliged to know the answer. The questions are meant to provoke thought, create emotional turmoil and inspire the student to find the answer. For the answers benefit the student, no one else. If the student refuses to find the answer, it is his loss, not the teacher's.

In the *Kathasaritsagar*, Vetal makes Vikramaditya wiser by asking him questions. The crematorium where the Vetal lives is the training room, where the past is processed for wisdom that can be applied in the future. Vikramaditya has to come to the Vetal if he wishes to serve his kingdom better. He has to come and then return. If Vikramaditya chose not to go to the crematorium or answer any question, it would be his loss not the Vetal's who is already dead. The Vetal must never go to Vikramaditya's kingdom, for he will end up haunting the land of the living.

When Lydia was appointed the head of the learning and development wing, she laid down some ground rules. Trainers were told not to herd participants into training rooms: they were free to come and go as they pleased. Learning was their responsibility, not the trainers'. They were not children who had to be disciplined. There was very little instruction on the part of the trainers; there were only questions asked and participants were encouraged to answer and analyse the reasons for the answers. Case studies were prepared using the knowledge of the organization itself. Sales, marketing, production, logistics and accounts officers were video-filmed and asked to present the common problems they faced and issues they expected to resolve so that everyone could share their thoughts on these. The focus was on practical work rather than theory, active answering rather than passive listening. Lydia put up a notice at the entrance stating, "Unless you speak we are not sure if you have learned anything."

We resist advice and instructions

While King Virata of Matsya was away chasing the king of Trigarta, who had stolen his cows, the Kaurav army took advantage of his absence and attacked the city. There was no one around to defend the city except the women and children. Everyone was frightened. "Do not worry, I will protect you," said the confident young prince, Uttar.

A eunuch called Brihanalla who taught dancing to the princess warned the prince that the Kauravs were a mighty force not to be taken lightly and that no single warrior could defeat them, except maybe Arjun. Uttar did not take too kindly to this comment. He admonished Brihanalla. "Know your place in the palace," he roared. Brihanalla apologized immediately. Unfortunately for the prince, there were no charioteers left in the city. "What do I do now? How can I ride into battle without a charioteer?" he whined. Brihanalla offered him his services, claiming to have some experience in charioteering. Though not happy to have a eunuch as his charioteer, the pompous prince, armed with a bow, rode out with Brihanalla to face the Kauravs in battle, cheered on by the palace women. When Uttar entered the battlefield and saw the enemy before him, he trembled in fear. Before him were great warriors, archers and swordsmen on horses, elephants and chariots. In a panic, Uttar jumped off the chariot and began running back towards the city. The Kauravs roared with laughter, further humiliating the embarrassed prince.

The eunuch-charioteer then turned the chariot around, chased the prince, caught up with him and drove him out of the battlefield into a nearby forest where she revealed that she was no eunuch but Arjun, the great archer, in disguise. "I will not tell your father about your cowardice but you must promise not tell anyone who I really am," said Brihanalla. An awestruck Uttar agreed.

And so, Brihanalla pushed back the enemy and Uttar returned to a hero's welcome. But the prince was not carried away by the praise; he knew the truth about himself. He was grateful to Arjun for revealing to him the truth about his martial abilities, without taking away his dignity.

This story from the Virata Parva of the Mahabharat provides an

important lesson in mentoring. Arjun is Uttar's mentor. Uttar imagines his capability and is ignorant about the true identity of his eunuch-charioteer until he is faced with a crisis. Arjun is mature enough not to humiliate the young, inexperienced prince, focusing instead on his growth. Students do not like being told what they can and cannot do. They need to discover it for themselves. Crisis usually helps.

When Dilip came back from business school with a business idea, his uncle Naresh agreed to fund him. "But it will not work," shouted Dilip's father, Mahesh. "I know," said Naresh, "He is young and wilful and will not listen to us. He has to figure it out himself. Besides we could be wrong. If he succeeds with the money I give him we all will benefit. If he loses, he will come back a seasoned, battle-scarred businessman."

Discourses never transform us

Just before the battle of Kurukshetra is about to begin, Arjun loses his nerve. He suddenly realizes the enormity of the situation before him. He is about to kill his kith and kin for a piece of property. He is consumed by guilt and shame. He throws his bow down and refuses to fight. This is when Krishna reveals to him the secret of life in a song thereafter known as the Bhagavad Gita. Enlightened by the wisdom, Arjun picks up his bow and prepares to fight. Or so we are told.

During the course of the war, Arjun loses his nerve time and time again. Krishna has to goad him on to kill Bhisma, the first commander of the Kaurav army. He is then reluctant to kill his teacher, Drona. He is shattered when his son Abhimanyu is killed. He finds it hard to kill the unarmed Karna even when Krishna advises him to. He is hardly the wise warrior, displaying equanimity in the middle of crisis.

We would like to believe that a training programme will transform people forever but it does not. An agreement with a professor does not mean one has understood the subject. What the professor says is smriti—the outer voice that can be spoken, but is not necessarily heard. What is ultimately heard is shruti—our inner voice, which is heard but can never be spoken.

> Haider has attended many leadership-training workshops. At the end of each workshop he feels charged and motivated. When it comes to actually leading people though he fails miserably. No one listens to him. Then one day, he asks himself, "Why should people follow me? What am I offering that makes me attractive?" As he ponders over the question, his understanding of himself and those around him improves. He is more interested in playing boss he realizes and not really in taking people along with him. Moreover, he is only interested in his goals with no interest in the goals of others. This stems from his fear of being ignored. The more he introspects, the more the frameworks he's learned in the classroom start making sense. The smriti becomes shruti. And the penny drops.

Emotional turbulence increases the probability of internalization of wisdom. But only the probability. There is no guarantee.

Crisis increases the chances of learning

As Ram, Vishnu is king in the Ramayan, but as Krishna, he is kingmaker in the Mahabharat. With Krishna's help the Pandavs built the city of Indraprastha. But as soon as he is gone, the Pandavs gamble this kingdom away. Thus, they learn that having a kingdom does not necessarily make one a king. A yajaman is determined not by what he has or what he does, but by who he is.

The vana-vaas or forest exile that strips the Pandavs of all their status, wealth and power is a time for learning. They realize that in the forest they are neither kings nor princes, just predator or prey. Emotional turmoil makes them more receptive to new ideas. Arjun is defeated in a duel by a kirata or tribal (Shiva in disguise) and learns that skill has nothing to do with social status. Bhim is unable to lift the tail of an old monkey (Hanuman in disguise) and learns to never underestimate those you encounter. A stork (Yama in disguise) asks questions and Yudhishtir answers them; the answers are subjective not objective, but they are his answers and Yudhishtir stands by them, thus learning that in order to be a decisive leader he must take decisions and not be paralyzed by doubt.

In their final year of exile, the Pandavs, former kings, live in another king's palace disguised as servants. This is not humiliation but rather darshan: they are seeing how the world looks from the bottom of the pyramid.

At the end of the exile, Krishna goes to the Kauravs to negotiate peace. The point is not to punish the villain but to invoke the Narayan in him so that he realizes the value of coexistence and generosity. Unfortunately, Duryodhan refuses to part with even a 'needlepoint of land'. This territorial behaviour makes Duryodhan an animal, a pack leader not a yajaman. Since he behaves like a beast he needs to be killed by any means. Krishna declares war.

The final lesson is imparted during the war itself. What is the goal of the war: to win back the kingdom or to expand the gaze? The war, like any other, has terrible consequences that the Pandavs have to face. They have to kill their elder (Bhisma), teacher (Drona), brother (Karna) and suffer the death of their own children. They learn the cost of being territorial.

In the forest, the varna of the Pandavs changes. They are no longer

conditional leaders. They become unconditional leaders who conduct the yagna not to dominate or domesticate the devatas for their own benefit, but to uplift them for everyone's benefit. In the war, this growth in varna is severely tested.

During interviews, Arvind only asks candidates to talk about their failures. He wants to see how they reacted in adverse situations. Did they bemoan the loss of Lakshmi and Durga, or did they gain Saraswati to enable future success? As far as Arvind is concerned, the tathastu of Saraswati is most available during vana-vaas when we feel we have failed in the system and find ourselves out in the wilderness with no direction or purpose.

Power play underlies the process of teaching

When Vishnu approaches Bali as the child Vaman and asks for three paces of land, it is in the third step that he turns into a giant. With the first two paces he covers all that Bali possessed. "Now where do I place my foot to claim my third pace?" he asks. Bali bows and offers his head. Vishnu shoves him to Patala, the nether regions where asuras belong.

Why does Vaman turn from dwarf into giant? Is it to dominate Bali and show him who the alpha is? Is it to domesticate Bali and compel him to respect cosmic rules? Or is it to make Bali open his eyes: make him realize that the answer to life's problem is not in Narayani (the availability of resources), symbolized by the gift of three paces of land but in Narayan (the human potential), symbolized by the dwarf's ability to become a giant?

The answer rests with Bali: how does he receive Vaman's action, Vaman's intention notwithstanding. Bali's bowing could be indicative of his surrender to Vishnu, his submission to the rules, or a genuine expression of gratitude following the expansion of his mind. Only he knows.

> Sandeep was a successful businessman who insisted that his son Vikas use public transport till he finished college. He wanted his son to learn the realities of life, learn that wealth and power are privileges and not entitlements. Unfortunately, Vikas does not see things that way. His friends would tease him every time they saw him at the bus stop; their parents had provided them with drivers and cars. Vikas felt his father was old fashioned and stingy. Sandeep never understood why there was so much a distance in his relationship with Vikas.

Supply will always be less than demand.
I thought charity would solve all problems, not create dependence.
Rather than have people rely on you for things why don't you make them self-reliant?
I submit to your greatness.
Don't submit, just open your mind.

To teach, we have to learn to let go

While searching for Sita's whereabouts Hanuman sets aflame the city of Lanka of his own volition. This displeases Ram as he had no desire to hurt the residents of Lanka for the crime of their king. Not wanting to displease Ram ever again, Hanuman swore never to take any decision without consulting Ram.

This absolute obedience became so intense that it alarmed Jambuvan, the wise bear, who also served in the army of animals raised by Ram to defeat Ravan and liberate Sita. When Hanuman was being given instructions on how to find the Sanjivani herb that could save Laxman from certain death after being injured in battle, Jambuvan told Ram, "Make sure to tell him clearly that he has to come back with the herb after he's found it. Otherwise, he will find the herb and simply wait by the mountain in complete compliance." This was not good, Ram realized. The situation had to be rectified.

As is related in the Adbhut Ramayan, during the course of the war, Ravan's cousin Mahiravan, a sorcerer, managed to abduct both Ram and Laxman and took them to Patala. Only Hanuman had the intellectual and physical prowess to rescue them. He had to rely on his own wits, as there was no Ram around to instruct him. He was on his own. Jambuvan realized this situation was of Ram's own making. Hanuman was being forced to rise to the challenge.

At one point during the rescue mission, Hanuman had to simultaneously blow out five lamps located in five corners of Patala. He solved this problem by sprouting four extra heads: that of a boar, an eagle, a lion and a horse. With these five heads he could blow out the five lamps easily. Eventually, Hanuman succeeded in rescuing Ram. He had been transformed from an obedient servant to an astute, independent decision-maker. He had been transformed from being a Ram-bhakt to Mahavir, from god to God, worthy of veneration in his own right. Ram had thus created a leader.

A time comes in every leader's life when he has to create leaders around him. This involves making one's team members competent enough to take independent decisions. This is not easy, as every decision has consequences,

not all of which are acceptable to a leader. It demands tremendous restraint and maturity on a leader's part to not intervene and change the decision taken by a junior.

Hanuman's decision to burn Lanka displeased Ram. And so after that, Hanuman stopped taking decisions. To rectify the damage done, Ram had to remove himself from the scene so that Hanuman could rediscover his decision-making abilities. A leader need not agree with a junior's decision. They are two different people and so may not see the same situation in the same way. But to imagine that a subordinate will think just like them, is many a leader's folly.

> Sanjeev's brilliant decision-making abilities have resulted in his becoming a partner in a consulting firm at a very young age. Now he has to nurture his managers and nudge them to take on more responsibilities. One of his managers, Sebastian, decided to follow up on the status of a business proposal with a client on his own. "Why did you do that?" shouted Sanjeev, "It could put them off." Another time, Sebastian gave a half-day's leave to a management trainee who was feeling unwell. "Why did you do that?" screamed Sanjeev, "There is so much work to do." After this, not wanting to upset his boss further, Sebastian stopped taking decisions independently. He only did what Sanjeev told him to do. During appraisals, Sanjeev said, "You need to be more proactive," much to Sebastian's astonishment and irritation. As a result of his own actions, Sanjeev is surrounded by obedient followers and not leaders.

Only when teachers are willing to learn does growth happen

Shiva is self-contained. So he has no desire to open his eyes to the world. With great difficulty, Gauri makes him open his eyes. She has questions that only he can answer. Shiva reveals why thoughts matter over things, and gaze over skills. As Gauri clarifies her doubts, Shiva begins to appreciate the fear that prevents a Brahma from letting go of things and skills, of all things tangible, of his limited worldview. The conversation provokes empathy in Shiva, transforming him into Shankar-Shambhu, the benevolent one.

Education and learning tend to be linear. In education, the burden of teaching rests with the teacher. In learning, the burden shifts to the student. Both education and learning can be made cyclical, especially in business, when the trainer and the mentor gives Vidyalakshmi and gets Sharda in return, even without the active participation of the participant. The yajaman can learn from the devata even if the devata refuses to learn from the yajaman. The yajaman can learn what makes a devata curious and eager for knowledge and what stops him from being curious and eager. This learning reveals to him the human condition, widens his gaze, makes him a more dependable and understanding yajaman.

In business, it is easy to get cynical about people's ability to learn and think that the only way to get work done is by dominating or domesticating others with rules and systems, by using reward and punishment to coerce them into being ethical and efficient. This approach only reveals impatience and a closed mind.

If we are convinced we know everything there is to know about the world, we create a world with little understanding of humanity, where humans are just animals to be controlled and directed. A society thus created, one without faith, is no society at all. It is a warzone waiting to explode.

To understand why people refuse to do as they are told, why they defy and subvert the system, we need Sharda. To get Sharda, the yajaman has to give Vidyalakshmi freely and introspect why the devata resists receiving it, why he would rather obtain fish than learn to fish, why he would rather be dependent and complain about others instead of taking responsibility and becoming dependable.

Ravi compares his mining business to collecting water from a well. When there is a high demand in the market, he widens the bucket and when the demand is low, he narrows it. With this approach of his, he is revealing that he looks at his organization as a mere bucket, a thing. People are just tools to be used as long as they are useful. And then he wonders why, despite being hugely successful, no one is his family looks up to him or cares for him. They fear him, and obey him, but do not appreciate him. He is not in a happy place and will continue to be unhappy if he doesn't widen his gaze to learn and grow.

Growth in thought brings about growth in action

As Vishnu goes about preserving the world, provoking everyone to expand their gaze, we discover how each of his avatars is based on the learning from previous avatars:

- As Matsya, the small fish, who is saved from the big fish by Manu and who saves Manu from pralay, he learns that humanity needs to learn moderation and balance. The helpless cannot be helped at the cost of the environment; the act of feeding must be accompanied by the encouragement to outgrow hunger.

- This leads him to become Kurma or the turtle who upholds the churn that functions only when force is balanced by counter-force, when both parties know when to pull and when to let go. Then he observes the animal nature of man that makes him aggressive, territorial and disrespectful of the boundaries of others.

- In the next avatars of Varaha, the boar, and Narasimha, the man-lion, he uses force to overpower and cunning to control the animal instinct. This does not stop the rise of Bali, who believes that all of life's problems will be solved by distributing wealth. Vishnu learns that humanity needs to expand its gaze from things to thoughts, from Narayani to Narayan.

- So Vaman, the priest, becomes Parashuram, the warrior-priest, who tries to instruct humanity on the value of thoughts over things. When instruction does not work, he becomes Ram, leading by example. But then that leads to pretenders who value rules in letter, not spirit. This leads to the birth of Krishna.

- In the final two avatars, Vishnu breaks the system, almost acting like Shiva, the destroyer, passively withdrawing as a hermit (Shramana, sometimes identified with the Buddha), or actively destroying it like a

warlord as Kalki. The point of the destruction is to provoke wisdom.

- With culture gone, nature establishes itself in all its fury. The law of the jungle takes over. The big fish eat the small fish until Manu saves the small fish and reveals that there is still hope for humanity. In this act of saving the fish, humanity displays the first stirrings of dharma, the human potential, motivating Vishnu to renew his cycle once more.

Vyas who put together the Mahabharat and the Purans is described as throwing up his hands in anguish over why people do not follow the dharma that benefits all. Vishnu, on the other hand, is never shown displaying such anguish. The transformation of Brahma is not his key performance indicator. Following dharma is not necessary. It is desirable. If not followed, the organization will collapse, but nature will survive and life will go on. So Vishnu smiles even though Brahma stays petulant.

Birendra believes his father Raghavendra is a successful man because he has made a lot of money. However, for Raghavendra money is not the objective but the outcome of intellectual and emotional growth. He began as a clerk in a small chemical company. He learned new skills and understood how the world worked, gradually becoming more and more successful in every task he undertook. He became an executive, a manager, even a director of his firm before he decided to break free and become an entrepreneur. His learning continued as he decided to mentor more companies as an investor. Before long he became the owner of many industries, but never ceased to learn, observing what made people give their best and what made them insecure. This knowledge made him a better negotiator and deal-maker. He shares his ideas freely and creates opportunities for people to grow, but very few see Saraswati the way he does. Naturally, they are neither as successful nor as content as he is.

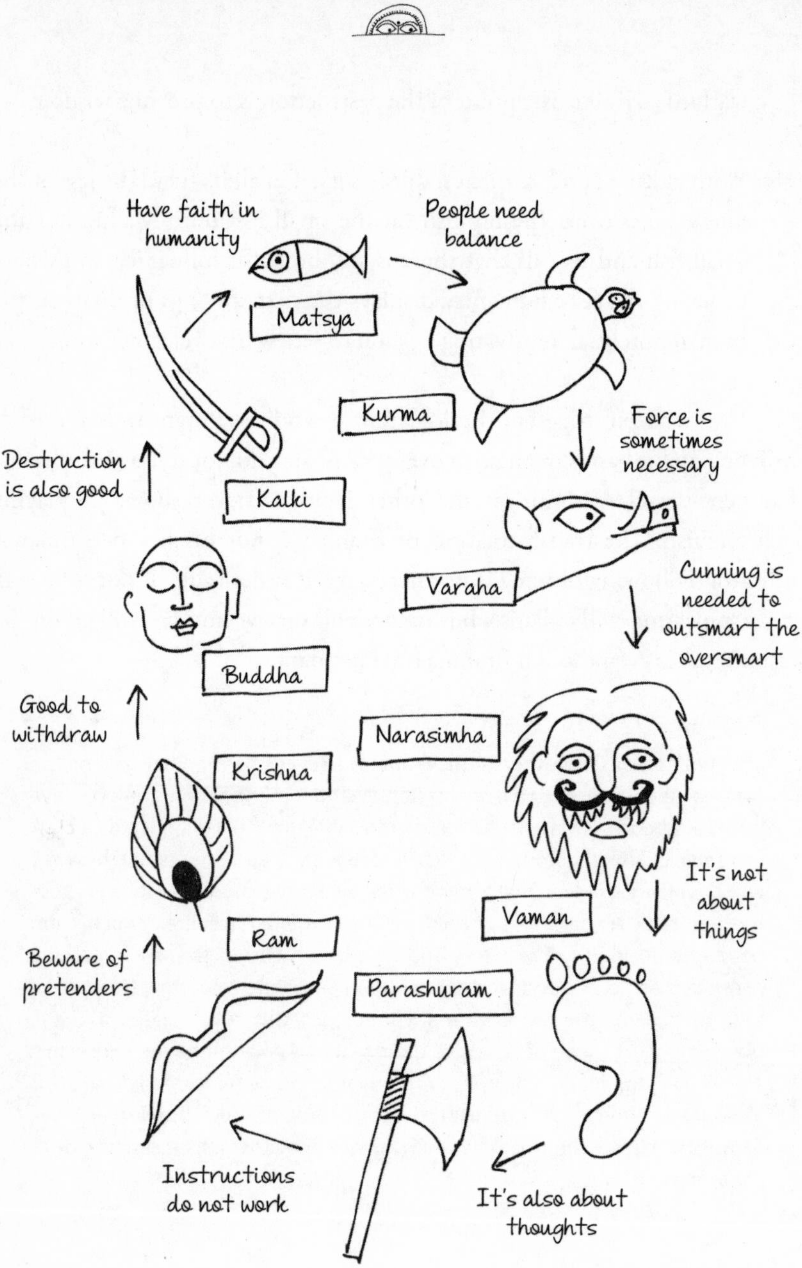

Have faith in humanity

Matsya

People need balance

Kurma

Force is sometimes necessary

Varaha

Cunning is needed to outsmart the oversmart

Narasimha

It's not about things

Vaman

It's also about thoughts

Parashuram

Instructions do not work

Ram

Beware of pretenders

Krishna

Good to withdraw

Buddha

Destruction is also good

Kalki

To provoke thought, we have to learn patience

The way Shiva provokes thought is very different from the way Vishnu does. Brahma chases his daughter Shatarupa, which is a metaphor for human attachment to belief. In fear, we cling to the way we imagine the world and ourselves. Shiva beheads Brahma for this. Shiva also beheads Daksha for valuing the yagna over people. Beheading is a metaphor for forcing the mind to expand.

Shiva wants Brahma and Daksha to shift their focus from Narayani to Narayan. But both stubbornly refuse to grow. Shiva's insistence only frightens them further. In exasperation, Shiva shuts his eyes to Brahma and his sons, allowing them to stay isolated like ghosts trapped by Vaitarni, unable to find tirtha. Frightened deer and dogs bark in insecurity and seek shelter from the rather indifferent Shiva.

Shiva is called the destroyer because he rejects Brahma's beliefs, beheads him and holds his skull in his hand in the form of Kapalika. In contrast, Vishnu is called the preserver as he allows Brahma his beliefs, gives him

shelter on the lotus that rises from his navel and waits for Brahma to expand his gaze at his own pace and on his own terms.

Vishnu keeps giving the devata the option to change, changing his strategies with each yagna, different avatars for different yugas, sometimes upholding rules, sometimes breaking them, hoping to provoke thought in the devata, to make him do tapasya until shruti is heard.

Like a mother gently persuading her child, Vishnu shows him two things: a wheel (chakra) and a conch-shell (shankha). The wheel represents the repetitive nature of prakriti and sanskriti: the changing seasons and the cycle of booms and busts that haunt the marketplace. The conch-shell represents the imagination that can spiral outwards in wisdom or inwards in fear.

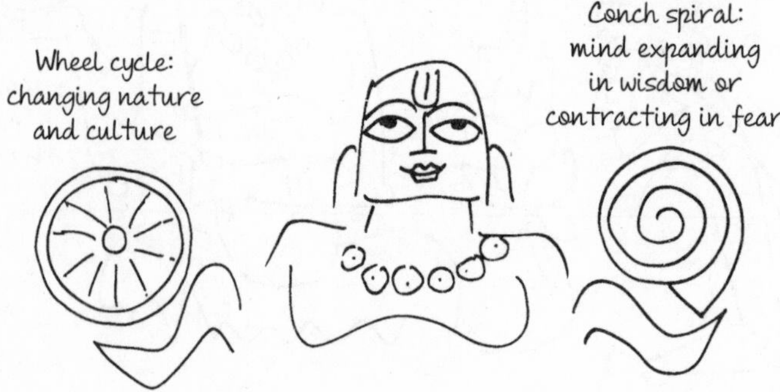

If the devata expands his gaze, the yajaman grows in faith. If the devata does not expand his gaze, the yajaman grows in patience. Either way, the yajaman grows. He sees more, he becomes more inclusive. He does not frighten away investors, talent, or customers who naturally gather around this patient, accommodating being. Thus Lakshmi walks his way.

All her working life, Maria has heard Kamlesh scream, "You will not understand. Just do what I tell you." She has been his secretary for twenty years and she knows that Kamlesh is a brilliant man who wants to share his knowledge with the world, but he has very little patience. As chief designer, he tries hard to explain his designs to his team but they just do not get it. He wins numerous awards and so many designers want to work with him, but while they work with him, few really try and appreciate what makes Kamlesh so brilliant. Kamlesh's thoughts are spatial, not linear. He sees patterns and thinks on his feet, changing ideas constantly, relying very much on instinct. He tries to explain this 'process' but it is very difficult to articulate. When those around him are not able to catch up with him, he loses his temper, shouts at them, calls them names and throws them out. Maria has been able to figure him out enough to know how to work with him. While she does not understand his design work, she knows how to get his administrative work done. She knows he is not as nasty as people think he is. He is like Shiva, quick to temper, easy to please, demanding too much of his students, unable to see that the world does not have the same line of sight as he does. The only other person who understands Kamlesh is Hamir, the head of the art department at the university. "Kamlesh," he says, "Why do you get angry? They will learn when they are supposed to. You just have to provide the input. Do not expect any output. I know it is frustrating but after teaching for thirty years I realize students will follow their own path. They will indulge you by obeying you. The point is not to get them to obey; the point is to inspire them to expand their own mind for their own good. If they don't, who loses?" So saying Hamir smiles.

Kama's Vision Statement

Drishti, observing objective reality

Divya-drishti, observing subjective reality

Darshan, observing the subject

Yama's Balance Sheet

There is nothing right or wrong in this world. There is only cause and consequence. That is why accountability and responsibility matter.

Closures are a time for introspection

Eventually, every yagna comes to an end. The yagna-shala or the ritual precinct is set aflame and the leftovers cast in the river. In the same way, when a person dies, his body is cremated and the ashes thrown in the river, for the body is the yagna-shala where we perform tapasya, the inner yagna of imagination. The fire and water that humanity consumes to establish culture, end up consuming the human.

After the cremation, food is offered to crows. The sound of the cawing crows, "Ka, Ka," is akin to the sound of, "Why? Why?" in Sanskrit, compelling the yajaman to introspect. Why do we conduct the yagna? For Lakshmi, Durga or Saraswati?

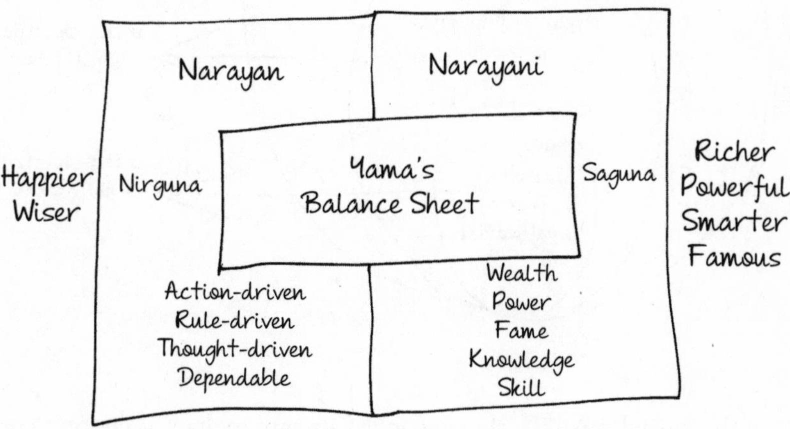

Humans can find meaning in wealth as well as power, in thoughts as well as things. That is why the subject artha-shastra, which literally means the philosophy or quest for meaning or Saraswati, also means economics (quest for Lakshmi) and politics (quest for Durga). Life is all about purush-artha, validating our humanity, which springs from imagination.

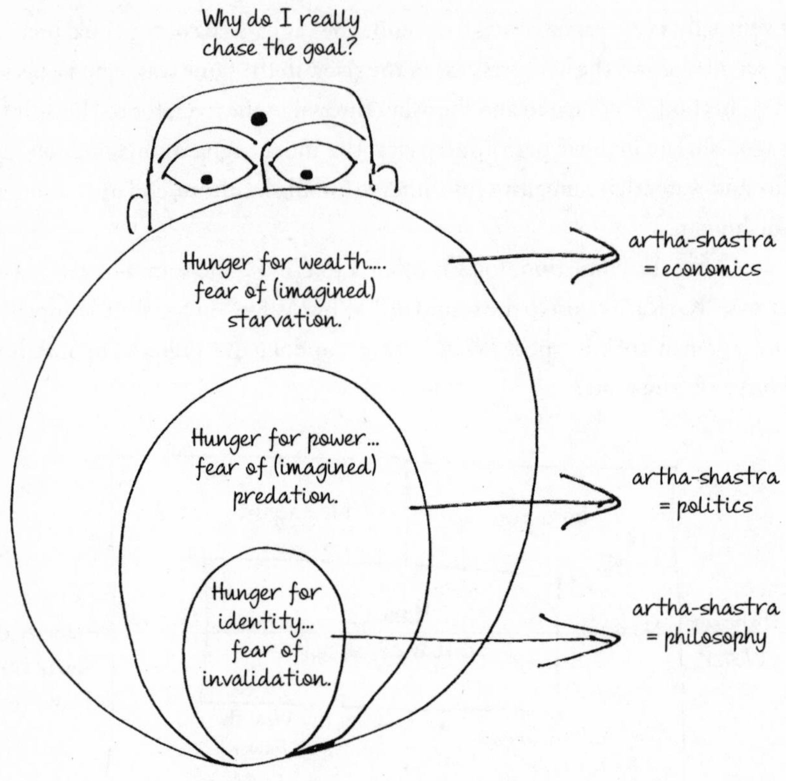

The funeral ritual is a choreographed attempt to draw attention to our unique abilities to find meaning, and to ask us what we have done with them. Death compels us to ask these questions. That is why Yama, the god of death, is also called Dharma, the god who validates human existence.

Yama, the meticulous record-keeper, is also the god of accounting who makes his way to every yajaman's house on Yama Dvitiya, the last day of Diwali, when new account books replace old ones. He wants to know if Lakshmi is happy in the ranga-bhoomi or held captive in the rana-bhoomi. He wants to know because he is Lakshmi's brother and concerned about his sister's welfare. Yama Dvitiya is therefore more popularly known as Bhai Dooj.

Yama wants to know if the yagna has had any impact on us? Is it still about resources or about potential? How much Narayan has been realized? Is the yajaman Indra or Vishnu?

Yama knows that the mere presence of Lakshmi makes no yajaman a Vishnu. Does the yajaman chase Lakshmi or attract her? What does Lakshmi mean to him? Is it the means to survival, a surrogate marker of power, or merely an indicator of his personal growth?

The answers to Yama's question will be subjective. By being honest while answering the question, the yajaman will impress no one and by being dishonest, he will fool only himself.

Any attempt to objectify the answer, or quantify it, and seek external validation, will destroy it. Some things, like trust, happiness, wisdom and patience cannot be measured. The act of measuring destroys their meaning, which is another reason why the god of accounting also serves as the god of death.

Pallavi learnt Hindustani classical music from a renowned musician, one who had succeeded both commercially as well as critically, earning national awards. His music school was legendary. Yet, as a person he was bitter, insecure, angry and jealous of young talent, promoting his sons and ignoring other talented disciples. Pallavi realized that the fabulous music that uplifted the souls of the audience had not uplifted the musician in his own lifetime. The yagna had generated a lot of Lakshmi and Durga, and the yajaman had even extracted a lot of Saraswati but it had failed to awaken Narayan.

Who we include as a devata reveals the meaning we give ourselves

We can start a business for many reasons: because it is the family trade, because we want to be rich, because we want to be answerable to no one, because we want to create opportunities for others and meaning for ourselves, or because we have no other source of income.

- When it is a debt to repay, a burden to bear, it is the belief of Daksha. Here, there is only talk of duties and responsibilities, not of rights, of what we owe the world not what the world owes us.

- When it is a debt to reclaim, a battle to be won, it is the belief of Indra. We believe the acquisition of Lakshmi and Durga will liberate us from fear. This belief is shared by devas and asuras, as well as by yakshas and rakshasas who are constantly indulging themselves, fighting, hoarding and grabbing. Here, there is always talk of rights, and entitlements, fairness and justice, never duties and responsibilities. Like Ravan and Duryodhan, we assume the world owes us something.

- Shiva does not believe in debts. He owes no one anything and no one owes him anything.

- Vishnu repays his debt the moment he incurs one. The transaction is instantaneous at the moment of exchange. The balance sheet is always balanced, with no expectations or obligations, no rights or duties. The business reveals to the yajaman how dependent he is on wealth, status, power and privilege. He strives to outgrow every fear that makes him dependent.

Debt can be understood as a dance. For whom do we dance? The apsara dances for the pleasure of Indra, because she has been been told by Daksha that it is her duty; she has no choice; in pleasing Indra lies her validation.

Indra dances for no one as he feels it is not his duty; in fact, to dance for others is beneath his dignity. Shiva who is Nataraj, the lord of dance, dances because he feels like it, with eyes shut, for his own pleasure, unmindful of the joy he is giving those who watch him. Vishnu who is Natawar, the performer, dances because he wants to entertain and because the reactions of the audience entertain him. He is in ranga-bhoomi. There is no pending credit or debit carried forward. The past does not drag. The future does not propel. There is no goal to reach, as every moment is perfect.

Shailendra works hard to be the best surgeon in the world. He loves the fame that comes with recognition. He is motivated by a vision of the future. Trevor competes with him because he refuses to be second in any race. It is a battle he has to win. Chang, another colleague, also works hard because not working fills him with boredom which makes him anxious. Shila, the most recent resident to join the department, works hard because she wants to prove she is as good as the men. None of them work because it brings joy to suffering patients even though that is the reason they state when the media interviews them. Nor do they work because they enjoy it. If they do enjoy their work, it is incidental. Each one has yet to realize his Narayan potential.

The resources we see reveal what we give meaning to

What we seek depends on what we can see, and what we see depends on how much potential we have realized. Shiva is often depicted as Ardhanareshwar, the half-woman god. The male half of Ardhanareshwar represents our potential and the female half represents resources. Without potential (Shiva), resources have no meaning. And without resources (Shakti), potential is useless, which is why without Shakti, Shiva is called shava or corpse. When our potential rises, we see more.

Drishti reveals Lakshmi, divya-drishti reveals Durga, darshan reveals Saraswati too, which is why, in Jain mythology, the heroic vasudev demands action, the chakravarti leads with rules and only the wise tirthankar outgrows violence and finds peace through thought.

In the Ramayan and Mahabharat, the sons of Brahma (Ravan and Duryodhan) are busy coping with fear by seeking Lakshmi and Durga in tathastu, while Vishnu (Ram and Krishna) keeps smiling as the darshan of the other in each and every engagement lets Saraswati gush out of his neo-frontal cortex, improving his understanding of the world and himself, enabling him to be at peace even in situations of conflict. Wisdom reveals that Lakshmi is often a surrogate for Durga and a compensation for the lack of Saraswati.

In every interaction, be it with an investor, employer, employee, auditor, regulator, customer or vendor, there is something to discover about our animal and human nature. We learn how we imagine the Other to be predator or prey, and how others imagine us to be the same. In ignorance, we behave like animals, choosing to dominate and establish pecking orders and territories. In wisdom, we invoke the human in each other and work towards mutual happiness. Sometimes, this means letting go of things and allowing the Other to win. When the Other gains Lakshmi and Durga, we gain Saraswati.

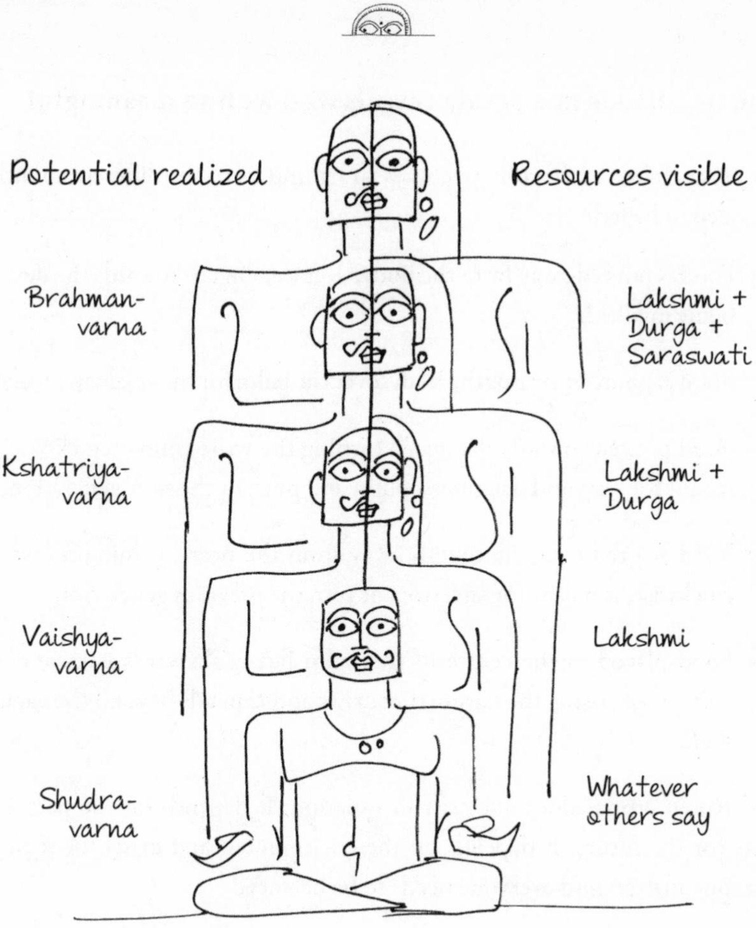

Potential realized | Resources visible

Brahman-varna | Lakshmi + Durga + Saraswati

Kshatriya-varna | Lakshmi + Durga

Vaishya-varna | Lakshmi

Shudra-varna | Whatever others say

After Janardan hired people from other BPOs, he noticed a great divide between the old team and the new one. The old team kept advising the new team to shed the baggage of their previous companies and embrace the culture of the company they had joined. Janardan could see the tension between the two groups. Culture had become a battle to be won, a burden to bear. Culture was being seen as static. One culture was being seen as superior to the other. The culture and company were being valued over individuals. Janardan smiled. He realized he had a team that sought Durga, not Saraswati. There was still much potential to realize.

Who we include as a devata reveals who we find meaningful

In a yagna, food is offered in five ways to remind us of the different mouths that need to be fed:

- Food is poured away from the body, over the fingers, towards the devata being invoked.
- Food is poured towards the body, over the palm for the yajaman himself.
- Food poured towards the heart, turning the wrist counterclockwise, is meant for sons and daughters, putra and putri or the next generation.
- Food poured over the thumb away from the heart, turning the wrist clockwise, is meant for ancestors or pitr, the previous generation.
- Food placed in the centre of the palm facing skywards is meant for animals or pashu, the nature that exists and expands beyond the yagna-shala.

An enterprise does not exist in isolation. It depends on the past and exists for the future. It depends on the environment and exists for society. Everyone matters and everyone needs to be balanced.

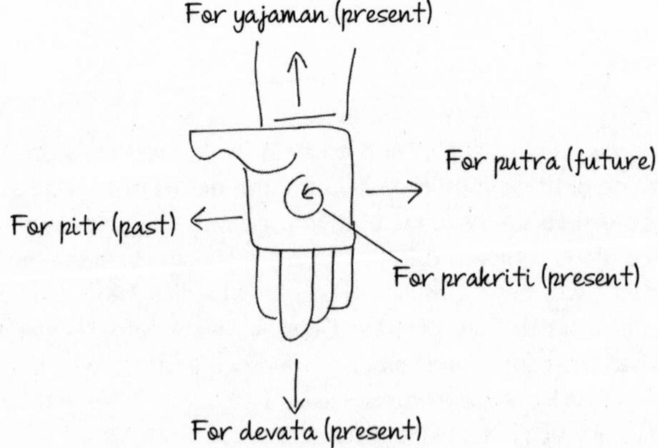

If too much is given to the devata, too little remains for the yajaman and vice versa. If too much value is placed on the past, there will be no innovation. If too much value is paid to the future, mistakes of the past will come back to haunt us. If culture matters more than nature, then one day nature will be destroyed, and with it culture. If nature begins to matters more than culture, then the point of being human is lost. He who preserves all five is Vishnu, the preserver. He creates an ecosystem where there is enough affluence and abundance to satisfy all.

When Ramson started his retail company he told everyone that the customer is god and everything must be done to give the lowest price to the customer. In the past five decades, the company has grown in size making it the darling of the stock exchange. But few notice that this has been done at a terrible cost. The low prices of goods has led to ridiculous consumption patterns in consumers, low wages and poor benefits to employees. Moreover, overproduction to ensure large scale demand and low prices has damaged the environment, and led to the outsourcing of vendors and related business to other countries resulting in unemployment. The only one to be fed by this yagna is Ramson. By focusing on one devata, he has denied food to everyone else.

How the devata sees the yajaman reveals the gap in meaning

Does business create the businessman, or is it the other way around?

Every yajaman is convinced he is either father of the yagna, or the entitled benefactor of the tathastu, but it is the devata who decides if the yajaman is an incestuous, abusive father, an unworthy groom, or a beloved worthy of courting and following. The devata is the darpan or mirror that reveals the gap between how we imagine ourselves and how the world imagines us.

- If the devata feels controlled and judged, the yajaman is like Daksha, who does not let his daughter, Sati, choose her own groom. Sooner or later, Sati's chosen groom, Shiva, will behead him.

- If the devata feels ignored, it means the yajaman is being seen as Indra, who treats his queen like a mistress with a sense of entitlement rather than responsibility. He will find Sachi going to another groom, the asura.

- If the devata fearlessly provokes the yajaman to be more understanding, the yajaman is being seen as the wise Shiva lost in his own world, who needs to be coaxed by Gauri to open his eyes and indulge other people's gaze: help those in the crowded bazaar of Kashi see what he can see from the lofty peaks of Kailas. The devas and asuras may fight over amrit; but only Shiva has the maturity to drink the poison, without demanding compensation or seeking motivation.

- If the devata feels no resentment despite being treated as Renuka, beheaded for having just one adulterous thought; or as Sita, exiled because of street gossip; or as Radha, abandoned when duty calls; or as Draupadi, helped without obligation or expectation, the yajaman is being seen as trustworthy Vishnu whose acts are driven by wisdom and not fear, who does not seek to dominate or domesticate the world

around him, but rather finds validation in helping every devata grow at his own pace. If talent, investors and customers chase the yajaman, he is Vishnu for sure.

If she is my daughter...I have to let her go to a worthy groom.

If she is my mistress...I cannot expect her to be faithful.

If she is my wife...I better be worthy of her.

If she is my sister...I have to be there for her.

If she is my friend...I can be there for her.

If she is my mother...I have to learn to be independent.

Ratnakar is rather curt and tends to be impolite, yet the people who work for him love him. They know that in his heart he wants everyone to grow. He is constantly checking if people have learned more, earned more, done more. To the new worker he asks, "Have you gained more skills?" To the old worker he asks, "Have you taught your skills to another? Why not? Don't you want a promotion or do you want to be a labourer all your life?" To the supervisor he asks, "Do you know how to read account books and balance sheets? Why not? Do you want this department to make losses? Do you want it to be shut down?" To the person who leaves his company, "I hope you are leaving for a better place and not because you are unhappy here." Ratnakar's sharp words seek to stir the Narayan potential in everyone. For people around him, he is Vishnu and they trust him.

The tathastu we give reveals the meaning we seek

Tathastu or what we give in exchange for what we have received can be of three types:

- Dakshina, which is a fee for goods and services received.
- Bhiksha, which is conditional charity that makes the yajaman feel superior.
- Daan, which is unconditional charity that makes the yajaman wise.

Dakshina is exchanged for Lakshmi, bhiksha for Durga and daan for Saraswati. Only daan creates ranga-bhoomi, not the other forms of tathastu.

	What you get	What you give	Type of tathastu
1.	Lakshmi	Lakshmi	Dakshina
2.	Durga	Lakshmi	Bhiksha
3.	Saraswati	Lakshmi	Daan

On the day they had to go their separate ways, two childhood friends took an oath that they would always share their possessions with each other. In time, one rose to wealth while the other was reduced to abject poverty. The poor friend, driven to desperation, decided to seek the help of his rich friend, reminding him of their oath. The story takes different turns in the Mahabharat and the Bhagavat Puran.

In the Mahabharat, the rich friend is Drupad, king of Panchal, and the

poor friend is Drona, a priest. On his arrival, Drona acts familiar with the king, reminding him of his childhood promise and expects at least a cow from Drupad, almost as if it were his right. Drupad does not take to this kindly and tells Drona, "Childhood promises cannot be taken so seriously: we were equals then, but now we are not. As king, it is my duty to help the needy. Ask for alms and you shall get them." Drona is so humiliated that he leaves Drupad's court, learns the art of warfare, teaches it to the princes of the Kuru clan, and as tuition fee demands that they procure for him one half of Panchal so that he can be Drupad's equal. When this is achieved, an angry Drupad seeks from the gods two children: a boy who will kill Drona and a girl who will divide and destroy the Kuru clan that helped Drona.

In the Bhagavat Puran, the rich friend is Krishna, who lives in Dwaraka, and the poor friend is Sudama, a priest. Not wanting to go empty handed, Sudama forsakes a meal so that he can offer a fistful of puffed rice to his friend whom he is meeting after several years. Krishna welcomes Sudama with much affection and orders his queens to bathe and feed him. Sudama feels awkward asking his friend for a favour, especially during their first meeting in years. He keeps quiet. When he returns home, he finds, to his surprise, gifts of cows and grain and gold waiting at his doorstep.

The mood in the Mahabharat story is full of rage. Drupad can give daan but offers bhiksha instead. Finally Drona takes dakshina from his students to satisfy his hunger. What is simply about hunger initially becomes an issue of status, for Drupad not only denies Lakshmi but also strips Drona of Durga by insulting him. Both sides speak of rights and duties, blaming and begrudging each other. All this culminates in a war where both Drupad and Drona die, none the wiser.

The mood in the Bhagavat Puran story is full of affection. Krishna gives daan. He gives Lakshmi and Durga and in exchange he receives Saraswati. He observes Sudama's wisdom: how by starving himself he creates a svaha of puffed rice, transforming his meeting into a yagna with Krishna as the devata; how he does not make the receipt of tathastu an obligation for he is sensitive to the context that the current situation is very different from the childhood one. Krishna observes that Sudama knows he can claim no rights

over Krishna nor impose any obligations on him. Sudama reveals to Krishna that it is possible for people to be generous and kind, even in abject poverty.

Sudama presents himself, without realizing it, as an opportunity for Krishna to give away his wealth voluntarily and unconditionally. Krishna does so without being asked because he is sensitive enough to realize how poor and helpless his friend is. That he expects nothing from Sudama indicates Krishna's economic and emotional self-sufficiency. Thus, he becomes a mirror to human potential.

In the Mahabharat story, Drona and Drupad end up in the rana-bhoomi because each is convinced the other is wrong. In the Bhagavat Puran story, Sudama and Krishna are in the ranga-bhoomi where each respects the mask imposed by society but is still able to do darshan of the human being beyond this mask—the human being who can seek help and offer help.

Mani has two sugar factories. As far as he is concerned, he is doing his workers a great favour by giving them jobs. Without him, they would be jobless. He wants them to be eternally grateful to him. He even wants his son to be grateful as he is getting a huge inheritance on a platter. Mani is giving bhiksha to all and by doing so strips them of power. Naturally everyone resents Mani. The workers would rather have their dues fairly paid as dakshina, for they help Mani generate Lakshmi. Nobody is learning anything from the exchange; there is no daan to be seen anywhere.

We alone decide if we need more meaning, another yagna

Hindus, Jains, Buddhists and Sikhs believe in rebirth. Rebirth is what distinguishes the mythologies of India from the rest of the world. When the word 'rebirth' is used even the most learned people immediately think of physical rebirth. However, for the great sages of India, rebirth referred to physical, social and mental rebirth owing to the three bodies of every human: sthula-sharira, karana-sharira and sukshma-sharira, nourished by Lakshmi, Durga and Saraswati.

- The rebirth of the physical body is a matter of faith, not logic. It can neither be proved nor disproved.

- The rebirth of the social body is not under our control, as it is impacted by social vagaries: the rise and fall of individual and market fortunes. With this comes a change in personality, which is temporary.

- The rebirth of the mental body is a matter of choice. We can spend our entire lives imagining ourselves as heroes or martyrs. Or we can seek liberation from these finite imaginations by realizing that these are stories we use to comfort ourselves. No one knows what the truth really is. All we can do is let our mental body die at the end of the previous yagna and allow it to be reborn at the start of the next yagna, with a little more sensitivity, recognizing that every devata imagines himself as hero or martyr, not villain.

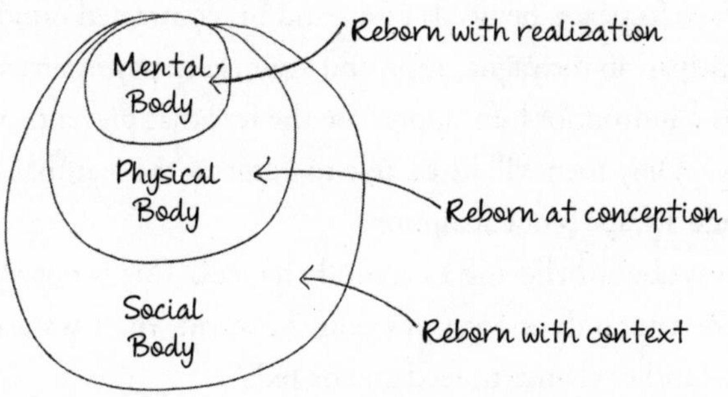

Shyamchandra is seventy years old but he continues to go to work. His wife tells him to slow down but he refuses to. "Remember those five years when I had no job and we were nearly on the streets. That should never happen again," he tells her. But that was thirty years ago. Since then work has been pouring in. The social body went through death and rebirth but Shyamchandra's mental body has not expanded. It has instead contracted in fear. He feels always like prey that will be attacked and ambushed anytime. Those around him see him as a predator who will not let anyone else work. He is the great banyan tree which will nurture nothing under its shade. In his mind, Shyamchandra sees himself as a victim. He does not trust the world around him. He clings to it as Brahma clings to Shatarupa, fearing abandonment. He refuses to see otherwise. All his wife can do is watch him in despair and support him with affection, hoping that one day wisdom will dawn.

In the Mahabharat, Arjun loses his nerve and refuses to fight the battle, not because he fears death or the infamy that will come from killing his kith and kin. More than the physical body, it is his social body that is threatened by the war. He seeks comfort and motivation, Durga, more than Lakshmi, in that moment of crisis.

But his charioteer, Krishna, gives him Saraswati instead: exhorting him to expand his mental body. Krishna reveals the Narayan potential by presenting his cosmic form: the vishwarup. Arjun, who is nara, sees in Krishna the entire universe, extending to infinity in the eight directions; all of time, the past, the present, the future; every deva, asura, yaksha, rakshasa, prajapati and tapasvi. Within Krishna, all worldviews are included.

If Arjun seeks peace, he needs to expand his contracted mind. For this, he has to participate in the yagna, again and again, keep paying attention to the hunger of those in front of him, appreciate the fear that prevents others from being inclusive. Only then will he be able to outgrow the fear that makes him want to exclude. Escape is not an option.

Rebirth is about believing in second chances. This is not the one and only life. There is not only one way of seeing the world. There is always another opportunity, another chance to feed and be fed.

The yagnas will never end. As long as humanity exists, there will always be hunger to satisfy, resources to generate and potential to realize. With every successive yagna, every devata can become a yajaman, and every yajaman, a bhagavan.

He who believes in infinite lives will also have infinite patience, for there is no single goal to reach, only one's gaze that has to keep expanding. It is this human ability that the rishis acknowledge when they join their palms, bow their heads and say, "Namaskar."

When the mind expands, Lakshmi follows. This is the essence of Business Sutra.

Bhagavan
↑
Yajaman
↑
Karta
↑
Karya-karta
↑
Devata

Business Sutra Vocabulary

With new words are created new worlds, as they are vehicles of new ideas. They enable the process of expanding the mind.

	Business context	Conventional context
aarti	adoration of the Other	waving of lamps around the face
agni	that which is used to tame and control nature	fire god
Amravati	the ideal goal where all needs are met without effort	Indra's paradise
ankush	a tool used for pushing people to do their job, and pulling them back	elephant goad
Arjun	one who argues too much, shooting counter questions like arrows when questioned	the third Pandav who is a skilled archer
ashram	a stage in one's career	stage of life
asura	one who feels his entitlement has been denied, resulting in rage and ambition	eternal enemies of the devas
avasarpini	pessimistic gaze	waning period of an era
avatar	role adapted to the context for the benefit of the Other	descent of Vishnu
bali	what is destroyed in the process of creation	sacrifice
bhaav	emotion underlying action	intent
bhagavan	a being who is not hungry but pays attention to others' hunger	a being who is never hungry but feeds others
bhaya	insecurities	fear
Bhim	One who wants to act rather than think	the second Pandav who is very strong
bhog	that which satisfies hunger	consumption
Bhoj	a leader who balances creativity with accountability	a legendary king
Brahma	subject of the subjective truth	the creator

	Business context	Conventional context
brahman	he of the infinitely expanded mind	being with expanded imagination that includes all other imaginations
brahmana	mindset that keeps expanding to appreciate, even include, other people's prejudices	priest or philosopher
brahmanda	imagined reality	subjective world
chakravarti	the king who controls his kingdom with rules	emperor of the world
Chandra	one who is very moody and has favourites	the moon god
Chaturbhuj	the one who multitasks	another name for Vishnu indicating he has four arms
chaval	the outcome	uncooked grains of rice
Chintamani	that which satisfies every wish	wish-fulfilling jewel of paradise
Daksha	one who is obsessed with rules	the patron of the yagna
darpan	the Other whose behaviour reflects who we really are	mirror
darshan	observing the subject of subjective reality	gaze
deva	he who sees what comes to him as entitlement	Brahma's sons who live in luxury above the sky
devata	he who responds to the transaction initiated by the yajaman	the deity being invoked
divya-drishti	observing subjective reality	special sight
doodh	topline	milk
Draupadi	one who has to deal with multiple bosses and subordinates	the common wife of the five Pandavs
drishti	observing objective reality	vision
Durga	power that grants security and authority	goddess of war
Duryodhan	the pretender, the mimic	villain of the epic Mahabharat
dushama	bust	negative period

	Business context	Conventional context
Gandhari	cruel self-righteous parent who is indifferent to his/her child's imagined fears	mother of Duryodhan
Ganesha	one who can easily wear many hats and so communicate between many departments	the elephant-headed god who removes obstacles
Gangu-teli	the one doing a monotonous job	legendary oil presser
garud-drishti	strategy, wide vision, long-term thinking	bird's eye view
Gauri	organization based on rules	the domesticated form of the Goddess Kali
ghee	the personal income emerging from profit	clarified butter
Goloka	sustainable happy business	paradise of cows
Go-mata	sustainable source of income	sacred cow
go-pala	leader who creates a sustainable source of income	cowherd
Gobar-ka-Ganesh	he who does what he is told to do with no view of his own	legendary dumb character
grama-deva	the manager who adapts principles of the centre to the realities of the periphery	village god
Halahal	the negative output of any action	poison that comes with nectar
haldi	that which removes negative energy	turmeric
Hanuman	he who obeys unconditionally and without question	the monkey who serves Ram and is worshipped in his own right
Indra	he who wants high return on investment always	king of devas
ishta-devata	one who grants us personal favours	personal god
jati	the certificates of society	caste based on profession
Kailas	where there is no hunger	abode of Shiva
Kali	marketplace with no regulatory control	the wild form of the Goddess Gauri
Kalpataru	that which satisfies every wish	wish-fulfilling tree

	Business context	Conventional context
Kama	right-brain activity, creativity, which does not like structure	god of desire
Kamadhenu	that which satisfies every wish	wish-fulfilling cow
karana-sharira	social body created by designations and equity	social body
karma	consequences of actions	the cycle of cause and consequence
karta	the one who gives the directive	a leader
karya-karta	the one who follows the directive	a follower
Kauravs	those who stubbornly refuse to learn	the hundred brothers led by Duryodhan who oppose the five Pandavs
Krishna	he who breaks rules to help others grow on their terms	cowherd avatar of Vishnu
kshatriya	he who does everything to be the dominant one	a warrior
kshira-sagar	market of possibilities	the ocean of possibilities
Kubera	the one who hoards	king of yakshas
kula-devata	one who grants us departmental favours	the family god
kumbha	that which turns natural wealth into personal wealth	pot
kumkum	that which collects and contains positive energy	vermilion powder
kupamanduk	know-it-all	someone who does not realize how narrow his gaze is
kurma	a leader who balances forces and counterforces	the turtle form of Vishnu
Lakshmi	wealth	goddess of wealth
makkhan	bottomline	butter
Matsya	a leader who seeks shelter for the weak against the strong	the fish form of Vishnu
matsya-nyaya	rule of the sea where big fish eat small fish and the small fish survive by being slippery	jungle law

	Business context	Conventional context
maya	measurement that creates a false sense of certainty, security and order	delusion
Mitti-ka-Madhav	he who does what he is told to do with no view of his own	folk character
Nakul	one who looks pretty but delivers nothing	the fourth Pandav who is very handsome
nara	one who has yet to evoke Narayan	a human being
Narad	he who makes people insecure by comparing and contrasting	trouble-making sage
Narasimha	he who outwits the oversmart	man-lion form of Vishnu
Narayan	human potential	God
Narayani	resources	Goddess
nirguna	not measurable	intangible
Pandavs	students who have made mistakes but are open to learning	the five protagonists of the epic Mahabharat
parashu	analysis	axe
Parashuram	leader who punishes rule-breakers sternly	the warrior-sage form of Vishnu
pasha	synthesis	string
prakriti	material world	nature
pralay	end of an organization or a market	the end of the world when everything dissolves into the sea
purush	imagination	humanity
Radha	leader who lets talent go without begrudging them	the milkmaid who is the beloved of Krishna
rakshasa	one who takes things by force	demon who grabs
Ram	he who follows the rule at any cost to help others grow on their terms	the royal form of Vishnu
rana-bhoomi	competitive environment	warzone
ranga-boomi	joyful environment where everybody grows	playground
rangoli	a pattern of thought	rice flour patterns drawn at the entrance of the house every morning

	Business context	Conventional context
Ravan	he who breaks the rule for his growth at the cost of others	king of rakshasas
rin	burden of obligation and expectation	debt
rishi	one who has more insight than others	seer who can see what others do not see
saguna	measurable	tangible
Sahadev	one who only speaks when spoken to even though he knows solutions to problems	the youngest Pandav who was very wise and never spoke unless spoken to
sanskriti	culture	society
Saraswati	human imagination	goddess of knowledge
sarpa-drishti	tactic, narrow-vision, short-term thinking	snake vision
sattra	an organization with many processes	a complex set of multiple yagnas
Shakti	inborn strength, capacity and capability	goddess of power
Shankar	he who is content and sensitive to others	another name of Shiva
Sharda	knowledge of purusha	goddess of wisdom
Shekchilli	dreamer with no accountability	folk character who dreams
Shiva	he who is independent but withdrawn from the world	God who destroys
shruti	personal ideas that cannot be shared	inner voice that is heard but cannot be spoken or transmitted
shudra	he who does not think for himself and so mimics others	labourer, slave
smriti	public ideas that are exchanged	outer voice that is spoken or transmitted but not necessarily heard
sthula-sharira	how we appear physically to others	the physical body
sukshma-sharira	how we imagine ourselves	the mental body
Surya	one who is radiant and attracts all attention	the sun god

	Business context	Conventional context
sushama	boom	positive period
svaha	input	this of me I offer
Swarga	Indra's paradise	another name for Amravati
swayambhu	one who has outgrown fear and is independent	self-created
tapasya	introspection, contemplation, analysis	the practice of churning tapa (mental fire)
tathastu	output	so be it
tirtha	empathizing, connecting, appreciating other people's subjectivity	the ford, the shallow riverbed that connects two riverbanks
tirthankar	one who understands the power of thoughts	Jain sage
Tri-loka	three worlds occupied by all humans	earth, atmosphere, sky
Upanishad	sitting together having a meaningful illuminating conversation	philosophical deliberations that form the final part of the Veda
utasarpini	optimistic gaze	upwards movement of time
Vaikuntha	workplace where everything comes together without conflict	Vishnu's abode in the middle of the ocean of milk
vaishya	he does everything for a tangible profit	merchant
Vaitarni	that which isolates us from others	the river that separates the land of the living from the land of the dead
Vaman	he who grows big and thus makes the Other feel small and insignificant	dwarf avatar of Vishnu
Varaha	he who uses force to overpower the Other	boar avatar of Vishnu
varna	mindset	colour of the mind
vasudev	one who is action driven	the hero who is a man of action who seeks wealth

	Business context	Conventional context
vetal	facilitator who asks questions that provoke thought, but does not know the answer	the teacher who never goes to the student and who provokes discomforting reflections
Vidyalakshmi	knowledge and skills that help us generate wealth and secure power	information, knowledge and skills, often mistaken for wisdom
Vikramaditya	the student who goes to the teacher	a legendary king
Vishnu	he who grows on his terms by enabling others to grow on their terms at their pace	God who preserves
Vishwarupa	the ability to be anyone and do anything	cosmic form of God
yagna	the process of exchange	Vedic fire ritual
yajaman	the one who initiates the offer of exchange	patron
yaksha	one who hoards	Brahma's son who hoards
Yama	left-brain activity that is highly structured	god of death
Yashoda	caring parent who is sensitive to the child's imagination	Krishna's mother
yoga	outgrowing hunger	alignment
Yudhishtir	upright but naïve leader	the eldest Pandav
yuga	context made of time, space and people	era

Index of Sutras

How to reject this book

"*Business Sutra* is THE truth."

"This is too theoretical, not practical."

"Which university endorses this?"

"Is there any organization where this has been proven to work?"

"Spiritual mumbo-jumbo."
(Note: The word 'spiritual' is not part of *Business Sutra*)

"How exotic!"

"This is Hindu right-wing propaganda."

"See, all wisdom ultimately comes from India."

"So this is how business should be done in India."

"This idea is too complex and confusing."

"I have always been practicing this."

"My grandfather used to practice this."

"So what does the author want me to do now?"

"Devdutt Pattanaik will solve my problems."